Legislative Politics in Latin America

This theoretically inspired study explores legislative politics in Argentina, Brazil, Chile, and Mexico. Instead of beginning with an assumption that these legislatures are either rubber stamps or obstructionist bodies, the chapters provide new data and a fresh analytical approach to describe and explain the role of these representative bodies in these consolidating democracies. For each country the book provides three chapters dedicated, in turn, to executive–legislative relations, the legislatures' organizational structure, and the policy process. The analytical focus of each section, however, remains the same: the role of institutional factors (including the allocation of policy-making authority between the executive and legislative branches of government; the number of relevant parties in the legislature; and the structure of electoral incentives) in shaping the patterns of legislative behavior.

Scott Morgenstern is Assistant Professor in the Department of Political Science at Duke University. Professor Morgenstern has held a visiting professor position at CIDE (Centro de Investigación y Docencia Económicas) in Mexico and served as a visiting researcher at the Instituto de Cienica Politica, Uruguay.

Benito Nacif is Research Professor at CIDE (Centro de Investigación y Docencia Económicas) in Mexico. Professor Nacif's academic distinctions include the British Foreign Office and Commonwealth Scholarship (1990–1992).

Cambridge Studies in Comparative Politics

General Editor
Margaret Levi   *University of Washington, Seattle*

Associate Editors
Robert H. Bates   *Harvard University*
Peter Hall   *Harvard University*
Stephen Hanson   *University of Washington, Seattle*
Peter Lange   *Duke University*
Helen Milner   *Columbia University*
Frances Rosenbluth   *Yale University*
Susan Stokes   *University of Chicago*
Sidney Tarrow   *Cornell University*

Other Books in the Series

Continued on page following Index

Legislative Politics in Latin America

Edited by

SCOTT MORGENSTERN
Duke University

BENITO NACIF
CIDE

CAMBRIDGE
UNIVERSITY PRESS

PUBLISHED BY THE PRESS SYNDICATE OF THE UNIVERSITY OF CAMBRIDGE
The Pitt Building, Trumpington Street, Cambridge, United Kingdom

CAMBRIDGE UNIVERSITY PRESS
The Edinburgh Building, Cambridge CB2 2RU, UK
40 West 20th Street, New York, NY 10011-4211, USA
477 Williamstown Road, Port Melbourne, VIC 3207, Australia
Ruiz de Alarcón 13, 28014 Madrid, Spain
Dock House, The Waterfront, Cape Town 8001, South Africa

http://www.cambridge.org

First published 2002

Printed in the United Kingdom at the University Press, Cambridge

Typeface Janson Text 10/13 pt.   *System* QuarkXPress [BTS]

A catalog record for this book is available from the British Library.

Library of Congress Cataloging in Publication Data

Legislative politics in Latin America / edited by Scott Morgenstern, Benito Nacif.
       p.   cm. – (Cambridge studies in comparative politics)
    Includes bibliographical references (p.) and index.
    ISBN 0-521-79219-3 – ISBN 0-521-79659-8 (pb.)
       1. Legislative bodies – Latin America – Case studies.   2. Legislative power – Latin
America – Case studies.   3. Executive power – Latin America – Case studies.   4. Party
discipline – Latin America – Case studies.   I. Morgenstern, Scott.   II. Nacif, Benito,
1965–   III. Title.   IV. Series.
JL963 .L43 2001
328′.098–dc21   2001025807

ISBN   0 521 79219 3   hardback
ISBN   0 521 79659 8   paperback

Contents

Contents

Tables and Figures

Tables

Tables and Figures

Figures

Contributors

Barry Ames
Department of Political Science
University of Pittsburgh
4L01 Forbes Quad
Pittsburgh, PA 152060

Octavio Amorim Neto
Rio de Janeiro Graduate Research
  Institute
Rua da Matriz 82
Rio de Janeiro, RJ 22260-100
Brazil

Ma. Amparo Casar
Division de Estudio Politicos
Centro de Investigacion y Docencia
  Economicas
Carretera Mexico – Toluce 3655
Col. Lomas de Santa Fe
Mexico DF, 01210
Mexico

John M. Carey
Department of Political Science
Washington University, St. Louis
Campus Box 1063
One Brookings Drive
St. Louis, MO 63130

Gary W. Cox
Department of Political Science
University of California, San Diego
9500 Gilman Drive, 0521
La Jolla, CA 92093

Kent H. Eaton
Woodrow Wilson School
Princeton University
Princeton, NJ 08544

Mark P. Jones
Department of Political Science
Michigan State University
East Lansing, MI 48824-1032

John Londregan
Department of Political Science
University of California, Los Angeles
3351 Bunche
Los Angeles, CA 14702-1180

Scott Morgenstern
Department of Political Science,
  Box 90204
Duke University
Durham, NC 27704

Ana María Mustapic
Universidad Torcuato Di Tella
Minones 2177
Buenos Aires, 1428
Argentina

Benito Nacif
Centro de Investigacion y Docencia
  Economicas
Lomas de Santa Fe
Careterra Mexico – Toluca 3655
Mexico, DF, 01210
Mexico

Contributors

David Samuels
Department of Political Science
University of Minnesota
Minneapolis, MN 55455

Peter M. Siavelis
Politics Department
Wake Forest University
Box 7568
Reynolda Station
Winston-Salem, NC 27109

Jeffrey A. Weldon
Dept. de Ciencia Politica ITAM
Rio Hondo #1
Col. Tizapan San Angel
01000 Mexico, DF
Mexico

Preface and Acknowledgments

Before 1997 few were studying the Mexican Congress, let alone other legislatures in Latin America. In 1996, however, the opposition parties in Mexico were poised to wrestle the PRI for control of the Congress for the first time, which they succeeded in doing the following year. Understandably, this generated tremendous interest in legislative politics not only among academics, but also in the business world, the press, and the general public.

At that time the two of us were working in the Centro de Investigación y Docencia Económicas (CIDE) in Mexico City. Blanca Heredia and Carlos Elizondo, the academic secretary and general director of CIDE respectively, charged the two of us with organizing an international conference of our own design. We both had recently finished dissertations related to legislative politics and realized that bringing in other experts could provide the field much fuller descriptions and richer analyses than our own individual work. Further, Mainwaring and Shugart had been working on their volume on presidentialism in Latin America, and we saw an opportunity to complement their valuable study.

Our first challenge was in defining the scope of our study. In this we relied on the División de Estudios Politicos (Political Studies Division) of CIDE, where we first presented our ideas. The first drafts of the proposal covered many countries and themes. We were forced, therefore, into a tradeoff between depth and breadth. We opted for the former, as it allowed us to add theoretical rigor to studies of Latin American politics. Having made this decision, we settled on addressing two main theoretical issues, executive–legislative relations and legislative organization, with a third section showing how these issues shape the policy process.

Our theoretical bent stems from our training in American politics, based on David Mayhew's general model of the U.S. legislature and Joseph Schlesinger's theory of political ambition. These works have been important cornerstones of studies of the U.S. Congress, since they have shown how simple assumptions about legislators' reelection drives shape politics. However, since they focus on just one case, they hide several assumptions about the nature of the party system, the constitution, the electoral system, and the reelection interests of legislators.

These "hidden" assumptions become variables in a comparative model. We therefore chose our four cases, Argentina, Brazil, Chile, and Mexico, to test their impact. The most prominent variable gleaned from the U.S. models is the reelection-seeking goal of legislators. In Latin America no country has reelection rates as high as those found in the United States, but Chile has the region's highest rates. At the other end of the spectrum is Mexico, where immediate reelection is prohibited. Argentina and Brazil lie at other nodes on the continuum, and thus these cases presented themselves as prime suspects for our study. These countries also provide important variance on our other variables, most importantly the shape of the party and electoral systems.

Our contributors, of course, share this methodological focus. This has allowed us to provide comparable chapters on each of the four countries for each of the three themes. As such, the volume combines depth of knowledge about the four cases as well as tests of our primary variables across four major Latin American countries.

In producing this volume we have incurred many debts. Foremost we must thank CIDE for its financial and moral support. The Center for International Studies at Duke University also provided key financial support for the project. The Fredrich Eber Foundation deserves a special mention for the important financial support from the early stages of the project. Also supportive were the Legislative Studies Committee (Comisión de Estudios Legislativos) and the Institute for Legislative Studies (Instituto de Estudios Legislativos) of the 57th Legislature of the Mexican Chamber of Deputies.

On the intellectual side, our primary thanks must go to an anonymous reviewer who provided almost 40 single-spaced pages of comments. Alex Holzman and Cambridge University Press were very encouraging and helped us focus our revisions. Finally, Lewis Bateman at Cambridge gave us the last necessary push to revise and improve some key sections.

Party Names and Other Acronyms and Abbreviations

Party Names

Argentina

Alianza	Alianza para el Trabajo, la Justicia y la Educación (Alliance for Work, Justice and Education)
FG	Frente Grande (Large Front)
FR	Fuerza Republicana (Republican Force)
Frepaso	Frente País Solidario (Front for a Country in Solidarity)
MODIN	Movimiento por la Dignidad y la Independencia (Movement for Dignity and Independence)
PA	Partido Autonomista (Autonomist Party)
PDC	Partido Demócrata Cristiano (Christian Democratic Party)
PDP	Partido Demócrata Progresista (Progressive Democrat Party)
PI	Partido Intransigente (Intransigent Party)
PJ	Partido Justicialista (Justicialist Party [Peronists])
PSD	Partido Socialista Demócratico (Democratic Socialist Party)
PSP	Partido Socialista Popular (Popular Socialist Party)
UCeDé	Unión del Centro Democrático (Union of the Democratic Center)
UCR	Unión Cívica Radical (Radical Civic Union)

Brazil

PDS	Partido Democrático Social (Democratic Social Party)
PDT	Partido Democrático Trabalhista (Democratic Labor Party)
PFL	Partido da Frente Liberal (Party of the Liberal Front)
PL	Partido Liberal (Liberal Party)
PMDB	Partido do Movimento Democrático Brasileiro (Party of the Brazilian Democratic Movement)
PP	Partido Progressista (Progressive Party)
PPB	Partido Progressista Brasileiro (Brazilian Progressive Party)

PPS	Partido Popular Socialista (Popular Socialist Party)
PRN	Partido da Reconstrução Nacional (Party of National Reconstruction)
PSB	Partido Socialista Brasileiro (Brazilian Socialist Party)
PSDB	Partido da Social Democracia Brasileira (Party of the Brazilian Social Democracy)
PST	Partido Social Trabalhista (Social Labor Party)
PT	Partido dos Trabalhadores (Worker's Party)
PTB	Partido Trabalhista Brasileiro (Brazilian Labor Party)

Chile

PPD	Partido por la Democracia (Party for Democracy)
PS	Partido Socialista (Socialist Party)
RN	Renovacion Nacional (National Renovation)
UDI	Union Democratica Independiente (Democratic Independent Union)

Mexico

PAN	Partico Acción Nacional (National Action Party)
PRD	Partido de la Revolución Democratica (Party of the Democratic Revolution)
PRI	Partido Revolucionario Institucional (Institutional Revolutionary Party)
PT	Partido de Trabajo (Labor Party)
PVEM	Partido Verde Ecologista de México (Green Party)

Other Acronyms and Abbreviations

CEDI	Centro de Estudios para el Desarrollo Institucional (Center for Studies for Institutional Development)
CEN	Comite Ejecutivo Nacional (National Executive Committee)
CLP	Comisión de Labor Parlamentaria (Committee of Parliamentary Work)
CMO	Comissão Mista de Planos, Orçamentos Públicos e Fiscalização (Joint Committee for Planning, Public Budgets and Oversight; Brazilian budget committee)
CONASUPO	Compañía Nacional de Subsistencias Populares (National Company for Public Subsistence)
CRICP	Comisión de Régimen Interno y Concertación Política (Committee for Internal Regulations and Political Concertation)
DGI	Direccion General Impositiva (Director Tax General)
DNU	Decree of Necessity and Urgency
DSV	double simultaneous vote

Party Names and Other Acronyms and Abbreviations

FOBAPROA	Fondo Bancario de Proteccíon al Ahorros (Banking Fund for the Protection of Savings)
GC	Gran Comisión (Great Committee)
IMF	International Monetary Fund
INJ	Instituto Nacional Juvenil (National Youth Institute)
ISI	Import-substituting industrialization
M	District Magnitude
GAO	General Accounting Office (Contaduria Mayor de Hacienda)
MC	Member of Congress
MCDs	Mexican Chamber of Deputies
NUDs	Necessary and Urgent Decrees
PEMEX	Petróleos Mexicanos (Mexican Petroleum)
PR	Proportional Representation
SEGPRES	Ministerio Secretaría General de la Presidencia (Ministry of the Secretary General of the President)
SMD	single-member district
VAT	Value Added Tax

1

Towards a Model of Latin American Legislatures

SCOTT MORGENSTERN

Ambition, channeled by incentives and institutions, drives politics. Ambitious politicians lead coups and palace takeovers in nondemocracies and engineer election victories and votes of no-confidence in consolidated democracies. In democratic situations, however, these leaders are constrained by party and electoral institutions, constitutions, federal arrangements, and various societal factors. While ambition and political institutions have long driven much research on the United States and other developed democracies, the turbulent histories of Latin American nations have not lent themselves to parallel analyses. In recognition of democracy's movement toward consolidation in much of the region, this book adapts the questions and hypotheses generally applied to studies of the United States and other Western consolidated democratic systems to the analysis of legislative politics in Argentina, Brazil, Chile, and Mexico.

An important change in Latin America is the high value that most voters and politicians profess to place on democracy. At the same time, however, many recent Latin American presidents (maybe not unlike their predecessors or even their U.S. counterparts) have railed against obstructionist, corrupt, or ineffective legislatures. Fujimori used this excuse to close the Peruvian Congress, and Menem in Argentina and Collor in Brazil sought to govern without involving their legislatures. In fear that they would undo his economic reforms and bleed the budget, Pinochet emasculated the Chilean Congress before allowing a transition to civilian rule, and Chavez overtook the odious Venezuelan Congress by (illegally) organizing a plebiscite to create a constituent assembly, which eventually subsumed the Congress. These experiences have helped to create a view that the Latin American legislatures are at best irrelevant to the policy process, if not venal and destructive. *The Economist*, in a single issue for example, argued

1

that the Venezuelan Congress would "happily avoid the responsibility of having to pass several tax bills" and that Brazilian President Cardoso had to "brow beat Congress into approving long-languishing reforms."[1] While more cautious, recent academic work has not loudly disputed this view and has often focused on how presidents avoid or undermine the legislature.

While many of the criticisms have validity, the representative wings of these governments have not been limited to negative participation. The legislatures' positive roles in peace negotiations (as in Mexico), tax reform (in Mexico and Argentina), economic reform (in Brazil), or uncovering corruption (again in Brazil) are not examples of aberrant behavior.[2] Neither is their involvement in interbranch bargaining. But, this more prosaic pattern of politics – the alternative to presidential decree-wielding – has drawn little attention.

In recognition of the importance of legislative politics to the democratic process, this book seeks to redress this oversight. In our effort we focus on legislators' ambitions, since we hope to better understand not just the degree to which the legislatures are overrun by the presidents (which is less than sometimes assumed), but also the source of their behavioral patterns. This book, then, has theoretical and empirical goals. The primary empirical question is, How do legislatures function in the new democratic period? Further, even if legislatures were weak in the past, how and why have their roles changed, and how do these roles differ across Latin America? Theoretically, even if we accept the notion that the president holds the single most important elected position in Latin America's politics, we still want to understand why the legislatures are not more assertive. More specifically, how does variance in partisan, electoral, and constitutional arrangements affect the legislatures' structure and function? In short, we have chosen to study Latin America's legislatures out of a belief that, although they may not take the most prominent role in the policy process, democratic politics revolve around their most representative bodies. It is therefore not possible to gain an understanding of the nature of politics in these countries without a careful analysis of their legislatures.

The purpose of this chapter is to examine whether and how models of Western democratic legislatures that are based on assumptions that politi-

[1] February 6, 1999, pp. 33–34.
[2] *The Economist* again provides a good example. Their reports about these issues show clear surprise with the positive legislative role (see, for example, November 6 and 27, 1999).

cians rationally follow their ambitions are applicable to our cases. As in studies of developed countries, we do assume that politicians in the four countries under study here are rule-bound, adhering to a given set of rules implied by the particular constitutional context. The politicians thus see only electoral paths to executive and legislative offices, and they see these offices as the source of policy change. This does not imply that the bureaucracy, the central bank, the International Monetary Fund (IMF), or even the military are uninvolved. It means, alternatively, that their pressures are registered as electoral threats, not as threatened military coups. When "democracy has become the 'only game in town'" and recourse to coercive force is only a remote possibility, comparativists award the label "consolidated democracy" (Linz and Stepan 1996. p. 5).

This book focuses on Argentina, Brazil, Chile, and Mexico, countries that if not already consolidated are moving clearly in that direction. Since 1997, the approval of Mexico's budget has been characterized by interbranch bargaining and a highly spirited and public debate centered on social spending and economic theory, a far cry from the executive-dominated politics that prevailed for over 60 years. Recent workers' demonstrations in Argentina were met with police forces and legislative demands on the administration instead of calls for military action. Chile's 1997 elections saw some slippage of their center-left coalition, but also the naming of Pinochet's replacement. Pinochet's arrest in Britain in 1998 brought some demonstrations and a short boycott of the Congress by the political right, but democracy was never truly threatened. And in Brazil, "political survival" now refers more to patronage politics and elections than to pacifying the military.[3]

In moving past the period when politicians did not expect democratic institutions to last, we are safe in applying Western-style assumptions that politicians will respond to incentives inherent within a democratic system. The authors in this book thus look at the structures (such as the party system), rules (such as electoral rules, veto provisions, and prohibitions on reelection), and incentives (such as an interest in reelection) that drive democratic legislative politics by acting on individual legislators. Of course, other factors, such as ideology, resource limitations, international economic pressures, and domestic social exigencies, also push on legislators. This model, then, is like the toy airplane discussed by King, Keohane,

---

[3] The term political survival comes from Ames (1987). See Ames' studies on legislators' strategic budgetary amendments (1994, 1995).

3

and Verba (1994). Like the toy, we are representing just a piece of reality with the full understanding that our model does not capture all of the complex conjunction of forces acting on legislators. Still, the model serves as a very useful representation, highlighting a crucial set of forces that influence the behavior of legislators and legislatures.

In sum, we have chosen to study legislative politics in four Latin American countries where politicians adhere to their constitutional frameworks and work without (or at least with a greatly reduced) fear of military intervention. This basic similarity with Western democracies justifies an in-depth study of Latin America's democratic institutions and encourages us to employ the outline of a model that has gained a wide application in studies of Western legislatures. We draw most heavily on studies of a comprehensively studied legislature that, like the Latin American cases, operates within a presidential regime: the U.S. Congress.

Although we rely heavily on models of the U.S. Congress since it is a highly studied presidential regime, we also find that models of multiparty parliamentary systems have interesting parallels with the multipartisan Latin American legislatures. Models of multiparty parliamentary systems generally focus on coalition governments that arise in the wake of the executive's lack of a parliamentary majority. This is the same situation that we find in much of Latin America. Of course the parliamentary systems differ in at least one fundamental way from their Latin American counterparts: Since legislators' tenure in office is related to their continued collective support of the executive, models of parliaments can often assume that legislators in the executive's coalition have an interest in avoiding conflict with the executive. Still, just like a prime minister, a president must command the support of a majority in the legislature to ensure passage of his legislation.[4] This fundamental similarity leads us to draw on the European models in our effort to create a general model of legislative politics that is useful in the Latin American context.

The remainder of this chapter first describes the principal questions, many of which are derived from studies of the U.S. Congress, that have driven the studies in this volume. In so doing, it explains the three themes – executive–legislative relations, parties and legislative structure, and

---

[4] There are some exceptions. When the president has constitutional decree powers, for example, he can avoid the legislature. It is quite questionable, however, whether a president could continue to decree legislation without considerable legislative support (see Carey and Shugart 1998).

policy studies – around which the book is organized. Throughout this volume the authors take the assumption common in U.S. models that politicians everywhere are ambitious. However, other assumptions in the U.S. model are not directly applicable to other cases. The second half of this introduction, therefore, dissects the U.S. models in a search for independent variables (such as career goals, party alignments, the electoral system, and constitutional structures) that the models disguise as assumptions. In addition to the assumption about ambitious politicians, these variables guide the subsequent chapters. They all show how the tremendous range of values on these independent variables accounts for differences in the legislatures' relations with their executives, their organizational structures, and their policy roles. In the concluding chapter, I collect the wealth of information from the case studies to display, compare, and contrast the full range and effects of these variables.

The Questions and Dependent Variables

In part because they have been overshadowed by presidents and frequently closed by militaries, Latin American legislatures have received limited study and are not well understood. Therefore, to explain their organization and activity it is necessary to first generate a view of what we are explaining. There are many different angles from which to view these legislatures, as studies of the current and historical U.S. Congress bear witness. Each angle uncovers a different aspect of the full picture. One study cannot hope to integrate all of these aspects into a single universal vision, but we do hope to identify several key perspectives.

At their base, studies of the U.S. Congress focus on the translation of interests – be they of the president, citizens, interest groups, bureaucrats, or legislators – into policy. To explain these competing demands, scholars have undertaken three types of studies related to the legislature: studies of executive legislative relations; studies of political parties and the structure of the legislature; and studies of the policy-making process.

This book is organized around these three themes. Unlike most collections, however, we do not try to answer these questions by offering single case studies on individual countries. Instead, we offer three independent studies for each of our four cases. We have less geographic coverage, but the tradeoff has yielded an important depth in the analysis that would be unattainable in the standard single-chapter format.

Questions About Executive–Legislative Relations

Whether focusing on narrow policy outcomes – such as tariff rates (Schnattschneider 1935), budget deficits (McCubbins 1991) – or tax policy (Birnbaum and Murray 1988) – or theoretical issues – such as the effects of campaign finance laws (Sorauf 1992) or the issue of reelection (Mayhew 1974; Carey 1996) – studies of the U.S. Congress safely assume that legislators are in powerful positions to pursue policy changes to further their goals. There has been little reason to pay heed to a question often raised about Latin American legislatures: Does the legislature play an important policy role?

In Latin America, many casual and academic observers alike assume that legislators often forego their constitutional powers, abdicating in favor of the executive. In part this perception stems from studies done while dictatorships ruled much of Latin America. Kornberg and Musolf (1970), for example, cite Packenham's study of Brazil in questioning whether some of the legislatures' "principal function of is now, or will be in the future, one of enacting legislation" (p. 8). Excepting Chile, Costa Rica, and Uruguay, Astiz (1973) and Mezey (1979) classify the Latin American legislatures as "marginal" and "rubber-stamp legitimizers," respectively. More recent work also questions the importance of the legislatures. O'Donnell's (1993) oft-cited and influential paper purports that Latin American democracies are a "new species," characterized by presidents who view courts and legislatures as "nuisances," not a vital part of a democratic polity. This view is reinforced by Linz's (1994) proclamations about the winner-take-all nature of presidential systems and the recent spate of studies that focus on the presidents' excessive use of decree powers, especially in Argentina under Menem, Brazil under Collor, and Peru under Fujimori.[5] The very useful contribution (and the rest of their collection) by Mainwaring and Shugart (1997) is a partial exception in that they take the president's legislative support into account in explaining the variation in presidential systems. Still, in focusing on the presidents' legislative powers, they have left aside a full analysis of the legislature itself.

---

[5] While the introduction to their volume on decree powers carefully sets up the limitations of decree powers, the focus of Carey and Shugart's (1998) interesting volume is the presidents' use of these powers. See the chapters by Ferreira Rubio and Goretti on Argentina, Power on Brazil, and Schmidt on Peru. Also see the chapters by Mainwaring (on Brazil) and Jones (on Argentina) in Mainwaring and Shugart (1997).

Towards a Model of Latin American Legislatures

Given this general perception of limited influence, if not irrelevance, a first goal of our book is to examine the ways in which the legislatures *do* involve themselves in the policy process. To this end, the chapters in the first part of the book develop a number of indicators of legislative activity. It is difficult, however, to fully grasp a legislature's role, since, as Cox and I argue in the epilogue, legislatures can assert themselves proactively or reactively. Further, it is often difficult to discern the legislature's policy influence, since, in addition to overtly proposing or killing legislation, it can discreetly lobby for favorable executive proposals or amend bills to its liking. In Huber's (1996) study of the French legislature, for example, he finds that presidents use restrictive amendment procedures to keep pre-arranged deals from falling apart. Thus it appears that the legislature is not amending bills, but in reality the negotiations took place before the legislation formally arrived at the legislature. In short, if a legislature is effective working behind the scenes, congressional floor activity may not be a good indicator of the legislature's influence.

This empirical problem is evident in spatial and delegation models of executive–legislative relations. For example, following Romer and Rosenthal's (1978) classic model, if the executive is the agenda-setter, he will propose the policy nearest her/his ideal point that the legislature will accept. The reverse is also true; when the legislature proposes a policy, it will choose in order to maximize its utility and still insure against an executive veto. In either case the second player would appear weak, since its best response is to accept the policy proposal. The player is not weak, however, since the proposal was based on the first player's anticipation of what the second player would accept.

On top of these methodological problems, studies of Latin American legislatures must face the stereotype that the primary policy role of these institutions has been either neglect and acquiescence or obstructionism. The methodological problems have not slowed rigorous analyses of the U.S. Congress, and they should not force us to shy away from such studies of this crucial democratic institution in consolidating democracies. Further, our studies show that the legislatures, at least today, do much more than obstruct executive policy; and even if the historical examples of intransigence were the legislatures' primary contribution to policy, we should ask why the legislatures are relegated to such a policy role.

The four chapters in the book's first part (and others) confront the methodological challenges and give evidence that these legislatures are highly relevant to policy outcomes. These studies look at how presidents win legislative support for their policy proposals and the degree to which the legislatures seek to initiate their own policies or modify those of the executive. In so doing, they provide evidence that Cox and I use in our epilogue to argue that, although none of the legislatures approaches the consistent policy strength of the U.S. Congress, none are perilously weak either. In terms of policy-making power, we classify these legislatures as generally "reactive," as opposed to "proactive." This implies that, while the legislatures rarely initiate legislation, they are often involved in negotiating over policy issues behind the scenes and vetoing or amending executive initiatives.

To support this general view, the authors in the first part discuss the methodological problem of hidden influence and also present several types of indicators of the legislatures' policy roles. Argentina is a case in point. Mustapic argues that the president must use numerous tools to deal with this "potentially recalcitrant" body. The presidents (Menem in particular) have been lucky to have at their disposal institutional powers and the ability to dole out ministerial and other jobs. She also argues, however, that part of the legislature's acquiescence has been due to the situation of economic and political crisis facing the nation.

In spite of these presidential powers, Mustapic argues that the legislature can and does disrupt the executive's policy priorities by simply failing to convene for sessions. She also shows that the legislature has been proactive enough to invite relatively frequent presidential vetoes.

Siavelis also notes the challenge of identifying quantifiable expressions of legislative influence in Chile. As a partial response he documents the high percentage of legislation that requires more than the legal minimum of steps (*trámites*) to pass through the legislature, as well as portrays data about legislative initiatives. He further argues that institutional structures (such as the legislature's ability to set the agenda and a ministry-level office of interbranch relations) and norms (such as the presidents' willingness to meet with Congressional leaders) have helped cement the legislature's influence.

There have been two primary and conflicting concerns about the Brazilian legislature. On the one hand, Mainwaring, Linz, and others who denigrate multipartism worry that Brazil's fractious legislature will be inefficient and likely to thwart attempts at reform. On the other hand, some studies, particularly those of the Collor years,[6] fear the Brazilan president's

---

[6] Cardoso, too, has issued numerous decrees.

ability to avoid legislative interference, thus chancing a move in the direction of "delegative democracy" (O'Donnell 1993).

While the second concern should not be dismissed, presidents have not been free to emit decrees without restriction. The most important legislation during Cardoso's term, including constitutional changes to allow for reelection of the president, pension reform, and administrative changes, have gone through the regular legislative process. It seems likely that other controversial legislation would also require legislative assent to avoid significant uprisings. Further, as Carey and Shugart (1998) note, the legislature is empowered to reject decrees, and recent changes have shut off the important loophole that allowed presidents to reissue decrees once their effectiveness formally ended.

In this vein, Amorim Neto's study focuses on the first issue, asking how Brazilian presidents gain legislative support in a legislature housing few of their co-partisans. He answers that particularly weak presidents, like Collor, have relied on decrees to avoid legislative roadblocks. Other presidents, however, have built support through the careful distribution of cabinet posts. He then shows a solid relation between a party's support for executive initiatives, that party's unity, and its representation in the cabinet.

Until very recently, the Mexican Congress has been the epitome of weakness. De la Garza's (1972) study well characterized most views of this institution. He found no significant policy role for the Mexican Congress and thus focused on its role in legitimating the regime. Casar's study here finds evidence that the long-languid legislature is undergoing profound changes. "The post-1997 Congress," she notes, "has already stopped and altered several important executive initiatives, affecting social security legislation, fiscal measures, and the peace accords in Chiapas." There is also quantitative evidence of the change, such as the dramatic rise in the rate of approval for bills sponsored by legislators.

Questions About Parliamentary Parties and Legislative Organization

Mayhew (1974) wrote, "If a group of planners sat down and tried to design a pair of American national assemblies with the goal of serving members' electoral needs year in and year out, they would be hard pressed to improve upon what exists" (p. 81). Studying the legislature's organization, then, is a reflection of the institution's locus of power. The power of committee chairmanships, for example, reflects the individualistic nature of the U.S. Congress. The legislative structure also has implications for the

9

representation of interests, the type of policy that may ultimately survive the process, and the legislature's ability to carefully scrutinize the executive branch. As such, the goal of Part III is to characterize the structure of the Latin American legislatures and explain why they do not follow the organizational path illuminated by the U.S. Congress. In explaining the issues that the chapters address, I will focus on three themes that are prominent in the American literature: procedural coalitions, committee systems, and floor voting patterns.

Procedural Coalitions Most legislative decisions are determined by majority rule. The basic question, therefore, is, Who joins the majority? Is the group stable or changing? Further, we might expect that "procedural coalitions" – those legislators who join to elect legislative leaders, approve voting rules, select staff, and dole out committee assignments, or generally organize the legislative business – may be quite different from those who form around particular policy initiatives.[7]

Models of the U.S. Congress explain how the majority party operates as a "cartel," monopolizing procedural advantages in the legislative process (Cox and McCubbins 1993; Aldrich 1995). These advantages unquestionably allow substantial influence in the content of legislation and the distribution of resources. This implies that we should expect that procedural coalitions also form in other countries – as appears to be the case in Europe (Doring 1995). Several of the studies in this volume therefore investigate how variance on the party structure or other variables affects the shape of the power structure in the Latin American legislature.

Nacif's careful look at the governing committee of the Mexican Congress best exemplifies this type of study. His chapter details how the Institutional Revolutionary Party (PRI) used its majority position to control the legislative process until the recent rise of the opposition. He also explains how these changes have affected the legislature's procedural coalition. Until a 1991 reform, the PRI leadership made decisions without much regard for other parties. However, since the reform, the parties have been able to negotiate for their share of committee posts, including chairs and other leadership positions.

The other chapters in Part III also follow this line of inquiry. Carey argues that the electoral alliances form procedural coalitions in Chile. He states,

[7] This definition follows Jones (1968) and Cox and McCubbins (1993).

"In conjunction with the traditional parties, they organize nominations for legislative elections, the legislative committee system, and floor voting."

In Argentina, Jones describes the Peronist or Justicialista Party (PJ), which held a complete or near majority as the prime mover in the legislature. He explains that the party designates its own and a chamber leader, who together operate with relative autonomy, given the high level of party discipline. A set of important resources available to the leaders, in turn, reinforces the party discipline.

Ames' chapter is largely a study of the lack of a procedural coalition in Brazil, in that party leaders are too weak to overcome dissension within their ranks. Samuels' view is that state delegations there play an important role in organizational and agenda issues. He presents evidence that, while partisanship determines the distribution of positions in committees generally, and in particular the joint budget committee, the committee structure privileges state delegations.

Committee Systems   Since membership on key committees is a highly valued political resource in the U.S. Congress, and control of committee seats is a key source of power for party leadership, studies of the committee system have contributed greatly to our understanding of the decision-making process in the legislature. The U.S. models emphasize the degree of autonomy of the committees from the party leadership (Cox and McCubbins 1993; Gilligan and Krehbeil 1990; Lowi 1979). Although their interpretations of similar data vary tremendously, this large body of literature has defined the way in which we think of personalistic and party politics. From these studies we have learned of the revolving doors in the iron triangle (Lowi 1979), the power of committee and subcommittee chairs (Jones 1968; Rohde 1991), and finally the reason why party leaders have some sway over rank-and-file members (Cox and McCubbins 1993).

Similar questions about committee systems in Latin American legislatures have not been asked. Some of the studies in this volume therefore make a first stab. Nacif's study, for example, looks specifically at the hierarchical nature of the committee structure in the Mexican Congress. Carey's study discusses the importance of seniority in Chile's lower house, and Londregan looks at the structure of voting in the labor committee of the Chilean Senate. Unlike the U.S. Congress, individual legislators are not the organizing powers of these legislatures. Still, these studies support Mayhew's contention about the way in which the committee structure reflects the goals of those empowered to shape the institution. In the

Mexican case, the committees further the goals of the majority party. Both Casar and Nacif also show that the PRI's loss of majority control, in turn, has brought about important changes in the composition and function of the committees. In Argentina, Mustapic argues that leaders use assignments to generate support, both within and among parties. Further, since reelection rates are low, the number of committee posts has grown to provide leaders more posts to offer to pliant legislators. In explaining the inordinate weight of the executive, it is telling that the executive has formal representation in the committee meetings. Jones furthers this line of inquiry. His study gives preliminary evidence of the power of the House President in Argentina, who in consultation with party leaders determines how to distribute committee assignments and leadership positions. He notes that these are important decisions since, as in the United States, some committees are much more valuable to legislators than others. The power structure is further evident in a leadership committee composed of the chamber president and vice presidents, along with party leaders, who set the legislative agenda and determine who will participate in debates. Next, as noted previously, Samuel's study of Brazil (in Part IV) suggests that the committees support state, not partisan, interests. In Chile, where reelection is more common, Carey reports that a seniority system is in place in the lower house. Moreover, there is a hierarchical relationship among committees, as all finance bills – even in the Senate, where the Concertación lacks a majority – must past through committees staffed by party leaders. Still, in spite of this organizational mechanism, Carey is careful to point out that committee leaders' power is limited in that their agendas are often overridden by the president. Londregan's study (also in Part IV) adds more to our knowledge of the Chilean committee system, with a focus on the Senate. Interestingly, he finds that while seniority is important, the parties, and not the individuals, hold the seats. As such, the membership is somewhat fluid – and the changes can have dramatic impacts on the outputs from the committees.

Floor Voting Coalitions Floor voting is the ultimate indicator of a party's behavior because it helps to identify a party's policy direction and coherence, policy coalitions, and the willingness of a party to work with the executive. Further, party unity, which results from a combination of disciplinary resources available to leaders and ideological coherence among legislators, can indicate the degree to which voters can think of parties as collectively responsible for a policy outcome. As such, the sources of party unity (or lack thereof) have been perennial themes in literature in both the American and comparative traditions. The undisciplined U.S. Congress is blamed for the high influence of special interests and general waste in the federal budget (c.f. Fiorina 1989; Lowi 1969). Parliamentary systems have generally done a better job at maintaining voting unity, due to the threat of early elections and the executive's use of cabinet posts to maintain support (Laver and Shepsle 1990; Laver and Schofield 1990). Bowler, Farrell, and Katz (1999), in the first text-length study of the subject, however, remind us of the faction-riddled Italian parliament. Contributors to their volume then discuss the factors that strain and support party unity as well as the effects of unity on interpartisan relations, the maintenance of coalitions, relations with party activists, formation of role of party unity, and other factors in a variety of European countries.

Due to its centrality to our understanding of the inner workings of a legislature, the patterns of floor voting are a focus of most of the studies in this book. Amorim Neto, for example, follows the literature on parliamentary democracies and argues that the Brazilian presidents (among others) have also used cabinet posts to gain legislative support. Ames also focuses on party unity in Brazil, testing a multivariate model. His model supports a theory about the role of reelection incentives, the importance of the party to a legislator's reelection, the pork barrel, and state politics in explaining whether legislators will stick with their parties. For Chile, Carey devises a unique indicator of legislative unity that takes into account the relative importance of a bill and absenteeism. He then uses this indicator to show that the Chilean parties generally revolve around the two primary coalitions. And finally, Weldon's chapter on Mexico (in Part IV) explains how power came to be concentrated in the presidency, which implied the loss of autonomy of individual legislators and the rise of strict party discipline.

Questions for the Policy Studies

As Birnbaum and Murray's (1987) study exemplifies, case studies of the policy process are very helpful in illustrating the dynamics of executive–legislative relations and highlighting the importance of the legislature's organization. The fourth part of the book seeks to provide a similar synthesis of these themes.

Several themes are common to these four studies: the role of the electoral system; the importance of party discipline; and the dominant, but not

13

supreme, role of the president. In discussing tax reform in Argentina, Eaton's chapter shows that legislators' regional ties, which are a function of the electoral system, generated opposition to the president's proposed plan. He concludes that, while the legislature's role is "reactive," most literature clearly underestimates its policy significance. Eaton's chapter also speaks to the themes of executive–legislative relations, as well as the importance of the legislature's organization. In particular, he illustrates how the president's loyalists in the legislature controlled the agenda to advantage Menem's policies, and how the Peronist (Justicialist) Party (PJ) used its procedural advantages to pass the reforms.

Samuel's study of Brazil focuses on the budget process, its reform, and legislators' efforts to procure pork-barrel resources. For Samuels, executive–legislative relations are less important, but legislator–governor relations and the committee structure play central roles. The governors, he explains, control many resources that are crucial to the political careers of the legislators. This has moved legislators to structure the committee system, which determines which interests are rewarded, to favor states over parties.

Londregan's study stands out somewhat from the others in that it focuses on the Labor Committee in the Chilean Senate and in particular on the role of the nonelected senators. As independents who are not generally interested in reselection, these senators are relatively free from electoral and party pressures, and, as a result, ideology drives their voting decisions. The study also highlights the importance of the committee system structure. Given that the senators do not hold their committee seats permanently, and given that the committees are quite small (just five people), any individual changes can determine policy outputs.

Finally, Weldon's study, as noted earlier, focuses on the budget process in Mexico. His more historical look first asks how, in light of the legislature's significant constitutional prerogatives, the president came to dominate the budget process. Power was not concentrated in the presidency until 1928, but the presidents did enjoy decree powers and procedural advantages that marginalized the legislature's participation. Once presidents had won "metaconstitutional powers," the legislature stopped blocking or amending the presidents' budgets, and the presidents therefore stopped using procedures that evaded the legislature.

Weldon's chapter also shows how the PRI's recent loss of its dominant position has interacted with the constitutional structure in affecting the committee structure and the budget process. For example, instead of over-

representation on committees and control of all chairs, the new system allocates chairs proportionally to parties and ended the excessive power of chairs over the agenda (including whether a meeting would be held) and the chair's extra vote in the case of ties. Finally, Weldon's chapter is very useful in detailing the importance of technical issues that are often the focus of studies about the U.S. Congress. For example, he explains how parliamentary rules in Mexico limit the ability of legislators to suggest amendments. In addition, he describes two interesting controversies about the budget stemming from obscurity in the constitution. Not only does the constitution fail to specify the budget's "reversion point" (i.e., the amount that would be spent in the absence of a budget), but it also leaves as dubious the president's ability to veto the budget legislation, since the budget bill is technically not a law (since it does not go through the Senate).

Assumptions and/or Independent Variables: Goals, Strategies, Parties, and Power

A second broad goal of this book is to move toward a general model of legislative politics and test the impact of several variables on legislative politics. Models purporting to explain congressional politics in the United States rely on several implicit and explicit assumptions regarding (a) legislator goals, (b) strategies to obtain those goals (which are based on the electoral system), (c) the distinctive party configuration, and (d) the given constitutional balance of power. A general model cannot make the same assumptions, even with regard to the most basic assumption about U.S. legislators' drive for reelection.

Mayhew's (1974) description of the "electoral connection" is perhaps the most straightforward statement of how ambitions determine legislative behavior. That model, and its extensions by numerous other scholars, explains the impact of the legislators' goal of reelection and their strategies to attain it. Mayhew uses the model to explain how legislators build the legislative machinery in "single-minded" pursuit of their goal: reelection. Fiorina (1989) uses the model in developing a theory to explain the growth of the bureaucracy; Lowi (1969, 1979) uses it to explain why legislators seek seniority and expertise in committees; and Aldrich (1995), Cox and McCubbins (1993), and Rohde (1991) use it to explain the growth and sustenance of political parties. Each of these authors points out that while legislators may have other important goals, they assume that the

15

proximate goal is fulfilling their static ambition. That is, in order to fulfill any other goal, legislators must first win reelection.

The goal of reelection is the first, and for many the most important, implicit assumption in these models. The assumption of "static ambition" (Schlesinger 1991) is supported by statistics that show an extremely high rate of reelection to the U.S. Congress. But, as the case studies detail, rates of reelection are relatively low across our Latin American cases. In our cases they run the gamut, from the prohibition of immediate reelection in Mexico to a small minority returning to their seats in Argentina to Brazil, where 70% of the legislators seek reelection but many fail, and to Chile, where a large majority seek and win reelection. This implies that we cannot employ the assumption of reelection – or static ambition – across all cases. Instead, our general model must consider the implications of following other career paths, such as through the state or federal bureaucracy, higher elected jobs, or a return to private business.[8]

The second basic assumption in the U.S. model regards the strategies for fulfilling reelection goals. Since they are dealing with just the U.S. case, U.S. scholars are safe in taking for granted the electoral system. That is, they implicitly assume that legislators compete under plurality rule in single-member districts. Further, if there is any internal competition, it is only in primaries (and there, incumbents are generally free from strong challengers). In addition, these authors rightly assume that laws or party rules place no important restrictions on a candidate's nomination. These assumptions lead the studies to focus on how candidates work to gain a plurality of their district's votes and are generally unconcerned with the candidate nomination process or intraparty competition.

As in the case of static ambition, the strategy assumptions are inapplicable in a comparative study. Some candidates must compete against their co-partisans during general elections, others must win the favor of party leaders to win a spot on the ballot, and others who sit atop their party's proportional representation list need only worry that their party wins a small fraction of the vote. Electoral and party rules, then, become independent variables in a comparative study of campaigning strategies. Further, if legislators are uninterested in reelection, then although the general model of ambition theory should consider how they won election

---

[8] Career paths of Mexican politicians have received the most academic attention. See Smith (1979) and Camp (1983) for the most detailed studies. On Brazil, see Samuels (this volume and 1998).

in the first place, the theory must also consider strategies for fulfilling other goals, such as loyalty to a governor in return for access to the state bureaucracy.

A third background assumption in U.S. models is that there are two stable political parties. This assumption is most crucial to Cox and McCubbins (1993), who assume that the majority party monopolizes the decision-making structure of the legislature to serve its own interests. While these same incentives to form a majority party (as explained by Aldrich [1995] and Cox and McCubbins [1993]) may exist universally, the partisan structure of other countries varies tremendously.

The fourth assumption is that presidents and legislators operate under the U.S. Constitution. That is, the president can only veto a bill in its entirety, the legislature can override a presidential veto by a two-thirds vote of both houses, the president cannot officially initiate legislation, the legislature can amend the budget and other bills without restriction, and so on. This assumption of course fails in a comparative context.

In sum, models of the U.S. Congress based on the ambitions of the legislators implicitly interact a large number of variables. A similar comparative model, therefore, must identify these variables and account for the interactions. A multivariate model would first differentiate the U.S. and most Latin American legislators based on their static or progressive ambition. A full model could also divide the legislators according to their motivation for entering the legislature (power, prestige, or policy concerns) and where their ambition might lead them (state or federal elected political careers, state or federal appointed positions, private business, etc.). The model would then have to account for different numbers of parties, the relationship of the parties to the executive, and the internal unity of those parties. Also, different constitutional arrangements that affect the relative power of the legislatures would have to be quantified. Finally, after specifying each of the variables, the model would have to allow for interactions among multiple combinations of the variables. For example, while the electoral system may well have an independent impact, its impact is surely mediated by the party and constitutional systems.

Specifying these independent variables and considering their interactions is an important goal of this book. We also seek to specify the dependent variable, the legislatures' policy role, by looking at executive–legislative relations and the policy process. These variables, however, do not lend themselves to cross-national multivariate quantitative models, and instead point to the need for careful, theoretically motivated case studies. For this reason, as opposed to descriptive histories, the following chapters examine the implications of different combinations of the variables that we have identified on key aspects of legislative politics. In investigating different pieces of this model, our contributors show that the Latin American legislators (a) are not homogeneous reelection seekers, (b) follow different strategies into office, (c) are restrained by different constitutional arrangements, and (d) operate within vastly different party alignments. As a result, the Latin American legislatures do not look or act like the U.S. Congress. I take up this discussion in the conclusion, borrowing the wealth of data provided in the following chapters to compare the countries along these various dimensions and to consider the effects that our authors attribute to them. Then, in the epilogue, I join Gary W. Cox in exploring a general typology of legislatures based on the information from the case studies. In a further move towards identifying the dependent variable, we propose that the U.S. Congress belongs at one end of a continuum labeled "proactive," while the Latin American legislatures belong closer to the other end, labeled "reactive." This is only a first step towards a general model, however, since, as is clear in the case studies, there is a great deal of variability among countries, and even across time in a single country.

Summary

In spite of their vital democratic functions, Latin American legislatures have escaped careful scrutiny. To begin to rectify this oversight, the assembled authors adapt pieces of the Mayhewian model of the U.S. Congress (and its extensions) to these cases. The chapters in this volume all apply the most basic assumption in these models, that legislators' ambitions drive their behavior. However, assumptions about the specific goals that legislators hope to attain, and how they might attain them, become independent variables in a comparative model. Even the foremost explicit assumption in the U.S. model – legislators' proximate goal of reelection – is not directly applicable. As a model based on politicians' ambitions would predict, the result of different values on these variables results in legislatures with very different functions and organizational forms.

In this book we cannot claim to develop a full model, but we do investigate conjunctions of variables affecting legislative structure and behavior. Since we cannot start to judge the impact of any independent variable without a notion of the final product, much of our effort is spent describing the Latin American legislatures and evaluating their political roles. The parts of this book are set up to identify three specific features of the legislatures, namely, their roles and relationships with the president, their internal organizational structures and their policy roles. The chapters go much further, however, in that they also posit causal relations tying the outcomes that they describe with reelection drives, the electoral and party systems, constitutional prerogatives, and other variables. Thus, in addition to offering important insight into the inner workings of the particular cases, each chapter provides an example of how to adapt and apply U.S.-style models to a comparative context. Together the chapters provide much of the initial analysis necessary for building a comparative theory of legislatures in presidential regimes within a rational choice framework, and, as such, this volume should give directions for further research on the structure and function of the representative institutions in Latin America's new and consolidating democracies.

PART I

Executive–Legislative Relations

2

Oscillating Relations: President and Congress in Argentina

ANA MARÍA MUSTAPIC*

This chapter analyzes executive–legislative relations in Argentina from the inauguration of democracy in 1983 through 1995, when Carlos S. Menem finished his first term in office. We will enter into this theme by investigating the principal risk to executive–legislative relations in presidential regimes: institutional paralysis.

Juan Linz and other critics of presidentialism have called attention to the risks of institutional paralysis, which they argue originate from the principle of division of powers and fixed electoral calendars. These factors, therefore, are inherent in the institutional structure of presidentialism. In effect, the principle of division of powers, which originates from the independent election of the executive and the legislative branches, generates autonomous powers armed with mutual vetoes. On top of this, the rigidity that stems from fixed electoral periods prevents a change of leadership, even during crisis situations, as well as the forced retirement of popular leaders. This argument leads to important questions about the two postdictatorship Argentine presidencies, both of which contained the seeds propitious for generating institutional paralysis. On the one hand, President Alfonsín faced a divided government and President Menem lacked an absolute majority in the Chamber of Deputies.[1] On the other hand, the country faced crisis situations including military rebellions and hyperinflation. Nevertheless, Argentina has not experienced harmful episodes of gridlock.

* I thank Scott Morgenstern, Natalia Ferretti, Juan Carlos Torre, and the anonymous reviewers for their very helpful suggestions and comments. I also thank the Antorchas Foundation for financing that facilitated my participation in the conference that gave rise to this project.
[1] An absolute majority in the chambers is important because that is the quorum required for sessions to begin.

23

These facts suggest that the critique of Linz and his followers requires a more careful specification of the conditions necessary to engender gridlock.[2] First, independent election of the two branches should not generate gridlock where presidents can count on a reliable majority in the Congress. I will therefore argue in the following that the risks of immobilism become active only when factors external to the institutional design of presidentialism intervene. In particular, I will stress the importance of electoral results and incentive structures that favor party discipline. Second, the risks that the fixed mandate creates are relieved if the executive has the capacity to generate the necessary parliamentary support. This capacity relies not only on the personal qualities of the leader, but also on two other factors that influence executive–legislative relations: access to institutional powers and partisan resources that can help the president discipline legislators.

The "hyperpresidentialist" reputation of the Argentine political regime led many analysts to emphasize the formidable institutional resources of the president. By issuing, for instance, the so-called *decretos de necesidad y urgencia* (decrees of necessity of urgency), the president can avoid gridlock. From this perspective, the distribution of power is strongly inclined in favor of the executive, leaving the Congress in a subordinate role. In this chapter I want to highlight the incidence of other factors. My thesis is that factors other than just the strong institutional powers have allowed the two postdictatorship presidents in Argentina (in particular Menem) to avoid confrontation with the legislature. In particular, I argue that the partisan resources as well as leadership resources provided by the crisis situations have also played vital roles in checking the level of interbranch conflict. When these last factors count, the Congress is not merely a passive actor, as its possible actions are unavoidable in working to avoid gridlock.

In order to develop this thesis, this chapter proceeds as follows: In the first section, I set the stage by arguing that the potential for gridlock has been high in Argentina. This leads to my primary puzzle about why presidents have been able to avoid serious confrontations with the legislature. This answer takes two parts. First I discuss the president's vast institutional powers that have helped him frequently to avoid or overcome a potentially recalcitrant legislature. Then I ask why the president has been able to

---

[2] For a reassessment of Linz´s conclusion about the risks of presidential systems and the mechanisms that mitigate gridlock, see Morgenstern and Domingo (1997).

count on continuous support in the legislature or, from the legislature's point of view, what motivates legislators to generally refrain from defection. The support of the president, I argue, has three sources: party payoffs in terms of leadership and legislative posts; Argentina's bipartisan system; and crisis situations. In the third section I analyze the manner in which these factors influence executive–legislative relations. The fourth and final section, then, concludes.

The Framework: A Potential for Gridlock

At least three factors can generate a gridlock situation. The first is a distribution of institutional power that does not assure the president the majority necessary to govern, and the second is the effects of decentralization in the legislative process and certain procedural mechanisms that create obstacles to decision making. Lastly, decentralized organization of political parties can also present important challenges to leadership by the president.

Divided Government

The fear of gridlock has been on the agenda since the very return to democracy of Argentina in 1983, because electoral results led to problematic configurations of power. Indeed, the two presidencies between 1983 and 1995, that of Raúl R. Alfonsín (1983–1989) and that of Carlos S. Menem (1989–1995) did not have an absolute majority in one of the two chambers of Congress. The distribution of institutional power under the presidency of the radical R. Alfonsín fits the definition of a divided government. The Senate was in the hands of the main opposition force, the Partido Justicialista (PJ), and after the legislative elections of 1987 he also lost his absolute majority in the Chamber of Deputies. Menem's first government had no absolute majority in the Chamber of Deputies either. Only after 1995, when Menem was reelected thanks to the constitutional amendments of 1994, did he have an absolute majority of Justicialist legislators in the two chambers. Tables 2.1 and 2.2 present the makeup of the chambers by political party and legislative period.

Veto Gates, Institutional Mechanisms

In addition to the lack of a majority, other institutional characteristics have made gridlock a potential threat: first are the several mechanisms linked

Table 2.1. *Makeup of the Chamber of Deputies by period and political party.*

	Alfonsín's Presidency			Menem's Presidency		
	1983–1985	1985–1987	1987–1989	1989–1991	1991–1993	1993–1995
UCR	129 (50.8)	129 (50.8)	113 (44.5)	90 (35.4)	84 (32.7)	83 (32.3)
PJ	111 (43.7)	101 (39.8)	103 (40.5)	121 (47.7)	116 (45.0)	126 (49.0)
Others	14 (5.5)	24 (9.4)	38 (15)	43 (16.9)	57 (22.2)	48 (18.7)

Table 2.2. *Makeup of Chamber of Senators by period and political party.*

	Alfonsín's Presidency		Menem's Presidency	
	1983–1986	1986–1989	1989–1992	1992–1995
UCR	18 (39%)	18 (39%)	18 (39%)	11 (23%)
PJ	22 (48%)	22 (48%)	22 (48%)	30 (63%)
Others	6 (13%)	6 (13%)	6 (13%)	7 (15%)

to the legislative process that can impede decision making. One of these devices is the refusal by the legislators to provide a quorum. For sessions to begin there must be an absolute majority of legislators present, and their deliberate absence therefore brings down the session. Sometimes, it is a weapon used by the opposition, especially when the government has no absolute majority. On other occasions, it is the weapon of the governing party legislators to air their disagreement. Although it is not possible to discriminate among the sessions that failed due to deliberate absences and those that failed for other reasons, in the period 1983–1995, 26.5% of the sessions scheduled by the Chamber of Deputies did not take place. Disaggregated by presidencies, 65 sessions failed during the government of Alfonsin and 130 between 1989 and 1995.[3] Table 2.3 provides this data on annual bases.

Second, the legislative process in the Argentine Congress, as in the United States, has a decentralized structure. In other words, its work is organized through standing committees. The routine passage of bills, once they have been presented in the office of the secretary of the chambers,

[3] For the period 1983–1993, see Schinelli (1996).

Table 2.3. *Canceled sessions due to a lack of quorum in the Chamber of Deputies (1983–1995).*

Year	# Canceled	Year	# Canceled
1983	–	1990	23
1984	5	1991	27
1985	10	1992	18
1986	9	1993	17
1987	12	1994	14
1988	25	1995	19
1989	16	**TOTAL**	195

Source: N.G. Molinelli, V. Palanza, and G. Sin, 1999. *Congreso, Presidencia y Justicia en Argentina*. Buenos Aires: CEDI – Temas.

begins with referral to one or more committees. As a result, there are multiple potential veto gates for presidential legislation.

Party's Decentralized Organization

Low party cohesion and the potential discipline problems that this entails are a third factor that might foster institutional paralysis. The organizational structures of the two main Argentinean parties, the UCR and the PJ, increase the possibility of observing such an outcome.

Both parties have decentralized organizations and democratic rules of competition for the election of their authorities and candidates. The decentralized structure arose in response to constitutional provisions that stipulate that each of the provinces is a plurinominal district. The parties reproduce these divisions, leading to two great authority structures: one national and the other provincial. In turn, the provincial organization of the parties reproduces the electoral units in the different provinces – tied to the provincial electoral laws – each one led by its authorities. Thus, both parties exhibit internal power fragmentation, which is strengthened by the fact that neither the UCR nor the PJ are ideological parties in the European style.

Where the nomination of the main authorities and candidates is concerned, primaries are held both in the UCR and the PJ.[4] In the case of the

---

[4] For more details, see the chapter by Mark Jones in this volume.

UCR, they are closed primaries with the participation of only affiliated members. In the PJ, however, for the nomination of candidates, apart from closed primaries, various district organizations have adopted the system of open primaries.[5] In addition, both parties have clauses in their rules – albeit with a 25% barrier – that grant representation to minorities in both the party authority structure and in the makeup of the list of candidates. As a result of these organizational characteristics and rules on internal competition, the national leadership of both parties is invariably supported by a coalition of regional leaders, on whom the balance of power in the organization depends; at the same time, regional leaders depend on their own regional coalitions. The mechanisms of nomination control are thus decentralized, and they ultimately rest in the hands of those in a position to mobilize members and sympathizers.[6] As a consequence, those politicians who succeed in obtaining a popular election post are also accountable to the latter.

Within this framework, even legislators from the president's own party have several important reasons to consider breaking with their party leadership or president. First, few are reelected – the reelection rate for lower house members oscillates between 15 and 29%[7] – and thus legislators should be relatively unconcerned with the president's ability to thwart their electoral goals. Second, the frequent internal party realignments, especially around electoral periods, imply that legislators' political careers are not tied to any particular leader. Third, as noted previously and as Eaton's chapter in this volume makes clear, regional concerns sometimes clash with national policy, and thus legislators must weigh presidential loyalty

[5] The changes in the rules on internal competition in the PJ came into effect beginning in 1987, with the triumph of the "renovating" current, whose aims included the democratization of the party.

[6] On many occasions internal elections, though called, do not materialize. This happens when the leaders reach an agreement and end up presenting a single list of candidates. The monetary cost and organizational effort implied by calling elections is an important disincentive. Even when there is an agreement, the place of the candidates on the list is also a function, though not exclusively, of the weight of the different leaders as regards their ability to mobilize affiliates. In some provinces, the PJ has tried to resolve the problem of internal competition by modifying the provincial electoral laws and by adopting the Uruguayan system of lists. This allows a party (list) to present different sublists of candidates. The votes for the sublists are summed with others in the party to to determine, firstly, the number of candidates that the party obtained. To assign the positions, unless there is only one, they are distributed in proportion to the votes obtained by the sublists. With this system, intraparty competition is resolved in the interparty electoral arena.

[7] Saiegh (1997a).

28

versus regional influences when voting. Fourth, when presidents for whatever reason deviate from the main course of their policies, they at least face vocal opposition by party loyalists. Thus, ideological divides are a final reason why we would expect legislators to oppose a president's policy initiatives.

Avoiding Gridlock

We have underscored the fact that no outstanding gridlock has occurred in Argentinean executive–legislative relations, despite the numerous circumstances that would have led us to expect otherwise. During the Alfonsín administration, such conflictual laws as the Beagle Treaty – which put an end to the border dispute that took Argentina to the brink of war with Chile in 1978 – and the laws of *obediencia debida* and *punto final* associated with the trial against the military's violation of human rights were passed. The bill declaring the need for constitutional reform and most of the state reform policies promoted by Menem was also passed into law, despite its obvious departure from traditional Peronist ideology. Thus, executives have shown an ability to avoid gridlock. In the next section, we focus on three resources that allowed Alfonsín and Menem to avoid gridlock: institutional power, partisan resources, and crisis situations.

A Strong Executive Veto Power and "Necessity and Urgency Decrees"

A primary reason that Argentina, especially under Menem, has avoided gridlock is that their presidents (at least Menem) have been able to use the powers of his office effectively to combat legislative opposition (if not simply for convenience). The most important of the powers have been decrees of necessity and urgency (DNUs) and the item veto.

DNUs are an expedient tool that the president can employ to influence policy outcomes and avoid the legislature. These decrees are regulations dictated by the executive through which decisions are made that normally can only be taken through an act passed by Congress. The 1853 Constitution did not authorize them because the only exceptional measures that it recognized, the state of emergency and federal intervention, were designed to face the main threat visible at the time: resistance by provincial powers. In any case, if serious situations arose that were not contemplated by the Constitution, the presidents were supposed to have recourse to mechanisms that are constitutionally questionable only in exceptional circumstances.

It is plausible to suppose – taking into account the agitated political history of Argentina – that exceptional circumstances did arise on 25 occasions in 130 years. This is the number of decrees of necessity and urgency counted for the period 1853–1983 by Ferreria Rubio and Matteo Goretti in their work.[8] The ten DNUs signed by president Alfonsín between 1983 and December 1989 could, but with reservations, be considered to have been in the context of serious emergencies. Meanwhile, the 166 DNUs signed by president Menem highlighted a leaning toward an autocratic government strategy.[9] To enforce it he had the support of the Supreme Court, which was opportunely "packed" through irregular procedures. In a ruling adopted in 1990, the Supreme Court issued its doctrine on the matter: The decrees of necessity and urgency are valid as long as they are dictated in response to situations of extreme gravity that endanger the continuity of the state or imply social breakdown.[10] This ambiguous wording opens the way to all sorts of interpretations and therefore to presidential discretion.

The strategic advantages of DNUs are obvious. The president dictates a decree, and if legislators react with an act repealing it, the president can veto their decision.[11] He only needs, for example, the support of one-third of the senators to impose his will over that of the rest of Congress. The question that immediately springs to mind is, if the PJ almost had a majority in Congress, why did the president use these decrees so often? The first answer concerns expectations of resistance by the president's own legislators against the policies if they (the policies) were subjected to routine legislative procedure. However, among these numerous decrees there were many, such as, for example, the television transmission of soccer games or the donation of asphalt cement to Bolivia, that should not have

---

[8] Delia Ferreria Rubio and Matteo Goretti (1996, 1998).

[9] In fact, Ferreira Rubio and Goretti counted 336 decrees in all, 166 recognized as such by the executive itself and 170 not recognized but which the authors, after careful analysis, feel should be considered decrees of necessity and urgency. Since the criteria used to include them could give rise to controversy, we preferred to consider those recognized by the executive, which is in itself a more than significant figure. Nevertheless, I agree with the authors that it is insufficient to rely on the executive's discretion to classify the decrees. Our analysis therefore assumes minimum values for this mechanism.

[10] The Case of Luis Peralta versus the State, the Ministry of Economics and the Central Bank. CSJN, 27/12/1990.

[11] In fact, this did happen. See Ferreria Rubio and Goretti (1996).

Table 2.4. *Presidential vetoes.*

Initiative	Alfonsín	Menem
Executive	1 (2.0%)	30 (27.5%)
Congress	48 (98.0%)	79 (72.5%)
Total vetoes	49 (100%)	109 (100%)

caused major conflict. This is what leads to the label of an autocratic style of government.

In sum, the decrees of necessity and urgency clearly avoid the legislature's participation and thus help eliminate gridlock. The costs of forming a parliamentary coalition to revise the presidential decision are extremely high, because it is very difficult to generate enough support for an override.[12] Moreover, on many occasions the decrees lead to irreversible situations about which legislators can do nothing. The president thus can govern with the disciplined behavior of only a minority of his own party. Recurring to decrees of need and urgency reveals that the president's leadership over Congress is weak, especially when the intention is to introduce innovative policies as Menem did. But, at the same time, he is sufficiently strong to prevent the formation of an opposition coalition in the parliament.

A second presidential tool that helps to avoid gridlock is the item veto. In Argentina the president has two kinds of veto, a total veto and an item veto. The latter, not explicitly recognized in the Constitution until its reform in 1994 but established in practice, authorizes the promulgation of an act without the vetoed sections.[13] When comparing the total number of vetoes, the first thing to note is the major difference that can be seen between Alfonsín's government and Menem's.[14] President Alfonsín vetoed 48 acts (7.59% of the total); Menem did so on 109 (12%) occasions. This difference between the administrations is also outstanding if vetoed acts are broken down by initiative. Data on presidential vetoes are summarized in Table 2.4.

[12] A special majority of two-thirds.
[13] The president does not have to veto an entire article; he may veto only part. This form of the partial veto was called by one deputy a "particle veto" (Interview with UCR Deputy, Raúl Baglini).
[14] This section is based on Mustapic and Ferretti (1995).

The most revealing figure in the table is the greater number of vetoes of initiatives emanating from the executive itself by Menem's government. In comparative terms, it shows that there have been more disagreements between the president and the positions adopted by his party in Congress. Let us look more closely at this question.

All of the vetoes of executive initiatives were item vetoes. The use of the item veto basically means that the executive, for whatever reason, did not manage to bring the process of negotiation to a satisfactory conclusion in Congress. In the case of Menem, many of these acts have been linked to structural reform policies, such as, for example, the privatization of state gas, electricity, and oil (YPF) companies and the retirement pensions system. On some aspects of bills the legislators acted autonomously and the president, in turn, using the item veto, refused authorization for part of what had been negotiated in Congress. The item veto is a most useful means to further the executive's goals when the president lacks a majority in the legislature and is therefore forced to negotiate with other parties. The possibility of the item veto thus gives the executive a mechanism to preserve, albeit in a diminished capacity by the intervention of Congress, its own initiative. It is, however, a powerful tool that tips the executive–legislative balance toward the former. President Menem was forced to use this power more often than president Alfonsín.

Partisan Resources

Presidents cannot make permanent decisions through decrees of necessity and urgency. Legal requisites, for example, mandate that they inform Congress about their decisions. This is where party discipline becomes relevant. Argentine academics and journalists largely agree that the political parties behave in a highly disciplined way. The work by Mark Jones on roll-call votes, the first to study them, confirms this impression: The level of discipline shown by Argentine political parties is high.[15] The numbers on this point are convincing but not conclusive. Since political parties are internally heterogeneous, one key question that must also be examined, especially where the party of government is concerned, is the ease or difficulty with which the president, as party leader, may obtain disciplined behavior from his legislators. Despite the obvious advantages it confers on the executive, the use of item vetoes is also evidence of unyielding con-

[15] See the chapter by Mark Jones in this volume.

gressional behavior. In this section we pursue a twofold objective. First, we use three indicators – voting behavior in committees, presidential vetoes, and veto overrides – to show that the executive has found it difficult to discipline legislators, especially during the Menem administration. Second, notwithstanding the fact that discipline is a troublesome topic, we will analyze two control mechanisms that parties use to maintain unity: the distribution of selective incentives and partisan identity.

Discipline as a Problem Aside from the journalistic coverage of executive–legislative relations, we can analyze voting patterns in the committees to identify some signs of conflict between the two branches. Before embarking on this analysis, it is important to note two caveats. First, analyses of voting patterns must underestimate the true level of conflict since they cannot differentiate legislators' strategic absences that imply opposition from excused absences that do not imply opposition. Second, the analysis deals only with bills that legislators vote on, and thus many that would otherwise have generated significant dissent are left off the agenda. Thus, the analysis that follows underestimates the level of executive–legislative conflict.

There are few floor votes in the legislature, but the committee reports offer a very clear (though still limited) window into party voting patterns. It is well known that the more restricted world of the committee favors agreements and that decisions taken by consensus are more easily abided. Indeed, the predisposition toward agreement is the ruling trend predominating in the committees.[16] Once the bill has been dealt with in committee, the body gives its opinion in reports.

Those cases in which the members of the committee belonging to one party sign different reports or express their disagreement on the majority report may be considered examples of indiscipline. The information that we have is as follows. Of the 588 committee reports on executive initiatives during the government of Alfonsín, only on 5 (0.85%) occasions did legislators from his party not vote with the majority; the PJ did so 7 (1.19%) times. During Menem's presidency, with votes on 709 reports, the PJ did not respect the party line 34 (4.79%) times and the UCR, 15 (2.11%). Although votes in committees are a weak indicator because our information concerns only reports on bills that were passed – these

---

[16] Interviews with different parliamentary advisors confirm that the first thing sought when a bill is introduced is a decision "by consensus" among the members of the committee.

Table 2.5. *Vetoes of initiatives presented by members of Congress, by political party.*

Legislative Initiative	Alfonsín	Menem
Only opposition parties	27 (PJ, others 60%)	25 (UCR, others 35%)
Only president's party	10 (UCR, 22%)	22 (PJ, 31%)
Government party and others	8 (UCR, others 18%)	25 (PJ, others 35%)

divisions did not affect policy outcomes – in comparative terms it is useful, because it offers a first indicator of the UCR's greater cohesion as a governing party.

Regarding presidential vetoes of Congressional initiatives, Table 2.5 presents legislators' initiatives broken down into bills presented by opposition legislators, by legislators from the president's party, and, finally, by joint bills with the participation of legislators of the ruling party.[17]

Table 2.5 makes it obvious that president Alfonsín used the greatest percentage of vetoes, 60%, as a mechanism to control opposition proposals. President Menem, for his part, used an almost equal proportion of vetoes for opposition initiatives, 35%, and for those of his party, 31%. Moreover, he vetoed more acts in which the PJ was involved. In effect, if we add the 31% of vetoed proposals that PJ legislators presented alone to the 35% of vetoes in the case of initiatives that PJ legislators presented jointly with other parties, the figure reaches 66% as compared to 40% (22% plus 18%) for Alfonsín. Therefore, his veto was used mainly to control initiatives in which legislators from his own party participated.

The number of veto overrides is another indicator of the difficulties faced in achieving party cohesion around the presidential leadership. In this sense, it must be made clear that for an override to be successful, a special majority of two-thirds of the members present in both chambers must be reached.[18] Therefore, the challenge is to overcome two barriers: the numerical one and that of party discipline. It is no surprise that between 1862 and 1985 there were only 12 overrides.[19] Under the

[17] This table does not include the acts that brought together more than one bill presented by different legislators – in both presidencies they account for 6% of all of the initiatives vetoed (three and five acts, respectively) – nor those of the Bicameral Committee, a category valid only for the Menem government, with 3% (two acts).

[18] It must be remembered that sessions begin with a quorum requirement equal to one-half plus one of the members in the chambers.

[19] Guillermo Molinelli (1986).

Table 2.6. *Number of positions and members on the front benches of the blocks.*

Year	UCR		PJ	
	Positions	Members	Positions	Members
1984	5	14	8	10
1987	5	15	16	24
1988	8	13	22	24
1989	8	13	24	32
1990	11	16	14	14
1992	13	13	16	16
1993	8	13	17	17
1994	8	16	19	19
1995	8	16	18	18

government of Alfonsín, Congress overrode only one veto whereas during Menem's first presidential term, Congress overrode 11 vetoes. Once again, here we can see the greater differences between President Menem and his party and Congress. The PJ found it more difficult to reconcile itself with the presidential point of view.

Distribution of Selective Incentives Given that discipline is not at all guaranteed, parties resort to the distribution of selective incentives as a mechanism to rebuild party unity. The party's power fragmentation is evident in the composition of the front benches of the parliamentary parties. Here the effort made by parties to reach a balance between different party lines becomes obvious. This search for equilibrium is reflected in the elastic organization of the parliamentary party leadership. Indeed, to overcome problematic situations, the parliamentary parties will take the drastic measure of creating new positions, multiplying, for example, the number of vice presidents, creating offices, designating heads and deputies, and so on. In Table 2.6 we show this phenomenon, which is more common in the PJ.

The appointment of authorities in the committees is also another balancing act to ensure the cohesion of the party. The importance to the parties of being able to distribute selective incentives is evident in the increase in the number of committees, as can be seen in Table 2.7.

Table 2.7. *Number of standing committees by chamber.*

Year	Chamber of Deputies	Year	Chamber of Senators
1983–1985	26	1983–1986	29
1985–1987	28		
1987–1990	31	1987–1991	32
1991–1992	35	1992–1995	40
1993–1995	39		

Bearing in mind the low reelection rate of legislators, the increase in the number of committees is hardly in response to the need to generate greater "expertise" and professionalization. Although this can be seen in some committees, and we will come to this shortly, the criteria governing their composition mainly responds to the need to satisfy the demands of the different party lines by distributing the clientelistic resources that Congress has available. At the same time, it responds to the governing party's need to garner support from other parties when it is not backed by a majority. Committee chairs are one of the most visible means of exchange among parties. The Movimiento Popular Neuquino, for instance, has held the Senate's Energy Committee chair since 1988, even though it only musters two Senate and two lower chamber seats.[20]

The parliamentary party leader is charged with the handling of these resources, which allows him some degree of control over the legislators.[21] However, the party leader's ability to control legislators through selective incentives is somewhat constrained in the first place by the degree of consensus that he can achieve among his partisans in the chamber. In the second place, it is subjected to acceptance by the president of the chamber. This reference to the parliamentary party leader allows us to comment on his role in executive–legislative relations. When his party is in office, the parliamentary party leader becomes extremely important because one of his main functions is to act as a link between the executive and his party in Congress. A clear indication of this function is provided by his partic-

[20] On the topic of provincial parties in Congress, see Sin and Palanza (1997).
[21] Formally, the makeup of legislative committees is a prerogative of the House chairman, but he follows the instructions of parliamentary party leaders. He intervenes actively only when deciding the distribution of chairs per party – according to chamber rules chairs are distributed proportionally among parties – and in case of conflict.

ipation in weekly cabinet meetings.[22] He plays an active role since, by definition, he must promote the president's initiatives. On the one hand, he must convince his legislators; on the other, he must report on the position of the legislators to the cabinet and, finally, he must negotiate with leaders of the other parties. Here it should be remembered that the party leaders plus the House chairman make up the Legislative Works Committee that is tasked with setting the parliamentary agenda. Although as an implicit rule priority is given to the executive's initiatives, when there is no absolute majority in the House negotiations are more difficult and the success of moves is not always guaranteed.[23] Unlike the situation that Cox and McCubbins describe, where U.S. legislative leaders can sometimes stay away from conflictive interbranch issues, in the Argentine case the leaders have to face conflicts because they are the president's negotiators.[24] This is the extra leadership demanded by the position, a task not without its tension and frustration.

Equally important are the chairmen of committees that are key to the working of the government. These include the Budget and Treasury Committee. This committee is one of the few that does not observe the general rules on duration in the position and "expertise." Between 1983 and 1995 we find a nucleus of legislators from both the UCR and the PJ who have served on it either continuously or intermittently.[25] In addition, its members include former provincial economy ministers. Apart from dealing with the budget, fiscal policy, and any bill involving spending, the committee has played a central role in decisions linked to the reform of the state promoted by Menem. This committee, and especially its chairman, interacts with officials from the executive and especially with the Economics Ministry on a daily basis.[26]

Both the parliamentary party leader and the chairmen of the most important committees lead us to the "president's men" in Congress. This does not mean that they are necessarily part of his closest circle. Under

[22] This practice was introduced by president Menem. The UCR, while in opposition, has decided to include block leaders in party directorship meetings (Interview with national Congressman Federico Storani, UCR Parliamentary Party Leader).
[23] Interview with national Congressman Federico Storani, UCR's Parliamentary Party Leader.
[24] Cox and McCubbins (1993).
[25] One of the few veterans in Congress is O. Lamberto, PJ Deputy and member of the committee for thirteen years and its chairman since 1990.
[26] Interview with Oscar Lamberto, PJ National Congressman.

Alfonsín's government, César Jaroslavsky, who was the party leader in the Chamber of Deputies until even after the end of the presidential mandate, was aligned in the same internal current as the president. However, the two PJ leaders up until 1995, José L. Manzano (1984–1991) and Jorge Matzkin (1991–1998), did not belong to the president's group of loyal men.[27] These leaders, together with the chairmen of the most important committees, have been in the chamber for the greatest number of years.[28]

We have reviewed some of the mechanisms that are employed to foster party discipline in Congress, but these are certainly not the only mechanisms available to parties. When the party wins presidential elections, the national leadership has valuable resources at its disposal with which to strengthen its support coalition, from the distribution of positions, for instance in the cabinet, to mechanisms of economic pressure that the management of state resources puts within its reach.[29] The decentralized structure of party authority thus becomes more centralized. On the other hand, in the opposition, the party leadership tends to be weak and subject to challenges because the selective incentives within its reach are few. Only an electoral victory can help to reestablish the power of the leadership of the opposition party. In turn, the defeat of the governing party opens the gates to internal readjustments.

Distribution of Collective Incentives   Political parties organize, at least at the moment of their creation, around certain principles of solidarity that allow them to pursue collective goals and offer to their members a sense of political identity. Through history, the political identities of the main parties, the UCR and the PJ, were so pervasive that it is difficult to entertain the idea of a Peronist switching to radicalism, or vice versa. Dissidents, however, might consider a third option. Yet, their ability to compete would then be hampered, for the structure of opportunities is laden in favor of the UCR and the PJ, the only two parties with national presence. Consequently, the trend toward polarization in presidential elections and the basically bipartisan format that concentrates competi-

---

[27] Neither is the current leader of the block, Humberto Roggero.

[28] However, their continuance is subject to the ups and downs of party competition. Neither César Jaroslavsky nor Jorge Matzkin managed to get included in the electoral lists of their respective provinces when their mandates were up for renewal. Matzkin was compensated by the president with a deputy minister's post in the national cabinet.

[29] These are particularly useful with regard to the provincial leaders.

tion around two families has one main effect: to operate as a device regulating the level of indiscipline of legislators. Compared for example with what goes on in the Brazilian party system, dissidents in Argentina have fewer incentives to threaten extreme measures such as breaking away from the party, forming another parliamentary grouping – that would make just another opposition grouping – or join the other side. In any event, this behavior has been more frequent in the PJ, but even here dissidents have eventually backtracked and returned to their original political party.[30]

The peculiar government-opposition dynamic that the Argentinean party system promotes reveals itself in the behavior of the opposition party. Opposition status fosters party discipline, despite the fact that the opposition party's leadership controls less resources and is thus more vulnerable. This alone can act as a mechanism of discipline, as happened with the five blocks that the PJ split into when in opposition under Alfonsín's government. When it came to votes, the five blocks voted as one. For the opposition party to be seen as an alternative government, it must show a united front on government initiatives. Being in opposition makes things easier, since unlike the governing party, it can choose when to act. In this sense it must be remembered that, unlike what happens in many parliamentary regimes where the opposition plays a mainly symbolic role, in a presidential regime it may participate in the decision-making process when the government does not have an absolute majority. It can be in a position both to veto government proposals and to block debate or participate in preparing bills.

On the one hand, when the opposition party controls one of the chambers, as happened under the Alfonsín government, its greater veto power may be a factor that helps to keep the governing party together. On the other hand, when the opposition's power is not so strong, as happened between 1989 and 1995, and it can only sometimes exploit the quorum – not permitting the number required for sessions to begin – it opens in the

---

[30] The most conspicuous case is that of PJ's ex-Senator Octavio Bordón. In 1995, he ran for president in coalition with Frepaso, and his vote count exceeded that of the UCR. However, he returned to the PJ after a short time. Frepaso might be the exception, although it appeared as the consequence of a division in 1990 of only eight PJ congressmen who purported to regroup Leftist political forces. However, the success of this type of move is uncertain, subject as it is to the changing conditions of the political and electoral playing fields. Nowadays, Frepaso has entered an alliance with the UCR due, among other things, to its weak national presence.

ranks of the governing party a space for differences to be aired. Because the quorum strategy must be used wisely due to its unpopularity, negotiations with the opposition can be the occasion to introduce individual points of view.[31] These differences may be one of the reasons why the UCR and the PJ demonstrated different levels of discipline under their respective governments.

Crisis Situations

Finally, we consider the use of the crisis strategy as a mechanism that avoids gridlock. As has been stated by various authors, crises bestow on the president new power resources that can be employed to circumvent conflictive situations. In certain occasions, crises can generate support for policies that would otherwise have been resisted. The Alfonsín administration passed the laws of *obediencia debida* and *punto final*, which marked a deviation from certain aspects of the government's human rights policy, in spite of strong reactions within Alfonsín's own party.[32] The immediate backdrop against which these decisions were taken was a military revolt and its menace to the recent process of democratization. Something similar happened under Menem's administration and the economic crisis that ensued due to the Tequila effect during the first quarter of 1995. The social security reform, for example, which had elicited such arduous negotiations just a short time before the crisis, was rapidly modified to mirror the government's original proposal.

In other instances, the crisis produces an even more portentous effect: to open the doors to delegation of power. This happened under the climate of social unrest produced by hyperinflation in 1989. On this occasion legislators, including those from the opposition party, agreed on temporarily delegating power to the executive through the Administrative Emergency Act and the Economic Emergency Act. As a result, President Menem could take advantage of a powerful array of economic, fiscal, and organizational powers with which to face the crisis. Later, he resorted to these powers to bring about the deep economic reforms that Argentina underwent in the 1990s.

---

[31] To persist with a blocking strategy is not a tool that favors the opposition, because to public opinion it seems to obstruct the action of a government elected by the majority of the people.

[32] On this topic, see Acuña and Smulovitz (1995).

An alternative way of garnering support is related to what American commentators refer to as "going public." This occurs when a president, facing an adversarial Congress, appeals to public opinion through the so-called "nonbinding plebiscite" (*plebiscito no vinculante*). This institutional innovation appeared during the process that led to the approval of the Beagle Treaty, also known as the Peace Treaty, with Chile. President Alfonsín promoted this treaty but faced enormous resistance by PJ senators. In order to avoid gridlock, the president decided to mobilize public opinion, resorting to the unforeseen mechanism of a nonbinding plebiscite. Given that the 1853 Constitution did not include any instruments of direct democracy, it was decided that constitutional legality required that the plebiscite would not compel legislators to stick to its result. Despite the nonbinding outcome, since voting in elections is mandatory, the level of participation in the plebiscite was quite high and vehemently in favor of approving the treaty. These results tilted the balance in the Senate, where the treaty was finally approved, albeit only by one vote. During the Menem administration, the threat to call a nonbinding plebiscite made possible the approval of the law that declared constitutional reform necessary. This tactic was effective because it induced the agreement with the UCR that led to the 1994 constitutional reform.

Executive–Legislative Relations in Argentina

We have so far analyzed the varied resources that the president commands in order to face potential gridlock. Undoubtedly, when the president resorts to decrees of necessity and urgency, the Congress becomes a marginal actor. The president, however, cannot rely on these decrees as the sole means to further policy implementation. Menem's privatization policy, for example, unavoidably required laws passed by Congress. In these cases, the role of Congress can never be ignored, although it is limited to giving legitimacy to the initiatives of the executive when, in principle, it could block them or revise them. In consequence, Congress is much more active than what conventional wisdom accepts.

It is certainly not up to the Congress to initiate government policies; that is the president's job. This is such an undisputed topic that the 1994 constitutional reform did not even consider the possibility of introducing mechanisms that could give priority to the legislative initiatives of the executive or limit the time devoted to them, as happened, for example, in Chile and Brazil. The old mechanism was retained, giving control of the agenda to the Parliamentary Works Committee in each chamber. However, the fact that Congress does not initiate public policy proposals does not mean that it cannot play a part in the decision-making process, either by modifying proposals, delaying their passage, or blocking them.[33]

Regarding changes to presidential initiatives introduced by legislators, we get a general overview by looking at the following data. Out of 190 bills submitted by the executive during Alfonsín's administration, 125 (65%) were modified in Congress; during Menem's tenure, this proportion fell to 50% (87 modified bills out of a total 165).[34] More specifically, case studies of privatization policy, fiscal policy, pension system reform, or the medicine patents act passed under the Menem government underscore the substantial role played by Congress in modifying executive bills.[35] In addition, with respect to the rate of approval for bills initiated by the executive, the statistics are as follows: President Alfonsín won approval of 69% of the bills presented to Congress and Menem 60%.[36] Stated alternatively, between 30 and 40% of the presidential initiatives did not win congressional approval.

Despite the fact that Congress never initiates government policy, its participation in legislative production is relatively high. Table 2.8 illustrates this fact. This high number of bills promoted by legislators reveals a certain active role played by Congress. What lies behind this high degree of participation in law making?[37] The explanation lies partly in the fact

---

[33] As Jean Blondel (1970) says, between the Congress' power of initiative and the preventive power with which Congress dissuades the government from proposing policies, there is the role of the legislatures as a reaction to government initiatives. This reactive role varies between total acceptance of the government's proposals to their rejection, giving rise to different degrees of "viscosity" in the legislative process.

[34] This does not include laws related to foreign policy – treaties, agreements, covenants, etc. – that, due to explicit constitutional prohibition – cannot be modified, only approved or rejected.

[35] On this subject see the chapter by Kent Eaton in this book. Among others, see also Alonso (1998), Etchemendy and Palermo (1998), Gerchunoff and Torre (1996), Llanos (1998), and Palermo (1995).

[36] Source: Molinelli, Palanza, and Sin (1999).

[37] It could be maintained that Menem's 166 decrees of need and urgency should be added to his legislative initiative. This is a pertinent argument. However, if we take into account that international treaties are, constitutionally, the exclusive initiative of the executive, it could be argued in turn that this would overrepresent the participation of the executive. For example, under the government of Alfonsín, 40% of the initiatives were treaties; under Menem's government it was 26%. If we exclude treaties from the analysis, the participation by the legislature in initiatives was greater (around 60%) under the government of Alfonsín and about the same, if we include decrees, under the government of Menem.

Table 2.8. *Bills passed by initiative and presidential period.*

Initiative	1983–1989	1989–1995
Executive	338 (52.4%)	386 (46%)
Congress	307 (47.6%)	449 (54%)
Total Acts	645 (100%)	835 (100%)

that Congress controls the parliamentary agenda. Although, as we mentioned, Congress gives priority to the initiatives of the executive, it does not neglect those of the legislators themselves.[38] Another factor that makes legislators' participation easier is that the areas that they cover do not compete with government policies. A quick look at the bills that became law offers the following panorama: There are multiple transfers of land and buildings from the nation to the municipalities, the creation of courts, some constructions of highways, declarations of special holidays (Tango Day, Harvest Festival), installation of monuments, regulation of specific labor sectors, and so on. Indeed, this concentration on microinitiatives closely matches the parochial and individualist reputation that Congress is tarred with in textbooks, but this is still an indicator of the representative function that legislators carry out as part of the relations that they maintain with the social fabric. It is in this sense that its role can be evaluated as active. That this is a duty of any legislator is evidenced by the fact that all of the parties, led by the governing party, manage to pass initiatives that they have penned either on their own or jointly with legislators from other parties. Table 2.9 makes the point forcefully.

It has to be noted that Congress uses its constitutional powers to the utmost when it comes to its own initiatives aimed primarily at satisfying sectorial or regional interests.[39] Veto overrides illustrate this point. For instance, the only veto override approved during Alfonsín's presidency was for an act that benefited a group of 100 bankers fired following a 1959 strike. Under the government of Menem, two veto overrides were related to the creation of federal courts: One declared the territory of the province of Santa Cruz a disaster zone due to the eruption of Mt. Hudson, another

---

[38] If we use the average number of days before a bill is passed into law as an indicator, we see that for both administrations it took Congress 267 days to sanction executive-initiated bills, whereas bills introduced by legislators were sanctioned after 369 days.

[39] Mustapic and Etchemendy (1998).

Table 2.9. *Passage of bills initiated by members of Congress.*

Party	1983–1989	1989–1995
UCR	112 (43.6%)	101 (23.2)
PJ	77 (30%)	181 (41.6%)
OTHER	15 (5.8%)	50 (11.5%)
UCR-PJ	29 (11.3%)	36 (8.3%)
UCR-PJ-OTHER	14 (5.4%)	40 (9.2%)
UCR-OTHER	6 (2.3%)	7 (1.6%)
PJ-OTHER	4 (1.5%)	20 (4.6%)
TOTAL	257 (100%)	435 (100%)

benefited soccer clubs, another the preparation and sale of foot-and-mouth vaccine, and so on. Given that these acts were introduced by legislators and had a limited scope, the veto override was less dramatic than could be supposed basically because government policies are not frustrated. In fact, only one veto override under Menem's government, the medicine patents act, was politically important.[40]

We see, then, that the Congress has behaved in accordance with the function assigned to it in the constitution, as an expression of society's diversity of interests. That is, the legislature clearly functions as a representative body. As the constitution also indicates, the formulation of policies with national importance and the general functioning of the government remain in the hands of the president. This division of labors between the executive and the legislature could be seen as an equilibrium point, balancing autonomous action by the legislators and loyalty to the presidential leadership that party membership demands.

Conclusiones

This chapter has tried to show how Presidents Alfonsín and Menem, in spite of working in a party and institutional framework that could gen-

---

[40] The legislative passage of this act presented by the executive was highly tortuous. Congress vetoed it "partially," meaning that it accepted some of the vetoed sections and insisted on its version in others. Once the insistence was passed and became law, the executive decided not to proceed with publication in the *Official Gazette*. Therefore, the act could not come into effect. After the executive had negotiated with Congress about the passage of another act that corrected part of what had been passed, the president finally ordered that it be published in the *Official Gazette*.

erate government immobilism, have avoided these risky situations. The argument has been that three factors have contributed to the reduction of the centrifugal tendencies and interbranch confrontations: strong presidential powers, the parties' capacity to distribute selective and collective incentives, and the country's crisis situation.

In light of the analysis it is possible to underline two points about the executive–legislative relations. First, the evidence presented here is not consistent with the image of legislators' behavior that is subordinated to presidental initiatives. In effect, when the president unilaterally decides to use his strong institutional powers he faces tougher challenges in Congress. This has been more visible in Menem's administration, where the president has found it more difficult to discipline his own ranks.[41] Further, the president's significant legislative powers do not imply that such powers can be used at will. One of the reasons that Menem was able to use his DNU powers so frequently was that the opposition did not have majority control of either house of the Congress. If they had had the power to veto initiatives in either house, as the PJ had in the Senate during Alfonsín's government, Menem's use of the DNU tool would surely have been much more moderate. If he had tried to emit a significant number of decrees while faced with low legislative support, he would have generated great hostility, thus affecting his ability to rely on the legislature's cooperation for the approval of routine bills.

Second, we acknowledge that the executive–legislative relationship changes continuously. Under some circumstances, the balance is decidedly tilted in favor of the executive; at other times, it leans in favor of the legislature. The oscillatory nature of executive–legislature relations stems from an incentive structure that generates two different superimposed logics, the logic of presidentialism and the logic of parliamentarism. On the one hand, constitutional powers and political parties consolidated the preeminence of the president as the leader of government and party, as happens in parliamentary systems. Thus we would expect governing party legislators to be loyal to the president and opposition party legislators to behave in a nonobstructionist manner. On the other hand, the division of powers and checks and balances, which are characteristic of presidentialism, combined with the internal heterogeneity of the parties grant legislators a margin of autonomy in limiting presidential leadership. In this

---

[41] Juan Carlos Torre (1996) has emphasized that, when in government, Peronists act as a political regime in itself, i.e., it behaves simultaneously as government and as opposition.

framework there is space for bargaining and negotiation, and we expect the president to take into account the interests and preferences of legislators. This tension between the parliamentary and the presidential components is well illustrated in a declaration by Humberto Roggero, the Peronist party's parliamentary party leader. As he was leaving a cabinet meeting convened to discuss fiscal policy, he declared to journalists: "Although we legislators belong to the ruling party (*somos oficialistas*), we are also deputies."[42] In other words, while legislators owe loyalty to the president because he is their party leader, they could not avoid representing the interests and preferences of their own electorate. In this respect, the Argentinean case is halfway between the European "party government" style and the "conditional party government" of the United States described by Cox and McCubbins.[43]

The analysis requires one final comment about party discipline. Party discipline habitually refers to legislators who vote the same way in the Congress. Nevertheless, in the case of governing parties, it takes on a more specific meaning. A disciplined governing party is, above all, one that is in a position to impede explicit challenges to the presidential leadership. The president's and the majority party's resources that guide the legislative process serve this purpose. For example, formal dissent from committee reports or the ability to present a minority report are mechanisms that permit legislators to vent their intraparty differences without affecting the discipline of the president's bloc. At the same time, the ability to recall a bill presented to Congress permits the president to avoid a possible defeat in Congress. Such defeats are precisely what a governing party tries to avoid. Not surprisingly, then, explicit defeats are exceptional occurrences. In fact, there was only one such case during each of the two presidencies: the labor reform law under Alfonsín's presidency, which was rejected in the Senate, where he lacked a majority, and the tax law under Menem's government, which was rejected by the lower house. Therefore, only the opposition complains that bills that do not win approval in the committees do not reach the congressional floor, or that Congress deals only in general session with two types of bills: those that win unanimous approval and those contentious bills on which the legislature divides along party

---

[42] Declaración de Humberto Roggero, PJ Parliamentary Party Leader. *La Nación*, February 12, 1998.
[43] Cox and McCubbins (1993). See also Cox and Morgenstern, this volume.

lines.[44] At almost all costs, the governing party wants to avoid self-wounding defeats – which could happen if only a few of its legislators join the opposition to reject a proposed bill. The governing party therefore works to assure that these types of projects will not reach the floor. In synthesis, the president can be confident that his legislators will not openly question his leadership; he cannot hope, however, that they will unconditionally support his policies.

[44] Interview with Marcelo Stubrin, representative for the UCR. In Mora Yazbeck Jozami, "Legisladores oficialistas y Poder Ejecutivo en Argentina: la construcción de la disciplina. Un estudio de caso," B.A. Thesis, Universidad Torcuato Di Tella, June 1999.

3

Presidential Cabinets, Electoral Cycles, and Coalition Discipline in Brazil

OCTAVIO AMORIM NETO*

Introduction

Recent works on Latin American presidentialism (Amorim Neto 1998; Deheza 1998; Thibaut 1998) indicate that the frequency of coalition governments in this area is higher than expected by comparative theorists of this system of government (Jones 1995; Lijphart 1992; Linz 1994). While such a finding reveals that Third World presidential democracies are able to devise extraconstitutional means by which the crisis proclivity of minority presidents can be overcome, it remains to be seen whether multiparty presidential cabinets can work as parliamentary-style coalitions that in general display a high degree of unity on the floor of parliament and operate in conjunction with the executive to promote legislation.

Brazil is a good starting point to tackle this question. There is an ongoing debate in the comparative presidentialism literature about Brazil's prevalent pattern of government formation. On the one hand, Abranches (1988), Deheza (1997, pp. 192–230), and Meneguello (1998) contend that all Brazilian presidents appoint coalition governments. On the other, Amorim Neto (1994, 1995) and Thibaut (1996, pp. 282–321) caution against a loose application of the concept of coalition government to presidential systems and argue that other types of cabinets also have been formed in this country. While Abranches, Deheza, and Meneguello simply

* This work was supported by FAPERJ under grant number E-26/150.194/98-BOLSA. I thank Gary W. Cox, Arend Lijphart, Fernando Limongi, Scott Morgenstern, and Benito Nacif for their helpful comments on earlier drafts of this chapter. The usual disclaimer applies. I also thank Argelina C. Figueiredo, Fernando Limongi, and Jairo Nicolau for kindly sharing their data sets on the 1989–1998 legislative roll calls in Brazil.

count the number of parties drafted into the cabinet to assert their coalitional status, Amorim Neto and Thibaut also look at cooptation strategies (as opposed to coalition ones) employed by presidents in their dealings with political parties and social actors, and the recruitment criteria of individual ministers. However, all of these five authors provide only illustrative evidence as to whether legislative policy making is actually associated with the type of cabinet chosen by the chief executive. The type of presidential cabinet does not hinge only on whether it is single-party or multiparty and whether it commands a majority of legislative seats. Presidential cabinets also vary according to how well parties are represented in the cabinet. Students of coalition politics in Europe provide a wealth of evidence showing that parties joining coalition governments as a rule receive ministerial payoffs proportional to their legislative weight (Browne and Franklin 1973; Budge and Keman 1990, pp. 88–131; Laver and Schofield 1990, pp. 164–194; Schofield and Laver 1985, 1990). Yet, in presidential regimes, given that presidents are constitutionally free to design the cabinet as they see fit, they may appoint a multiparty cabinet but not reward the parties based on a proportionality rule. What is the consequence of such a coalition-building strategy? Will it generate lower rates of legislative support to the president by the cabinet partners? Does a fair distribution of cabinet posts to parties help boost the support to the president?

As long as those questions about the role of the cabinet in influencing legislative voting patterns remain improperly answered, any effort to establish whether multiparty cabinets in Brazil or in any other presidential systems actually work as parliamentary-style coalitional arrangements will arouse justified skepticism. After all, as Sartori (1997, p. 161) correctly puts it, "The problems of presidentialism are not in the executive but in the legislative arena." In this chapter I seek to analyze the impact of how cabinet posts are distributed to parties on the latter's legislative behavior in Brazil in 1989–1998 using roll-call data. The effects of other relevant variables on legislative behavior, such as the elapsing of the president's term and the ideological diversity of the cabinet, will also be checked.

The period 1989–1998 provides a suitable setting to test the impact of cabinets on legislative behavior in a single country, as there has been important variance on both the legislative behavior and cabinet membership across and within presidential terms. As presidents frequently appoint different cabinets over their terms, I can investigate how cabinet changes affect legislative behavior by holding constant many intangible factors that affect presidents and legislators. Further, as discipline rates in Brazil vary across parties and over time, we can test for the impact of cabinet composition on these rates.

A key to executive–legislative relations in Latin America rests on the ability of presidents to cobble together majorities to support policy initiatives. Coalition behavior in presidential regimes, however, is an understudied aspect of Latin American politics. This chapter is thus an attempt to improve our knowledge of coalition behavior in Latin American presidential systems by means of a case study. It will also provide an extension of the literature that has focused on the Brazilian parties' loose discipline (Amorim Neto and Santos 2001; Limongi and Figueiredo 1995[1]; Mainwaring and Liñán 1998) and the president's use of budgetary resources and agenda-setting powers to obtain legislative support (Amorim Neto and Santos 2001; Limongi and Figueiredo 1998; Santos 1997).

The chapter will proceed as follows. In the next section I propose a quantitative measure to tap the degree of coalescence of presidential cabinets based on the distribution of ministerial portfolios to political parties. A coalition cabinet is defined as featuring at least two parties and a high degree of proportionality between the parties' cabinet shares and legislative weights. The application of that indicator to Brazil shows that there is a substantial variation in the degree of coalescence of cabinets in this country. In the third section I briefly describe Brazil's institutional structure in 1985–1999 and show how it relates to the politics of cabinet formation. Using time-series analysis, the fourth section checks the impact of the degree of proportionaliy between cabinet shares and legislative weights plus two variables relating to the ideological makeup of cabinets and the elapsing of the president's term on coalition discipline using roll calls taken in 1989–1998. The tests show that coalition discipline is mainly a function of the degree of cabinet coalescence and the elapsing of the president's term. In the fifth section I provide party-specific tests of support to the executive, demonstrating that the support given to presidents by Brazil's largest parties depends on their ministerial payoff ratio, the elapsing of the president's term, and, to some parties, on their ideological distance from the chief executive. The sixth and last section concludes.

---

[1] It should be noted that Figueiredo and Limongi assert that Brazilian parties are actually fairly disciplined and behave in a predictable manner.

The Degree of Coalescence of Presidential Cabinets

In this section my goal is to propose an indicator based on the partisan distribution of ministerial portfolios that will allow us to measure the coalescence of presidential cabinets and to provide the criteria to pin down when a new cabinet is formed.[2] Coalescence will be understood here as a continuous variable: The higher the proportionality between the parties' cabinet shares and legislative weights, the more coalescent the cabinet. Based on this notion of coalescence, in the next section I will check empirically whether more coalescent cabinets are associated with higher legislative discipline of cabinet parties.

Can presidential cabinets work as coalitional arrangements as in parliamentary systems? In principle, yes. But, it is not enough for politicians from at least two parties to simply join the cabinet. As Laver and Schofield (1990, p. 130) contend, a coalition means that there must be a *binding agreement* between those parties. However, the authors are considering parliamentary systems in this definition, and coalition agreements do not work in the same way in presidential systems. Politicians from different parties may be appointed ministers by a president, but this does not mean that the parties endorsed those appointments. That is to say, their appointment does not necessarily bind their parties to support the president in the legislature (Mainwaring 1993). Moreover, one could argue that a president may strike one binding agreement with party X and a second binding agreement with party Y; yet those agreements may very well not bind parties X and Y to each other. But one thing is the formation of a coalition cabinet, another thing is coalition governance. Even in a parliamentary regime a well-cemented coalition cabinet may unravel in a short period of time due to inter- or intraparty conflicts, and this does not signify that the cabinet was not a coalition when it was formed. So, to avoid the conceptual confusion between coalition formation and coalition governance, I posit that a coalition cabinet in a presidential system simply requires an agreement over cabinet appointments between the president and more than one party. The question then becomes, does the design of a coalition agreement affect coalition governance as evinced by the legislative behavior of cabinet parties? In this chapter I argue that the answer is positive, and that if coalition agreements provide for a proportional

---

[2] For an analysis of the application of this measure to cabinets in 10 Latin American countries, see Amorim Neto (1998, ch. 3).

distribution of cabinet shares relative to legislative weights, coalition parties should display a disciplined behavior toward the president on roll-call votes.

How do we observe empirically that an agreement was actually struck? We would have to obtain historical and/or newspaper accounts of the negotiations over all appointments made to appoint a cabinet. This procedure would be too time-consuming. Moreover, even if a researcher were able to collect accounts of the appointments of all ministers, many deals actually cut by presidents and party leaders would go unnoticed because of the secrecy that often surrounds political negotiations. She would thus have to make judgment calls to classify some cabinets. Such procedures would often result in *ad hoc*-ery, which would certainly hurt the analysis' reliability.

It is nonetheless possible to avoid such pitfalls by making some plausible assumptions about what constitutes an agreement over cabinet formation and relying solely on the basic information available on cabinet ministers, namely, their party affiliation (if any), appointment and dismissal dates, and the legislative weight of their parties. Thus, I assume that if a president and more than one party reach a coalition agreement over the composition of the cabinet, the parties receive ministerial portfolios in a measure that is roughly proportional to their legislative weight. By this logic, proportionality in cabinet shares is the equilibrium solution for the bargaining problems faced by presidents and parties regarding the division of the executive pie.[3] Actually, students of parliamentary regimes have demonstrated empirically that coalition payoffs in Europe are distributed according to the legislative size and bargaining power of the parties (Browne and Franklin 1973; Budge and Keman 1990, pp. 88–131; Laver and Schofield 1990, pp. 164–194; Schofield and Laver 1985, 1990). Additionally, I posit that the degree of coalescence of presidential cabinets is a continuous variable. Hence, the proportionality norm will be employed here as a yardstick to identify the degree of coalescence of cabinets. Ministerial allocations deviating from proportionality should therefore be seen as a characteristic of cabinets displaying lower levels of coalescence. The assumption here is that the more cabinet shares deviate from proportionality, the less coalitional is the cabinet.

---

[3] I am using the concept of equilibrium in the technical game-theoretic sense of a Nash equilibrium, that is, a situation in which no actor has an incentive to move unilaterally.

To account for the relationship between cabinet shares and legislative weight, I propose a mathematical indicator called Cabinet Coalescence Rate (call it CABINET). It is based on the index of proportionality devised by Rose (1984) to measure the amount of deviation from proportionality between seats and votes that a given election produces. Here ministries and seats take the place of seats and votes. The index's formula is

$$CABINET = 1 - \frac{1}{2} \sum_{i=1}^{n} (|S_i - M_i|)$$

where M_i is the percentage of ministries that party i receives *when the cabinet is appointed* and S_i is the percentage of legislative seats that party i holds in the total of seats commanded by the parties joining the cabinet *when the cabinet is appointed*.

In order to arrive at the coalescence rate for a given cabinet, we add the absolute value of the difference between the percent of ministries and the percent of legislative seats for all parties joining the cabinet, whether or not these parties hold legislative seats, and for all ministers, whether party members or not, and then divide the total by 2. Subtracting the result from 1 yields the coalescence rate. The index varies between 0 (no correspondence between ministerial payoffs and legislative seats) and 1, which defines an upper limit of perfect correspondence between cabinet shares and legislative weights. Any departure from this upper limit is detected. To work properly, the index requires that at least one minister be a partisan. If all ministers were nonpartisans, the index would yield the value of 0.5, a result that does not match the meaning of a partly coalitional cabinet. So in the case of a ministerial distribution with no partisans, 0 should be assigned simply as its coalescence rate.

The values obtained with this index express a relation between the information available to the analyst – the percent of ministers belonging to a given party and that party's share in the total number of legislative seats nominally commanded by the party labels included in the cabinet. That is to say, CABINET measures how the distribution of cabinet posts is roughly weighed vis-à-vis the dispersion of legislative seats *across the legislative contingent of the parties joining the executive*. Consider, for example, the following hypothetical case.

Table 3.1 reports a 100-seat legislature divided among three parties, A, B, and C, and a cabinet comprising 10 portfolios. The president allocates two portfolios to A, six to C, and appoints two independent ministers. A

Table 3.1. *Hypothetical example of how to calculate the cabinet coalescence rate.*

Legislative Parties	Cabinet Shares	$S_i(\%)$	$M_i(\%)$	$|M_i - S_i|$
A = 20 seats	2	0.31	0.2	0.11
B = 35 seats				
C = 45 seats	6	0.69	0.6	0.09
	Independent	0	0.1	0.1
	Independent	0	0.1	0.1
Total = 100 seats	10 portfolios			0.4

Cabinet Coalescence Rate = $1 - 1/2*0.4 = 1 - 0.2 = 0.8$.

and C together command 65 seats; therefore S_A is 0.31 (= 20/65), S_C is 0.69 (= 45/65), and the independent ministers each score 0 on S_i. As for the percentage of portfolios (M_i), A has 0.2, C has 0.6, and each independent minister has 0.1. The sum of all $|M_i - S_i|$ values is 0.4; this result divided by 2 gives us 0.2, which subtracted from 1 leaves 0.8. This result tells us that the allocation of portfolios in this cabinet deviates from perfect proportionality, but the correspondence between cabinet shares and legislative seats is still high.

Although CABINET does capture much information, there are two concerns. First, note that it assumes that all cabinet posts are of equal value. In the real world of politics they are not. Some cabinet posts are often more important than others. The finance ministry is always a good example. However, any procedure to quantify the different political value of cabinet posts would hardly be reliable and would always be open to criticism. For instance, if we were to use the budgetary appropriations allocated to ministries to measure their relative political value, a highly prized post such as the foreign office would score very low in Brazil, in particular, and in Latin America, in general. So while recognizing that assuming equal political value for all ministries is an imperfect solution, I contend that it is more reliable than any effort to quantify such a value.

Second, CABINET assumes that a party's bargaining power is directly proportional to the size of its legislative delegation. There may be some circumstances under which a small party can successfully demand that it be overrepresented in the cabinet so as to join it. This is likely to happen in pure parliamentary regimes because the survival of the government in office depends on the tolerance of legislative parties. However, in pure presidential systems such as Brazil, small parties' ability to extract dispro-portional concessions is severely reduced, owing to the president's fixed term of office.

Cabinet Change

Presidents in a pure presidential system are constitutionally entitled to freely dismiss their ministers. Hence, new cabinets may be formed over a president's term. How do we identify them? Three criteria are applied to distinguish a new presidential cabinet:

1. the inauguration of a new president;
2. a change in the party membership of the cabinet; and
3. a change of more than 50% in the identity of individual ministers.

The first criterion is obvious. In presidential systems the inauguration of a new presidency represents a wholesale change in the executive branch because the executive power is vested solely in the head of the state. The second criterion is required because CABINET is centered on the party makeup of the executive, and any change in it constitutes of necessity a new cabinet. The third is included because, in a presidential system, as individual ministers must ultimately run their portfolios according to pres-idential goals, a major change in the identity of ministers may also repre-sent a major change in the way in which the president wants to run the executive branch and the way in which he deals with the parties and the legislature.

Military Officers in the Cabinet Finally, I consider high-ranking mili-tary officers, who, as a rule, are appointed to head the Army, Navy, and Air Force Ministries in Brazil as independents. However, only the Army Ministry will be included in the calculations. The reason for this simplifi-cation is to avoid an overestimation of nonpartisan ministers.

Presidential Cabinets in Brazil Table 3.2 provides the coalescence rate and other indicators of the cabinets appointed by the four presidents in 1985–1999. As the data show, there is a substantial variation in the coa-lescence rates in Brazil, ranging from a minimum of 0.22 (Franco's fifth cabinet) to a maximum of 0.62 (Franco's first cabinet). Based on their values on CABINET, one can hardly say that the last cabinets of Sarney

Table 3.2. *Presidential cabinets in Brazil (1985–1998).*

President and Cabinet	Period in Office	Parties Represented in the Cabinet	Cabinet Coalescence Rate	President's Party and its (% of Seats)	Cabinet's Nominal Size (% of Seats)	Ideological Range of the Cabinet	% of Nonpartisan Ministers
SARNEY I[a]	(03/85–02/86)	PMDB-PFL-PTB-PDS	0.66	PMDB (41.8)	93.5	1.0	18.0
SARNEY II	(02/86–01/89)	PMDB-PFL	0.64	PMDB (44.7)	69.3	1.0	14.0
SARNEY III	(01/89–03/90)	PMDB-PFL	0.41	PMDB (35.4)	53.3	1.0	35.0
COLLOR I[b]	(03/90–10/90)	PMDB-PFL-PRN	0.40	PRN (5.1)	50.3	1.0	60.0
COLLOR II	(10/90–01/92)	PFL-PDS-PRN	0.40	PRN (5.1)	29.6	0	60.0
COLLOR III	(01/92–04/92)	PFL-PDS	0.30	PRN (6.0)	26.2	0	60.0
COLLOR IV	(04/92–10/92)	PFL-PDS-PSDB-PTB-PL	0.46	PRN (6.0)	43.7	1.5	45.0
FRANCO I	(10/92–01/93)	PMDB-PFL-PSDB-PTB-PDT-PSB	0.62	No party	61.6	1.5	20.0
FRANCO II	(01/93–05/93)	PMDB-PFL-PSDB-PTB-PDT-PSB-PT	0.59	No party	67.4	2.0	38.0
FRANCO III	(05/93–09/93)	PMDB-PFL-PSDB-PTB-PSB	0.51	No party	53.3	2.0	38.0
FRANCO IV	(09/93–01/94)	PMDB-PFL-PSDB-PTB-PP	0.48	No party	58.6	1.5	52.0
FRANCO V	(01/94–01/95)	PMDB-PFL-PSDB-PP	0.22	No party	55.3	1.5	76.0
CARDOSO I[c]	(01/95–04/96)	PSDB-PMDB-PFL-PTB	0.57	PSDB (12.1)	56.3	1.5	32.0
CARDOSO II	(04/96–12/98)	PSDB-PMDB-PFL-PTB-PPB-PPS	0.60	PSDB (15.8)	76.6	1.5	32.0

[a] This cabinet was appointed by president-elect Tancredo Neves (PMDB), who fell ill on the eve of his inauguration. He came to die 38 days later without ever being sworn in.

[b] I disregarded the first minister of Agriculture appointed by Collor, Joaquim Roriz (PST), because he stayed in office for only 14 days.

[c] Cardoso's minister of Culture, Francisco Weffort, was affiliated with the PT when he took office in January 1995. However, he bolted this party soon after his appointment. Hence I decided not to include the PT as one of the parties represented in Cardoso's cabinet.

Source: CPDOC (N.d.), *Ministros de Estado da República*, Rio de Janeiro: Fundação Getúlio Vargas, and data provided by Antônio Octávio Cintra and José L. M. Dias. Additional sources: for Sarney: *Keesing's Contemporary Archives*, vol. 31, n. 6, 1985, pp. 33642–33650; *Veja*, February 12, 1986, pp. 16–21; *Veja*, January 11, 1989, pp. 34–36; for Collor: *Veja*, March 14, 1990, pp. 26–31; *Veja*, April 15, 1992, pp. 18–26; for Franco: *Veja*, October 7, 1992, pp. 34–49; *Jornal do Brasil*, August 20, 1993, p. 2; *Jornal do Brasil*, August 21, 1993, p. 4; *Jornal do Brasil*, August 29, 1993, p. 12; for Cardoso: *Istoé*, January 4, 1995, pp. 21–2.

and Franco and those appointed by Collor are coalition cabinets, whereas the first cabinet appointed by Sarney and the two cabinets appointed by Cardoso are certainly so. In the next section I briefly review the institutional structure of Brazil's presidentialism so as to relate it to the politics of cabinet formation.

The Institutional Structure of Presidentialism in Brazil

In March 1985 a civilian president, selected by an electoral college composed of congressmembers and six representatives from each state legislature, was sworn in after 21 years of military dictatorship, and a protracted transition started in 1974. One of the first acts of the new regime was to confer constitution-making powers to the Congress to be elected in November 1986. This Congress was inaugurated in February 1987, and it was only able to promulgate a new constitutional text in October 1988. So between March 1985 and October 1988 the political system operated under the provisions of the 1967 Constitution enacted by the military. These provisions provided for a pure, strong presidential regime under which the president had total control over the executive branch and could govern by decree almost unhampered by legislative checks (Pessanha 1997, ch. 3). If Congress failed to deliberate on the decrees issued by the executive in 30 days, they were considered approved.

After the promulgation of the 1988 Constitution, Brazil's presidentialism displayed the following features.[4] The president is elected by majority rule, with a runoff between the two top tickets if no candidate obtains more than 50% of the valid votes in the first round. From 1985 to 1994, the presidential term was five years. In 1994, the term was reduced to four years. In June 1997, the Congres approved, for the first time in its history, a constitutional amendment allowing presidents to run for one consecutive term. The 1988 Constitution grants the chief executive the power to issue a partial and total veto over bills; the ability to initiate legislation with monopoly of initiative over many policy areas; the power to freely appoint and dismiss cabinet ministers; and the prerogative to adopt *medidas provisórias* (provisional measures) with the immediate force of law. Provisional

---

[4] In this chapter I will delve only into the problems of legislative fragmentation and presidential powers, leaving the question of federalism aside. Readers interested in the latter topic should consult the works of Abrucio (1998), Dias (1997), Mainwaring (1997), and Samuels and Abrucio (1997).

measures must be submitted immediately to Congress, and if not converted into law within 30 days, they lose effectiveness. Although Article 62 states that provisional measures may be issued only to deal with urgent and relevant matters, they have actually become the presidents' most preferred policy-making instrument, particularly for the implementation of economic policy. Figueiredo and Limongi (1997a, p. 144) show that, in 1988–1995, 1,249 provisional measures were issued. Yet it should be noted that, out of this total, 862 were basically reiterated versions of measures that Congress failed to consider within 30 days of their issuance. Such a high rate of re-issued provisional measures is a clear sign that this constitutional weapon tempts presidents to act unilaterally and to overstep their legislative powers (Power 1998).[5]

Multipartism

A key factor affecting executive–legislative relations in any democratic polity is the partisan distribution of power in the legislative branch. According to a survey of 54 democracies (Amorim Neto and Cox 1997, pp. 169–170), in the 1980s Brazil had one of the most fragmented legislatures in the world. For many analysts, such a high level of fragmentation cripples the decisiveness of the political system (Lamounier 1994; Mainwaring 1995), thus seriously hurting the country's prospects for democratic consolidation. As a measure of legislative fragmentation I use the conventional Laakso and Taagepera index of effective number of parties (1979), the formula of which is

$$N = 1/\sum x_i^2$$

where x_i is the percentage of seats held by the i-th party with representation in the lower chamber. Table 3.3 reports the effective number of legislative parties in Brazil in 1985–1999.

In the period from 1985 to 1992, the fragmentation of Brazil's lower chamber almost tripled (from 3.2 to 9.4). It is true that it declined from 1986 to 1987 and stabilized from 1996 to 1999, but the central trend for the whole period is one of dramatically increasing fragmentation. In the 1985–1999 period the mean size of the president's party was 12.3% of the

---

[5] Other summaries of the 1988 Constitutions can be found in Carey, Amorim Neto, and Shugart (1997) and Mainwaring (1997).

Table 3.3. *Effective number of legislative parties (1985–1999).*

1985	1986	1987*	1988	1989	1990	1991[a]	1992	1993	1994	1995*	1996	1997	1998	1999*
3.2	3.3	2.8	4.1	5.5	7.1	8.7	9.4	8.5	8.2	8.1	7.1	6.9	6.8	7.1

[a] First year of a new legislature elected the previous year.
Sources: Nicolau (1996, p. 72), *Folha de São* (a São Paulo–based daily newspaper), "O Novo Congresso," (October 10, 1998), p. 1; *Folha de São*, "A Nova Câmara dos Deputados," In *Eleições 1998–Caderno Especial* (October 10, 1998), p. 2; and data provided by Bolívar Lamounier.

lower chamber seats. High fragmentation in Brazil resulted from the combined effects of two factors: the electoral decline of the two largest parties of the military period (the PDS and PMDB), and unrestrained party switching on the part of federal deputies (Lima Júnior 1993; Nicolau 1996).[6]

How does legislative fragmentation affect presidentialism? Many authors have already delved into this question (Mainwaring 1993; Mainwaring and Shugart 1997; Jones 1995), and the tenor of their conclusions is one: The higher the legislative fragmentation, the weaker the president's party support. The data in Table 3.3 show that Brazil provides compelling evidence to this effect.

How does the institutional structure of presidentialism relate to coalition formation in Brazil? Using data on 75 cabinets appointed by 57 presidents in 10 Latin American countries in the 1946–1995 period, Amorim Neto (1998, ch. 3) has demonstrated that cabinet coalescence is a positive function of the size of the president's party and a negative function of whether the constitution grants the president the power to issue decree laws. The larger the size of the president's party, the higher CABINET. The power to issue decrees, in turn, leads to a lower CABINET. The link between the size of the president's party and CABINET is that presidents

[6] Additional comments on Brazil's impressive rates of party switching are in order. Table 3.3 shows that legislative fragmentation varies within a single legislature. Party switching is the main cause of this fact, because it alters the partisan distribution of seats during a single legislature. When changing parties, deputies either go to older labels or create new ones. According to Nicolau (1996, p. 65), 64.6% of the members of the legislature elected in 1994 have switched parties at least once since 1980. Some deputies change their party affiliations even twice in the same legislature. Party switching reached its peak in the late 1980s. The effective number of legislative parties that emerged in the 1986 election was 2.8. However, due to party switching, it jumped to 4.1 in 1988, to 5.5 in 1989, and to 7.1 in 1990, the last year of this legislature.

59

with strong party support tend to make policy mostly through statutes. They thus build more coalitional cabinets to solidify support in the legislature. Presidents with weak party support prefer policy-making strategies other than statutes, so they use cabinet appointments for other purposes, such as to reward cronies or to bring policy expertise into the executive branch. Likewise, presidents with decree authority are prone to make policy with this unilateral instrument, which does not necessitate high rates of CABINET. Unlike in 1946–1964, all Brazilian presidents had decree authority in 1985–1999. So, much of the variation in CABINET in this period is explained by the size of the president's party. For example, Collor's cabinets scored so low on CABINET in part because his party commanded a very small share of lower chamber seats.

The Impact of Presidential Cabinets on Legislative Voting

In order to analyze the impact of CABINET on coalitional behavior in the legislative arena, we need to find a valid measure of the latter. Legislators behave in a coalitional fashion when the members of the same coalition act as unity. There are two key legislative arenas in which coalitional behavior can be readily observed, namely, committees and the assembly's floor. The second is certainly the most relevant, because the decisions there often convey the assembly's last word on policy. Also, a greater number of representatives are required for floor decisions to be made than for committees. That is to say, the floor offers a more representative sample of the whole legislature than do committees.

Further, the assembly's floor is the best arena to observe the degree to which coalition agreements over cabinet composition are actually binding on legislative parties. Consider a comparison between presidential and parliamentary regimes. To begin with, in presidential systems interbranch cooperation is harder to achieve than in parliamentary regimes. This is ultimately due to the fixed term of office of both the president and the assembly. Such a provision ensures that the chief executive does not have to resign in case a government-sponsored bill is defeated, nor can the assembly be dissolved in case of an executive–legislative deadlock. Members of governing parties in presidential systems therefore feel much freer to vote against the executive on the assembly's floor than their counterparts in parliamentary systems. If the latter wish to do so, the prime minister can always threaten to resign, probably triggering a snap election, whose consequence may be the defeat of the governing parties. Anticipating this outcome, backbenchers, as a rule, prefer to transfer their eventual conflicts with the cabinet to arenas other than the house of parliament. In this sense, prime ministers have a strong weapon to induce compliance from their rank-and-file *as far as floor behavior is concerned*. That is why roll-call decisions in parliamentary systems are usually a foregone conclusion, with the cabinet line almost always having the final say. Only on a few and extraordinary occasions can one observe backbenchers voting against the cabinet on the parliament's floor.

By this logic, roll calls are not the best evidence for the analysis of legislative discipline in parliamentary systems. Legislative discipline (or conflict) in parliamentary regimes is best observed in party caucuses and conventions and in cabinet meetings, where the party line is formed, and where divergent preferences can be safely given free rein. In these arenas a compromise between the cabinet position and those of individual legislators is often reached so that bills taken to the floor stand a very low risk of defeat. In most presidential regimes, particularly those in which party discipline is not tight, as in Brazil and the United States, however, roll-call votes are characterized by a great deal of uncertainty for the reason stated above. Separation of powers poses a serious commitment problem to presidents in their dealings with legislators, and this problem is clearly reflected in floor behavior. In view of this fact and the loose discipline of Brazilian political parties, roll-call votes will be used to test the legislative impact of presidential cabinets.

Some observations about the rules governing roll calls in Brazil are in order. According to the standing orders of the Chamber of Deputies, motions can be decided by three kinds of voting procedures: secret vote, voice vote, and roll-call vote. A secret vote requires a two-thirds quorum and is designed to decide on the establishment of investigation committees and the impeachment of presidents, legislators, and judges. The voice vote is the most frequently employed decision rule. For a voice vote to be valid, a minimum of 50% + 1 of deputies should be present on the floor. But voice votes can be taken without the lower chamber's steering body checking whether a majority is present. However, if after a voice vote some deputies consider that the minimum quorum required for the vote to be valid had not been met, they can request a quorum counting. Any quorum counting request supported by at least 6% of the lower chamber membership triggers a roll-call vote.

Hence, in Brazil, roll calls provide opposition legislators with an opportunity to make decisions by majorities more costly – because preferences have to be publicly disclosed, which is not the case with voice votes – and slower – because the majority has to vote twice on the same bill. So roll calls constitute an important obstructionist tool in the hands of the opposition. This means that roll calls are a good site to observe party conflict and coalition discipline in Brazil in particular.[8]

Data

I have considered all roll calls taken in the Chamber of Deputies in 1989–1998 for which there was information on the preferences of the president. The reason for looking at only these roll calls is straightforward: Since this section's goal is to check the extent to which legislators affiliated with the parties represented in the presidential cabinet take unified action, roll calls that convey some information on the president's agenda are the most valid ones for this purpose.

Ascertaining the president's position is straightforward in Brazil due to a provision entitling presidents to appoint a so-called government leader in the Chamber of Deputy. The role of this leader is to communicate the president's preferences over legislative bills to party leaders and legislators and negotiate with them. Before a roll call is taken, the government leader is asked by the chair of the lower house to announce the executive's position on the matter to be voted on.

Four hundred and twenty roll calls for which there was information on the government leader's position were found in 1989–1998. This period covers the last two years of the 1987–1990 legislature; all years of the 1991–1994 and 1995–1998 legislatures; the last year of the Sarney administration; the entire presidencies of Collor and Franco; and the first term of Cardoso.

The Dependent Variable: Coalition Discipline of the Cabinet Parties

Coalition discipline is here defined as the degree of coalition unity on voting decisions (call it COAL). Because my focus is on the behavior of parties with politicians appointed to the cabinet, I measure coalition discipline as follows:

[8] In countries where party discipline is tight, as in Venezuela in the 1959–1993 period, the analysis of roll-call votes is meaningless (Coppedge 1994b).

COAL = % of *the total legislative membership of the cabinet parties* voting in accordance with the orientation of the government leader on each roll call.

Note that this measure assumes that abstention and absence are also forms of noncooperative behavior vis-à-vis the government. If we were to assume that the only form of noncooperative behavior on the part of individual deputies vis-à-vis the government leader is when the former vote explicitly against the recommendation of the latter (e.g., the government leader recommends that deputies vote aye, and a deputy affiliated with one of the cabinet parties votes nay, or vice versa), then we would be overestimating coalition discipline.

For example, suppose that a presidential cabinet is composed of parties A, B, and C. Party A holds 60 legislative seats; party B, 30; and party C, 10. In a given roll, 54 legislators of party A were present; 37 voted aye, and 17 voted nay. Twenty-four legislators of party B turned out to vote; 20 voted aye, and 4 voted nay. As for party C, 8 responded to the roll call, with 4 voting aye, and 4 voting nay. Now suppose that we know the position of the government leader, and that she oriented the cabinet parties to vote aye. If abstention and absence are discounted, the coalition discipline of the cabinet parties on this roll call is $(37 + 20 + 4)/(54 + 24 + 8) = 61/86 = 0.71$. However, if we include abstention and absence in the denominator, the coalition discipline rate is $(37 + 20 + 4)/(60 + 30 + 10) = 61/100 = 0.61$.

Finally, as many authors have emphasized (Bond and Fleisher 1991; Carey 1999; Limongi and Figueiredo 1995; Mainwaring and Pérez Liñán 1998; Riker 1959) not all roll calls are meaningful for coalition behavior and party conflict. Roll calls on which there is consensus or near consensus are less relevant than those on which the sizes of the majority and the minority are close. Likewise, roll calls with a low attendance can also be said to be less relevant than those with high attendance. Therefore, a clear criteria of roll call relevance must be set up, taking into account both vote closeness and attendance. The solution adopted here is to estabish a cutoff point based on the indicator of roll-call "critical-ness" proposed by Carey (2000). The formula of a roll call's critical-ness is

CRITICAL-NESS = ATTEND * CLOSE,

where

Table 3.4. *Summary statistics of coalition discipline, support to the president, per cabinet in Brazil (1985–1998).*

President and Cabinet	Number of Roll Calls	Discipline Coalition		PMDB's Support to the President		PFL's Support to the President		PSDB's Support to the President	
		Mean	Std. Dev.	Mean	Std. Dev.	Mean	Dev. Std.	Mean	Std. Dev.
SARNEY I	n.a.	n.a.	n.a.	n.a.	n.a.	n.a.	n.a.	n.a.	n.a.
SARNEY II	n.a.	n.a.	n.a.	n.a.	n.a.	n.a.	n.a.	n.a.	n.a.
SARNEY III	4	.52	.26	.46	.25	.65	.30	.19	.27
COLLOR I	18	.63	.17	.53	.21	.73	.21	.35	.31
COLLOR II	41	.51	.19	.45	.25	.55	.21	.35	.30
COLLOR III	1	.55	–	.02	–	.60	–	.00	–
COLLOR IV	8	.63	.13	.34	.29	.65	.29	.25	.30
FRANCO I	10	.70	.10	.76	.10	.65	.14	.83	.11
FRANCO II	11	.54	.20	.60	.21	.42	.27	.70	.22
FRANCO III	13	.55	.19	.60	.24	.49	.23	.66	.25
FRANCO IV	1	.44	–	.50	–	.33	–	.58	–
FRANCO V	2	.48	.08	.50	.01	.35	.19	.81	.06
CARDOSO I	82	.71	.16	.64	.17	.75	.19	.77	.18
CARDOSO II	133	.70	.12	.63	.15	.77	.12	.77	.13

– does not denote that the party was not in the Cabinet.
Source: Roll-call data provided by Argelina C. Figueiredo, Fernando Limongi, and Jairo Nicolau.

ATTEND = % of legislators voting,
CLOSE = 1 − (2∗|0.5 − %aye|),
%aye = #aye/entire lower chamber membership.

Only roll calls on which there is at least 0.6 of legislators voting and on which at least 0.2 of legislators dissent from the majority will be included. Plugging those numbers into the above formula will yield the following value of CRITICAL-NESS:

$$\text{CRITICAL-NESS} = 0.6 * \left[1 - \left(2 * |0.5 - 0.8|\right)\right] = 0.6 * [1 - 0.6]$$
$$= 0.6 * 0.4 = 0.24.$$

This means that for a roll call to be selected it has to score at least 0.24 on Carey's indicator of critical-ness.[9] By applying the 0.24 cutoff point, the final sample was reduced to 324 meaningful roll calls. Table 3.4 displays

[9] According to Carey, because some votes require extraordinary majorities to pass, the index of roll-call critical-ness should be adjusted accordingly. For example, if an extraordinary threshold is set at 0.67 of the entire membership of the legislature, this value should be used in the place of 0.5. In Brazil there are three types of majorities: simple majority (for

the mean values and the standard deviations of COAL per cabinet along with individual parties' support to the president (defined in the next section).

The Key Independent Variable: Cabinet Coalescence

The key hypothesis to be tested is the following:

H1. *The more coalescent the cabinet, the more disciplined the behavior of the legislators belonging to the cabinet parties on roll calls.*

This is expected to be so because a cabinet with a high coalescence rate reflects a judicious allocation of ministerial posts to the parties by the president. Such an allocation is very likely to bring the parties drafted into the cabinet to a more consistent support of the executive. So I expect that the cabinet coalescence rate will have a positive sign in the regression equations.

Other Relevant Independent Variables: The Elapsing of the President's Term and the Ideological Range of the Cabinet

Underlying the cabinet coalescence rate is the assumption that parties are office-seeking actors. However, as is forcefully argued by Strom (1990a), parties have another two fundamental concerns, namely, vote maximization and the pursuit of policy goals. How do vote and policy seeking affect coalition discipline in the context of Brazilian politics?

Given that in pure presidential regimes the president's term is fixed, as the term elapses the value of holding ministerial posts for parties declines over time as concerns with office seeking give way to vote maximization (Altman 1998; Amorim Neto and Santos 2001). By this logic, larger opposition factions should emerge inside the legislative contingent of cabinet parties as the president's term comes to an end. Therefore, coalition unity should also ebb over time. So the second hypothesis to be tested is

H2. *As the president's term elapses, coalition discipline on roll calls declines.*

To operationalize the elapsing of the president's term, I simply count the temporal distance in days between the day that a roll call is taken and

standard bill proposals), absolute majority of the entire membership of the legislature (for votes on bills regulating constitutional articles), and a 0.6 majority of the entire membership (for constitutional amendments). As I do not have reliable information on the type of majority required for each roll call, I opted for a compromise solution, 0.5, which means that an absolute majority is being required.

the constitutional end of a given administration (call this variable ELAPSE):

$$ELAPSE = T_e - T_r,$$

where T_e is the day that the president's term constitutionally ends and T_r is the day that a roll call is taken.

For example, if a roll call on a bill is taken on the ninetieth day of a five-year presidential term (total of 1,825 days), this roll call's score on ELAPSE is $1,825 - 90 = 1,735$. I expect this variable to have a positive sign. That is to say, early in the president's term, when the distance between the days that roll calls are taken and the presidency's expected end are larger, coalition unity should take on higher values.

What about policy concerns? Although Brazil's largest parties (those often drafted into the cabinet) are usually seen as mostly clientelistic organizations, they also have an identifiable ideological profile (Figueiredo and Limongi 1995; Kinzo 1993; Mainwaring 1999, pp. 88–135) that affects their electoral coalition strategies (Schmitt 1999) and legislative behavior (Figueiredo and Limongi 1995). If this much is true, then the ideological diversity of the cabinet should impact on coalition discipline. Cabinets joined by highly ideologically diverse parties should display lower levels of coalition discipline than cabinets composed of ideologically homogeneous partners. For example, a cabinet joined by two centrist parties (a highly homogeneous coalition) is very likely to generate higher rates of coalition discipline than a cabinet composed of three parties, one centrist, the other center-right, and the third center-left.[10] This is so because the coordination of cabinet parties' preferences is much more difficult to achieve under the latter cabinet than under the former. Thus, I surmise that

H3. *The more ideologically diverse the cabinet, the lower coalition discipline on roll calls.*

To operationalize the cabinet ideological diversity I measure the ideological distance between the furthest-left and the furthest-right cabinet

---

[10] Note that ideological diversity is a key government attribute to explain cabinet survival in parliamentary democracies (Warwick 1994, pp. 49–74). Tsebelis (1995) argues that the same variables that explain the breakdown of presidential democracies also account for cabinet termination in parliamentary democracies, namely, the number of partisan veto points and the heterogeneity of preferences. However, if we assume democratic stability, coalition discipline as a function of the ideological diversity of the cabinet is presidentialism's functional equivalent of cabinet survival in parliamentarism.

parties (call this variable IDRANGE). How is it measured? Following Coppedge (1997) and Mainwaring (1999), I measure this by assuming that the most salient cleavage that divides Brazilian parties is the classic left–right one. Additionally, these two authors place Brazilian parties on the five standard positions along the left–right dimension, namely, left, center-left, center, center-right, and right.[11] Drawing on a similar procedure adopted by Coppedge, I further posit that the distance between each contiguous position is 0.5. Thus, if a cabinet is joined by a center, a center-left, and center-right party, its score on IDRANGE is the distance between the latter two parties, that is, 1.0. IDRANGE varies bewteen 0 and 2; 0 is the IDRANGE value for all cabinets whose parties are all placed on the same ideological position, and 2 is the value for all cabinets being joined by both a left and a right party:

$$\text{IDRANGE} = |P_{fl} - P_{fr}|,$$

where P_{fl} is the ideological position on the left–right dimension of the furthest-left party represented in the cabinet and P_{fr} is the ideological position on the left–right dimension of the furthest-right party represented in the cabinet.

Note that IDRANGE is an imperfect indicator of ideological diversity because it does not take into account the ministerial share held by each ideological block represented in the cabinet. An ideal measure would have to include both the ideological positions and the ministerial shares of all ideological blocks represented in the cabinet in the same way as Coppedge (1998) does to calculate the effective number of ideological blocs in Latin American party systems. However, it is impossible to apply such a measure owing to the high percent of nonpartisan ministers in Brazilian cabinets. The only reliable method to identify the ideological position of nonpartisan ministers is experts' surveys. Unfortunately, there are no experts' surveys on the ideological position of Brazilian ministers.

Table 3.2 shows that no cabinet formed in 1985–1999 was all occupied by partisan ministers, and that the percent of nonpartisan is high in many cabinets. For example, Franco's last cabinet had 76.0% nonpartisan ministers; Collor's first three cabinets, 60.0%; and Cardoso's two cabinets,

---

[11] According to Coppedge (1997) and Mainwaring (1999), the ideological position of all 12 of the parties that joined the cabinet at least once since 1985 is the following. On the left: PT, PSB, and PPS; on the center-left: PSDB, and PDT; on the center: PMDB; on the center-right: PTB; and on the right: PFL, PDS, PP, PL, and PRN.

32.0%. One way to reduce the error of not considering the ministerial share of each ideological position represented in the cabinet is to apply IDRANGE only for parties holding more than one cabinet post or at least 5.0% of the lower chamber seats. It is better to use these arbitrary but plausible relevance criteria than to overestimate the weight of tiny parties in the cabinet ideological diversity. Let us thus restate the definition of IDRANGE: It measures the ideological distance between the furthest-left and furthest-right cabinet parties that meet one of the two relevance criteria. Table 3.2 displays the IDRANGE for all cabinets in 1985–1999.

All in all, the resulting regression equation takes the following form:

$$COAL = \beta_0 + \beta_1 CABINET + \beta_2 ELAPSE + \beta_3 IDRANGE + \varepsilon. \quad (1)$$

Results

The regression results are displayed in Table 3.5. In Model 1, the full model, both CABINET and ELAPSE were found significant at the 0.01 level in a one-tailed test. IDRANGE was not statistically discernible from zero, and it came with the wrong sign. A second model was run without IDRANGE on the right-hand side of the equation. CABINET and ELAPSE remained significant at the same level as in the first model. In a

Table 3.5. *The determinants of the coalition discipline rate (in accordance with the president's preferences) of cabinet parties (1989–1998)*[a].

Dependent Variable: Coalition Discipline of the Cabinet Parties				
Independent Variables	Model 1	Model 2	Model 3	Model 4
Constant	.107	.094	.258***	.503***
	(.803)	(.079)	(.066)	(.039)
CABINET	.874***	.930***	.727***	
	(.164)	(.122)	(.158)	
ELAPSE	.00007***	.00008***		.00003
	(.00002)	(.00002)		(.00002)
IDRANGE	.012		.003	.098***
	(.024)		(.024)	(.019)
Adjusted R-squared	.151	.153	.130	.078
Number of observations	324	324	324	324

[a] Standard errors are indicated in parentheses.
*** $\rho > 0.01$; ** $\rho > 0.05$; * $\rho > 0.1$.

third model, ELAPSE was dropped. In this model CABINET continued to be significant at the 0.01 level, and IDRANGE was again not found significant and came with the wrong sign. I checked whether IDRANGE had a multicollinearity problem by correlating it with CABINET and ELAPSE. IDRANGE and CABINET were found to be highly correlated (a 0.75 correlation). So a fourth model was run without CABINET on the right-hand side of the equation. ELAPSE was not found significant. However, IDRANGE had for the first time a significant effect on coalition discipline but, again, came with the wrong sign.

Given the employment of time-series data, I checked for autocorrelation by regressing the unstandardized residuals on its lags and all other explanatory variables for the four models. No autocorrelation problem was detected in either case.

Why did IDRANGE fail to be significant? With all probability, because it is too crude a measure. So only when a more refined indicator is available will the impact of the ideological diversity of Brazilian cabinets be properly checked.

At any rate, which model do we choose? Model 2 is clearly the best because the coefficients on the independent variables are the highest, their significances are also the highest, and it has the highest adjusted R-squared (albeit just a bit higher than that of Model 1). Holding ELAPSE constant in this model, a unit increase in CABINET is approximately associated with a unit increase in cabinet coalescence. So, for example, if a president changes a government scoring 0.4 on CABINET to one scoring 0.6, an increase of 0.19 in cabinet coalescence should be observed. Holding CABINET constant, the coefficient on ELAPSE indicates that if a roll call is taken when there are still 1,000 days (approximately three years) for the president's term to elapse, coalition discipline should increase by .08 relative to a roll call taken by the end of the term.

The meaning of the results are clear-cut: Cabinets with a higher coalescence rate maximize the coalition discipline of governing parties, and coalition discipline decreases later in the president's term.

Party-Specific Tests of Support to the President

In this section I provide party-specific tests of support to the president. Let us first glance at the most relevant governing parties.

On the center of the left–right dimension the key player is the *Partido do Movimento Democrático Brasileiro* (PMDB – Party of the Brazilian

Democratic Movement). In spite of its marked electoral decline since 1988, it was Brazil's largest legislative party from 1985 to 1996. It held the presidency under José Sarney in 1985–1990. Table 3.2 indicates that the PMDB was represented in all but 3 of the 14 cabinets appointed in 1985–1998.

On the right, the *Partido da Frente Liberal* (PFL – Party of the Liberal Front) stands out as the most relevant party. It became the second largest party in 1986, and since 1997 it has been the largest one, having participated in all presidential cabinets appointed since 1985.

Finally, the *Partido da Social Democracia Brasileira* (PSDB – Party of the Brazilian Social Democracy) was created in 1988 during the National Constituent Assembly as a breakaway from the PMDB. It is a center-left organization and has been an increasingly important party since the election to the presidency of one of its leaders, Fernando Henrique Cardoso, in 1994, and his reelection in 1998. It became the third largest legislative party in 1995, and after the 1998 races it is the second largest one. The PSDB was first drafted into the cabinet by president Collor in 1992. Since then this party has always occupied key ministerial posts.

I hypothesize that individual parties will cooperate with the president if they see positive benefits for doing so. These benefits can imply serving career ambitions, winning pork, or passing favored policy initiatives. One way to assure a share of the benefits is for party politicians to take cabinet positions. In order to keep their posts, I assume that cabinet ministers must work to assure the support of their party for the president. Further, individual legislators should share in the pork barrel if their leader maintains the cabinet post. Thus, I expect that

H4. *The better the cabinet representation of a party, the stronger its support to the president on roll calls.*

I test this hypothesis by looking at individual parties' support to the president as a function of the degree to which they are awarded with an at least fair ministerial payoff. The dependent variable will be operationalized as the percent of the whole lower chamber delegation of a given party voting in accordance with the orientation of the government leader on legislative roll calls (call it SUPPORT):

$SUPPORT_i$ = % of the whole lower chamber delegation of party i voting with the government leader on a given roll call.

Note that SUPPORT, like COAL, accounts for all forms of non-cooperative behavior vis-à-vis the president (as represented by his leader on the floor). That is, abstentions and absences are also included in the denominator.

Ministerial payoff, the key independent variable, will be measured as the ratio of a party's percent of ministerial posts to its percent of seats in the legislative contingent of the cabinet parties (call it PAYOFF). Its formula is

$$\text{PAYOFF}_i = M_i/S_i.$$

(M_i and S_i are defined in the previous section.)

So if a party is allocated 0.35 of ministerial posts, and this party holds 0.60 of the seats in the cabinet parties' legislative contingent, its score on PAYOFF is 0.35/0.60 = 0.58. If a party does not receive any cabinet post, its score on PAYOFF is obviously zero. I expect that PAYOFF will have a positive sign. Table 3.6 displays the PAYOFF values for the PMDB, PFL, and PSDB for all cabinets appointed in 1985–1998.

Table 3.6. *Ministerial payoff ratio of the PMDB, PFL, and PSDB (1985–1998).*

President and Cabinet	PARTIES		
	PMDB	PFL	PSDB
SARNEY I	1.17	0.54	0.00
SARNEY II	0.71	0.51	0.00
SARNEY III	0.44	0.35	0.00
COLLOR I	0.19	0.53	0.00
COLLOR II	0.00	0.32	0.00
COLLOR III	0.00	0.30	0.00
COLLOR IV	0.00	0.45	0.50
FRANCO I	0.57	0.64	1.41
FRANCO II	0.58	0.51	1.31
FRANCO III	0.46	0.40	0.78
FRANCO IV	0.38	0.44	0.86
FRANCO V	0.13	0.27	0.25
CARDOSO I	0.27	0.49	1.40
CARDOSO II	0.13	0.56	1.10

Source: The same as for Table 3.2.

Additionally, the variable ELAPSE, tapping the impact of the electoral cycle on coalition discipline, will also be included in the party-specific tests, as in the tests with aggregate measures of coalition discipline and cabinet coalescence. Again, I expect that ELAPSE will have a positive sign. That is to say,

H5. *As the president's term elapses, a party's support to the president on roll calls declines.*

Finally, the ideological distance between individual parties and the president is clearly a factor that should affect the former's willingness to support the latter. The hypothesis in this case is similar to H3:

H6. *The larger the ideological distance between a party and the president, the weaker the former's support to the latter on roll calls.*

To operationalize the ideological distance between party and president, it is first assumed that the ideological position of the president is that of his party. How plausible is this assumption? Obviously, in the real world of politics presidents differ ideologically from their parties. In general, the reality of power makes presidents more conservative than their party when the latter leans to the left. This is the case of President Cardoso and his Party of the Brazilian Social Democracy. The opposite is also true: When the president's party is right-leaning, the chief executive tends to look more progressive. A good example is President Juscelino Kubitscheck, who ruled Brazil in 1956–1961, and whose policy stances seemed to be to the left of those of his conservative PSD. At any rate, a president's party label can be said to provide a reliable clue as to the central trend relating to presidential preferences over a myriad of policy goals. I posit that the distance on the left–right scale between the president's ideological position and that of the party can be depicted by the following formula:

$$\text{DIST} = |P_{\text{pres}} - P_i|,$$

where P_{pres} is the ideological position on the left–right dimension of the president's party and P_i is the ideological position on the left–right dimension of party i.

For example, the ideological distance between a center-right president and a center-left party is 1.0. The only Brazilian president who poses an operational difficulty to DIST is Franco. When he took office in October 1992 he was not affiliated with any party. However, during most of his career he was affiliated with the PMDB, having bolted this party just before his name was placed on Fernando Collor's presidential slate in 1989. During his presidency, Franco took mostly centrist, moderate positions, just like his former party. Thus, equating Franco's ideological position to that of the PMDB would not be an egregious violation of reality.

All told, the equation representing the additive effects of the independent variables relating to a party's office, vote, and policy concerns on its support to the president on rolls calls is as follows:

$$\text{SUPPORT}_i = \beta_4 + \beta_5 \text{PAYOFF} + \beta_6 \text{ELAPSE} + \beta_7 \text{DIST} + \varepsilon. \qquad (2)$$

Results

Table 3.7 reports the party-specific regression results. For the PMDB, all three independent variables were found to be significant and came with the right sign. Holding all else constant, if the PMDB's payoff ratio jumps from 0.5 (meaning that only half of the party is properly represented in the cabinet) to 1.0 (a perfectly proportional representation in the cabinet), the party's support to the president should increase by 0.22; if a roll call

Table 3.7. *The determinants of individual parties' support to the president's preferences (1989–1998)[a].*

Dependent Variable: Support to the President of Individual Parties

Independent Variables	PARTIES		
	PMDB	PFL	PSDB
Constant	.355***	.224***	.583***
	(.074)	(.079)	(.065)
PAYOFF	.447***	.664***	.174***
	(.049)	(.160)	(.055)
ELAPSE	.0001***	.00007**	−.00003
	(.00003)	(.00002)	(.00003)
DIST	−.097*	.076***	−.148***
	(.051)	(.024)	(.051)
Adjusted R squared	.139	.158	.434
Number of observations	324	324	324

[a] Standard errors are indicated in parentheses.
*** $\rho > 0.01$; ** $\rho > 0.05$; * $\rho > 0.1$.

is taken when there are three years before the end of the president's term, the PMDB's support to the president should increase by 0.1 relative to a roll call at the end of the term; and if a centrist president is replaced by a rightist one, the PMDB's support should decline by 0.1.

As for the PFL, PAYOFF, ELAPSE, and DIST, they all had a significant effect on SUPPORT, although at different levels of significance (0.01, 0.05, and 01, respectively). However, DIST came with the wrong sign, thus confirming the null hypothesis. With all else constant, if the PFL's payoff ratio goes from 0.5 to 1.0, the party's support to the president should increase by 0.33; a roll call taken three years before the elapse of the president's term should see the PFL's support to the president increase by 0.07 relative to a roll call at the end of the term.

Finally, in regard to the PSDB, only PAYOFF and DIST were found to be significant (both at the 0.01 level) and came with the right sign. With all else constant, if the PSDB's payoff ratio jumps from 0.5 to 1.0, the party's support to the president should increase by 0.09; and if a centrist president is replaced by a rightist one, the PSDB's support should decline by 0.15.[12]

Why did DIST come with the wrong sign for the PFL? Students of conservative politics in Brazil (Hagopian 1996; Power 2000) assert that this party is an essentially clientelistic organization. Parties of this kind are chiefly concerned with the benefits of office. Thus it is no wonder that it joined all of the cabinets appointed since 1985. Therefore, the positive sign on DIST in the PFL's regression equation and its statistical significance can be said to be spurious.

Finally, why did ELAPSE have no significant impact on the PSDB's support to the president? Among Brazil's largest parties, the PSDB is certainly the one with the strongest ideological commitments. It is much less clientelistic than the PFL and less heterogeneous than the PMDB. Therefore, it can be argued that once the PSDB decides to support or not a government (it did not join either the Sarney or Collor's first three cabinets), its pattern of relationship with the chief executive will be stable over the president's term. Therefore, a variable tapping the elapsing of the latter is bound to have no significant impact on this party's support to the president.

In short, the legislative support given to presidents by Brazil's two largest parties, the PMDB and PFL, is mainly determined by their min-

---

[12] No autocorrelation problem was found in any of the regressions.

isterial payoff ratio and the elapsing of the president's term. In the case of a more ideological party such as the PSDB, the ideological distance between president and party also plays a key role, and the elapsing of the president's term has no significant effect on the party's support to the chief executive.

Conclusion

Let us now return to the question posed in the introduction: Can multiparty presidential cabinets work as coalition arrangements in parliamentary regimes? The analysis of the Brazilian case provided in this chapter allows the following conclusions. First, a presidential cabinet joined by politicians from two or more parties should not be assumed to constitute a coalition executive. Only cabinets displaying a high correspondence between cabinet shares and the parties' legislative weights (relative to the legislative contingent of the cabinet parties) can be regarded as such in a strict interpretation of the term coalition. Second, a judicious allocation of cabinet posts to parties based on the proportionality norm, particularly if it is early in the president's term, approximates the legislative behavior of the parties joining a multiparty presidential cabinet to that of coalition partners in a parliamentary regime. That is, higher coalition unity on legislative votes should be observed under presidential cabinets featuring those attributes. Third, more ideological parties display a more consistent coalition behavior over time.

How generalizable are those findings? With all probability, they should hold up for any presidential system in which parties are either not perfectly disciplined or factionalized, and where executive patronage in the form of cabinet positions is an important political currency. So, data availability permitting, Equations (1) and (2) can well be applied to countries like Bolivia, Chile, Colombia, Ecuador, pre-Fujimori Peru, and Uruguay. They should not be valid for countries like pre-Chávez Venezuela, because of the perfect discipline of its parties, and the United States, owing to the little importance of cabinet posts for political parties.

How does coalition discipline help presidents? First of all, it is important to note that the fact that a Brazilian president happens to count on a more disciplined legislative coalition due to his judicious allocation of cabinets posts to parties does not mean that he has a stable majority in Congress. Table 3.2 shows that almost all cabinets in Brazil nominally command a majority in the lower chamber. Yet Brazilian presidents are always striving to achieve legislative majorities. However, if the president's legislative contingent behaves in a disciplined fashion, this certainly helps the president negotiate a majority with opposition parties because he may bargain with them from a firmer launching base. That is why presidents who apppoint more coalescent cabinets tend to be the most stable in Brazil.

The example provided by President Fernando Collor de Mello (1990–1992) is illustrative in that respect. When he took office in March 1990, his party in the Chamber of Deputies, the PRN, commanded only 5.1% of the seats. His legislative situation was thus quite difficult in terms of party support and was further complicated by the generalized perception that he was too far to the right of the political spectrum. Had he wanted to form a stable legislative majority, he would have had to make an enormous number of concessions to the largest parties. However, Article 62 of the Constitution empowered him to issue decrees with the force of law (the so-called provisional measures). On his inauguration day, he made his policy-making strategy clear: He decided to face the hyper-inflation crisis in which Brazil was enmeshed since 1987 exclusively by means of decrees. He signed no less than 36 decrees in his first 15 days in office (and 163 during 1990)[13] and appointed a cabinet composed mostly of cronies and technocrats.

Collor kept governing by decree during the first year and the beginning of the second year of his term, despite growing dissatisfaction with the way in which he was handling his relationship with Congress and with the overall performance of his government. Dissatisfaction was so great that in April 1991 Congress nearly approved a bill (the so-called Nelson Jobim Bill) that regulated and constrained the issuance of decrees by the executive. According to Power (1998, p. 211):

Although Jobim and his allies did not succeed in redefining Article 62 of the Constitution, their effort seems to have resonated among Collor and his advisers. While the Jobim Bill was being considered by Congress in February, March, and April, Collor did not decree a single MP [provisional measure].... Based on the experience of his first year in office, his restraint was astonishing. It is difficult to avoid the conclusion that the president imagined his good behavior might save him from having his decree power reduced by an act of Congress.

In a certain sense, the vote on the Jobim Bill was a turning point in the Collor presidency. In 1991 he only signed 8 decrees as compared to 163 in 1990, indicating a steady decline in his legislative support. Yet

[13] Data provided by Jorge Vianna Monteiro.

throughout 1991 Collor resisted negotiating an agreement with opposition parties so as to improve executive–legislative relations, and insisted on dealing with Congress at arms' length. This impasse had the effect that 1991 was a year during which little was done to address Brazil's main problem, hyperinflation. In December 1990, the monthly inflation rate was 16.0%; in December 1991, it was 23.3%.[14] In January of 1992, Collor reshuffled his cabinet to bring more solid support from some conservative parties to his government.[15] We can easily understand why he flagrantly failed to do so: The cabinet scored only 0.30 on the coalescence rate. By the first quarter of 1992, there were disquieting signs that Collor's government was completely failing. Monthly inflation rates were still above 20.0%. His popularity was eroding: In March 1992, a nationwide poll showed that only 15.4% of the respondents considered his government good or very good, as compared to 35.3% in August 1990, 23.3% in March 1991, and 20.4% in August 1991.[16] Moreover, charges of corruption against cabinet ministers and presidential advisers were increasingly making the headlines. It was clear that Collor needed above all to boost his support in Congress to be able to initiate a new, more successful phase of his presidency. By late March 1992, Collor dismissed the whole cabinet and, for the first time in his presidency, publicly avowed that he was opening negotiations with political parties to form a governmental majority in Congress.[17] He ended up forming the most coalescent cabinet of his whole presidency (CABINET = 0.46), thus finally trying to effectively obtain more legislative support by a more sensible allocation of cabinet posts to political parties. Had Collor not been impeached, it can be said that his new cabinet would probably have performed better in terms of

[14] Data provided by the Department of Economics of the Catholic University of Rio de Janeiro.
[15] See *Veja* (a Brazilian weekly magazine), "Faxina em Casa: Collor demite Alceni e Chiarelli, cria um ministério para Bornhausen e convoca o PFL para dar um novo desenho político ao governo" [Cleaning the House: Collors dismisses Alceni and Chiarelli, creates a portfolio for Bornhausen, and calls the PFL to give a new political shape to the government], (January 29, 1992, pp. 18–24).
[16] These poll data were provided by the Centro de Estudos de Opinião Pública (CESOP) of the University of Campinas.
[17] See, for example, *O Globo* (a Rio de Janeiro–based daily newspaper), "Collor dissolve o Governo: irritado com denúncias diárias de corrupção, presidente inicia reforma ampla do ministério" [Collor dissolves the Government: irate with daily corruption charges, the president begins a major cabinet change], (March 31, 1992, p. 3), and *Folha de São Paulo* (a São Paulo–based daily newspaper), "Governo tenta compor base partidária" [Government tries to form a party base], (March 31, 1992, p. 11).

coalition support than the previous ones. Obviously this kind of expost speculation should always be read with a grain of salt. One wonders why he took so long to change his cabinet so as to obtain more legislative support. A plausible reason is that he was aware that under an actual coalition cabinet the policy-making autonomy that he had enjoyed in his first year in office would be seriously curtailed. At any rate, the case of Collor shows a clear, if loose, connection between the interaction of cabinet coalescence and coalition support. This sort of example could be multiplied to other Brazilian and Latin American presidents, which is what the quantitative analysis in the chapter shows.

4

Exaggerated Presidentialism and Moderate Presidents: Executive–Legislative Relations in Chile*

PETER M. SIAVELIS

Introduction

With few exceptions, the scholarly study of Latin American legislatures has been tangential to the wider study of the executive branch and presidential authority. This is the case primarily because of the real disparities in power between branches of government in the region, but also because legislative branches have traditionally been perceived as either "rubber stamps" or impediments to the efficient execution of presidential policies.[1] More recent literature treats legislatures more seriously, but still tends to focus on the executive side of the interbranch equation.[2] This is, of course, due to the overwhelming strength or perceived strength of Latin American presidencies in many postauthoritarian democracies. Yet, scholars should not commit the same error again, simply revisiting the theme of executive predominance without a closer examination of the real and important role that legislatures play in the region.

Even in academic work that expresses a specific intent to examine Latin American legislatures, the president seems ultimately to end up playing the starring role. Part of the reason that presidents receive so much

---

* The author is grateful for useful comments, criticisms, and suggestions from Scott Morgenstern, Benito Nacif, and an anonymous reviewer for Cambridge University Press.

[1] For example, Stokes (1959), in his chapter, "The Subservient Legislature," contends that in Latin America, "Executive–legislative relations have been characterized by executive dominance and legislative subservience" (p. 412). This sort of interpretation was typical until relatively recently.

[2] See Shugart and Carey (1992) and Mainwaring and Shugart (1997). Close's (1995) edited volume is a partial exception, though many of the chapters do not depart significantly from the focus on the executive side of the equation. What is more, the Chilean case study (Nef and Galleguillos 1995) is constitutionally rather than empirically focused.

attention in work on legislatures is the very way in which legislative power is measured. As much as one tries to avoid it, a discussion of the legislature inevitably returns to a discussion of the executive branch, given the intricate and intimate relation between the two and the fact that legislative power is often conceptualized as the amount of influence that assemblies can exert over executive actions, in both the spheres of legislation and administrative oversight. Indeed, in a recent work on Latin American legislatures, Needler (1995, p. 156) contends that, "In the sense of formal constitutional attributions of power the legislature is stronger where the president is weaker," positing a direct and zero sum game between the branches of government. The formal focus on the balance of power between the branches of government often overlooks the real potential influence that legislatures can have. What is more, this type of focus often leads one to zero in on one branch or the other, without a thorough enough examination of interbranch connections or how the balance of power between the president and legislature can in some situations make for a positive sum game. The balance of interbranch power is also more malleable and dependent on other variables like the party distribution of seats in the legislature than students of institutional politics have suggested. Finally, focusing on the formal powers of the president and Congress presents a static view of legislative power that ignores the reality of shifting influence depending on the partisan power of each branch of government and the nature and extent of presidential support in Congress.

This chapter takes these considerations into account to analyze executive–legislative relations in postauthoritarian Chile, focusing on the connections between the branches of government, rather than on one branch of government or the other. It considers both institutional connections and less formal avenues of communication and interaction between the branches of government. It seeks to provide an analysis of the additional elements other than the simple formal power of the presidency that have been at the root of recent Chilean presidents' ability to successfully pursue their legislative agendas, without resorting to the extraordinary measures that they are provided. It also underscores how the legislature has been influential despite superficial evidence that would suggest otherwise.

In addition to recognizing the necessity of a shift in focus in the work on executive–legislative relations in Chile, this chapter also addresses some puzzling theoretical questions. Recent comparative work on Latin American political institutions suggests that presidential systems characterized by very strong executives are more likely to experience difficulties in terms of democratic governability (Mainwaring and Shugart 1997; Shugart and Carey 1992). Postauthoritarian Chile presents something of a puzzle in this regard. Despite working within what has been characterized by scholars as one of the most powerful presidencies in the world, the first two postauthoritarian governments represent models of what should be done by executives in transitional political situations. Does this suggest that Chile's military authorities were successful in designing a successful institutional formula for presidentialism? Why have some of the problems associated with very strong presidential systems not emerged? Why have presidents not more aggressively employed their wide range of powers?

This chapter contends that while Chile's institutional structure is characterized by an exaggerated presidential system, its two postauthoritarian presidents, Patricio Aylwin and Eduardo Frei, have been decidedly moderate and measured in the use of presidential prerogatives. Thus, it is important to differentiate between the constitutional and political powers of Chilean presidents and to analyze the extent to which the balance between the two has shaped how presidents employ their prerogatives in practice. The chapter argues that the unique characteristics of the party system, the extent of presidential support in the legislature, and the political situation created by the democratic transition have provided incentives for presidents to avoid resorting to the use of extreme presidential power. In the process, the legislature has emerged as a more powerful and significant actor than it might be in other contexts. In situations of crisis, when presidents face more significant partisan challenges to their authority, or where the possibility of establishing working majorities is more remote, it is likely that presidential prerogatives would be more aggressively employed. The legislature would, in turn, be less influential, and interbranch relations would likely be characterized by some of the problematic features described by the critics of strong presidentialism.

First, the chapter argues that, despite the overwhelming power of the president in constitutional terms, many of the prerogatives associated with the office have not been used or have been less significant than one might expect. This reality is a product of party alignments in the Chamber of Deputies and Senate, and the very nature of transition politics.

Second, the chapter argues that, while many of the statistics presented make it appear that the legislature is very weak, they mask the formal and informal influence that Congress and individual members of Congress can have within the new institutional framework for executive–legislative relations erected by the first postauthoritarian government. While these avenues of influence were created to facilitate interbranch relations, they also somewhat paradoxically mask the real influence that Congress and individual legislators have had.

Finally, this chapter underscores that legislative influence is more variable than has been suggested, even by those analysts who recognize the importance of the partisan powers of presidents, and that legislative influence is partly a function of the size of the pro-governmental majority. The chapter suggests that Chile's less than unified government has actually enhanced the power of the legislature in a surprising way. Had the president a majority in both houses, he may have had little incentive to cultivate support from members of Congress, given the expectation that his legislation would simply pass. Alternatively, given an intransigent Congress more dominated by the opposition, the president may have had an incentive to employ more aggressively his wide range of powers. Nonetheless, given that Presidents Aylwin and Frei had a majority in the Chamber of Deputies and could negotiate a majority in the Senate, the influence of Congress as a whole was enhanced. Thus, the degree of legislative influence varies according to the distribution of government-opposition seats in the legislature and appears to have been maximized by a less than unified, though not intransigent, Congress. In short, presidents had incentives to negotiate, rather than attempting to impose their will.

The chapter begins by analyzing the formal structure of interbranch relations and how it was transformed from the preauthoritarian era. The second section of the chapter goes on to show how the new constitutional balance of power between the branches of government has, indeed, tilted the formal balance of legislative power in favor of the president. This section presents data on the origin and speed of consideration of legislation during the Aylwin administration. The third section discusses the extent to which postauthoritarian presidents have employed their prerogatives to affect the legislative process, focusing particularly on urgency provisions, the national budget, and the extent to which legislators have influenced laws passed during the first two postauthoritarian presidencies. The fourth section analyzes the party system and features of the democratic transition, asking how they have affected the functional balance of power between the branches of government. It analyzes how the extent of presidential support in Congress influenced the incentives for executives to employ extraordinary powers. The chapter concludes with a discussion of the significance of these findings in terms of the long-term evolution of executive–legislative relations in Chile.

The Transformation of Executive–Assembly Relations in Chile: The 1980 Constitution

Unlike most other legislatures in Latin America, Chile's National Congress stood out historically as a body with significant powers and influence. It played a central role in the country's long experience with democracy, both as a deliberative body and as an institution for the resolution of conflict in Chile's sometimes-fractious multiparty system.[3] Executive–legislative relations in particular formed an important axis of political negotiation in the country.

Despite the important role played by Congress in the historical development of Chilean democracy, the president has always been an important legislator, with the ability to dominate the legislative process given his agenda-setting ability, budgetary dominance, and areas of exclusive initiative.[4] Indeed, Shugart and Carey's (1992) cross-national study of presidential systems ranks Chile's 1925 Constitution along with that of 1980 as among the most presidential of systems in the world. Although the Chilean institutional structure has been characterized in the modern era by constitutionally strong presidents, the necessity of coalition-building within Chile's divided and sometimes polarized party system at times diluted their power, given the need to moderate policies in order to satisfy coalition partners. In the best of times, presidents attempted to build multiparty governing coalitions. In times of crisis, they often resorted to extraordinary and sometimes extraconstitutional means to achieve their goals.[5]

Following the country's almost 17-year experience with authoritarian rule, legislative authority was substantially undermined by a new

---

[3] For a discussion of the multifunctional contribution of Chile's legislative branch to democratic governability, see Gil (1966), Siavelis (1997a), and Valenzuela and Wilde (1979). Agor (1971) underscores the important role of the Chilean Senate, and particularly Senate committees during the country's democratic evolution.

[4] On the evolution of the power of the presidency under the 1925 Constitution, see Frei et al. (1970)

[5] The Allende administration is usually cited as that most characterized by this type of extraconstitutional executive action, given the distribution of party power in Congress that made it difficult for Allende to pass legislation, but also impossible for the Congress to impeach him. Nonetheless, Allende's actions are only the most graphic representation of what was a recurrent problem in Chile when presidents lacked legislative majorities.

constitution approved in 1980 and a series of reforms designed to reinforce the powers of the Chilean president. Although consonant with the overall historical evolution toward increased presidential power in the country, the formal structure of interbranch relations in postauthoritarian Chile has changed significantly.

In terms of the concrete balance of power between the branches of government, in postauthoritarian Chile the president has been the most important legislative actor, and perhaps the most important legislator.[6] A complete discussion of the formal and informal advantages accorded to the president is beyond the scope of this chapter and has been provided in work by this author and others (Arriagada 1984, 1992; Cea Egaña, 1992; Nef and Galleguillos 1995; Siavelis 1997a). In brief, the 1980 Constitution provides the president exclusive initiative in all matters relating to taxation and the creation of new public agencies and employment therein. Presidential exclusive initiative also applies to any bills creating or changing the terms of entitlement programs and social security, and any proposals dealing with collective bargaining procedures. The national budget proposed by the president automatically becomes law in 60 days if Congress fails to approve it. The president also has the right to declare legislation urgent in any phase of its consideration and to declare extraordinary sessions of Congress, during which only initiatives of the executive branch may be considered (Constitutional Articles 62–64). Finally, the executive branch has access to a much higher quality of expertise and informational resources than the legislative branch, providing it with an advantage in terms of drafting quality legislation (see Siavelis 1997a, pp. 332–335). All of these powers have provided postauthoritarian presidents an upper hand in the legislative process.

Legislative Success: Who Gets What Passed, and How Fast?

Despite the existence of exaggerated presidentialism in Chile and the potential for executive domination, fluid contact, cooperation, and consultation have characterized interbranch relations during the first two postauthoritarian presidencies. There have been few instances of outright conflict between the branches of government. A wide array of important

---

[6] This assertion is qualified, of course, by the discussion presented in the following. The functional legislative powers of presidents are dependent on the partisan powers on which they can rely.

Table 4.1. *Comparison of presidential and legislative initiatives 1990–1993.*

	Presidential Initiatives					
	1990	1991	1992	1993	Total	Percent
Introduced	161	157	175	144	637	100.0
Completed	150	128	112	57	447	70.2
Pending	11	29	63	87	190	29.8
	Congressional Initiatives					
	1990	1991	1992	1993	Total	Percent
Introduced	137	156	148	88	529	100.0
Completed	35	22	10	2	69	13.0
Pending	102	134	138	86	460	87.0

Source: *Congreso de Chile* (1994).

legislation was proposed, passed, and promulgated. This is especially impressive given the challenges faced by the first two governments in resurrecting democratic politics, creating new governmental authorities, and attempting to dismantle some of the most authoritarian aspects of the military government's institutional legacy. Nonetheless, and despite what will be argued in the following concerning the influence that legislators can have, it has been the president who has played the dominant role in legislating since the return of democratic politics, at least in quantitative terms.

During the Aylwin administration, it is clear that the president exercised overwhelming control over the legislative agenda and, given his prerogatives, had a great deal more success than legislators in securing the passage of his initiatives.[7] During the four *legislaturas* (1990–1993) of the Aylwin administration, a total of 1,166 bills were presented. Table 4.1 presents a breakdown of the composition of initiatives based on whether they originated in the executive or legislative branch.

Of the 1,166 bills presented, 529 were presented by members of Congress and 637 were presented by the executive branch. The president both

---

[7] This section of the chapter relies exclusively on data from the Aylwin administration. It is difficult to analyze similar data from the Frei administration, as the available data are not yet complete. Nonetheless, a necessarily impressionistic reading suggests that Frei's record does not differ substantially from that of Aylwin.

Table 4.2. *Forms of completion for presidential and legislative initiatives 1990–1993.*

	Presidential Initiatives					
	1990	1991	1992	1993	Total	Percent
Law	139	110	105	50	404	63.42
Withdrawn	9	12	6	6	33	5.28
Defeated	2	3	0	1	6	0.94
Other	0	3	1	0	4	0.62
Pending	11	29	63	87	190	29.83
Total	161	157	175	144	637	100.0

	Congressional Initiatives					
	1990	1991	1992	1993	Total	Percent
Law	14	13	7	2	36	6.80
Withdrawn	3	4	1	0	8	1.50
Defeated	6	1	2	0	9	1.70
Other	12	4	0	0	16	3.02
Pending	102	134	138	86	460	86.96
Total	137	156	148	88	529	100.0

Source: Congreso de Chile (1994).

presented more proposals and was much more successful in maneuvering bills through the legislative process. Table 4.1 also summarizes whether the initiatives completed their entire cycle of consideration, otherwise known as all of their *trámites* (shuttles – or steps in the legislative process). Of the 637 proposals presented by the executive branch, 447, or about 70%, completed the entire legislative cycle, irrespective of whether they became laws or not, while only 69 out of the 529 proposals presented by members of Congress were considered, or only 13%. The remaining legislation remained on the calendar for the following year.[8]

In terms of the total rate of passage for legislation, Table 4.2 presents a breakdown of the number and percentage of laws passed. Of the 1,166 laws introduced and summarized in Table 4.1, 440, or 38%, became law. Nonetheless, the president was much more successful in securing the passage of legislation than members of Congress. Of the 440 initiatives

[8] Some of this legislation was subsequently withdrawn, as will be discussed later.

Table 4.3. *Length of consideration: Comparative measures of presidential and congressional initiatives.*

	Duration (days)			
	Average	Minimum	Maximum	Median
Presidential Initiatives	205	2	1190	149
Congressional Initiatives	487	3	1169	448
Both	228	2	1190	158

Source: Congreso de Chile (1994).

passed, 404, or 92%, originated in the executive branch, while only 36 originated in Congress.

Even the rate of passage for bills that were duly and completely considered was quite low if they originated in the legislative branch. Of the 69 bills presented by members of Congress that completed their *tramitación*, only 36, or 52%, were converted into law. What is more, of those projects proposed by members of Congress that were still pending, 385 (of the 460 total), or 83.6%, were *sin tramitación* at the end of Aylwin's term of office, meaning that members of the chamber had been made aware in writing of the bills' introduction, but that the legislation had not yet left the committee stage. In contrast, only 89, or approximately 50%, of the pending presidential initiatives could be characterized as *sin tramitación*.[9]

In terms of speed, presidential initiatives were much more likely to travel quickly through each of the *trámites* necessary for passage. Table 4.3 summarizes the comparative amount of time that it took presidential and legislative initiatives to complete the entire legislative process.

The president's initiatives that became laws took an average of 205 days to complete all of the steps in the legislative process, while legislative initiatives averaged 487 days to complete all of their *trámites* – more than twice the time it took for executive initiatives. Thus, it appears that a crucial indicator of whether or not legislation is passed, and how quickly

[9] While 50% without *tramitación* may seem to suggest legislative blocking power, it is crucial to bear in mind that these 89 initiatives constitute a fraction of the total (637), the majority of which (447) have been approved. This and all other data cited in the text are from *Congreso Nacional de Chile* (1994) unless otherwise noted. The data summarize all legislation, including that characterized in the following as less than significant.

it moves through the legislative process, is where it is introduced. Executive initiatives are much more likely to be considered, and move more quickly through the legislative process.

What is more, executive initiatives during the Aylwin administration were rarely rejected by Congress. During the four years of the Aylwin administration, only six initiatives were defeated. These data should be interpreted cautiously. Both Aylwin and Frei avoided presenting major legislative and constitutional reform initiatives that were unlikely to pass. Both have also withdrawn legislation when it appeared likely that it was in trouble.[10] What is more, and as will be discussed in the following, presidents are also much less likely to have legislation rejected when they can rely on a legislative majority of their own coalition in one chamber and a near majority in the other. Nonetheless, the data still point to a great deal of intracoalitional cooperation, the absence of a great deal of institutional rivalry, and, most importantly, enormous influence for the executive branch in the legislative process.

Time and legislative success are not the only important variables when measuring the legislative balance of power. It is important to consider also the substance of legislation. Simply passing a high number of initiatives quickly says little about their legal or substantive importance for the country. Many of the presidents' initiatives were weighty and substantial in terms of content and influence.[11] On the other hand, few congressional initiatives were of a great deal of significance for the legal or constitutional future of the country. Appendix 4A.1 provides a compilation of legislation proposed by members of one of the two chambers of Congress that became law. Of the initiatives promulgated 14, or 39%, dealt with the establishment of monuments to important national political and literary figures, the granting of citizenship, local scholarships, or the designation of holidays. Two initiatives, or 5%, were laws delegating power or authority to the president or minister in particular areas. Thus, of the limited number of legislative initiatives that became law, 44% were less than significant.

[10] Both controversial bills and those withdrawn given lack of support were often the ones necessitating an extraordinary majority. There are three distinct types of legislation with three levels of quorums necessary for passage. Presidents were most likely to withdraw legislation that required extraordinary majorities.

[11] They include the creation of several agencies at the ministerial level, local government reform, tax reform, and a number of other important initiatives related to the democratic transition. See Siavelis (1997a, pp. 336–337) for a summary.

The rest of the laws dealt with issues of national scope, although not necessarily with issues of the same magnitude that characterized executive initiatives.[12] As the summation presented in Appendix 4A.1 suggests, the only real significant legislation proposed by members of Congress was that raising the legal age of adulthood, and some substantial changes to the penal code.

The legislative record of the Aylwin administration is especially impressive given that the president lacked a legislative majority in the Senate. While the government has indeed garnered an elective majority in the Senate in all elections since the return of democracy in 1989, the existence of nine "institutional" senators (*designados*) appointed by the outgoing Pinochet government has tilted the balance of control in the Senate toward the opposition, for both the Aylwin and Frei administrations.[13] Tables 4.4 and 4.5 summarize the level of coalitional support in Congress during the last three legislative periods.

Powerful Presidents and an Influential Congress: The Transitory Politics of Consensus

Given the unequal distribution of prerogatives between the branches of government and data measuring the legislative balance of power between the president and the legislature, there is a strong temptation to simply conclude that the Chilean legislature is insignificant to the legislative process and, indeed, a rubber stamp for executive initiatives, as earlier literature on Latin American legislatures suggested. The reality that the

[12] I was unable to determine the substantive content of 3 of the 36 congressional initiatives, as they were not provided in the summation issued by the Offices of Information of the Congress, the source of these data. Nonetheless, percentages presented here are based on a total of 36 laws.

[13] The Pinochet government appointed the first set of institutional senators. For subsequent governments, according to the Constitution, the president appoints two senators, the National Security Council four, and the Supreme Court three. Nonetheless, the influence of the right in the appointment process goes farther than it appears at first glance, given the limitations on the pool of candidates from which senators can be drawn, a requirement that four of the senators must be former commanders of the armed forces, and the reality that Pinochet appointees continue to be represented in governmental institutions that choose senators not designated by the president. This influence is likely to decrease as officials appointed by the democratic government work their way through the system.

Table 4.4. *Distribution of seats in the Chilean House of Deputies by party – 1989, 1993, 1997 (N = 120).*[a]

Year		1989 Number of Seats	1989 Percent Seats	1993 Number of Seats	1993 Percent Seats	1997 Number of Seats	1997 Percent Seats
Concertación		72	60%	70	58.3%	70	58.3%
	PDC	39	32.5%	37	30.8%	39	32.5%
	PS	18	15%	15	12.5%	11	9.2%
	PPD	7	5.8%	15	12.5%	16	13.3%
	Other	8	6.7%	3	2.5%	4	3.3%
Unión Por Chile[b]		48	40%	50	41.7%	47	39.2%
	RN	32	26.7%	29	24.2%	23	19.2%
	UDI	14	11.7%	15	12.5%	17	14.2%
	Other	2	1.7%	6	5%	7	5.8%
Individual and others not on major lists						3	2.5%

[a] There was a great deal of fluidity in party identification after the 1989 election, given limitations on the registration of parties imposed by the outgoing government and problems with individual candidate registration. The breakdown of party identification for Tables 4.4 and 4.5 represents the parties that candidates eventually joined, not necessarily the label under which these candidates ran in the election.

[b] This pact in previous elections has also been known as Democracia y Progreso and Unión por el Progreso.

Source: Siavelis (2000).

Senate was dominated by the opposition, but seems not to have been obstructionist, would tend to confirm that the legislature is not very influential. However, conclusions of this sort are premature and probably incorrect. It is important to subject both the use of executive authority and the extent of the assemblies' influence in the governing process to some scrutiny. Careful analysis suggests that, while the characterization of exaggerated presidentialism in constitutional terms is correct, in practice other variables have shaped the way in which presidents have chosen to act and the range of powers that they have had the incentives to employ. What is more, analysis of less formal activity by legislators also suggests that the legislature is more influential than a concrete reading of the Constitution or organic law of the Congress would suggest.

Table 4.5. *Distribution of seats in the Chilean Senate by party, 1989, 1993, 1997 (N = 47 [38 elected, 9 appointed for 1989, 1993], N = 48 [38 elected, 9 appointed, 1 former president] for 1997).*[a]

Year		1989 Number of Seats	1989 Percent Seats	1993 Number of Seats	1993 Percent Seats	1997[b] Number of Seats	1997[b] Percent Seats
Concertación		**22**	**46.8%**	**21**	**44.7%**	**20**	**41.7%**
	PDC	13	27.7%	14	29.8%	14	29.2%
	PS	4	8.5%	4	8.5%	2	4.2%
	PPD	1	2.1%	2	4.2%	4	8.3%
	Other	4	8.5%	1	2.1%	0	0%
Unión Por el Progreso		**25**	**53.2%**	**26**	**55.3%**	**27**	**56.3%**
	RN	13	27.7%	11	23.4%	7	14.6%
	UDI	2	4.2%	3	6.4%	5	10.4%
	Other	1	2.1%	3	6.4%	5	10.4%
	Appt.[c]	9	19.1%	9	19.1%	10	20.8%
Unión Progresista del Centro						1	2.1%

[a] Only one-half of the Senate is elected every four years.

[b] General Pinochet stepped down as commander in chief of the armed forces in 1997 and assumed a life-long Senate seat. He is included with the appointed senators after this date and is counted when calculating the percentage of total seats after 1997.

[c] Appointed senators have no obligation to support the right. Nonetheless, they are listed along with this sector given that evidence from voting records suggests that they usually do, and that they provide effective veto power for the right on especially conflictual legislation. One of the appointed senators during the Aylwin administration died in office and was not replaced, so only eight appointed senators served during his term.

Source: Siavelis (2000).

Urgency Provisions: A Powerful Presidential Tool? A Matter of Time or Influence?

Scholars have often cited the importance of the president's urgency prerogatives when discussing the Chilean presidency. Indeed, I have argued in other places that urgency powers are an important tool for presidents (Siavelis 1997a). However, is the root of success in the legislative arena the president's ability to declare urgencies? What determines the greater likelihood of the president having his initiatives converted into law? Data from the Aylwin administration suggest that, although urgency powers may be

Table 4.6. *Legislation introduced according to urgency and branch of origin (1990–1993)*.

	Presidential Initiatives					
	1990	1991	1992	1993	Total	Percent
With urgency	80	95	108	92	375	58.9
Without urgency	81	62	67	52	262	41.1
Total	161	157	175	144	637	100.0
	Congressional Initiatives					
	1990	1991	1992	1993	Total	Percent
With urgency	9	7	9	6	31	5.9
Without urgency	128	149	139	82	498	94.1
Total	137	156	148	88	529	100.0

Source: Congreso de Chile (1994).

significant in constitutional terms, or potentially important given certain partisan constellations, during the Aylwin administration they had less of an effect than one might expect.

The Chilean president has broad powers to declare legislation urgent at most stages in the legislative process. Although urgency powers were originally designed to be employed in extraordinary situations so that pressing legislation crucial to the country's future would be expedited, presidential urgency power has become a standard legislative tool for Chilean presidents. There are three levels of urgency: *simple urgencia, suma urgencia*, and *discusión inmediata*, each with different requirements concerning the speed with which presidential initiatives must be considered (The Political Constitution of the Republic of Chile, Article 71 and Organic Law of the Congress Articles 26, 27, and 28).[14] The president can also declare urgent bills presented by deputies or senators in order to expedite their consideration. This was done rarely during the Aylwin administration. Of the 529 bills presented by members of Congress, only 31 were declared urgent by the president. At the same time, as Table 4.6 shows, a

[14] The requirements for time of consideration in either chamber of Congress are 30, 10, and 3 days, respectively, for a *simple urgencia*, a *suma urgencia*, and a *discusión inmediata*.

Table 4.7. *Length of legislative consideration of presidential initiatives according to urgency.*

	Duration (Days)			
	Average	Minimum	Maximum	Median
With urgency	203	2	871	134
Without urgency	208	3	1190	160

Source: Congreso de Chile (1994).

little under two-thirds of presidential initiatives were designated urgent at some point in their consideration.[15]

Despite the fact that urgency powers were instituted to speed up the consideration of legislation deemed important for governing the country, in reality the president employed urgency powers to give priority to his own initiatives. The simple term urgency suggests a call for immediate attention and that time is crucial. The data presented in Table 4.1, which show the relative legislative success of each of the branches of government, would seem to suggest that urgency has given the president an advantage. However, the real test to determine the effect of urgencies is to analyze and compare the fate of *executive* initiatives with and without declared urgencies. Although counterintuitive, there is little appreciable difference in the speed of consideration or the legislative success rate for executive initiatives designated as urgent and those not. It appears that the branch of origin, then, is much more important than urgency declaration in terms of the passage of legislation.

Table 4.7 compares the amount of time required for legislation with origin in the executive branch to complete all of its *trámites*. Data from the Aylwin administration clearly demonstrate that the declaration of a presidential urgency made little difference in terms of whether an executive initiative would be approved. With declared executive urgency, bills

---

[15] One should treat these statistics with caution, as particularly good legislative initiatives often find their way into a bill proposed by the president. In addition, the president is known to monitor legislation and often proposes initiatives that are quite similar to those presented by members of Congress. It is very difficult to determine for which bills this is the case, given that much legislation emerges from consensus between legislators and representatives of the executive branch.

Table 4.8. *Summary of approval rate for executive initiatives with and without urgency (1990–1993).*

Presidential initiatives	With urgency	Without urgency	Total
Approved	240 (64%)	164 (62.6%)	404
Pending withdrawn	135 (36%)	98 (37.4%)	233
Total	375	262	637

Source: Computed by the author from data from *Congreso Nacional de Chile* (1994).

took an average of 203 days to consider and pass, compared to 208 days without urgency.

What is more, if one compares the overall percentage of presidential bills that were converted into law based on whether or not the president employed urgency powers, it appears that these powers do almost nothing. Table 4.8 summarizes these data.

Of the 637 total initiatives presented by the president, 375 were declared urgent and 262 were not. Nonetheless, the approval rating for both sets of legislation is virtually the same. Legislation declared urgent had a 64% approval rate while legislation without urgency had an approval rate of 62.6%.

Do urgencies then have no effect? What is intriguing about the answer to this question is that when urgencies are considered separately it seems that urgency does something to expedite the consideration of particular bills by the legislature. When broken down into distinct types (whether it is a *simple urgencia*, a *suma urgencia*, or a *discusión inmediata*) the level of urgency seems to have bearing on the likelihood that legislation is approved. Of the presidential initiatives with *discusión inmediata*, 92% were converted into law, while the rate of passage for *suma urgencia* and *simple urgencia* was 73% and 56%, respectively. These bills were also considered more quickly, and the speed of consideration was directly related to the level of urgency.

These data present a number of puzzles. When the data comparing legislative success and speed of consideration for executive and legislative initiatives are considered separately, it appears that urgency helps the president secure the passage of his initiatives. However, when only executive initiatives are considered it appears that urgency powers have little global effect, until they are disaggregated by type.

Executive–Legislative Relations in Chile

It is difficult to determine what to conclude from what seems contradictory data. Clearly, a number of other variables can help to explain the inconsistency between the global effect of urgencies and their effect when broken down into distinct types. It is quite conceivable that certain types of more universally acceptable legislation are more likely to be considered for *discusión inmediata*. The president might designate legislation as such when passage looks simple, in order to move it quickly through all of its *trámites*. What is more, the overall influence of the president, and the other legislative- and agenda-setting tools at his disposal, may also help to explain the variance in the data. The president would clearly have used the *discusión inmediata* designation for the legislation that was most important to him, and would likely have applied the other tools at his disposal to expedite the consideration of his pet legislation. Presidential urgency has been interpreted as an important tool in the arsenal of the Chilean president, but it is only one of those tools.

However, the overall (and perhaps not completely realized) power of the executive branch may do more to explain the disparity in the rates of passage of legislation with distinct branches of origin. Herein lies the most likely (and important in terms of the argument of this chapter) explanation for the seemingly minimal effect of urgency declaration: Presidents have been very flexible in the use of urgency powers, and the legislature has been successful in securing time extensions in order to more carefully consider legislation.[16] Officials within the executive branch often have been asked by congressional leadership to withdraw or change the level of urgency of particular pieces of legislation in order to be assured of the overall coherence and passage of the ruling Concertación coalition's legislative package.[17] Presidents in most circumstances respect those requests in the interests of coalition maintenance and the furtherance of their

---

[16] That said, presidential urgency has affected the quality of legislation, at least according to members of Congress. In interviews with legislators, 96.7% of the deputies agreed that presidential urgencies negatively affect the quality of legislation. Several deputies noted that it will probably be necessary to relegislate in a number of key areas, given that declared urgencies prevented the careful elaboration of legislation, both in terms of substance and legislative technique. Interview data cited in this article are based on a series of over 70 interviews with deputies, senators, and members of the executive branch in 1992 and 1993. A party-representative sample of 25% of the membership of each of the chambers was interviewed.

[17] Interviews with Cesar Ladrón de Guevara, Santiago, April 28, 1993, Judicial-Legislative Division, Ministerio Secretaría General de la Presidencia, Patricio Zapata, Ministerio Secretaría General de la Presidencia, May 7, 1993.

legislative agendas. Data on the actual speed of consideration of legislation with designated urgency show that very few urgent proposals are actually considered within the time periods established by the organic law of the Congress. Of those bills designated with simple *urgencia* in their *primer trámite*, only 17% completed this cycle in the required 30 days, and only 23% with such a designation in their *segunda trámite* did so. For those designated with *suma urgencia* (10-day completion requirement) these figures are 45% and 52%, respectively, for each of the *trámites*, and for *discusión inmediata* (3 days), these figures are 75% and 81% (Congreso Nacional de Chile 1994, pp. 39–52). This suggests that the president was willing to withdraw and change levels of urgency, or at the very least accept the fact that Congress would often fail to consider legislation within the timing parameters set out in the organic law. Urgencies form a part of the overall equation of constitutional executive dominance that has yet to come into play. With a change of coalitional and political circumstances urgency powers may become a more important tool for presidential agenda-setting and in turn may enhance the potential for interbranch conflict.

Thus, partisan considerations, the constellation of party power, and coalitional and transitional politics have helped to ease the president's legislative task and have created few incentives for the strict and inflexible exercise of presidential urgency powers.

Presidential Budgetary Dominance?

The 1980 Constitution provides the president with strong budgetary powers. Article 64 states, "The Budgetary Law Proposal must be submitted to the National Congress by the President of the Republic at least three months prior to the date on which it should become effective; should it not be passed by Congress within sixty days from the date of its submittal, the project submitted by the President of the Republic shall enter into force."[18] Just as the urgency power described previously seems like a powerful tool in the presidential arsenal that has yet to be employed, despite the president's budgetary authority, neither postauthoritarian president has been tempted to simply impose his version of the budget. Budgetary negotiations are particularly illustrative of the influence that Congress, and especially the opposition, can have in informal ways not set out in the Constitution or in organic laws. Despite strong control over the

---

[18] All translations were undertaken by the author.

national budget, both Aylwin and Frei have worked constructively with members of Congress to hammer out an agreement.[19] Presidents also routinely consulted with members of their own parties, and indeed with opposition parties in and outside of Congress.[20] Every year since the return of democracy the president has signed the version of the budget passed by Congress.

Budgetary success for presidents still lies in negotiation, and the success of negotiation hinges on all sides having a certain measure of influence. How does this influence take shape? Legislators have been successful in altering the initial proposals of the president, although in terms of overall percentage of the budget the change is minor. Baldez and Carey (1996) found that, for the four years that they analyzed, the final budget varied by less than 1% from the initial proposal.[21] However, final budget-numbers are not the whole story in terms of legislative influence over budget-making. For particularly important legislation like the budget (but also for other important initiatives) active lobbying takes place by legislators in both the proposal and consideration stages. Thus, the demands of the presidents' *coreligionarios*, coalition partners, and opposition are often incorporated into the presidents' proposal. During consideration, the president maintains constant contact with the legislative leadership of both his own party and the opposition.

Since the return of formal democracy in Chile the primary conflicts that have emerged in budget negotiations between the government and the opposition have been centered in the areas of social spending and the rate of overall government expenditure. The interbranch negotiations for the 1997 and 1998 budgets reflect the dynamic of negotiation described previously in terms of the ways in which these conflicts were resolved. While in both instances the government's initial budget proposals for the most part prevailed, the opposition was able to extract some concessions from the executive. In coming to an agreement on the 1997 budget, the opposition criticized the government for its failure to both manage and rein in social spending, for a lack of transparency in discretionary spending, and for general mismanagement in the disbursement of public funds. Through negotiations with the government, the opposition UDI (Unión Demócrata Independiente) was able to extract agreements setting a limit

[19] For a discussion of the budget-making process in Chile, see Baldez and Carey (1996).
[20] Impressionistic readings of budget negotiations in the press suggest this.
[21] Baldez and Carey (1996) analyze the 1991 and 1993–1996 budgets.

on discretionary spending from the public treasury and measures to enhance transparency and efficiency in spending, including external audits to evaluate bidding and contracting procedures. Finally, the government and a congressional conference committee (*comisión mixta*) on the budget agreed to select 20 social subsidy programs for evaluation during 1997 to determine whether they should be continued.[22]

Similarly, only 3 days away from the expiration of its 60-day consideration period, the 1998 budget agreement was sealed in November 1997. For this set of budget negotiations the government was again criticized for excessive and irresponsible social spending, and for insufficiently addressing the transparency issues brought up in the previous year's budget negotiations. In particular, opposition senators pointed to insufficient budget cuts for the National Youth Institute (INJ) in the Chamber of Deputies' budget proposal. The opposition also contended that the government had reneged on its promise to evaluate the social subsidy programs discussed in the 1997 budget negotiations. As in the case of the previous year, a compromise proposal was reached by cutting the agencies' budget, albeit to a lesser degree than set out in the Senate version of the budget proposal. What is more, the government agreed to redouble its oversight of social subsidy programs and to consider an additional 40 programs for systematic evaluation and potential elimination.[23]

Why would the president subject himself and his party to such arduous negotiations if he could conceivably wait it out and see his budget take effect? From the most basic perspective, the passage of a budget law in this manner would create a great deal of potential uncertainty. The Constitution and organic law are unclear on the exact process that would be followed should the president's proposal fail to be approved by Congress. If the president's budget proposal becomes law automatically, does this refer to the budget set out in the *original* executive proposal, or one that has been subject to modifications during negotiations? There are additional questions concerning whether the president can veto a budget law as passed by Congress, because a presidential veto is never mentioned in Article 64, which deals with the budgetary process.[24] However, there are

---

[22] Alhough it contained many of its proposals, the main opposition party Renovación Nacional (RN) refused to sign the agreement.

[23] For a recounting of these budget negotiations see, *La Epoca*, November 26, 1997, and *El Mercurio*, September 30 and November 21, 1996.

[24] See Baldez and Carey (1996) for a discussion of this uncertainty.

a number of other important realities that make such unitary presidential action on the budget unlikely.

First, both Aylwin and Frei have had an interest in seeking agreement and consensus on the budget given the party distribution of seats in Congress. Presidents had little to gain from unilaterally trying to impose budgets. If budget proposals existed in isolation and the processes of budget-making and legislating were not an iterated game, it would make perfect sense for the president to simply sit back and wait for the 60-day limit on congressional action to expire. Nonetheless, given that neither postauthoritarian president has been afforded the luxury of a majority in the Senate, after the budget, the president must continue to legislate and rely on at least a few votes of the opposition or institutional senators in order to have a viable legislative program.[25] Although the complete opposition has not in every case joined in approving the budget, the failure of a president to attempt to negotiate a solution to at least some of the opposition's objections could have resulted in a legislatively moribund president. In this sense, with a majority in both chambers the president may have been able to impose his budgetary agenda by attempting to compel coalition discipline. Similarly, with a very large opposition majority in the Senate, the president may have been tempted to also impose his agenda by simply letting the 60-day period established for the consideration of the budget expire. Given their proximity to a working majority in the Senate, both presidents avoided these strategies and instead sought to negotiate and cajole rather than resort to strong-arm tactics.

Thus, the coalitional situation just described, with presidents a few votes short of a majority in the Senate, made for a situation in which the presidents sought to insure the integrity of their legislative programs by avoiding the imposition of presidential budgets. With a distinct correlation of party forces, or in situations in which immobilism has come to characterize interbranch relations, the president would probably be tempted to act in a more unilateral fashion on the budget and to more vigorously employ executive powers.

Second, legislators cannot change the president's proposal very much. By subjecting the budget proposal to congressional scrutiny, the president

---

[25] Although institutional senators deny automatically voting with the right, on matters of importance like constitutional reform and the status of the military, institutional senators have invariably lined up with the opposition.

is unlikely to lose much of what he or she wants. Given the constitutional limitations on congressional budgetary action set out in the Constitution, legislators cannot propose additional spending to that set out in the budget proposal, nor can they move spending between categories. However, according to Article 64, legislators do have the power to cut spending programs. Nonetheless, for members of Congress there is little incentive to exert pressure for decreased spending; there is still a strong incentive for Chilean legislators to bring home pork.[26] However, given budgetary limitations on personalistic proposals set out in the Constitution, legislators have few mechanisms to do so. Supporting presidential proposals for services or concrete infrastructure development projects allows legislators to at least point to these initiatives as proof that they are advocates for their constituents. This dynamic, again, may change as partisan alignments change.

What is more, legislators cannot propose reductions to budgetary allotments guaranteed by permanent law. These include the areas limited by rules regulating the executives' areas of exclusive initiative and constitutionally mandated allotments for certain areas of expenditure, like the military's guaranteed and legally designated quota of a portion of state copper revenues. This leaves very few areas for legislators to cut. Legislators are loath to reduce the expenditures that do remain, because these are often entitlements and capital purchases.

Finally, from the perspective of interbranch (as opposed to interparty) rivalry, it appears that members of Congress are satisfied with a president with strong budgetary powers. Indeed, in a party-representative sample of legislators interviewed during the Aylwin administration, 93% of the deputies agreed that the president should maintain the prerogative of exclusive initiative for the budget. There was a consensus among legislators that, without centralized budgetary control in the executive branch, particularistic spending initiatives of individual legislators could break the national budget. Legislators appear to have an expectation that the executive should play the dominant role in the budgetary process. This basic predisposition makes the presidents' job easier and provides fewer incentives for the employment of extraordinary executive power.

[26] For a discussion of this reality, see Siavelis (1997a). For a discussion of the importance of personalism in Chilean historical perspective, see Valenzuela (1978) and Valenzuela and Wilde (1979).

Presidential Decree Authority

While the issue of presidential decree authority has received detailed attention in recent literature,[27] very little has been written on decree authority in postauthoritarian Chile. First, decree authority is limited in the Chilean case. The president has the ability to issue decrees with the force of law during a period of one year with a specific delegation by Congress (Article 32–22). Second, although the scope of the presidential decree is, indeed, limited, it has also been underestimated in the literature on the Chilean presidency. The president need only consult the Congress when declaring a state of siege; states of assembly, emergency, and catastrophe can be declared without consulting Congress.[28] What is more, the president also has the ability to "exercise the statutory authority (*potestad reglamentaria*) in all those matters which are not of a legal nature, without prejudice to the power to issue other regulations, decrees or instructions which he may deem appropriate for the enforcement of the law" (Article 32, No. 8). Although not decree authority as it is usually understood, as noted, the president also has effective decree authority over the budget in certain situations, and Congress cannot increase expenditures nor make transfers between categories of spending.

However, most importantly, the political situation in which postauthoritarian presidents have operated has not necessitated the use of decree authority. Both presidents have been able to rely on a coalitional majority in the lower chamber and a near majority in the upper chamber, so situations in which it would be necessary to employ extraordinary executive powers have never materialized. This is not to suggest that the president and assembly have identical preferences. Rather, the sensitive and precarious nature of the democratic transition and the continued necessity of coalition building to pass legislation have also encouraged presidents to be moderate and measured in the choice of strategies to pursue their initiatives and provided legislators important incentives for negotiation. The muted and moderate nature of political discourse, the politics

---

[27] See Carey and Shugart (1998).

[28] To declare these states of exception the president must seek the approval of the National Security Council (CSN), made up of the president of the republic, the president of the Senate, the president of the Supreme Court, and the four commanders in chief of the armed forces. While this represents a check on presidential decree authority, it is a limited one given the council's composition.

of *democracia consensual*, and the necessity of coalition maintenance have made for an environment of consensus, rather than conflict, between the executive and legislative branches. In short, presidents have had little reason to contemplate the use of decree authority.

The Legislature as an Influential Actor

The data presented throughout this chapter seem to suggest that legislators have little if any influence over the legislative process beyond acting as a rubber stamp. This is an erroneous conclusion, which several realities contradict. Measures of legislative success and time of consideration are not the only indicators of potential avenues of influence for Congress. What is more, an analysis of the formal powers of legislatures based on the zero-sum type of equation set out in the introduction is not entirely accurate. The relative power of legislatures and the influence of individual legislators depend on a wide array of variables, some of which have already been suggested or explicitly discussed here.

One of the tasks of legislatures is to improve legislation through collective deliberation. No data exist measuring the extent to which legislation is changed in wording or substantive content as it passes through the legislative process. It is quite difficult to pinpoint when changes to legislation are made and by whom. There were some concrete measures of legislative influence during the Aylwin administration, including the fact that 46% of the legislation passed through more than two *trámites*, suggesting that a modification of proposals was occurring in one of the two chambers.

Nonetheless, less quantifiable evidence suggests that members of Congress do have an important role in the legislative process. There are other avenues of influence for legislators, some of which are dependent on formal institutional structures, some informal, and some that are a function of the partisan composition of the legislative and executive branches.

First, in formal terms, legislators affect the legislative process and laws in other ways than simply voting and carrying out their constitutionally mandated legislative roles. A series of new institutions and ministries was created in the aftermath of the authoritarian regime and during the first democratic government to ease relations between the branches of government, given the delicate and transitional nature of politics. Many of these institutions were innovations of the Aylwin administration that were consciously designed to coordinate and ensure the coherence of the activities of the new government, thus underwriting the integrity of the democratic transition. One of the most important has been the Ministerio Secretaría General de la Presidencia (SEGPRES). SEGPRES was an administrative creation of the authoritarian government that Pinochet relied on as a coordinating secretariat of the military government's cabinet. With the return of democracy, the secretariat was elevated to the ministerial level, and five separate divisions that did not exist during the authoritarian government were created.[29]

The most important in terms of executive–legislative relations are the Division of Political-Institutional Relations and the Judicial-Legislative Division. The former is responsible for coordination between the executive branch and social organizations, and during the first two postauthoritarian presidencies has dealt principally with relations between the government and political parties. The latter researches and elaborates presidential bills, studies those presented by legislators, and is responsible for maintaining frequent contact and fluid interchange between the branches of government. This division is often referred to as the *cocina* (kitchen) of the legislative process, but it does much more. It also coordinates and serves as a clearinghouse for *oficios* (official requests for information) sent by legislators. Given the president's success in dominating the legislative process in the postauthoritarian period, the Judicial-Legislative Division is one of the most important centers of the legislative process in Chile. The division maintains an office in the Congress in Valparaíso, with three full-time staff members charged with representing the executive branch in Congress and with coordinating the president's agenda with the activities of parliamentarians of the governing coalition.

Both of these divisions have served as crucial formal interlocutors in interbranch relations. They maintain constant contact with legislators and monitor the direction of opinion, providing the president with information concerning the likelihood that his legislative agenda will fare well in Congress. The president can also be provided this information directly from the opposition. According to SEGPRES officials, when drafting the president's legislative agenda, the staff is usually quite aware of legislators' stances on particular issues, and legislation is often adjusted accordingly in order to attract sufficient votes.

---

[29] The others in addition to those discussed here include the Division of Inter-ministerial Coordination, the Research Division, and the Executive Division.

Representatives of the executive branch are also formally represented within the legislative process in testifying before the general assemblies of each of the chambers of Congress and at the committee level. Here executive branch officials get a feeling for the general mood in the legislature and the members' attitudes toward the president's legislative program. Executive proposals are surely influenced by this exposure.

Members of Congress also help set the legislative agenda, both formally and informally. There are a series of interparty connections that link executive institutions and the Congress. At the beginning of every legislative session officials of the executive branch meet with both chambers of Congress to set legislative priorities for the year.[30] For example, in June 1997, Secretary General of the Presidency Juan Villarzu met with legislators and other ministers to decide on a list of obsolete executive initiatives to be removed from the legislative docket. Each of the committees of the two chambers was asked to provide the president with a list of items for which members would recommend withdrawal.

Informal meetings between the representatives of the executive branch and legislators have also been the norm. Legislators of governing parties meet with high-level officials within the ministries working in the same substantive area to discuss what type of legislation is necessary and should be incorporated into the executives' program.[31] Representatives from ministries and legislative committees in the same substantive areas continue to meet after the proposal stage to discuss aspects of bills later in the legislative process. In cases where particularly important legislation is being considered, like the annual budget, the president often meets with legislators of the committee discussing the legislation.

However, more important in terms of making conclusions concerning long-term trends (and as will be discussed in detail later), the partisan composition of the legislature during the first two postauthoritarian governments made the presidents' legislative tasks much less arduous and gave legislators more influence. While presidents have been almost assured approval of their initiatives in the Chamber of Deputies, they were forced to negotiate in the Senate, where they lacked a majority, as Tables 4.4 and 4.5 summarized. This meant that the government often entered into formal and informal negotiations with the opposition to reach

---

[30] Interview with Cesar Ladrón de Guevara, advisor, Judicial-Legislative Division of the Ministry of the General Secretary of the Presidency, Santiago, April 28, 1993.
[31] Interview, Carlos Carmona, April 23, 1993.

agreements and construct working majorities for the most controversial legislation.

Informal negotiations among parties of the Concertación are difficult to quantify, and it is even more difficult to determine the influence of the opposition. Nonetheless, though it appears that the president is doing everything legislatively, governing and opposition deputies do have some influence. As an official in SEGPRES contended, the government recognizes that members of the opposition often have something to offer, given that their perspective is distinct from that of the government in terms of both the problems facing the country and the potential solutions to them.[32] More realistically, the president could not pass anything without some consultation with the opposition. Hence, the executive branch often engaged the opposition in extensive discussions on particularly controversial legislation. This reality even prompted some members of Aylwin's own coalition to suggest that he "went over their heads" to negotiate directly with the opposition. In interviews undertaken during the Aylwin administration with a party-representative sample of legislators, 44% of the government deputies and 50% of the opposition deputies agreed with this contention. The most often cited example of this type of behavior was Aylwin's direct negotiations with business leaders and members of the opposition in arriving at an agreement on Chile's 1990 comprehensive tax reform.

With a different constellation of party forces in the legislature, these types of negotiations might have been less productive. Despite a strong presidency during Chile's first extended period of democracy between 1925 and 1973,[33] presidential power was circumscribed by the exigencies of coalition building in Congress.[34] Given PR and multipartism, presidents were forced to hammer out agreements with opposition parties in Congress to ensure the passage of legislation. Both postauthoritarian presidents have had the advantage of a coalition majority in one chamber and the ability to negotiate a majority in the other. Thus, it has been much easier for presidents to legislate without extensive interparty wrangling. When future presidents find themselves lacking congressional majorities, presidential initiatives are less likely to make their way through Congress so smoothly.

[32] Interview, Cesar Ladrón de Guevara, April 28, 1993.
[33] On the 1925 Constitution see Bravo-Lira (1985) and Campos Harriet (1969).
[34] For a discussion of this reality and a breakdown of congressional support for all presidents between 1932 and 1973, see Valenzuela (1994, pp. 110–127).

All of these structures, institutions, and norms have enhanced the influence of Congress. In terms of the argument of this chapter, they have also made the presidents' jobs easier and provided them with few incentives to resort to the extraordinary powers of the presidency.

Party Politics, Presidential Power, and the Future Executive–Legislative Relations

As has been repeatedly stressed throughout this chapter, much of the legislative success of postauthoritarian Chilean presidents seems to be attributable to the constellation of partisan forces in Congress and the dynamic of inter- and intracoalition cooperation forced by the democratic transition. The efforts of the authoritarian regime to engineer a majority through the use of an electoral law designed to benefit the right, and the appointment of nine senators designated by the outgoing authoritarian regime, deprived the governing Concertación alliance of its electoral majority (see Carey, this volume; Guzmán 1993; Rabkin 1996; Siavelis 1991; Siavelis 1997b; Siavelis and Valenzuela 1996). While the president could rely on a coalitional majority in the Chamber of Deputies, each had to cultivate the support of a few of the individuals across the aisle in the Senate, either from the opposition or from among the *designados*. Referring to the pre-coup party system, Valenzuela (1978, p. 17) contends that the legislature remained significant given the absence of party giants capable of dominating politics. Presidential influence was based on the ability of executives to negotiate both within their working coalitional alliances and with the opposition.[35] The existence of a Concertación majority in the chamber and a near majority in the Senate provided both presidents Frei and Aylwin the luxury of circumstances unique in Chilean history. Negotiating and legislating have been much easier. Despite the legislative power and agenda-setting ability formally granted the president by the 1980 Constitution, presidents have governed without employing them to the fullest extent possible.

The exercise of presidential authority during the Aylwin and Frei governments has also been checked in the interests of intracoalitional harmony. Coalition maintenance for the Concertación depended on fluid contact and negotiations, as well as the incorporation of distinct party

---

[35] For a breakdown of these coalitions, see Valenzuela (1994, pp. 123–125).

platforms into a coherent governing agenda. The original Concertación alliance was made up of 17 parties whose interests had to be reconciled. While the 1988 plebiscite exerted a unifying force on the then opposition, purposeful efforts to find a common programmatic denominator and then negotiate other aspects of policy were crucial to coalition maintenance and the integrity of the democratic transition. Most illustrative of this dynamic has been the negotiated distribution of ministry posts. During both the Aylwin and Frei administrations, the various ministries were divided among the parties of the Concertación. What is more, in most ministries the vice minister was from a different party of the coalition than the minister. This provided party leaders insurance that their programmatic concerns would be incorporated into the legislative agenda of the Concertación and their interests taken into account.

This dynamic also extended into the legislative arena. Presidents who dominated the legislative process would be accused of not respecting coalition agreements.[36] Executives walked a fine line, and the full use of presidential authority would signal a deviation from this line.[37]

The nature of postauthoritarian political competition and transitional politics also helped the presidents to succeed in the advancement of their legislative agendas, and provided few incentives for resorting to extraordinary powers. First, the unfolding of the democratic transition has been crucial to interparty and intracoalitional cooperation within both the governing and opposition coalitions (Siavelis 1997a). Throughout the course of interviews undertaken with legislators during the Aylwin presidency, few failed to refer to the "special time" or "special context" of the transition as having an important effect on their behavior and relations with the president. Second, the very nature of Chile's plebiscitarian transition, and the drawing of a clear line between a coherent, unified and well-structured government and opposition, made negotiation less complicated for the president. Given predictable and durable coalition patterns, combined with the formal and informal consultative mechanisms described

---

[36] Indeed Frei was accused of violating this spirit of the Concertación. See *Latin American Weekly Report*, 20 January 1994: 20.

[37] The importance of this reality is evident in the constant comparison of the leadership styles of Aylwin and Frei by party leaders and in the press. While Aylwin is portrayed most often as a consensus-builder, Frei is accused of a more Christian-democratic centered and less consensus-minded style of leadership. The latter has been accused of undermining the bases of trust underwriting coalition functionality and maintenance.

previously, presidents knew where they stood in terms of votes and understood the necessity of marshalling support, and how much support was necessary for initiatives to succeed.

Conclusion

This chapter presented a number of paradoxes and seeming contradictions. It has argued that the Chilean presidency is undeniably very strong in formal constitutional terms. Comparative evidence suggests that these types of systems have the potential to stymie the legislative process and lead to problems of governability (Mainwaring and Shugart 1997). However, empirical evidence from the Chilean case suggests that presidents have had a great deal of success in imposing their legislative agendas both in terms of substantive content and timing, and that relations between the branches of government have been characterized by cooperation and moderation. It does, indeed, appear as if the president has the upper hand in legislation, but this does not mean that the operational dynamic of exaggerated presidentialism has been tested. Indeed, it is quite conceivable that the problems of exaggerated presidentialism have not yet emerged because Chile has yet to have a president that has incentives to use the full arsenal of presidential power. The constellation of formal presidential powers combined sets the stage for executive domination of the legislative process. Nonetheless, presidents may not have the incentives to take advantage of these powers to the extent that the Constitution would permit, given the idiosyncrasies of particular political situations and partisan configurations, and the nature and size of presidential contingents in Congress.

In addition, despite the presidents' legislative success, the chapter suggests that Congress has been quite relevant to the legislative process. However, this is not to suggest that the legislature is strong or that the authoritarian regime's institutional legacy is the optimal framework for Chilean democracy. On the contrary, given that both the unique circumstances of the democratic transition and the constellation of party forces that it produced have begun to change, presidents may in the future have incentives to employ the extraordinary powers that they are provided by the Constitution, and the often predicted problems of governability may materialize.

Also paradoxical is the reality that a divided (though not intransigent) Congress actually provided the legislature more influence, and provided the president a strong incentive to avoid the potentially damaging use of the extreme presidential powers accorded the office by the Constitution. With a clear majority the president could have probably bypassed Congress and relied on the party discipline and good will generated by the transition to simply initiate executive policy. Alternatively, with an intransigent opposition in both houses, the president most likely would have been tempted to use the powers granted him by Chile's hyperpresidentialist Constitution. However, given the constellation of forces in the two houses, presidents could best achieve their goals through negotiation, while simultaneously avoiding poisoning the legislative well. Presidents had more to gain from a combined strategy of cajoling, convincing, and accommodating the opposition than from an imperial imposition of their constitutionally vested authority. The sensitivity of the transition provided an additional incentive for such a course of action. These realities provide support for Cox and Morgenstern's (this volume) conclusion that presidential strategies toward the legislature are partially a function of the extent of pro-government support in the legislature, though this is certainly not a linear relationship. Jones' (this volume) discussion of Argentina provides additional evidence to support this contention. Chile's presidents thus have been "coalitional" in Cox and Morgenstern's terms, though there is certainly no guarantee that future presidents will act in a similar fashion and remain in this category.

Indeed, with a transformed pattern of representation in Congress, these incentives will be less important. Recent institutional reform in Chile makes it more likely that such a transformation in the balance of partisan power will take place in the future. Given the nonconcurrence of presidential and legislative elections, it is more likely that presidents will be forced to govern without a legislative or coalitional majority.[38] Presidential elections are held every six years and congressional elections are held every four.[39] Tapia Videla (1977) notes with reference to the historic nonconcurrence of elections in Chile that "the president had to win two elections to govern" (p. 459). Given the timing and sequencing of elections in Chile, this will still often be the case.

Despite the constitutional power of presidents, the Chilean Congress for the long term will continue to influence the legislative process in

---

[38] In February 1994, Congress approved a constitutional reform that shortened the presidential term from eight to six years.

[39] Senators serve 8 year terms. One-half of the elected members of the Senate face election every four years.

important ways. The question is whether this influence will be a positive one based on negotiation and consensus or a negative one based on veto power. A shift in partisan composition combined with an end to the special context of the democratic transition can in a paradoxical way make the Congress either more or less influential in situations in which presidents lack congressional majorities. Congress will be less influential if presidents choose to employ their full range of powers and bypass the legislative branch. Alternatively, in the same situation, Congress has the potential to be more influential, given its very real capacity to act as a veto on presidential power, and to make it very difficult to govern. Thus, for the long term, the consolidation of democracy in Chile depends on enhanced influence for Congress to institutionalize the incentives for interbranch negotiations, upon which the success of Presidents Aylwin and Frei was based. These incentives were very much a function of the immediate postauthoritarian political situation and the correlation of partisan powers that the composition of Congress helped to produce. However, reforms to the formal powers of the presidency can help to institutionalize a formal dynamic that was in large part dependent on somewhat transitory partisan variables. By reducing the scope of presidential powers, executives will be forced to take the difficult, but ultimately more productive, road of taking into account and incorporating Congress' interests throughout the legislative process, roads that Alywin and Frei took, albeit for different reasons. At the same time, a stronger legislature will force executives to negotiate with the legislature and take fuller account of the demands of Chile's numerous parties, rather than simply imposing presidential agendas through the use of exaggerated presidential powers.

Appendix

Table 4A.1 *Summary of legislation with origins in the legislative branch promulgated as law during the Aylwin administration (1990–1994).*

	Law number/ Boletín number	Date	Material	Origin
1.	18.992 0057-06	8/16/90	Empowers the president of the republic to determine the limits of *comunas* indicated and to renew faculties listed.	Chamber

	Law number/ Boletín number	Date	Material	Origin
2.	18.996 0083-04	9/5/90	Authorizes the erection of monuments in memory of Edmundo Pérez Zujovic.	Chamber
3.	19.013 0131-04	12/17/90	Authorizes the erection of monuments in memory of Jorge Alessandri Rodríguez.	Chamber
4.	19.014 0126-04	12/17/90	Authorizes the erection of monuments in memory of Eduardo Frei Montalva.	Chamber
5.	19.051 0196-04	4/1/91	Authorizes the erection of monuments in memory of Luis Bossay Leiva.	Senate
6.	19.064 0070-06	7/9/91	Protects the norms set out in Law 6.071 concerning horizontal structures and existing buildings in open markets, meadows, markets, and slaughterhouses as indicated.	Chamber
7.	19.092 0325-04	11/14/91	Authorizes the erection of monuments in memory of Caupolicán in the city of Temuco.	Chamber
8.	19.094 0427-04	11/14/91	Modifies Law numbers 17.288 concerning national monuments, and 18.918 of the Organic Law of the National Congress.	Senate
9.	19.099 0156-07	12/5/91	Establishes norms for the granting of birth certificates for the ends therein established.	Chamber
10.	19.101 0055-04	12/11/91	Establishes norms concerning academic and nonacademic personnel of institutions of superior education indicated, which ceased to function in virtue of Article 13 of Law number 18.768.	Chamber

(continued)

Table 4A.1 (*continued*)

	Law number/ Boletín number	Date	Material	Origin
11.	19.135 044-05	5/5/92	Modifies Law number 18.768, with respect to the distribution of income from the betting industry	Chamber
12.	19.150 0722-06	7/7/92	Modifies time limits indicated in Law number 19.130, which modified the Organic Law of Municipalities.	Chamber
13.	19.164 0386-07	9/2/92	Modifies Penal Code and Penal Procedures Code with the intention of strengthening legitimate defense; abolishes Law number 17.010.	Chamber
14.	19.189 0476-07	12/31/92	Modifies Article 66 of the Penal Procedures Code, with respect to notifications.	Chamber
15.	19.203 0121-08	2/24/93	Establishes time limit indicated for energy supplier or consumer cooperatives.	Senate
16.	19.204 0483	2/5/93	Modifies Articles 84, 138, and 139 of the Penal Procedures Code.	Chamber
17.	19.205 344-04	2/6/93	Authorizes the erection of monuments in memory of Jaime Guzmán Errázuriz.	Senate
18.	19.206 0151-04	3/18/93	Modifies Law number 18.681, concerning scholarships for Aysén, Isla de Pascua, and Juan Fernández.	Chamber
19.	19.215 0624-07	5/17/93	Modifies Article 505 of the Penal Procedures Code.	Chamber
20.	19.216 0387-04	5/19/93	Authorizes the erection of monuments in memory of Claudio Arrau León.	Chamber
21.	19.218 0768-04	5/19/93	Establishes a "Day of Solidarity" as a tribute to the priest Alberto Hurtado Cruchaga.	Chamber

	Law number/ Boletín number	Date	Material	Origin
22.	19.219 0615-04	5/20/93	Authorizes the erection of monuments in memory of Radomiro Tomic Romero.	Chamber
23.	19.221 0066-07	6/1/93	Establishes 18 as the legal age of adulthood and modifies all legal codes and statutes indicated.	Senate
24.	19.223 0412-07	6/7/93	Perfects codes relative to computer technology.	Chamber
25.	19.225 0399-07	6/22/93	Modifies Article 201 of the Civil Procedure Code and Article 448 of the Penal Procedure Code.	Senate
26.	19.232 0037-07	8/4/93	Modifies Article 163 of the Tax Code.	Chamber
27.	19.241 0625-07	8/28/93	Modifies indicated articles of the Penal Code and of Law 18.314 (concealment and rape).	Chamber
28.	19.244 0351-04	9/3/93	Authorizes the erection of monuments in memory of the poet Pablo Neruda.	Chamber
29.	19.245 0825-03	9/4/93	Establishes norms relative to jurel processing and modifies the Fishing and Agricultural Law.	Senate
30.	19.258 0496-04	11/4/93	Authorizes the erection of monuments in memory of the poet Gabriela Mistral in La Serena and Vicuña.	Chamber
31.	19.265 1016-09	12/10/93	Authorizes the Directorate of Viability of the Ministry of Public Works to obtain and ship the necessary equipment listed therein.	Senate
32.	19.266 1093-07	11/22/93	Grants honorary Chilean citizenship to religious leader Antonio Ronchi Berra.	Senate
33.	19.273 0273-06	12/9/93	Modifies Decree Law 1.094 of 1975 concerning the exit of resident foreigners.	Chamber and Senate

5

Executive–Legislative Relations: The Case of Mexico (1946–1997)

MA. AMPARO CASAR*

Variance in the balance between the executive and the legislature has a major impact on democratic stability and on the presidential system's performance. In addition, in the case of Mexico – a country that has recently moved into an environment of political plurality – the changing relation and balance between the governmental branches may be of the utmost importance in drafting some of the aspects of the pending state reform.

Analyzing executive–legislative relations in Mexico poses certain difficulties that are not found in other case studies. First, there is the wide gap between formal and informal powers of the executive. Owing to the long dominance of the official party (the Partido Revolucionario Institucional, PRI), presidents in Mexico have been far more powerful than what one would gather from an analysis of only their constitutional prerogatives. I will show in this chapter that these extraordinary informal powers do have institutional roots. They derive, I argue, from the party and electoral systems and the incentives that these have created, not from the abuse of power or usurpation of powers by the presidency.

A second difficulty is posed by the fact that the Mexican political system is still moving. Most analysts date the liberalization of the political system to 1978, when the first serious electoral reform since 1963–1964 was enacted. Nonetheless, it was not until 1988 when the Chamber experienced the first profound change in its composition, a change that deprived the president's party from the two-thirds majority needed to alter the Constitution. Almost 10 years later and after 68 years of a long-standing hegemonic, quasi-single or overdominant party system, the 1997 congressional elections produced a much more plural system, in which control of the

* I am indebted to Cecilia Martínez Gallardo for the research work done for this chapter.

Chamber of Deputies is now shared among three principal parties (47.8% of the seats for PRI, 24.2% for PAN, and 25.2% for PRD). This change allows, at least as a precondition, the alteration of the balance of power between the executive and the legislative branches of power. The fact that the president's party lost its majority in Congress also means that formal powers will begin to play a larger role as a determinant in executive–legislative relations.

The questions relevant to the analysis of executive–legislative relations may not have changed in 1997, but the answers certainly have. While we may offer some more or less clear-cut explanations regarding the determinants of the relation and why they operated in favor of the executive during the period of dominance by the PRI, we must be much more tentative regarding the period in which Congress began to house an important number of representatives from other parties. Drawing on other countries' experiences, the recent changes in the Mexican political system and the behavior of the different parties in the chamber in the last legislative terms, in this chapter I will suggest possible directions that this new relation may take.

Drawing on the work of Shugart, Carey, and Mainwaring (1992, 1997), there are three types of power that define the interbranch balance:

- legislative powers of the executive,
- executive powers of the legislature,
- partisan powers of the executive.

In the next section I explain that the formal powers – presidential lawmaking powers and the legislature's executive powers – have changed somewhat over the years. These formal changes have generally strengthened the formal authority of Congress. Nonetheless, I argue, they have had a minimal impact as compared with the more recent changes brought about by the alteration in the structure of political opportunity and the new composition of Congress. The latter two factors cut into the president's power over his party and, as a result, the historically quiescent rubber-stamp Congress transposed itself. Since 1997, the Mexican Congress has stopped and altered several important executive initiatives, affecting social security legislation, fiscal measures, and the peace accords in Chiapas.

In what follows I begin with an overview of executive–legislative relations before the opening of the system, based on an analysis of the three types of power identified previously. I then discuss the transition period, focusing on the causes that are altering the traditional executive dominance over members of Congress. My conclusions, again, stress the debasement of presidential informal powers as a consequence of the new structure of political opportunity.

Congress and the Executive in the Period of the PRI Hegemony: An Unbalanced Relation

Although there are few in-depth studies that offer hard empirical evidence about the activities of Congress and the behavior of legislators, the picture that emerges from historical analyses of executive–legislative relations is one of absolute domination by the executive (see the next section), of a Congress that has not been up to the powers granted to it by the Constitution, and of a Congress that has had a poor performance regarding its law making and oversight authority. In this section I argue that the explanation to this fact does not lie in an unbalanced constitutional distribution of power between the two branches, but rather in other features of the political system that have greatly increased the scope of presidential power.

The Congress and the Constitution

A brief review of the Congress' powers will readily show that the constitutional ordering of the legislative power establishes the independent origin and survival of Congress, allows it to perform the two basic roles for which it was created, and endows it with the means to do so.

First, the president cannot dissolve the legislature nor compel its action. The independent origin and survival of Congress is "guaranteed" by the Constitution.[1] Next, the law-making authority is ample enough and, of the three branches, the legislative is the one with the greatest number of

---

[1] Articles 41 and 50–61 regulate the Constitution and composition of Congress. Following the essential characteristics of presidential regimes, maximum separation regarding origin and survival is observed. The terms of the legislature are fixed and in no way contingent on the confidence of the executive. To these constitutional articles one must certainly add the electoral law that regulates in a very detailed way the procedures of competition and the distribution of seats. The importance of electoral laws and those that regulate competition cannot be underscored, for through them the division of powers established by the Constitution can be greatly altered.

prerogatives in the economic, political-administrative, judicial, and social spheres (see the Appendix). Third, provisions for checking the executive appear sufficient and adequate enough to make good the division of powers and to serve the countervailing purpose.

The Mexican Constitution is famous for its hundreds of amendments in its 80-year history, but what is less well-known is that a principal target of these reforms has been the powers of Congress (Article 73) and its chambers (Articles 74 and 76). Of the over 300 reforms as of 1997, more than 50 correspond to these three articles. Although there are cases where reforms have decreased the powers of Congress vis-à-vis the executive, most have increased them.[2]

The Constitution and the reforms grant the Congress the power to provide specific direction to policy through legislation and to oversee the policy implementation and regulatory acts of the executive. While these powers are counterbalanced by the president's array of legislative powers (which include veto powers, the right to initiate legislative proposals, rule-making authority, and decree powers) the Mexican president is not extra-ordinarily strong on paper. In short, it would be misleading to conclude that the Mexican Congress is *constitutionally* impaired or poorly equipped[3] to act as an autonomous power.

---

[2] Orozco Henríquez (1988, pp. 27–39 and 50–110) gives a detailed account of the evolution of the powers of the Mexican Congress and of the executive. Reforms increasing the power of the executive correspond, mainly, to the first two decades after the Constitution was drafted. Among those reforms whose purpose was to strengthen the executive, the following stand out: allowing reelection for the president (reforms of 1927 and 1928 but reversed in 1933); extending the presidential period to six years; enhancing the administrative system under control of the executive; and expressly delegated powers under paragraph 2 of Article 131. However, the legislative branch has increased its powers more relative to the executive. There is not enough space to give a detailed account of the extension of powers of Congress, but the following may serve as examples: right of the Permanent Commission to convene Congress to hold extraordinary periods; extending the terms served by congressmen from two to three years; right to call before Congress the secretaries of state as well as directors and managers of state enterprises; a number of controls over administrative and economic matters; the establishment of two instead of just one congressional term; and, very importantly, several electoral reforms. More recently, autonomy was granted to the Bank of Mexico and to the Federal Electoral Institute, subtracting from the direct control of the executive these two institutions. It is imperative to mention that, beginning in 1997, the Major of Mexico City, which was an appointment reserved to the head of the executive, became a popularly elected post.

[3] This does not mean in any way that the legislative branch of government cannot and should not be strengthened through constitutional reform.

The "Classic" Legislature in Operation

In spite of its constitutional powers, the Congress in postrevolutionary Mexico appears as a weak and subordinated institution. Weakness and subordination are patent in the domains where congressional action is expected. Congress in Mexico has played a rather poor role in law making. It is not only that congressmen are seldom initiators of law proposals, but also that they do not play the role of stopping or substantially amending those bills sent by the executive.[4] In fact, there are very few studies on the behavior of Congress regarding initiatives from the executive. Of these, all present evidence for congressional weakness. Gonzalez Casanova's (1965) study finds that in 1935, 1937, and 1941 every bill (100%) sent by the executive to Congress was approved unanimously. The average number of executive initiatives passed unanimously in the period 1943–1961 was 77%, and the average opposition to initiatives was never over 5%.[5] In another study, Goodspeed (1955) records some important initiatives that were blocked in the early postrevolutionary years (1917–1934), and although he accepts that those years saw a more combative Congress, he nonetheless concludes that it had a subordinate role vis-à-vis either the strong man or the president. Regarding the budget, an area where the Chamber of Deputies has the last word, Wilkie (1967) reached the following conclusions: "From 1918 to 1928 there was only one change in the budget submitted by the President and approved by the House, and this amounted to only .1%"; "[Generally] the President could ignore the House and decree his budget in case of an emergency as was done in 1919, 1920, 1921, 1922 and 1924"; "the 30s witnessed the last congressional budgetary modifications of any extent in Mexico." In 1932 and 1937, the president's initiative was changed by about 1%, and in 1934 it was revised by 6%." [Then] from 1939 to 1953 modifications of .1% to .2% were made . . . [Since that time] Congress has abandoned its role as

---

[4] Although a compliant Congress, that is, a Congress that supports permanently all or most initiatives from the executive, is not proof enough of powerlessness or subordination, it is nonetheless striking that, term after term, over four decades Congress records a minimum of rejected or substantially reformed pieces of legislation.

[5] It is difficult to say how accurate the figures presented by González Casanova are. There is evidence, for example, that Cárdenas' initiative regarding the trade unionization of federal public employees was delayed twice by Congress. In the end it was approved in 1938, but it took the dismissal of those members of Congress who opposed the proposal (Goodspeed 1955, pp. 131–132).

overseer of expenditure since 1954, except for a moment of daring in 1960 when it upped projections by .1%" (p. 17). He adds that "presidential flexibility to disturb federal funds is maximum" given the existence of a permanently compliant Congress (p. 19).

The general image is then that initiatives have traditionally passed either unamended or with minor amendments that might have been deemed necessary to incorporate the interests of certain sectors (within the same "revolutionary family") that had not been taken into account initially.

Congressional checking of presidential powers has not been a practice either. As stated previously, the legislative branch was endowed with specific and direct powers to check executive acts. This authority covers different areas that go from confirmation of appointments to the power to indict (impeach) the head of the executive for high treason or severe offenses against the common order. However, history records that Congress has seldom made use of them. Maybe the most striking example is the disuse of Congress' power to oversee the executive budget (Article 74, frac. IV). Although the General Accounting Office officially depends on Congress, it has *always* approved the budget, even when it was clear that the executive had ignored the approved budget. Carpizo (1978, p. 149) cites the example of 1976 when the executive "borrowed on the credit of the nation" 48.4% in excess of what had been authorized by Congress. No action was taken by Congress in spite of the unconstitutionality of this behavior.

There are other examples. As recently as 1988–1989 the opposition parties in the Chamber of Deputies,[6] making use of a constitutionally endowed right, requested an investigation of the Federal Electricity Commission and PEMEX. But, in a manner that was judged unconstitutional, the PRI deputies decided to block the request.

Finally, there is the area of the delegation of powers. Article 49 clearly prohibits the delegation of legislative powers to the executive, except in the case of Article 29, which deals with emergency situations that require the suspension of constitutional guarantees and to regulate foreign commerce (Article 131). In 1951, Article 49 was amended to include an extra provision further limiting the delegation of extraordinary powers to

---

[6] Article 93 establishes that 25% of the deputies may request that a commission be set up to investigate the state of a federal agency or state enterprise.

119

legislate.[7] In spite of these constitutional prohibitions, cases of delegation of powers during the early postrevolutionary period abound. Most of the time, delegation did not observe the constitutional prescriptions. From 1917 to 1940, all presidents made use of this recourse more than once. Moreover, they used the extraordinary powers granted by Congress not only for the purposes for which the empowerment was made, but also to legislate in as varied areas as education, industry, building of infrastructures, and penal and civil codes (Goodspeed 1955).

After the Cárdenas period (1934–1940), only once has Congress invoked Article 29 to grant the executive legislative powers (and that was during the Second World War). However, Congress has continued to delegate powers that are deemed unconstitutional by specialists. The case of the *Ley de Ingresos de la Federación para el Ejercicio Fiscal de 1978* (Income Law) can be taken as a good example of delegation. This law authorized the executive to acquire and spend 50 million pesos in internal debt and 44.5 million pesos in external debt to cover the spending needs of the 1978 budget. This same law authorized the executive to undertake additional financing if, according to the president, there are extraordinary circumstances that may require him to do so (Carpizo 1978, p. 145). Carpizo rightly states that this ordering violates the Constitution and exemplifies Congress' abdication of its "power of the purse."

This brief account demonstrates how the Mexican Congress has repeatedly been unwilling or unable to carry out its constitutional mandate. What explains this failure? More specifically, how can we reconcile the claim that Congress is a reasonably well-built institution (constitutionally speaking) with the evidence that far from supporting the separation of powers principle, the Congress has repeatedly forfeited its central roles of

---

[7] Specifically, the amendment prohibits delgation except for the provisions of the second paragraph of Article 131. Paragraph 2 of this article states that the executive may be empowered by Congress to increase, decrease, or abolish tariff rates on imports and exports that were imposed by Congress itself, and to establish others, and likewise to restrict and to prohibit the importation, exportation, or transit of the articles, products, and goods when he deems this expedient for the purpose of regulating foreign commerce, the economy of the country, the stability of domestic production, or for accomplishing any other purpose to the benefit of the country. It adds that, the executive himself, in submitting the fiscal budget to Congress each year, shall submit for its approval the use that it has made of this power. Constitutionalists have judged this article as unconstitutional and, we may add, as an abdication of the power of Congress in one of the main areas where it could have checked presidential power.

law making and checking the executive? The source of this weakness must be found in extraconstitutional factors.

Explaining Congressional Weakness

In practice, formal powers are far from sufficient to uphold an autonomous behavior, and, unless certain political conditions are met, the way is paved for the encroachment by the executive on the legislature either by way of delegation or abdication.

As Weldon also argues in his contribution to this volume, two factors – large PRI majorities and loyalty of those majorities to the president – largely explain the Congress' unfulfilled constitutional role and its delegation or abdication of powers to the executive.[8] Both factors have to do with the executive's penetration into the representative role of Congress. The executive has guaranteed the large legislative contingents and their loyalty by setting up a structure of incentives that make it in the interest of congressmen to serve the interests of the executive. Put another way, by gaining control over representation the executive set the conditions for Congress to abdicate its law-making and checking powers.[9]

Since the foundation of the PRI in 1929, the competitiveness of the political system was severely restricted through subjecting political participation outside the "mainstream" to overwhelming obstacles and by legally enhancing the executive's control over electoral matters.[10] Through political means first, and through more effective and legal means with the passing of the 1946 Electoral Law, the manipulation of electoral results and the decisions regarding who could participate and how participation was to take place were put staunchly under the control of the executive. With it, the main characteristics of the Mexican electoral and party systems were established for years to come: centralization of political and electoral processes in institutions controlled by the executive, a party system

---

[8] Weldon cites three factors, "unified government, party discipline, and the recognition of the president as party leader." As the first two relate to the last, I prefer to think of two factors, with the prerequisite that the party is under the president's control.

[9] With this argument I am discarding the idea that the executive has usurped the powers of Congress. Usurpation refers to acts of the executive where it circumvents or bypasses Congress. The rule in Mexico has been that of delegation or of abdication, not of usurpation.

[10] For an interesting discussion of the development of the "official" party from the date of its creation (1929) until its transformation into the well-known PRI, see Weldon, this volume.

composed of several parties with slight chances of getting substantial shares of power, and the systematic manipulation of elections.[11] By tightening the conditions for competition and participation, by establishing highly unequal conditions, and by gaining control over the agencies in charge of organizing elections, large congressional majorities for the president's party were assured.

The party system that resulted was characterized as hegemonic, quasi-single, or overdominant. In other words, the majority party could not be effectively opposed – whether in the electoral arena or in the arenas of representation – either by any other single party or a coalition of two or more parties.[12]

From 1946 until 1963, when the first serious electoral reform was passed, opposition seats in the House of Representatives amounted to 4.7% on average. Between this last date and the 1977–1978 reform, the opposition held 17% of the chamber. From 1979 until 1987, the presence of the opposition reached 26.3% of the seats on average (see Table 5.2 below). Not only did the PRI hold the absolute majority, until 1988 (when the opposition won 48% of the seats) the PRI controlled at least two-thirds of the legislative seats, ensuring an unencumbered alteration of the Constitution.

Large congressional contingents for the president's party are not, however, sufficient to ensure an interbranch balance of power that favors the executive. Three other features combine to strengthen the position of the executive vis-à-vis Congress: (i) a highly centralized and disciplined party capable of controlling nominations; (ii) the concurrence of presidency of the country and presidency of the party in the same person; and (iii) the no-reelection clause. These characteristics coupled with few opportunities of career advancement outside the PRI due to the low level of competitiveness of the system constitute a clear case of a set of institutions and norms generating incentives for congressmen to behave as if they had only one constituency, the president, and to create an unbalanced

[11] An extensive description of this system and its evolution can be found in Molinar (1991).

[12] The number of parties with representation in Congress from 1949 onwards was as follows: four in 1949, five in 1952, four in 1955, and five in 1958 and 1961. Thereafter and until 1979, only three opposition parties were able to survive the new law and the party system would consist of four parties: PRI, PAN, PPS, and PARM. The average number of parties jumped from four in the 1964–1978 period to 8.3 in the 1979–1985 period (see Molinar 1991, p. 51, and Lujambio 1991, p. 15).

relation between the executive and Congress *independently* of the formal powers granted to each of them by the Constitution.[13]

Successive electoral reforms (six since 1978) have affected the old equilibrium based on very large legislative contingents for the president's party and a high degree of party discipline, which together translated into high levels of support for the executive's programs. Through their effects on the party system, these reforms have also altered the president's partisan powers to control nominations, control the fate of career advancement of congressmen, and enforce discipline (these powers, which have been key to the president's powers in practice, are discussed in the next section).

In sum, what we find in the period of stability of the political system is an array of institutional and partisan factors that combined to yield an interbranch balance of power that greatly favored the executive. The transition has not substantially modified the formal powers of the executive, but it has eroded his partisan powers and thus will lead to the revalorization of formal powers and, most probably, to a redressing of the balance of power between the executive and Congress.

Let us now turn to a more detailed analysis of the factors that determine the interbranch balance in the case of Mexico.

Factors that Determine the Interbranch Balance of Power

The President's Legislative Powers

The legislative powers of the Mexican president do not present themselves as extraordinary if compared to other presidential countries in Latin America and do not seem to place the executive in an advantageous position vis-à-vis Congress (Casar 1997).[14] In fact, in terms of the constitutional provisions concerning the president's power of initiative, his veto

---

[13] For the development of this argument see Casar (1997), where it is argued that the executive in Mexico was able to successfully penetrate and subordinate the rest of the political institutions and to establish a *unitary government*. The causal roots of this process are traced back to the setting up of a noncompetitive structure of access and distribution of power that allowed the executive not only to establish a hegemonic party system, but also to preside over internal party affairs. For a similar view regarding the importance of the president being the head of the ruling party and its discipline, see Weldon (1997 and this volume).

[14] See Table 14.8 in Morgenstern's conclusion, or, for a more detailed comparison, see Mainwaring and Shugart (1997).

powers, and his budget prerogatives, the Mexican Congress stands out as a strong institution.

The power of initiative is shared among the president, federal, and local or state legislators. The right of exclusive introduction is granted to the head of the executive only in regard to the budgetary field, where the executive must submit the revenues law and the spending budget on an annual basis. However, unlike the legislatures in Brazil, Chile, Costa Rica, pre-1991 Colombia, and Uruguay, the Mexican Congress has unrestricted authority to amend the budget.[15]

The executive in Mexico is endowed with both a package and a partial veto,[16] but its use is restricted to legislation that "is not of the exclusive competence of one of the chambers." This implies that the chief executive cannot veto the expenditures part of the budget, since it only passes through the lower house. Both types of vetoes are also restricted by the possibility of overrides, though the override requirements are quite stiff (two-thirds of the votes in both houses) (Article 72).

The Mexican president is also endowed with decree powers of different kinds and importance. A first type of decree power is essentially regulatory (Article 89). In the case of Mexico this power should not be disregarded, because although regulatory measures must be subordinated to the law, the laws leave the executive significant discretion to decide on different means and forms to do so, not to mention how and when to enforce the codes.

A second and stronger variant is that where the authority to legislate by decree is delegated by Congress. The Constitution establishes two such cases: the case of states of emergency in which, according to Article 29, the president is allowed to suspend liberties and Congress may grant extraordinary legislative powers; and the case of Article 131, which allows Congress to delegate legislative powers to increase, diminish, or suspend export and import tariffs and to restrict or even forbid imports, exports, and transit of goods whenever the executive may deem it necessary.

---

[15] Here a word of caution should be introduced. If we take the revenues law, we will find that on an annual basis it empowers the chief executive to authorize additional amounts of revenues when, on the executive's perception, there are extraordinary circumstances that may call for such need. Constitutionalists agree that this practice is unconstitutional and a clear symptom of Congress' abdication in this area (Orozco Henríquez 1993, p. 209, and Carpizo 1978, p. 145).

[16] The Constitution does not speak of partial and total veto, but Article 72 (a) states that "A bill or proposed decree rejected in whole or in part by the executive shall be returned. . .".

A third variant is where legislative power is constitutionally granted to the executive as in certain health issues in which the president has the power to issue decree laws (Article 73, fr. XVI).

Thus, all in all, the Mexican Constitution establishes that the executive is able to perform legislative functions in the following cases: regulatory or statutory rights, in states of emergency, regarding health issues, international treaties (Article 76, fr. I), and economic regulation according to Article 131. Some of these presidential powers to legislate are directly endowed by the Constitution (statutory rights, sanitary measures), others must first be delegated (legislate in emergency situations), while others are subject to either ratification or subsequent approval (international treaties and economic regulation).

Finally, it is important to mention that, in contrast to other presidential systems, the head of the executive in Mexico does not have two other important legislative powers: (a) the power to call referenda or plebiscites, and (b) the power to convene Congress to extraordinary sessions (Article 67 endows this prerogative to the *Comisión Permanente del Congreso*).

As stated earlier, there has been an important disjunction between these moderate formal powers and the Mexican president's ability to dominate Congress. There are a number of indicators that can help us to explore the extent of this historical domination and the recent changes. First, to analyze measures of legislative capacity, I will examine the origin and approval rates of bills, and the extent to which executive-initiated bills are modified. We do not yet have a time series that can account for the whole period under consideration, but the data gathered in the last few years serve as a good approximation to the legislative powers of the president.

First, as in other Latin American countries, the executive has been the major bill-initiator. Figures of approval rates are not yet readily available, but those gathered in the last few years are striking. From selected years of the period 1940–1970, De la Garza (1972) concludes that no executive bill was defeated on the floor. He rightly mentions that this does not mean that all executive bills were passed or went unammended. The chamber did not act on several and it filed others. De la Garza does not provide figures for the total number of initiatives in these years. Nonetheless, he indicates that in contrast to 143 approved bills that originated in the Chamber of Deputies, the executive managed to get the approval for 664 bills.

In the more recent period, 1982–1988, figures reveal that although many more bills originated in the legislature, the rate of approval for

Table 5.1. *Initiatives introduced and approved by the Chamber of Deputies (1982–1988).*

	Legislature			
	1982–1985		1985–1988	
Source	Introduced	Approved	Introduced	Approved
Executive	155	151 (.97)	188	186 (.99)
Chamber of Deputies	197	13 (.07)	352	37 (.1)
PRI deputies	17	10 (.59)	70	9 (.13)
Opposition	180	3 (.2)	282	26 (.09)

Source: Nacif (1995).

presidential projects was close to 100%, while barely one-tenth of the legislative bills won approval (Table 5.1).

While these figures cannot account for the content of the bills, they still provide a rough indicator of legislative capacity and provide clear evidence that the president is the dominant political player. This has resulted from the president's control of the PRI, the size of the PRI legislative contingent, and the party's strict discipline toward the head of the executive. Now that the PRI's dominance in the legislature has eroded, we should therefore expect a new pattern of politics.

The composition of Congress, in particular of the Chamber of Deputies, favored the president's party for nearly six decades. Until the 1988 legislative elections, the opposition parties never won, taken together, over 30% of the seats in the Chamber, nor a single seat in the Senate. Table 5.2 shows the evolution of the lower chamber from 1946 to 1985.

Things changed when the atypical 1988 election subverted all expectations. The PRI lost 20 percentage points of the votes in the presidential election and 15 percentage points in the Chamber of Deputies' election. This resulted in the president's party losing for the first time the majority needed to alter the Constitution and in getting only nine seats over the simple majority needed to pass laws. The 1991 midterm elections reversed the trend of PRI losing seats. It recovered 12 percentage points and held 64% of the Chamber. In 1994, the opposition held 40% of the Chamber and 26% of the Senate. Finally, the 1997 legislative elections produced the first divided government in PRI's history, with 261 (52.2%) seats for the opposition and 239 for the PRI (Table 5.3).

Table 5.2. *Representation in the Chamber of Deputies (number and percentage of seats held by party, 1946–1985).*

	1946	1949	1952	1955	1958	1961	1964	1967	1970	1973	1976	1979	1982	1985
PRI	141	142	151	153	153	172	175	177	178	189	195	296	299	289
%	95.9	96.6	93.8	94.4	94.4	96.6	83.3	83.5	83.6	81.8	82.3	74	74.8	72.3
Opposition	6	5	10	9	9	6	35	35	35	42	42	104	101	111
%	4.1	3.4	6.2	5.6	5.6	3.4	16.7	16.5	16.4	18.2	17.7	26	25.3	27.8
TOTAL	147	147	161	162	162	178	210	212	213	231	237	400	400	400

Source: Rodríguez Araujo (1985), Barquín (1987).

Table 5.3. *Representation in the Chamber of Deputies (number and percentage of seats held by party, 1988–1997).*

	1988	1991	1994	1997
PRI	260	320	300	239
%	52	64	60	47.8
Opposition	240	180	200	261
%	48	36	40	52.2
TOTAL	500	500	500	500

Source: Memoria Primer Periódo Ordinario de Sesiones (1988); Memoria del Proceso Electoral Federal de 1991 (1991); La Voluntad de Nuestro Pueblo (1994); Estadística de las Elecciones Federales (1994, 1997).

The opposition's growing presence in the legislature has had an impact on legislative politics. First, there has been a marked change in the number of bills initiated in the legislature (rising from a few dozen in the 1950s and 1960s to a few hundred), and, importantly, the rate of approval of initiatives coming from the Chamber of Deputies has passed from just 7% in 1982–1985 to 25% in 1991–1994 (though falling again in the subsequent two sessions).[17] This change clearly represents the growing opposition, since the opposition is by far the more active as an initiator of bills. It is also telling that it was precisely during the periods when the PRI's control was most limited – 1988–1991, when it had only 52% of the Congress, and 1997–2000, when it had less than 50% – that the executive submitted far fewer bills than in other years.

[17] The figures on initiatives are drawn from the research done by Cecilia Martiínez Gallardo for her BA thesis, "The Evolution of the Committee System in the Chamber of Deputies, 1824–1997."

The consequences of the gradual loss of control by the PRI and the more plural composition of Congress can be already observed both in the origin and in the rate of approval of initiatives. Bill introduction by legislators in Congress rose sharply as opposition parties gained greater spaces in the Chamber of Deputies, passing from 209 in 1988–1991 to 493 in 1997–2000. Approval of initiatives has also suffered changes. Although the executive retained a rate of approval close to 100% until 1997, it diminished to 86% when the president's party lost the simple majority needed to pass ordinary bills. On the other side, the rate of approval of initiatives coming from legislators jumped from 7% in 1982–1985 (Table 5.1) to 20% in 1997–2000 (Table 5.4).

While these statistics do not provide conclusive evidence of substantial changes, they do point to a beginning in the transformation of executive–legislative relations. Further, the statistics overstate the executive success, since the presidents may withhold controversial legislation. This legislative power of resistance may explain the lower number of executive bills in these years. One key example comes from the 1988–1991 period, when, in the absence of the required two-thirds majority required for constitutional changes, Salinas' fear of defeat led him to postpone the introduction of reforms that were to alter longstanding traditions such as state–church relations, agrarian property rights, and the economic and financial institutions of the state. Similarly, during the first legislature of Zedillo's administration (1994–1997) the president faced some difficulty rallying not only the opposition's support, but also that of his own party. This was the case with two important presidential initiatives: one referring to the privatization of the petrochemical industry and the other one

Table 5.4. *Initiation and approval of bills, 1988–2000.*

| | Legislature | | | | | | | |
| | 1988–1991 | | 1991–1994 | | 1994–1997 | | 1997–2000 | |
Source	Introduced	Approved	Introduced	Approved	Introduced	Approved	Introduced	Approved
Executive	85	82 (.96)	84	82 (.98)	56	55 (.98)	37	32 (.86)
Legislators	209	49 (.23)	117	20 (.17)	151	21 (.13)	493[a]	99 (.20)
PRI	19	6 (.31)	32	10 (.31)	19	7 (.36)	80	16 (.20)
Opposition	190	43 (.23)	85	10 (.11)	132	14 (.11)	413	83 (.20)

[a] Bills presented by legislators of more than one party are not included.
Source: Nacif (1995), Cuadernos de Apoyo, SIID, Cámara de Diputados (1991–1994), Gaceta Parlamentaria (1997–2000), Diario de Debates (1997–2000).

that modified the pensions system of the country. In both cases, and with the projects already in Congress, the president had to modify his original position to get the initiatives approved.

From 1997 to 2000 President Zedillo faced a situation of divided government, and further changes occurred. Lacking the simple majority to pass ordinary laws, Zedillo was forced to systematically negotiate with – instead of ignore – the opposition. This applies to all pieces of legislation that the president introduced but was more evident and important in the case of the three budget bills introduced in 1997, 1998, and 1999. Since Mexico lacks an escape valve in case the budget is not approved, the government had to reach an agreement with one or more political parties if it wanted to avoid a budgetary crisis that in turn could lead to a constitutional crisis. In fact, for the first time since the consolidation of the political system in the 1940s, the budget was not approved during the ordinary sessions of Congress, and three extraordinary periods as well as moving far from the initial preference of the executive were needed before the necessary coalition could be built. It seems clear that even in the absence of a reform in the distribution of formal powers, the dominance of the executive over the legislative branch has already suffered as a result of the altered composition in Congress.[18]

In addition to these examples about specific pieces of legislation, the new plurality in the Congress has led to organizational changes that have a good chance of making Congress more democratic and institutionally stronger. An example here is the participation of the opposition in the committee system within the Chamber of Deputies. In the past, the PRI's majority in Congress allowed that party to control the committee assignment process, and, since it dominated each committee and held all of the committee chairs, it generally excluded the opposition from committee work. It was not until 1988 that the PRI gave up the presidency of 4 out of 39 committees, with another 8 following in 1991 and 16 more in 1994.[19] In the second half of Zedillo's term (1997–2000) the opposition forced a resolution on the PRI fraction to divide the presidencies of committees and their composition in proportion to the seats held by each party. This

[18] For a further discussion of executive–legislative relations in the first divided government, see Casar (2000).

[19] Information on the committee system has been taken from Lujambio (1995a, pp. 183–204). For a comparative analysis of committee systems in Latin American presidential regimes, see Casar (1998).

Table 5.5. *Chamber of Deputies' committee presidencies (1988–1997).*

Legislature	PRI	PAN	PRD	Other
1988	35	2	–	2
1991	37	3	2	3
1994	32	9	6	1
1997	28	14	14	4

Source: Lujambio (1995), Reforma (1997).

resolution resulted in the distribution of committee presidencies shown in Table 5.5.

These developments showed that Congress – especially the Chamber of Deputies – was beginning to acquire an importance that would not have been dreamt of just a few years earlier. Again, it is clear that these changes were the result of the opposition having gained bargaining power vis-à-vis the union of the PRI and the executive.

The Legislature's Oversight Powers

Congress in Mexico has few powers regarding the appointment and dismissal of high-level public servants. The executive in Mexico can freely appoint and dismiss most of the cabinet members and other close collaborators. There are three categories of presidential appointment power: appointments in which no constraints are provided (secretaries, attorney general,[20] head of government of the capital city,[21] attorney general of the capital city, and other employees not included in the following restrictions); those that need the Senate's approval (diplomatic agents and general consuls, colonels, and other high officials of the National Army, Navy, and Air Force, the supreme court ministers, and the superior employees of the treasury); and those that have to be appointed in accordance with secondary laws that rule over the National Army, Navy, and Air Force. Of these, the practice of approving the top employees of the treasury is simply

[20] The 1994 reforms changed this appointment power. As of the year 2000, the Senate will have to ratify the naming of the general attorney.
[21] This important appointment power has recently (1996) been withdrawn from the presidency. Since 1997, the citizens of the capital city have been empowered to elect their head of government.

not observed; the rest are observed, but cases of conflict over appointments have been exceptional.

Like all other presidential constitutions, the Mexican version provides for the possibility of ousting the president in extreme situations. Although ambiguous regarding the situations under which the president can be dismissed, Article 108 states that the chief executive, while in office, can be indicted only for treason to the nation (*patria*) and serious common crimes (*delitos graves del orden común*). The procedure is that the Chamber of Deputies must make an accusation before the Senate, which in turn has the right, through resolution of two-thirds of the members present, to impose the ensuing sanction.

The Mexican constitutional order does not provide for either votes of censure or no-confidence. However, there are three norms that refer to the legislature's executive power. The first is that cabinet members – among other top public servants – can be summoned by Congress if this body should need information regarding the activities of the departments headed by them or when a particular law is being discussed (Article 93). This prerogative does not imply either the possibility of Congress issuing a public statement or that of recommending, let alone prescribing, the dismissal of the incumbent. Since the purpose is only to get information and the decision on the course of action to follow remains with the executive, there is no real curtailment of the latter's power of naming his cabinet.[22]

A second oversight power granted to the legislature is detailed in Articles 108–111, which are dedicated to the responsibilities of public servants, as well as political, administrative, and penal offenses. Political offenses are said to be those through which acts of public servants may go against the public interest. This is, again, a very general precept and, in spite of its regulation through the *Ley Federal de Responsabilidades de los Servidores Públicos* (Article 7), its interpretation remains the authority of Congress.[23]

---

[22] During the first five decades after the revolution (1920 to 1970), this power was rarely deployed. Thereafter, beginning with President Echeverría (1970–1976), both chambers have been regularly summoning most members of the cabinet to question them on their policy areas. Although Congress may not issue any binding decision regarding the dismissal of a cabinet member, this power can be effectively used to either strengthen or weaken the stand of a minister.

[23] The *Ley Federal de Responsabilidades de los Servidores Públicos* typifies the following: attacks on democratic institutions and on the republican, representative, and federal forms of government; grave and systematic violations of individual and social guarantees; attack of the freedom to vote; infringement of the Constitution or federal laws; and grave or systematic violations of plans, programs, or budgets of the public administration.

Public servants accused of such offenses will be subject to *political judgment* and its sanction: dismissal and disqualification to carry out public functions. Again, in order to proceed, the Chamber of Deputies must accuse the incumbent before the Senate. The Senate will then decide by two-thirds of its present members whether the incumbent is guilty and sanctions are to be applied. Since 1946, no member of any presidential cabinet has ever been subject to political judgment while in office.

Next, the Mexican Congress appears to have free (constitutional) reign, not only to oversee, but to control the budget. As noted earlier, the Congress' authority to approve, modify, or reject both the income and expenditures pieces of the budget (*Ley de Ingresos and Presupuesto de Egresos*) gives it much more authority than most of its Latin American counterparts and constitutes a powerful instrument to intervene in policy formation. The only significant constraint here is that the Constitution prescribes a balanced budget. Potentially even more important, according to most interpretations, the president does not have veto authority over the expenditure side of the budget, because it is a bill that has to be approved only by the Chamber of Deputies.[24]

In spite of the congressional power of the purse, while the PRI held the majority, it chose not to make use of it. I have already quoted Wilkie's work, which shows that Congress has been absolutely compliant to the president's budgetary projects. More recent studies confirm this view. From 1970 to 1993, the *Presupuesto de Ingresos* was always approved mainly with the votes of the president's party and with little or no modifications. This pattern, however, was broken in 1997. The installment of a divided government opened the possibility of gridlock in relation to the budget if no coalition could be formed.[25] Congress (or one of its chambers) had to vote five laws in budgetary matters: the Value Added Tax (VAT) Law, the *Miscelánea Fiscal*, the *Ley de Ingresos*, the *Ley de Coordinación Fiscal*, and the *Presupuesto de Egresos*. In the first round, both the VAT Law and the *Miscelánea* were defeated on the floor. In the second round, the VAT Law was defeated again. The *Ley de Ingresos* and the *Presupuesto de Egresos* were

---

[24] For a discussion of this issue, see Weldon in this volume. The 1997 debate of the budget project opened the discussion about what would happen in case Congress rejected the presidential bill. There were rumors about the possibility of the president attempting a veto. However, since the project was finally approved, it is still not clear whether the Supreme Court would have sustained the presidential veto or ruled against it.

[25] It also opened the discussion on the interpretation of the Constitution in budgetary matters and of the need to reform it to avoid future deadlocks.

approved at the last minute with a coalition of PRI and PAN in favor and the votes of PRD, PVEM, and PT against. Finally, the *Ley de Coordinación Fiscal* was approved almost unanimously (four abstentions).

In addition to its power to shape the budget bill, as noted earlier, the Congress is endowed with the power to supervise, through a committee drawn from its body (the *Comisión de Vigilancia*), the correct performance of the functions of the General Accounting Office (GAO). Through auditing the government agencies, the GAO is to elaborate an annual statement confirming whether the executive has exercised the spending budget according to the criteria and amounts stated in the law.

As noted, historically the GAO has not been an effective legislative agent. Data on its recent activities are very scant. Ugalde (1996) concludes that the performance of the GAO has been poor whether we attend to the recommendations issued by this body or the sanctions imposed by it.[26] The increased assertiveness of the legislature in other areas suggest that this body may gain greater notoriety now that is not under the control of the PRI.

Finally, the last paragraph of Article 93 (added in 1977) allows Congress – by a petition of 25% of the deputies or 50% of the senators – to convoke special commissions to investigate the workings of decentralized organisms and state-owned enterprises. The use of this power has been severely curtailed by the PRI majority in Congress in a manner that has been judged unconstitutional. According to Ugalde (1996), between 1977 and 1995 the chamber attempted to create a commission on seven occasions. Three attempts were successful (TELEX 1979, Banpesca 1989, and CONASUPO 1995), but the other four attempts were blocked through dubious means.

All in all we see that, during the PRI's long reign, Congress has not employed much of the authority conferred to it in regard to oversight functions and that the executive has rarely found obstacles to his actions by way of the effective checks that Congress can provide. The recent changes, however, suggest that Congress will take a much more active role in the future. This and the preceding section show that, although formal powers did not determine executive–legislative relations during the

---

[26] He found that, from a total of 2,800 audits performed in the 1975–1988 period, only 257 sanctions were decreed but has no data on whether these were, in fact, imposed. On the other hand, only around half of the recommendations issued to the audited agencies were attended to.

longstanding period of PRI dominance, they will become crucial in defining the balance of power in the years to come. This increased role for the Congress will be reinforced, as I argue in the next section, by the weakening of the president's partisan powers.

President's Partisan Powers   A large legislative contingent is insufficient to guarantee the president's power over Congress. The loyalty of members of Congress to the president is also crucial in determining the balance of power between the two branches of government. In the case of Mexico, the president's partisan powers have guaranteed the president enormous autonomy to govern without fear of significant checks or oversight from the Congress generally or the PRI majority specifically.

The Mexican president's partisan powers – that is, his power to control members of the PRI – have resulted from a number of factors, many of which have eroded with the growing level of competition. First, the growing competitiveness has eliminated the high degree of certainty of success for PRI candidates and opened new opportunities for politicians to dissent or exit the party without jeopardizing their political (or economic) careers. Second, the PRI's control over the selection of candidates to office at all levels is being replaced in many areas with primaries and local control.[27] As a result of these two changes, the PRI is losing its ability to ensure the level of loyalty that it once demanded.

The first effect of the new competitive context has been to diminish the incentives for legislators to cooperate or to assume a subordinate position, because the capacity to control patterns of career advancement has been greatly reduced. Until very recently, the structure of political opportunities of the country was practically dominated by PRI candidates and the distribution of available offices was clearly under the control of the executive. But recently, in addition to the growing number of seats that the opposition has won in Congress, the PRI has lost control of numerous governorships, mayors' offices, and municipality governments, as well as the assemblies associated with these executive posts. The formal size of the structure of political opportunities is equal to the number of offices

---

[27] The nonimmediate reelection clause – especially in a context of very reduced competitiveness – has also been a crucial factor in weakening the party, for it does not allow congressmen to develop an independent and continuous base of support. I will not develop this point, for, as yet, this institutional feature is still in place and so are its consequences. The rate of reelection for the 1934–1997 period was 13.3% (Campos 1996).

available at any point in time; and the distribution of them among parties is strongly related to the competitiveness of the system and to the prevailing electoral rules. Table 5.6 shows the size of this structure and the dominance and gradual loss suffered by the PRI.[28]

The evolution of this structure and of the position of the PRI within it shows the impact of the growing competitiveness of the system in the dominant party. The political consequences of this change cannot be underestimated. While in 1982 the PRI held over 90% of the elected country's posts, in 1994 this number dropped to 62% and to 54% in 1997. Moreover, the drop was so steep that, in spite of an absolute increase of almost 700 available posts, the PRI held about 1,000 fewer offices in 1997 than in 1982.

Of course, loyalty and discipline can also be solicited by promising future jobs in nonelective offices, of which the president controls thousands. However, as the system becomes more competitive there is ever less guarantee that the PRI will continue to win the presidency, and thus the nonelective careers of PRI supporters are also threatened.

To this it must be added that, in the event of a PRI candidate not winning a nomination, he or she does have an exit option that was very limited in 1982 and practically nonexistent a decade earlier. As a result, costs of defection from the president have declined. In fact, a considerable number of PRI members have taken the exit option over the last 10 years, helping to strengthen opposition parties.

In addition to the reduction of electoral certainty and exit options, control by the executive over the selection of candidates is also being transformed by the growing competitiveness of the system. The Mexican electoral system affects the control over nominations in two ways. On the one hand, it determines whether candidates require a nominator's seal of approval; on the other, it determines to what degree control of this seal is an effective tool for leaders (Morgenstern 1997, pp. 12–13). In Mexico, both of these variables conjoin to give maximum importance to the nominator.

Mexico belongs to that kind of system where there is an official nominator of candidates. The system does not allow candidates to participate without party approval. Although electoral laws do not regulate intraparty rules for the selection of candidates that are to run for elective

---

[28] To these elected posts one would have to add the large number of administrative posts available for the executive to distribute.

Table 5.6. *Structure of political opportunity (number of popularly elected posts, 1982–1997).*

	1982			1988			1994			1997		
	Total	PRI	%	Total	PRI	%	Total	PRI	%	Total	PRI	%
Presidency	1	1	100	1	1	100	1	1	100	1	1	100
Senate	64	64	100	64	60	94	128	95	74	128	76	59
Deputies	400	296	74	500	260	52	500	300	60	500	239	48
Governorships	31	31	100	31	31	100	31	28	90	32	25	78
State legislatures	589	448	76	809	558	69	984	590	60	1,078	550	51
Mun. presidencies	2,394	2,322	97[a]	2,387	2,148	90	2,412	1,520	63	2,418	1,354	56
Total	3,479	3,162	91	3,792	3,058	81	4,056	2,534	62	4,157	2,245	54

[a] This figure is approximate because it excludes the municipalities of four states for which I could not find the relevant information.

Source: Own elaboration from Becerra et al. (1996), Crónica del Gobierno de CSG 1987–88 and 1988–94, Carpizo and Madrazo (1984), Crespo (1996), Estadísticas de Elecciones Federales (1995), Reforma, Centro Nacional de Desarrollo Municipal, SEGOB (1997), Casar M.A., The Sources of Presidential Authority in Post-Revolutionary Mexico, PhD. Thesis, University of Cambridge, 1997.

office,[29] they forbid the presentation of independent candidates, that is, of candidates with no party label or one that is not formally registered. Additionally, since there is no intraparty competition, the role of the nominator is even more effective.[30]

The PRI's internal party regulations clearly favor the strength of the selector as against voters (as in the case of systems that mandate primaries or allow intraparty competition), or even party members.[31] Formally, the PRI involves its political council, a national convention, and its mass base in the selection of candidates. Nonetheless, in all cases, the National Executive Committee (CEN) has the authority to approve the *convocatorias* for the selection of candidates and thus the authority to decide on the method of selection. In practice, no candidate can hope to win the nomination and advance his or her political ambitions without the support of the Central Executive Committee of the PRI and, since this party structure is controlled by the head of the executive, no *priista* is able to advance in his or her political career and move among the different tiers of the party – party organization, legislative party, and party in the administration – without the blessing of the president.[32]

In spite of having a system that gives the nominator a crucial role and places in his/her hands an effective tool to enforce discipline, we can still predict that the opening of the system to competition will not only affect the strength of the nominator, but may even alter the position of the head of the executive as the "supreme nominator." Increased competition is bound to alter both control of candidate selection and discipline for two main reasons: first, because the "exit option" can readily be used if a PRI member is not blessed with a nomination; and, second, because in a competitive context the nominator is forced to select a candidate with good

---

[29] Within presidential regimes, the United States and Colombia exemplify two systems in which no "nominator's seal of approval" is needed, in the first case because primaries effectively replace it and, in the second, because parties cannot prevent candidates or lists from participating in an election under any label they like (Morgenstern 1997, p. 13).

[30] Mexico's electoral system is a mixed one in which 300 deputies are elected on a plurality basis and 200 under proportional representation. These last are chosen from a closed list, thereby enhancing the role of the selector. Although in the case of the 300 deputies elected under the principle of plurality, the representatives are more closely tied to the voters, the impossibility of getting a nomination without the party label and the nonimmediate reelection clause mitigate the importance of the voters and increases that of the nominators.

[31] The role of party members in the selection of candidates is enhanced in parties where a variety of a primary among party affiliates is held. That has been the case in the Partido de la Revolución Democrática (PRD) for some selection processes.

[32] For a study on the formal rules of candidate selection, see Langston (1996).

chances of electoral success, that is, he or she is constrained by the expected preferences of voters. The changes in the Mexican political system are still too recent to yield definite conclusions, but there is some empirical evidence that these arguments do indeed apply.

As argued before, the exit option has been taken by a considerable number of *priistas* over the last ten years.[33] Although exit from the party is not always explained by failure to win nomination, this reason figures prominently in the most recent resignations from the PRI. This was the case of Raúl Castellanos (Oaxaca); Juan José Roca, Juan José Rodríguez Pratts, and Manuel López Obrador (Tabasco); Rosa María Martínez Denegri, Guillermo del Río, Yolanda Valladares and Layda Sansores (Campeche); Iván Camacho (Chiapas); Luis Eugenio Todd (Nuevo León); and José Ortiz Arana (Querétaro). All of these were local PRI leaders who on average had over 17 years of affiliation and participation within the PRI. To these cases one must add the group led by Cuauhtémoc Cárdenas (originally the Corriente Democrática, now the PRD), which split from the PRI in 1987, purportedly over a disagreement of this group with the nomination processes of the party.[34] Finally, Manuel Camacho, the former Mayor of Mexico City, split when he failed to get the party nomination for the presidency and is now forming his own political party.

Regarding the nomination of governor candidates, the contrast between the Salinas and Zedillo terms is also revealing. Centeno (1994, pp. 91, 92, and 169) shows that, even before the 1991 elections, almost one-third of the governors had worked with Salinas in the IEPES and SPP prior to 1988 and had close personal ties with him. Zedillo faced five gubernatorial elections in 1995 (Jalisco, Guanajuato, Yucatán, Baja California, and Michoacán) and seven more in 1997 (San Luis, Colima, Campeche, Sonora, Nuevo León, Querétaro, and, for the first time in postrevolutionary history, the Federal District itself). Not one of the candidates that

---

[33] A thorough inspection of *Proceso* weekly journal for the 1987–1996 period yields a figure of around 30,000 *priista* defectors. This figure is extremely inflated, for it accounts not only for *priistas* who had regularly participated in the party (what is called *militancia*) but rather for sympathizers or "clienteles" of party leaders that left the PRI and claim that their followers are leaving the party. Examples of this kind of defectors are the allegedly 5,000 *priistas* in Tabasco that left the PRI when Manuel López Obrador resigned from the party and affiliated with the PRD or the 4,000 that abandoned the party when José Mendoza was favoured over Irma Piñeiro in Oaxaca (Proceso No. 915, May 16, 1994).

[34] There are several accounts of the causes of this important split from the PRI. The most comprehensive ones are Bruhn (1993) and Garrido (1993).

ran for the governorships in 1995 or 1997 belonged to Zedillo's camarilla,[35] worked for him in previous years, or formed part of his personal
network. Moreover, after 1997 the PRI adopted an altogether new way of
selecting candidates – primary elections – for gubernatorial posts, further
checking the traditional power of the executive to name governors. This
was the case in 13 of the 17 gubernatorial elections held in 1998 and 1999.
The same can be said about the removal of governors. While Salinas used
his partisan powers to remove or reassign more than a dozen governors,
Zedillo is said to have been unable to remove Governor Madrazo from
Tabasco in spite of a media campaign against him and the demonstration
of fraud in the electoral process that secured him the governorship.

It is possible to interpret these events in a number of ways. One is that,
in the face of the opening of the system and in order to attain as many
votes as possible, the president himself made a personal decision, if not to
democratize the selection process, at least to allow more leeway to the PRI
apparatus, especially at the local level. This interpretation is based on the
repeated assertions by the president regarding the "healthy distance"[36]
between the PRI and the head of the executive and the idea that he will
impose "no directives" on the party from Los Pinos (the presidential
residence).[37]

Another interpretation is that he no longer has the power to impose
candidates of his own liking and, if he did, would face a rebellion from different sectors of the party. This argument was upheld by political journalists to explain several gubernatorial candidacies. For example, (a) a
candidate (Cervera Pacheco) who was considered a hard liner, undemoc-
ratic, and unfavorable to Zedillo "won" the nomination for the state of
Yucatán; (b) the incumbent governor of Sonora (Manlio Fabio Beltrones)
was able to impose his candidate (López Nogales) over Bulmaro Pacheco,
who was considered the candidate of the "center"; and (c) in Campeche,
a local candidate (Gozález Kuri) received the nomination against Carlos
Sales, who was favored by Zedillo.

---

[35] A camarilla is a hierarchically organized faction.
[36] The idea of the president maintaining a "healthy distance" from the party was originally
advanced by Zedillo in a meeting with the state party presidents on August 3, 1994; but
it derives from a speech given by Colosio on March 6, 1994, in which he demanded that
the government should stop assuming the responsibilities that belonged only to the party
(Intervención de Luis Donaldo Colosio durante el Acto Conmemorativo del LXV Aniver-
sario del PRI el 6 de marzo de 1994).
[37] Speech by Zedillo at the XVII PRI National Assembly, September 22, 1996.

These few examples show that the once unquestioned power of the president to choose and impose candidates of his liking is being eroded.[38] Furthermore, the fact that PRI-elected governors do not perceive that they owe their posts to Zedillo casts some doubts on the prospect that governors will in the future prove nearly as compliant with the wishes of the head of the executive as they have had reason to be in the past. In short, the basis for sustaining the traditional unobstructive behavior and discipline that governors have shown toward the head of the executive is rapidly disappearing.[39]

Further evidence of the changing relation between the executive and the party can be drawn from the last General Assembly of the PRI (September 1996). There is some dispute over just what occurred at this assembly,[40] but the clear end result was that the party imposed a number of restrictions on the nomination process and over the requisites that candidates must fulfill before being nominated.

The most important general resolution of the assembly regarding candidate selection was to require that any PRI presidential or gubernatorial candidate have held a post in the party structure itself *and* have previously held an elective office.[41] This need not mean that the head of the executive has been dispossessed of his unwritten right of being the ultimate "selector," but considering that none of the last five presidents would qualify under these rules, the change has definitely reduced the universe from which the president can choose.[42]

---

[38] I deliberately speak of the erosion rather than the withering of this power because there are important examples where the president's will still prevails over the party. The most striking one is, without doubt, the designation of the head of the National Executive Committee.

[39] This point is of the utmost importance because all governors have a seat in the Consejo Político Nacional and, since the party reforms of September 1996, this is the body in charge of selecting the future PRI presidential candidate.

[40] For a review of the assembly see González Compeán (1996).

[41] Article 144 of the new statute states that candidates for the presidency and the governorships must demonstrate that they have "been a party cadre, a party leader and have held elective office through the party, as well as having ten years of militancy" (PRI, Comité Nacional Ejecutivo, *Documentos Básicos*, 1996).

[42] Moreover, the changes have reduced the chances of the so-called technocrats (or other party outsiders) in attaining the most important executive posts. These changes, along with the resolution of abandoning "social liberalism" – Salinas's ideological legacy to the party – and reassuming "revolutionary nationalism," are deemed to be victories of the politicians over the technocrats.

It must be pointed out, however, that the methods of selection themselves did not change and that the current system still supports a determinant role for a "selector" with the necessary tools to induce discipline. Further, the ultimate formal authority to nominate candidates remains within the CEN, for it is this party organ that has to approve and authorize the convocatorias for the selection of candidates (Article 153) at all levels. Traditionally, through the unwritten rules of the PRI system, this authority passed in practice to the head of the executive and constituted one of the bases of stability within the PRI and of the disciplined submission shown by the party toward the executive. With the changes in the electoral competition system, the conditions are being set for the party to assume the role of determining who the candidates will be, and thus transforming its prior subordination to the president. In any case, there are signs that point to the future strengthening of the party structure or, as Colosio would have had it, of the party "assuming the responsibilities that belong to it."

Although some analysts have questioned the importance of the new competitive context in the recent changes in the PRI[43] and in the relations between party and executive, I have sought to demonstrate the preeminent importance of these factors. Even the outcome of the XVII Assembly cannot be understood without considering the increased competitiveness of the system and the very serious electoral challenges that the PRI has faced in the period since Zedillo assumed the administration in December 1994. It is also clear that party discipline is crucial to presidential power. The president's ability to enforce discipline is under threat, and, as a result, the balance of executive–legislative relations may therefore tip away from the once-dominant Mexican president.[44]

Conclusions

Constitutional powers do not allow us to qualify the Mexican president as exceptionally powerful. Neither do they allow us to differentiate between

---

[43] Hernández (1996) holds that the major variable in explaining the recent changes and difficulties that the PRI is facing is the lack of clarity in the president's handling of the PRI.

[44] In addition to other cases in this book, see the revealing case studies of the relationships between presidential strength and party discipline in Brazil and Venezuela by Mainwaring (1997) and Crisp (1997).

the period of hegemony of the PRI and the more recent period in which the president's party has lost the overwhelming majorities that it used to enjoy. The real difference between Mexico and other systems had always been the nature of the party system, which was based on the uncompetitiveness of the political system or, to put it more strongly, on the nonobservance of the principle of electoral sovereignty.

Under what we commonly termed the "classical period," Mexico had a quasi-single party system that guaranteed very large majorities for the president's party. This, combined with an extremely high degree of discipline that resulted from the president's strong partisan powers, resulted in a balance of power that favored the executive to such a point that the autonomous action of Congress was effectively annulled.

The still mild (but potentially great) transformations observed in executive–legislative relations have been more the consequence of the opening of the political-electoral system than of any change in the formal powers of these two branches. From 1978 to 1996, Mexico enacted six electoral reforms. These reforms have helped to move Mexico toward a true electoral democracy by limiting fraud and improving the chances for opposition electoral victories. The result has been a substantial change in the structure of political opportunity and, consequently, a depletion of the president's partisan powers. As a result, characterizations of the postclassical period will likely depict the end of Mexico's subservient legislature.

Appendix: Congress' Constitutional Powers

Economic

- To levy the necessary taxes to cover the budget.
- To levy taxes on foreign trade, on the utilization and exploitation of natural resources, on institutions of credit and insurance companies, and on public services under concession or operated directly by the federation.
- To levy special taxes on electric power, tobacco, gasoline, and other products derived from petroleum, matches, *maguey* products, forestry exploitation, and beer.
- To create and abolish public offices and to fix their salaries.
- To fix the bases on which the president may borrow on the credit of the nation; to approve such loans and to acknowledge and order payment of the national debt.

- To legislate throughout the republic on hydrocarbons, mining, the motion picture industry, commerce, games of chance and lotteries, credit institutions, electric and nuclear power, and financial services, and to establish a single bank of issue and to enact labor laws.
- To enact laws on economic and social planning.
- To enact laws on the promotion of Mexican investment, regulation of foreign investment, and the transfer of technology.
- To examine the public account (*cuenta pública*) that the executive branch must submit to it annually.
- To approve the annual budget of expenditures (Chamber of Deputies).

Political–Administrative

- To make all laws that shall be necessary and proper for carrying into execution the powers of the three branches of government.
- To admit new states and territories into the Federal Union and to form new states within the boundaries of existing ones.
- To legislate on all matters concerning the Federal District except those reserved to the Legislative Assembly.
- To issue the Federal District's statute of government.
- To legislate in regard to the Federal District's public debt.
- To grant leaves of absence to the president.
- To constitute itself as an electoral college and designate the citizen who is to replace the president as either an interim or provisional substitute.
- To accept the resignation from office of the president.
- To declare war.
- To approve the suspension of guarantees, declared by the president, in the event of invasion, serious disturbance of the public peace, or any other event that may place society in great danger.
- To make laws that regulate the organization, maintenance, and service of the armed forces, navy, and air force.
- To prescribe regulations for the purpose of organizing, arming, and disciplining the National Guard.

Social

- To establish, organize, and maintain throughout the republic rural, elementary, superior, secondary, and professional schools and schools for scientific research, of fine arts, and of technical training.
- To enact laws and coordinate actions on environmental issues.

Judicial

- To define crimes and offenses against the federation and to prescribe the punishments to be imposed.
- To grant amnesties for crimes within the jurisdiction of the federal courts.
- To constitute itself as a grand jury to take cognizance of crimes and offenses of the officials that the Constitution expressly designates.
- To enact laws for the establishment of administrative tribunals.

Oversight and Appointment

- To ratify the appointment of the attorney general, ministers, diplomatic agents, consuls general, superior employees of the treasury, colonels, and other superior chiefs of the National Army, Navy, and Air force (Senate).
- To designate the ministers of the supreme court from a list submitted to it by the president (Senate).
- To review through the General Accounting Office (*Contaduría Mayor de Hacienda*) the strict observance in the exercise of the approved budget (Chamber of Deputies).
- To supervise, through a committee drawn from its body, the correct performance of the functions of the General Accounting Office (Chamber of Deputies).
- To name the chiefs and employees of the General Accounting Office (Chamber of Deputies).
- To set up committees to investigate the performance of decentralized agencies and parastatal firms.
- To call before Congress and acquire information from the heads of ministries, decentralized agencies, and parastatal firms.

Political Parties and Legislative Structure

6

Explaining the High Level of Party Discipline in the Argentine Congress*

MARK P. JONES

Politicians and academics consider party discipline in the Argentine Congress to be (comparatively) very high (Jones 1997a; Molinelli 1991; Mustapic and Goretti 1992). While the conventional wisdom of high levels of party discipline is nearly universal in Argentina, there have been no empirical studies of roll-call voting behavior during the post-1983 era and virtually no structured attempts to explain the principal sources of this high level of discipline.

This chapter has two goals. First, undertaking the first analysis of roll-call votes in the post-1983 period, it underscores the comparatively high levels of party discipline in the Argentine Chamber of Deputies. Second, it identifies the primary determinants of this highly disciplined voting behavior.

Argentine Political Institutions

Argentina is a federal republic consisting of 23 provinces and a semi-autonomous federal capital.[1] It has a presidential form of government with

* Support for this research was provided by the National Science Foundation (grant SBR-9709695), the Centro de Estudios para el Desarrollo Institucional (CEDI) de la Fundación Gobierno y Sociedad, and the Michigan State University Political Institutions and Public Choice Program. I thank Pablo Ava, Rodolfo Bernardini, Miguel De Luca, Alberto DiPeco, Susana Dri, Marcela Durrieu, Alberto Föhrig, María Cristina Fra Amador, Ariel Godoy, Guillermo Molinelli, Teresa Moreno, Valeria Palanza, María Teresa Pianzola, Sebastian Saiegh, Gisela Sin, Rossana Surballe, María Inés Tula, Cristina Vallejos, and the staff of the Legislative Reference Division of the Argentine Congress for their tremendous assistance during the research portion of this study. John Carey, Gary Cox, Miguel De Luca, Scott Morgenstern, Benito Nacif, and the participants at the February 1997 Centro de Investigación y Docencia Económicas (CIDE) conference on "Legislatures in Latin America" provided many valuable comments on earlier drafts of this chapter.
[1] The national territory of Tierra del Fuego achieved provincial status in 1990. For stylistic

a bicameral legislature and since 1983 has represented one of Latin America's most vibrant and successful democracies.

The Argentine Chamber of Deputies has 257 members, who are elected from multimember districts (the 23 provinces and the federal capital) for four-year terms.[2] The deputies are elected from closed party lists using the d'Hondt divisor form of proportional representation. In the event that a deputy dies or resigns during office, he/she is replaced by the next person on the party list who has not yet occupied a Chamber seat.[3] One-half (127 and 130) of the Chamber is renewed every two years, with every district renewing one-half of its legislators (or the closest equivalent).

The 24 provinces receive a number of deputies in proportion to their respective populations, with the following restrictions: (1) that no district receive fewer than five deputies, and (2) that no district receive fewer deputies than it possessed during the 1973–76 democratic period. As a result of these rules, the least populous provinces (Catamarca, La Pampa, La Rioja, San Luis, Santa Cruz, and Tierra del Fuego) are highly over-represented in the Chamber. For example, the least populous quartile (i.e., those six provinces listed above) contains 3.9% of the population yet possesses 11.7% of the Chamber seats (and 25% of the Senate seats).[4] In contrast, the country's most populous province (Buenos Aires) is highly underrepresented. Buenos Aires accounts for 38.7% of the national population but only holds 27.2% of the Chamber seats.[5] Two of the other most populous provinces, Córdoba and Santa Fe, are moderately underrepresented, with 8.5% and 8.6% of the population and 7.0% and 7.4% of the seats, respectively. The other large district, Capital Federal, is slightly overrepresented (9.1% of the population and 9.7% of the seats) due to point (2) above. The current distribution of seats was carried out using the 1980 census. While a new allocation of seats should have been conducted

---

reasons it and the federal capital (Capital Federal) will generally be referred to as "provinces" in the remainder of the text.

[2] Prior to 1991, the Chamber had 254 deputies (three were added after Tierra del Fuego became a province). In 1983 all 254 deputies were elected at the same time.

[3] Intramandate turnover is relatively common in Argentina. Between 1985 and 1997, an average of 13% of the legislators were replaced by alternates every two-year legislative period (Molinelli, Palanza, and Sin 1999).

[4] For an analysis of political and economic consequences of this overrepresentation, see Gibson, Calvo, and Falleti (1999).

[5] If the 257 Chamber seats were allocated based purely on population (with each province receiving one seat at the minimum, as in the United States), then the province of Buenos Aires would have 99 deputies instead of the 70 that it currently possesses.

following the 1991 census, this has not occurred, and it is unlikely to occur anytime in the near future.

The Senate is composed of 72 members, with every province (and the federal capital) represented by three senators.[6] Until 2001 these senators will continue to be elected indirectly by the provincial legislatures (one-third of the Senate was renewed in 1998), with the stipulation that no one party can occupy more than two of a province's seats in the Senate.[7]

Every Argentine province has its own Constitution with a directly elected governor and legislature. The provincial governments are very important political entities, controlling relatively large budgets and exercising influence over vital areas of public policy such as education, health, and public safety. Furthermore, the principal locus of partisan competition in Argentina is at the provincial level, making a strong base in the provinces vital for electoral success at the national level. After the president and a few key national government ministers, the most powerful political actors in Argentina are generally the governors.

The Argentine Party System

Since the return to democracy in 1983, the two dominant political parties in Argentina have been the Partido Justicialista (PJ, also known as the Peronist Party) and the Unión Cívica Radical (UCR).[8] The level of support for these parties has however varied considerably during this period, with

---

[6] Prior to the 1994 constitutional reform, all of the country's 22 provinces (23 after 1990) and its federal capital were represented by two senators. Senators were elected indirectly for nine-year terms by the provincial legislatures using the plurality formula, except in Capital Federal, where they were selected via an electoral college. By lottery two-thirds of the Senate began in 1983 with either three- or six-year initial terms, with no province having two senators on the same cycle.

[7] In theory, the provincial legislatures had very little latitude in this choice. In 1998, for example, any senate seat being renewed should have gone to the plurality party in the provincial legislature. The only exception was if this party already held two seats, in which case the seat would have gone to the second largest party in the provincial legislature. In all cases the party would choose its candidate, who would then be ratified by the provincial legislature. Unfortunately, however, the constitutional article governing this process was not very well written and was subject to distinct interpretations by the political parties, provincial legislatures, and the Senate. This led to some serious conflicts (mostly in 1998) in a few (although certainly not most) instances (e.g., the 1998 elections of senators from Chaco, Corrientes, and Jujuy). In most instances, the PJ-dominated Senate appeared to use the interpretation for each specific case that best suited the interests of the PJ.

[8] For general overviews of the Argentine political party system, see the important contributions of Manzetti (1993) and McGuire (1995).

the UCR in particular experiencing a wide degree of fluctuation in terms of the support that it received at the polls (see Table 6.1). In the Chamber of Deputies the UCR's presence has ranged from a high of 51.2% seats between 1985 and 1987 to a low of nearly half that amount (26.5%) between 1997 and 1999. The PJ's legislative presence throughout this period has remained more stable, ranging from a high of 51.2% (1995–1997) to a low of 38.9% (1999–2001).

In addition to the PJ and the UCR, other important actors in the Chamber are the small center-right provincial parties that tend to compete in only one province (where they are often the dominant, or main opposition, party).[9] Many of these parties provided votes for the administration of President Carlos Menem (1989–1999) in the legislature in exchange for benefits for their respective provinces as well as for ideological reasons (Sin and Palanza 1997).[10]

Finally, an additional party, Frepaso (Frente País Solidario), recently has had a great deal of electoral success. Frepaso is an alliance of parties (Frente Grande [FG], Partido Socialista Popular [PSP], Partido Socialista Demócratico [PSD], Partido Intransigente [PI], and Partido Demócrata Cristiano [PDC]) that is dominated by the FG (e.g., FG members currently [2000] occupy all of the Frepaso Cabinet posts and over three-quarters of Frepaso's seats in the Chamber).

For the 1997 Chamber election Frepaso and the UCR presented a joint list (Alianza para el Trabajo, la Justicia y la Educación [Alianza]) in 14 provinces. In 1999, the Alianza presented a single presidential candidate (Fernando de la Rúa of the UCR) as well as a joint legislative list in 23 provinces. With the election of President De la Rúa (1999–   ), Frepaso

---

[9] Between 1989 and 2001, the provincial parties that held seats in the Chamber of Deputies were Acción Chaqueña; Partido Autonomista (PA), Partido Liberal, and Partido Nuevo of Corrientes; Movimiento Popular Jujeño; Partido Demócrata of Mendoza; Movimiento Popular Neuquino; Partido Popular Rionegrino; Partido Renovador de Salta; Cruzada Renovadora, Desarrollo y Justica, and Partido Bloquista of San Juan; Partido Demócrata Progresista (PDP) of Santa Fe; Fuerza Republicana (FR) of Tucumán; and Movimiento Popular Fueguino. The PA, PDP, and FR held the status of national parties during most or all of this period, although, with the partial exception of the PDP's limited electoral success in Capital Federal, their electoral support was for all intents and purposes limited to a single province.

[10] Also important (particularly during the 1989–1993 period) was the support of the now moribund center-right Unión del Centro Democrático (UCeDé). Roll-call analysis indicates that the UCeDé deputies generally supported the Menem administration's neoliberal initiatives in the Chamber. The UCeDé's record of support for other Menem administration initiatives was, however, much more mixed.

and the UCR now co-govern Argentina, albeit with Frepaso the junior partner in the governing coalition.

Roll-Call Votes in Argentina

In Argentina, one-half of the legislature is replaced on December 10 of every odd year. This study employs roll-call data from the 1989–1991, 1991–1993, 1993–1995, and 1995–1997 legislative periods (December 10 of every odd-numbered year to December 9 of the following odd-numbered year).[11]

The Argentine Chamber of Deputies possesses an electronic system of voting by which a deputy, from his/her seat, can utilize a key and then press a button with the vote then registered on an electronic scoreboard on the Chamber wall. The other common method of voting involves a simple show of hands (normally used for nonconflictual votes).[12]

A nominal vote can be taken in two ways. The most common way is for the votes to be recorded from the electronic voting system. The other, more traditional, method is to pass a paper list around the chamber in alphabetic order. Nominal votes are rare and are generally only taken on conflictual issues where party leaders want to use them to enforce discipline and on controversial issues where deputies or parties want their vote (or the votes of others) to be public knowledge. A final use of the nominal method is for votes related to the Chamber rules or specific constitutional duties of the Congress (i.e., impeachment proceedings, constitutional reform).

A nominal vote is taken when a motion for a nominal vote has been made and then supported by at least one-fifth of the deputies in attendance.[13] Nominal votes are recorded in the *Diario de Sesiones de la Cámara*

---

[11] Only 39 roll-call votes were taken during the Alfonsín presidency (1983–1989) (this excludes a small number of roll-call votes employed in some years for the election of Chamber authorities). This comparative lack of roll-call votes is suggestive of the greater level of UCR party discipline, which made the need for the use of roll-calls to enforce party discipline less necessary. It is also the consequence of the deputies' relative lack of experience in parliamentary procedures, the more consensual leadership style of the President of the Chamber between December 1983 and July 1989 (Juan Carlos Pugliese), and the UCR's minority position in the Senate (which necessitated a greater level of prior interparty negotiation than was the case under Menem) (Mustapic and Goretti 1992).

[12] Information on the Chamber rules comes primarily from Schinelli (1996).

[13] When the nominal vote is constitutionally mandated, no such motion is required. Furthermore, on rare occasions nominal votes have been taken based on the discretion of the presiding president, a practice that is not mentioned in the Chamber rules. In none

Table 6.1. *Percentage of seats held, by party.*

| | Chamber of Deputies, 1983–2001. | | | | | | | | |
Political party	1983–1985	1985–1987	1987–1989	1989–1991	1991–1993	1993–1995	1995–1997	1997–1999	1999–2001
Partido Justicialista	43.7	40.6	42.9	50.0	50.2	50.2	52.1	46.7	38.9
Unión Cívica Radical	50.8	51.2	46.1	37.0	33.1	32.7	26.9	26.5	33.1
UceDé	0.8	1.2	2.8	4.7	4.3	2.0	0.8	0.4	
Center-right provincial parties	3.2	4.3	5.9	7.1	9.3	9.3	8.2	9.3	9.3
Center-left and left parties	1.6	2.8	2.4	1.2	2.0				
MODIN					1.2	2.7	1.6		
Frepaso						3.1	9.7	16.0	14.0
Acción por la República								1.2	4.7
Total	100.1	100.1	100.1	100	100.1	100	100	100.1	100
	254 seats	254 seats	254 seats	254 seats	257 seats	257 seats	257 seats	257 seats	257 seats

Senate, 1983–2001

Political party	1983–1986	1986–1989	1989–1992*	1992–1995	1995–1998	1998–2001
Partido Justicialista	45.6	45.6	54.4/54.2	62.5	55.7	55.7
Unión Cívica Radical	39.1	39.1	30.4/29.2	22.9	28.6	30.0
Center-right provincial parties	15.2	15.2	15.2/16.7	14.6	14.3	12.9
Frepaso					1.4	1.4
TOTAL	99.99	99.99	100/100.1	100	100	100
	46 seats	46 seats	46/48 seats	48 seats	70 seats	70 seats

* In 1990 the then national territory of Tierra del Fuego achieved provincial status. The province elected two senators in early 1992.

Note: All seat totals are based on election results and do not account for minor seat changes due to defections during the congressional term of a deputy or senator. These defections are, however, relatively infrequent and minor in scope. For the PJ in a few instances, parties that represent PJ splinters at the provincial level are included with the PJ total above. Included with the PJ and UCR totals are those candidates from other parties (e.g., PI, PDC) elected on the PJ/UCR lists (this is not, however, done for the 1997 and 1999 Alianza lists). Center-right provincial parties effectively compete in only one province. They tend to occupy the center-right/right portion of the ideological spectrum. For the 1993–1995 period the Frepaso entry consists of seats won by FG, PSD, and PSP candidates in 1991 and 1993. The UCR and Frepaso presented joint lists in the Chamber elections of 1997 (14 districts) and 1999 (23 districts), lists that in some provinces were joined by center-right provincial parties such as the Partido Renovador de Salta, Cruzada Renovadora, and the Partido Bloquista. While allies of the Alianza, these parties do not belong to the supra-Alianza coordinating block in Congress. They are included above with the other center-right provincial parties. Since December 10, 1995, two senate seats (one belonging to the PJ and the other to the UCR) from the province of Catamarca have not been occupied (see note 48 for more information).

153

de Diputados de la Nación.[14] There are no exact data on what proportion of all votes taken during a given year are nominal, but it is doubtful that nominal votes account for more than 5% of the votes.[15]

During the 1989–1991, 1991–1993, 1993–1995, and 1995–1997 periods there were 103, 66, 96, and 64 roll-call (i.e., nominal) votes taken, respectively. Of these respective votes, 78, 48, 47, and 45 were considered to be moderately controverted (at least 20% of the Chamber deputies present voted for the losing option of yes or no) (Mainwaring and Pérez Liñán 1997) and distinct from other bills voted on that day (e.g., not a re-vote on the same bill). These 218 votes form the basis of this study's roll-call vote analysis.

Several different types of votes are conducted in the Argentine Chamber (e.g., votes on bills, votes on articles within bills, votes on motions, votes on recommending the impeachment of judges to the Senate, votes on temporarily departing from the Chamber rules). Most of these votes require a majority of only a plurality of those voting, while others require a majority of two-thirds or three-quarters of those voting. A few remaining votes are based on a percentage of the 254/257 Chamber members (either two-thirds or an absolute majority). Of the 218 votes examined here, 144 were decided on the basis of a plurality vote, 46 on the basis of a two-thirds vote, 20 on the basis of a three-quarters vote, six on the basis of a two-thirds vote of the entire Chamber, and two on the basis of an absolute majority vote of the entire Chamber. It should be noted that, in addition to these voting rules, the Chamber cannot take a vote without a quorum, which is equal to 50% + 1 of the total number of legislators. For the period 1983–1991 the number necessary to achieve a quorum was 128, while between 1991 and 1996 the number was 130. Since late 1996 the number has been 129.[16]

---

of these occasions, however, did any deputy object to the president's decision to hold a nominal vote.

[14] Data for the 1995–1997 period were still incomplete as of December 2000, since the Diarios de Sesiones for August 20 through December 9, 1997 had not yet been published.

[15] Fennell (1974) found that very few contested roll-call votes (with contested defined as roll calls where at least 5% or more of those voting opposed the majority) took place during the 1900–1966 period. The mean number of contested roll calls during each two-year period was 42, while the median was 27. Smith's (1974) meticulous analysis revealed that, during the 1904–1955 period, 1,712 roll-call votes took place. Of these 1,712, 1,052 were defined by Smith as contested (i.e., at least 10% of those deputies voting took the minority position). Other than for the election of Chamber authorities, no roll-call votes were held during the 1973–1976 democratic period.

[16] Under the current rules, more legislators must be present than absent. When all legislators are in office, this signifies a minimum number necessary to achieve a quorum of 129.

For every session of the Argentine Chamber of Deputies an attendance list is compiled. There are five principal categories: Present, On Leave, On Leave (vote on leave pending Chamber approval), Absent with Notice, and On an Official Mission. For those voting, there are three categories: Affirmative, Negative, and Abstain.[17] Deputies who at some point were present at the session but were not on the Chamber floor at the time of the vote (or chose not to vote) are considered in this study to be Present But Not Voting.

Party Discipline in the Argentine Chamber

Table 6.2 provides information on the relative and absolute discipline of the principal political parties (i.e., those with more than 10% of the Chamber seats) during the four legislative periods between 1989 and 1997. Given the low proportion of roll-call votes, these percentages should not be directly compared to those in other countries. At the most these data provide information on one extreme of party discipline in Argentina, expressing the levels of discipline on those votes that on average generate the most conflict within one or both of the major parties.[18] All of the other normal caveats related to the analysis of roll-call vote data (see Ames, this volume) apply as well.

Relative discipline was calculated as the percentage of party members voting who voted with the majority of the party. Absolute discipline was calculated as the percentage of party members present at the session (at any time) who voted with the majority of the party.[19] For the absolute discipline calculations, in a few cases a plurality of the party chose to absent itself from the Chamber floor (i.e., Present But Not Voting). In these cases

---

[17] A deputy technically must obtain permission from the Chamber to abstain. Most do not bother and abstain from the vote without seeking permission (although for most votes fewer than 5% of those voting abstain). However, in the event that those abstaining could have changed the outcome of a vote, the result of the vote generally is annulled and a new vote taken. Often abstentions in the roll-call list are due to errors in the electronic voting system, which are rectified later in the debate by the deputies employing their right to correct an erroneous recording of their vote.

[18] I do concur though with Ames' (this volume) assessment that, based on our Argentine and Brazilian roll-call data, party discipline is noticeably higher in Argentina.

[19] For example, in a vote where the majority of the party voted "yes," the relative discipline score would be calculated as: party members voting yes/(party members voting yes + party members voting no). For this same vote the absolute discipline score would be calculated as: party members voting yes/(party members voting yes + party members voting no + party members abstaining + party members present but not voting).

Table 6.2. *Party discipline in the Chamber of Deputies, 1989–1997.*

PARTY	1989–1991		1991–1993		1993–1995		1995–1997	
	Relative Party Discipline	Absolute Party Discipline	Relative Party Discipline	Absolute Party Discipline	Relative Party Discipline	Absolute Party Discipline	Relative Party Discipline	Absolute Party Discipline
Partido Justicialista								
mean	94	72	97	74	98	83	97	70
median	97	73	99	76	99	85	99	73
Unión Cívica Radical								
mean	98	72	98	74	96	67	94	66
median	100	73	100	74	100	71	100	70

Note: Only those parties that held more than 10% of the chamber seats during the term are included. Number of roll-call votes included in the analysis: 1989–1991 (78), 1991–1993 (48), 1993–1995 (47), 1995–1997 (45).

this choice was considered as the numerator to calculate the absolute level of party discipline.

The relative discipline levels are extremely high for both parties.[20] They indicate that it is extremely rare for a PJ or UCR deputy to vote against his/her party in the Chamber. This is not surprising, since, during this period, every Tuesday night (sessions normally took place on Wednesday and at times on other days such as Thursday) or on other nights as needed the PJ and UCR blocs met (separately of course) and established the way that the party would vote the next day(s); or perhaps better said, the party leadership informed the deputies, with levels of debate varying from intense to subdued, what the party position (for the PJ, a position that during this time period normally was strongly influenced by President Menem) would be.[21]

Those party members who strongly oppose the position taken by the party generally will leave the floor at the time of the vote or less frequently will register their abstention. Only on rare occasions, and usually only when the legislator is voting as part of an organized larger group such as a provincial or regional (e.g., Patagonia) delegation, an intraparty faction (e.g., Duhaldistas [i.e., followers of Eduardo Duhalde, Buenos Aires governor between 1991 and 1999]), or an ideological group (e.g., PJ deputies from the labor unions) will legislators actively register a "No" vote in the Chamber.[22]

Thus, the most common method of opposing the majority party position on a vote is to absent oneself from the floor at the time of the voting. This pattern of behavior is detected in the data in Table 6.2 with absolute discipline scores that are without exception significantly lower than the relative discipline scores.[23] Ideally, we would like to be able to also include in this "Present But Not Voting" category some of those legislators who

[20] The respective unweighted and weighted unity scores for the 1989–1991 period based on all 103 votes are Partido Justicialista (0.87 and 0.86) and Unión Cívica Radical (0.94 and 0.95). The unweighted and weighted unity scores were calculated following the method recommended by Carey (this volume).

[21] This party position was also often influenced by the governors (particularly from the PJ) who generally exercise a considerable amount of control over the voting behavior of their copartisans in the province's Chamber delegation.

[22] A recent (1997) example would be the "no" vote cast by most of the PJ Patagonian deputies in opposition to President Menem's proposed deal with Chile to resolve the "Hielos Continentales" border dispute.

[23] Obviously not all deputies coded as "Present But Not Voting" were absent due to their opposition to the party-mandated action on the vote in question. Many were absent due to factors that had nothing to do with what was occurring on the Chamber floor.

failed to attend the session, since a few undoubtedly were engaged in similar behavior. Unfortunately this cannot be done due to the inability to distinguish between deputies who were absent for valid reasons (e.g., illness, family crisis, transportation problems, district emergency) from those who were absent out of a desire to miss the vote.

Bills that were likely to result in serious voting divisions in the PJ, and thus which might have led to the PJ majority being rolled on the Chamber floor, were generally not brought up for a vote during the 1989–1999 period.[24] As will be discussed later in the chapter, as the majority party the PJ was able to exercise nearly complete control over the legislative agenda between 1989 and 1999.[25]

Explaining the High Levels of Party Discipline[26]

This high level of relative party discipline in the PJ and UCR stems primarily from the relationship between the party and the political careers of

[24] Notable exceptions were those bills that were urgent and indispensable for the economic reform program (at least prior to 1997). However, some of these bills were brought up not to actually obtain the bill's passage, but rather to appease either the International Monetary Fund or the U.S. government when they were pressuring for the passage of a specific piece of legislation (e.g., a new labor law or a new patent law).

[25] See Cox and McCubbins (1999) for an excellent discussion of this type of behavior by majority parties. This agenda control also indicates that we should be cautious in using presidential vetoes as a measure of serious indiscipline, vis-à-vis the president's policy preferences, by the PJ legislative bloc. As noted, between 1989 and 1999 no legislation was passed without the majority support of the PJ in the Chamber and Senate. Given this majority support (as well as the near-universal willingness of the UCR, Frepaso, and a few minor parties to override Menem's vetoes) it is noteworthy that between 1989 and 1997 only 13 of 79 full and 7 of 84 partial vetoes were overridden. While the legislative coalition that passed the vetoed legislation initially could have easily overridden all of the vetoes, only 16.5% and 8.3% of the respective presidential vetoes were overridden (Molinelli, Palanza, and Sin 1999). There are certainly multiple explanations for this failure to override (particularly for the partial vetoes); however, the most salient is that the PJ congressional leadership did not wish to override the veto. While they were willing to pass legislation that Menem opposed (a mild form of protest), they were sufficiently responsive to the wishes of their president so as to not actually override his veto. In the end, Menem obtained his desired legislation while the PJ legislators in some instances partially avoided responsibility for its unpopular components. However, when the PJ legislators decided to override a presidential veto, they did so in a near unanimous (i.e., highly disciplined) manner. In fact, of the 19 Chamber overrides of Menem's vetoes between July 1989 and August 1997, in only two instances did the percentage of PJ legislators opposing the override surpass 5% (13% and 20%), with the mean and median percentage of these legislators voting to override 97% and 98%, respectively.

[26] I am currently carrying out a Centro de Estudios para el Desarrollo Institucional (CEDI) de la Fundación Gobierno y Sociedad sponsored study of the determinants of legislator

legislators in Argentina. First, the provincial-level, and to a lesser extent the national-level, party has a great deal of control over a legislator's access to the ballot, and hence their opportunity for reelection. Second, most legislators pursue political career pathways that are strongly linked to the party. Third, legislators who consistently vote against their party are likely to be expelled. Once expelled, legislators normally (with the partial exception of the recent experience of some Frepaso deputies) have a difficult time achieving either reelection or pursuing a career elsewhere in politics due to the lack of an alternative viable political party to join.

Fourth, linked to the previously mentioned career-related factors, party discipline in the legislature is also the product of the congressional party leadership's ability to determine the amount of resources/opportunity that a legislator has to engage in in political entrepreneurship at both the provincial and national levels. Regardless of the legislator's career ambition (discrete, static, or progressive), these resources are vital to the fulfillment of his/her career goals (Schlesinger 1966).

Finally, distinct from the previously mentioned career-driven explanations, being a Peronist (PJ) or Radical (UCR) is a fundamental part of many deputies' personal identity and social relations. To be expelled from the party (likely in the face of frequent indiscipline) thus carries consequences for the deputy beyond mere political career concerns.

Legislator Access to the Ballot and PJ and UCR Intraparty Politics[27]

Mainwaring and Shugart (1997) list three key features of electoral laws that influence the level of party discipline in a country: (1) pooling of votes among a party's candidates, (2) control over who runs on the party label, and (3) control over the order in which candidates are elected from the party list. In Argentina, deputies are elected via closed party lists and thus for this office votes are pooled. This encourages deputies to engage in behavior that enhances the electoral prospects of their party (Molinelli 1991).

Three important party groups exercise influence over the formation of the party lists (i.e., affect who runs on the party list and what order they

---

roll-call voting behavior in the Argentine Chamber between 1989 and 1997. This multi-variate study is comparable in many respects to that of Ames in this volume.

[27] This section draws heavily from Jones (1997a) and De Luca, Jones, and Tula (2000).

occupy) for the election of Chamber deputies: the national party organization, the district-level party organization, and the district-level rank-and-file party members (i.e., party affiliates). Both the PJ and the UCR are divided into 24 district-level party organizations (corresponding to the 23 provinces and the federal capital).[28]

National party organization: When a party's leader (de facto if not also de jure) is the president, he/she has the ability to influence local party leaders through threats of fiscal or administrative reprisal/promises of fiscal or administrative reward, or in very extreme cases the threat or real (albeit extremely rare) occurrence of the direct intervention of a province governed by a copartisan (i.e., where the national government assumes direct control of the provincial government).[29] Thus, when the leader of a party is also the president, the national party organization has a greater degree of influence over who runs on the district-level party lists and the order they occupy than has the national organization of the party out of power.

The national party, even when its leader is not the president, has two important powers that can be employed to influence the district-level party organizations. First, the national party can intervene district-level party organizations and take over their governance.[30] Both the PJ and, to a lesser extent, the UCR national party organizations have employed this mechanism, or the threat of it, to influence party-related events at the district level. This strategy is however risky, because it can potentially adversely affect the party's electoral performance in the intervened dis-

[28] I do not discuss Frepaso here due to this study's primary focus on the 1989–1997 period (Frepaso has only been a major legislative actor since December 1997) as well as to the inchoate nature of the Frepaso alliance, which makes any effort to analyze its internal functioning very difficult. For example, it still is not clear if the relevant political unit to analyze is the Frepaso alliance, or Frepaso's constituent parties (e.g., FG, PSP, PSD, PI, PDC). Furthermore, during the 1997–1999 period Frepaso had elements that rendered it very undisciplined (its status as an alliance of different parties and its lack of a significant party apparatus) and at the same time other elements that allowed it at times to be extremely disciplined (Frepaso's electoral success depended in large part on the considerable popularity of its two most prominent leaders, Graciela Fernández Meijide and Carlos "Chacho" Alvarez, thereby endowing them [especially Alvarez] with considerable power vis-à-vis the behavior of their co-partisans) (Abal Medina 1998).

[29] Between 1983 and 2000 there were only five distinct national government interventions of provinces (Molinelli, Palanza, and Sin 1999). Four of these interventions (Catamarca 1991, Corrientes 1992–1993, Santiago del Estero 1993–1995, Tucumán 1991) took place during the Menem presidency (1989–1999), while the final intervention (Corrientes 1999–) took place at the beginning of the De la Rúa presidency (1999–).

[30] It also has the power to expel or suspend individual party members.

trict.[31] Second, the national party has control over the use of the party label (Jones 1997a).

District-level party organization: The ability of the national party to influence district-level party officials also depends on the relative strength and unity of the district-level party organization. Best able to resist national party influence and defy national party authority are those district-level organizations where the party leadership enjoys a high level of popularity with the party rank-and-file and strong control over the district-level party organization. Least able to resist national party influence and defy national party authority are those district-level organizations where different party tendencies (one of which is often linked to the national party organization) are in conflict, with no single faction possessing secure control of the district party organization. Also, other factors held constant, the more important a district is electorally to the party, the better able its local party organization is to resist national party pressures.

In districts where prominent party leaders are highly unified (often under the hegemony of one individual), the district-level organization has a great deal of control over who runs on its list and what order they occupy. In districts where the local party leaders are not highly unified, the local party organization's ability to influence who is on its list and what order various candidates occupy is reduced.

For example, one can contrast the PJ candidate selection processes in San Luis and Capital Federal. In San Luis, Adolfo Rodríguez Saa (PJ) has been governor continuously since 1983. The San Luis PJ has never held a primary election to select its Chamber candidates, with Rodríguez Saa and his close advisors generally determining who occupies a position on the legislative list.

In contrast, the PJ in Capital Federal (the district where the absence of a strong and unified PJ party leadership is most evident) has held primaries to select its candidates in every election but 1983 (when it used a party assembly). In a reflection of the importance of the district-level party organization, it is telling that even "outsider candidates" strongly supported by

---

[31] For example, in 1991 the PJ intervened its district-level party organization in the province of Catamarca to replace the province's PJ leadership. In the congressional (and provincial) elections of 1991, the displaced PJ members formed their own independent list that competed against both the UCR as well as an official PJ list. The displaced group won 37% of the votes and one congressional seat while the official PJ list won only 14% of the votes and no seat. Furthermore, a UCR-led alliance was able to take advantage of the PJ's internal division and win the election for provincial governor.

President Menem such as Erman González (the head of the 1993 Chamber list) and Daniel Scioli (the head of the 1997 Chamber list) had to compete in primary elections against a list of candidates backed by a portion of the Capital Federal PJ party organization.[32] That is, Menem was unable to impose his candidates, even in the district where the PJ party organization is the weakest. The lists headed by González and Scioli eventually won in relatively competitive primary elections (González's list won 60% of the vote and the runner up 30% while Scioli's list won 50% and the runner up 39%).[33]

Rank-and-file party members: The rank-and-file party members most commonly have an opportunity to influence who is on the party list and what order they occupy (within the constraints imposed by the use of closed lists in the primary elections) in two instances. First, when the national-level party organization and district-level party organization disagree over the composition of the party list and cannot come to an agreement among themselves, the rank-and-file (when the national party does not impose a list) is generally called on to make the decision (e.g., the 1997 PJ Capital Federal primary, where the Menem-supported list headed by Scioli competed with, and defeated, a list backed by the dominant local factions of the PJ). The other (often related) instance where the rank-and-file plays an important role in the list formation process is when the district-level party organization is divided and cannot agree on a common list (e.g., the PJ primary in Jujuy in 1998, where two lists competed, each backed by a different set of pro-Menem Jujueño politicians).

In sum, three distinct party groups influence who runs on a party's list and what order they occupy. The national party's influence on candidate selection is greatest when (1) the president (de facto if not also de jure) of the party is also the president of the nation and (2) the district-level party elites are not unified. The district-level party organization's influence is greatest when (1) the party's president is not the president of the nation and (2) the district-level party elites are unified. The rank-and-file party members' influence is greatest when there is disagreement over the list composition (1) between the national- and district-level party organiza-

---

[32] González, a childhood friend of Menem, was a long-time member of Menem's inner circle. González had occupied important posts in his gubernatorial administration in La Rioja as well as in his presidential administration. At the time of his 1993 candidacy, he was the Minister of Defense. Scioli was a moderately popular sports figure and a political amateur.

[33] Under the Capital Federal PJ's primary allocation formula, the respective runner-up list in each election received the fourth, eighth, and twelfth positions on the PJ list.

tions and/or (2) within the district-level organization. However, in the list creation process, for any given election all three groups either directly or indirectly exercise some degree of influence over the construction of the party's legislative list. However, the degree of this influence varies considerably.

As would be expected (although not assured) in a country where the provinces possess a considerable degree of autonomy, the provincial branches of the Argentine political parties tend to play a preeminent role in the electoral process at the district level (Jones 1997b). The provincial branches normally enjoy a significant amount of autonomy in regard to activities such as the creation of party lists and the formation of electoral alliances at the district level. This is not to say that the national party is not an important actor in the electoral process at the district level; on balance however, the provincial branches are dominant.

Methods of candidate selection in Argentina: Three distinct methods of candidate selection were employed by the PJ and the UCR during the 1983–1999 period: elite arrangement, assembly election, and direct primary. The first category includes a variety of types of elite arrangements, ranging from the imposition of a list by a provincial-level caudillo (e.g., a powerful governor) to a list that emerged out of a negotiation among provincial party elites. Instances where this single list was presented to the party electorate in an uncontested primary are also categorized as an elite arrangement. The second category encompasses those lists that were the product of a formal provincial party assembly in which delegates to the assembly (themselves directly elected by party members) elected the candidates.

The final category includes only those cases where two or more lists competed in a direct election. The electorate for this contest can be either party members alone or party members and a selection of nonmembers. In this latter category, the nonmembers allowed to vote range from those not affiliated with any party (referred to as independents in Argentina) to all registered voters. The two most common primary methods in Argentina are elections restricted to party members only (referred to as closed primaries) and primaries restricted to party members and independents (referred to as open primaries).[34]

---

[34] Even where primaries are held, the party will at times change the order of candidates on the list that emerges out of the primary process. These changes are, however, virtually always carried out with the consent, albeit at times grudging, of all of the affected individuals.

The PJ has progressively increased its use of direct primaries to select its candidates for national deputy. Since 1989, over one-half of the PJ lists have been the product of primaries, with a high of two-thirds reached in 1993. At the same time, the percentage of lists that emerged out of an elite agreement has declined steadily since 1983. The election of legislative candidates by a party assembly was not a common method in the PJ during this period.

In sum, since the late 1980s, the norm in the PJ increasingly has been to select legislative candidates via the use of primaries. Furthermore, as the 1990s progressed, the PJ has favored the use of open primaries over closed primaries; since 1997, over two-thirds of the PJ's primaries have been open.

The UCR's experience with direct primaries is distinct from that of the PJ. Unlike the PJ, which very rarely held primary elections to choose legislative candidates prior to 1985 (Levitsky 1998), the UCR has a long history of using primary elections (De Luca, Jones, and Tula 2000).[35] During the post-1983 period, the UCR's use of primaries to select its legislative candidates reached a zenith in 1991, when 83% of the provincial branches held primaries to select their candidates, but fell to a post-1983 low of 38% in 1999.[36] Like the PJ, in recent years the UCR has also increasingly employed open primaries in place of closed primaries, although this development has progressed at a slightly slower pace.

Chamber deputy reelection rates: The reelection rate of Argentine Chamber deputies is comparatively very low (Jones, Saiegh, Spiller, and Tommasi 2000). Thus, a focus on the rules governing the election of deputies can only partially explain the behavior of legislators. Since the return to democracy in 1983, the average reelection rate for Chamber deputies has been 20%, ranging from a high of 29% in 1985 to a low of 15% in 1995.[37] As of 2000, there was only one deputy, Lorenzo Pepe (PJ,

[35] The failure of most provincial branches of the UCR to employ primaries to select their legislative candidates in 1983 stemmed much more from the relatively rushed nature of the democratic transition process than from any lack of internal democracy.

[36] This nadir is in part the product of the complications involved in presenting a joint list with Frepaso and other parties (as part of the Alianza). Because the UCR would in the end need to negotiate the list positions with Frepaso and the other parties, there was a tendency to bypass the primary process in many provinces due to the uncertainties surrounding this final stage (e.g., it was unclear what positions the candidates in the UCR primary would actually be competing for). This reduction in the use of primaries may however be merely associated with the initial stages of the formation of the Alianza, and thus we may very well see an increased use of primaries by the UCR in future elections.

[37] For additional information on the reelection of deputies in Argentina, see Molinelli, Palanza, and Sin (1999) and Saiegh (1997b).

Buenos Aires), who had served in the Chamber of Deputies continuously since 1983.

The PJ and UCR are relatively similar in terms of their reelection rates for the 1985–1999 period, although the UCR deputies have been reelected at a slightly lower rate than their PJ counterparts. This lower reelection rate is due in part to the general UCR party rule (which is presently being eliminated from the district-level party's statute in most provinces) that requires incumbents to win two-thirds of the vote in the intraparty primary election to gain the right to run for reelection. While this requirement can be met relatively easily via a negotiated agreement with opposing intraparty forces, it nonetheless represents an additional hurdle faced by the UCR deputies that is not confronted by their PJ counterparts.

There are three principal reasons for this relatively low Chamber reelection rate in Argentina. First, to be reelected legislators must compete at the intraparty level to obtain a spot on the party list. The data in Table 6.3 indicate that during the 1989–1999 period an average of 26% of all deputies surpassed this first hurdle. This number, however, only includes those deputies who both desired reelection and obtained a position on the party list. The number that actually desire reelection is considerably higher, but unfortunately very difficult to measure accurately.[38] It also should be noted that sitting deputies normally do not occupy places on the party list from which they stand no realistic chance of election.[39] Thus this average of 26%, with a few exceptions, reflects the percentage of deputies who were able to achieve a list position from which they had a good possibility of election.

Second, due to the vagaries of electoral politics, every election several deputies who occupy relatively high positions on the party lists are not elected as a consequence of the sagging electoral fortunes of their party. For example, between 1989 and 1999, one-quarter of those incumbents who obtained a position on the party list did not achieve reelection, in

[38] Preliminary analysis by De Luca, Jones, and Tula (2000) of those instances in which primary elections were held indicates that there is a noteworthy number of sitting deputies (between five and ten in every election during the 1990s) who compete in, but lose, a primary election.

[39] The one exception would be where the deputy competed in, and lost, a primary election but at the same time obtained a sufficient number of votes to obtain a place on the list, albeit not a position from which they could hope to be elected. In these instances the deputy most often remains on the list, because dropping out would likely be interpreted as an attempt to undermine the party's success in the general election.

Table 6.3. *Reelection to the Chamber of Deputies, 1989–1999.*

	Number of Seats Being Renewed	Number of Incumbents Presenting	Number of Incumbents Reelected	Number of Seats Being Renewed	Number of Incumbents Presenting	Number of Incumbents Reelected
Party	1989			1991		
Partido Justicialista	48	12	11	62	12	10
Unión Cívica Radical	65	12	11	46	5	3
UCeDé	2	1	1	5	4	2
Provincial Parties	7	5	4	9	5	3
Other Parties	5	1*	1*	5***	2	1
Total	127	31 (24%)	28 (22%)	127	28 (22%)	19 (15%)
	1993			1995		
Partido Justicialista	66	12**	11**	63	10**	9**
Unión Cívica Radical	41	8	3	43	6	3
UCeDé	6	2	0	3	1	1
Provincial Parties	11	5	3	14	4	2
Other Parties	3	2	1	7	2	2
PJ Defectors		4	1		3	2
Total	127	33 (26%)	19 (15%)	130	26 (20%)	19 (15%)
	1997			1999		
Partido Justicialista	66	21**	14**	69	15	9
Unión Cívica Radical	41	14	12	28	7	7
UCeDé	1	0	0	1	0	0
Provincial Parties	10	2***	2***	12	4	3
Frepaso				20	9	9

Party	Number of Seats Being Renewed	Number of Incumbents Presenting	Number of Incumbents Reelected	Number of Seats Being Renewed	Number of Incumbents Presenting	Number of Incumbents Reelected
Other Parties	9	3***	2***			
PJ Defectors		2	1			
Minor Party Defectors		2	0			
Total	127	44 (35%)	31 (24%)	130	35 (27%)	28 (22%)

* Includes one deputy from the Partido Intransigente who was elected on a PJ list in 1989.
** PJ figures do not include defectors who ran for office on the list of another party. All of the successful PJ defectors were elected on a Frente Grande/Frepaso list.
*** Does not include defectors (one from Frepaso and one from the MPJ) who ran for office on the list of another party.
**** Includes four deputies from minor parties who were elected in 1987 on either a UCR or PJ list. The percentages of deputies who achieved reelection for the eight elections held since 1985 are 1985 (29), 1987 (22), 1989 (22), 1991 (15), 1993 (15), 1995 (15), 1997 (24), 1999 (22).

many cases due to the reduced level of support received by their party at the polls.

Third, the political careers of most politicians do not involve extended stays in the Chamber of Deputies. Instead of possessing static ambition, a large majority of deputies possess progressive ambition, with a much smaller number having discrete ambition. In the cases of either static or progressive ambition (and even in a few instances discrete ambition), party loyalty influences deputies' future career prospects.

Political Careers in Argentina[40]

Prior empirical research on the career pathways of Argentine politicians during the post-1955 era does not exist.[41] An initial analysis, however, indicates that the career pathways of Argentine Chamber deputies during the post-1983 period are extremely party-oriented. Virtually all deputies arrive

[40] The analysis in this section is based on extensive interviewing with political elites, detailed archival research, and the consultation of three valuable recent sources (Argento and Gerschenson 1999; Sinatra and Veléz 1994; Veléz 1997).
[41] However, excellent studies of the career pathways of Argentine members of Congress between 1889 and 1955 are provided by Cantón (1966) and Smith (1974).

Table 6.4. *Last post held by deputies (class of 1991–1995) prior to assuming office.*[a]

| | Percentage Distribution of Deputies | | |
Position	Total	PJ	UCR
Provincial Legislator	29	15	50
National Deputy	17	20	12
Mayor	10	11	9
National Executive Branch[b]	9	12	5
Provincial Executive Branch	8	14	0
Party Activity	5	6	2
Private Activity	5	6	2
Prov. Party President (only post)	4	2	7
Governor	3	3	2
Municipal Councilor	3	2	5
Union Leader	3	3	2
Vice Governor	3	5	0
Career Diplomat/Party Activity	1	0	2
Federal Judge	1	2	0
National Senator	1	0	2
TOTAL NUMBER OF DEPUTIES	108	64	44

[a] Includes elective or appointive posts held up to two years prior to 1991.
[b] Includes appointees to the Attorney General's office and political ambassadors.

to the Chamber having previously occupied an elective, appointive (in a national or provincial executive branch), or party post. Following their tenure in the Chamber, an equally high percentage continue in elective, appointive, or partisan posts. The consequence is a very strong link between the careers of legislators and their relationship with their party. Without continued good party ties, deputies will not have success in their political careers. Maintenance of these good ties requires, among other things, normally following the party instructions for voting in the Chamber.

Table 6.4 provides information on the last elective, appointive, party, or other post held by PJ and UCR deputies prior to the start of the 1991–1995 congressional term.[42] Table 6.5 provides information on the

[42] Only PJ and UCR deputies who served more than a year during the 1991–1995 period are included in the analysis population. Minor party members who were elected on either a PJ or UCR list (normally as part of a provincial level alliance) are not included.

Table 6.5. *Post held by deputies (class of 1991–1995) as of mid-1998.*

Position	Percentage Distribution of Deputies		
	Total	PJ	UCR
Party Activity	20	9	37
National Deputy	16	17	14
Private Activity	12	12	12
Provincial Legislator	9	9	9
National Senator	8	6	12
Provincial Executive Branch	8	9	7
National Executive Branch*	7	12	0
Union Leader	5	8	0
Defector	3	3	2
Deceased	2	3	0
Prison/Fugitive	2	3	0
Business Association President	1	2	0
Career Diplomat/Party Activity	1	0	2
Governor	1	0	2
Mayor	1	2	0
Municipal Councilor	1	0	2
Prov. Party President (only post)	1	2	0
Vice Governor	1	0	2
Vice President	1	2	0
TOTAL NUMBER OF DEPUTIES	108	64	44

* Includes appointees to the Attorney General's office and political ambassadors.

same posts held by these deputies two-and-a-half years after the end of their term in office (i.e., as of mid-1998).

Nineteen posts are included in the tables, covering the gamut of the positions occupied by these individuals before and after the 1991–1995 term. The national-level posts included are vice president, national executive branch (i.e., the individual held an appointive post in the National Executive Branch), national deputy, and national senator. The provincial level posts include: governor, vice governor, provincial party president (that is, a person who held no post other than the presidency of the party at the provincial level), provincial executive branch, and provincial legislator. The municipal level posts are mayor and municipal councilor. The remaining categories are business association president, career diplomat/party activity, union leader, party activity (no formal high-level position was held, but the person was actively engaged in party activities and held a lower level party post), and private activity (the person was not engaged in any noteworthy partisan activity nor did they hold any elective or appointive position). Finally, three categories are exclusive to the post-1995 careers: deceased, prison/fugitive, and defector (i.e., the person defected to another party between 1991 and 1995).

Table 6.4 details the last position held by the deputies of the 1991–1995 legislative class prior to their assumption as national deputies. Of the 108 deputies, all but 6 (6%) held either a governmental (appointive or elective) or party position (e.g., as a national-, provincial-, or municipal-level party official) prior to their election as deputy.[43] The most prominent penultimate post among these deputies was provincial legislator (29%).[44] One-half of the UCR deputies were provincial legislators prior to assuming office in 1991. Other common positions held by these individuals immediately prior to 1991 include national deputy (17%), mayor (10%), functionary in the National Executive Branch (9%), and functionary in a Provincial Executive Branch (8%).

Table 6.5 indicates that, after the deputies of the 1991–1995 class completed their term in office, an overwhelming majority continued a career path that was tightly linked to their respective party. Of the 108 legislators, as of mid-1998, 82 were in positions that were strongly influenced by their party ties/position within the party. Of these 82, 50% held elective office at the national, provincial, or municipal level; 29% were active solely as party leaders at the provincial, county, or municipal level; while 21% occupied appointive posts in the national or provincial executive branches.[45]

The remaining 26 legislators can be divided into three groups. First, are those six in posts (five union leaders and one business association president) with a high political content, where ties to the PJ were an integral

---

[43] The position of union leader, particularly for Peronists, is for all intents and purposes a party position.

[44] Furthermore, between 1983 and 1991, of the 108 deputies, 40 (37%) at one time held the post of provincial legislator.

[45] With a few exceptions a party leadership position at the county or municipal level does not carry with it any type of salary. These posts do however provide the individual with a considerable amount of political power, and it is furthermore quite common for many of these local-level leaders to receive some type of salary through an appointive post in the national, provincial, or municipal executive branches or in the national, provincial, or municipal legislatures.

part of their position.[46] Second, are those seven who, because of prior events, could not continue in any of the elective, appointive, or party posts. They are the two deceased individuals, the prisoner (prior to his incarceration he occupied an important post in the National Executive Branch), the fugitive, and the three deputies who defected to another party (all three continued to be active in politics, one as a national deputy). Third, in sum, only 13 of the 108 (12%) deputies actually voluntarily departed from the political scene. Moreover, even after having left politics, many of these 13 individuals continued in careers in which their success was aided by their political connections and good relations with fellow party members.[47]

Further evidence of the progressive ambition held by many chamber deputies is provided by an analysis of the previous careers (of PJ and UCR politicians only) of national senators during the 1995–1998 legislative period, of gubernatorial candidates between 1991 and 1999, of governors elected between 1991 and 2000, and of major party presidential and vice presidential candidates between 1989 and 1999. The post of deputy is clearly used as a springboard to higher offices by a substantial number of politicians.

Of the 59 PJ and UCR national senators, as of March 1996, 36% had previous experience as national deputies (see Table 6.6).[48] Over one-quarter (28%) of the PJ senators had previous experience as deputies, while 50% of the UCR senators previously occupied a seat in the lower house. Furthermore, the position of national deputy was the most common position held by senators immediately prior to assuming office (see Tables 6 and 7). Fifteen percent of the PJ senators and 35% of the UCR senators were Chamber deputies immediately prior to their election as senator. None of the senators were political amateurs.

[46] Indicative of the political nature of this latter post (Business Association President), in 1999 this person was elected vice governor of the province of Santa Fe.
[47] Two examples are a former PJ deputy from Misiones who owns an industrial dry-cleaning service that receives a substantial portion of its revenue from contracts with the provincial and municipal governments and a former UCR deputy from La Pampa who is a lobbyist for one of Argentina's main telephone companies. Of the remaining 11 former deputies, at least 2 (each of whom has a long history of activity in partisan and elective positions) were not politically active strictly due to their poor health.
[48] These senators assumed office between December 1989 and December 1996. Due to a political impasse between the Catamarca provincial legislature, the PJ candidate for senator in Catamarca (Ramón Saadi), and the Senate, Catamarca had only one of its three senators in office between December 10, 1995 and December 9, 2001.

Table 6.6. *Percentage of PJ and UCR senators (1995–1998) who held these positions during the post-1983 democratic period.* *

Position	Total	PJ	UCR
National Deputy	36	28	50
Provincial Minister	22	26	15
Provincial Legislator	20	21	20
Mayor	15	18	10
Governor	10	10	10
Natl. Exec. Branch (2nd tier)	9	8	10
National Senator (a prior term)	9	5	15
National Minister	8	3	10
Vice Governor	7	8	5
Prov. Exec Branch (2nd tier)	2	3	0
Municipal Councilor	2	0	5
TOTAL NUMBER OF SENATORS	59	39	20

* Only positions held prior to their assuming office as senator for their present term are included.

Note: Second tier refers to executive-branch officials who are not cabinet members.

The position of deputy has also been a frequent launching pad for runs at the governorship in Argentina. Of the 128 competitive PJ and UCR candidates who ran for the office of governor between 1991 and 1999, 28% were deputies at the time of their candidacy.[49]

In general, the pattern of deputies running for governor is more common in the UCR (38% of the UCR's candidates were national deputies, as opposed to 20% for the PJ). This is primarily the product of deputies being the most prominent UCR politicians in many provinces. Since the UCR held relatively few governorships during the 1987–1999 period, it is logical that far fewer of its candidates were sitting governors or provincial cabinet members.[50] As Table 6.8 indicates, a considerable proportion of PJ gubernatorial candidates (27%) were sitting governors running for reelection.[51]

[49] A similar pattern can be observed among the four non-UCR gubernatorial candidates presented by the Alianza in 1999; three were sitting deputies while the other was a sitting senator (and former deputy).

[50] For the periods 1987–1991, 1991–1995, and 1995–1999 the UCR held two, four, and five governorships, respectively. In contrast, during these same three respective periods the PJ held 17, 14, and 14 governorships.

[51] Of the 28 times since 1983 that PJ and UCR incumbent governors (who had been elected) were eligible to seek reelection, in all but one instance (when a 77-year-old governor

Table 6.7. *Percentage distribution of PJ and UCR national senators (1995–1998) by the position they held immediately prior to being elected.* *

Previous Position	Total	PJ	UCR
National Deputy	22	15	35
Provincial Legislator	14	15	10
Provincial Minister	12	15	5
Mayor	10	13	5
President of Prov. Party**	9	5	15
Governor	9	8	10
Natl. Exec. Branch (second tier)	7	8	5
Vice Governor	5	8	0
National Senator (in a prior term)	5	3	10
Party Activist (second tier)	3	5	0
National Minister	3	3	5
Prov. Exec Branch (second tier)	2	3	0
TOTAL NUMBER OF SENATORS	59	39	20

* If no position was held at the time of election, then the most recent position was used, provided that it had been held within two years of the election.
** Only position held. Where a party president held an elective or appointive office, that post is used.
Note: Second tier refers to executive-branch officials who are not cabinet members and to party activists who are not president of the provincial party.

Table 6.9 provides information on the previous political experience of the 40 PJ and UCR members who were elected governor between 1991 and 1999. Of these 40 individuals, 40% had occupied the post of National Deputy at some point between 1983 and their election as governor, with the next most common posts held previously by these governors being mayor (25%) and national senator (23%).

While I have focused primarily on the post of deputy in the previous discussion, it is important to note the general importance of a politician's career path within the party to becoming a PJ or UCR candidate for the office of governor, senator, or deputy. While there are instances when a person with no prior political experience (either as an elective or appointive official or as a party leader) has obtained the candidacy of the PJ or UCR, these instances are extremely rare.[52] The recent history of PJ

decided to step down so his son could run for governor) the governor has run for reelection. In 24 of these 27 elections the incumbent was victorious.

[52] Recall that only 6% of the PJ and UCR deputies from the class of 1991–1995 were political amateurs and that none of the PJ and UCR senators for the 1995–1998 period were political amateurs.

Table 6.8. *Percentage distribution of PJ and UCR gubernatorial candidates (1991–1999) by the position they held when running for office.*

Position Held	Total	PJ	UCR
National Deputy	28	20	38
Governor	20	27	12
Mayor	15	16	14
National Senator	11	17	4
Provincial Legislator	9	1	17
Provincial Minister	4	6	2
Party Activist (second tier)	4	1	7
Amateur**	4	6	2
Vice President	2	3	0
Prov. Party Pres.***	2	0	4
Vice Governor	1	1	0
Natl. Exec. Branch (second tier)	1	1	0
National Minister	1	0	2
Total Number	128	70	58

* If no office was held when they ran for office, but they did hold an office within two years of the election, then this latter position is included. In provinces where the PJ and UCR candidates were the top two finishers in the gubernatorial election, both candidates are included. In those provinces where either party's candidate (assuming they presented one) finished third or lower in the election, the candidate is included only if they were generally regarded as viable. In provinces that used the double simultaneous vote for the gubernatorial election, only the party candidate who received the most votes (i.e., the intraparty plurality winner) is included. Because the Capital Federal held only one "gubernatorial" election during the 1991–1999 period, the potential number of elections for the period is 1991 (23), 1995 (24), and 1999 (23). Only the first 1991 Corrientes election is included. The 1993 and 1997 Corrientes elections are included in the 1995 and 1999 categories, respectively.

** This category includes people with no prior partisan political activity in an elective, partisan, or appointive post.

*** Only position held. Where a provincial party president held an elective or appointive office, that post is used.

and UCR candidacies for the country's most prominent political posts after the presidency (i.e., for the governorships) is especially telling in this regard. Only 4% (6% for the PJ and 2% for the UCR) of the gubernatorial candidates can be classified as having no prior political experience.[53] Thus the well-known successful 1991 gubernatorial candidacies of the political amateurs Jorge Escobar, Ramón "Palito" Ortega, and Carlos

---

[53] Furthermore, in two of these five instances, the candidate previously had been actively involved as a supporter of an election campaign.

Table 6.9. *Percentage of the 40 individuals elected governor for the PJ and UCR between 1991 and 1999 who held these positions during the post-1983 democratic period.*

Position	Total	PJ	UCR
National Deputy	40	43	33
Mayor	25	25	25
National Senator	23	29	8
Vice Governor	10	11	8
Vice President	5	7	0
Governor Since 1983**	5	4	8
Total number of Individuals	40	28	12

* Included are the 40 PJ and UCR candidates who won their gubernatorial election between 1991 and 1999. During this period many governors from both parties won more than one term in office. These individuals are only included once. Only positions held since 1983, but prior to their election as governor, are included.

** At the time of their election as governor in 1991, two governors had occupied the post of governor continuously since 1983. One of these governors (Adolfo Rodríguez Saa) has occupied the governor's office in San Luis continuously since 1983, with his current term running until 2003.

Reutemann should be viewed as extremely uncommon events that prove the general rule: To become a PJ or UCR candidate a person must have at least some prior experience in an elective, appointive, or party office.[54]

The prominence of the post of deputy in the career path of politicians is also reflected among the presidential and vice-presidential candidates in the three post-1983 presidential elections. Of the three relevant tickets in 1989, one featured a presidential candidate who was a sitting deputy (Alvaro Alsogaray of the Alianza de Centro). Two of the three vice-

[54] All three of these PJ candidates were encouraged to run, and then actively supported, by Menem. However, only in Tucumán was Menem able to impose his candidate (Ortega), thanks to the intervention of the local PJ party organization (as well as that of the province). In San Juan Escobar had to compete in a primary against an important district-level faction, while in Santa Fe Reutemann had to face other PJ candidates in the first stage of the province's double simultaneous vote (DSV) electoral system. Escobar won his primary with 50% of the votes (the runner up won 40%) while Reutemann easily won the first DSV stage (i.e., the intraparty election) with 70% of the votes (the runner up won 14%).

presidential candidates were sitting deputies (Eduardo Duhalde of the PJ and Alberto Natale of the Alianza de Centro), while the other was a former deputy (Juan Manuel Casella of the UCR).

Of the three relevant presidential tickets in 1995, two had vice-presidential candidates (Carlos "Chacho" Alvarez of Frepaso and Antonio María Hernández of the UCR) who were sitting deputies. The other vice-presidential candidate (Carlos Ruckauf of the PJ) as well as two of the presidential candidates (José Octavio Bordón of Frepaso and Horacio Massacessi of the UCR) were former deputies.

In 1999, all three major presidential candidates (the Alianza's Fernando de la Rúa, the PJ's Eduardo Duhalde, and Acción por la República's Domingo Cavallo) had previous experience as national deputies, with Cavallo a sitting deputy at the time of the election. One of the three vice-presidential candidates, the Alianza's Carlos "Chacho" Alvarez, was a sitting national deputy. Thus, of the nine major presidential and vice-presidential candidates between 1989 and 1999, six and seven, respectively, had held the office of national deputy.[55]

Two important points can be drawn from this analysis of legislators' political careers. First, only a small fraction of deputies are able to pursue a career as a national deputy.

Second, most deputies are involved in a career path within their political party that requires the maintenance of their good standing within the party. The nature of these career pathways varies considerably. Some individuals begin as mayors, move on to a post as national deputy, and finally reach the Senate. Others are second-tier party activists who spend one term in the Chamber (normally placed on the list by a powerful sponsor within the party) and then go back to their province either to continue their work within the party or to hold a position in the provincial executive branch or provincial legislature. Still others start as a provincial leg-

---

[55] The former number takes on added significance when one considers that the remaining three presidential candidates lacked any opportunity to be a chamber deputy during the post-1983 period while one of the remaining two vice-presidential candidates (the PJ's Ramón "Palito" Ortega in 1999) was a sitting national senator. From the start of the post-1983 democratic period these three presidential candidates continuously occupied an office that was clearly superior to that of national deputy. Carlos Menem (PJ candidate, 1989, 1995) was Governor of La Rioja from 1983 to 1989 and president from 1989 to 1999. Eduardo Angeloz (UCR candidate, 1989) was Governor of Córdoba from 1983 to 1995. It is worth noting that all of the PJ and UCR presidential candidates were sitting governors (or in De la Rúa's case as mayor of Capital Federal, a de facto governor) at the time of their candidacy (Menem's initial candidacy). The most competitive third-party candidate during this period, Bordón, was a former (1987–1991) PJ Governor of Mendoza.

islator, eventually arriving as a national deputy, and then either return home (from which they may return to Buenos Aires as a national deputy in the future) or move on to the Senate.

In all cases however, the common denominator for these deputies is that to pursue their desired career pathway, they must maintain a good relationship with the party. One of the pre-requisites to maintaining this good relationship is the adherence to party rules and codes of conduct, one of which is voting the party line in the legislature. While the provincial or internal party faction to which the deputy belongs may at times mandate/recommend a vote against the party line, when these suggestions are not provided, the deputy must (barring a good explanation in the presession evening bloc meeting) vote the party line. While the party leadership is willing to tolerate a modest amount of indiscipline, too much indiscipline (particularly if it is not part of a larger political battle, such as that between different factions or provincial delegations within the party) is very likely to create serious problems for the deputy's political future.

The data demonstrate convincingly that the political careers of these politicians remain firmly linked to the party. Whether they remain in the legislature, move on to the national or provincial executive branches, or return to their province to continue their militancy in the party, these politicians' careers are directly influenced by their relationship with their party. Thus, by maintaining a relatively disciplined voting record in the Chamber, these legislators also maintain their good standing within the party at both the national and provincial levels.

Expulsion/Defection

A deputy who consistently votes against his/her party will eventually be expelled. Knowing this, most deputies who are consistently at odds with their party will defect (i.e., jump before they are pushed). There are three principal types of defection: defect and form your own unipersonal bloc, defect with others and create your own new party, and defect to another party. With the possible exception of a few recent defections from the PJ to Frepaso and from Frepaso to the PJ (the latter defections via the now essentially defunct PAIS [Política Abierta para la Integridad Social]), the latter behavior has been extremely rare in the post-1983 period, due in large part to the existence (until the 1994 emergence of Frepaso) of only two relevant political parties (the PJ and the UCR). Defections from the

PJ to the UCR, and vice versa, are extremely rare, for ideological, historic, and personal reasons.

Therefore, legislators who defect/are expelled have generally found themselves in the political wilderness, with moribund political careers. A few have tried to create their own party, but in virtually all instances have not had any electoral success. In addition to the basic problem of obtaining electoral support (combined with the lack of institutional and financial resources with which to campaign), these legislators also need to surpass institutional obstacles, such as obtaining official recognition of their party.[56] Obtaining party status at the district level requires, among other bureaucratic hurdles, providing the National Election Board with the official adhesions [i.e., voters who are registered as members of the proto-party] of a number of registered voters equal to, at the minimum, 0.004% of the province's registered voters (Gómez de la Fuente and Pérez Colman 1995). In the end, most of these defectors have either left politics or eventually returned to their former party, albeit at a level beneath that which they occupied prior to their departure.

Indeed, this was the situation in which many of the members of the "Grupo de los Ocho" (Movimiento Peronista) found themselves following their defection from the PJ.[57] Their political careers were saved by the fortuitous circumstances of the 1993 PJ–UCR "Pacto de Olivos," which paved the way for the constitutional reform that facilitated President Carlos Menem's reelection. At the same time, the Pacto de Olivos deeply discredited the UCR's status as a reliable opposition to the PJ (Jones 1997a; McGuire 1997; Olivera 1995). This strategic error by the UCR allowed many of these former PJ deputies to restart their political careers via the electoral success of the FG in the 1994 Constituent Assembly elections.[58]

---

[56] For information on the extremely prominent role played by the Argentine political parties in the financing of electoral campaigns, see Olivero (1994).

[57] The Movimiento Peronista was formed in late December of 1990 by eight defectors from the PJ.

[58] The UCR's strategic error should be seen as a necessary, but not sufficient, explanation for the success of the FG (Cheresky 1994; Novaro 1998). The FG's novel discourse/ message and positive public image were in large part responsible for its long-term success. One can contrast the trajectory of the FG with that of MODIN (Movimiento por la Dignidad y la Independencia), a right-wing party led by Aldo Rico. Like the FG, MODIN was a small party with limited popular support that enjoyed success in the 1994 Constituent Assembly elections. In contrast to the FG's subsequent success, however, MODIN failed to win any seats in the 1995 and 1997 Chamber elections and for all intents and

Internal Legislative Organization

The previous sections examined the sources of discipline that stem from the importance of a legislator's relationship with his/her party for reelection or a postlegislative career. This section examines the important role of the party leadership in the Chamber in influencing the behavior of legislators.

The principal organizing unit in the Argentine Chamber is the party bloc. All parties with three or more members constitute a bloc, with a president and any other authorities they wish to designate (the PJ and UCR party directorates have several other officers and members).[59] Once designated, the party leader generally enjoys a considerable amount of autonomy, although this does not imply that he/she does not need to negotiate with the other deputies/factions in his/her party.

The following discussion focuses on the topic of party leadership in the PJ and the UCR. Minor parties are excluded, because during the 1989–1999 period they held very few seats in the chamber, and thus had internal dynamics that are very distinct from those within the PJ and the UCR.[60]

When discussing the blocs, it is important to place this discussion within the political context of the 1989–1999 period. First, the PJ was the dominant force in the Chamber, enjoying either an absolute majority or near-majority of the legislative seats. As such it operated in a rather hegemonic manner, both in the allocation of committee positions as well as in the construction of the legislative agenda in the Chamber Rules Committee (Comisión de Labor Parlamentaria [CLP]).[61] Furthermore, whereas the leadership of the UCR was firmly held by one person, the Chamber party leader, the PJ Chamber party leader at times partially had to share

---

purposes ceased to exist as a viable force when Rico and his closest followers joined the PJ in early 1998, after Rico was elected mayor of the Buenos Aires municipality of San Miguel as a PJ and MODIN fusion candidate.

[59] Parties that enjoy bloc status do not lose it if their membership drops to one or two members (De Riz and Feldman 1990).

[60] An exception is the Frepaso bloc since December 1997. Even after this date, however, the functioning of the Frepaso bloc continues to be somewhat distinct, primarily for the reasons discussed in note 28.

[61] While the CLP operates in part based on consensus, every party leader possesses a number of votes equal to the size of his/her bloc in the Chamber. When a disagreement occurs, the majority position will almost always prevail.

his leadership of the PJ bloc with the President of the Chamber.[62] Between July of 1989 and December of 1999 the Chamber president was Alberto Pierri (PJ, Buenos Aires).

The party leader possesses several important resources at his/her disposal with which to influence legislator behavior. These resources are committee/bloc assignments, budgetary resources, and control over the flow of legislation.

A deputy wishing to further his/her political career, and/or be an effective legislator, requires resources. Independent of whether the deputy wishes to be reelected, move on to higher office, return to their previous status as an important local leader, or have a successful tenure as a legislator prior to returning to private activity, resources are required. All deputies are aided in their efforts to the extent that they can maintain an active presence in the province (which requires money/resources), achieve media exposure, and be seen as actively working on behalf of the province and/or the nation. The party leader in turn has a great deal of influence on the ability of a legislator to achieve these goals.

All legislators in Argentina receive a base disbursement of approximately $5,000 U.S. dollars a month to pay the salaries of their staff.[63] Given the combined need to maintain a presence in their province and the demands of their legislative tasks, this amount is generally insufficient. The party leader, however, can be of great assistance in terms of additional staff in three respects: a committee leadership appointment, an appointment on the party directorate, and the use of his/her own budgetary resources to finance more staff.

Every two years following the assumption by the legislators elected during the partial renovation, committee positions are allocated among the parties by the President of the Chamber in rough proportion to the percentage of seats held by the parties in the Chamber. At the same time, based on the distribution of forces in the Chamber, the president also

---

[62] Furthermore, throughout this period both the PJ party leaders (José Luis Manzano [1985–1991], Jorge Matzkin [1991–1997], Humberto Roggero [1997–]) and Pierri had to contend with the overarching power of President Menem.

[63] The deputies actually have the right to hire a set number of people at differing fixed-pay scales (e.g., secretary, advisor category three). Virtually all deputies informally or formally divide these salaries among a larger number of staffers. The reader should be aware that the cost of living in Argentina during the latter half of the 1990s was roughly equivalent to that in Washington, DC. For additional information on legislator staff and budgetary resources, see Molinelli, Palanza, and Sin (1999) and Pellet Lastra (1992).

decides (in consultation with the presidents of the various party blocs) which committee leadership positions (president, vice president, secretary) correspond to which parties. Once this allocation has been decided, the leadership of each of the parties determines how its committee assignments will be allocated.[64]

While the party leader must engage in a great deal of negotiation and respect informal rules in this allocation, he/she maintains considerable latitude in determining who receives which committee assignments. These assignments are important in four respects: additional staff allocations, media exposure, additional budget resources, and possibilities for favor-trading.

With a few minor exceptions, every committee president receives extra resources for staff salary that amount to approximately 50% of the base allocation received by each legislator. In addition, the committee president has at his/her disposal the permanent staff assigned to the committee. Committee vice presidents and secretaries also receive additional resources for staff salary that amount to approximately 25% of the base allocation received by each legislator.

Not all committees are created equal. Of the 45 Chamber committees (as of the 1997–1999 legislative period), some are highly valued whereas others are not.[65] The benefits provided by the different committees can vary. Some (such as Impeachment and Foreign Affairs) provide a great deal of media exposure, whereas others (Budget and Finance, Constitutional Affairs, Energy and Fuel, General Legislation, Justice) provide opportunities to influence important legislation, while finally others (Budget and Finance, Education, Housing, Joint Library of Congress) provide additional opportunities to acquire resources for a deputy's own political activities and for favor-trading with other deputies. Conversely, many committees provide little opportunity for the receipt of any of the above benefits (e.g., Culture, the Disabled, Drug Addiction, Population and Human Resources, Senior Citizens).

The chief arbitrator in the biennial battle for committee posts within the party is the party leader. This provides the leader with considerable leverage over the behavior of individual legislators.

---

[64] Technically the Chamber president makes all committee appointments. However, in virtually all instances with opposition parties, and in most instances with the PJ, Pierri respected the nominations made by the respective party leaders.

[65] In addition to these 45 committees there are also quite a few joint (i.e., with the Senate) and special investigative committees.

The party leader also can influence the amount of resources that legislators receive through a variety of other mechanisms. (1) By appointing a legislator to the party directorate in the Chamber, the party leader insures that the legislator will receive an increase in staff salary of approximately 25% over base. (2) The party leader has at his/her disposal a moderate amount of additional staff resources that he/she can allocate at his/her discretion. (3) Every bloc leader receives from the Chamber a modest disbursement of money each month in proportion to the number of deputies in the bloc (approximately $1,000 per deputy). These funds provide an additional resource that the party leader can distribute among deputies for office, staff, and political-related expenses.[66]

Prior to all legislative sessions, the legislative agenda is programmed by the Chamber Rules Committee. The members of this committee are the Chamber president, three vice presidents, and the presidents of all of the recognized blocs in the Chamber (or their designated alternates).[67] This committee decides which bills will be treated during the session, who will speak during the floor debate, the hours of the session, and so on. Important for our discussion here is the role of the party leader as the principal advocate for the legislation sponsored by his/her party's members and his/her role in influencing who are the principal participants during the oral debate on the floor. Thus the president of the party is a very important gatekeeper vis-à-vis the ability of legislation (presented by one of his/her co-partisans) to reach the floor. If a party leader so desires, he/she can generally keep any co-partisan's bill off the floor (particularly the PJ leader during the 1989–1999 period). The same is true for a deputy's participation in debates, which is determined in large part by the party leader. In addition, the party leader's role as gatekeeper also extends, albeit more indirectly, to the committee level, where his/her party's principal leader on

[66] All legislators receive a base amount of resources for the granting of subsidies to nonprofit and governmental institutions (approximately $18,000–$20,000 in 1998), of pensions to individuals (approximately $1,200 per month all together [a sum that is almost always divided among several individuals], including medical coverage), and of a small number of modest scholarships to university students. They also receive a limited number of plane tickets and bus passes, the former of which normally they or their staff either use or trade in for their cash equivalent and the latter of which are often distributed to individuals in their provinces who need to travel to Buenos Aires or to colleagues in the party who need to travel on party-related business.

[67] Normally the only people from the major parties who attend these meetings are the first and or second vice presidents of the bloc. The respective party leaders (i.e., the party presidents) generally attend only when the former group has been unable to resolve a complicated or controversial issue.

the committee is able to influence the treatment of legislation within the committee, and who owes, in part, his/her position to the party leader (Goretti and Panosyan 1986).

While all deputies have the right to propose that a bill be discussed on the floor, without the support of the party leadership these proposals almost always are quickly defeated. Similarly, while deputies can at times participate in the debate even when they have not been scheduled as speakers (assuming that someone yields time to them), without party support the extent of this participation is normally quite limited in those instances where it takes place.

The Personal/Historical Factor

In addition to the above-mentioned career-related incentives, to fully understand the high levels of party discipline one must also comprehend the strong personal and historical ties that many deputies have to their party. A large majority of PJ and UCR deputies have been active in partisan politics since their mid to late teens. Many of the current PJ and UCR deputies, especially the Peronists, suffered extreme levels of persecution during the 1976–1983 military dictatorship due to their partisanship. A smaller, yet significant group of current deputies (primarily Peronists) suffered similar duress during the 1955–1973 period. Being a Peronist or a Radical is therefore a very important part of many deputies' personal identity. Similarly, a large part of their social network is within the party.

Therefore, for many deputies consistently voting against their party, and in turn facing the possibility of expulsion, is not a decision to be taken lightly. For them the decision to remain a Peronist or a Radical is much more than a simple rational calculation of costs and benefits vis-à-vis their political career. This personal factor is thus an important final, albeit non-institutional, determinant of the high levels of party discipline in the Argentine Chamber.

Finally, at least within Peronism, there is a strong tradition of loyalty to the party leader and to the party hierarchy in general. Many Peronists (although fewer than in the past) still view Peronists who leave the party as traitors. Thus, this tradition of loyalty within Peronism acts as a further constraint on at least some politicians who might consider breaking with the party. The restraining effect is both internal (i.e., they would consider themselves to be engaging in treasonous activity) and external (they would in all likelihood receive sanctions in the form of hostility from many of their former comrades).

Conclusion

Party discipline in the Argentine Chamber of Deputies is relatively high. This high level of discipline stems primarily from a combination of the institutional rules governing elections and intralegislative organization in Argentina. These rules, combined with a majority of legislators possessing progressive ambition, helps in large part to explain the rarity of legislators voting against their party's position on the Chamber floor.

7

Party Discipline in the Chamber of Deputies

BARRY AMES

Although political parties are key actors in all legislatures, their roles vary enormously. In Great Britain and Argentina, parties are the main players, and the legislative game can be understood with few references to individual deputies. No one would argue that Brazil's legislative parties have the strength of Argentina's Peronists or Britain's Labor Party. Nonetheless, leaders of Brazil's congressional parties organize the legislative calendar, participate in legislative negotiations, and mediate between individual deputies and ministers.

This chapter adapts theories of legislative parties to the Brazilian case. The first section demonstrates that Brazilian presidents, while powerful, are far from dominant. From the administration of José Sarney through the first government of Fernando Henrique Cardoso, most executive proposals come out of the legislature highly modified or fail to come out at all. Why do presidential proposals so seldom emerge unscathed from the Congress? Do party leaders, especially leaders of parties that are nominally part of presidential coalitions, really oppose these proposals? If, instead, party leaders are simply unable to marshal their troops to support these bills, why are backbench deputies so reluctant?

The answers lie in the nature of Brazil's legislative parties. The second section reviews the theoretical literature on legislative parties, a literature based mainly on the U.S. experience. This dscussion demonstrates that Brazil ought to be a case of "conditional party government." Given Brazil's electoral rules and its federal structure, influence should flow from the bottom up, from party members to leaders, not from the top down. Arguments about the flow of influence in legislative parties depend, in the final analysis, on leaders' ability to compel backbenchers to follow their lead. The third section utilizes roll-call votes to test a multivariate model of the

185

probability that individual deputies cooperate with their parties. A key indicator of party strength is the ability of party leaders to compel their members to follow the leadership's vote recommendations. A second, less direct indicator comes from the success of individual deputies in garnering local public works or control over job nominations, what scholars of American politics call "pork barrel." The higher the price leaders pay to buy support, the weaker the party. These indicators of party strength are embedded in a model that also includes measures of individual electoral security, ideology, seniority, constituency characteristics, and career background. The empirical analysis presented in the fourth section demonstrates that party recommendations (and the punishments and rewards that accompany them) rarely matter very much in determining cooperation or defection. In the end, the presidents' weakness stems less from the recalcitrance of party leaders than from their inability, even with lavish pork-barrel spending, to persuade deputies to support presidential proposals.

Do Presidents Dominate?

Presidential success is commonly measured by assessing the approval rates of presidential initiatives on roll-call votes. In any legislative setting, this technique is problematic. First, to the degree that roll calls reflect only those issues actually coming to a vote, they exemplify the classic problem of "nondecisions." If congressional opposition is too strong, a presidential proposal may never face an up or down vote. A presidential trial balloon can generate such fierce opposition in the legislature that the president gives up, never sending a formal proposal to the Congress.[1]

Roll-call measures of party unity also fail to reflect the *costs* of gaining party backing. Presidents and party leaders pay these costs in combinations of pork and substantive policy concessions. Roll calls, in other words, really represent the *end point* of negotiations among presidents, party leaders, and rank-and-file deputies. What is needed, and what is usually lacking, are head counts – executive-branch leaders' estimates of the direction in which individual deputies are leaning, estimates made during the process of negotiation.[2]

---

[1] In Brazil, two well-known examples include Collor's proposal for administrative reform and Sarney's attempt to impose tuition at federal universities. Both quietly disappeared, never to arrive at Congress's door.

[2] Sullivan (1987) has analyzed head-count data for some issues during the Eisenhower years.

A third limitation stems from the possibility of fundamental differences between the political processes generating roll calls and those generating other types of congressional decisions.[3] Without question, committees and voice votes on the floor make many key decisions in the Brazilian Congress.[4] Furthermore, roll calls are notoriously subject to "bandwagon" effects. In most congressional votes, 80% of the deputies support the winning side.[5] An eight-to-two ratio implies neither that four-fifths of the deputies supported the original proposal nor even that four-fifths support the final bill. In fact, overwhelming victories occur even when only bare majorities are really supportive. Such bandwagons develop when indifferent deputies trade support as part of cross-issue logrolls, or when they join the winning side in the hopes of gaining an advantage on future votes. If a proposal has undergone, between its original form and final passage, significant concessions to congressional opposition, and if the proposal then passes with 80% approval, either enormous bandwagon effects are operating or the proposal's authors badly overestimated the concessions needed to obtain majority support.

In an important new research development, Brazilian scholars have begun using legislative roll calls to assess presidential success and party strength. In recent essays, Fernando Limongi and Argelina Figueiredo (Figueiredo and Limongi 1997b; Limongi and Figueiredo 1995, 1996) analyze roll calls taken from 1988 (the end of the Constituent Assembly) through 1994.[6] To approximate the concept of the party agenda, these authors concentrate on votes where party leaders made explicit recommendations (*encaminhamentos*) to their members. Adopting the Rice index of party discipline, in which the minority percentage is subtracted from the majority percentage for each party on each vote, Limongi and

---

[3] In the U.S. Congress, it is clear that leaders exert influence in varying ways in these differing settings. Interest group representatives, moreover, have varying degrees of access. After intensive research, VanDoren concluded that "the processes that determine committee and voice-vote decisions are different from those that determine roll-call decisions" (1990, p. 311).

[4] Moreover, the Brazilian Congress has adopted rules deliberately hindering the use of roll calls.

[5] In addition, few roll calls occur when ideological blocks oppose each other. If we group the PSDB and PMDB together in one block and the PFL, PTB, and PDS in another, we find that majorities of these two blocks opposed each other on only 35 of 473 regular Chamber votes (1988–1996) and on only 5 of 77 emergency measure votes (1988–1992).

[6] The findings of Figueiredo and Limongi have gained considerable attention in Brazil, even in the popular press. See Barros and Silva (1995, pp. 1–8).

Figueiredo find that even in the weakest parties an average of 85% of the members vote the same way.[7]

Figueiredo and Limongi admit that Brazil's electoral system fosters individualism on the part of legislators and hinders "accountability" between party and voter (Limongi and Figueiredo 1995, p. 498). In spite of the electoral system, they argue, the legislature's internal rules allow "party leaders [to] control the work agenda and limit the area open to the individualistic strategies of deputies and senators" (p. 500). Party leaders, as a result, dominate party followers. Arguments linking the electoral system to party weakness stop, in this view, at the Chamber door.[8] For Figueiredo and Limongi, Brazilian parties take predictable, coherent ideological positions and are serious legislative actors.

The findings of Figueiredo and Limongi are controversial among students of Brazilian politics. As the only truly empirical research, their work must be taken as the conventional (if somewhat beleaguered) wisdom, but questions remain. What level of party unity, in comparative terms, makes a party disciplined? True, Brazil's parties have discipline scores (Rice indices) in the 80s. Are these high numbers? Cross-country assessments, as I will subsequently demonstrate, are risky, but even a direct comparison leaves Brazil's parties well below some neighboring countries. Argentine party unity has traditionally been over 98% and Argentine party leaders achieve these high levels of party voting with neither the pork-barrel wooing of deputies nor the substantive legislative concessions that occur in Brazil.[9] Venezuela, at least until recently, is another example of a polity with parties vastly more disciplined than those of Brazil.

Implicit in any judgment about the comparative discipline of Brazil's parties is an assumption of *ceteris paribus*. Scholars begin with certain questions of primary interest, typically hypotheses linking such concepts as presidentialism versus parliamentarism, single-member versus multimember electoral districts, or open-list versus closed-list proportional representation. Then, to make cross-national comparisons of party strength,

---

[7] Figueiredo and Limongi follow the common convention of calling this indicator "cohesion." Following Tsebelis, I refer to deputies voting together as "discipline" or "unity." Parties are "cohesive" when deputies agree on substantive policy questions. (See Tsebelis 1995).

[8] Similar arguments about party weakness have been made by Mainwaring (1993, 1999), Lima Junior (1993), Lamounier (1994a), and Castro Santos (1997). On the side of the "preponderant executive" see also Diniz (1995).

[9] Personal communication from Mark Jones. Chilean discipline seems equally high.

they assume that the remaining institutional contexts are equivalent. Suppose that we seek to test the hypothesis that closed-list proportional representation yields higher levels of party unity than open-list proportional representation. The logic of causal inference naturally requires the assumption that other institutional rules are constant across the different party systems. Is this assumption reasonable? When deputies easily switch parties, for example, the concept of party discipline may be illusory. If party leaders attempt to punish dissenters, deputies jump to another party. Discipline for the party losing members then rises. Given a sufficient number of alternative parties for defectors to join, unity for the receiving parties need not fall (Mainwaring and Liñán 1997). During the Sarney administration, the Brazilian Democratic Movement (PMDB) lost members to the Brazilian Social Democratic Party (PSDB) on its left and to the Liberal Front Party (PFL) on its right. In the short run, overall discipline rose. Where members easily switch, in other words, the concept of party itself is a moving target.

In Brazil these caveats represent real problems, not merely theoretical objections. Consider the problem of nondecisions. Any judgment of the strength of presidents presupposes knowledge, as a starting point, of the president's agenda. How is it possible to know what proposals presidents would send to the Congress if they thought passage was remotely possible? Although certain ideas may go unmentioned because they have no chance of passage, most reasonable proposals are at least aired in the media. Utilizing the *Latin America Weekly Report: Brazil*, the *Economist Country Report*, and the *Gazeta Mercantil*, I constructed an inventory of all presidential proposals from 1990 to 1998.[10] Although the results are not amenable to quantitative measures, they are, nonetheless, quite revealing. *Many important proposals, though aired in the media, never arrive at Congress's door.* Faced with powerful congressional opposition, President Collor gave up his attempts to eliminate the state oil monopoly, control state and municipal finances, end free university education, and eliminate lifetime tenure for government employees.[11] Itamar Franco never sent Congress

[10] Although my inventory undoubtedly missed some proposals, their inclusion would only strengthen the argument that many proposals are "dead before arrival." A more complete treatment would include the effects of judicial interventions. For an extensive analysis of the role of the judiciary in hampering presidential initiatives, especially in the economy, see Castro Santos (1997).

[11] These proposals were all part of the *emendao*, The National Reconstruction Project, first proposed on February 14, 1991.

his fiscal-reform program or his plan for a wealth tax.[12] Fernando Henrique Cardoso abandoned his drive to install a mixed public–private pension system.[13] Although his economic team regarded tax reform as crucial to its stabilization program, the president sent no tax-reform proposals to the Congress during his first term. FHC also made no effort to push through the political–institutional reforms that he had long advocated. *Among the proposals that do arrive at the Congress, many never reach a vote.* Collor's proposals for new wage-adjustment indices failed without ever coming to a vote.[14] Franco's November 1993 package of emergency tax increases met a similar fate.[15] *Long delays are common.* Pension-reform and administrative-reform proposals arrived in the Congress at the beginning of Cardoso's first term, but they received final approval only at the beginning of his second term, four years later. *Little gets through the Congress without substantive concessions to individuals, to narrow economic interests, or to states.*[16] As Castro Santos points out (1997, p. 348), "the essential medium of exchange [between governors, their state delegations, and the executive] is the rollover of state debts." Fernando Collor was forced to roll over US$70 billion in debt that states owed to the central government before the Congress would approve an increase in the personal income tax ceiling.[17] Itamar Franco had to agree to an accord pegging monthly wage rates to inflation before the 11 state governors would resume repayments on billions of dollars that they owed to the central government.[18] Approval of Franco's plan to cut government expenditures, a key part of his stabi-

[12] The president's call for "full and lasting fiscal reform" was made on October 21, 1992. His attempt to tax those with assets over US$2 million came on November 25, 1993.

[13] The Minister of Social Welfare proposed a mixed system of public and private pensions on February 18, 1995.

[14] Collor's first proposal to establish a new index for calculating "wage losses" was made on June 25, 1990. In March 1991, the Collor administration proposed a minimum wage of US$66. Congress ultimately approved a minimum of US$77.

[15] In addition to the failed wealth tax proposal, the Franco administration had proposed an increase in income tax rates for those earning over US$1,500 per month.

[16] In early April 1997, the Chamber passed, by one vote, the president's proposal on administrative reform. The one-vote majority was achieved by doubling the ceiling on the maximum retirement benefit receivable, but just for retired parliamentarians. On April 13, the president disavowed the agreement, putting the proposal itself in doubt. The proposal was finally approved in late 1998, but its effects were substantially delayed because Brazilian law prohibits the hiring or firing of government employees six months before or after an election. Since the next election occured in October 1998, no one could be fired until after April 1999.

[17] In January 1992, Congress rejected Collor's proposal to raise the income tax ceiling to 35%, even though Collor had already agreed to the state and municipal debt rollover.

[18] These negotiations occurred in late August 1993.

lization program, required government concessions on debts of the rural caucus.[19] In the first administration of Fernando Henrique Cardoso, the government's critically needed social-security reform approached final passage only after a four-year struggle that required a substantial weakening of the original proposal as well as significant outlays in pork-barrel spending.[20]

The inability of presidents to force their agendas through their legislatures is common, of course, in all democracies and, in particular, in presidential sytems. Still, Brazilian presidents seem particularly crippled. If the supposedly all-powerful president is really far from all-powerful, attention should turn to the sources of presidential weakness. Is the problem simply that the multiplicity of parties creates an excess of veto players, thereby hindering any policy constituting a movement away from the status quo? Or does the problem lie in the propensity of deputies to defect from the wishes of their party leaders?

The Concept of the Legislative Party

Why do legislative parties exist?[21] Even where party identification is weak (surely the case in Brazil), enough voters have at least vague conceptions of parties and their records, so that party labels affect reelection chances.[22] Legislators need the party label to take advantage of partisan electoral tides.[23] Thus, legislative parties exist as solutions to collective action

---

[19] In 1999, I interviewed a high-ranking member of Finance Minister Cardoso's economic team. He confirmed his personal involvement in negotiations with the rural caucus and with state governors. These negotiations did not include party leaders.

[20] The pessimistic interpretation above notwitstanding, some proposals do survive congressional scrutiny unscathed. Economy-opening measures, including tariff reduction and deregulation, have a high success rate, with especially strong support from the PFL's neoliberal wing and from northeastern deputies, who benefitted less from state intervention in the economy. The drive to privatize state-owned enterprises has moved equally smoothly. Here state governors, needing the revenue generated by enterprise sales to cover their deficits or to reduce the fiscal pressure on the central government, joined neoliberals and northeasterners.

[21] For a comprehensive discussion of the theoretical bases of legislative parties, see Bowler, Farrell, and Katz (1999), especially Chapter 1.

[22] Remember, however, that in Brazil, where turnover between legislative sessions can surpass 50%, the goal of reelection is necessarily broader – including election to other offices and possible reelection to legislatures in the more distant future – and is not shared by all deputies.

[23] Most observers would regard the PMDB's growth in 1986 and the PSDB–PFL alliance's surge in 1994 as partisan tides.

problems. Parties help prevent, in Gary Cox and Matthew McCubbins' (1993) language, such "electoral inefficiencies" as the overproduction of particularistic legislation and the underproduction of legislation with collective benefits.

The strength of central authority in a party depends in part on the strength of individuals' motivations to defect. These motivations, in turn, depend on deputies' ties to their constituencies, the homogeneity of those constituencies, their ideological positions, and other factors. As a result, a finding that party membership predicts the voting of individual legislators does not establish the strength of the legislative party. Members may vote together because they share common beliefs about an issue, because their electoral constituencies are similar (Fiorina 1974, pp. 2–3), or because they engage in logrolls or policy alliances.[24]

Cox and McCubbins (1993, pp. 4–5) review three distinct ways in which scholars of the U.S. Congress conceptualize the legislative party. As floor *voting coalitions*, parties have little systematic influence on prefloor (committee) behavior. Partisans of this view utilize discipline on roll calls as a measure of party strength. As *procedural coalitions*, parties organize the House, make rules, and establish committees, but seldom do parties assume responsibility for policy. As conditional *legislative parties*, leaders' actions depend on the support of party members on a case-by-case basis. Influence flows from the bottom up, and party leaders take responsibility only when there is widespread policy agreement among the party's members. By contrast, in such countries as Great Britain and Argentina, influence flows from the top down, and the rank-and-file grants automatic support within some range of acceptability to the leadership.

The empirical evidence marshaled by Cox and McCubbins for the U.S. case supports the model of a conditional party government. What does this mean for the assessment of party strength? In their view, a measure of party strength should combine the size of the party's agenda with the party's discipline in support of its leadership on that agenda. The party agenda is all roll calls, where (a) the leadership has a position and (b) where the other party either has no position or is opposed. When both parties have positions, and when these positions are opposed, the roll call is a party

---

[24] Cox and McCubbins describe the policy alliance between urban democrats supporting farm subsidies and rural democrats supporting food stamps. When this alliance, which party leaders merely facilitate, breaks down, the decline in average party loyalty is an indicator of the part of cohesion created by intraparty logrolls. See also Kingdon (1981).

leadership vote. Discipline on such votes is the strongest test of party strength.

Scholarly understanding of the U.S. Congress helps to provide knowledge about party strength in Brazil. In other writings (Ames 1995a, 1995b, 2001), I have demonstrated that Brazil's electoral system produces a legislature with lots of weakly disciplined parties. Such a legislature is likely to be good at distributing pork, but it will have trouble making laws on issues of a truly national scope. These difficulties matter less where presidents dominate their legislatures. But when key proposals in an executive's program require approval by a bicameral legislature, congressional obstructionism becomes a serious problem.

In retrospect, this argument remains incomplete. Brazil's legislature does, of course, shelter many parties. But while the nation's electoral rules clearly produce individualistic deputies motivated to resist discipline, until recently there has been no evidence from the legislature itself establishing the relative discipline of parties. Moreover, discipline (the propensity of party members to vote together) must be distinguished from coherence (the agreement of members' preferences on policy issues). Greater coherence means that, for any given number of parties, it will be *harder* to reach a legislative decision departing from the status quo (Tsebelis 1995).

Imagine an electoral structure in which deputies owe their seats and their political futures totally to party leaders.[25] Such deputies have no choice: They must delegate power to party leaders in exchange for access to "party goods." But suppose that sitting deputies have automatic places on party slates, that voters cast votes for individual candidates rather than party labels, and that fund-raising is completely centered on candidates. Now deputies can choose. They delegate to party leaders a portion of their freedom to make individual bargains and a portion of their freedom to vote with their constituency's interest. Legislators do so in exchange for a combination of individual and party goods surpassing what they can achieve individually. For some deputies – particularly those who do not dominate their constituencies, who share their electoral base with party colleagues, or who compete with deputies from other parties – the trade-off is an easy one: They need the party. For others, the party is marginal. Such deputies concede autonomy only after adequate compensation.

A finding, therefore, that a party's deputies vote together cannot prove that influence between party leaders and deputies necessarily flows from

---

[25] Coppedge's (1994) portrait of pre-1991 Venezuela fits this description.

the top down. Instead, this phenomenon may denote the occurrence of a successful bargaining process in which nearly all deputies are satisfied with their individual payoffs. In a sense, the best predictor of the amount of bargaining likely to occur is the structure of electoral rules, because these rules determine party leaders' control over the ballot as well as deputies' propensities to negotiate with party leaders and with the executive. Brazil's electoral rules, without question, produce a plethora of deputies motivated to drive hard bargains.

In this political context, roll-call analyses can measure legislative parties' strength only within a multivariate model. Figueiredo and Limongi's work, while truly pioneering, is essentially univariate: The only variable is the level of unity of each party in the Chamber of Deputies. To make inferences about the strength of party leaders, it is necessary to assess the importance of other determinants of party voting, including ideology, constituency characteristics, pork-barrel benefits, and seniority.

A Model of Cooperation and Defection from Party Majorities

Motivation to Defect

Deputies desert their parties when they have motivation and autonomy. Motivations can be both ideological and electoral. *Ideological* motivation means that on a given issue a deputy's preferences differ from those of the party majority. These preferences may be predictable on the basis of the deputy's political career or personal background, but they are analytically distinct from the interests of the deputy's constituency. In 1995 (before the 1995–1998 legislative session), Maria das Graças Rua constructed a six-point left–right ideological scale. This measure, formulated from surveys of deputies and from background information, is reasonably free from contamination by actual votes, but it can be utilized only in the 1995–1998 period. For earlier legislatures, deputies' links to ARENA (the right-wing political party created by the military dictatorship) serve as a crude indicator of conservatism.[26]

Electoral motivations, which come from demands made by the constituencies that deputies represent, are more complex. "Constituencies" in Brazil include the actual voters who put deputies into office, the interest

---

[26] See the work of Tim Power (1997a, 1997b), who contributed the Graça Rua scale. I combined these two indicators by standardizing them both.

groups and lobbies financing them, and their states' governors. Given Brazil's combination of open-list proportional representation and regionally specialized vote bases, defining a voting constituency is far from easy. It is possible to say, however, that deputies with more concentrated (or clustered) votes ought to have closer links to their voters; hence, they will have greater motivation to defect when their constituents' interests diverge from the party position.[27] At the same time, these deputies will need to deliver pork-barrel programs to their constituents to ensure political survival. *Local* politicians, whose political careers include a stint as mayor or councilperson, are likely to emphasize their independence from party control.

The "primacy of reelection" assumption typically made by students of American politics is inapplicable to Brazil. While some deputies want long parliamentary careers, many others see the Chamber of Deputies as a mere stopover. Their immediate objective is a mayoral post, a run at the governorship, or even a return to private business. For these deputies, and for many who do seek Chamber careers, state governors are figures to reckon with. The ability of governors to influence the voting behavior of their delegations varies across the states as a function of social, historical, and demographic factors (Ames 2001). In general, however, cooperation should be higher when a deputy represents the same party as the state governor.

Motivations are only part of the cooperation-defection story; equally important is the *autonomy* that allows defection. Deputies who are electorally less vulnerable, that is, less subject to partisan tides, are clearly better able to go their own way. One measure of electoral vulnerability is postelection rank in the party list. A deputy ranking first in the list has enormously more freedom of action than a deputy coming in at the bottom. Deputies with a greater share of the votes cast for candidates of their party, or with more seniority, are also more autonomous.[28] Finally, a

[27] The concepts of concentration and domination are explained more fully in Ames (1995a, 1995b, 2000). Note that the unit of observation for determining dominance and concentration is the municipality. Deputies run at-large in states, but the vote is reported in municipalities, which are themselves important political units. Operationalizing concentration begins with V_{ix}, candidate i's share of the total vote cast in each municipality. A statistical measure called Moran's I utilizes a "nearest-neighbor" matrix – a matrix recording that municipalities share common borders – to assess the *spatial* distribution of those municipalities where the candidate does well, that is, where V_{ix} is high. These municipalities can be concentrated, as close or contiguous neighbors, or they can be scattered.

[28] Note, however, that seniority is also correlated with leadership positions, which may make defection much more difficult.

central determinant of individual autonomy is the degree to which deputies dominate their constituencies. Dominance means that a deputy gets a high share of the total vote cast in the municipalities that are important to that deputy; hence, that deputy dominates.[29] Deputies who dominate their voters fear no competition from other parties or from members of their own party. If they change parties, their voters change with them. These party-transcending ties to voters come from an individual's charisma, family tradition, or reputation as an effective leader as well as from deals that the deputy makes with local politicians. In either case, domination allows deputies to thumb their noses at party leaders.

The behavior of dominant deputies is complicated by their greater ability to "claim credit" for public works that they deliver to their electoral bases. Greater dominance leads to more activity in such pork-seeking activities as the submission of budgetary amendments. Deputies who share their constituencies with other deputies have much less incentive to attract public projects to their bases, because such legislators cannot claim exclusive credit. This relationship, however, is curvilinear. At some level of dominance, deputies have such control that their seats are safe and their incentives to fight for voters decline. In sum, the relationship between dominance and defection is linear in terms of autonomy from party control, but it is U-shaped in terms of the relationship between dominance and the deputy's need for pork barrel.

This formulation is implicitly interactive. Three autonomy measures – domination, seniority, and rank – work in concert with vote concentration, the electoral indicator of the potential desire to defect. More defections should be expected among deputies with concentrated votes when (1) they dominate their constituencies, (2) they rank high in postelection vote outcomes, and (3) they attain greater seniority.

No one who follows Brazilian politics doubts that pork-barrel programs and control over appointive jobs are the mother's milk of legislative majorities. Every crucial piece of legislation seems accompanied by the "liberation" of grants plus a spate of appointments to party loyalists. Pork-barrel

[29] Technically, domination begins with the calculation, for every candidate in each municipality, of V_{ix}, candidate i's share of all of the votes cast in municipality x. Each candidate's *municipal dominance* is the candidate's share of the total votes cast for members of all parties. These shares represent the candidates' dominance at the municipal level. Now we use V_{ix} to calculate D_i, the average dominance for each candidate across all of the state's municipalities, *weighted by the percentage of the candidate's total vote that each municipality contributes*. Candidates with higher weighted averages tend to "dominate" their key municipalities; those with lower weighted averages "share" their key municipalities with other candidates.

programs strongly affected voting in the Constituent Assembly of 1987–1988. Between 1988 and 1993, the Chamber's internal rules allowed deputies to propose unlimited budget amendments, but a major scandal (involving millions of dollars in kickbacks from construction companies) led the Congress to reform the amendment process. Current rules allow each deputy amendments up to a fixed amount, roughly US$ 1.5 million. These amendments are essentially under the deputy's control. The new rules might seem to weaken presidential autonomy, since the money cannot be increased or decreased, but in fact the system simply changed. The executive branch still has to transfer the funds, that is, to sign the checks. In practice, the executive has proved willing to speed up or hold back disbursements for individual deputies. Whether the executive seeks the cooperation of deputies from parties supporting the government or the defection of deputies from parties in opposition, speedy disbursements are an appropriate tactic. Utilizing data from SIAFI, the national online accounting system, I calculated, for each year, the ratio of each deputy's actually disbursed funds to the average disbursed funds for all members of the Chamber. The resulting variable measures the pork-barrel favoritism of each deputy.

It might be expected that if pork leads to party cooperation (limiting the discussion, for simplicity, to progovernment parties), a positive sign will be found on the pork variable – that is, more pork leads to more cooperation. In a dynamic sense this is certainly correct, but cross-sectionally it might be wrong. Suppose that the government concentrates its pork on deputies tending to vote no. Some gratefully change their votes to yes, while others remain obstinate. Compared to those who are so progovernment that they need no bribes, the opportunistic deputies are still less likely to cooperate, even though they are more cooperative than they would have been without the pork. Hence the sign on the coefficient of the pork variable could be negative even though pork induces deputies to increase their party cooperation. In terms of the overall hypothesis regarding party strength, however, the size of the pork coefficient is crucial. The greater the importance of pork as a determinant of cooperation, the weaker is the party's control over individual deputies.

Party Strength and Encaminhamentos

It is now possible to categorize the sources of party voting consensus. Party discipline can be a consequence, on the one hand, of pork inducements,

197

constituency demands, and common policy preferences, or, on the other, of the influence of party leaders. The key to party strength as a determinant of cooperation and defection is the importance of the recommendation, or *encaminhamento*, of party leaders. On most votes, party leaders suggest to their members how they should vote. Just before votes are cast, the Chamber president calls on each party leader for this recommendation. Leaders respond with "yes," "no," or "the vote is left open."[30]

Parties frequently recommend votes in situations where the outcome, given that normally opposed parties are on the same side, is a foregone conclusion.[31] In fact, a majority of all recommendations occurs on votes that are essentially uncontested. In such cases, dissent has few consequences for the leadership (or for party followers), since the vote cannot be lost. On contested recommendations, the chances of losing are much greater. A party's membership might live with a few dissenters, but as defections increase, tolerance for free riders drops. If defections are very numerous, of course, it becomes unclear whether the leadership recommendation has much impact on the members.

The central tests of party strength, then, are the coefficients of the variables measuring party leaders' recommendations on contested and uncontested votes. If neither is significant, party unity in voting does not result from leadership sanctions. If the recommendation variables are significant in both kinds of votes, deputies accept party leadership as long as it remains noncoercive; that is, party leaders avoid unpopular recommendations on contested votes, because they know that members will reject such recommendations. If the coefficient on contested votes is significantly greater than the coefficient on uncontested votes, then we will conclude that party discipline matters: Deputies respond to leadership recommendations when they are crucial to the ultimate outcome of the vote.

---

[30] *Encaminhamentos* are not intended to force members to cast a particular vote; such compulsion is very rare and normally follows a party membership vote to "close the question." Sometimes a leader responds to the Chamber president's question with "the vote is left open, but the leader votes . . .". I coded such recommendations as "open."

[31] The analysis excludes votes where more than 90% of the deputies cast the same vote; i.e., votes classed as "uncontested" have at least 10% dissent from the majority position. For the PMDB, PFL, and PSDB, I defined a recommendation as uncontested if each party made the same recommendation as the other two. For the PDT, a recommendation equal to that of the PFL was uncontested. For the PPB (formerly called the PDS or PPR), uncontested recommendations were equal to those of the PDT and the PFL. Inclusion of variables for both contested and uncontested recommendations does not imply a full set of dummies, because the null case ("0") is the condition of no recommendation at all.

Are All Votes Created Equal?

On many Chamber votes, individual cooperation and defection have little importance in terms of overall results, either because the vote is purely procedural or because the outcome is overwhelmingly one-sided. As a result, in a manner similar to Carey (this volume) I weighted the 635 included votes by the number of deputies voting and by the closeness of the vote. For ordinary simple-majority votes, the weight was calculated as:

(Total Voting/Chamber Total)
$\times (1\ ((2 \times \text{Yes Total Voting})/\ \text{Total Voting})).$

On constitutional issues, those requiring three-fifths of each chamber, the formula was:

(Total Voting/Chamber Total) $\times (12 \times \text{abs}((308\ \text{Yes})/\text{Chamber Total})).$

Absentee Deputies

Most roll-call analyses simply delete deputies who fail to vote, counting them neither for nor against. In Brazil, at least, it is quite certain that party leaders hold a different view. On the basis of interviews with leaders of every major party, it is clear that party leaders know who failed to vote and why they failed to vote. Absentees lacking a good reason (medical leave, critical local political commitment) are regarded as defectors, especially on constitutional issues where 308 votes are needed for passage.

I obtained lists of deputies absent from the Chamber for "legitimate" reasons, including medical leaves or acceptance of executive-branch posts. After removing these deputies from the analysis for each day of official leave, the remaining absentees were coded "present." I then took the most conservative approach possible, reclassifying these "present but not voting" deputies only on the issues where their votes were most crucial. Thus, on constitutional issues I switched these deputies from "present" to "defect."[32]

---

[32] Suplentes are not included in the analysis, because electoral and biographical information was generally lacking for them.

Analysis

Why Do Deputies Cooperate or Defect?

For every recorded vote in the Chamber between 1988 and 1996, I created a dichotomous variable called "Cooperate." This variable measures the agreement or disagreement of each deputy with the majority of that deputy's party.[33] The cooperation variable was then regressed, using a logistic specification, on the independent variables discussed earlier. The resulting regressions take the form:

Cooperation = Contested Recommendation
    + Uncontested Recommendation + Pork Share
    + Rank in Post-Election List + Share of Party Vote
    + Municipal Dominance + Vote Concentration
    + Terms Served (Concentration × Rank)
    + (Concentration × Term)
    + (Concentration × Dominance)
    + Ideology + Local Career
    + Governor of State from Deputy's Party
    + Incumbent Seeking Reelection.

The model was implemented separately for each of six parties: on the right, the Liberal Front Party (PFL), the Brazilian Labor Party (PTB), and the Brazilian Progressive Party (PPB); in the center, the Brazilian Democratic Movement (PMDB) and the Brazilian Social Democratic Party (PSDB); and on the left, the Democratic Labor Party (PDT).[34] The unit of observation, then, is the individual vote, cooperating or opposing the party majority, of each deputy. Separate regressions were run for two periods: all post-1991 votes (utilizing a dummy variable for the 1995–1998 period), and just the 1995–1998 administration of Fernando Henrique Cardoso.[35] The regressions were also implemented, in each period and for

---

[33] Note that a member can be in different parties on different votes. A few members have three or more party affiliations over the course of these votes. There are only a few cases in which a majority of a party voted against the recommendations of the party's leaders.

[34] The model was not applied to the Workers Party (PT) because party unity in the PT is so high that the logistic broke down. The model was also applied to the Brazilian Labor Party (PTB), but the paucity of observations produced more unstable (though not contradictory) results.

[35] SAS "Proc Logistic" was utilized for the regressions. The procedure provides tests for collinearity and overdispersion as well as various checks on the residuals. Collinearity was

each party, with absentees counted as missing or, on constitutional super-majority votes, as defectors.

No single table can include 24 separate regressions, and I have spared the reader the burden of 24 separate tables. Tables 7.1–7.6 present one regression – the whole period model with absentees included – for each party. The Appendix contains the results (for each party) with absentees always counted as missing.[36] All of the regressions attain high levels of statistical significance, and numerous variables reach high levels of significance in each regression. In other words, the basic model tested here, while far from a complete explanation of party cooperation and defection, is persuasive.

Logistic models are appropriate when a dependent variable is limited to dichotomous values, as in "yes" or "no," "cooperate" or "defect." To evaluate the whole model, each table provides a series of statistics analogous to those utilized in ordinary least squares. Thus the "–2 log likelihood" is equivalent to the total sum of squares, and the "model chi-squared" is equivalent to the regression sum of squares, with the associated probability interpretable as in an F-test. The "Max-rescaled Rsquared" is the percentage of variance explained, adjusted, for the number of parameters in the model. Interpreting the individual coeffecients is similarly straightforward. The unstandardized parameters give the degree of change in the dependent variable for a unit change in an independent variable, but the change is not linear with respect to the independent variable; that is, the slope of the curve varies depending on the value of the independent variable. The odds ratio (actually the antilog of the unstandardized coefficient) is the number by which we would multiply the odds of a deputy cooperating on a given vote (the probability divided by 1 minus the probability) for each one-unit increase in the independent variable. An odds ratio greater than 1 means that the chances of cooperation increase when the independent variable increases; an odds ratio less than 1 means that the chances of cooperation decrease. The standardized estimates enable us to judge the importance of any independent variable in comparison to all of the others.[37]

occasionally a problem, though never in the case of the leadership vote recommendations, but little can be done except to interpret individual coefficients cautiously. Overdispersion, however, was present. Overdispersion was corrected with the deviance criterion, thus increasing the standard errors of the uncorrected regression. Various residual diagnostics, including the C criterion and the hat matrix diagonal, were examined for outliers and observations of extreme influence. None had any visible effect on the coefficients. For an introduction to logistic models, see Liao (1994).

[36] Results from other periods are available from the author.

[37] Standardizing causes variables to have the same mean and standard deviation. The coef-

Table 7.1. *Cooperation and defection among PFL deputies: 1991–1998.*

	Dependent Variable: Cooperation with Party Majority (Absentees Included)			
Variable	Unstandardized Parameter Estimate and Probability Level	Standard Error	Standardized Estimate	Odds Ratio
Cardoso Administration (1995–1998)	−0.3873	.2043	−0.0477	.679
Contested Party Recommendation	.1657	.1499	.0254	1.180
Uncontested Party Recommendation	−0.3476**	.1386	−0.0587	.706
Share of Pork Disbursements	−0.3960***	.1065	−0.0776	.673
Rank in Postelection List	1.7097***	.3386	.1569	5.527
Share of Total Party Vote	.0953	2.0308	.0011	1.100
Dominance of Key Municipalities	3.1012***	.7578	.1386	22.224
Concentration of Vote	.1574***	.0313	.3825	1.170
Concentration × Rank in List	−0.1123**	.0385	−0.1444	.894
Concentration × Terms Served	−0.0004	.0067	−0.0028	1.000
Concentration × Dominance	−0.4057***	.0925	−0.3067	.666
Ideology	.2775**	.1069	.0629	1.320
Terms Served	.0528	.0605	.0281	1.054
Local Political Career	−0.2654*	.1381	−0.0437	.767
Governor from Same Party	.3204*	.1594	.0586	1.378
Incumbent Seeking Reelection	.3917**	.1544	.0568	1.479

−2 log likelihood = 2019.4; model chi-squared = 455.3, $p < .0001$; correctly predicted = 63.9%; $N = 13,101$; * $p < .05$, ** $p < .01$, *** $p < .001$. $R^2 = .0342$, max-rescaled $R^2 = .1984$.

Table 7.2. *Cooperation and defection among PMDB deputies: 1991–1998.*

Dependent Variable: Cooperation with Party Majority (Absentees Included)				
Variable	Unstandardized Parameter Estimate and Probability Level	Standard Error	Standardized Estimate	Odds Ratio
Cardoso Administration (1995–1998)	−.9400***	.2014	−0.1150	.391
Contested Party Recommendation	.1937	.1339	.0302	1.214
Uncontested Party Recommendation	−0.2853*	.1235	−0.0483	.752
Share of Pork Disbursements	−0.4223***	.0850	−0.9467	.656
Rank in Postelection List	.1997	.3564	.0206	1.221
Share of Total Party Vote	2.8314**	1.1202	.0621	16.969
Dominance of Key Municipalities	3.5046***	.8855	.1388	33.268
Concentration of Vote	.1729***	.0297	.4228	1.189
Concentration × Rank in List	.0232	.0337	.0360	1.023
Concentration × Terms Served	−1.0101	.0103	−0.0570	.990
Concentration × Dominance	−0.4962***	.0852	−0.3786	.609
Ideology	.3289***	.0986	.1394	1.481
Terms Served	.3928***	.0986	.1394	1.481
Local Political Career	.007230	.1173	.0014	.765
Governor from Same Party	−0.2677**	.1284	−0.0484	.765
Incumbent Seeking Reelection	.3776***	.1145	.066391	1.459

$-2 \log$ likelihood = 2,348.6; model chi-squared = 337.7, $p < .0001$; correctly predicted = 68.1%; $N = 14,224$; * $p < .05$, ** $p < .01$, *** $p < .001$. $R^2 = .0235$, max-rescaled $R^2 = .1363$.

Table 7.3. *Cooperation and defection among PSDB deputies: 1991–1998.*

Dependent Variable: Cooperation with Party Majority (Absentees Included)			
Variable	Unstandardized Parameter Estimate and Probability Level	Standard Error	Standardized Estimate	Odds Ratio
Cardoso Administration (1995–1998)	−0.7415**	.3008	−0.0633	.476
Contested Party Recommendation	−0.0308	.1721	−0.0044	.595
Uncontested Party Recommendation	−0.2999	.1614	−0.0488	.741
Share of Pork Disbursements	−0.5192***	.1280	−0.1101	.595
Rank in Postelection List	2.5151***	.3528	.3066	12.368
Share of Total Party Vote	14.2774***	2.4760	.1999	999.0
Dominance of Key Municipalities	2.4301*	1.0115	.1040	11.360
Concentration of Vote	.1432***	.0317	.4075	1.154
Concentration × Rank in List	−0.2093***	.0342	−0.4889	.811
Concentration × Terms Served	−0.0067	.0108	−0.0387	.993
Concentration × Dominance	−0.0381	.0869	−0.0267	.963
Ideology	−0.2411	.1362	−0.0533	.786
Terms Served	.1406	.0880	.0523	1.151
Local Political Career	−0.0622	.1509	−0.0116	.940
Governor from Same Party	.9257***	.1580	.1800	2.524
Incumbent Seeking Reelection	−0.3957**	.1599	−0.0668	.673

−2 log likelihood = 1,543.5; model chi-squared = 429.9, $p < .0001$; correctly predicted = 66.3%; $N = 10,723$; * $p < .05$, ** $p < .01$, *** $p < .001$. $R^2 = .0393$, max-rescaled $R^2 = .2338$.

Party Discipline in the Chamber of Deputies

Table 7.4. *Cooperation and defection among PPB deputies: 1991–1998.*

	Dependent Variable: Cooperation with Party Majority (Absentees Included)			
Variable	Unstandardized Parameter Estimate and Probability Level	Standard Error	Standardized Estimate	Odds Ratio
Cardoso Administration (1995–1998)	−0.4469*	.2175	−0.0441	.640
Contested Party Recommendation	.2696*	.1255	.049700	1.309
Uncontested Party Recommendation	.5673*	.2490	.0576	1.764
Share of Pork Disbursements	−0.1170	.0991	−0.0272	.890
Rank in Postelection List	1.8857***	.3094	.2032	6.591
Share of Total Party Vote	−1.0858	2.3506	−0.0141	.338
Dominance of Key Municipalities	−2.7803**	1.0167	−0.1226	.062
Concentration of Vote	.0973***	.0242	.2379	1.102
Concentration × Rank in List	−0.2721***	.0443	−0.4320	.762
Concentration × Terms Served	−0.0281**	.0095	−0.1701	.972
Concentration × Dominance	.3848**	.1206	.1832	1.469
Ideology	.1489	.0898	.0541	1.161
Terms Served	.3246***	.0901	.1448	1.383
Local Political Career	−0.2148	.1325	−0.0405	.807
Governor from Same Party	.9368	.7068	.0395	2.552
Incumbent Seeking Reelection	.2626	.1408	.0438	1.300

−2 log likelihood = 1,698.6; model chi-squared = 261.2, $p < .0001$; correctly predicted = 66.6%; $N = 9,024$; * $p < .05$, ** $p < .01$, *** $p < .001$. $R^2 = .0285$, max-rescaled $R^2 = .1462$.

Table 7.5. *Cooperation and defection among PDT deputies: 1991–1998.*

Dependent Variable: Cooperation with Party Majority (Absentees Included)			
Variable	Unstandardized Parameter Estimate and Probability Level	Standard Error	Standardized Estimate	Odds Ratio
Cardoso Administration (1995–1998)	.1889	.5957	.0194	1.208
Contested Party Recommendation	.4611*	.2155	.0888	1.586
Uncontested Party Recommendation	−0.1112	.2672	−0.0169	.895
Share of Pork Disbursements	−0.6556**	.2181	−0.1408	.519
Rank in Postelection List	.4559	.7348	.0563	1.578
Share of Total Party Vote	12.5580	9.2882	.1078	999.0
Dominance of Key Municipalities	3.6081	3.1463	.1557	36.898
Concentration of Vote	.1649	.1102	.2907	1.179
Concentration × Rank in List	.0225	.0982	.0302	1.023
Concentration × Terms Served	−0.0332	.0420	−0.1076	.967
Concentration × Dominance	−0.2491	.3356	−0.1463	.779
Ideology	.167437	.2682	.0443	1.182
Terms Served	.2276	.2066	.1033	1.256
Local Political Career	−1.0725**	.3457	−0.2067	.342
Governor from Same Party	1.3073	.8239	.1292	3.696
Incumbent Seeking Reelection	−0.1962	.3160	−0.0334	.822

−2 log likelihood = 540.7; model chi-squared = 131.7, $p < .0001$; correctly predicted = 68.9%; $N = 3,764$; * $p < .05$, ** $p < .01$, *** $p < .001$. $R^2 = .0344$, max-rescaled $R^2 = .2102$.

Table 7.6. *Cooperation and defection among PTB deputies: 1991–1998.*

Dependent Variable: Cooperation with Party Majority (Absentees Included)			
Variable	Unstandardized Parameter Estimate and Probability Level	Standard Error	Standardized Estimate	Odds Ratio
Cardoso Administration (1995–1998)	−0.6395	.4771	−0.0659	.528
Contested Party Recommendation	−0.7079***	.2075	−0.1368	.493
Uncontested Party Recommendation	−0.4101	.2563	−0.0570	.664
Share of Pork Disbursements	−0.0620	.1838	−0.0152	.940
Rank in Postelection List	−2.2549*	1.0933	−0.2059	.105
Share of Total Party Vote	24.6165***	5.7649	.2985	999.0
Dominance of Key Municipalities	5.9312*	2.6933	.2417	376.6
Concentration of Vote	.0224	.0568	.0452	1.023
Concentration × Rank in List	.3548**	.1139	.5247	1.426
Concentration × Terms Served	.0462	.0365	.2525	1.047
Concentration × Dominance	−0.7916**	.3117	−0.4671	.453
Ideology	.9967***	.2758	.2805	2.709
Terms Served	−0.1850	.2590	−0.0930	.831
Local Political Career	−0.5821	.3378	−0.0783	.559
Governor from Same Party	−1.5557**	.5726	−0.1511	.211
Incumbent Seeking Reelection.3299	.3415	.059522	1.391	

−2 log likelihood = 671.2; model chi-squared = 186.1, $p < .0001$; correctly predicted = 69.0%; $N = 3,474$; * $p < .05$, ** $p < .01$, *** $p < .001$. $R^2 = .0522$, max-rescaled $R^2 = .2385$.

Although Tables 7.1–7.6 are limited to one regression for each party, the discussion that follows considers models from both time periods and with absentee deputies counted both as missing and as defectors. The emphasis is on overall, cross-party patterns, with some attention paid to the results for each party. In each case, the crucial tests are the significance and direction (sign) of the unstandardized coefficients and the differences, within a given regression, in the sizes of the standardized coefficients.

Do Leadership Recommendations Matter?

In only two cases – the PFL with absentees excluded and the PPB with absentees included – do leadership recommendations on both contested and uncontested votes increase party cooperation. In Table 7.4, for example, the odds ratios demonstrate that recommendations on contested votes raise the chances of cooperation by 31%, while recommendations on uncontested votes raise the chances of cooperation by 76%. Note, however, that for these two parties the chances of cooperation are no stronger on votes that are contested rather than uncontested. Only in the case of the PDT is a positive recommendation on contested votes stronger than the recommendation on uncontested votes; that is, recommendations on contested votes increase cooperation by 59% while recommendations on uncontested votes have no significant effect. Moreover, recommendations clearly play a minor role, even for these three parties, in the *overall* determination of deputies' propensities to cooperate or defect. In Table 7.4, for example, the standardized coefficient (.0497) of the PPB's contested recommendation variable is smaller than the standardized coefficients of nine other variables, and it is one-ninth the size of the indicator of vote concentration. Overall, it appears that recommendations do not affect cooperation through threats of sanctions or promises of rewards. Party vote recommendations sometimes matter, in the sense that they guide deputies who respond to calls for party solidarity and who simply need to know how the party is voting.[38] But even when recommendations do matter, other factors far outweigh them in determining deputies' cooperation or defection.

ficients are then comparable, because the coefficient represents a change in the propensity to cooperate that results from a change of one standard deviation in the independent variable.

[38] In the U.S. context, a more elaborate version of this argument is found in Kingdon (1981).

Can Pork Buy Deputies' Cooperation? In other writings (Ames, 1995, 2001) I demonstrated that pork-barrel expenditures buy, or at least rent, congressional loyalty. In four of the six parties represented in Tables 7.1–7.6, the coefficient on the pork variable is negative and significant; for the other two parties the coefficient is weak but the sign is correct. The same effect appears when votes are restricted to the administration of Fernando Henrique Cardoso (1995–1998). The tables in the Appendix, however, demonstrate that the exclusion of absentee deputies (counting them as missing) produces a coefficient that is positive in all cases and significantly positive in three.

Why is there a difference in the results with absentees included and excluded? Note that absentee deputies have a propensity to defect. Their threat of defection establishes a claim on pork-barrel spending. Government and party leaders reward defectors, expecting greater cooperation on future votes. Overall, the government concentrates pork-barrel spending on those likely to defect. Pork-barrel spending can increase their rate of cooperation, but even afterwards they remain more likely to defect – producing a negative coefficient – than deputies who receive less.[39]

Parties in which influence flows from top to bottom, as in Venezuela's Acción Democratica, maintain discipline without individualized bargaining. This not so in Brazil, where pork-barrel spending is necessary to cement coalitions on practically any serious issue. In part, then, pork compensates for the party weakness revealed by the analysis of the leadership recommendation variables.

Electoral Strength, Constituency, Ideology, and Career Background

In nearly every case, low ranks in parties' postelection lists are associated with higher degrees of cooperation with party majorities.[40] These weak deputies cooperate, because doing so facilitates access to jobs and pork. Cooperation gives deputies a platform on which to stand when running for reelection in districts where they think the electorate cares about the party label. For the PSDB and the PFL, the effects of rank on cooperation are strikingly larger between 1991 and 1994 than between 1995 and

[39] Obviously this interpretation is tentative. A time-series model would offer a more appropriate test.
[40] The coefficient on the indicator of deputies' shares of an aggregate party vote was much less consistent. Due to the weakness of these coefficients and also to the high collinearity of the two variables, it seems reasonable to emphasize the effects of rank on cooperation.

1998. A weakening in electoral rank of one place for a PFL deputy increased the odds of cooperation by 5.5 times over the whole 1991–1998 period (see Table 7.1), while in the Cardoso years alone a decline of one place increased the odds on cooperation only 3.2 times. A similar rank decline in a PSDB deputy led to a 12.4-fold increase in the chances of cooperation over the whole 1991–1998 period (Table 7.1), but in the Cardoso years a similar decline resulted in merely a 3.7-fold increase in the chances of cooperation.[41] The PSDB opposed the government during most of the 1991–1994 period, but after 1994 the party became a key member of the governing coalition. The decline in the importance of rank for PSDB deputies suggests that the party label, not access to pork, motivated cooperation, because access to pork increased greatly post-1994. The PFL had an off-again, on-again relationship with the government before 1995 but, like the PSDB, participated in Cardoso's governing coalition.[42]

The complexity of the electoral rank-cooperation effect can also be seen in the case of the PDT. In the Cardoso years, with absentees counted as "defectors," rank had no effect on cooperation. But when absentees are counted as missing in the same period, then lower rank strongly increased cooperation. In the case of the PDT, no common objectives exist between party leaders and the executive. On the basis of interviews with PDT deputies, I believe that the executive targeted pork to weak PDT deputies to persuade them to avoid voting against the government; that is, in this situation not voting was preferable to the government than a vote with the antigovernment party majority.

What happens when deputies dominate their constituencies, that is, when they monopolize the votes cast for any candidate in the regions where they collect high proportions of their own total vote? For the PFL, PMDB, PSDB, and PTB, dominance is associated with greater party cooperation. Dominant deputies tend to be traditional types whose political careers are based either on their family's regional predominance or on their own deals made with scattered local (often rural) bosses able to deliver blocks of votes. For these deputies, continued electoral success requires delivering pork-barrel projects to their local intermediaries.

The only exceptions to the dominance–cooperation linkage were the PPB, where the link was significantly negative, and the PDT, which was positive but insignificant. I have no definitive explanation for these deviant

[41] These comparisons were made with absentees counted as "defectors" on supermajority votes, but the results are similar with absentees always counted as missing.
[42] This explanation does not work for the PPB. I have not figured out why.

party members. Since their parties took opposing positions on most government-sponsored proposals, the ideological positions of dominant deputies are not the motivating factor. Instead, the explanation might lie in the supracongressional leadership of these two parties. In both cases, a powerful presidential hopeful dominated the party, but neither (the PPB's Paulo Maluf nor the PDT's Leonel Brizola) controlled any pork. For deputies in these two parties, defecting from the party majority could be a tactic of political survival that only dominant deputies had the autonomy to pursue.

A much stronger constituency effect comes from the geographic concentration of the votes of individual deputies. Vote clustering has strong and positive effects on cooperation in nearly every party, time period, and absentee condition.[43] Given the assumption that the concentration of votes increases the accountability of deputies to their voters, it might be argued that this observation simply reflects popular support for executive initiatives. To some degree this is plausible, but issue-based links must be rare in Brazil, because the ties between voters and deputies are so weak and because deputies have little idea what constituents think. Instead, vote concentration means that deputies are simultaneously more likely to be able to claim credit for public spending directed to their constituencies and under more pressure to deliver.

Seniority produces small and inconsistent effects. The original hypothesis suggested that senior deputies, all other things being equal, have the autonomy to defect if they so desire. Conversely, senior deputies tend to get along by going along, and they may be thoroughly tied to the leadership. Many senior deputies hold some sort of minor leadership position.

Deputies with local political backgrounds did not cooperate or defect at different rates than other politicians, and governors did not consistently influence the deputies from their states. But deputies in states with PSDB governors were exceptionally cooperative, probably because three PSDB governors represented industrial states with similar economic problems and with close ties to the origins of the PSDB and to President Cardoso.[44] PFL governors, led by the powerful PFL machine in Bahia, also influenced their deputies in the direction of cooperation. PTB and PMDB deputies in states with governors from these parties seemed more likely to defect,

[43] The only negative relationship is found in one PDT case; but given the opposition status of the party, this is really confirmatory.

[44] The three PSDB governors included Eduardo Azeredo in Minas Gerais, Marcello Alencar in Rio de Janeiro, and Mário Covas in São Paulo.

211

but this finding may simply be a result of particularly fractious intrastate politics.

Incumbents seeking reelection consistently cooperated with their parties. Among the larger parties, only PSDB members cooperated significantly less often if they planned reelection campaigns. As Table 7.3 shows, PSDB deputies (with absentees included over the whole 1991–1998 period) cooperated at only 67% of their rate when they were not running for reelection. In the Cardoso period, their cooperation dropped to 52.2% of the rate of those not running for reelection. If the causal story behind this relationship is the currying of favor by deputies expecting to seek reelection, what explains the PSDB defections? Here, perhaps, are the consequences on its more left-of-center deputies of the PSDB's increasing neoliberalism. For those deputies whose constituencies are vulnerable to invasions from the left, usually from the PT, or who are ideologically uncomfortable with their party's rightward drift, defection may be a rational survival strategy. This argument once again suggests that the decision to seek reelection is causally prior to, and therefore affects, voting decisions.

Ideology is a moderately strong and fairly consistent force, but its effects at first glance seem counterintuitive. With the exception of the PDT, more conservative members within each party are more likely to follow party recommendations. If most legislation is aimed at the median legislator, then the conservative members of right-wing parties ought to be most disaffected and hence most prone to defect. Likewise, left-wing members of left-of-center parties ought to be most disaffected and prone to defection. Why do conservative right-wingers cooperate? In part, pork-barrel inducements overwhelm ideological disagreements. At the same time, ideological conformity with party programs fails to affect deputies' behavior because most Brazilian parties simply lack any sort of coherent programs.

Last, consider the three variables representing the interaction of clustering with electoral rank, seniority, and dominance. Contrary to my earlier prediction (that strong deputies with concentrated votes would defect), weak but concentrated deputies are the defectors. An examination of residuals shows that such deputies tend to share their electoral bases with other deputies.[45] Sharing limits their ability to claim credit for pork,

[45] A typical example of this kind of concentrated and shared electoral base is the municipality of São Paulo. While the whole state constitutes the legal electoral district, this single municipality effectively elects 20–30 deputies, or nearly one-half the state total. No can-

so currying favor with party leaders is pointless. However, their constituencies have higher levels of voter awareness and include cohorts of voters negatively affected by neoliberal economic policies. For weak deputies facing such voters, defection from the party yields a positive electoral payoff.

Clustered PFL and PMDB deputies who dominate their key municipalities defect more from their leaderships, but their counterparts in the PSDB cooperate more with the party. This finding is not surprising: Concentrated dominant PFL and PMDB types are mostly in the northeast and reflect the strength of traditional political families and deal-making.[46] For these deputies, the party label has little importance for their electoral futures. By contrast, concentrated dominant PSDB deputies usually have strong local backgrounds, often as mayors or state deputies from medium-sized communities. These deputies cooperate because party labels and pork access matter.[47]

Conclusion

Although Brazil's democratic presidents have an impressive range of formal and informal powers, they face constant and crippling difficulties in moving their agendas through the legislature. Some proposals never arrive at the Congress at all. Many proposals fail to come to a vote. Others cannot get out of committee. Proposals that survive the legislative process emerge disfigured by substantive concessions and weighted down by pork-barrel side payments. This chapter took the first steps in exploring executive–legislative relations in Brazil by searching for the microfoundations of congressional intransigence. I sought to resolve an apparent contradiction raised by two strands of research. One strand identifies the electoral system as the culprit, pointing to Brazil's combination of open-list proportional representation, high-magnitude electoral districts, unlimited reelection, and candidate selection at the level of states. This institutional

didate gets more than 10% of the municipality's votes, but all get 60–70% of their personal vote there.

[46] As we saw earlier in this book, Bahia is a state where the party label is quite important. Antonio Carlos Magalhães built his PFL machine on access to central government funds, and former state secretaries of programs such as health and education dominate his congressional delegation. I am indebted to Simone Rodrigues da Silva for help on this question.

[47] The combination of senior deputies with concentrated vote bases does not seem to affect cooperation.

213

structure should produce a legislature full of individualistic, pork-oriented deputies and weakly disciplined parties. But a second strand of research suggests that the sanctions and rewards wielded by party leaders are strong enough to counteract the fragmenting tendencies of the electoral system and produce legislative parties with very high levels of voting unity.

As in many political systems, votes on the floor of Brazil's legislature represent the culmination of a process of intensive bargaining among presidents, party leaders, interest-based caucuses, and individual deputies. Given the nation's institutional structure, Brazil should be a prime example of *conditional legislative parties*, where leaders' actions depend on the support of party members on a case-by-case basis and where influence flows from the bottom up.

In this setting, the analysis of roll-call votes requires a theory of legislative behavior that is necessarily multivariate. As a first step, I developed a model predicting cooperation or defection from party majorities. If the conditional party influence model is incorrect, if influence flows from the top down, party leaders ought to be able to persuade their members to follow leadership vote recommendations. Leaders too weak to compel cooperation can try to buy support with pork-barrel programs and job appointments directed at individual deputies. But many deputies have the autonomy and motivation to resist party leaders or to extract a high price for support. The freedom to resist ought to depend on electoral security, which in turn should be determined by a deputy's postelection rank, share of the party vote, legislative seniority, and municipal-level dominance. The motivation to resist should depend on ideology, constituency characteristics, and political background.

Applied to Brazil's six major parties in the 1991–1998 period, this model of cooperation and defection fares well. Overall, it provides persuasive evidence that party leaders lack the power to compel cooperation. Leaders make voting recommendations to their members, and these recommendations sometimes positively affect cooperation. But vote recommendations have no more effect on crucial, highly contested votes than on uncontested votes, and they have much less influence than constituency characteristics and pork-barrel spending.

Deputies cooperate at higher rates when they are weak electorally and when their constituencies are geographically concentrated. Electoral weakness makes deputies reluctant to surrender the benefits of the party label. Legislators may bargain hard for substantive compromises on legislation and may extract high prices in pork or appointments for support,

214

but in the end the party label helps defend deputies against interparty and intraparty competitors. When a deputy's constituents are geographically concentrated, they are more likely to know who their deputy is and more likely to demand results from their deputies. Given the absence of programmatic content in Brazil's parties, results implies pork.

The model's most notable misprediction resulted from the indicator of ideology. Brazil's parties do have broadly distinct ideological centers, even if the distinctions are very broad indeed. In general, however, conservative deputies cooperate more, regardless of the relationship between their party and the median legislator. I expected more defections from conservative members of right-wing parties and leftist members of left-wing parties. Perhaps the error lies in the use of a unidimensional indicator of ideology in a multidimensional voting space. It is also possible that legislators rarely care much about ideological questions, so their ideological predilections are overwhelmed by their need for pork.

Appendix

Table 7A.1. *Cooperation and defection among PFL deputies: 1991–1998.*

Variable	Dependent Variable: Cooperation with Party Majority (Absentees Excluded)			
	Unstandardized Parameter Estimate and Probability Level	Standard Error	Standardized Estimate	Odds Ratio
Cardoso Administration (1995–1998)	.7123***	.1530	.0955	2.039
Contested Party Recommendation	.3374*	.1424	.0518	1.401
Uncontested Party Recommendation	.3792***	.1148	.0658	1.461
Share of Pork Disbursements	.1134	.0908	.2231	1.120
Rank in Postelection List	1.0978***	.3265	.0974	2.998
Share of Total Party Vote	−1.7189	2.0150	−0.0188	.179
Dominance of Key Municipalities	2.4470***	.7104	.1087	11.554
Concentration of Vote	−0.0209	.0293	−0.0480	.979
Concentration × Rank in List	−0.0074	.0301	−0.0091	.993
Concentration × Terms Served	.0090	.0062	.0568	1.009
Concentration × Dominance	−0.1494	.0826	−0.1080	.861
Ideology	.2195*	.0994	.048983	1.245
Terms Served	.0217	.0585	.0113	1.022
Local Political Career	−0.3829**	.1287	−0.0610	.682
Governor from Same Party	−0.7149***	.1499	−0.1313	.489
Incumbent Seeking Reelection	1.17019***	.1458	.1688	3.222

−2 log likelihood = 2,864.1; model chi-squared = 4,990.6; $p < .0001$; correctly predicted = 65.3%; $N = 10,626$; * $p < .05$, ** $p < .01$, *** $p < .001$. Rsquared = .3748, Max-rescaled Rsquared = .7173.

Party Discipline in the Chamber of Deputies

Table 7A.2. *Cooperation and defection among PMDB deputies: 1991–1998.*

	Dependent Variable: Cooperation with Party Majority (Absentees Excluded)			
Variable	Unstandardized Parameter Estimate and Probability Level	Standard Error	Standardized Estimate	Odds Ratio
Cardoso Administration (1995–1998)	−0.4333*	.1926	−0.0578	.648
Contested Party Recommendation	.1420	.1462	.0223	1.153
Uncontested Party Recommendation	.1427	.1263	.0247	1.153
Share of Pork Disbursements	.5427***	.0867	.1234	1.721
Rank in Postelection List	.3045	.3757	.0309	1.356
Share of Total Party Vote	−4.2542***	1.0142	−0.0960	.014
Dominance of Key Municipalities	2.1994*	.9468	.0860	9.019
Concentration of Vote	.1714***	.0322	.4191	1.187
Concentration × Rank in List	−0.0486	.0368	−0.0768	.953
Concentration × Terms Served	.004293	.0112	.025358	1.004
Concentration × Dominance	−0.5651***	.0864	−0.4318	.568
Ideology	−0.0979	.1075	−0.0220	.907
Terms Served	−0.0208	.1010	−0.0074	.979
Local Political Career	.0709	.1316	.0131	1.073
Governor from Same Party	.5212***	.1405	.0910	1.684
Incumbent Seeking Reelection	.6612***	.1220	.1138	1.937

−2 log likelihood = 2,217.0; model chi-squared = 1,419.8; $p < .0001$; correctly predicted = 65.7%; $N = 11,471$; * $p < .05$, ** $p < .01$, *** $p < .001$. Rsquared = .1164, Max-rescaled Rsquared = .4285.

Table 7A.3. *Cooperation and defection among PSDB deputies: 1991–1998.*

Variable	Dependent Variable: Cooperation with Party Majority (Absentees Excluded)			
	Unstandardized Parameter Estimate and Probability Level	Standard Error	Standardized Estimate	Odds Ratio
Cardoso Administration (1995–1998)	−0.0455	.2397	−0.0043	.956
Contested Party Recommendation	.1154	.1732	.0163	1.122
Uncontested Party Recommendation	.3779**	.1368	.0631	1.459
Share of Pork Disbursements	.2492*	.1090	.0526	1.283
Rank in Postelection List	3.0055***	.3256	.3599	20.197
Share of Total Party Vote	4.9735*	2.1542	.0711	144.5
Dominance of Key Municipalities	−0.7839	.9498	−0.0334	.457
Concentration of Vote	.1909***	.0319	.5603	1.210
Concentration × Rank in List	−0.3665***	.0461	−0.8723	.693
Concentration × Terms Served	.0037	.0109	.0219	1.004
Concentration × Dominance	.2427**	.1507	.0609	1.311
Ideology	.2704	.1507	.0609	1.311
Terms Served	−0.1422	.0776	−0.0537	.867
Local Political Career	−0.1405	.1627	−0.0259	.869
Governor from Same Party	.5043**	.1712	.0962	1.656
Incumbent Seeking Reelection	.3941**	.1464	.0675	1.483

-2 log likelihood = 2,016.9; model chi-squared = 3,780.6; $p < .0001$; correctly predicted = 63.0%; $N = 8,757$; Rsquared = .3506, Max-rescaled Rsquared = .7241.
$^*p < .05$, $^{**}p < .01$, $^{***}p < .001$.

Party Discipline in the Chamber of Deputies

Table 7A.4. *Cooperation and defection among PPB deputies: 1991–1998.*

	Dependent Variable: Cooperation with Party Majority (Absentees Excluded)			
Variable	Unstandardized Parameter Estimate and Probability Level	Standard Error	Standardized Estimate	Odds Ratio
Cardoso Administration (1995–1998)	.2225	.1874	.0238	1.249
Contested Party Recommendation	−0.0500	.1250	−0.0093	.951
Uncontested Party Recommendation	.3612	.2422	.0380	1.435
Share of Pork Disbursements	.2222*	.1008	.0509	1.249
Rank in Postelection List	2.2678***	.4241	.2353	9.658
Share of Total Party Vote	−4.5867*	2.3663	−0.0576	.010
Dominance of Key Municipalities	−0.6940	1.0217	−0.0306	.500
Concentration of Vote	.0987***	.0259	.2430	1.104
Concentration × Rank in List	−0.3313***	.0461	−0.4970	.718
Concentration × Terms Served	.0129	.0099	.0732	1.013
Concentration × Dominance	.1765	.1219	.0838	1.193
Ideology	.4595***	.0960	.1574	1.583
Terms Served	−0.2526**	.0889	−0.1099	.777
Local Political Career	−0.1056	.1392	−0.0194	.900
Governor from Same Party	1.4454	.9917	.0627	4.243
Incumbent Seeking Reelection	.6431***	.1357	.1080	1.902

−2 log likelihood = 1,721.9; model chi-squared = 9,089.7; $p < .0001$; correctly predicted = 67.2%; $N = 7,504$; Rsquared = .1140 Max-rescaled Rsquared = .3857.
*$p < .05$, **$p < .01$, ***$p < .001$.

Table 7A.5. *Cooperation and defection among PDT deputies: 1991–1998.*

Dependent Variable: Cooperation with Party Majority (Absentees Excluded)

Variable	Unstandardized Parameter Estimate and Probability Level	Standard Error	Standardized Estimate	Odds Ratio
Cardoso Administration (1995–1998)	.3901	.4414	.0442	1.477
Contested Party Recommendation	.4134*	.2114	.0776	1.512
Uncontested Party Recommendation	−0.1339	.2687	−0.0196	.875
Share of Pork Disbursements	.2321	.1903	.0498	1.261
Rank in Postelection List	.5614	.6423	.0689	1.753
Share of Total Party Vote	−10.8177*	5.4370	−0.0959	0.000
Dominance of Key Municipalities	5.4832	3.1742	.2444	240.6
Concentration of Vote	.2643**	.1007	.4547	1.303
Concentration × Rank in List	−0.1142	.0861	−0.1566	.892
Concentration × Terms Served	−0.0222	.0392	−0.0731	.978
Concentration × Dominance	−0.5895	.3280	−0.3511	.555
Ideology	−0.4357*	.2229	−0.1147	.647
Terms Served	.3889	.2068	.1659	1.475
Local Political Career	−0.3144	.3408	−0.0585	.730
Governor from Same Party	.1723	.5442	.0187	1.188
Incumbent Seeking Reelection	−0.4927	.3389	−0.0841	.611

−2 log likelihood = 671.6; model chi-squared = 1,137.0; $p < .0001$; correctly predicted = 64.3%; $N = 2,995$; Rsquared = .3159 Max-rescaled Rsquared = .6969.
$*p < .05, **p < .01, ***p < .001$.

Party Discipline in the Chamber of Deputies

Table 7A.6. *Cooperation and defection among PTB deputies: 1991–1998.*

	Dependent Variable: Cooperation with Party Majority (Absentees Excluded)			
Variable	Unstandardized Parameter Estimate and Probability Level	Standard Error	Standardized Estimate	Odds Ratio
Cardoso Administration (1995–1998)	.5750*	.2840	.0637	1.777
Contested Party Recommendation	−0.1489	.1723	−0.0285	.862
Uncontested Party Recommendation	−0.0257	.2387	−0.0034	.975
Share of Pork Disbursements	.0252	.1646	.0060	1.026
Rank in Postelection List	−0.1765	.7465	−0.0160	.838
Share of Total Party Vote	7.1588*	3.6206	.0882	999.0
Dominance of Key Municipalities	−0.0495	1.8588	−0.0019	.952
Concentration of Vote	.1029*	.0420	.2035	1.108
Concentration × Rank in List	.1162	.0830	.1725	1.123
Concentration × Terms Served	−0.0115	.0162	−0.0670	.989
Concentration × Dominance	−0.1819	.2030	−0.1093	.834
Ideology	.0992	.1988	.0272	1.104
Terms Served	.1131	.1638	.0550	1.120
Local Political Career	−0.6169*	.2723	−0.0815	.540
Governor from Same Party	−0.7486*	.3371	−0.0741	.473
Incumbent Seeking Reelection	.4837	.2645	.088455	1.622

−2 log likelihood = 1,072.4; model chi-squared = 1,225.1; $p < .0001$; correctly predicted = 63.6%; $N = 2,917$; Rsquared = .3430 Max-rescaled Rsquared = .6292.
*$p < .05$, **$p < .01$, ***$p < .001$.

8

Parties, Coalitions, and the Chilean Congress in the 1990s*

JOHN M. CAREY

Chile's Congress has conventionally been regarded as among the most effective in Latin America in representing diverse interests and influencing policy. Analyses of Chilean politics prior to the 1973 coup consistently point to the strength of Chilean parties to support this evaluation. Valenzuela (1994), for example, argues for the adoption of parliamentarism in Chile largely on the grounds that its party system resembles those of western European parliamentary democracies. Mainwaring and Scully (1995) point to the stability of support for Chilean parties among the electorate, their ideological consistency, and the strength of national party organizations. In the 1990s, after the return to democracy, the central questions were whether and how the Chilean legislative party system is different from the preauthoritarian period, and what are the implications for the effectiveness of the Congress.

Accounts of Chilean politics at midcentury portray a system characterized by parties with widespread membership and activism at the grassroots, prominent parliamentary leaders, and highly articulated national policy agendas that were spread across a broad ideological spectrum (Scully 1995; Valenzuela and Wilde 1979). This portrait stands in sharp contrast to that of party systems in neighboring Argentina (McGuire 1994), Brazil (Mainwaring 1999), and Peru (Cotler 1994), where personalism and clientelism were endemic, weakening the ability of legislatures to act collectively and to compete with strong presidents in shaping policy.

* Comments on various manifestations of this chapter were offered by seminar participants at the Centro de Investigaciones y Docencia Económica in Mexico City, Harvard University, the Ohio State University, Duke University, and long-suffering graduate students at Washington University. Special thanks are due to Scott Morgenstern, for including follow-up questions for this chapter in his interviews with Chilean legislators and party officials in August 1998. All of the usual caveats apply.

In addition to portraying a highly institutionalized party system, the literature on Chilean politics emphasizes that coalitions among legislative parties were highly fluid (Agor 1971). Between 1932 and 1973, for example, Valenzuela (1994, pp. 123–125) identifies 19 separate coalitions among legislative parties in support of the eight presidents who served during this period.[1] The mean coalition lifespan during this period was thus 2.1 years, with the longest surviving coalition lasting five years, from 1932 to 1937. The Chilean Congress was a center of partisan compromise and dealmaking, and served as an effective counterweight to the presidency up through the 1960s. From the late 1950s through the early 1970s, however, a series of electoral and constitutional reforms undermined incentives for cooperation, both among parties and between the branches (Shugart and Carey 1992). In an increasingly ideologically polarlized environment, these reforms contributed to the stand-off between Salvador Allende's Popular Unity coalition and the parties on the right, which preceded the military coup of 1973 (Valenzuela 1994; Valenzuela and Wilde 1979).

The transition to democracy in Chile in 1990 raised a number of issues about the roles and performance of the newly reestablished legislature. General Augusto Pinochet's 1980 Constitution, even as amended in 1988, provides for a presidency with extensive formal powers, including the capacity to control the legislative agenda (Baldez and Carey 1999; Siavelis, this volume). The establishment of a large block of generally conservative, nonelected senators has served as a brake on policy changes and proposed institutional reforms (Arriagada 1994). With respect to the parties themselves, one question is whether the new, two-member district electoral system imposed by the outgoing military regime fundamentally alters the party system.

In this chapter, I argue that the post-transition Chilean legislative party system differs from the midcentury system portrayed in previous literature in at least one important way: Throughout the decade of the 1990s, it has been characterized by the stability and cohesiveness of the two main legislative coalitions – the *Concertación* on the center-left, and the coalition of

---

[1] Valenzuela does not define precisely what he means by coalition. Although he discusses efforts by presidents to ensure legislative support by naming cabinet ministers from a range of parties (pp. 119–120), he does not state explicitly that cabinet participation is his criterion for coalition membership. It appears that party statements of support for, or opposition to, the president determines what counts as a coalition (p. 122). How this is operationalized remains unstated.

the right.[2] The centrality of the coalitions to Chilean politics in the 1990s, moreover, is a product of the two-member district reform of the electoral system. The coalitions coexist with the party organizations that are their main component parts. In conjunction with the traditional parties, they organize nominations for legislative elections, the legislative committee system, and floor voting. In the first post-transition decade, the coalitions themselves have resembled parties composed of multiple factions. The composition of the first three congresses, by party and coalition, are shown in Table 8.1.

Throughout this chapter, I present data on political careers, the committee structure, and voting in the Chilean Chamber of Deputies since the transition to democracy. In order to make a conclusive case about changes in the party system, it would be necessary to provide analogous data for the pre-1973 period as well. Unfortunately, there is no systematic evidence from the earlier era of which I am aware. The bases of intertemporal comparison, therefore, are scholarly accounts of legislative politics in that period. The current data from Chile also provide the basis for cross-national comparison with the other Latin American legislatures examined in this volume. To the extent that we can draw conclusions about legislative capacity by examining legislative organization and the structure of political careers, as Morgenstern suggests in his introductory chapter, Chile is an ideal case for study because information on the Congress is readily available to scholars, including a number of excellent internet sites.

The chapter proceeds as follows. First I review the changes in the legislative electoral system established by the outgoing military regime, emphasizing the incentives that this created for cross-party coalitions. Next I review the early literature on the post-transition Chilean party system, focusing on divergent expectations and evaluations of levels of fragmentation and polarization. Then I begin an empirical analysis of legislative parties and coalitions throughout the first decade after the return to civilian rule, examining legislative careers, the committee system, and floor voting in turn.

---

[2] The coalition of the right has gone by a different name in each of the three post-transition elections: Democracy and Progress in 1989, Union for Progress in 1993, and Union for Chile in 1997. In every election, it has included a handful of independents and regional party candidates in a few districts, but over 90% of its nominations are awarded to candidates of either the National Renovation (RN) or the Independent Democratic Union (UDI).

Table 8.1. *Partisan and coalition representation of elected[a] legislators in post-transition Chile.*

Coalition	Party	1989 Chamber	1989 Senate	1993 Chamber	1993 Senate[b]	1997 Chamber	1997 Senate
Concertación	Christian Democrat (DC)	39	13	37	13 (4)	39	14 (10)
	Party for Democracy (PPD)	7	1	15	2 (2)	16	2 (0)
	Socialist (PS)	18	4	15	5 (3)	11	4 (1)
	Radical (PR)	6	3	2	1 (0)	4[c]	0 (0)
	Social Democrat (PSD)	0	1	0	0	0	0
	Independent (I-Conc)	0	0	1	0	0	0
Coalition Total		70	22	70	21 (9)	70	20 (11)
Right	National Renovation (RN)	32	13	29	11 (5)	23	7 (2)
	Democratic Independent Union (UDI)	14	2	15	3 (2)	17	5 (3)
	Center-Center Union (UCC)[d]	–	–	2	0 (0)	–	–
	Independent (I-Right)	0	1	4	3 (2)	9	6 (4)
Coalition Total		46	16	50	17	49	18 (9)
Alternative	Alternative Democratic Leftist Movement (MIDA)	2	0	–	–	–	–
Alternative	Center-Center Union Party (UCCP)[d]	–	–	–	–	1	0 (0)

[a] The entire Chamber of Deputies is elected. In the Senate, there are nine additional appointed seats, plus lifetime seats for former presidents who served six or more years in office.

[b] All 38 elected Senate seats were initially filled in the 1989 elections. Beginning in 1993, renewal of the Senate is staggered, and the standard term length is eight years. In 1993, 9 of the 19 districts held elections to renew their seats, while senators in the other 10 districts continued for the full, 8-year term. In 1997, these 10 districts renewed their senators. The numbers in parentheses represent the number of seats won (of those contested); the first number represents the total number of seats held in the Senate.

[c] The Radical and Social Democrat parties merged between the 1993 and 1997 elections to form the Radical Social Democratic Party (PRSD).

[d] The Center-Center Union ran candidates as part of the coalition of the right in 1993, but on its own lists in 1997.

Source: El Mercurio (12/13/93); http://www.elecciones97.cl/RESULTADOS/INFORME

The Transition and the Two-Member District Reform

In 1988, the government of General Pinochet lost a plebiscite on its continuation for another eight years by a margin of 56%–44%. Grudgingly accepting the defeat, the military government prepared to conduct open elections – the first in 16 years – in 1989. In doing so, the military government handed down a new electoral law, changing the manner of election for Congress.[3] Before the coup of 1973, legislators had been elected from districts ranging in magnitude from 1 to over 20, with a mean magnitude of 5.3 (Nohlen 1993). Beginning with the 1989 election, all elected legislators are chosen from two-member districts. The entire Chamber of Deputies is elected – with two members drawn from each of the 60 districts. The Senate is composed of both elected and nonelected members. The 38 elected members are drawn, two each, from 19 districts, for staggered eight-year terms. The Constitution of 1980 also provides for nine designated members – appointed respectively by the military (four), the Supreme Court (three), and the president (two) – and for lifetime senate seats for former presidents who have served six or more years in office.

As before the coup, the new system provides for open ballot lists. Voters simply indicate a preference for one candidate within a list of up to two candidates; all votes for candidates within each list are pooled together to determine the distribution of seats among lists; then seats are allocated to those candidates from seat-winning lists in the order of their individual vote totals. In Chile, the practical effect is that both candidates on a list can be selected only if that list more than doubles the vote total of the second-place list; otherwise, the top candidate from each of the first two lists is elected. Quite frequently, these are not the two top individual vote-getters.

Another key element of the new system is the cross-party coalition list. Electoral coalitions in the form of *apparentment* lists had actually been common in Chile and had encouraged cooperation across parties, until prohibited by an electoral law reform in 1958 (Valenzuela 1994). Under *apparentment*, allied parties nominate candidates and present lists that

---

[3] The military government also changed the method of presidential election. Until 1970, if no candidate won >50% in the first round, then Congress selected the winner from among the two top candidates. As of 1989, the two top candidates would compete in a run-off election if no one wins >50% in the first round. For discussions of the effects of this change, see Carey (1994, 1997).

appear separately on the ballot, but the vote totals of the allied parties are pooled before seats are distributed (Lijphart 1994). In the new Chilean system, coalition lists straddle the structure of typical party lists on the one hand, and *apparentment* on the other. Each coalition's candidates appear together on a list with the coalition's name at the top and the candidate's party's symbol beside her or his name below. This means that the coalitions must negotiate a common list of candidates in each district prior to the election. Given that the major coalitions have included more than two parties in each election, it also means that in every district some party(ies) must agree not to run candidates.

Under the two-member district system, intracoalition negotiations prior to each election over the distribution of candidates across districts have resembled the internal deliberations among factions within parties over list composition. Parties confront the need to trade their electoral presence in some districts, as well as the freedom to press policy priorities at odds with the larger coalition, in exchange for coalition membership. Negotiations over nominations and policy are therefore a constant source of tension within each coalition, but because only the top two lists can win representation in any district, the incentive to maintain the coalitions has so far prevailed.

Initial Evaluations of the Post-Transition Party System: Fragmentation and Polarization

Fragmentation

Proponents of the two-member district reform claimed that it would discourage fragmentation of the legislative party system, according to the well-known logic that low magnitude reduces the viability of small parties, thus decreasing the effective number of parties winning votes and seats (Cox 1997; Duverger 1954; Taagepera and Shugart 1989).[4] How one assesses this claim depends on whether one regards the traditional parties or the broader electoral coalitions as the relevant units of analysis.

Most of the current literature on Chile focuses on the traditional parties. The persistence of independent party organizations, public disagreements over policy, and the competing ambitions of presidential aspirants – all among parties within the same coalitions – are cited as evidence

[4] C.f. Laakso and Taagepera (1979) for a discussion of the concept of "effective number of parties."

Table 8.2. *Effective number of vote-winning parties/lists in the Chilean Chamber of Deputies.*

Year	1925–1973 (mean)	1989	1993	1997
Parties	6.82	7.83	6.29	7.12
Lists	6.82	2.56	2.25	2.52

Source: Siavelis (1997); Nohlen (1993); *La Época* (1997) "Jornada electoral."

that the coalitions are marriages of convenience at election time, whereas the parties are far more important as independent actors (Scully 1995; Siavelis 1997; Valenzuela 1994). On these grounds, the answer to whether the two-member district reform reduced the fragmentation of the Chilean party system is clearly no. Siavelis (1997) shows that, whether one simply counts the number of parties winning Chamber representation or relies on conventional concentration indexes, such as those of Laakso and Taagepera (1979) or Molinar (1991), the number of legislative parties has not declined in the post-transition era relative to midcentury. Siavelis (1997) and Scully (1995) also emphasize that, if one ignores coalitional alliances and divides Chilean parties, pre-coup and post-transition alike, into left, center, and right blocks, then the national vote shares of candidates from parties in each block show striking continuity across both periods.[5] Conversely, if one were to assume that the coalitions are the relevant units of analysis in the Chilean system, then the conclusion that fragmentation has been reduced would be inescapable. Table 8.2 compares the mean effective number of vote-winning parties and lists during the 1925–1973 period with the same statistic calculated across lists in the post-transition period. If the parties serve as the unit of analysis, there is no difference in system fragmentation across the two periods. If we calculate the index based on ballot lists (i.e., the post-transition electoral coalitions), the average drops from 6.86 to 2.44. The drop in fragmentation would be even greater if it were calculated on the basis of seat distributions in Congress rather than vote distributions. The bottom line here is that the conclusion that one reaches with respect to the effect of the two-member district

[5] Both authors note, correctly, that tallying national vote shares of parties from these hypothesized blocks is a dubious exercise, given that no party runs candidates in every district, and the very nomination decisions that determine how many votes each party actually competes for are endogenous to the coalition organizations themselves. The validity of national-level vote shares as measures of party system fragmentation, therefore, is suspect.

reform on fragmentation depends on what entities one counts. Although I do not suggest that the traditional parties should be disregarded, my emphasis here is on the importance of the coalitions in the post-transition Chilean Congress.

Polarization

Some proponents of two-member districts contend that the reform discourages extremism in electoral competition and legislative bargaining (Rabkin 1996). These accounts hold that coalition reputations are meaningful to voters independent of party labels, and that the existence of coalitions necessarily encourages moderation. For example, Guzmán (1993) contends:

Because the two-member district system rewards large majorities, parties will quickly tend to unite and coalesce into alliances to reach higher combined vote shares than they could win individually. This encourages parties to engage in negotiations that require moderation of their positions. In this sense, the coalitions that the system "forces" generate collective outcomes that reflect more than the individual support of each party. (p. 309)

In advancing the case that two-member districts encourages moderation, both Guzmán (1993) and Rabkin (1996) invoke Downs' (1957) well-known arguments about partisan competition in SMD plurality systems, arguing that Chile's move from high-magnitude to two-member districts is a step toward Downs' centrist result. Criticisms of this argument fall along both empirical and theoretical lines. Many experts on Chilean politics regard the persistence of traditional parties as conclusive evidence against the effects of the reforms (Scully 1995; Siavelis 1997; Siavelis and Valenzuela 1991, 1994). Valenzuela (1994), for example, states:

The key to understanding Chilean politics, even after a lengthy authoritarian interlude, is the existence of several important political currents with strong party representation and clear left, center, and right referents. The challenge for strengthening Chilean democracy is not the illusory and counterproductive attempt to destroy the party system or change the underlying ideological attachments of voters. The military government clearly failed in this endeavor. The challenge for Chile is to structure mechanisms to bridge the centrifugal realities of Chilean politics. . . . (p. 137)

The principal claim here is that the Chilean party system traditionally has had a tripartite character that persists despite the coalitions that the

229

two-member district reform makes imperative at election time. For Scully (1995) the

chief conclusion . . . is that the underlying patterns and tendencies within the Chilean political landscape are quite resistant to fundamental change. A key genetic feature, from the mid-nineteenth century on, is that party politics in Chile tends to divide among three fundamental politcal segments, right, center, and left.

The tripartite (or *tres tercios*) description of the party system refers both to voter attachments and to legislative behavior. Scully (1995) emphasizes the former when he shows that, in response to the survey question, "Do you feel closer to the right, left, or center?" the percentages of respondents who locate themselves in each category has been fairly stable, even from 1958 to 1993. Scully interprets these data as evidence that the party system is "still manifestly tripartite" (p. 133).[6] Alternatively, the tripartite description at times refers to historical patterns of coalitions among parties. Valenzuela (1994) distinguishes among blocks of parties on the left (Socialists and Communists), center (Radicals and Christian Democrats) and the right (Nationalists – formerly Liberals and Conservatives), emphasizing the fluidity in their patterns of coalition, both in presidential elections and behind common legislative programs, and arguing that these are impervious to the institutional reforms of the military regime.

The second line of argument regarding polarization under two-member districts draws on spatial theories of elections and cautions against overstating the analogy between Chile's system and the Downsian account of SMD plurality. Both Magar, Rosenblum, and Samuels (1998) and Dow (1998) establish formal models of electoral competition under two-member districts, emphasizing the importance of open lists in what are still multimember districts and rejecting the Guzman (1993) and Rabkin (1996) claims of parties/candidates clustering near the median voter. Both of these studies conclude that the new Chilean system encourages the two legislative candidates from within the same coalition in each district to stake out similar ideological positions, but for each pairing to diverge considerably from the center of the voter distribution. If extended to the national level, this would suggest coalitions that are internally cohesive but ideologically distinct from each other. My results suggest that this is an accurate description of the Chilean party system in the 1990s.

[6] He does not, however, consider whether the result is merely a product of the survey question, which is explicitly tripartite.

Legislative Careers

In the introductory chapter to this volume, Morgenstern makes the point that most prominent theories of legislative behavior work on the assumption that incumbents are motivated to sustain political careers. Students of the U.S. Congress, for example, where renomination and reelection rates are extraordinarily high, have grown accustomed to the assumption that, regardless of legislators' actual motivations, their behavior can be modeled as though they were pure reelection-seekers (Mayhew 1974). In Latin America, however, reelection rates vary substantially across countries, and in many cases the assumption that legislative behavior is primarily motivated by reelection is unwarranted (Carey 1996; Weldon 1997). Before we can generate any expectations about Chilean legislative behavior based on a theory of ambition, therefore, it is necessary to determine whether Chilean legislators seek to build careers in Congress itself, use Congress as a springboard for other public office, or leave politics altogether after serving in the legislature. If the primary career path is within the legislature itself, institutions that structure legislative behavior – such as committees, and party and coalition leadership – should be important to legislators and to the operation and effectiveness of the legislature as a whole (Cox and McCubbins 1993; Krehbiel 1991; Mainwaring and Scully 1995; Polsby 1968).

Electoral data from Chile since the transition show that most legislators seek careers in Congress, and that they can reasonably expect success along these lines. Tables 8.3 and 8.4 show re-nomination and reelection rates for the Chamber of Deputies, broken down by party and by coalition, for the 1989–1993 and 1993–1997 periods. Overall levels of reelection do not differ substantially, either across coalitions or among parties within coalitions.[7]

---

[7] In interviews, legislators and party officials from both coalitions agreed that the parties themselves are hesitant to deny renomination to incumbents who seek it (Canales 1998; Kuschel 1998). In large part, this is because incumbents tend to have personal reputations and name recognition that are important electoral assets in their districts (Melero 1998; Orpis 1998; Paya 1998). Of course, one's party endorsement is only the first step toward being renominated for the coalition, particularly within the Concertácion, where there are always more parties demanding spots on the ballot than the two nominations available in each district (Canales 1998). The slightly higher rate of incumbent renomination in the coalition of the right may be due to the fact that it is dominated in almost all districts exclusively by two parties.

232

Table 8.3. *Renomination and reelection rates to the Chilean Chamber of Deputies, 1989–1993.*

Coalition/Party	Incumbents[a]	Renominated	Renominated winners	Switched coalitions	Switched + Won	Senate nominees	Senate winners
Concertación	68[b]	47 (69%)	35 (51%) (74%)[c]	2 (3%)	0	3 (4%)	2
DC	38	28	21			2	1
PS	17	10	9			0	0
PPD	7	5	4			1	1
PR	6	4	1			0	0
Right	48	41 (85%)	35 (73%) (85%)	0	0	1 (2%)	1 (2%) (100%)
RN	32	27	23			0	0
UDI	14	13	11			0	0
Indpt.	2	1	1			1	1
MIDA	2	0	0	1 (50%)	1 (50%) (100%)	0	0
Total	118	91[d] (77%)	71[e] (60%) (78%)	3 (3%)	1 (1%) (33%)	4 (3%)	3 (3%) (75%)

[a] The number of incumbents does not always correspond exactly to the number of legislators elected by each party from Table 8.1, because of occasional party or coalition switches during the term, or because of deaths.

[b] The *Concertación* elected 70 deputies in 1989; of these, three died during the 1990–1993 term and two had not been replaced before the 1993 elections.

[c] When two percentages are shown, the first refers to the percentage of *all incumbents* and the second to the percentage of those in the column immediately to the left (e.g., % of those renominated who won).

[d] Two *Concertación* deputies ran as independents for the Alternative Democratic Left coalition in 1993. One who was elected on an independent left list in 1989 ran for the Socialist Party on the *Concertación* list in 1993. These three count toward the total number renominated but are not counted as having been renominated by their coalitions.

[e] The former independent who ran with the *Concertación* in 1993 won, but he is not counted as a renominated winner either as an Independent or for the *Concertación*.

Table 8.4. *Renomination and reelection rates to the Chilean Chamber of Deputies, 1993–1997.*

Coalition/Party	Incumbents	Renominated	Renominated winners	Switched coalitions	Switched + Won	Senate nominees	Senate winners
Concertación	70	47 (67%)	41 (59%) (87%)	1	1	6 (9%)	3 (4%) (50%)
DC	37	24	21	1	0	2	2
PS	15	11	10	0	0	3	1
PPD	15	10	9	0	0	1	0
PRSD	2	2	1	0	0	0	0
Indpt.	1	0	0	0	0	0	0
Right	50	37 (74%)	30 (60%) (81%)	1	0	11 (22%)	4 (8%) (36%)
RN	29	23	16	0	0	7	1
UDI	15	12	12	0	0	2	2
Indpt.	4	2	2	0	0	2	1
UCC	2	1	1	1	0	0	0
Total	120	85 (71%)	72 (60%) (85%)	2 (2%)	1 (1%) (50%)	17 (14%)	7 (6%) (41%)

In the 1993 and 1997 elections, around three-quarters of incumbents have been renominated for the Chamber within the same coalition, and three-fifths have won reelection. In addition, in each period, there have been a couple of incumbents who have switched lists, and in each period one of these has won reelection.[8] Finally, the number of deputies nominated to run for the Senate jumped from 4 in 1993 to 17 in 1997, although the rate of success dropped off. In both elections, more than 80% of the incumbent deputies have sought and secured nominations to run again for Congress, and about two-thirds have been successful.

Analogous figures for senators show that renomination rates are slightly lower, on average, and reelection rates are slightly below 50%. Given that senators tend to be older, that terms are eight years rather than four, and that progressive ambition does not lead senators to run for the Chamber, a lower rate of reelection-seeking and success is to be expected. This is confirmed by the data in Table 8.5.

The preceding tables demonstrate that it is entirely appropriate to apply theories premised on reelectoral ambition to the Chilean Congress. One other way to cut these data is to consider the overall levels of legislative experience that the reelection rates generate. As of the December 1997 election, in which the Chamber was renewed in its entirety and 20 of the elected Senate seats were contested, each Chamber seat has now been contested three times and each Senate seat twice. The composition of the Congress serving the 1998–2001 term is described in Table 8.6. As the reelection data suggested, levels of experience do not vary much across coalitions or among the major parties. The Chamber is about equally divided among those in their first, second, and third terms, and the Senate among those in their first and second terms and those with prior Chamber experience.

Substantial majorities of legislators in both houses, in both coalitions, and across all parties have prior legislative experience. If current reelection rates persist through the next few elections, the overall level of experience of the Chilean Congress will rise further. Given that every election spells four or eight years of service, current reelection rates suggest that the average tenure of Chilean legislators will quickly approach that of

[8] In all cases, these are deputies who switched into or out of one of the major coalitions to/from minor lists. In no cases has a deputy switched from one of the major coalitions to the other. The stability of party and coalition membership among legislators in Chile is striking, particularly in contrast to the frequency of party switching in Brazil (Desposato 1997).

Table 8.5. *Renomination and reelection rates to the Chilean Senate.*

Coalition/Party	1989–1993			1993–1997		
	Incumbents	Renominated	Renominated winners	Incumbents	Renominated	Renominated winners
Concertación	9	7 (70%)	2 (20%) (29%)	12	8 (67%)	6 (50%) (75%)
Christian Dem	4	2	1	9	6	6
Socialist	3	2	1	2	1	0
PPD	2	1	0	1	1	0
PRSD	2	2	0	0	0	0
Right	9	7 (88%)	6 (75%) (86%)	8	2 (25%)	2 (25%) (100%)
RN	5	6	5	6	1	1
UDI	2	1	1	1	1	1
Indpt.	2	0	0	1	0	0
Totals	18	14 (78%)	8 (44%) (57%)	20	10 (50%)	8 (40%) (80%)

Table 8.6. *Experience of the 1997–2001 Chilean Congress.*

Coalition/Party	Chamber of Deputies			Senate		
	First term	Second term	Third term	First term[a]	Second term[b]	Chamber experience[c]
Concertación	23 (33%)	27 (39%)	20 (28%)	7 (35%)	8 (40%)	5 (25%)
DC	16	10	13	5	6	3
PS	1	5	5	1	2	1
PPD	4	11	1	1	0	1
PRSD	2	1	1	0	0	0
Right	17 (35%)	11 (22%)	21 (43%)	6 (33%)	7 (39%)	5 (28%)
RN	8	4	11	0	6	1
UDI	4	3	10	2	1	2
Indpt.	5	4	0	4	0	2
UCCP	0	1	0	0	0	0
Total	40 (33%)	39 (33%)	41 (34%)	13 (34%)	15 (39%)	10 (26%)

[a] First elected in either 1993 or 1997, with no previous legislative service in the 1990–1997 period.
[b] First elected in 1989; then reelected in either 1993 or 1997.
[c] Served in Chamber of Deputies prior to the Senate.

members of the U.S. Congress. It is clear, then, that reelection matters to the vast majority of Chilean legislators and that the stability and experience of Congress provide an environment in which stable and effective legislative institutions can be expected to redevelop.

The Organization of Congress

Mesas

The fundamental institutions of both chambers of Congress are the executive boards (*mesas*) and the permanent committees, whose members are elected by majority votes in each respective chamber. The Chamber's *mesa* includes a president as well as a first and second vice president while the Senate's consists only of a president and a single vice president. The rules of both the Chamber and Senate establish that the *mesas* serve for four-year terms, and that they are not collegial bodies; rather, their powers are formally centralized in the presidents, with vice presidents substituting in case of the president's absence or sickness (*Reglamentos de la Cámara de Diputados*, Article 44; *Reglamento del Senado*, Articles 21,23). Christian Democratic Deputy Roberto León (1998), however, suggests more flexibility in how leadership of the *mesas* is exercised – at least in the Chamber – describing a negotiated agreement within the *Concertación* by which the presidency would rotate from the Christian Democrats to the Socialists, to the PPD, and back, over the four years of the current Congress. This sort of consensual power-sharing agreement, if it can be sustained, appears to be essential to the survival of the *Concertación*.

The authorities of the *mesas*, as outlined in the Chamber and Senate rules, run along the lines of those of most assembly directorates – they are responsible for communications between chambers, with the executive, and with the public; and they have some control over the legislative agenda and committee assignments. These latter two points are particularly important and warrant some more comments.

Regarding control of the legislative agenda, both chamber presidents are given some formal authority in the respective *reglamentos* – in the case of the Chamber, to determine what matters are subject to "immediate versus nonurgent dispatch" (Article 44:4), and in the Senate "to direct debate, distributing and ordering discussion of matters and limiting the number and duration of statements, when necessary to ensure the adoption of resolutions" (Article 23:2). *Mesa* presidents also direct the flow of

237

legislative traffic through discretion on the referral of bills to legislative committees, an authority that can affect the prospects for a proposal's success, depending on the committee's composition (Alzamora 1998; also cites on bill referral power in U.S. Congress). These measures of agenda control, however, are regularly overridden in practice by the president's constitutional authority to dominate the legislative agenda by declaring his proposed bills urgent, as Siavelis's chapter in this volume shows. Thus, although the formal agenda control of officers of the Chilean Congress *within* the legislature is akin to that found elsewhere, the existence of strong constitutional agenda powers in the executive mitigates the effectiveness of this authority by the *mesas* somewhat.

In both chambers, the *mesa* president considers requests from deputies, filtered through their respective *bancadas* (partisan blocs), for desired committee assignments, and then presents proposed committee rosters to the respective Chambers for ratification.[9] In interviews, legislators from various parties concurred that the process of committee assignments is consensual, and that *mesa* presidents honor the assignment requests from the various *bancadas* (Interviews with Kuschel and Mata 1998).

Committees

Most of the substantive policy-making work of Congress is conducted in the committees of each Chamber. Legislation introduced to each Chamber is routinely referred to one of the 17 permanent committees, where hearings are held and amendments are considered. Ordinary legislation can die in committee for lack of majority support, and the fate of bills on which

---

[9] There is a subtle, but potentially important, difference between the Chambers here. The Chamber rules determine that the president names all committee members "with the agreement of the Chamber" (Article 44:2). In the Senate, by contrast, "committee members are elected by the Senate at the president's proposal. . . . The president's proposals will not be debated and are tacitly approved if there are no objections." However, if the Senate president's proposal for a particular committee is rejected, the positions on that committee are filled in the next session by cumulative vote, whereby each senator is afforded as many votes as there are positions on the committee and may distribute these votes across candidates as s/he prefers, including allocating more than one vote to a particular candidate (*Reglamento*, Article 30). This particular voting method is frequently advocated as a means of preventing majorities from swamping the will of minorities with intense preferences (Guinier 1991). According to Senator Manuel Antonio Mata (DC), however, the committee assignment process has always been consensual enough that presidential proposals have not been challenged.

floor action is required (e.g., executive proposals under urgency provisions) is influenced by committee recommendations.

Permanent committees in the Chamber are composed of 13 members each and in the Senate, 5 members.[10] Availability on the Internet of Chamber committee membership for the 1994–1997 and 1998–2001 Congresses makes it possible to examine in detail patterns of committee assignment at the coalition, partisan, and individual levels. As with the powers of the *mesas*, there are slight inconsistencies between the formal rules of the Chamber with respect to the allocation of committee seats and actual practice. Article 213 of the *Reglamentos* states that the partisan composition of each committee shall proportionately reflect the partisan composition of the Chamber as a whole. This rule implies uniformity of partisan (and, of course, coalitional) composition across committees. Table 8.7, which presents data on Chamber committee membership from 1997, and then at the beginning of the 1998–2001 Congress, illustrates that such uniformity at the partisan level is not strictly maintained.

At the coalitional level, the *Concertación* maintains a majority, of either 7:6 or 8:5, on all committees at all times. At the partisan level, the proportionality rule is observed in the aggregate, but not in the particular, case for each committee. That is, the overall number of committee posts assigned to each party mirrors its share of Chamber seats, but there are many instances of particular committees in which proportionality across parties within coalitions is not observed.[11]

There is a change between the two Congresses in the distribution of committee chairs. In 1997, 5 of 17 were held by members of the opposition, whereas 10 of the remaining 12 were occupied by Christian Democrats. At the beginning of the 1998–2001 Congress, the majority coalition has asserted a near-monopoly over chairs, holding 16 of 17, while simultaneously distributing them more proportionally within the coalition itself. The columns Repeat, Reappointed, and Experience, respectively, indicate whether the same person held the chair for successive periods, whether the former chair (if reelected) still serves on the committee, and whether

[10] When amendments generate different versions of the same bill in each Chamber, the respective committee members, plus an additional eight senators (such that each Chamber has equal membership) participate on conference committees to resolve the differences and to report uniform legislation back to the respective Chambers for floor votes.

[11] It is noteworthy, however, that there is no evidence of parties specializing in issue areas that are of high salience to their constituencies – for example, of the Socialists dominating the Labor Committee.

Table 8.7. *Committee characteristics, Congresses of 1994–1997 and 1998–2001.*

Committee	Coalition Ratio Concertación:Right '94–'97	'98–'01	Partisan Ratios DC:PPD:PS:PRSD/RN:UDI:Indpt. '94–'97	'98–'01	Chair '94–'97	'98–'01	Repeat	Reappt	Members Experience	Reassigned
Finance Constitution +	8:5	7:6	4:2:2:0/3:2:0	5:1:1:0/3:2:1	UDI	DC	no	yes	yes	7/7 (100%)
Justice	7:6	8:5	4:1:2:0/4:2:0	6:2:0/3:2:0	DC	DC	no	yes	yes	7/8 (88%)
Health	8:5	7:6	4:2:2:0/3:2:0	4:2:1:0/2:3:1	PS	PS	yes	yes	yes	6/8 (75%)
Defense Educ., Culture, Sports	7:6	7:6	3:2:2:0/4:2:0	4:1:1:1/3:2:1	PPD	PS	no	–	yes	5/7 (71%)
Mining +	7:6	7:6	3:2:1:1/4:2:0	4:2:1:0/1:2:3	DC	DC	no	yes	no	7/10 (70%)
Energy	8:5	7:6	4:2:2:0/3:2:0	4:1:1:1/2:2:2	RN	RN	yes	yes	no	4/6 (67%)
Family Agriculture +	8:5	8:5	4:2:2:0/3:1:1	4:2:2:0/3:0:2	DC	PS	–	–	yes	6/10 (60%)
Fisheries Labor + Social	8:5	7:6	4:2:2:0/3:2:0	5:1:1:0/3:2:1	RN	DC	no	no	yes	7/12 (58%)

Committee	Seats 94–97	Seats 98–01	Composition 94–97	Composition 98–01	Chair 94–97	Chair 98–01	Reassigned	Experienced	Repeat	%
Security	8:5	8:5	5:1:2:0/3:2:0	4:2:2:0/3:2:0	DC	DC	no	no	yes	5/10 (50%)
Local Govt. + Planning	7:6	7:6	5:1:1:0/4:2:0	4:2:1:0/2:2:2	DC	DC	–	–	no	4/8 (50%)
Foreign Relations	7:6	8:5	4:2:2:0/5:1:0	4:1:1:1/3:3:0	DC	DC	–	–	no	3/6 (50%)
Nat. Resources, Eviron	8:5	8:5	4:2:2:0/3:1:1	4:2:2:0/1:1:3	PS	DC	–	–	yes	5/11 (45%)
Human Rights, Ctznshp	8:5	7:6	4:2:1:0/3:2:1	4:2:1:1/2:3:0	DC	DC	–	yes	yes	4/9 (44%)
Economy	8:5	7:6	4:1:1:1/4:2:0	4:2:1:1/2:2:1	PPD	UDI	no	yes	yes	3/7 (43%)
Public Works	8:5	8:5	4:2:2:0/3:2:0	4:2:1:1/3:1:1	PPD	DC	–	yes	yes	3/7 (43%)
Housing, Urban Dvpmt	7:6	7:6	4:1:2:1/4:1:0	4:1:2:1/3:1:2	DC	RN	–	yes	no	3/8 (38%)
Science + Technology	8:5	7:6	4:1:1:1/4:2:0	4:2:1:1/3:1:1	PRSD	DC	no	no	no	3/9 (33%)
Summaries	8:5 (8) 7:6 (9)	8:5 (10) 7:6 (7)	68:28:29:4/ 60:30:3	73:31:20:7/ 42:31:21	9:2:4:1/1:0:0	10:1:1:0/ 3:2:0	1/9[a] (11%)	7/9[a] (78%)	11/17 (65%)	82/135 (61%)

[a] Eight committee chairs from 1994 to 1997 did not return to the Chamber for the 1998–2001 period.

Repeat: Chair in 1998–2001 served as chair during 1994–1997 Congress.

Reassigned: Chair in 1994–1997 served on committee during 1998–2001.

Experienced: Chair in 1998–2001 served on committee during 1994–1997.

Source: http://200.9.122.8:80/html/comis/index.htm

241

the current chair served previously on the committee. Unlike in the United States, committee chairs do not normally retain their posts from one Congress to the next. Instead, the coalitions work out agreements by which committee chairmanships rotate (Kuschel 1998; León 1998). When they are reelected, however, they generally remain on the committee, and those selected as chairs generally have prior experience on the committee.

The importance of committee composition, and its relationship to the coalition structure of Congress, are best illustrated through an extended quotation from Deputy Andrés Palma (1996) (during the 1994–1997 Congress) with respect to budget legislation:

An agriculture bill might not go through the Agriculture Committee, but it has to go through the Finance (Hacienda) Committee if it affects the budget. That is, it will generally pass through Agriculture and then go to Finance; but if the bill came with urgency from the executive for immediate discussion, it would go straight to Finance without going through Agriculture, although the subject is agriculture, because it affects the budget. Because of this, we've been particularly concerned that the composition of the Finance Committee is 8–5 [*Concertación* – right] so that even the absence of a couple of legislators won't affect the transmission of [financial] bills. There will always be a *Concertación* majority there. If one is missing, OK, there's still – or better, even up to 6–5 – you could be missing two people without affecting the majority.

[In the 1993–1997 Congress] in the Senate, the standing Finance Committee is the only one . . . with a *Concertación* majority. That is, there are three from the *Concertación* and two from the opposition. [When an additional 8 senators are named to serve on the Joint Finance Commitee, to bring the numbers of representatives from each chamber to an equal 13] the other eight are named by votes in the Senate Chamber, more or less in proportion to the senators; and because there are eight, four come from the *Concertación* and four from the opposition; so the entire Senate contingent ends up 7–6. But in the previous [1990–1993] Congress it wasn't like this. At that time . . . the other eight were three and five, respectively, such that whole Senate contingent was 6–7. . . . At any rate, it doesn't matter what the distribution of senators is because the composition of the Chamber's contingent will give us a majority in the Joint Finance Committee.

Palma's extended analysis touches on some key points about the role of committees in legislative policy making. First, his primary concern is with the nature of committee majorities – both within each Chamber and in conference – in terms of coalition membership. Second, the Finance Committees in each Chamber play the role of control committees over a wide range of policy jurisdictions, by vetting all legislation that has an impact on the budget.

All of the above reflect on the level of experience and expertise that accumulate within the committee system. Committee expertise is widely regarded as an indicator of a legislature's capacity as an independent policy-making institution (Norton 1994; Polsby 1968; Schuttemeyer 1994; Strom 1990a). On the rationale that experience is a good measure of expertise, the committees in Table 8.7 are listed in order of the rate at which members from the first period who were reelected to the Chamber were reassigned for the second period. Thus, all seven Finance Committee members from 1997 who returned to the Chamber in 1998 were reassigned to Finance, seven of eight in the case of Constitution and Justice, and so on. The resulting rank order is consistent both with the accounts of Palma and other deputies (Kuschel 1998; León 1998) about the centrality of the Finance Committees, and with conventional intuitions about the complexity and salience of the various policy jurisdictions in Chile. The committees with the highest reassignment rates – Finance, Constitution, Health, Defense – all deal with complicated policy areas that have been heavily contested in the 1990s (Baldez and Carey, 1999; Weyland 1995).

The data presented thus far demonstrate that the Chilean Congress is highly professionalized – particularly for a young legislature – and that its committee system is accumulating substantial expertise, and is organized and dominated by the majority coalition. Within the comparative study of legislatures, these are all regarded as indicators of strong legislative capacity. The accounts reviewed thus far suggest the importance of coalitions in determining committee membership and performance, but they do not provide sufficiently fine-grained information to distinguish clearly the relative importance of the traditional parties versus the broader coalitions in making policy. To address that issue, I turn to the subject of floor voting in the Chamber.

Legislative Voting

The Unity Index

Academic studies of the U.S. Congress have long focused extensively on roll-call voting behavior, and particularly on levels of party discipline (Anderson, Watts, and Wilcox 1966; Brady 1973; Collie 1984; Cox and McCubbins 1993). Systematic analysis of partisanship and legislative voting in Latin America has begun only more recently, as legislatures have become more prominent in policy making and data have become more accessible (Ames 1997; Limongi and Figueiredo 1995, 1997; Mainwaring 1999; Mainwaring and Pérez Liñán 1997). In this section, I present an analysis of a dataset of all 215 votes recorded in the Chamber of Deputies' *Boletín de Sesiones*, from the 40 sessions of Legislatura Ordinaria (May 22 – September 9, 1997) and the 29 sessions of Legislatura Ordinaria No. 336 (September 30, 1997 – January 21, 1998). The main products of this analysis are indexes of voting unity within parties and coalitions, which can range from 0 (the party or coalition is evenly divided between voting "aye" and "nay") to 1.0 (the party or coalition is perfectly united, whether for "aye" or "nay"). The unity index is weighted according to the rationale that we should be more interested in cohesiveness the more critical the vote, and that both attendance by legislators and the overall closeness of the vote are indicators of *critical-ness*. Thus, in calculating the index, votes that are sparsely attended and/or lopsided one way or the other are discounted. The basic formula for measuring party or coalition unity on legislative votes is

$$\text{Weighted UNITY}_i \text{ index} = \frac{\sum \text{UNITY}_{ij}*\text{ATTEND}_j*\text{CLOSE}_j}{\sum \text{ATTEND}_j*\text{CLOSE}_j}$$

where

ATTEND_j = % of legislators voting on issue j
CLOSE_j = 1– %aye – %nay, for legislature as a whole on issue j[12]
UNITY_{ij} = %aye – %nay, within coalition or party i on issue j.

Thus, the extent to which unity on a given vote contributes to the overall index score depends on how heavily attended a vote is, and how close it is to a tie.[13]

---

[12] This formula is based on the assumption that a measure is approved as long as more legislators vote "aye" than "nay." In some cases, however, legislative procedures establish more stringent requirements for a measure's approval – e.g., an extraordinary majority of the entire Chamber's membership. In Chile, such supermajority requirements exist for changes to the Constitution and to organic law and are applied to ten of the votes included in the dataset analyzed here. The modified formula for calculating the unity index to accommodate such votes is discussed in Carey (n.d., Appendix C).

[13] Most of the votes in this dataset were sparsely attended and unsuspenseful. ATTEND was between 33% (the minimum quorum) and 50% of the deputies on almost half of the votes; and on almost half, the losing side attracted less than 10% support (yielding CLOSE scores between 0 and 0.2). It is noteworthy, however, that there is no correlation between ATTEND and CLOSE. Both variables, therefore, appear to bring to the weighted index independent and important information about the critical-ness of votes.

The motivation for and properties of the unity index are discussed at length in Carey (2000). For the present purposes, however, it is worthwhile to discuss briefly the use of legislative voting as a manifestation of party and coalition unity. In this volume, Ames makes a compelling case that, by the time legislation reaches a vote, either in committee or on the Chamber floor, much of the bargaining over its content may already have transpired, such that if party and coalition leaders have good information about legislators' preferences, voting outcomes themselves may be foregone conclusions. To the extent that leaders with control over the legislative agenda prevent votes on issues that they expect to be divisive within their parties and coalitions, measures based on recorded votes will overrepresent levels of unity.[14] Nevertheless, legislative voting is a central procedural element of all democracies, and there are good reasons to pay attention to the information that it reveals about parties and coalitions. First, leadership information about legislators' preferences is never perfect, so floor votes are not inevitably predetermined. Second, important votes often cannot be avoided despite the threats that they might pose to unity – for example, on legislation on urgent issues and annual budgets, or when qualified minorities are enfranchised to bring matters to the floor (Carey 2000). Third, patterns of division in floor voting can communicate to voters the relative positions of legislative actors; even unsuspenseful votes can convey important information about both unity within parties and coalitions and differences among them. Finally, although recorded votes have historically been unusual in most Latin American countries, suggesting skepticism of the accuracy with which they reflect general legislative dynamics, the recent adoption of electronic voting in a number of countries, including Chile, means that we can rely on recorded votes to provide a fairly complete picture of floor activity. In short, although a more complete portrait of legislative bargaining that encompasses action occurring off the floor, such as Ames provides for Brazil, would be preferable, there are theoretical and empirical reasons to take an interest in floor voting patterns.

The first cut is to examine index scores across the two major coalitions and their main component parties.[15] Table 8.8 provides a good deal of

---

[14] Of course, leaders may also tolerate *dis*unity when such behavior does not threaten the outcome of votes, implying a bias in measures of unity running in the opposite direction.

[15] For the 1993–1997 Congress, four candidates without party affiliations were elected as Independents on lists run by the coalition of the right, as were two candidates from the minor party, the Unión del Centro Centro (UCC). Two candidates from the Partido

Table 8.8. *Weighted UNITY scores for coalitions and parties.*

Coalition/Party	All votes	Economic	Social/ Military	Foreign Policy	Government Reform	Miscellaneous
Concertación	.69	.83	.71	1.00	.61	.97
DC	.75	.92	.75	1.00	.67	.94
PPD	.71	.89	.71	1.00	.61	1.00
PS	.77	.86	.76	1.00	.78	1.00
Right	.61	.67	.59	.49	.50	.48
RN	.68	.82	.63	.82	.70	.46
UDI	.78	.92	.78	.96	.73	1.00
Whole Chamber	.38	.50	.31	.84	.79	.90
N	215	96	66	14	31	8

information about the levels of unity within both coalitions and within the major parties of which they are composed, both for all votes analyzed and for subsets of votes coded by policy issue area.[16] The index scores reported for the whole Chamber give an indication of how hotly contested votes in each issue area were, with lower scores there indicating that votes tended to be more divisive. As one might expect, votes on foreign policy and on miscellaneous (e.g., approving construction of monuments to a nineteenth-century priest and a policeman killed in the line of duty; renaming a city park) were the most consensual, whereas votes on social and military issues, and to a lesser extent economic matters, were the most divisive.

At the level of coalitions and the parties that comprise them, the scores are higher within the parties than within the coalitions overall. This is to be expected if common party membership means *anything at all* as a predictor of legislative behavior. Arithmetically, the index score of any group

Radical (PR) and one from the Partido Democrática de la Izquierda (PDI) were elected on Concertación lists. For the purposes of calculating UNITY indexes, these legislators are included in the scores for each coalition. Separate indexes are calculated for each of the major parties within each coalition. Later, when indexes are calculated for cross-partisan blocks both within and across coalitions, only the members of the major parties are included.

[16] Roughly, a score of .700 indicates that 85% of the set of legislators in question voted together on votes of "average" *critical-ness*. The idea of an average, of course, entails that votes that are most divisive across the legislature as a whole are given the most weight, so scores should be interpreted cautiously.

cannot be higher than the mean of index scores of its component sub-groups, weighted according to subgroup membership.[17] Given this, it is remarkable how little difference there is between the overall cohesiveness of the coalitions and of their component parties – particularly within the *Concertación*, where cohesiveness at the coalition level is not much below that at the partisan level.

Table 8.8 also gives some idea about the relative divisiveness of different policy issues within each of the parties and coalitions. Both coalitions are relatively unified around economic issues, with the *Concertación* also highly unified on foreign policy and the few miscellaneous bills. Big differences between unity at the coalition level and at the level of component parties indicate issue areas that are internally divisive across parties within coalitions. For example, the two main parties within the coalition of the right are each highly cohesive on foreign policy votes, but the coalition as a whole is not, indicating stark differences at the partisan level on that issue area. The right is similarly (although not as starkly) divided on economic votes and on government reform votes. On the few miscellaneous votes, the UDI is perfectly united, whereas the RN is internally divided. In the *Concertación*, no issue area stands out as clearly dividing unified parties against each other within the coalition.

Unity Among Cross-Partisan Blocs

The next question is how we might draw on the unity index to learn about the relative importance of party versus coalition to explain legislative voting. Consider an alternative cut on the data, distinguishing among various cross-party blocs. Based on survey responses to questions about ideological placement from 94 of the 120 deputies in the 1994–1998 Chamber of Deputies (Rehren 1997), I suggest the following spatial map of party and coalition locations along a standard left–right dimension:

[17] If all parties within a coalition were precisely equally disunited on every vote in the dataset, then all of their UNITY scores would be equal, and would equal that of their coalition as a whole. On the other hand, if members of the same party were *at all more prone* to vote together than to vote with members of other parties within their coalition, then the UNITY scores of each party would be higher than that of the coalition.

It is also worth noting that the parties for which index scores are calculated make up the vast majority of members of each coalition, but not all. The handful of minor party legislators and independents in each coalition are included in the coalition scores. For independents and parties with lone legislators, it would be meaningless to calculate their party UNITY scores.

Socialist PPD DC   RN UDI

Concertación   Right

In the survey, legislators were asked to locate themselves, their own party, and finally each of the other major parties in the Chamber on a left–right ideological scale ranging from 1 to 10. The mean responses, by party, are reported in Table 8.9, with the number of respondents on which each score is based in parentheses. The scores are interesting on a number of counts. First, individual respondents – especially those on the right – tend to see themselves and their parties as more moderate than do their colleagues from other parties. The range of means for self-placement is only 3.8 points (2.9 to 6.7), whereas for placement for other parties it is 6.3 (2.5 to 8.8). Second, the relative self-placement and own-party placement by RN and UDI deputies are the reverse of the general evaluations by deputies about party locations, and of the conventional wisdom about Chilean politics, based on political debate, electoral platforms, and political history. Third, the distance between the adjacent parties across coalitions (whether one regards the RN or UDI as furthest left) is at least as large as the internal spread within either coalition.[18]

The ideological placements in Table 8.9 suggest substantial ideological cohesiveness among the parties within each of the major coalitions, an assessment that is supported by the unity scores in Table 8.8. Drawing on the same set of roll-call votes, Table 8.10 shows index scores calculated for legislators from every pair of parties, distinguishing according to whether the pairs are ideologically adjacent and whether they are members of the same major coalition.[19] Table 8.10 suggests that common coalition membership encourages unity in legislative voting over and above ideological adjacence or ideological distance. Within the _Concertación_, distance and adjacence appear to count for very little; the PS–DC unity score is effectively equivalent to those of the PS–PPD and the PPD–DC, despite the fact that the ideology scores place the PS and DC much further apart than

[18] On self-placement, the PS–DC distance is 1.6, exactly equal to the DC–UDI distance. On own party and other party placement, however, the intra-_Concertación_ distances are slightly smaller than those between the DC and the closest party in the coalition of the right.

[19] Because of the inconsistencies in the relative placement of the RN and the UDI, I simply put them both in the "adjacent" category to the DC on the right side of the _Concertación_, for the purposes of Table 8.10. None of the conclusions that follow would be affected by regarding one or the other parties as adjacent and the other not.

Table 8.9. *Ideological locations of Chilean legislators, by party, on 1–10, left–right scale.*

Mean legislator placement of:	PS	PPD	DC	RN	UDI
Self	2.9 (13)	3.6 (10)	4.5 (31)	6.7 (24)	6.1 (12)
Own party	2.6 (13)	4.3 (11)	4.4 (31)	6.6 (24)	6.4 (12)
Other parties	2.5 (81)	4.2 (83)	4.7 (63)	7.7 (70)	8.8 (82)

Source: Rehren (1997).

Table 8.10. *UNITY scores and ideological distances for cross-partisan blocs.*

		Same coalition			Different coalition	
	Parties	Ideological distance	Weighted UNITY	Parties	Ideological distance	weighted UNITY
Adjacent	PS-PPD	1.4	.83	DC-RN	2.5	.54
	PPD-DC	0.5	.80	DC-UDI	2.6	.56
	RN-UDI	0.6	.70			
Nonadjacent	PS-DC	1.9	.78	PS-UDI	4.4	.45
				PPD-UDI	3.1	.43
				PS-RN	4.0	.51
				PPD-RN	3.0	.55

either of the other pairs. At the same time, the unity index shows stark divisions across coalitions.

Ideally, we could evaluate the relative effects of ideological distance and coalition membership on unity between sets of parties by regressing $UNITY_{ij}$ on both $DISTANCE_{ij}$ and a dummy $COALITION PARTNER_{ij}$ variable. If the coalitions do not constrain the voting behavior of legislators, then the boundary between coalitions should not tell us any more about the voting patterns of deputies on opposing sides than does the ideological location of their respective parties alone. On the other hand, if the electoral coalitions are important, then unity between any two parties within a coalition should be greater than that between two parties that are not coalition partners, *controlling for ideological distance*. Statistical analysis is complicated, however, by the small number of observations as well as multicollinearity – distance and partnership are correlated at −.85, significant at .01. To determine whether coalition partnership provides any additional leverage over and above ideological distance, in explaining unity, I proceeded as follows:

- Using logistic regression, estimate the effect of distance on coalition partnership, saving the error terms.
- Using OLS, estimate the effect of distance and the error terms on unity.

The intuition here is that the error terms represent the component of coalition partnership that are *not attributable to* ideological distance. If the error terms help unity, this suggests that coalition partnership matters, over and above ideological proximity, to legislative voting. The results of the second regression (with standard errors in parentheses) are

$$UNITY = 0.828 - .092 * DISTANCE + .25 * ERROR\ TERM.$$
$$(.035)\quad (.013) \qquad\qquad (.066)$$

$N = 10$

Adj.R – squared = .88.

At the most basic level, these results demonstrate that legislators from the two main coalitions in Chile tend to vote with each other and that the coalitions also tend to vote against each other.

Discipline, Agenda Control, and Bicameralism

What are the mechanics that generate cohesiveness within coalitions, and polarization across them, in the legislature? Ideological spread is part, but not all, of the explanation. As Siavelis demonstrates in this volume, the executive's authority to control the legislative agenda may assist the *Concertación* in preventing votes on legislation that could potentially divide the coalition from reaching the Chamber floor. The executive's control over the budget, moreover, may provide resources that help to persuade, or co-opt, recalcitrant legislators to vote along coalitional lines (Baldez and Carey 1999). The fact that unity within the *Concertación* is higher than that within the coalition of the right suggests that control of the executive entails an advantage in generating coalitional unity.

Legislators themselves point to various sources of coordination and pressure to explain coalitional cohesiveness in floor voting. Most commonly, they point to coordination at the level of coalition leadership. In the *Concertación*, for example, leaders of each party and of the respective *bancadas*, along with key government ministers, meet each Monday in the presidential office building to plan strategy and negotiate the legislative agenda. The substance of these conferences is communicated both at subsequent weekly meetings of the individual *bancadas* themselves and among the entire *Concertación* cohort of legislators. Legislators generally emphasize the informational and consensus-building functions of such meetings, rather than strict coalitional *or* partisan discipline backed up by sanctions. In different interviews, Dep. Orpis (UDI) refers to both discipline at the coalition level (1996) and, later, to a more subtle "tacit agreement" within the coalition of the right on cohesiveness (1998). The Executive Secretary of the PPD *bancada* in the Chamber gives a similarly ambiguous account, referring to a "moral obligation to support the *Concertación*" and to "discipline," but downplaying the imminence of explicit sanctions against those who vote against the coalition (Canales 1998).

The coalition-level unity that is evident from the roll-call data may be a product either of discipline, which implies exerting pressure on deputies to vote together, or coordination of the legislative agenda. The interviews suggest that discipline at the coalition level is a function of moral obligation rather than sanctions imposed on maverick legislators. An alternative source of discipline is the electoral incentive under the two-member district system for candidates from the same coalition to stake similar ideological positions while distinguishing themselves from the candidates of the other main coalition, as implied by the formal models of Dow (1998) and Magar, Rosenblum, and Samuels (1998). The role that the coalitions play in coordinating the activities of their constituent parties is more clear and straightforward. The weekly *Concertación* meetings provide regular information to those who control the legislative agenda – the executive, the *mesas directivas*, the *bancadas*, and committee chairs – about what issues can be pushed through the legislative process with majority (or, where necessary, supermajority) support; and conversely, when legislation is potentially divisive enough that it should be kept off the Chamber floor. The polarization of the two main coalitions, together with their internal unity, demonstrate that the coalitions are either exerting pressure on their members to vote together, or else that they are determining what matters are put to decisions before Congress, or some combination of these. Whatever the balance between these two types of influence, the coalitions are clearly central actors in structuring congressional decisions.

A second implication, following from the cohesiveness of coalitions in the Chamber, is that the existence of nonelected senators means that much of the most important deliberation and negotiation within the legislature should take place between, rather than within, Chambers. In the absence of nonelected senators, Chile's would be an example of congruous bicameralism, in which one would expect majorities in each chamber to generate similar decisions, because the electoral systems for the Chamber and Senate are identical (with the caveat that Senate districts are larger) (Lijphart 1999). The nonelected senators, however, change things substantially. The initial cohort was appointed by Pinochet himself, and swung the Senate majority from the *Concertación* to the right. The result was that, for the first eight years after the transition, interchamber negotiations were the principle forum of bargaining and compromise in the Chilean Congress. This is underscored by Rossana Costa, an economist for a conservative think tank and lobbying organization, again with respect to budget legislation:

Q: How would you characterize the relationship between the Chamber and the executive with respect to the budget?

Costa: [In 1995], the Chamber reached an agreement with the executive and, because the opposition is a minority, there is no reason to debate anything. It's voted on and it's done. The source of compromise is the Senate, because there, in some cases it's necessary to reach an agreement with the opposition, and that's what produces negotiation, conversation, discussion – not in the Chamber.

The term of the original cohort of appointed senators ended in early 1998, at which point nine new senators were named, and the retired General Pinochet himself assumed his seat as a former president.[20] Because of the constraints of the appointment process discussed previously, the ideological bent of the group appointed in 1998 is still to the right of the *Concertación* majority among elected legislators, providing the coalition of the right with sufficient votes to block key *Concertación* initiatives in the Senate (*Santiago Times* 1999).

Conclusion

Prior to 1973, the Chilean Congress was long regarded as the most powerful legislature in Latin America, a forum for negotiation and bargaining among strong parties, and a significant counterweight to the executive

---

[20] Pinochet's subsequent arrest and detention in Britain later that year, on charges of human rights abuses brought by Spanish Prosecutor Baltazar Garzón, removed him as a direct legislative player in the Senate.

branch in shaping policy. Upon the return to democracy in 1990, the legacy of a long authoritarian hiatus, a new constitution that provides strong legislative powers to the president, and a new electoral system all raised questions about the role of Congress. Recent research confirms the importance of presidential agenda control in shaping policy outcomes (Baldez and Carey 1999; Siavelis 1998). Nevertheless, according to the standard criteria by which legislatures are compared, Chile's Congress is reestablishing itself as an unusually professionalized and technically competent legislature. Politicians endeavor – generally successfully – to build careers through reelction to Congress. They pursue these careers through parties and coalitions that have been stable throughout the post-transition period. Much of the substantive oversight and policy-making work of the legislature, moreover, is delegated to a set of standing committees, and stable membership on these committees (particularly those that deal with the most important policies) means that these intralegislative institutions are accumulating substantial policy expertise. All of these are widely regarded as signs of legislative capacity and autonomy.

Perhaps the most noteworthy characteristic of the Chilean legislature in the post-transition era, however, is the prominence of the two multi-party coalitions, particularly in contrast with accounts of the legislative party system during the pre-transition era. The establishment of coalitions was undoubtedly motivated by the electoral law imposed by the outgoing dictatorship, yet their impact on legislative representation suggests that they are more than marriages of electoral convenience. First, even if either of the major coalitions exploded tomorrow, they have already *both* proven far more durable than *any* legislative coalitions during the entire 1932–1973 period (Valenzuela 1994). Second, two major institutions that direct the work of the Chamber of Deputies – the *mesas directivas* and the committees – are organized on the grounds of coalition control. The *mesa* presidency is rotated under an agreement among the parties within the *Concertación*; and committee composition is marked by consistent coalition majorities, even while the formal rule of strict partisan proportionality is sometimes violated. Finally, coalitions structure how Congress as a whole will divide when it comes time to vote. To sum up, the electoral system encourages parties to coalesce; and the coalitions, in turn, matter to the way in which Congress operates and to the sort of representation that legislators provide.

9

Understanding Party Discipline in the Mexican Chamber of Deputies: The Centralized Party Model

BENITO NACIF

Throughout the long period of single-party dominance over the Mexican political system, the study of the legislature was exhausted by the study of the congressional delegations of the PRI (Institutional Revolutionary Party). Founded in 1929, the PRI maintained a long-lasting control of access to the vast majority of elected offices, which allowed it to monopolize the constitutional powers formally residing in the two houses of the Congress – the Chamber of Deputies and the Senate. The congressional opposition played a marginal role in the decision-making process, questioning presidential initiatives in floor debates but without any significant impact on policy outcomes.

Political analysts have identified two institutional aspects of the PRI congressional delegations that have had an enormous significance in terms of the operation of the Mexican political system as a whole. First, the real source of party leadership has not resided within the Congress itself but in the Presidency of the Republic. Second, PRI congressional delegations have regularly shown a high degree of party unity. According to Weldon (1997), as long as the PRI has had the majority in the Congress, presidential leadership and party discipline have provided sufficient conditions for executive dominance over the policy-making process. Casar (1999) argues that one of the distinguishing features of Mexican *presidencialismo* was that the enormous authority of the chief executive did not spring from his constitutional prerogatives but from his ability to mobilize at will the disciplined support of PRI congressional majorities. Unlike other Latin American chief executives, Mexican presidents are not allowed by the Constitution to introduce changes in legislation without active congressional approval.

Party Discipline in the Mexican Chamber of Deputies

While it has been well recognized that the dominant position of the PRI enabled the party to centralize its policy-making power, the mechanisms sustaining party unity and subordination to presidential initiatives within the PRI's congressional delegation have not been analyzed thoroughly. Political parties are often assumed to be monolithic units responding to a single source of leadership. And yet, as Ames demonstrates in his study of the Brazilian legislature (see his contribution to this volume), party discipline cannot be taken for granted, nor can the ascendancy of the president over contending sources of leadership within his own party.

Recent changes in Mexican politics have rendered the study of congressional parties even more important. Over the last two decades Mexico evolved from a single-party regime into an increasingly competitive three-party system. The growth of the opposition as a whole was produced by the expansion of the old center-right opposition party, the PAN (National Action Party) and the creation of a new center-left opposition party in 1989, the PRD (Party of the Democratic Revolution).[1] The persistent erosion of the PRI's political hegemony reached a turning point in the 1997 midterm congressional elections. For the first time since its foundation, the PRI was not able to win the majority of seats in the Chamber of Deputies.

The demise of PRI control over decision making in the Chamber of Deputies transformed the opposition parties from mere symbolic checks on the PRI majority into pivotal actors within the Congress. Accordingly, explaining party discipline and subordination to the President of the Republic within the congressional PRI is no longer sufficient to understand the making of policy in post-1997 Mexican politics. We need to incorporate congressional opposition parties into the analysis. Only through the understanding of how the PRI and the opposition parties operate in the Congress can we explore the impact of the new multipartisan balance of power on executive–legislative relations and the role of the Congress in the policy-making process.

The purpose of this chapter is to analyze the structure of institutional incentives and disincentives shaping the relationships between individual legislators and party leaders in the Mexican Chamber of Deputies. The central argument is that, while there are three relevant congressional

---

[1] In the three elections from 1991 to 1997, the main parties (PRI, PAN, and PRD) have concentrated more than 90% of the votes cast, and the number of relevant parties, measured by the Laakso-Taagepera index of effective number of components, evolved from 2.26 to 3.42.

parties or parliamentary fractions – as they are formally known – legisla-tors regularly operate as agents of their national party organizations. This is because party leaders outside the Congress control the nominations to legislative office and the future careers of lame-duck legislators, who are constitutionally prevented from running for reelection in consecutive terms.

As a consequence, the degree of party unity in the Mexican Chamber of Deputies is notably higher than in any of the other legislatures studied in this book. Once in office, individual members of the Chamber of Deputies face severe restrictions to take part in the selection of their own parliamentary leaders, who are primarily responsible to the national party organization. Party discipline depends on the potential sanctions to unco-operative behavior in terms of career-advancement opportunities. But the leaders of the parliamentary fractions also use their procedural powers to monitor and keep tabs on individual legislators throughout all stages of the law-making process, including committees.

To develop this argument, the chapter is organized as follows. The first section deals with the effect of electoral institutions on the career strate-gies of politicians seeking and holding office in the Chamber. The second section analyzes how prevailing career strategies mold the relationship between the national party organizations and individual legislators in the organization of parliamentary fractions. The third section studies the role of parliamentary fractions in solving the collective action problems that individual legislators face in the decision-making process. The fourth section deals with the delegation of power from parliamentary fractions to their contingents in committees. Finally, the last section shows how par-liamentary fractions control the flow of legislation from committees to the floor and coordinate vote-making majorities in the plenary.

Electoral Institutions and the Political Strategies of Legislators

The theory of political ambition asserts that the behavior of politicians is a response to their office goals (Schlesinger 1991). Of course, politicians pursue a variety of goals, including the implementation of their preferred policies. However, even for the policy-oriented politician, achieving office should be preeminent for two reasons: Gaining majority status in the leg-islature is usually a pre-condition to having the ability to introduce policy change. Second, surviving in politics may not be sufficient to attain the power to direct policy change, but it definitively increases the capacity of legislators to influence policy outcomes. The theory of political ambition anticipates that policy-oriented politicians will not behave in a substantially different way from office-seeking politicians.[2] It asserts that in the long run the politicians who do not attach sufficient importance to their office goals will be driven away from politics.

The possibility for politicians to achieve elective office depends on two factors – their personal reputation before the electorate and the collective reputation of the political party that nominates them (Cain, Ferejohn, and Fiorina 1987). The significance of the individual-reputation component is defined by the extent to which the personal characteristics of candidates matter in elections. The collective component of a politician's chances to achieve office is determined by the importance of the party label. Regularly, both the individual and the collective components are present in elections, but what is uncertain is their relative significance in determining a politician's chances to gain elective office. The key variables defining the relative importance of the party label *versus* the personal vote are the institutions that regulate competition for office between and within parties (Shugart and Carey 1992).

Members of the Mexican Chamber of Deputies (MCDs) are elected through a system that combines single-member and multimember districts. There are 300 *diputados uninominales* elected by plurality in single-member districts and 200 *diputados plurinominales* elected in five multimember districts. The number of single-member districts was fixed at 300 in 1977. Multimember districts, however, have experienced important changes in number and size. Legislation passed in 1977 set up four multimember districts with a magnitude of 25 each. Further changes in 1987 introduced one more multimember district and increased their magnitude to 40, bringing about an overall increase of 100 in the total number of seats elected in multimember districts (Nacif 1997).

Multimember districts (*circunscripciones*) have the same district magnitude, with each of them being entitled to elect 40 MCDs. Single-member and multimember districts are geographically overlapping and tied by the same ballot. The voter casts one single ballot that is subject to a double

---

[2] The ambition theory does not assume that political parties will constantly change their policy positions to capture electoral gains. Office-seeking strategies can also drive politicians to stick to a set of policies to gain credibility in the long term (Laver and Shepsle 1996).

counting that produces two seat-relevant vote totals. The first vote total determines who wins the plurality in the single-member district, and the second vote total serves to allocate seats in multimember districts.[3] Seats in multimember districts are assigned according to each party's share of the total votes cast within the district, this being the reason why they are also named proportional representation seats.[4]

There is a significant difference in the probability for individual candidates to gain office in the Chamber in single-member and multi-member districts. Candidates in single-member districts depend directly on the decisions made by the electorate. In the case of seats disputed in multimember districts, the likelihood of winning office also hinges on another factor – the candidate's position in the party slate. As the contest for proportional representation seats operates under closed lists, the candidate's position in the party slate is a decision taken in advance by the party organization that voters cannot alter.

One important restraint on individual politicians seeking office in the Chamber is that political parties control access to the ballots. The nomination by an officially registered political party is a legal prerequisite to run for federal office. By banning independent candidacies, this arrangement provides a source of power to political parties. Gaining official registration as a political party is a costly and time-consuming process that prevents politicians from seeking office in the Chamber outside registered parties. Electoral legislation also has granted political parties complete discretion to establish their own nominating procedures. Therefore, formal nominating rules vary substantially from party to party.[5] However, there is a pattern that is shared by all political parties in Mexico: Party organizations tend to be highly centralized. The party leadership residing at the National Executive Committees (CENs) has control over the assignment of the most valuable party candidacies. This pattern derives primarily from

---

[3] There is a third vote-significant total at the national level to determine which parties are entitled to take part in the allocation of seats disputed in multimember districts. The electoral threshold is 2% of the national vote. The current level was established in 1996, rising from the previous 1.5 level introduced in 1971.

[4] Two systems are employed to accord seats to political parties in multimember districts. First, a simple quota is calculated by dividing the total number of votes in the *circunscripción* by 40. The quota represents the number of votes that a party must gather to gain one multimember seat in the *circunscripción*. Second, once parties have been granted seats according to the quota system, if there are any seats left, they will be apportioned to the parties that have the largest remainder vote. The remainder is a portion of the quotient that is left after dividing the party's votes cast by the quota.

[5] For an analysis of changes in the PRI nominating rules and practices, see Langston (1996).

258

Party Discipline in the Mexican Chamber of Deputies

Table 9.1. *Experience in office of incumbent deputies (percentage of legislators).*

No. of terms	1982–1985	1985–1988	1988–1991	1982–1991
No experience	86.5	81.0	78.9	81.9
One	9.4	16.0	19.5	15.2
Two or more	4.2	3.0	1.6	2.9

Source: Nacif (1996).

the practice of office rotation imposed through the constitutional banning of consecutive reelection to the Chamber.[6]

The institution of nonconsecutive reelection is an important constraint molding the career strategies of politicians seeking and holding office in the Chamber. A forceful break of one term out of office clearly discourages legislators from pursuing reelection as a long-term career goal. To complete a three-term career in the Chamber takes 15 years, spending 6 of them out of office. Available information confirms that the prospect of three years in the wilderness for every term of service prevents politicians from pursuing long careers in the Chamber. As Table 9.1 shows, on average eight out of ten MCDs have no previous experience serving in the Chamber of Deputies. This renders Mexican deputies the most inexperienced legislators of the four Latin American countries studied in this book. The vast majority of politicians serving in the Chamber of Deputies work under the assumption that they will never return to this body. In the period from 1985 to 1991, an average of less than 10% of the outgoing legislators (50 out of 500) went back to the Chamber of Deputies after the compulsory one-term break (Lujambio 1995). The return rate dropped to nonsignificant levels for those serving a third term in the Chamber.

Nonconsecutive reelection also shapes the relationship between members of the Chamber of Deputies and their constituencies. A large-district magnitude together with the closed-list system might be sufficient to explain why the identity of the 40 candidates appearing in the party list for each multimember district has no significant influence in voters' decisions. Nonetheless, there are 300 seats elected by plurality in single-member districts where the conditions and the incentives to cultivate a

[6] The constitutional amendment prohibiting the consecutive reelection of elective officials serving in the Senate, the Chamber of Deputies, state legislatures, and municipal presidencies was introduced in 1933. See Nacif (1997) for an analysis of the causes and consequences of this institutional change.

personal vote are apparently present. But the inability to run for re-election inhibits the development of permanent links between incumbent legislators and their constituents. Even more, since candidates running for the Chamber are constantly changing, voters are unable to gather sufficient information about their personal characteristics.

Opinion poll surveys demonstrate that the vast majority of Mexicans do not know the name of their district's outgoing MCD, nor that of the candidate they are voting for. A survey conducted a few days after the 1997 elections showed that the percentage of respondents who were able to correctly recall the name of at least one of the candidates running for a seat in the Chamber of Deputies in their districts was only 17.9%. Those who had some form of contact with an MCD represented only 11.4% of those interviewed.[7] These figures indicate that the "visibility" of politicians seeking and holding office in the Chamber tends to be rather low. In addition, according to Cain, Ferejohn, and Fiorina (1987), visibility is necessary for politicians to have an independent standing in the electorate's mind. Clearly, party labels have the most significant influence on voting decisions, even though MCDs are elected in single-member districts. The overwhelming importance of party labels in elections to the Chamber renders individual politicians dependent on the party organization to achieve their career goals.

The prohibition of consecutive reelection also affects the way in which parties nominate candidates to the Chamber. By removing the incumbent from competition for party nominations, nonconsecutive reelection provides CENs with an open slate of candidacies to allocate among aspiring politicians. Of course, the ability of CENs to control the nomination process is restricted by nominating lobbies linked to the party organization. The characteristics of nominating lobbies vary from party to party. The PRI, for instance, operates through a system of quotas whereby affiliated unions, state party organizations, and other political associations compete for party nominations (Langston 1996). Nevertheless, nonconsecutive reelection enhances the potential influence of CENs in the assignment of slots in the party list of candidates, allowing for a considerable degree of centralization in the nomination process (Nacif 1997).

The prohibition of consecutive reelection instills what Schlesinger (1991) termed "progressive ambition" – the aspiration to attain an office

---

[7] The sample of the survey was representative of the population eligible to vote in the entire country. The survey is part of an international project known as the Comparative Study of Electoral Systems (CSES).

Table 9.2. *Previous office experience of elected senators, 1997–2000.*

Type of office	PRI	%	Opposition	%	Total	%
Federal deputy	31	(40.8)	21	(41.2)	52	(40.9)
State administration	12	(15.8)	6	(11.8)	18	(14.2)
Local deputy	6	(7.9)	6	(11.8)	12	(9.4)
Federal administration	10	(13.2)	2	(3.9)	12	(9.4)
Activities in the political party	5	(6.6)	4	(7.8)	9	(7.1)
Mayor	2	(2.6)	4	(7.8)	6	(4.7)
State judiciary	3	(3.9)			3	(2.4)
Governor	2	(2.6)			2	(1.6)
Municipal counselor	1	(1.3)	1	(1.3)	2	(1.6)
Others	4	(5.3)	7	(13.7)	11	(8.7)
TOTAL	76	(59.8)	51	(40.2)	127	(100.0)

Source: Sánchez Rebolledo (1999).

that is more important than the one a politician is currently seeking or holding. Progressive ambition among MCDs is encouraged by high turnout rates in other elective offices. In fact, all elective offices in Mexico have 100% turnout rate as they are either bound by nonconsecutive reelection or subject to a one-term life limit.[8] Given the position of the Senate in the hierarchy of office opportunities, Senate seats represent attractive elective office goals for outgoing MCDs. Table 9.2 shows that a significant number of Senate seats are allocated to outgoing MCDs. As many as 40% of the Senators elected between 1994 and 1997 served in the Chamber of Deputies before being nominated to the upper chamber. Up to 1994, the PRI controlled almost all office opportunities in the Senate. With the introduction of proportional representation seats, opposition parties have gained access to a regular share of Senate seats. This has enhanced the career potential of opposition politicians serving in the Chamber of Deputies, providing party leaders with a powerful instrument to reward the cooperative behavior of legislators.

Another attractive career goal for outgoing MCDs is state governorships. In fact, the position of a state governor in the hierarchy of opportunities is higher than that of a regular Senate seat. State governors are more powerful and have more resources than senators. Also, there are

[8] The president and state governors are bound by a life limit of one term. The prohibition of consecutive reelection holds for other elective offices, including federal senators and deputies, state deputies, and municipal presidents and counselors.

Table 9.3. *Previous office experience of elected governors,*
1976–1995.

Type of office	Governors	Percentage
Federal administration	45	35.7
Senator	30	23.8
Deputy	27	21.4
Mayor	11	8.7
State administration	2	1.6
Military	2	1.6
Federal judiciary	1	0.8
State judiciary	1	0.8
Not identified	7	5.6
TOTAL	126	100.0

Source: Camp 1992; México 1987, 1989, and 1992.

fewer state governorships than Senate seats, which means that the race for each state governorship is more competitive. MCDs have to compete with senators, high-ranking administrative officials, and mayors of important municipalities for their party's gubernatorial nomination. Yet, as Table 9.3 shows, from 1976 to 1995, 21.4% of the elected state chief executives served in the Chamber of Deputies before gaining the party gubernatorial nomination. This figure compares well with that of senators and high-ranking administrative officials. Up to 1989, state governorships were controlled totally by the PRI, but as local elections grew in competitiveness over the last decade the gubernatorial nomination of some opposition parties has become increasingly attractive for outgoing MCDs.

Politicians serving in the Chamber of Deputies also target offices of similar status, such as the mayoralties of important *municipios* and positions in state legislatures. With the introduction of proportional representation seats in state legislatures during the 1980s, opposition parties gained access to a regular share of positions to allocate among their cadre, including outgoing MCDs. The Mexico City Assembly, created in 1988, has become another important outlet for politicians seeking some continuity in their careers after a spell in the Chamber.

The political strategies of MCDs concentrate on opportunities where their chances to gain office are better. The probability of achieving office depends primarily on the electoral support for the party label. The reputation of individual candidates plays no significant role in the races for the

Senate, state legislatures, and the Mexico City Assembly. The personal vote is arguably gaining a new significance as levels of competitiveness rise in gubernatorial races. Accordingly, individual reputations are becoming more important in the quest for party nominations. Nevertheless, this is unlikely to substantially change the political strategies of MCDs. Making a name in state politics usually requires more than a spell in the Chamber. Even more, a successful bid for state governor cannot depend solely on the candidate's individual reputation; the backing of a vote-winning party label is necessary (Mizrahi 1999).

The party organization is also important in terms of the number of opportunities for career advancement. Parties are organizational networks linking rotating offices within which politicians advance their careers. The political ambitions of MCDs focus on offices where their party has either incumbency status or is well positioned to mount a realistic challenge to the incumbent. The greater the electoral strength of a political party across federal states the greater the number of available office opportunities for MCDs to capture. For this reason the party label is a collective good of central importance for all politicians seeking to advance their career under the same party.

In summary, although nonconsecutive reelection has a dispersing effect on career goals, MCDs can still be characterized as seeking external promotion to other elective office opportunities. While their office goals may vary substantially, the electoral strategies of MCDs tend to be very similar. MCDs depend on the party reputation to achieve office and advance their careers. Accordingly, MCDs do not have electoral incentives to go against the party line. On the contrary, we should expect party leaders to reward legislators serving to fulfill the party's collective interest. Uncooperative legislators may face powerful sanctions in terms of career opportunities.

The Parliamentary Fractions of Political Parties

Once individual politicians get elected to the Chamber of Deputies, they face strong incentives to join the parliamentary fractions of their political parties. Parliamentary party organizations are instruments to solve collective action problems. Decision making within the Chamber of Deputies affects the reputation of political parties before the electorate. Accordingly, political parties take positions on policy issues seeking relative gains in voter support and then demand that individual legislators follow the party line as the policy initiative passes through the Chamber. Legislators may disagree on specific positions taken by the party, but at the end of the day it is the party as a whole that remains responsible to the electorate. Individual legislators cannot be held accountable directly to their constituencies since they are forbidden to run for reelection; they are accountable through their parties.

In some ways, the logic of parliamentary party organizations in Mexico is not very different from that of legislative parties in the U.S. House of Representatives, as described by Cox and McCubbins (1993). They respond to the collective component of the career advancement probabilities of legislators from the same party. However, whereas in the U.S. House of Representatives legislators are primarily driven by the reelection goal, in Mexico existing institutions force politicians serving in the Chamber of Deputies to seek promotion to other offices as a means to surviving in politics.

Another important difference has to do with the relative significance of the individual and collective components of career advancement probabilities. The chances of attaining reelection for an average U.S. Representative depend primarily on their ability to maintain the "electoral connection" with their constituencies back in the districts (Mayhew 1974). Cooperation with the party is subordinated to cultivating a personal reputation. As a consequence, legislative party organizations tend to be decentralized and respond to what has been termed the "conditional party government" (Aldrich 1995; Cox and McCubbins 1993; Rohde 1992). Conditional party government is characterized by influence flowing from the bottom. The power of party leaders is thereby limited, because individual legislators have to retain a substantial degree of independence to respond to the specific demands of their constituencies (Rohde 1992).

Ames argues that the conditional party government also characterizes the relationship between party leaders and individual legislators in the Brazilian Congress. Even though reelection rates in the Brazilian Congress tend to be substantially lower than in the U.S. House of Representatives, electoral incentives and career advancement opportunities drive Brazilian legislators to cultivate local electoral constituencies. In other words, one sees different career goals but similar strategies for individual legislators to develop long and successful careers.

The Mexican Chamber of Deputies differs from the US House of Representatives both in the goals and the strategies of career advancement that individual legislators pursue. In the Mexican Chamber of Deputies, the chances of individual legislators to survive in politics and advance their careers depend primarily on the party's collective reputation. This provides the basis for the development of centralized party organizations, for centralization enables party leaders to protect the collective good shared by all members of the party. In contrast with the conditional party government, in the centralized party government model prevailing in the Mexican Chamber of Deputies, individual legislators preserve very limited autonomy with respect to the party leadership.

Another distinguishing feature of parliamentary fractions in the Mexican Chamber of Deputies is their lack of continuity. Parliamentary fractions are temporary associations. They dismantle at the end of the three-year term as their members are not allowed to run for reelection and are rebuilt from scratch at the beginning of the congressional session. This institutional restriction determines the relationship between the parliamentary fractions and the individual legislators. The authority of parliamentary leaders is constrained by the fact that they also are lame-duck legislators. Their political future may be promising, but it is uncertain. The leaders of the PRI parliamentary fraction are usually promoted to higher offices, such as state governorships, Senate seats, head of department in the federal administration, or high-ranking offices in the national party organization. The leaders of the parliamentary fractions of opposition parties also gain political promotion with regularity after service in the Chamber of Deputies. However, the available office opportunities for opposition parties to reward outgoing parliamentary leaders were limited compared with those of the ruling party.

Given the fact that the political futures of individual legislators lie outside the Chamber of Deputies, the leader of the parliamentary fraction has very little influence on their career prospects. In fact, it is the party organization, acting through the National Executive Committee (CEN), that controls the political future of all members of the parliamentary fraction. Parliamentary fractions operate in practice as agents of their respective CENs. The leaders of the parliamentary fractions are in charge of monitoring and enforcing the agency relationship that individual legislators maintain with the party organization throughout all of the stages of the legislative process within the Chamber of Deputies.

Leaders of parliamentary fractions in the Mexican Chamber of Deputies are primarily responsible to their respective CENs. The CENs have the prerogative to appoint the leaders of the party's parliamentary fractions. In fact, more than parliamentary leaders, the chairs of the parliamentary fractions are appointed party officials charged with protecting the interests of the national party organization. The CEN's prerogative to appoint the chairs of the party's parliamentary fraction is a by-product of its power over the nomination process. The chairs of the parliamentary fractions are pre-selected when the CENs prepare the list of candidates to the Chamber of Deputies. Politicians with the potential to serve as chairs of their party's parliamentary fraction are nominated to safe districts or top positions in the party slate of candidates to multi-member districts.

The role of legislators in selecting the chairs of the parliamentary fractions is in general very limited. The opportunity for legislators to organize parliamentary fractions independently of the CEN is in practice nearly nonexistent. The large majority (around 85% on average) of the members of the Chamber of Deputies have no previous experience serving in this body, and therefore they are not familiar with the complex parliamentary procedures of a 500-member assembly. Furthermore, their prospects of career advancement depend primarily on their connection with the party's CEN. As a consequence, members of the Chamber of Deputies play a merely ratifying role in selecting the leadership of the parliamentary fractions. In fact, the organization of the parliamentary fractions takes place even before the legislators meet for the first time.

The CENs of the parties represented in the Chamber regularly announce the names of the future leaders of the parliamentary fractions some time after the elections and before the new congressional session begins. The process takes place amidst much speculation by the press about possible candidates. Ratification by the members of the parliamentary fraction once the Chamber convenes is not a common practice among all political parties. In the case of the PRI, this formality is regularly obviated. Opposition parties, however, hold parliamentary fraction conventions to ratify the CEN's nomination, as the PAN has done regularly since the 1960s. The PRD's formal procedure to select the leadership of its parliamentary fractions in the Chamber of Deputies has varied substantially ever since this party was founded in 1989. Since 1994, the parliamentary fractions of the PRD have held elections to choose their own leadership. In spite of this procedure, however, the influence of the PRD's CEN in selecting the chair of the parliamentary fraction is overwhelming. Like the PRI, the PRD leaders' influence stems from the fact that the CEN

controls the nomination of party candidates to the Chamber, the lack of
information about the composition of the parliamentary fraction among
incoming legislators, and powerful career incentives to follow the party
line as defined by the CEN.

The PRI differs from opposition parties in another important respect
– it had sole control over the executive branch of government from 1929
to 2000. The regular existence of a PRIista president had a substantial
impact on the organization of the party. It provided an independent source
of leadership for the national party organization that, shortly after the
foundation of the party in 1929, sought to gain control of the CEN (Lajous
1979). In the mid-1930s the president of the Republic finally prevailed
over contending sources of leadership within the party (Garrido 1982).
Ever since, the CEN of the PRI has been subordinated to the federal Chief
Executive. The president of the Republic has been the actual head of the
national party organization with the power to appoint the chair of the
PRI's CEN. Presidential control over the PRI's national party organization transformed the PRI's parliamentary fractions in the Chamber of
Deputies into mere agents of the federal Chief Executive. Due to careful
screening, selection, incentives, and oversight, there was limited agency
slack. In effect, the administration defines the party program, and the
parliamentary fraction passes the legislative changes necessary for that
program to become the policy of the government.

Subordination of the CEN to the president of the Republic has been a
long-standing feature of the PRI organization. It is probably an equilibrium resulting from the enormous patronage resources controlled by the
Chief Executive and the political visibility of the presidential office. The
tendency of the presidential party to prevail over other sources of leadership within the national party organization is not completely exclusive to
the PRI. In opposition parties, once the presidential candidate has been
nominated, the chair of the party's CEN is reduced to a secondary position. Presidential candidates wield substantial leverage in the nomination
of party candidates to other elective offices, including the Chamber of
Deputies, the Senate, and state governorships. CEN chairs gain prominence within their parties as presidential candidates fail to win office. They
replace presidential candidates as the unifying figures within their parties.
Even then, as long as unsuccessful presidential candidates have the potential for a second run, they remain highly influential figures within their
parties, overshadowing the CEN chair.

Parliamentary Parties as Procedural Coalitions

Legislatures are collective decision-making bodies that operate through majority rule. The powers that formally rest with the assembly as a whole are in practice exercised by coalitions of legislators forming majorities on the floor. In analyzing the authority that a majority of legislators can exercise within the legislature it is important to distinguish substantive from procedural powers (Cox and McCubbins 1993; Jones 1968). Legislatures work through two different majorities – substantive majorities passing legislation on the floor, and procedural majorities organizing the legislature for business. Substantive majorities basically wield the law-making authority of the assembly. Procedural majorities are formed at the beginning of the session to capture the power to regulate the process of legislation and fill positions of influence within the Chamber.

In the Mexican Chamber of Deputies, parliamentary fractions coordinate the formation of decision-making majorities as they seek to capture the powers of the body to fulfill their collective goals. When a single party has a majority of seats, it can organize the Chamber for business and administer the process of legislation according to its interests. Single-party majorities have the authority to assign positions of influence such as committee memberships and chairs, as well as the ability to fix the legislative agenda by regulating the flux of bills from committees to the floor. Single-party majorities also translate their procedural power into substantive power as they control the formation of law-making majorities on the floor.

In the absence of a single-party majority, a coalition of parties is necessary to organize the Chamber and pass legislation. Multiparty procedural majorities allocate procedural advantages among members of the coalition. Members of the coalition use their procedural advantages to influence the substance of legislation. However, multiparty procedural majorities do not necessarily cooperate when it comes to passing legislation. Different law-making coalitions can be formed on the floor of the Chamber, even though the same multiparty procedural majority persists throughout the session.

Since parliamentary fractions coordinate decision making, the functioning of the Chamber of Deputies has primarily responded to changes in the partisan balance of power. Over the long-standing political hegemony of the PRI, the Chamber was ruled by a single-party committee – the *Gran Comisión* (GC). Formally, the authority of the GC was that of a committee on committees. Congressional rules endowed the GC with the power to staff standing committees and appoint administrative officials serving in the Chamber.[9] In practice, however, power was concentrated in the chair of the GC, who was, above all else, the leader of the PRI parliamentary fraction.

The GC had no direct involvement in floor activities. Congressional rules provided that the meetings of the Chamber's plenary be chaired by the Directive Board, composed of one chair and a variable number secretariats. The chair of the Directive Board was charged with presiding over floor debates and conducting voting procedures. However, the Directive Board was a rather weak body, as congressional rules have stipulated the monthly renewal of both the chair and the secretariats. In fact, the GC had exclusive authority to submit to the floor the consideration of the bill containing the list of the proposed legislators to fill monthly the rotating positions in the Directive Board. This meant, in practice, that the chair of the Directive Board was an appointee of the GC.

Members of the GC were not responsible to the Chamber's majority. They were elected by state delegations. Congressional rules even provided that, in the case of small state delegations with only two members, the GC representative was picked at random. The GC was not designed to operate as a party committee. Up to 1979, congressional rules did not recognize the existence of parliamentary fractions. However, as the PRI dominated state delegations, all members of the GC were members of a single legislative party. This political fact became more important for members of the GC than their formal link to state delegations. Practice turned into law as the new parliamentary procedures enacted in 1979 (*Ley Orgánica del Congreso de la Unión*) explicitly stipulated that the GC be formed by members of the majority party and chaired by the leader of that party.[10]

The first attempt to regulate the operation of congressional opposition parties came with the enactment of the *Ley Orgánica*, following the introduction of the 1977 electoral reform. It created the figure of

[9] The GC can be traced back to the rules of parliamentary procedure (*Reglamento para el Gobierno Interno del Gobierno Federal*) enacted in 1824. It persisted for more than one and a half centuries even though new parliamentary rules were introduced in 1897, 1934, and 1979. The dissolution of the GC was the result of the absence of a single-party majority in the Chamber after the 1997 elections.

[10] The *Ley Orgánica* of 1979 responded to the changes in the partisan composition of the Chamber brought about by the new electoral legislation introduced in 1977. The 1934 rules of parliamentary procedure (*Reglamento para el Gobierno Interior del Congreso de la Unión*) remained binding, although the *Ley Orgánica* had overruling authority.

"parliamentary fractions" to organize the congressional opposition, which grew in size and number of parties as a result of the introduction of 100 proportional representation seats. The *Ley Orgánica* granted parliamentary fractions a minimum of rights in the law-making process and vaguely defined the responsibility of the governing majority to provide them with offices, staff, and financial resources. The only requirement to form a parliamentary group was a minimum of four legislators, which has allowed tiny delegations of small opposition parties to operate separately as parliamentary groups.

The *Ley Orgánica* of the Congress did not provide any specific role in the process of governance to parliamentary groups. The GC, which began to be regarded as the embodiment of the PRI parliamentary fraction, retained its structure and powers, remaining the traditional governing organ of the Chamber. However, as the parliamentary fractions of opposition parties fought for a role in the activities of the Chamber of Deputies, the practice of government was adjusted. The congressional opposition claimed not only the right to take part in the floor debate, but it also demanded its share in the system of standing committees. Accordingly, floor proceedings and committee assignments regularly required negotiations between the PRI leadership and the parliamentary groups of opposition parties. The exchange of procedural agreements evolved into an increasingly necessary practice to maintain the Chamber in operation.

The expansion of proportional representation seats from 100 to 200 in 1987 brought about an increase in the size of the parliamentary fractions of opposition parties. The pressure to reform the old system of governance based on the GC grew as the PRI suffered a substantial loss of voter support in 1988. The PRI majority in the 54th Legislature (1988–1991) was reduced to only 10 votes, creating enormous difficulties in running the Chamber. The parliamentary fractions of opposition parties gained a position to force changes in parliamentary proceedings by adopting such obstructionist practices as walking out of Chamber meetings and convening apart from the PRI majority.

The 1991 midterm congressional elections returned a larger PRI majority (65 votes). But the Chamber was ripe for reform, and the new PRI leadership made a swift move to change the prevailing governing arrangements, seeking to prevent the radical obstructionism that characterized the 54th Legislature. The PRI leadership put aside the framework provided by the congressional rules. Drawing on the practice of procedural agreements negotiated between the parliamentary parties, the PRI drafted new rules for the operation and governance of the Chamber.

The "parliamentary agreements" of the 55th Legislature were hammered out first by the leaders of all of the parliamentary groups and then approved by unanimity in the plenary. They consisted of a short list of basic rules. The parliamentary agreements, though not having any legal status, provided a new institutional framework for the organization of the Chamber. The central innovation was the constitution of the new *Comisión de Régimen Interno y Concertación Política* (CRICP) – a small committee formed basically by the coordinators of each parliamentary fraction and presided over by the chair of the GC as leader of the majority party.

The CRICP took over the authority as committee on committees formerly resting on the GC. The CRICP preserved the PRI rule of the Chamber of Deputies. The leaders of the PRI presided over the new multiparty governing body, and the most important positions in the Chamber were reserved for the members of the PRI. The PRI still controlled every aspect of the law-making process. The arrangement was devised to gain the procedural collaboration of the opposition parties, without which majority rule could no longer operate. In the long term, the 1991 reform of the Chamber of Deputies provided a new framework for the government of an increasingly multipartisan body.

Nevertheless, despite immediate acceptance of the new parliamentary understanding, the CRICP was from the beginning a poorly defined institution. Its decision-making and voting procedures were not properly spelled out. In principle, the CRICP incorporated the leadership of all parliamentary fractions, but in practice the differences in size among legislative parties were huge, and therefore the vote of each party could not have the same weight. Therefore, the CRICP has had to operate through a system of weighted voting based on the size of the parliamentary fractions as floor majorities can reverse parliamentary agreements.

The 1997 midterm elections had important consequences in terms of the Chamber's governing arrangements. As the PRI lost its majority in the Chamber, the GC, being already reduced to a lesser status with the creation of the CRICP, received its *coup de grâce*. Since no party won the overall majority in the Chamber, the conditions to form the GC were not met. The PRI remained the largest parliamentary fraction, falling only 12 votes short of the overall majority. However, all opposition parties, including the PRD, PAN, the Green Party (PVEM), and the Labor Party (PT), joined together to form a new procedural majority. The coalition was known in journalistic jargon as the G-4.

The main goal of the G-4 was to suppress the procedural advantages that the PRI enjoyed. One of its first decisions was to change the constitution of the CRICP by limiting its membership to the leaders of the five parliamentary fractions, thereby crushing PRI predominance in this body. The G-4 also agreed that the CRICP would be presided over by an annually rotating chair, and that the leaders of the three main parliamentary fractions – PAN, PRD, and PRI – would alternate throughout the three-year session (Paoli Bolio 1997).

The compounded effect of the 1991 reform and the absence of a single-party majority after 1997 was the decentralization of procedural powers from the GC to the parliamentary fractions of all parties represented in the Chamber. As a consequence of the growing multipartisan balance of power, the parliamentary fractions of the opposition parties gained control over the assignment of a number of committee chairs according to their proportion of seats in the Chamber. As the PRI lost its majority in the Chamber, this was reflected in the composition of the standing committees, which in turn deprived the PRI parliamentary fraction of the ability to control committee activities and the flow of legislation to the floor.

Delegation to Committees

The rules governing the process of legislation in the Chamber provide that bills submitted for the consideration of the assembly be referred to committee for study and analysis before they are debated and voted on the floor. Internal procedures allow for exceptions when the Chamber determines that a bill is of "urgent and obvious resolution." However, as the decision to circumvent committees requires a two-thirds majority, normally legislative proposals are not expected to reach the floor unless they have been previously examined and reported on by the relevant committee.

Committees have the power to collect information through hearings and investigations. They are also invested with the authority to draft the actual language of bills and to report legislation to the plenary. Internal procedures also reinforce the role of committees by providing that what is debated and voted on is the bill as reported by committee, not as it was originally introduced in the Chamber. A central feature of committees reporting legislation to the floor is that they are permanent bodies, as their members enjoy security of tenure for the duration of the session. Accordingly, standing committees have jurisdiction over a specific policy area, which can be deduced from their denomination.

Staffing standing committees is perhaps the most important organizational task of the parliamentary fractions. Standing committees had to be formally constituted within the first 15 days after the session begins. Since the 1991 reform, the list of members of all standing committees, including chairs, and secretariats, is drafted by the CRICP and then submitted to the plenary for discussion and approval.[11] The party leaders sitting in the CRICP negotiate party shares of committee slots. By convention, committee slots are allocated according to party share of seats in the plenary. Proportionality, however, is just a rule of thumb. The PRI in the past and the G-4 coalition since 1997 have imposed some form of overrepresentation to guarantee control of decision making at the committee stage.

The 1991 reform of the Chamber also ended PRI monopoly over committee chairs and secretariats. Prior to 1991, the allocation of these positions was a family business sorted out through negotiations within the PRI parliamentary fraction. The practice adopted after the Chamber reform was to assign committee chairs and secretariats to each party in accordance with the size of their parliamentary fraction. This process has led to intense negotiations between party leaders sitting in the CRICP.

Party leaders coordinate the assignment of committee seats, secretariats, and chairs to members of their party delegation. The fact that standing committees, as their parent chamber, are reconstituted from scratch at the beginning of each session provides party leaders with enormous leverage in allocating committee slots. The absence of seniority claims or previous attachments to particular committees among incoming MCDs renders the party contingents in committees mere creatures of the leadership of the day.

Committee assignment discretion has an enormous significance in terms of the ability of standing committees to gain some degree of independence. Where standing committees have evolved into semiautonomous policy-making bodies, as in the U.S. House of Representatives, one of the foundations of this development has been the custom of seniority. Seniority guarantees reassignment to committee members and provides that chairs be given to members with the longest service on each

---

[11] Before the 55th Legislature (1991–1993) this was a prerogative of the GC.

committee (Smith and Deering 1990). Certainly, despite the system of seniority, political parties are able to exert some leverage in the committee assignment process and in the promotion to committee chairs (Cox and McCubbins 1993). Nevertheless, seniority rights operate as a significant institutional constraint on the party leadership.

Under PRI rule there was very little delegation of authority to committees in the Mexican Chamber of Deputies. The PRI leadership had the ability to circumvent committees to expedite the passage of legislation. Congressional rules stipulated that committee reports must have the endorsing signature of all committee members before they were referred back to the floor. When demanded by political expediency, the PRI leadership had the ability to draft committee reports and then circulate them among committee members to collect their signatures. In such cases, the committees did not have to convene at all for bills to be reported back to the floor, and their involvement in the process of legislation was reduced to a mere formality.[12]

It is difficult to say how extended this practice was. Apparently, it became less common as the involvement of opposition parties in committee activities grew. However, PRI contingents on committees worked under the close supervision of the party leadership, which had the capacity to control the timing and content of their reports. With most of the PRI legislation coming from the executive departments, the legislative PRI used Chamber committees as revising bodies (de la Garza 1972; Nacif 1995; Padget 1965). Committees held regular meetings with administrative officials of the executive departments, which had the responsibility of introducing and sponsoring changes of legislation. Amendments to executive bills at the committee stage were not unusual. Committees provided an opportunity to incorporate the requests of interest groups represented in the PRI that executive officials did not take into consideration in previous stages.

The G-4 coalition introduced some changes to the committee system. All committees were to have an equal size of 30 members. Some committees disappeared while new ones were created. The overall number of committees, however, did not change substantially. The number of committee chairs going to the parties forming the G-4 coalition grew. More importantly, the chairs of committees dealing with crucial pieces of legislation,

---

[12] Opposition MCDs used to complain that, as their signatures were not necessary for committee reports to reach the floor, they did not know of bills until these were referred back to the floor for debate (de la Garza 1972).

such as the budget and finance committees, were given to the PRD and PAN, the main parties in the G-4 coalition.

The lack of a single-party majority in the Chamber has rendered the committee stage more significant in terms of the end result of the legislative process. The disciplined endorsement of PRI committee contingents no longer guarantees the flow of legislation from committee to the floor. For bills to be reported back to the floor, the support of a multiparty majority is necessary. Accordingly, the exchange of agreements between parties to build law-making coalitions takes place at the committee stage.

However, the fact that committee reports are necessarily the product of multiparty negotiations does not mean that the independent influence of standing committees on the law-making process has increased. High levels of party discipline pervade all political parties, and basically the committee assignment powers of legislative party leaders remain unrestrained. Committee contingents continue to act as disciplined agents of their political parties. On issues affecting the party reputation, CENs define the parties' position and get directly involved in the negotiation of legislative deals. Committee contingents may contribute to define the party's position, but within the party the CEN takes the decision.

A case in point was President Zedillo's initiative to rescue the banking system, certainly the most controversial piece of legislation passed by the Congress during the second half of his administration. With the PRI 12 seats short of a majority in the Chamber of Deputies, the Zedillo administration had to negotiate its banking rescue program with the opposition parties. In the process, the whole policy was reshaped as several initiatives presented by potential coalition partners in the Chamber were incorporated to the original bill. However, the negotiations took place outside the Chamber itself. When a deal was finally struck between the administration and the PAN, the parliamentary fractions of the PRI and the PAN ratified it in the Chamber of Deputies, first at the committee stage and then on the floor. Despite the fact that legislators from both the PAN and the PRI protested their exclusion from the negotiation, party discipline prevailed on the floor. In the parliamentary fraction of the PAN, 12 out of 122 voted against the party line; in the PRI, only 5 out of 239 defied the leadership. But even the parliamentary fraction of the PRD, which voted against the bill, did not show any sign of independence from its CEN. Shortly after the initiative arrived at the Congress, the president of the PRD's CEN mounted a campaign against the banking rescue operation and issued orders to the parliamentary fraction to keep away from any negotiations with the administration.

Committees can have an independent influence on the process of legislation on nonpartisan policy issues. The conditions for committees to advance independent initiatives are, however, highly demanding. Committee proposals need the backing of a cross-party consensus to reach the floor and can prosper only if they are unopposed by the executive.

Agenda Control and Floor Voting Coalitions

One of the crucial powers that the PRI monopolized as long as it had the majority in the Chamber was the ability to control the traffic of legislation from committees to the plenary and the scheduling of bills on the floor. Formally, congressional rules require committees to report bills back to the floor within five days after committee referral. This restrictive provision, however, has survived only because it has hardly been enforced. In practice, committees operate as gate-keepers in the legislative process. Initiatives that lack the support of the majority are usually withheld indefinitely at the committee stage, a practice known in the journalistic jargon as sending a bill to the *congeladora* (the freezer).

The initiation of bills in the Chamber is a rather open procedure. The Constitution restricts the authority to introduce legislative proposals to the president of the Republic, state legislatures, and MCDs, but congressional rules guarantee committee referral to every bill that comes before the floor. It is within committees that legislative bills are dealt with on political considerations, compensating for the relative openness of the legislative process at its initial stage.

As head of the majority party in the Chamber, the PRI leader was in charge of monitoring bills through the committee system and shepherding them to the floor. The nature of his authority was procedural rather than substantive. He operated as the middleman in the regular interaction between the executive branch, where the leadership of the national party organization resided, and the legislative party. The role of the PRI legislative leader was to keep the parliamentary fraction united around the legislative program of the president and to prevent any interference in the law-making process. In practice, his task was to provide for efficiency in delivering the legislation demanded by the president. The large legislative majorities that the PRI enjoyed regularly, and the complete dependence

Table 9.4. *Agenda control in the Chamber of Deputies under PRI majority: The flow of legislative bills from committees to the floor in the 56th Legislature (1994–1997).*

Source	Referred to committee (#)	(%)	Reported to the floor (#)	(%)	Approved by plenary (#)	(%)	Report rate (%)	Success rate (%)
Executive	84	33.5	83	71.6	83	76.9	98.8	98.8
Financial[a]	12	4.8	12	10.3	12	11.1	100.0	100.0
Other	72	28.7	71	61.2	71	65.7	98.6	98.6
PRI	19	7.6	8	6.9	7	6.5	42.1	36.8
PAN	79	31.5	11	9.5	8	7.4	13.9	10.1
PRD	45	17.9	5	4.3	3	2.8	11.1	6.7
PT	8	3.2	3	2.6	3	2.8	37.5	37.5
State legislatures	2	0.8	2	1.7	1	0.9	100.0	50.0
Independent	12	4.8	2	1.7	2	1.9	16.7	16.7
Other	2	0.8	2	1.7	1	0.9	100.0	50.0
Total	251	100.0	116	100.0	108	100.0	46.2	43.0

[a] This category of bills includes the Federal Budget, the Public Revenue Bill, miscellaneous legislation linked to the Revenue Bill, and the Public Account Bill.
Source: SIID (1997).

of MCDs on the party organization to continue their political careers, made this task relatively easy.

The ability of party leaders to keep their parliamentary fractions together is best assessed by an analysis of roll-call voting (*votaciones por lista nominal*). Unfortunately, there are no records of roll-call voting in the Chamber of Deputies up to March 1998, when the electronic voting system was first introduced. The records produced ever since have not as yet been made available to the public. All that the analyst has to assess the significance of political parties in floor-voting behavior is what happens to a bill once it has been introduced to the Chamber.

Table 9.4 shows data on the process of legislation in the Chamber during the last three years of PRI dominance, coincident with the first half of President Zedillo's administration. The data confirm that opposition parties, especially the PAN and the PRD, took advantage of their ability to initiate legislation; they drafted half of the initiatives introduced to the Chamber. However, most of the bills initiated by opposition parties did not have any real chance to become law. Only a small number of these bills were actually reported to the floor, and the number of bills passed by the Chamber was even smaller.

Committee reports are regularly approved by the plenary. The small difference between bills reported to the floor and bills passed by the Chamber in most cases reflects negative committee reports that the plenary endorsed. A single committee report on a specific piece of legislation might contain negative reports on other initiatives dealing with the same subject.

The control of the PRI majority over the legislative agenda was reflected in the fact that nearly every single bill introduced by the executive made its way from committee to the plenary and was finally passed by the Chamber. Executive bills amounted to 76.9% of the total number of bills passed by the Chamber during the first half of Zedillo's administration. As the president was in practice the head of the PRI, executive departments were in charge of drafting the legislative program of the party. Accordingly, a rough estimate of the PRI's agenda control in the Chamber is the share of bills approved by the plenary of both the executive and PRI legislators taken together, which amounted to 83.4% during the 56th Legislature (1994–1997).

Table 9.4 separates financial bills from other executive initiatives. There are regularly four financial bills: the Budget of the Federal Government, the Public Revenue Bill, miscellaneous changes in legislation linked to the Revenue Bill, and the Public Account Bill. This type of legislation has a special constitutional status. Financial legislation is annually recurring and by constitutional provision can be initiated only by the president of the Republic. In the Chamber, financial bills go through the regular legislative procedure, except that they have to be scheduled according to constitutional deadlines. Nonfinancial executive bills provide a more accurate picture of presidential control over the Chamber's legislative agenda. Table 9.4 shows that even if we take out financial legislation, executive predominance was overwhelming.

PRI legislators were not very active in promoting changes in legislation. They initiated substantially less legislation than the opposition MCDs. The reasons for this pattern of behavior were twofold. On the one side, members of the PRI parliamentary fraction had no political incentives to play an active role as lawmakers competing with executive departments in the policy process. On the other side, MCDs were usually lacking in professionalism and expertise; the president of the Republic could rely on the more resourceful and technically competent administrative departments.

Table 9.4 also shows that more than half of the bills initiated by PRI legislators failed to pass the committee stage. This rate of committee report might seem low given the fact that the PRI had the majority in the Chamber. However, it only implies that the initiatives of individual PRI legislators did not regularly have the backing of the party leadership. In fact, they competed for it. The PRI leadership in the Chamber ensured that legislation reported by the committees was compatible with the agenda and policy goals set up by the president of the Republic.

Because the PRI lost its majority, the 1997 midterm elections had important implications in terms of agenda control in the Chamber. The formation of the G-4 coalition aimed at breaking the long-lasting PRI monopoly over the legislative process in the Chamber. The criteria to organize Chamber activities was no longer the expedient delivery of the legislation demanded by the executive. Instead, the main purpose of the G-4 coalition was to enhance the influence of opposition parties in the legislative process. Although the G-4 coalition had the majority in the Chamber, it was not able to legislate by itself because the PRI still controlled the Senate and the president could veto bills passed by the Congress.[13] However, opposition parties sought to strengthen their negotiating position by capturing procedural advantages in the Chamber.

Opposition parties shared a common goal in preventing a PRI-dominated coalition from gaining the power to organize the Chamber. The new parliamentary organization was to allow opposition parties to push legislation through the Chamber even against the PRI position. A case in point is the initiative to reduce the Value Added Tax (VAT) from 15 to 12.5% in December 1997. All opposition parties backed the VAT reduction bill. The Chamber passed the initiative against the PRI's vote. Subsequently, the PRI majority in the Senate rejected the bill and returned it to the Chamber. The G-4 coalition resorted to the Chamber's right to a second closure in the exchange of motions with the Senate, where the initiative was finally killed.[14] Opposition parties anticipated that the VAT reduction bill would not be enacted, but they used their new power in the Chamber to make their mark on public opinion by blaming the PRI

[13] The Congress can override presidential vetoes by qualified majorities of two-thirds.
[14] By constitutional provision a bill cannot be re-introduced during the same session after the revising Chamber has rejected it for a second time.

for the tough economic measures adopted by the Zedillo administration in 1995.[15]

However, opposition parties did not form the G-4 coalition to deal with the PRI as a single block and legislate by consensus. Opposition parties individually preserved their capacity to negotiate with the PRI to pass specific pieces of legislation. In fact, as the Chamber dealt with the annually recurring financial legislation initiated by the president – the budget and public revenue bills – the G-4 coalition split. The executive hammered out a deal with the PAN leadership to form a winning coalition with the PRI in the Chamber to pass the last three budgets and public revenue bills of the second half of the Zedillo administration.

Since the exchange of agreements between executive departments and opposition parties begins before the president formally initiates legislative proposals, data on the process of legislation does not fully capture the new role of opposition parties in the Chamber. Despite this, Table 9.5 shows that the loss of the PRI majority in 1997 had a substantial impact on the law-making process. The most remarkable change has been the substantial drop in the executive's share in bills reported to the floor and approved by the Chamber. During the first half of the Zedillo administration, 76.9% of the total legislation enacted by the Chamber of Deputies were executive-initiated bills. This figure plunged to 21.9% after the 1997 midterm elections. Now the PAN, an opposition party, equals the executive in its share of bills approved by the Chamber. If we take out financial bills, the executive's contribution to the total legislative output has been only 10.5%, less than that of the two major opposition parties individually. This represents a break with 70 years of presidential control over the law-making process. For the first time since the PRI came into being, the president of the Republic has not been at once both the Chief Executive and the chief legislator.[16]

The drop in executive-initiated legislation did not lead to any significant reduction in the overall legislative output of the Chamber of Deputies. If we take the number of approved bills as an indicator of leg-

---

[15] One of the consequences of the economic crisis set off by the devaluation of the Mexican peso in December 1994 was a substantial drop in tax collection. To correct public finances, President Zedillo sent to the Congress an initiative to increase the VAT from 10 to 15%. Amid widespread discontent in public opinion, the bill was passed by Congress thanks to the disciplined support of the PRI majority.

[16] For a quantitative study of executive dominance over the lawmaking from 1917 to 1940, see Weldon (1997).

Table 9.5. *Agenda control in the Chamber of Deputies without PRI majority: The flow of legislative bills from committees to the floor in the 57th Legislature (1997–2000).*[a]

Source	Referred to Committee (#)	(%)	Reported to the floor (#)	(%)	Approved by plenary (#)	(%)	Report Rate (%)	Success Rate (%)
Executive	29	6.5	25	20.0	23	21.9	86.2	79.3
Financial[b]	13	2.9	13	10.4	11	10.5	100.0	84.6
Other	16	3.6	12	9.6	12	11.4	75.0	75.0
PRI	48	10.8	11	8.8	11	10.5	22.9	22.9
PAN	118	26.6	30	24.0	23	21.9	25.4	19.5
PRD	114	25.7	24	19.2	19	18.1	21.1	16.7
PT	19	4.3	8	6.4	7	6.7	42.1	36.8
PVEM	30	6.8	7	5.6	6	5.7	23.3	20.0
State Legislatures	29	6.5	6	4.8	4	3.8	20.7	13.8
Independent	8	1.8	2	1.6	2	1.9	25.0	25.0
Committees	17	3.8	3	2.4	3	2.9	17.6	17.6
Other	31	7.0	9	7.2	7	6.7	29.0	22.6
Total	443	100.0	125	100.0	105	100.0	28.2	23.7

[a] The data presented in the table refer to bills originated in the Chamber of Deputies from September 1, 1997, to April 26, 2000.
[b] This category includes the Federal Budget, the Public Revenue Bill, miscellaneous legislation linked to the Revenue Bill, and the Public Account Bill.
Source: http://gaceta.cddhcu.gob.mx/

islative production,[17] there is no significant difference between the first and the second halves of the Zedillo administration. The 56th Legislature (1994–1997) approved a total amount of 108 bills, whereas by the time this research was conducted the 57th Legislature (1997–2000) had already passed 105 bills, despite the fact that one and a half months of ordinary session were pending. What prevented the drop in legislative production was a substantial increase in the ability of opposition parties to get their initiatives through the Chamber. As Table 9.5 shows, opposition parties have initiated one out of every two bills approved by the Chamber.

The loss of the PRI majority in the Chamber of Deputies did not produce deadlock in the law-making process as a regular outcome. The success rate of executive-initiated legislation decreased from 98.8% in the first half of the Zedillo administration to 79.3% in the second half. This

[17] The total number of bills passed by the legislature is a poor measure of the legislative production. Bills are counted as though they were equal despite the fact that they differ substantially in extent and significance.

is still a respectable success rate for a president who does not have the majority, one that dispels the image of an obstructionist opposition in the Chamber. However, the fact that the president retained a high success rate during the second half of his administration was achieved at the expense of a substantial drop in the number of bills presented by the executive. Nonfinancial bills initiated by the executive went down from 71 to 16.

Apparently, presidential response to the loss of the PRI's majority was institutionally induced self-restraint and accommodation. The chief executive refrained from initiating legislation when organizing multiparty coalitions was too costly. At the same time, the PRI allowed opposition parties to take a greater part in law making in exchange for their cooperation in passing executive-initiated legislation. In the end, the growth of legislation sponsored by opposition parties could not have been possible without the active support of the PRI majority in the Senate.

Conclusions

The main argument developed in this chapter is that legislators in the Mexican Chamber of Deputies conform to the centralized party government model. The defining characteristic of a centralized party government is that individual legislators have a very small margin of autonomy with respect to the party leadership. As a consequence, the degree of party unity tends to be rather high, with leaders controlling access to resources and opportunities within the legislature. Another crucial aspect of the centralized party government in the Mexican Chamber of Deputies is that party leadership resides outside the legislature, with the head of the national party organization – the National Executive Committee (CEN). Individual legislators have very little say in the election of the chair of the party's parliamentary fraction.

Individual legislators, in fact, act as agents of the national political party that nominated them to office. Once in office, they join the party's parliamentary fraction seeking to gain promotion to positions of influence within the Chamber of Deputies, and to improve their chances of career advancement once the legislature dissolves. The chairs of the party's parliamentary fractions are in charge of monitoring and enforcing the principal–agent relationship between the national party organization and the individual members of the Chamber of Deputies. Their central task is to guarantee that individual legislators cooperate with the advancement of the collective goals of the party as defined by the CEN. The powers of parliamentary party chairs depend on whether the party has a majority status.

Normally, parliamentary party chairs control the assignment of the party's share of committee seats and chairs, and the allocation of resources such as staff. Of course, if the parliamentary fraction has a majority status, the powers of the chair increase substantially. They gain the power to assign the most valuable positions in the legislature and control of the administrative apparatus of the Chamber. But above all, they can regulate the traffic of legislation from committees to the plenary and guarantee party control over the law-making process. A significant consequence of centralized party government in the Chamber is limited delegation of authority to committees. Committee members owe their positions to party parliamentary chairs and lack incentives for specialization and the development of expertise. After all, the Chamber of Deputies is only a temporary station in their political careers.

The structural sources of centralized party government lie in the institutions molding the career strategies of politicians seeking and holding office in the Chamber of Deputies. As are all elected officers in Mexico, legislators are prohibited from running for reelection in consecutive terms. Accordingly, they seek to continue their political careers by moving to other elective offices outside the Chamber, such as state governor, senator, state legislator, and municipal presidencies. However, in seeking political survival, MCDs lack electoral incentives to build an individual reputation separate from that of the party. They depend on the collective reputation of their party to expand the number of office opportunities to which they can realistically aspire. The party reputation is a collective good of paramount importance for individual politicians to lead successful careers.

Centralized party government in the Chamber of Deputies developed during the long-lasting period of single-party dominance. In fact, one of the central institutions underpinning centralization within party parliamentary fractions – the constitutional prohibition of consecutive reelection – was introduced in the early 1930s as part of a strategy to weaken the political links between legislators and local constituencies and concentrate power in the national leadership of the single hegemonic party. However, the development of a more competitive party system has not changed the relationship between individual legislators and their parties. If anything, the growth of opposition parties was accompanied by institutional changes that increased the powers of the national party leaders.

A centralized party government in the Chamber of Deputies has had profound implications in terms of executive–legislative relations in Mexico. As long as the PRI had the majority, it virtually assured the subordination of the Chamber of Deputies to the president of the Republic. Through their control of the party apparatus, the PRI presidents were able to prevent any interference with their legislative program. Neither the members of the PRI parliamentary fraction nor the opposition parties had any significant impact on the final result of the law-making process.

As the PRI lost its majority in the Chamber, the centralized single-party model of government crumbled. However, what emerged after the collapse of PRI rule in the Chamber was not an entirely new model of government. The degree of centralization within parliamentary factions remained unaltered. The subordination of parliamentary factions to the leadership of their national party organization has also persisted. And yet, an important process of dispersion of power from the PRI to the opposition parties took place as a consequence of the 1997 elections. The centralized single party government gave way to a centralized multiparty government in the Chamber of Deputies, as opposition parties became pivotal actors in the law-making process.

A centralized multiparty government in the Chamber transformed executive–legislative relations in Mexico. Despite the fact that President Zedillo had the support of the PRI majority in the Senate and the power to veto bills passed by the Congress, legislative initiatives needed the backing of multiparty majorities in the Chamber to succeed. As a consequence, the capacity of opposition parties to influence the law-making process increased dramatically, breaking the long-lasting dominance of the Chief Executive over the Congress.

PART III

Legislatures and the Policy Process

10

Fiscal Policy Making in the Argentine Legislature*

KENT H. EATON

If political ambition drives politicians, as this volume argues, then legislators should intervene in the policy process in ways that are calculated to advance their careers. In Argentina, due to features of the electoral system that are described in Jones' chapter, the keys to career advancement are held by the leaders of the parties to which legislators belong. In the main, legislators' career prospects are enhanced by toeing the party line on policies endorsed by the national party leadership. However, while Argentine parties are quite disciplined and hierarchically organized around a national political leader, provincial party leaders enjoy substantial autonomy over candidate selection within their own districts.[1] Consequently, in seeking to cultivate ties to both provincial and national party leaders, governing party legislators sometimes face a conflict between the interests of the provinces that they represent and the national party line as it is articulated by the president.[2] To date, scholarship on Argentina has emphasized the extent to which strong national party identities in the legislature undercut

---

* Research for this chapter was supported by the Fulbright Foundation and the Woodrow Wilson International Center for Scholars.
[1] Whether provincial party leaders support the national party leadership is largely a function of factional disputes within the party. Factions typically take shape as provincial party leaders cluster around the various governors jockeying for support as the party's next presidential standard bearer. In President Menem's second term, for example, different brands of intraparty opposition to his leadership were organized by Governors Eduardo Duhalde of Buenos Aires, Néstor Kirchner of Santa Cruz, and Arturo Lafalla of Mendoza.
[2] How individual legislators negotiate this potential conflict depends on their specific career goals, in particular whether they seek to further their careers via other elective or appointive offices at the federal or provincial level. For example, governing party legislators who aspire to appointive offices at the federal level would do well to support the president's policies aggressively in the legislature, while legislators who anticipate running for governor may calculate that a more oppositional stance makes better sense.

legislators' loyalty to their provinces of origin (Frías 1980; Pírez 1986). In contrast, this chapter shows that legislators successfully demanded important changes in the president's fiscal policy proposals in response to some of their provincial concerns. One implication is that the Argentine legislature plays a more relevant though still clearly reactive role than is commonly acknowledged in the literature.

In comparative perspective, since Argentine legislators cultivate relations with both national and provincial party leaders, their electoral incentives combine elements of the Brazilian and Mexican electoral systems. In Brazil, national parties do not exert much influence over legislators' careers, and ambitious legislators instead focus their policy-making efforts on acquiring fiscal benefits for the states that they represent. Despite recent and ongoing changes, the national governing party in Mexico exerts nearly total control over the career prospects of legislators, who consequently face few incentives to defend their states' interests in the legislature. In a sense, Argentina occupies a space between these two extremes: On the one hand, political ambition is generally channeled within disciplined and powerful national parties, yet on the other hand, ambition sometimes encourages legislators to pursue provincial interests in a way that challenges the executive and forces policy compromises.

Fiscal policy making is a particularly interesting arena to explore the implications of this hybrid incentive structure for actual legislative outcomes. When legislators meet to decide who shall pay taxes and how the revenues shall be distributed among the different provinces that serve as their electoral districts, the potential for conflict between their ties to national and provincial party leaders often becomes explicit. Conflict over the incidence of taxation and the distribution of fiscal revenues has a lengthy history in Argentina, serving as one of the critical issues that pitted unitarians against federalists in the long nineteenth century. More recently, the issue gained renewed salience during Carlos Menem's first term as president (1989–1995), during which period Argentina experienced a fundamental transformation in its public finances. Politicians redesigned both the structure of taxation and the distribution of tax revenues between the federal government and the provinces (Eaton, forthcoming). With respect to the tax structure, Menem proposed and the legislature approved a shift away from narrow tax bases and complicated rate schedules toward a simpler system centered on a few broadly based taxes, principally the Value Added Tax (VAT). These changes in tax policy played a central role in Argentina's striking transition from hyperinflation to macroeconomic stability. As a result of such changes, tax revenues increased from 14.7% of the GDP in 1989 to 19.4% in 1994.[3] Given the institution of revenue sharing with the provinces begun in 1935, this surge in tax revenues automatically increased the size of fiscal transfers to the provinces. Once tax reform was in place, however, Menem successfully negotiated a series of measures that reduced the provinces' legal shares in tax revenue.

While the executive branch initiated these changes and served as the main protagonist of fiscal reform, a full explanation of policy change must address the role played by legislators from the governing Peronist party. In general, Peronist legislators supported these reforms because delivering fiscal stability was critical for the success of Peronism as a governing party and thus valuable to individual Peronist legislators. Despite this general support, however, legislators were sometimes successful in insisting on modifications to benefit their provinces, several of which I discuss in this chapter. Evidence of substantive policy compromises and interbranch bargaining is important because it suggests the need to temper conclusions about congressional subservience and hyperpresidentialism in Argentina.

In addition to analyzing the content of legislators' participation in policy making, this chapter argues that the president and Peronist party leaders enjoyed important procedural advantages in the assembly in getting these fiscal reforms legislated. This supports the point in Cox and Morgenstern's concluding chapter that, in contrast to U.S. presidentialism, Latin American systems are characterized both by greater presidential control over the legislature's internal agenda and by greater integration between the executive and legislative branches of the party. Since 1990, President Menem has served as president of a party that held a comfortable majority in the Senate and until 1997 a near majority (or better) in the lower chamber.[4] In practice, these majorities enabled the president to control each chamber's presidency. Shortly after Menem's election, legislators from the

---

[3] While some of this increase is due to the onset of macroeconomic stability after 1990, much of it is due to a shift in legislation toward broader tax bases and fewer tax rates. In their econometric model, Durán and Gómez Sabaini (1995) estimate that 50% of the increase in VAT revenues, now the most important tax in terms of revenue generated, is due to base broadening, 25% due to higher rates, and 25% due to macroeconomic stability. The figures for tax revenue come from Taachi (1995, p. 881).

[4] In the critical legislative session of 1989–1991, there were 120 Peronist deputies, 8 short of a majority (there were 254 deputies in that session). Alliances with the Unión del Centro Democrático (Ucedé), with its 11 members, gave the Peronists a working majority on the most controversial economic reforms.

"menemista" wing of the party were elected to preside over each chamber – Alberto Pierri in the lower Chamber, thanks to an alliance with minor opposition parties, and the president's brother Eduardo Menem in the Senate.[5] These individuals enjoyed considerable leeway in organizing the business of Congress via agenda-setting and floor-voting procedures. Since the fiscal reforms proposed by Menem represented a fundamental break with past policies and provoked some dissension within the party, the procedural prerogatives of the Chamber presidents were often important in limiting the scope of congressional amendments.

Through his status as president of the party, Menem also enjoyed significant though not unlimited authority over the individuals who led the Peronist delegation of legislators in each chamber. In the lower chamber, José Luis Manzano of Mendoza province initially served as head of the Peronists and was later replaced by Jorge Rubén Matzkin of La Pampa province.[6] Like Pierri and Eduardo Menem, the careers of both were closely tied to the success of Carlos Menem as president. After completing their service as head of the Peronist delegation, each was rewarded for his efforts on behalf of the president with a high-level position in the Interior Ministry – Manzano as Minister and Matzkin as Vice Minister. In the Senate, Alberto Rodríguez Saá of San Luis province was elected head of the Peronist block. As a Senator who entertained presidential ambitions of his own, Rodríguez Saá was generally less supportive of Menem's agenda than Manzano and Matzkin in the lower chamber and embraced a somewhat stronger stance in defense of the provinces.[7] For the most part, Peronist Chamber presidents and legislative party leaders served Menem well by employing the many procedural prerogatives that came with the party's majority status.

---

[5] In Argentina, while the vice president serves automatically as president of the Senate, the Senate elects one senator to serve as provisional president, and this individual effectively leads the body.

[6] Although both had been allied earlier with the "renewalist" wing of the party that supported Antonio Cafiero over Menem in the 1988 Peronist presidential primary, each became an important advocate of Menem's economic agenda in office.

[7] Rodríguez Saá was one of only two Peronist senators who in 1993 voted against Menem's proposed revision of the constitution to allow presidential reelection. He then left the party and retired from politics in 1994, only to reenter political life in 1997 by founding a provincial opposition party, the Partido Unión y Libertad. Thus, while opposition to Menem undermined Rodríguez Saá's future within the Peronist Party, it did not terminate his political prospects in San Luis province, where he subsequently emerged as a front runner in the 1998 gubernatorial race.

This chapter is made up of the following four sections. First, I present the most salient features of Argentina's fiscal structure before the initiation of reform in 1989 and discuss revenue-sharing procedures between the federal and provincial governments. This background helps to make sense in the second section of the political goals that Menem pursued by proposing tax reform. In the third section, I focus on legislative committees as sites where legislators may breach party discipline in response to their provincial concerns. The fourth section discusses three different floor votes to illustrate how leaders of the Peronist party exercised their authority over internal assembly procedures.

Argentina's Fiscal Structure Before Reform

Understanding the political stakes associated with fiscal reforms in the 1990s requires first evaluating the fiscal system that Menem and the Peronist-controlled legislature inherited in 1989.

Narrow Tax Bases, Special Tax Rates, and Poor Tax Collection

As is the case with many late industrializers, policy makers in Argentina have been aggressive in their use of the tax system to fulfill a variety of purposes other than simply generating revenue. These multiple purposes included industrial promotion, income redistribution, regional development, and, more generally, the construction of political support coalitions. During Argentina's experience with import substituting industrialization (ISI), federal tax incentives were granted to promote certain types of expenditure, sectoral categories, and, finally, geographic locations as well.[8] Through scores of laws, decrees, and regulations, promoted companies and those who invested in them received deductions, deferrals, and partial or total exemption from income, trade, and general sales taxes. Successive democratic and military governments added fresh tax breaks in line with their particular economic and political objectives.

Loading up the tax system with a variety of different incentives made it very difficult for the tax collecting agency (the *Dirección General Impositiva* or DGI) to administer them. Tax bureaucrats adapted by spreading their resources thinly, rather than focusing on the application of simple,

---

[8] For the details of these different incentive programs, see Azpiazu and Basualdo (1990), López Murphy et al. (1981), and Macón (1985).

broad-based taxes that are levied at only a few different rates. In addition to the difficulty of monitoring a tax structure that was riddled with special rates and exceptions, the content of these exceptions was subject to a great deal of volatility. As governments with very different ideological orientations and political support bases alternated in power through short and recurring cycles of coups and elections, tax bureaucrats were required constantly to learn and implement new rules. Political instability served to shorten the tenure of the directors-general, who ran the DGI and increased the need to appoint individuals who could bring political support to the administration, whether or not they could bring the appropriate technical background to the position.[9]

Whatever the changing rationale for the use of tax breaks, their cumulative effect was to narrow the bases of modern consumption and income taxes and to complicate the tax system. According to the World Bank, by 1987 virtually all investment activity was subsidized through the tax system at a cost approaching 3% of the GDP.[10] Narrow bases and complicated rate schedules created an enormous scope for collusion between evaders and corrupt tax collectors. In a vicious cycle, anemic revenues forced policy makers to further complicate the tax system by legislating emergency, ad hoc tax handles to close the fiscal gap. Narrow tax bases and complicated rate schedules were thus implicated in some of Argentina's most entrenched economic problems in the ISI era: chronic budget deficits, heavy government debt, and high inflation. By the late 1980s, individually rational attempts to avoid or evade taxes had seriously undermined collective welfare by triggering hyperinflationary episodes that brought economic activity to a virtual standstill.

Tax Revenue Sharing Between the Federal and Provincial Governments

Beginning in 1935, the Argentine provinces delegated to the federal government exclusive authority to determine and collect taxes that the Constitution had either reserved for provinces (such as direct taxes) or jointly assigned to both federal and provincial governments (such as nontrade, indirect taxes). Using criteria that national legislators legislate, the federal treasury then automatically divides the revenues that it collects from these

[9] Raúl Cuello (1996), and personal interview, August 15, 1996.
[10] World Bank 1993, p. 39.

taxes between the federal government and the provincial governments. In contrast, proceeds from trade taxes, the inflation tax, and a few other special taxes are not shared automatically with the provinces. Although widely criticized as an arrangement that has undermined Argentine federalism, provincial politicians supported this system of centralized collection and automatic revenue sharing as a solution to the serious problems of double taxation and base migration experienced by the provinces before 1935.[11]

Under democratic periods of government, representatives to the national legislature have sought to defend the interests of their provinces in the revenue-sharing system. In particular, it is striking to observe how the provinces' share of revenues relative to the federal government's has been repeatedly ratcheted up under successive democratic governments (from 17% to 21% in 1946, 34% in 1959, 42% in 1963, 48.5% in 1973, and 57.8% in 1988) and frozen or reduced under military government, precisely when congressional checks were inoperative (Nuñez Minana and Porto 1982, 1983; Eaton 2001b). As successive electoral laws have increasingly overrepresented the poorer and sparsely populated provinces in the Chamber of Deputies, the criteria selected by legislators to divide up tax revenues among the provinces have become increasingly redistributive (Porto 1990). As Table 10.1 shows, the criteria endorsed in the latest (1988) Revenue-Sharing Law clearly favor the nonadvanced provinces, many of which are very important to the Peronist party in electoral terms. During the legislative session of 1989–1991 that approved Menem's centerpiece value added tax reform, a great majority of Peronist senators (92.6%) and a slight majority of Peronist deputies (50.5%) represented these nonadvanced provinces. For these legislators, endorsing Menem's proposed shift away from trade and inflation taxes toward a broadly based consumption tax pleased the national party leadership and furthered provincial interests as well. For Peronist legislators from the advanced provinces, the vote was more complex. On the one hand, supporting the shift toward taxes that are shared with the provinces would increase the absolute size of fiscal transfers to their own provinces. On the other hand, in the absence of changes that would make revenue sharing less redistributive, a vote for tax reform would also effectively increase fiscal

[11] For an analysis of the risks and opportunities posed by delegation, see Kiewiet and McCubbins (1991).

Table 10.1. *Provincial shares of population, product, and revenue transfers versus the electoral importance of the provinces to the Peronist Party.*[a]

	Provincial Share of Total Population	Provincial Share of Gross Provincial Product (GPP)	Provincial Share of Federal Revenue Transfers (1988 Law)	# and % of Total Peronist Deputies from each Province (1989–1991)	# and % of Total Peronist Senators from each Province (1989–1991)
Type of Province	100	100	100	115 (100%)	27 (100%)
Advanced	67.4	71.1	44.03	57 (49.5%)	2 (7.4%)
Buenos Aires	43.6	42.4	22.00	35 (30.4%)	0
Córdoba	9.4	10.1	8.90	8 (6.9%)	0
Mendoza	4.8	5.8	4.18	4 (3.5%)	0
Santa Fé	9.6	12.8	8.95	10 (8.7%)	2 (7.4%)
Nonadvanced	32.6	28.9	55.97	58 (50.5%)	25 (92.6%)
Low Density	5.2	7.8	9.3	13 (11.3%)	6 (22.2%)
Intermediate	12.8	11.4	19.17	18 (15.7%)	8 (29.6%)
Underdeveloped	14.6	9.7	27.50	27 (23.5%)	11 (40.8%)

[a] Population figures are based on 1985 data, GPP data based on 1980 figures, and data on Peronist seats are based on the 1989–1991 legislative session. I have not included representatives from the federal capital in these calculations because revenues for the capital come from the federal government's share in tax revenues and I am concerned here with how the provincial share in tax revenues is divided up between individual provinces.
Source: República Argentina, *Cámara de Diputados: Su Composición y Comisiones* (1989) and World Bank (1990, p. 24).

subsidies for other provinces at the expense of their own, more advanced provinces.[12]

Although automatic revenue sharing bolstered support in the legislature for the tax reforms that Menem proposed, it also presented him with a variety of economic and political problems. For example, automatic revenue transfers to the provinces threatened macroeconomic stability at the national level and fiscally independent governors threatened the president's ability to condition aid to the provinces on political support for his agenda. To maintain macrostability and to preserve political power, then, the president proposed a series of changes that increased his discretion

---

[12] To rectify the particularly disadvantageous position of Buenos Aires province in the distribution of tax revenues, in March 1992 the national legislature approved a special fund for Metropolitan Buenos Aires (*fondo del conurbano*) that set aside 10% of the income tax revenues for Buenos Aires before tax revenues were divided up among the provinces.

over revenue transfers. The principal instruments used to substitute discretion for rule-based transfers were the two fiscal pacts that Menem negotiated with the provinces in 1992 and 1993. The net effect of these pacts was to link revenue transfers to progress by the provincial governments toward a series of federally defined economic reforms. Menem strategically used side payments to build support among the governors for these pacts and then presented them to the legislature as *faits accomplis* (Eaton 2001a). In contrast to the governors' acquiescence to the fiscal pacts, however, the record suggests that legislators were more successful in holding Menem to the letter of the law, stipulating a broad set of taxes to be distributed automatically with the provinces. In many of the policy episodes discussed in the following, the executive branch proposed reserving for the federal government revenues that would be produced by changes in tax bases and rates. Peronist legislators responded by agreeing to some of these changes in tax bases and rates in exchange for modifications that explicitly increased provincial shares in the proceeds.

The Proposal Stage: Menem as Tax Policy Entrepreneur

Proposals for the transformation of Argentina's tax structure clearly originated and took shape in the executive branch, reflecting Menem's pronounced need to achieve fiscal stability and the legislature's generally weak capacity in the area of economic analysis and revenue forecasting. When chief executives are elected in the dire fiscal circumstances that prevailed in Argentina in 1989, whether they are motivated by reelection or more programmatic policy agendas, increasing tax revenues is a necessity. Menem's successful attempt in 1994 to change the constitutional limit of one presidential term attests to his great interest in reelection upon taking office in 1989, particularly given the political capital and substantive compromises that this change required on his part.[13] Menem's reelection prospects depended largely on his ability to deliver macroeconomic stability, a collective good that he, as the only politician elected in the nationwide electoral district (via an electoral college), was uniquely poised to

---

[13] In exchange for agreeing to support the reform of the Constitution to allow presidential reelection, the opposition Radical Party exacted a number of important changes designed to limit presidential power and strengthen the legislative branch. Subsequent to the 1994 reform, however, the Peronist-dominated legislature proved slow to pass the enabling laws that would put into effect a number of these changes.

provide. Thus Menem's reelection depended on fiscal stability, which in turn depended on comprehensive tax reform: broadening tax bases, flattening tax rates, and improving tax collection in a marked shift away from the particularism that had characterized Argentina's ISI-era tax structure.

If Menem's election in a national electoral district amidst fiscal crisis explains his role as a protagonist of sweeping tax reform, international and interest group pressures help to explain his decision to focus on the Value Added Tax as its most important component. International pressures to emphasize consumption taxes came in indirect and direct forms. Indirectly, the globalization of capital markets since the 1970s has encouraged governments to compete for investments by lowering income tax rates while relying more heavily on consumption taxes. More directly, Vito Tanzi, the Director of the Fiscal Department of the IMF, played a critical role in pushing the VAT as opposed to a traditional, turnover sales tax, participating in early executive branch meetings to this effect.[14]

With respect to domestic interest group pressures, Menem's need to shore up support among agricultural interests, which were traditionally antagonistic toward Peronism, ruled out a significant role for export taxes. The agricultural sector proposed a general VAT rate of 15%, with a special rate of 5% for newly included goods and exemptions for agricultural products at the first stage of production. The principal industrial lobby, *Unión Industrial Argentina*, resisted these special exemptions while Bunge y Born, the powerful multinational to which Menem's then economy minister belonged, advocated a turnover tax instead of the VAT.[15] Menem skillfully mediated these pressures by agreeing to a lower but single VAT rate of 13% in exchange for a broader base that included agricultural goods. After insisting first on a broad base, Menem was then successful in gradually increasing the VAT rate to 15.6% in November 1990, 16% in February 1991, 18% in August 1991, and 21% in March 1995.

Apart from transforming the VAT into Argentina's main revenue generator, Menem and his top economic advisors also proposed eliminating many of the emergency, ad hoc taxes that had been legislated over the

---

[14] For a description of these indirect pressures, see Tanzi (1995). For a description of Tanzi's direct role, see *Clarín*, October 14, 1989, and *Página 12*, September 20, 1989.

[15] In 1989, Néstor Rapanelli was picked from among the top officials at Bunge y Born to serve as Menem's economy minister as a symbol of the president's commitment to the sort of liberal economic reforms that such multinationals had long advocated. Nevertheless, as economy minister, Rapanelli supported the VAT reform despite the vigorous opposition of Bunge y Born.

years. Repealing taxes on items like debt instruments, stamps, and equity transfers promised to make the tax system more efficient, less intrusive in the investment decisions of economic actors, and easier to administer. Despite this general goal, however, Menem continued to rely heavily on tax handles and excise taxes for revenue because it took a number of years for the VAT to become fully established. For example, the tax on minimum assets was proposed and legislated in 1989 as a measure that would guarantee contributions from corporations that had successfully avoided or evaded income tax liability. Finally, in addition to gradually eliminating tax handles, a high-level panel of experts met to study tax reform in August and September 1989 and recommended a series of organizational changes in the tax collecting bureaucracy. Composed of past directors-general of the DGI, the panel proposed endowing the tax collecting side of the Finance Secretariat with greater institutional autonomy from its expenditure side.[16]

Once the president decided on the general contours of tax reform, he faced a series of strategic choices over how to transform these proposals into actual pieces of legislation. Most importantly, he could either pursue statute changes in the legislature or attempt to legislate his reforms by issuing what are known as Necessary and Urgent Decrees (DNUs). In their study of these decrees in Menem's first term, Ferreira Rubio and Goretti find that the largest number of DNUs issued by the president in fact pertained to tax policy, and they conclude that "the government used taxation by DNUs as a means to redirect economic policy fundamentally."[17] At the same time, many of the most important and controversial fiscal reforms, such as the broadening of the VAT base, were passed by the legislature. Despite his use and abuse of decrees, Menem often found statute changes attractive because they would make future reversals of his policies harder to effect (Corrales 1997). Menem enjoyed enough support in the assembly to believe that it would legislate his reforms essentially intact, though in many cases his preference for statute changes required him to accept some congressional modifications in favor of the provinces. As a further counterweight to the emphasis often given to Menem's decrees, the decision to decree a policy did not always protect the president

---

[16] This panel was headed by Raúl Cuello, who became the first Secretary of Public Revenues, and included former Directors-General Krieger Vasena, Petrei, Massat, and Malacorto.

[17] 22% of the DNUs issued between July 1989 and December 1993 (69 out of a total of 308) concerned tax policy. See Ferreira Rubio and Goretti (1998).

from the input of legislators, even though the legislature failed to act on most DNUs.[18] A case in point is the legislature's modification of a decree establishing the solidarity tax discussed in the following.

When Menem decided to pursue a statute change, he subsequently had to decide whether to submit the bill to the upper or lower chamber. His strategic choices in this regard reflect this volume's larger point about the institutional determinance of policy outcomes. Menem's tax bills were usually introduced into the lower chamber, which the Constitution identifies as the chamber of origin for tax legislation. Since much of the early economic emergency legislation took the form of omnibus bills that combined tax and nontax content, however, identifying the appropriate Chamber of origin was often a matter of some controversy.[19] Some tax reform proposals were introduced in the Senate, where the Peronist party had a higher share of seats throughout Menem's first term as president. This is important since the chamber of origin has procedural advantages over the chamber of revision, which needs to muster a two-thirds majority to insist on its version of a bill in the event that the chambers pass different versions.[20]

Fiscal Policy Making in Congressional Committees

Each year, before the legislature opens its regular session, a preparatory session is held to elect each chamber's president and vice presidents.[21] Subsequently, the leaders of each party block name individual legislators

---

[18] As Ferreira Rubio and Goretti acknowledge, many of these DNUs conformed to rather than clashed with the policy preferences of the Peronist legislators.

[19] The Economic Emergency Law of September 1989 was introduced in the Senate even though it included important changes in tax policy, including the suspension of tax incentives. Although the Radical-dominated lower chamber had agreed not to obstruct Menem's policies when he took office six months ahead of schedule, Menem saw the Senate as a more attractive chamber of origin due to the Peronist majority there.

[20] The chamber of origin only needs a simple majority to defend its version of the bill against the revising chamber. In a few cases, when the Senate intruded on the deputies' constitutional prerogative by initiating tax legislation, the deputies responded by vetoing the legislation. For example, when the Senate revised the social security bill passed by the deputies in 1991, it incorporated several new changes to the administrative procedures regulating tax collection, which the lower chamber refused to approve despite substantive support by Peronist deputies for the measures. See *Diario de Sesiones de la Cámara de Diputados de la Nación*, July 31/August 1, 1991, pp. 2029–2045.

[21] If no election is held, the chamber's president from the previous session continues in the position.

to specific committees. Seniority plays little role in these assignments, due to the high turnover among the legislators, and the provincial delegations of each party compete for spots on the most important committees. Alhough the rules of each chamber stipulate that committee members themselves elect the committee chair, in practice it is the party block that decides which of its members will chair the committees that the party controls.[22] During Menem's first term, Peronist legislators chaired the two most important committees for fiscal policy: the Finance and Budget Committee in the lower chamber and the Budget Committee in the Senate.[23] These committee chairs enjoy important procedural advantages on the floor of each chamber.

Once legislators are named to committees, they generally face few incentives to become policy experts due to low reelection rates in Argentina. While committees tend to be underfunded, understaffed, and unable to initiate complicated fiscal bills on their own, the record discussed in the following suggests that membership on the Budget Committee can be a valuable resource for legislators who are interested in producing tangible benefits for their provinces. In discussing tax bills proposed by the president, committee members from the governing party did not enjoy a great deal of autonomy from party leaders but nevertheless could at times use their membership either to improve the provincial share in tax revenues or to lessen the impact of harmful measures on their provinces. Despite the fact that Menem often used his partial veto power to undercut deals made in the legislature by Peronist legislators (Mustapic and Ferretti 1995), most of the modifications designed to defend provincial finances were in fact not vetoed.

During the regular session that begins once all committee assignments are made, the chamber president meets once a week with the heads of all of the party blocks to decide scheduling matters, including which committees should treat which bills.[24] Although this is usually very straightforward, a chamber president who opposes a bill can slow it down

---

[22] Articles 106 and 107 of the *Reglamento del Honorable Senado de la Nación*.

[23] Jorge Matzkin initially served as chair of the Deputies Budget and Finance Committee (*presupuesto y hacienda*). When Matzkin became head of the Peronist party block, Oscar Lamberto of Santa Fé province gave up his chairmanship of the Banking Committee (*finanzas*) to take over the Budget and Finance Committee, reflecting its high status in the hierarchy of committees. In the Senate, Alberto Rodríguez Saá served as head of the Budget Committee.

[24] They meet in the Parliamentary Labor Plenary (*Plenario de Labor Parlamentaria*).

considerably and potentially alter its content by maximizing the number of committees asked to report on the bill. Once a committee receives a bill, committee members who belong to the governing party write a majority report (*dictamen de mayoría*), with their individual names appearing at the end of the report, while members of the opposition party write and sign a dissenting report (*dictamen de minoría*).[25]

While committees are the places where legislators can participate in the legislative process in the most detailed way, for some of the more important fiscal reforms in recent years congressional committees played no formal role in the legislative process. This is because two-thirds of the legislators present in any given session can vote to bypass the committee stage entirely and base plenary discussions on the president's proposed bill (*sobre tablas*), in which case the Chamber as a whole is said to convert itself into a committee. For example, at the request of party leaders and over the opposition of the Radical Party, Peronist legislators voted in September 1989 to skip over the committee stage and discuss Menem's VAT reform proposal directly. Using the president's proposed bill as the basis for discussion expedited the reform and enabled Menem to set the parameters for debate on his centerpiece fiscal reform.

Not all attempts by Peronist party leaders to bypass the committee stage succeeded, however. In September 1989, party leaders tried a similar maneuver to expedite the discussion of reforms that would improve the bureaucratic implementation of the new tax policies. Specifically, Menem proposed making tax evasion an offense punishable by prison and thus subject to the penal code. The reform received a great deal of attention in the press and legislators insisted on studying the bill in committee first. Ultimately, Peronist legislators voted stiff increases in penalties for tax evasion but denied the president's request to give evaders mandatory prison sentences.[26] In the following paragraphs, I discuss three other cases in which the Peronist members of the Budget Committees of both cham-

---

[25] Any individual legislator on the committee can also partially dissent from the majority or minority report. Since floor votes are not recorded unless legislators agree to vote nominally, these signatures on committee reports can serve as an indicator of whether bills received support from both main parties. This is the device used by Mustapic and Goretti (1992) in their analysis of the cross-party alliances common under the Alfonsín administration.

[26] According to a high-level official in the Economic Ministry, politicians were worried that the backlash produced by throwing "all of Buenos Aires in prison" would have undermined the effort to crack down on tax evasion. Personal interview, August 7, 1996.

bers made substantive changes to the fiscal bills proposed by the president. These cases are representative of a basic dynamic at play in fiscal policy: In each, the committees exacted benefits for the provinces in exchange for legislative support for changes in tax policy.

The Economic Emergency Law

The economic emergency law of September 1989, together with the reform of the state law of August 1989, were central to Menem's attempt to stabilize the economic crisis that he inherited from the previous administration on taking office five months ahead of schedule in July 1989. The Senate was the first to discuss the economic emergency bill, which included a variety of topics including foreign investment rules, Central Bank autonomy, and budget cuts.[27] An important component of this omnibus bill was the suspension of tax incentives for investment in four special provinces that had been granted under Argentina's industrial promotion laws. These incentives had come to represent huge fiscal losses for the national treasury as scores of companies either relocated part of their business to these provinces or, more commonly, did so on paper. The president originally proposed terminating 100% of the tax benefits granted to enterprises located in the provinces of Catamarca, La Rioja, San Juan, and San Luis. Peronist senators on the Budget Committee were able to successfully modify this proposal. Rather than terminate benefits, these senators reported a bill in which these benefits would be suspended for a six-month period of time, reserving for the president the right to extend this for another six months. In addition, the committee reduced the scope of the suspension to only 50% of the benefits rather than 100%, as Menem had requested. Significantly, a disproportionately high percentage of senators on this committee (3 out of 11) represented one of the affected provinces.[28] In addition, one of these Senators, Rodríguez Saá, was then serving as head of the Peronist block in the Senate and chair of the Budget

---

[27] This omnibus bill was promulgated as Law 23,697.

[28] These were Horacio Bravo Herrera from San Juan, and Oraldo Britos and Alberto Rodríquez Saá from San Luis. While 27% of the members of the Budget and Finance Committee were from one of these provinces, senators from these four provinces represent only 17% of the total number of senators. Furthermore, two of the three Budget Committee members were senators from the province (San Luis) that had been most aggressive in granting tax incentives. *Diario de Sesiones de la Cámara de Senadores de la Nación*, August 8/9, 1989, pp. 1468 and 1520.

Committee. In exchange for these modifications, which effectively benefited the four special provinces at the expense of the other provinces, the
committee approved the other important parts of the bill, including a liberalization of the foreign investment code that proved even more radical
than changes undertaken by Economic Minister Martínez de Hoz during
Argentina's military government of 1976–1983.

Legislating the Solidarity Tax

As one of his first attempts to tackle the fiscal chaos he inherited from the
previous government, in August 1989 President Menem decreed the so-
called solidarity tax of between .5% and 2% on income earned by a large
number of companies in the hyperinflationary environment of 1988.[29]
Although many, including the ranking Radical member of the Deputies'
Budget and Finance Committee, considered this evidence of the president's
unconstitutional protagonism in tax policy, the legislature ratified this tax
in September 1989, though not without making important changes that
benefited the provinces. In the version of the bill decreed by the president
and approved by the Chamber of Deputies, 93% of the revenues produced
from this tax would go to the Ministry of Health and Social Action, with
7% set aside for social emergencies in the provinces. These provincial funds
would be divided according to an index that ranks the provinces according
to their levels of basic unsatisfied needs (*necesidades básicas insatisfechas*). This
meant that 93% of the revenues produced by this tax would be distributed
at the discretion of the national executive through his health minister.

Led by Rodríguez Saá, the Peronist-dominated Senate Budget Committee fundamentally reworked the rules that would be used to distribute
revenues from this tax. The committee proposed channeling 99% of the
proceeds from the tax to a National Solidarity Fund that would in turn
automatically distribute the revenues between the national and provincial
governments according to transparent criteria established in the 1988
Revenue Sharing Law. This meant that 57% would go to the provinces,
42% to the nation, and only 1% (as opposed to 93%) would be subject to
discretionary executive branch transfers.[30]

---

[29] Decree 400/89, *Boletín Oficial*, August 4, 1989, p. 4. This was passed as Law 23,740.
[30] The committee further altered the bill to specify that, with its share of the revenues from
this tax, the federal government would be responsible for issuing "solidarity bonds" in the
federal capital and the then national territory of Tierra del Fuego. See *Diario de Sesiones
de la Cámara de Senadores de la Nación*, September 27, 1989, pp. 2578, 2584, 2585.

In addition to making transfers automatic, the Senate Budget Committee also modified the criteria approved by the lower chamber to distribute revenues from the solidarity tax among the provinces. Reflecting the fact that a majority of deputies represent one of the four industrially advanced provinces where poverty is highly concentrated, the lower chamber favored the use of the basic unsatisfied needs index, because this index would translate into larger transfers. In contrast, the great majority of senators represented the nonadvanced provinces. Thus, the Senate Budget Committee voted to divvy up revenues from the solidarity tax by using the criteria of the 1988 Revenue Sharing Law, which favors the nonadvanced provinces at the expense of the advanced ones.[31] Although the Senate was the chamber of revision for this bill, it was able to muster the two-thirds majority necessary to insist on its version of the bill since 36 of the 46 senators (78%) represented nonadvanced provinces.

Distributing Revenues from Excise Taxes

As a stop-gap measure to close the fiscal deficit in December 1989, Menem proposed replacing taxes on net wealth and capital gains (*beneficios eventuales*) with a tax on minimum assets of 1%. According to this new tax handle, all enterprises, regardless of size and profit levels, would pay a tax equivalent to 1% of their assets.[32] In addition to the minimum assets tax, the bill modified various excise taxes and established emergency taxes on cars, yachts, and financial services and entities. While the Budget and Finance Committee of the lower chamber approved the minimum assets tax exactly as proposed by Menem, it introduced significant changes to the distribution of revenues from excise taxes. For example, the committee changed the distribution of revenues from the tax on tires, though not its rate, which the executive proposed at 27%. In the executive's proposal, 4% of this 27% would be automatically shared with the provinces, and 23%

---

[31] On the floor of the Senate, legislators from the sparsely populated but electorally over-represented Patagonian provinces were particularly hostile to the basic needs index. These provinces fare poorly under the index due to their relatively high per-capita GDP. As Senator Solari Yrigoyen from the province of Chubut remarked, the basic needs index harms Patagonian provinces by not considering distances, harsh climate, and lack of communication. Opposition to this shift by Senator Gass from Buenos Aires province can be understood in light of the fact that, given the concentration of poor households in Buenos Aires, the province would fare better under the basic needs criteria. Ibid., p. 2578.

[32] This measure was passed as Law 23,760.

would be channeled to the National Highway Fund to be distributed at the discretion of the chief executive. The committee changed this distribution so that all of the revenues from the tax on tires would be shared with the provinces according to criteria established in the 1988 Revenue Sharing Law, as would the revenues produced by the tax on lubricant oils. Although seemingly minor, these changes were important for provinces given that the tire tax alone produced an estimated $200 million per year.[33]

The committee also modified the distribution of fuel tax revenues, though this was later vetoed by Menem.[34] In the president's proposal, revenues from the fuel tax in excess of a fixed sum would be channeled toward the national treasury. In the bill that the committee reported, the Peronist leadership built support for the rate increase by stipulating that excess revenues would be divided between the national and provincial social security systems. Thus Menem's partial veto allowed greater executive discretion over the distribution of fuel tax revenues to the provinces and, as Mustapic argues in this volume, undermined the ability of party leaders to construct deals in the legislature.

Fiscal Policy Making on the Chamber Floor

Once a bill is reported by the Budget Committee, a member of the governing party from the committee (usually the chair) then shepherds the bill through the debate on the floor of the Chamber. As provided in the Constitution and specified in the rules of each chamber, voting occurs in two phases. First, the bill reported by the committee is voted in a general up or down vote (*aprobación en general*). Second, the bill is then disaggregated and voted article by article (*aprobación en particular*), allowing individual legislators to oppose certain articles of the bill even if they supported the bill in the general vote.[35] The Chamber president decides exactly how to package votes on the floor and may choose to divide arti-

[33] *Diario de Sesiones de la Cámara de Senadores de la Nación*, December 7, 1989, p. 3280; *Diario de Sesiones de la Cámara de Diputados de la Nación*, November 23, 1989, pp. 4735, 4736, and November 30, 1989, p. 5682.

[34] *"Mensaje del Poder Ejecutivo," Boletín Oficial*, no. 1465, December 14, 1989.

[35] The constitutional reform of 1994 changed these rules, presumably to expedite the legislative process. Under Article 79 of the reformed Constitution, after approving a bill in the general vote, an absolute majority of the members of each chamber can vote to delegate to the relevant committee the authority to modify particular articles. Observers of the Argentine legislature worry that this will make policy making even less transparent since floor proceedings, unlike committee meetings, are recorded in the *Diario de Sesiones*

cles up into their specific component parts for highly disaggregated votes. Since the governing Peronist party controlled the Chamber presidencies, party leaders were able to use this agenda-setting authority in the service of legislating President Menem's reforms. Specifically, when the party block senses opposition to a particular point, it can have the Chamber president disaggregate the voting. This makes it possible for dissenters within the party to reject specific elements of the bill without threatening broader changes to the legislation. Thus the ability to package votes helps the governing party to accommodate and contain internal party opposition to various fiscal policy changes.

In voting a bill article by article on the floor of each chamber, the committee chair who is in charge of the bill, or an individual delegated by the chair, has the authority to accept or deny modifications on the spot. If the committee chair accepts a modification, the chamber then votes to approve or reject it. Thus the committee chair is able to retain tight control over the amendment process, which it exercises in consultation with the Chamber president and the head of the governing party block in each chamber, who typically meet before the floor vote to decide what if any types of amendments will be accepted. In practice this has proved to be an important procedural advantage for the governing party, particularly in conjunction with its authority over the packaging of votes. By strategically accepting some of the amendments that Peronist legislators proposed on the floor to benefit their provinces, Peronist party leaders built support within the party for the fiscal reforms requested by Menem.

A separate rule that enhances the ability of the Peronist party leadership to control floor proceedings is the stipulation that roll-call votes must be held if supported by a mere one-fifth of the members present. On controversial matters, when governing party legislators may prefer not to record their votes, members of opposition parties are often able to impose roll-call votes. Although leaders of the governing party generally do not like to publicize internal divisions, on important matters roll-call votes have allowed them to enforce discipline over party backbenchers.

The three following policy episodes illustrate these points about fiscal policy making on the floor of the legislature. Similar to modifications at

---

and thus are more exposed to public scrutiny. Advocates of this change disingenuously argue that the modification of particular articles is "scientific or technical" and not political, and thus best undertaken by policy experts in committees and not on the floor. See Dromi and Menem (1994, p. 287).

the committee level, when party discipline ruptures on the floor of the legislature, it is often the result of legislators seeking to defend provincial interests. Also, similar to modifications in committee, amendments on the floor to defend provincial interests occur not just in the Senate but in the lower chamber as well. That the lower chamber has modified some fiscal bills in defense of provincial public finances makes sense given the career paths of many deputies, but it is at odds with the research on Argentine federalism that identifies the Senate as the only Chamber where provincial interests are likely to be represented.[36]

Exempting Cargo Transport from the VAT

Having agreed in January 1990 to extend the VAT to a broad range of formerly exempt goods, Peronist deputies in September 1990 considered Menem's proposal to apply the VAT to services as well.[37] Apart from the inclusion of newspapers, radio, and television programming, the part of this bill that met with the greatest opposition from Peronist legislators was the inclusion of cargo transport in the VAT. In the debate over this exemption, representatives from both major parties and from various interior provinces voiced concern that extending the VAT to cargo transport, in addition to existing highway tolls, would destroy "regional economies," a term that legislators used to refer to the more remote and less developed provinces.[38]

Jorge Matzkin, leader of the Peronist block, and Oscar Lamberto, Peronist chair of the Budget Committee, responded by explaining that, since transportation is an intermediate service, applying the VAT to cargo transport would not increase the final cost to consumers of products from distant provinces. Given the credit–debit features of the VAT, producers in interior provinces would be able to claim the VAT that they pay to transport their goods as a fiscal credit. As for truck drivers, the Peronist

---

[36] See, for example, Bidart Campos (1993, pp. 373–376), Frías (1980, pp. 47–49), and Pírez (1986, pp. 97–101).

[37] This bill was promulgated as Law 23,871.

[38] The comments of Peronist Deputy Luis Saadi from the interior province of Catamarca are representative as he complained that the extension of the VAT to cargo transport would further harm the ability of producers in his province to compete with the advanced provinces. *Diario de Sesiones de la Cámara de Diputados de la Nación*, September 5/6, 1990, p. 2285.

leadership argued that, once included in the VAT system, they could deduct the VAT that they were already paying on their trucks, tires, and parts from the VAT that they would now have to collect and deposit in the DGI for transporting goods. Defenders of interior provinces did not accept this reasoning, arguing that the majority of trucks used to transport goods from interior provinces were small-scale operations and did not operate within the VAT system (so-called nonregistered contributors). Since nonregistered trucks could not deduct VAT payments as fiscal credits, legislators from the interior feared that truckers would pass on this cost increase to producers in the form of higher transport fees.[39]

Due to the structure of the bill reported by the Budget and Finance Committee, the Peronist Party leadership had reason to worry that strong opposition by the Peronist rank-and-file to the specific issue of cargo transport would complicate the approval of other, less controversial elements of the bill. Specifically, Article 5 of the bill presented a detailed list of different services to be exempt from the VAT. According to the list proposed by the president, the VAT exemption for transport would be limited to the transportation of passengers and international cargo, leaving domestic cargo transport to be covered by the tax. Fearing the defeat of the entire article over this one issue, which would considerably alter the bill as it was proposed by the executive branch, Peronist leaders decided to disaggregate the article into its many component parts.[40] This led to 21 separate votes rather than a single vote on the entire list of exemptions. As seen in Table 10.2, which shows the substance of the 21 votes and their results, most of the particular service exemptions were approved by solid majorities. In contrast, legislators rejected the limited exemption of passenger transport, which is line item 5.j.12 in the table.

As indicated in Table 10.2, Peronist legislators from the interior provinces who favored a broader exemption for cargo transport voiced their opposition mostly by leaving the floor and not voting at all. For the first 20 votes, the number of legislators voting oscillated between 190 and 201. This number dropped to 156 when it came time to vote for the limited transport exemption. In addition to those Peronist legislators who contributed to the defeat of this limited exemption by simply leaving the floor, 10 Peronist deputies actually stayed and voted against the bill. This

[39] Ibid., p. 2285.
[40] For Matzkin's motion specifying how he wanted the vote to be packaged, see Ibid., p. 2269.

Table 10.2. *How deputies voted on a list of services that would remain exempt from the VAT.*

Type of service to receive exemption		Yes vote	No vote	Abstain	Total voters
5.a	Books and pamphlets (*folletos*)	140	48	4	192
5.b	Special paper for bank notes	151	40	3	194
5.c	Stamps	151	40	3	194
5.d	Lottery tickets	157	39	4	200
5.e	Gold specie sold by official entities	164	27	8	199
5.f	Metal coins as legal tender	158	27	15	200
5.g	Ordinary natural water and sales to final consumers of bread and milk	161	24	15	200
5.h	International cargo and passenger transport	144	29	26	199
5.i	Sales of goods by institutions covered under Law 21.526[a]	155	28	17	200
5.j.1	Services provided by government	168	22	8	198
5.j.2	Insurance services	162	35	2	199
5.j.3	Services provided by private educational establishments	104	90	4	198
5.j.4	Services related to the teaching of handicapped students in private educational facilities	122	66	11	199
5.j.5	Services provided by religious institutes	172	23	5	200
5.j.6	Services provided by union-financed health centers (*obras sociales*)	170	18	11	199
5.j.7	Services provided by medical and paramedical assistants in hospitals and clinics	102	90	9	201
5.j.8	Funeral services	162	31	8	201
5.j.9	Services provided by stock markets that are organized as civil associations	160	20	10	190
5.j.10	Tickets to shows of the following variety: artistic, scientific, cultural, theatrical, musical, singing, dancing, sporting, and circus events	163	22	7	192
5.j.11	Production and distribution of movies shown in cinemas and on TV	150	28	12	190
5.j.12	The transport of passengers by land or by water. Transport by school bus, tour bus, or chauffeur is not exempt, nor is the transport of cargo not accompanied by passengers	74	81	1	156

[a] Law 21.526 covers a variety of financial entities.

was sufficient to result in the defeat of the limited VAT exemption.[41] Four of the Peronist legislators who voted did not represented the interior provinces, and another three were affiliated with the "Group of Eight" dissident Peronists who ultimately left the party over the direction of Menem's economic reforms.[42] Most Peronist legislators from interior provinces who wanted to expand the VAT exemption to include cargo transport participated by leaving the Chamber.

The defeat of the limited exemption for passenger transport in effect meant that all passenger and cargo transport would be included in the VAT. This would be hugely unpopular with the public and thus an unacceptable outcome for the governing party. Since this reversion point was less attractive to the Peronist leadership than a blanket exemption for all transport, it agreed to a much broader exemption of transport than was initially proposed by either the Budget and Finance Committee or the executive branch. Despite being a "sub-subpoint" of an extensive omnibus tax bill, the outcome of this debate over the exemption of transport services was of great importance for the president's tax agenda, because exempting all cargo and passenger transport meant not only considerable foregone revenue, but also a VAT system that would be more difficult to administer and easier to evade due to the inclusion of greater exemptions.[43]

Increasing the Tax on Minimum Assets

In late 1990, a hyperinflationary outburst left the federal government scrambling for revenues and resulted in the replacement of Ermán González with Domingo Cavallo as Economy Minister. Subsequently, in February 1991, President Menem submitted an omnibus tax bill to the legislature at the center of which was an increase in the tax on minimum assets from 1% to 2%. Notable in the congressional debates over this increase was the extent to which Peronist Party leaders and administration officials appealed to legislators' identities as representatives of their provinces by

[41] Ibid., p. 2286. Of the 156 deputies who voted, 81 voted against the committee's report (most of whom were Peronist), 74 voted for it, and 1 abstained.

[42] These three rebels included Franco Caviglia, Juan Pablo Cafiero, and Hector Gatti. The latter two were reelected as Frepaso party legislators in 1995.

[43] The deputies also successfully insisted on this broader exemption in modifying the executive's version of the bill that became Law 24,073, which would have limited the exemption to passenger transport. *Diario de Sesiones de la Cámara de Diputados de la Nación*, March 11, 1992, p. 6051.

emphasizing the greater revenue sharing with the provinces that would result from this bill. Cavallo explicitly appealed to provincial interests by stating, "If you approve this reform this week, next Monday it will be published in the *Boletín Oficial*, next week the executive can start implementing the legislation, and by the last week of this month the provinces will begin receiving a very significant amount of revenues enabling them to pay provincial salaries and pensions on time."[44]

Early 1991 was a low point for Menem's administration: Eighteen months into his term, the president had still failed to deliver macroeconomic stability. In hindsight, Cavallo's selection as Economy Minister clearly represents a turning point that ushered in a period of strong economic growth with price stability. But in February 1991, in the context of renewed hyperinflation and in the run up to congressional elections in October, Peronist legislators were anxious about approving a tax increase. A particular concern was that growing inflation would erode the real value of revenue transfers. Consequently, during the article-by-article vote on this bill, Peronist party leader Jorge Matzkin accepted a proposal by backbenchers to change the distribution of revenues from this tax. In the bill submitted by the president and reported by the Budget and Finance Committee, the criteria from the 1988 Revenue Sharing Law would be used to divide up the revenues, meaning 57% for the provinces and 42% for the federal government. Matzkin accepted an amendment that reserved 50% of the tax revenues for the provinces alone and that distributed the remaining 50% according to the Revenue Sharing Law. This increased the provincial share in the proceeds of this tax from 57% to 79%.[45] The support of Peronist deputies for an increase in this tax handle thus came at a price in the form of fewer tax revenues for the federal government at a time when it urgently needed these revenues.

In addition to changes in the distribution of revenues from the minimum assets tax, Peronist deputies also successfully modified the criteria used to distribute tax revenues belonging to a transitory fund for provincial fiscal disequilibria. Thus, while the deputies approved the executive's proposal to distribute 64% of the fund among eight needy provinces, they stipulated that the remaining 36% for the other provinces

---

[44] *Diario de Sesiones de la Cámara de Senadores de la Nación*, February 16, 1991, p. 5363. The increase in the tax rate on minimum assets was promulgated as Law 23,905.

[45] *Diario de Sesiones de la Cámara de Diputados de la Nación*, February 14/15, 1991, pp. 4617–4618.

would be distributed not by executive discretion but according to the Revenue Sharing Law. Before this change, to receive revenues from this fund, provinces had to adhere to fiscal adjustment plans and limits on the salaries of provincial public sector officials. After this shift toward less discretion, all provinces were guaranteed to receive some assistance from the fund.[46]

Raising the VAT Rate to 21% Without Sharing the Proceeds

As part of the federal government's attempt to maintain fiscal stability in the fallout of the Mexican tequila effect, Menem proposed in March 1995 to raise the VAT rate for one year from 18% to 21%.[47] According to his proposal, however, to sustain the hard-won fiscal equilibrium of the federal government, the proceeds of this increase would not be shared with the provinces. To overcome the opposition of legislators who correctly argued that this contradicted the 1988 Revenue Sharing Law, the leader of the Peronist Party in the lower chamber agreed to insert an article that obligated the federal government to distribute grants to the provinces amounting to approximately US$1.2 billion to help finance the reform of provincial state banks.[48] This article established no objective criteria to govern how these funds would be distributed among needy provinces, which suggests instead that political discretion by the executive branch would serve as the distribution mechanism. Thus, in the words of one opposition legislator, "this law takes revenues away from the provinces and then partially restores them, but only to provinces that obey."[49]

Unlike earlier measures that diverted tax revenues from the provinces, this attempt in 1995 forced the governing party leadership to confront a new set of rules adopted in the 1994 Constitutional reform. To protect provincial shares of tax revenues against presidential discretion, these new rules stipulated that the executive branch could divert revenues from the automatic sharing mechanism only if an absolute majority of the total members of each chamber approved the change.[50] In other words, the

---

[46] *Diario de Sesiones de la Cámara de Diputados de la Nación*, February 14/15, 1991, p. 4626.

[47] This increase was legislated in Law 24,468. The VAT has remained at 21% ever since, due to various extensions.

[48] *Boletín Oficial*, March 23, 1995, pp. 1, 2.

[49] See the speech of Senator Genoud, *Diario de Sesiones de la Cámara de Senadores de la Nación*, March 16, 1995, p. 886.

[50] See the third clause of Article 75 of the reformed Constitution governing the legislation of *asignaciones específicas*.

support of a majority of the members present on the floor would no longer be sufficient. The new rules particularly strained Peronist party discipline in the lower chamber, where, in order to pass this change in revenue distribution rules, the party leadership needed to turn out affirmative votes by almost the entire Peronist block. Hoping to expose divisions in the governing party over this controversial measure, opposition legislators provided the necessary votes to impose a roll-call vote in the Chamber.

When the deputies first voted on the article that would raise the VAT rate to 21%, 128 legislators voted yes, 63 voted no, and 6 abstained. This was one vote shy of the 129 votes needed to approve the measure with an absolute majority. Since the law regulating congressional procedures requires legislators to ask the Chamber president for permission to abstain, and since the number of legislators abstaining would affect the vote outcome, Chamber President Pierri conducted a second vote. The second vote resulted in a worse outcome for the governing party, with 126 voting yes, 68 voting no, and 10 abstaining. After this vote, a disagreement in strategy developed between Pierri and Matzkin, the head of the Peronist block. Matzkin tried to obfuscate the issue of the special majority needed for this bill, but Pierri insisted on holding a third vote. Since Pierri held formal authority over the voting procedures, a third vote was held in which 136 legislators voted yes, 68 voted no, and only 1 abstained. Four Peronist deputies who abstained in the first vote voted yes in the third vote, while three switched their votes from no to yes.[51]

Thus, in this policy episode, the menemista president of the lower Chamber aggressively enforced party discipline through the use of repeated votes and nominal voting procedures. With respect to the electoral cycle, this enforcement of party discipline is particularly interesting because the vote occurred just two months before the 1995 elections. At this phase of the electoral cycle, Peronist legislators were in a tough spot: They feared that raising the VAT to 21% in an already recessionary environment might undermine the party's performance in the congressional race, but they also feared recriminations by Menem and other party leaders in the event that they refused to comply with the rate hike. Considering the widespread social upheaval caused by provincial public sector deficits in 1995 and 1996, the ability of Peronist Party leaders to force legislators to divert revenues from the provinces is particularly noteworthy.

---

[51] For the record of these three votes, see *Diario de Sesiones de la Cámara de Diputados de la Nación*, March 15, 1995, pp. 591, 592, 598.

Conclusion

To place the Argentine legislature and its fiscal policy performance in comparative perspective, two salient points deserve emphasis. First, depending on their specific career paths, which may vary significantly, ambitious legislators in Argentina cultivate relationships with the national and provincial party leaders who are likely to influence their careers. The fiscal policy implications of ambition, then, are that governing party legislators remain quite disciplined in supporting the president's proposals, although they often try with some success to defend provincial public finances against these proposals. Although this clashes with the popular image of a rubber-stamp legislature, the congressional record shows that Peronist legislators did in fact amend Menem's fiscal reform proposals.

The second point concerns the procedural advantages that redound to the governing party when it also enjoys a majority in the legislature, an electoral outcome that is more likely in Argentina than in many other multiparty Latin American democracies (Jones 1995). The leadership of the governing party can structure the business of Congress to accommodate some of the provincial interests of governing party legislators without letting these modifications significantly threaten the president's overall fiscal policy agenda. As the policy cases analyzed in this chapter show, these procedural advantages did not prevent Peronist legislators from inserting amendments to benefit the provinces, but rather enabled the party leadership to structure the amendment process.

An important comparative point is that when party discipline is breached in Argentina, this occurs not because legislators seek to deliver tax breaks to specific constituents in a personalized fashion, as in the United States. Instead, breaches reflect attempts to negotiate loyalty to two sets of party leaders, national and provincial. The contrasts with Mexico and Brazil are instructive. In Mexico, as Weldon's chapter shows, the enormous metaconstitutional powers that the president held over individual legislators between 1937 and 1997 resulted in few incentives for legislators to try to insert fiscal benefits for their home states into the federal budget. During this period, influence over the career prospects of governing party legislators was concentrated in the person of the Mexican president to a degree that considerably exceeded the influence that Menem held in Argentina. Influence over legislators' careers is more decentralized in Argentina than in Mexico, and this is reflected in Argentina in the greater incidence of attempts by legislators to alter fiscal policy to benefit their provincial electoral districts. These attempts pale in comparison, however, to the pork-barreling efforts of Brazilian legislators that Samuels documents in his chapter. The Brazilian president exerts little influence over the career prospects of individual legislators, unlike his Argentine and Mexican counterparts. Instead, electoral incentives are predominantly state-based, encouraging ambitious legislators to bring home fiscal benefits to the states and municipalities where they anticipate continuing their careers.

My analysis is based on only those policy changes that were made after the president proposed legislation. As the rule of anticipated reactions suggests, legislators may have input in more hidden ways. My analysis does not capture the changes for which legislators lobbied behind closed doors in the design phase of fiscal reform, nor does it capture changes that the president may have endorsed in anticipating legislators' preferences. By focusing on only cases where provincial modifications were made, I do not mean to overstate the importance of these changes in Argentina's overall reform experience. The basic reality remains that Peronist legislators enthusiastically accompanied Menem on his most important statute changes and also accepted most of his DNUs. Instead, the focus on modifications to benefit provincial interests is meant to show that, in fiscal policy, there is often great tension between these interests and the concerns of the federal executive, and that this tension sometimes results in important policy changes. Traditionally, Argentine scholars have emphasized the extent to which representatives to the national legislature fail to represent specific provincial interests because they are too disciplined by the national parties to which they belong. Yet if this were entirely the case, then none of the modifications discussed in this chapter would make any political sense.

As a final point, though Argentine legislators do not tend to stay in the legislature for very long, and thus face few incentives to become policy experts on legislative committees, this failure to institutionalize the legislature should not be equated with the failure of the legislature to influence policy making. Progressive ambition on the part of most legislators certainly undermines the ability of the legislature to initiate changes in fiscal policy and to interact in the policy process as an equal partner to the executive branch. Yet committees do not need to be highly institutionalized for legislators to be able to participate meaningfully in the policy process, as the cases discussed in this chapter reveal.

11

Progressive Ambition, Federalism, and Pork-Barreling in Brazil

DAVID SAMUELS

This book aims to relate legislators' political ambitions with various aspects of electoral politics and the policy process. In this chapter, I discuss how Brazilian federal deputies' careerist motivations are related to the process of pork-barreling in the yearly budget. In Brazil, the executive branch proposes the budget. Legislators add pork-barrel amendments to this proposal and then pass the budget back to the executive branch. However, the president possesses a line-item veto, so during the budgetary year Brazilian federal deputies spend a significant portion of their time seeking to convince the president to release funds that they want directed to their constituents.

Ames (1995) argued that Brazil's electoral system, which encourages candidates to ignore their parties and campaign on individualistic grounds, encourages all deputies to engage in pork-barreling, and he suggested that deputies devote so much attention to pork-barreling because they want to bolster their chances of winning reelection. However, in other work (Samuels 1998) I questioned whether pork-barreling provides reelection-minded deputies with significant electoral benefits and found no statistical relationship between a deputy's pork-barreling success and his or her subsequent electoral success.

This finding leaves us with a puzzle: If pork-barreling in Brazil provides no clear electoral return, then why do so many deputies devote so much time and energy to it? To reach an answer, we must discuss two distinct notions of political careerism: *static* ambition and *progressive* ambition. A deputy who exhibits *static* ambition seeks to build a career within the legislature. In contrast, *a progressively* ambitious deputy seeks to *leave* the Chamber after serving only one or two terms and continue his or her political career at the state and/or municipal level. As I have shown elsewhere

(Ibid.), comparatively very few Brazilian deputies seek long-term legislative careers. The assumption that Brazilian deputies, like their counterparts in the U.S. House of Representatives, are "single-minded reelection seekers" (Mayhew 1974) therefore cannot be true. In contrast, over two-thirds of the deputies do continue their careers in politics at the subnational level after leaving the Chamber.[1] Thus, we may instead assume that *progressive* ambition motivates Brazilian federal deputies.

Once we consider that very few Brazilian deputies seek to build a long-term career in the Chamber, we can derive hypotheses that contrast the expected behavior of a *statically* ambitious deputy with a *progressively* ambitious deputy. For instance, if deputies exhibited static ambition, then we might suppose that they would seek pork to ensure repeated reelection. This would leave the finding that pork does not help reelection (Samuels 1998) quite puzzling. However, if we supposed that deputies attempt to use pork for other purposes, then the puzzle can be solved.

I argue that pork serves deputies' *progressive* ambition and thus conditions their legislative behavior, both indirectly and directly. First, pressure from subnational actors pushes deputies to favor subnational interests in the budget process. State-based political forces weigh heavily on deputies' decisions. Deputies respond to this pressure because they know that their future careers depend on building good relationships with state-level political actors. Unlike their relationship with national political parties, the "shadow of the future" is long for deputies' relationships with subnational actors.

Deputies' progressive ambition also directly shapes their pork-barreling activity. Progressively ambitious deputies engage in distinct pork-barreling strategies that are aimed at improving their chances of winning an *extra*congressional political position, not at ensuring repeated reelection. When we take these two factors into account, there is little reason to expect a strong relationship between pork-barreling and reelection in Brazil. Because deputies are not primarily motivated by winning repeated reelection, they have not designed a constituency-service system that will help them achieve that goal. Instead, they have designed a system that helps them advance their *progressive* ambition goals.[2]

---

[1] In contrast, most U.S. House representatives, who epitomize legislators with *static* ambition, simply retire from politics or go into private-sector activities after leaving the House (Herrick and Nixon 1996).

[2] For additional details, see Samuels (1998, ch. 6, 2000).

This chapter is organized as follows: In the next two sections, I provide evidence that subnational forces have pushed deputies to reshape the budget process in their favor. I explain how deputies have structured the budget committee to reflect state-level political interests in particular, and then I describe how deputies have transformed the process of pork-barreling to also heavily favor state-level interests. Subsequently, I provide evidence demonstrating how progressive ambition directly shapes deputies' pork-barreling strategies. The last section concludes.

Why Deputies Have Moved to Favor Subnational Interests in the Budget Process

Although access to the budget does not appear to help deputies individually develop long-term congressional careers, they do spend a good deal of time seeking pork. In this section I first discuss how state-level pressure in particular has pushed deputies to strategically structure the budget committee (officially known as the Joint Committee for Planning, Public Budgets and Oversight [*Comissão Mista de Planos, Orçamentos Públicos e Fiscalização*, or CMO]) to reflect spatially defined political interests, in particular state-government actors. I then discuss how the process of pork-barreling has evolved to favor state-based political interests.

Structure: State "Representation" on the Budget Committee

The CMO was first installed after the promulgation of Brazil's new democratic constitution in 1988. The way in which members of the Brazilian Congress set up the CMO reflects both their desire to limit national partisan influence in budget policy and their strong ties to subnational political institutions and agents. Thus, while party representation proportionally determines the initial distribution of seats on the CMO (as it does with all committees), *parties have no role in the formulation of budget priorities and no role in the negotiation of budget amendments.* Instead, the structure of the CMO privileges *states'* political interests. First, the CMO privileges all states because it is a joint committee of Congress, and, second, it privileges certain states over others by overrepresenting Brazil's poorer states, which comprise a majority of both houses of Congress and where state-level political organization is strong.

Jointness The CMO is a joint committee of Brazil's National Congress; deputies and senators serve as co-equals. The presidency of the CMO

Table 11.1. *Malapportionment in the Brazilian Congress,*
1998.

Region	% Chamber	% Senate	% Population
Center-West	8.0	14.8	6.4
Northeast	29.4	33.3	29.2
North	12.7	25.9	6.8
Southeast	34.9	14.8	42.5
South	15.0	11.1	15.1

Source: Nicolau (1996) and Mainwaring and Samuels (1999).

switches from a deputy to a senator each year. Neither the Senate nor the Chamber has an independent budget committee – only the CMO analyzes, modifies, amends, and votes on the executive's proposal before the final vote in a joint session of Congress. The CMO's jointness favors state interests because as the budget is being prepared and analyzed, deputies and senators do not meet in partisan groups, but as state delegations. As several politicians confirmed, jointness thus transforms deputies into "mini-senators," because deputies and senators work together as a state delegation to defend both the individual amendments of *all* MCs (Members of Congress) from their state as well as defend their *state's* delegation amendments, which the entire delegation submits as a group (see the following).[3]

Malapportionment   Malapportionment in the CMO also tends to favor state-level interests in the budget, because it tends to favor the states where state-level political forces have historically been particularly strong. As Table 11.1 shows, Brazil's Congress overrepresents the poor, less-populated states of the country's Center-West, North, and Northeast regions. Table 11.1 provides the percentage of seats that the states in each region have in each Chamber and the percentage of the country's population in each region. If the percentage of seats in either Chamber exceeds the percentage of the population, the region is overrepresented.

Table 11.1 reveals that the states in the relatively wealthier Southeast and Southern regions are underrepresented, while the states in the three poorer regions are overrepresented. The three less-developed regions had

[3] Interviews with Lidia Quinan, Waldeck Ornellas, and Antônio Carlos Pojo do Rêgo.

Table 11.2. *Malapportionment and CMO membership.*

	1992	1993	1994	1995	1996	1997	1998	1999	Avg.
% Poor senators	83.3	80.0	71.4	85.0	78.3	82.1	85.7	90.4	*82.0*
% Rich senators	16.7	20.0	28.6	15.0	21.7	17.9	14.3	9.6	*18.0*
% Poor deputies	57.8	63.3	58.7	54.1	48.1	62.2	60.0	55.6	*57.5*
% Rich deputies	42.2	36.7	41.3	45.9	51.9	37.8	40.0	44.4	*42.5*
% Poor total on CMO	64.2	67.5	63.4	61.7	57.8	67.6	66.7	64.2	*64.1*
% Rich total on CMO	35.8	32.5	36.6	38.3	42.2	32.4	33.3	35.8	*35.9*

Sources: Brasil, Senado Federal, Secretaria-Geral da Mesa (1991–1997, 1999) and Brasil, Congresso Nacional (1998).

50.1% of the Chamber seats, 74% of the Senate seats, and 54.3% of the seats overall in the 1995–1998 legislature.

Because the Chamber and Senate vote jointly on the budget, we might suppose that the CMO would reflect the division of seats in the joint plenary session: That is, the poorer regions would get 54.3% of the seats. However, the CMO exacerbates the overrepresentation of poorer states. Table 11.2 breaks the membership of the CMO down according to whether the senators and deputies on the budget committee were from the "poor" regions or the "rich" regions and reveals that, on average, Brazil's poorer states send about 81% of the senators and about 58% of the deputies to the CMO, for an overall average (%POORTOTAL) of 64% of the CMO seats. This means that the budget committee is about 20% more malapportioned than the Chamber.

The three poorer regions dominate the CMO because they can. As noted previously, the states in these regions already possess an absolute majority of the joint session of Congress. The reason that MCs from these regions desire to dominate the budget committee is because the states in these regions have historically been relatively more dependent on federal government support than states in the South and Southeast, and because municipal interests in these states are less prominent and less well articulated in contrast to state-level political interests. Consequently, MCs from these regions are likely to receive more intense pressure from their state governments to obtain resources. To achieve this goal, MCs from these regions attempt to dominate the budget committee. In addition, because relatively fewer deputies from the poorer regions turn to municipal-level

319

politics on leaving the Chamber, their own career ambitions tend to favor state-based political interests.

Process: How and Where Congress Targets Pork

Not only does the structure of the CMO privilege state-level interests – certain state-level interests in particular – but the *process* of pork-barreling does so as well, in two ways. First, MCs have come to organize at the *state* level to submit and approve budget amendments, instead of simply submitting them as individuals. Second, whether as individuals or organized as a state delegation, MCs have also come to target a good portion of budgetary pork to state governments, as opposed to only municipal governments.

How MCs Target Pork Ames (1995b) highlighted MCs' capacity to present budget amendments as individuals, and when Congress set up the budget amendment process in 1988 only individual MCs could submit amendments. However, MCs have altered the amendment submission and approval process several times over the last decade, limiting their own individual involvement and increasing activities as members of organized groups, in particular as state delegations. Table 11.3 relates the *number* of amendments (not their relative amounts – see the following) submitted since 1992 by agent (Brasil, Senado Federal, 1997).

After 1991, the number of amendments that MCs submitted as individuals has declined. Several groups of MCs have been allowed to submit amendments: state and regional delegations, congressional committees, parties, executive-branch agencies, and groups of more than 30 MCs, independently of party. Currently, individual MCs, the president of the CMO, permanent congressional committees, and state and regional delegations can submit amendments. Interestingly, despite giving parties the right to submit amendments in two years, parties only submitted eight amendments: three each by the leftist Workers' Party and Democratic Labor Party and two by the conservative Liberal Party.

The raw numbers of submitted amendments do not relate the relative *amounts* of money that these actors target. Tables 11.4 and 11.5 presents this information for both submitted and approved amendments as a percentage of the total value of all amendments, providing strong evidence of the increasing weight of state delegations in recent years (Brasil, Senado Federal, 1997–1999).

Table 11.3. *Budget amendments by agent, 1992–1999.*

Agent	Number of amendments submitted per year							
	1992	1993	1994	1995	1996	1997	1998	1999
Individual MC	73,642	20,826	13,915	22,664	10,403	10,348	8,533	7,572
Congressional Cmte.	–	257	9	28	517	1,018	537	361
Executive Agency	–	–	–	84	–	–	–	–
Party	–	1	–	7	–	–	–	–
Regional Delegation	–	–	–	–	28	27	26	–
State Delegation	–	1,407	–	468	279	271	245	272
Group of >30 MCs	–	108	–	–	–	–	–	–

Source: Brasil. Senado Federal, 1997–99.

Table 11.4. *Percent value of all submitted amendments, by submitting agent.*

Agent	1992	1993	1994	1995	1996	1997	1998	1999
Individual MC	100	63.9	99.8	88.7	54.3	57.6	27.8	26.3
State Delegation	–	34.0	–	8.4	21.9	32.7	69.5	70.9
Congressional Committee	–	0.4	0.2	0.0	5.4	4.5	1.1	2.8
Party	–	0.1	–	2.0	–	–	–	–
Regional Delegation	–	0.0	–	–	3.8	5.2	1.5	0.0
>30 MCs	–	1.6	–	–	–	–	–	–
Executive Agency	–	–	–	1.9	–	–	–	–

Source: Author's Compilation, from Brasil. Senado Federal. 1997–1999.

Table 11.5. *Percent value of all approved amendments, by submitting agent.*

Agent	1992	1993	1994	1995	1996	1997	1998	1999
Individual MC	100	71.1	X	42.4	30.5	32.5	33.5	58.5
State Delegation	–	25.4	X	46.1	58.9	60.6	48.8	32.1
Congressional Committee	–	2.4	X	0.0	1.3	2.3	15.0	5.9
Party	–	0.1	X	0.0	–	–	–	–
Regional Delegation	–	0.0	X	–	9.4	4.6	2.7	–
>30 MCs	–	1.1	X	–	–	–	–	–
Executive Agency	–	–	X	11.5	–	–	–	–

X = no approved amendments.
Source: Author's compilation, from Brasil. Senado Federal. 1997–1999.

These tables demonstrate that while individual MCs initially accounted for 100% of both submissions and approvals, by 1998 individual amendments accounted for less than 10% of the value of all submissions, and only about 25% of the value of all approved amendments (in 1999, individual deputies obtained most of the value of approved amendments, but as we will see in the following, they mostly targeted these amendments to state governments). On the other hand, the amounts that state delegations have submitted and approved has increased dramatically. I explain this transformation in what follows.

Where MCs Target Pork Where do MCs target their pork, whether as individuals or members of a state delegation or congressional committee? Several scholars have focused on deputies' propensity to target municipalities, highlighting deputies' "localistic" behavior (Ames 1995; Mainwaring 1999). Do members of Congress target only municipalities? Amendments can target municipal, state, regional, national, or "exterior"

Table 11.6. *Percent value of submitted amendments.*

Target	1992	1993	1994	1995	1996	1997	1998	1999
% to Region	0.7	15.0	3.3	1.6	7.5	6.3	1.9	2.6
% to States	7.4	38.6	22.3	39.4	43.8	38.8	59.5	40.7
% to Municipalities	91.8	46.4	74.4	59.0	48.7	54.9	38.5	56.7

Source: Author's compilation, from Brasil. Senado Federal. 1997–1999.

Table 11.7. *Percent value of approved amendments.*

Target	1992	1993	1994	1995	1996	1997	1998	1999
% to Regions	13.3	8.2	X	1.6	7.9	3.8	1.0	0.6
% to States	46.9	42.4	X	45.0	47.5	46.9	68.4	75.3
% to Municipalities	39.8	49.5	X	53.4	44.6	49.3	30.5	24.0

X = no approved amendments.
Source: Author's compilation, from Brasil. Senado Federal. 1997–1999.

government agencies such as embassies. For a number of reasons, I exclude from consideration amendments targeted to national and exterior programs.[4] Table 11.6 demonstrates that over the last 10 years the portion of submitted amendments targeted at specific municipalities has declined, while the portion targeted to states (and even regions) has increased. Regardless of *how* MCs target pork – whether individually or in groups – currently about half the value of all submitted amendments are targeted at states, not regions or municipalities.

The trend to favor state programs becomes even more pronounced when we consider not only what MCs *submit* to the CMO, but what the CMO actually *approves*. Table 11.7 shows that the trend to favor states is even more pronounced at this second stage of the budget process. Currently, most of the value of approved amendments is targeted at states (no amendments were approved for the 1994 budget).

Finally, at the most important and final stage of the budget process, the "execution" stage, when the executive branch releases funds, states are also highly favored over municipalities. I only have information on executed amendments for 1993–1998, provided in Table 11.8 (no amendments were approved in 1994, meaning that none were executed, and only 39 amendments were executed in 1995).

[4] See appendix 7.2 of Samuels (1998) regarding national and exterior amendments.

Table 11.8. *Percent value of executed amendments.*

Target	1993	1994	1995	1996	1997	1998
% to Regions	2.3	X	0.0	7.4	1.5	0.6
% to States	71.1	X	92.3	58.1	68.6	75.2
% to Municipalities	26.7	X	7.7	34.4	29.8	24.2

X = no executed amendments.
Source: Author's compilation, from Brasil. Senado Federal. 1997–1999.

Although MCs sometimes target municipalities, nearly all of the money that is actually released goes to state-level projects. This means that while individual MCs may spend some time and effort targeting municipalities – as Ames argues – when push comes to shove they tend to prioritize amendments that their *state's* government will implement, not municipal governments.

In sum, the current budget amendment process tends to downplay the ability of individual deputies to see their amendments, often targeted to their municipal vote bases, approved and executed. On the other hand, state-delegation amendments and amendments directed more generally at states tend to have a better chance of approval and execution.

Evolution of the Amendment Process

Why have MCs limited their individual involvement in the amendment process? Four factors explain why MCs have altered the budget process. First, Brazil's continuing fiscal crisis has limited MCs' ability to extract resources from the federal government. For individual deputies, supply is tight while demand remains high, and few deputies have the political "weight" to extract funds from the executive branch on their own. To have a chance to play *any* role, deputies must organize collectively to concentrate their political weight. Tellingly, MCs have not chosen to organize along partisan lines, but instead have organized along *state* lines.

Second, high demand for pork caused administrative chaos. When the number of amendments submitted in 1991 and 1992 swamped the CMO and impeded its ability to finish its work on time, the budgets were delivered late (Sanches 1993). The executive used this delay to its advantage, manipulating funds at will while Congress dallied. To prevent this, MCs chose not to reduce the president's authority, but instead limited the number of amendments that individual MCs could submit.

Third, submission of over 70,000 amendments a year pulverized the resources available for pork-barrel projects. Many projects require multiyear funding, but with no multiyear guarantees, MCs' submissions resulted in literally thousands of small, unfinished projects dotting the Brazilian landscape. Moreover, projects often require counterpart funds and technical capacity for completion and implementation, but nearly all municipalities are too poor to put up even the small counterpart funds requirement (10% of the total in the three poorer regions, 20% else-where) (Sanches 1993), and few municipalities can pay for technical staff. Because many individual amendments lacked funding and technical support, they provided deputies with little political return (*Folha de São Paulo*, 6/2/96).

Fourth, the absence of party control, administrative chaos, and most MCs' complete lack of knowledge of budgetary techniques allowed a small clique of MCs to grab control over the pork supply. In the absence of significant peer oversight, these "Cardinals" of the budget process began to hog larger pieces of pork, and sometimes took bribes to direct pork a certain way. This practice was mostly eliminated following directly on the heels of Congress' impeachment of President Fernando Collor in the fall of 1992. After the impeachment, Congress turned its investigative skills on itself and exposed a scandal in the budget committee that resulted in the spring of 1993 in the expulsion of seven deputies, with five more resigning before expulsion votes could be taken (INESC 1993a, 1993b).

Given the first three factors, the scandal finally pushed MCs to streamline the budget process. Fearing another scandal, Congress passed the 1994 budget entirely without amendments, and in 1995 Congress implemented selected parts of an investigative committee's recommendations (the recommendations went much further and included eliminating individual amendments altogether). MCs aimed to tie their hands to each others' by institutionalizing and prioritizing collective amendments (from states, regions, and permanent committees), reducing the weight of individual amendments, and reducing the power of the CMO's leadership. They limited the power of the committee leadership positions (rapporteurs and subrapporteurs), reduced the maximum number of amendments an individual could submit to 20 (a 1993 resolution had set the limit at 50), and forced themselves to prioritize ten of these, and they required that three-quarters of a delegation sign each state-delegation amendment

(*Folha de São Paulo* 12/6/96; Greggianin 1997; *O Estado de São Paulo* 12/15/96; Sanches 1996).[5]

The Sources of State-Based Pressures

Why did MCs choose to particularly benefit states in the budget amendment process? Given the administrative chaos and corruption in the budget process, one might suppose that eventually a crisis would push MCs to reform. However, nothing mentioned previously predicts any particular modification. To understand why MCs ended up privileging state delegations and reducing their individual involvement, I return to my argument about political ambition and the pressures that legislators face from subnational political actors. On the one hand, one can understand pressure for individual MCs to target *municipalities* relatively easily. The municipality is the unit of government closest to the voters, and most deputies maintain ties to local vote brokers or have their own local organizations. If a deputy makes his or her career at the municipal level, pork can maintain or expand a vote base.

Yet MCs ultimately chose to reduce their own individual ability to target submissions to municipalities (or elsewhere), and relatively fewer amendments are even *approved* that target municipalities (see Table 11.7). Understanding why all deputies face pressures to promote state-based interests is more complex. One reason why deputies must support state governments is that many of them come from and continue their careers at the state level. These deputies have developed and desire to maintain clienteles within the state bureaucracy and tend to favor state interests over municipal or national partisan interests.

Second, we should consider the impact of what is called *governismo* in Brazil, a tendency for politicians to support whoever is in government once an election has been decided. At the state level, *governismo* has historically been particularly strong. After a gubernatorial election, politicians seek to distance themselves from the losing candidates and strengthen their ties to the winner, because he or she will control the state-level purse strings and access to jobs in the state bureaucracy, with very few checks and balances. These political tools provide the governor with considerable power over both municipal mayors as well as federal deputies. Mayors need gov-

---

[5] Interviews with Waldeck Ornelas, Lidia Quinan, João Henrique, Onofre Quinan, Milton Mendes, Jacques Wagner, and Antônio Carlos Pojo do Rêgo.

ernors because they cannot govern without state-government assistance in many important policy areas such as public security, primary and secondary education, health care, and infrastructural investment.

For their part, because much federal pork is channeled through state governments, and because they also often seek pork or jobs for their cronies at the state, not federal level, federal deputies also depend on close ties to state government officials. As noted in Table 11.7, over two-thirds of all government pork typically is sent to state governments. Once in a state government's hands, the federal government loses influence over the ultimate destination of the funds; the governor can distribute the funds according to his or her own (political) criteria.[6]

In practice, both Congress and the president have little room to alter this situation, because economies of scale and municipalities' lack of technical know-how limit the amounts that could be earmarked for municipal pork. As one senator put it, "Municipalities are not viable agents for infrastructural investment. States are the agents that can operate in these areas, they have better technical capacity."[7] As in the United States, the state and federal governments in Brazil take responsibility for infrastructural investment in such politically credit-worthy activities as road-building, dam construction, bridge-building, and construction and upkeep of schools and hospitals. In Brazil, few municipalities have a tax base that would allow them to develop their infrastructure independently. Instead, the state and federal governments typically undertake most municipal and statewide development programs. While MCs can only direct small-scale projects to their municipal bases, state governments undertake much higher impact projects. Knowledge of this reality shapes MCs behavior; they know that to bring home the really valuable political bacon, they must have good relationships with those in power at the state level.

Moreover, even when the federal government spends money for public-works projects, often the state government plays a large role through counterpart funds. This is the case with many of the projects in President Cardoso's much-ballyhooed "Brazil in Action" investment program. In one instance, Cardoso's Minister of Mines and Energy, Eliseu Padilha, traveled to São Paulo in an attempt to publicize the president's efforts on behalf of the state. Instead of returning to Brasília with news that his boss

---

[6] Interviews with Antônio Carlos Pôjo do Rego, Yeda Crusius, Aglas W. Barrera, and Mara José de Macedo.
[7] Interview with Waldeck Ornellas.

received significant political credit, São Paulo Governor Mario Covas forced Padilha to sit through a speech in which Covas noted that, in all of the projects that Padilha cited, including a major rail bridge, the widening of an important highway and a "beltway" project to ease traffic congestion in the city of São Paulo, the state government would spend *more* money than the federal government (*O Estado de São Paulo* 9/5/97). Fortunately for Padilha, Cardoso and Covas were close allies. In other states the governor's capacity to spend and claim credit could prove embarrassing to the president.

In addition to obtaining federal pork, governors can also access their own coffers to distribute pork-barrel goods and can decide which municipalities and which politicians to benefit with the political credit. Nearly all mayors lack such capacity and depend instead on state and federal funds. Deputies in all of Brazil's regions recognize that state-government resources provide the governor with powerful tools that can be used as political "carrots" or "sticks." One deputy from the poor northeastern state of Piauí lamented that, "In my first term, the governor was my political opponent. So, I was practically impeded from realizing my goals."[8] Deputies from relatively wealthier states also recognize the governor's influence. One deputy from the southern state of Rio Grande do Sul claimed that, "In order for a deputy to have visibility in his state, either he's allied with the governor, or he's in the [leftist] opposition and is extremely competent. Because, if he has nothing to offer, the mayors say 'this town is off-limits to you, don't come here'."[9]

We might suppose that deputies with municipal-level electoral bases would feel relatively free of state-government pressures. However, one deputy from the state of São Paulo, which has several relatively wealthy municipalities, affirmed that his state's governor still controls resources that ambitious politicians desire:

A deputy often needs the governor for his own reelection. In areas such as health care, public security, road-building, and elsewhere, the power of the governor is considerable. He can make or break somebody's election. He'll put a road in the deputy's region that the deputy wants, give the deputy the power to nominate the head of education in the area, or the health post. Or he could turn against someone. He's got a lot of strength.[10]

[8] Interview with João Henrique.   [9] Interview with Yeda Crusius.
[10] Interview with Alberto Goldman.

In short, federal deputies recognize the political power of the state governor. No deputy wants to be on the governor's "bad side," as the governor could shut off access to politically life-sustaining jobs and pork-barrel funds, or direct such resources to a deputy's rival. While governors are often seen patrolling the halls of Congress and the executive-branch ministries, lobbying for pet projects or additional decentralization of funds, their efforts need not always be so overt. Because of the weight of the state government in all deputies' careers, and deputies' reluctance to shift such weight to national entities such as the president or political parties, deputies have incentives to protect and even amplify the weight of state-based political interests in the budget process.

Short supply, administrative chaos, and a corruption scandal pushed Brazil's Congress to revise the budget-amendment pork-barreling process. Because many deputies face pressures to support the incumbent governor (independently of their or the governor's partisan affiliation) and because many of them also desire to continue their careers at the state level, deputies have strong incentives to support state-level interests in budgetary matters. This implies that if pressured to reform the budget process, they ought to favor state interests, as opposed to purely local, partisan, or other interests. In fact, this is what they have done since 1988. In the next section, I describe the major innovation since 1988: the state delegation amendment, whereby all deputies and senators from each state come together to make pork-barrel submissions on behalf of their state. This process reduces deputies' *individual* credit-claiming ability and benefits the state governor.

Submission and Approval of State Delegation Amendments

In the last few years state delegation amendments have received a growing share of the available budgetary pork. At all stages of the budget process, these amendments impede individual credit-claiming. Instead, the governor plays a key role, and MCs must share the credit. Each state delegation may submit 20 amendments per year. In a series of meetings the delegation members negotiate and decide how to prioritize 10 amendments, which the CMO subsequently approves automatically. While a delegation could allow members to divide up submissions among its representatives individually, interviews confirmed that all MCs from the state (deputies and senators) are typically involved in the negotiation process, regardless of party, and that the governor plays a crucial role in the articulation of delegation priorities.

329

State-based political divisions proportionally determine how the delegation divvies up its 10 priority amendment proposals. A "government and opposition" logic at the state level dominates the division of state delegation amendments, *not* a purely state-level partisan logic, and certainly not a *national* partisan logic. What matters is whether the MC is "in" or "out" of power at the state level. For example, in Bahia, one Workers' Party deputy (in opposition to the current governor) explained that "The group that supports the current governor is in the majority, so they took seven amendments, and the opposition in the state got three amendments."[11]

Deputies and senators also explained that the governor influences the delegation amendment submission process. Governors provide a coordinating role for the state delegation (not only in the budget area). Because they control a well-developed bureaucratic machine that can assess statewide political demands more efficiently than an often-fractious state congressional delegation, they take the lead in the state delegation amendment submission process. In many cases, the governor seeks counterpart funds for a pet project, or simply seeks additional pork-barrel funds to use for his own political benefit. Generally, depending on his or her political group's degree of domination of the state, the governor sets the priorities for the state delegation amendments (Greggianin 1997, p. 15).

MCs agree that state delegation amendments limit individual credit-claiming, and that they force all MCs to take responsibility for the state's budget success.[12] One deputy stated that delegation amendments are

A form of self-control, self-patrolling. We start with 20 suggested amendments. Then we say, for example, 'Hey, this one is really to benefit that construction firm.' So that one gets thrown out, it's not approved.[13]

Another deputy added that

More and more we are realizing that because of the dispersion of resources, these projects often never get finished. So nothing gets built, and you have no dam, no road, or no electricity. So, we've united to make our demands as a bloc, even though the political benefits of the project might be inevitably divided among members of the delegation.[14]

At the execution phase for state delegation amendments, the MCs' situation is more difficult than for their individual amendments because they

---

[11] Interview with Jacques Wagner.
[12] Interviews with Onofre Quinan, Gonzaga Mota, Antônio Pojo do Rego, and Waldeck Ornellas.
[13] Interivew with Milton Mendes.   [14] Interview with João Henrique.

have to share credit both with the "executor" of the amendment, the governor, as well as with other deputies and even senators. When federal money goes to a state, the state government executes the project, not the federal government. State-government officials, primarily the governor, claim the credit.

Governors claim the credit because they, not deputies, decide where to spend the money that state delegation amendments provide. One deputy described the situation: "The state delegation submits an amendment, for example, for 'sanitation improvements in the state of Goiás,' but the governor determines which municipalities will be included in this program."[15] It should come as no surprise that state-level politics "matters" here. As one high official in the Ministry of Planning put it, "You have some states where the governor exerts almost complete control over the delegation amendments. The governor's group is politically hegemonic, and he divides up the pie . . . typically, there will be some kind of 'agreement' on where to distribute these funds."[16] That is, mayors and deputies allied with the governor will gain preferential treatment. Deputies rely on mayors to maintain their local support networks. Because the state governor controls a wide variety of resources that mayors need, he consequently influences federal deputies as well.

As might be expected, in some cases the governor's involvement in the submission and execution phases of state delegation amendments leads to friction between the governor and "his" state delegation. For example, in 1996, deputies from the state of Minas Gerais threatened to retract the power that they had delegated to the governor to decide the state's delegation amendments. One deputy complained that, after giving the governor essentially a blank check, with the understanding that the funds would be distributed across the state, the governor had instead used the amendments to further his electoral goals by distributing money only to municipalities run by his allies (*Estado de Minas* 10/22/96).

Despite the obvious tension in the relationship, since 1988 MCs have not overhauled the pork-barrel system to their individual benefit. Instead, they have delegated *greater* power to governors in the pork-barrel process. This appears puzzling: If the governor is so powerful, and has so many tools to use against deputies, why do deputies allow such a situation to persist and promote it? Despite the difficulty in claiming credit individually, they do so in their own interest: Their long-term careers depend on

---

[15] Interview with Sandro Scodro.   [16] Interview with Antônio Carlos Pojo do Rêgo.

cultivating tight links with state government actors. They cannot afford to be on the "outs" at the state level at any point during their careers, because doing so might bring their careers to a premature end.[17]

The changes in the pork-barreling process since 1988, specifically the institutionalization of the state delegation amendment, have tended to favor state government interests. In contrast, deputies have done little to insure that pork will help them win reelection. To benefit from pork-barreling, a deputy must be close to state government officials, primarily the governor, and cooperate with other deputies from his or her state, including deputies from other parties. This holds for *all* deputies, now that opposition parties such as the PT, PDT, and PSB have won several state-houses. However, deputies might differ in the degree to which they support state and/or municipal governments with pork, depending on their personal career motivations. I explore this possibility in the next two sections.

Pork and Progressive Ambition (1): Running for Statewide Office

I have argued that Brazilian deputies do not use pork for "static" ambition, that is, to hold onto a seat in Congress. Instead, pork serves deputies' "progressive" ambition. Deputies use pork to pave their future noncongressional career paths, at the state or municipal level. In this section, I demonstrate that deputies who seek *state-level* elected positions strategically employ pork differently than do deputies who do not seek such positions, and that political variables also influence pork strategy *within* the group of state-office-seeking deputies.

Hypotheses: The Links Between Pork and State-Level Progressive Ambition

What would we expect to see if those deputies who choose to run for state-level office (governor, vice governor, or senator) attempt to use the pork-barrel to improve their chances of electoral success? Two ways to distinguish this type of progressive ambition through analysis of pork-barreling strategy exist, both of which compare where deputies who run for statewide office target pork against where deputies who do not run for statewide office target pork. Deputies can submit amendments to benefit

[17] This is less true for leftist candidates.

the state government, or to benefit municipal governments.[18] Given their previous job experience, for example as State Secretary of Public Works, a deputy might already exercise some influence within the state bureaucracy, and directing pork to the state government could thus serve as a strategy to maintain support. On the other hand, a deputy might target the state government in an attempt to *build* support within the state bureaucracy. Thus, first, I hypothesize that deputies who run for statewide office ought to pave their way by submitting more pork to state government agencies in the election year.

Second, we can explore the degree to which deputies spread their pork around. As Ames (1995b) has described, because the entire state serves as the electoral district in Brazil, deputies can "concentrate" their votes in one or a few municipalities, or obtain a "dispersed" vote pattern, getting just enough votes in many municipalities to win. Ames argued that deputies use pork to seek out new voters in their rivals' bailiwicks. However, that finding may be a function of progressive, not static, ambition: Let us suppose that Deputy X and Deputy Y each win election at time t by concentrating their votes in ten municipalities. At time $t + 1$, Deputy X runs for reelection and Deputy Y runs for governor. What kind of pork-barreling strategy might we see for each politician? Ames might hypothesize that Deputy X would submit amendments to 12 municipalities, his original 10 plus 2 others where votes might be found. Ames implies nothing about what Deputy Y would do.[19]

Deputy Y's best strategy for a run for statewide office is to spread pork around to a much greater extent than a deputy who runs for reelection. A deputy who runs for statewide office must construct a much broader clientelistic base of support than a deputy running for reelection, because winning executive office requires winning a plurality race, while winning reelection requires winning only a public relations race in large multimember districts. Mayors and other local bigwigs serve as vote brokers, so a deputy running for statewide office ought to attempt to broker more pork and develop relatively more ties to local officials than a deputy running for reelection.

[18] They can also benefit national or regional entities, but I ignore that possibility here.

[19] I recognize that deputies who run for statewide office would not be counted in the same group as deputies who run for reelection, and thus one would not include the former set of deputies in an analysis of incumbency-minded deputies' pork strategies. However, the point remains: Even deputies running for reelection may be planning a longer term investment in developing statewide contacts, in the hope that a statewide career opportunity opens up.

Table 11.9. *Average percentage value of amendments submitted to benefit state government, per deputy, 1991–1998.*

	1991	1992	1993	1994	1995	1996	1997	1998
Overall Average %	**19.3**	**14.1**	**20.9**	**23.4**	**13.6**	**6.0**	**3.6**	**5.6**
Standard Deviation	26.2	21.2	24.5	26.8	23.7	17.3	14.0	18.3
Avg. if Run State	**20.9**	**16.9**	**22.1**	**30.0**	**10.8**	**4.9**	**1.5**	**5.3**
Standard Deviation	24.4	24.3	26.5	25.1	20.3	12.2	4.6	19.5
N	37	37	44	37	30	30	31	33
Minimum %	.06	0	0	0	0	0	0	0
Maximum %	88.6	98.5	89.4	78.6	82.7	48.8	23.3	100.0
Avg. if Not Run State	**19.1**	**13.8**	**20.7**	**22.7**	**13.9**	**6.1**	**3.7**	**5.3**
Standard Deviation	26.4	21.0	24.2	26.9	23.9	17.6	14.5	17.8
N	430	425	392	351	444	439	450	480
Minimum %	0	0	0	0	89.5	95.2	100	100
Maximum %	100	95.32	97.44	100	0	0	0	0

Source: Author's compilation, from Brasil. Senado Federal. 1997–1999.

Testing the Hypotheses   To test these two hypotheses, I used the budget amendments from the 1991–1994 and 1995–1998 legislatures. At the end of the 1994 term, 47 deputies (9.3%) ran for governor, vice governor, or senator. At the end of the 1998 term, 32 ran for statewide office. I first hypothesized that deputies who run for statewide office ought to attempt to "pave their road" to statewide electoral success with pork by submitting relatively more pork to the state government, in particular during the election year. Table 11.9 provides, for deputies who submitted amendments, the average percentage of *all* deputies' pork submissions to benefit the state government, and also separates *deputies who ran* for statewide office from those who *did not run* for statewide office and provides the same averages (Brasil, Senado Federal, 1997–1999).

While there is some evidence that deputies in the 1991–1994 legislature who ran for statewide office did target their state government, and that the difference was most pronounced during the election year, the evidence does not support this contention for the 1995–1998 legislature. Why is this the case? Two factors explain the difference.

First, the changes in the budget amendment process since 1994 that have increased the weight of state delegation amendments (see above) parallel the decrease in *all* deputies' average submissions to their states. Many fewer individual MCs targeted their state government in the 1995–1998 legislature than did previously, because all MCs were working much harder as members of state "teams" to deliver pork to their state. For example, in

1995, 194 of the 513 deputies targeted some portion of their amendments at the state level. This number dropped to 111 in 1996, 71 in 1997, and remained at 73 in 1998. In some states, deputies may refrain from individually submitting amendments to their state because a collective system is now employed. This explains why deputies now target a much lower percentage of their pork to states as individuals.

The second factor is that fewer deputies ran for statewide office in 1998, and those who did run had relatively few incentives to target the state. Two elements pushed the number of deputies running for statewide office in 1998 down: the fact that state governors could run for reelection starting in 1998, and the fact that the senate election was for only one seat in each state, as opposed to two in 1994. These two factors constrained deputies' career options.

When there was no incumbent running for reelection, deputies could target the state government with pork in the election year knowing with certainty that the incumbent would not be controlling the state government in the next year. With a favored incumbent running, deputies have less certainty that the pork that they target to the state will not be used by the incumbent *after* the election.

The presence of incumbent governors on the ticket also eliminated the "favorite son (or daughter)" candidates from the pool of deputies. Previously, if a deputy running for statewide office was of the governor's party (or coalition), he or she might have been considered the "favorite son" candidate. In fact, in 1994, while all deputies who ran for statewide office submitted on average 30% of their pork to benefit the state government, "favorite children" candidates for statewide office, defined as those who run on the party label or in the party coalition of the incumbent governor, sent 40% of their pork to the state.

Favorite children candidates attempted to play on the advantage of incumbency – not their own, but of their political group's back in the state. They sent more money to the state government, believing that their allies' control over the state machine would help them to win statewide office. On the other hand, candidates who ran for statewide office but who were on the "outs" at the state level attempted to go "under" the state machine relatively more. They focused relatively more attention on municipalities to construct their statewide political coalition.

A second indicator of deputies' state-level progressive ambition is the extent to which deputies who run for statewide office spread their pork around to their state's mayors. If my argument is correct, then we ought

Table 11.10. *Average percentage of municipalities to which deputies submitted amendments as a percentage of all municipalities in the state, 1991–1998.*

	1991	1992	1993	1994	1995	1996	1997	1998
Overall Average %	**14.8**	**10.1**	**10.8**	**14.2**	**8.5**	**9.4**	**8.8**	**6.1**
Standard Deviation	19.1	13.3	14.7	18.0	12.9	13.8	13.5	9.0
Avg. if Run State	**18.9**	**12.8**	**10.3**	**19.7**	**9.6**	**11.1**	**10.4**	**6.6**
Standard Deviation	24.6	8.4	11.7	19.9	13.3	12.5	11.6	4.7
N	37	37	44	37	28	27	32	28
Minimum %	0.5	0.8	0.5	0.2	0	0	0	0
Maximum %	98.6	33.9	66.7	93.3	63.6	54.5	54.5	16.5
Avg. if Not Run State	**14.4**	**10.1**	**10.9**	**13.6**	**8.1**	**9.2**	**8.7**	**6.1**
Standard Deviation	18.5	13.7	15.0	17.8	11.5	13.8	13.6	9.2
N	407	416	387	340	423	418	434	430
Minimum %	0.02	0.1	0.3	0.4	0.2	0	0	0
Maximum %	100	100	100	100	100	100	100	100

Source: Author's compilation, from Brasil. Senado Federal. 1997–1999.

to see deputies who run for statewide office strategically submitting pork to benefit relatively more municipalities in their state, regardless of the extent to which their own vote base is concentrated or dispersed. Table 11.10 provides the average percentage of the municipalities in their state that deputies targeted for each year.

In three of the four years in the 1991–1994 legislature, deputies who ran for statewide office in 1994 targeted more municipalities. This difference is statistically significant at the .01 level in 1994, when deputies who ran for statewide office targeted almost 50% more municipalities on average than did deputies who did not run for statewide office. In the 1995–1998 legislature, deputies who eventually ran for statewide office targeted only a slightly higher percentage of their states' municipalities. As with my previous measure, the transformations in the budget process since 1995 that benefited state governments have tended to limit MCs' ability to target large numbers of municipalities. Prior to 1995, deputies could submit 50 amendments each, but starting that year they could only submit 20 each. This reduction necessarily restricts the number of municipalities to which MCs can submit amendments.

Summary

I hypothesize that, in general, progressive ambition ought to shape deputies' pork-barreling strategies. Specifically, I hypothesized that deputies who run for statewide office ought to exhibit different pork-barreling behavior from deputies who do not run for statewide office. Prior to 1995, I showed this to be the case: Deputies who ran for statewide office tended to direct more pork to the state government as opposed to municipal governments, in an attempt to build up support within the state bureaucracy. They also tended to attempt to "spread" their pork around to a greater number of municipalities, in an attempt to build a wide coalition of local-level political bosses in preparation for the statewide plurality election. However, once MCs deliberately changed the amendment process to favor state-based interests, those who aimed to run for statewide office had fewer incentives and less ability to favor states.

Pork and Progressive Ambition (2): Running for Mayor

In the previous section I demonstrated that deputies with state-level progressive ambition attempt to distribute pork differently from other deputies. In this section, I demonstrate that the same can be said about deputies who seek *municipal* posts.

Hypotheses: The Link between Pork and Municipal-Level Ambition
What would we expect to see if deputies who choose to run for mayor sought pork to improve their chances of winning? All deputies can submit amendments to benefit municipalities. However, deputies may choose where to submit, and how much to submit to each municipality. Let us suppose that Deputy X and Deputy Y both obtained 4,000 votes in municipality 1, and 1,000 votes in municipality 2, at election t. Subsequently, Deputy X decides to run for mayor in municipality 1, whereas Deputy Y seeks only to maintain her current vote base in municipality 1. If both deputies had ten amendments to submit, Deputy X might "concentrate" his pork and submit all of his amendments to municipality 1, whereas Deputy Y might divide up her amendments proportionally according to where she obtained votes, that is, eight in municipality 1 and two in municipality 2. Deputy X seeks to use pork to maximize his vote totals in municipality 1 because he needs to win a plurality race for mayor, whereas Deputy Y seeks only to maintain her level of support in each municipality. *Ceteris paribus*, deputies who run for mayor ought to "concentrate" their amendments in the municipality where they run for mayor.

Due to Brazil's electoral cycle, we can posit a corollary hypothesis. Municipal elections are held at the midterm of the legislative term:

Legislative elections were held in 1990 and 1994, municipal elections in 1992 and 1996. I hypothesize that deputies who run for mayor should exhibit the "concentration" strategy *only during the municipal election year*. Deputies who win the mayoral race do not continue to submit amendments following the election because they must vacate their congressional seat. Deputies who *lose* the mayoral race, on the other hand, should continue to submit amendments, either to run for reelection as deputy, to switch to a run for statewide office, or to seek some other political position. Thus, while during the municipal election year these mayoral losers should concentrate their amendments, after the municipal election that they should deconcentrate their amendment submissions to reestablish links to clienteles that they had ignored, or to strategically seek out electoral support elsewhere.

Testing the Hypotheses   For each deputy who ran for mayor ($N = 85$ or 17% of the total in 1992 and 107 or 21% of the total in 1996), I tracked the amount of money sent to the municipality where the deputy ran for mayor as a percentage of the total amount of the amendments that that deputy submitted. If my hypotheses are correct, we ought to see a jump in the amount sent to this municipality during the election year (1992 and 1996) and a subsequent decline as deputies deconcentrate their amendment submissions in an attempt at political survival. Table 11.11 provides the findings (Brasil, Senado Federal, 1997).

Table 11.11 shows unequivocally that deputies who run for mayor exhibit a clear pork-barreling strategy. During the municipal election year, they direct pork where they are campaigning. For example, in 1992, for the 1993 budget (which would be in effect during the subsequent mayoral term), deputies running for mayor attempted to direct almost four times

Table 11.11. *Value of amendments submitted to "their" city as a percentage of the total by deputies running for mayor, 1991–1998 (municipal election years 1992 and 1996).*

Year	1991	1992	1993	1994	1995	1996	1997	1998
% To City	10.1	38.0	17.6	16.3	32.6	38.5	17.6	17.0
Minimum	0	0	0	0	0	0	0	0
Maximum	100	100	77.0	60.7	100	100	100	73.3
Std. Dev.	27.5	35.2	21.6	15.0	27.3	30.9	20.7	20.4
N	75	78	51	45	101	96	73	73

Source: Author's compilation, from Brasil. Senado Federal. 1997–1999.

as much pork to the municipality where they wanted to serve as mayor as they had the previous year. Following the election, deputies who lost then clearly changed strategies and deconcentrated their amendment submissions.

A similar pattern holds for deputies in the 1995–1998 legislature who ran and lost in the 1996 election. Although 1996 also exhibits an increase over 1995, the difference is not so stark (and is not statistically significant). The explanation for this is that deputies were already concentrating their submissions in 1995, because of changes in the amendment submission process in 1994 (see above) that limited deputies to 20 amendments each. Given this limitation, deputies had less leeway to spread their amendments around their state in the first year of the legislature. Thus, deputies who planned to run for mayor in 1996 had to begin their strategy earlier. If they lost, the data again clearly show that deputies deconcentrated their amendment submissions in 1997 and 1998 to adopt a different strategy.

I hypothesized that deputies who run for mayor ought to use the pork-barrel to further their goals. They ought to concentrate their pork submissions more heavily in the city where they run for mayor, and we ought to observe this phenomenon during the second year of the legislature. Through an examination of deputies' amendment submission strategies, I confirmed these two hypotheses. This provides additional confirmation that progressive ambition distinctively shapes Brazilian deputies' pork-barreling behavior.

Conclusion

An understanding of the impact of Brazilian deputies' *progressive* ambition allows us to answer the question that I raised at the beginning of this chapter: If deputies cannot effectively use budgetary pork to secure a congressional career, why do they spend so much time seeking pork? I argued that we can explain the structure and process of the Brazilian budget only by assuming that deputies are motivated by progressive ambition, as opposed to static ambition. Specifically, I argued that because extralegislative political forces affect deputies' long-term careers, deputies have strong incentives to favor state- and municipal-level governments in the budget process. In addition, I hypothesized that deputies who plan to seek state- or municipal-level office during or at the termination of a legislative term will exhibit different pork-barreling strategies from deputies who choose not to make such a move. Through an examination of the structure and process of the amendment submission process in Brazil, I confirmed these hypotheses.

This finding has tremendous implications for how we understand the link between pork-barrel politics and the "electoral connection" in a comparative perspective. Without careful attention to legislators' goals, we may arrive at an erroneous explanation for legislators' behavior, and thus also not arrive at a proper understanding of why it is that legislators pursue pork and how they attempt to use the perquisites of their office to further their careers. Explanations of pork-barreling that pay closer attention to legislator motivation will provide better understandings of the glue that holds together patron–client ties, the dynamic behind presidential coalition-building efforts within the legislature, and the relationship between national and subnational governments in terms of budget process and fiscal policy.

12

Appointment, Reelection, and Autonomy in the Senate of Chile*

JOHN LONDREGAN

Introduction

Biologists can learn a great deal about plants and animals by studying how they adapt to harsh "fringe" habitats such as the desert or the tundra, evolving body structures that either shed or conserve heat, and coloration that blends into the background hues of scorched earth or snow. In a similar way, students of legislative politics can learn a great deal by studying legislatures in the "fringe habitat" of an ongoing democratic transition.

The Chilean Senate exists on the edge of democracy, operating under a constitution written in 1980 under the auspices of that country's former military government. The Senate includes 38 elected members, and during the period under study it also included 8 or 9 nonelected senators appointed by the departing military regime.[1] The "binominal" system used to choose the elected senators has some "fringe features" of its own: it virtually guarantees that the party list that comes in second in each of the two member Senate districts gets one of the two seats in contention. Between the appointed senators and the electoral system, legislators friendly to the former military government control a majority of the Senate. The opposition-controlled Senate looms over the legislative process like a robber baron's castle overlooking the Rhine, and legislative initiatives must stop and pay tribute.

While the rules for choosing its members were designed to produce a Senate majority sympathetic to the former military government, they have

* I am grateful to Scott Morgenstern, to serminan participants at CIDE and UCLA, and to two anonymous referees for very constructive comments on earlier versions of this work.
[1] The number varies because one of the nine appointed senators died in 1990 and was not replaced until 1998.

the unintended side effect of creating a "natural experiment" on the impact of selection rules on legislative behavior. In this chapter I compare the voting records of the appointed senators with the corresponding votes of their elected counterparts to assess several hypotheses about the legislators' motives.

The first of these hypotheses about the policy goals pursued by Chile's elected parties (and the institutional senators) is advocated by Carey, who contends that Chile has a de facto two-party system, with the *Concertación* coalition and the main alliance among the parties of the right each behaving like a single political party.

A second hypothesis is a more extreme version of the first. It posits that an ideologically homogeneous "right" confronts an equally monolitic "left." I will refer to this as the "bipolar" hypothesis.

Legislators' policy positions are influenced by two avenues: screening and the prospect of reelection. Lott (1992) finds evidence that the U.S. parties screen candidates sufficiently that retiring members of the House of Representatives maintain the issue positions that they established during their careers. When the eight-year term of the cohort of senators appointed by Pinochet's government lapsed, all were replaced by fresh appointees. To the extent that the appointed senators foresaw that they would not be renewed[2] or were indifferent to the prospect of reappointment, either because of advanced age[3] or individual disposition,[4] we would expect them to advocate the policy positions that they genuinely preferred.[5] This is certainly what they claimed to be doing.[6] If indeed the appointed senators were constrained only by their policy preferences, the policy positions that they advocated while in office can tell us about how effectively Pinochet screened the people he appointed to the Senate. In

---

[2] Institutional Senator William Thayer correctly saw no prospect that President Eduardo Frei would reappoint him when his term expired (Interview with the author, May 1997).

[3] Former Supreme Court Judge Carlos Letelier was already an octogenarian when he was appointed to the Senate in 1990!

[4] Institutional Senator Olga Feliú reported having declined invitations from both of the major parties on the right to seek a second Senate term as an elected member (Interview with the author, May 1997).

[5] The one clear exception to this rule is Sergio Fernández, Pinochet's former Minister of the Interior, whose successor was to be chosen by Christian Democrat Eduardo Frei. Fernández sought, and won, election as an elected senator. While still an appointed senator, Fernández cosponsored "pork-barrel" legislation favoring his future constituency.

[6] One of the appointed senators, William Thayer, asserted that "I seek that I should have the most reasonable position" rather than looking to defend a particular ideology (Interview with the author, May 1997).

particular, we can use the voting records of the institutional senators to test the hypothesis that Pinochet succeeded in appointing nine "preference clones" pursuing a common policy agenda. I shall refer to this third hypothesis as the "Pinochet clones" hypothesis.

The first section of this chapter describes the data: roll-call votes cast during the Aylwin period, March 1990 to March 1994, during the second readings of bills by the Senate Labor Committee.[7] I go on to present an overview of the statistical model used to estimate members' issue positions. I discuss the important challenge to the interpretation of roll-call votes as "sincere," as articulated by Ames in this volume. Ames' cogent criticisms apply to votes cast in the Senate Chamber and are the reason that no estimates based on the Chamber as a whole are included in this analysis. However, votes cast in committees are largely immune from the specter of strategic voting that haunts the parent Chamber, because of the difficulties in casting strategic votes and manipulating the agenda, while the estimator that I use improves on the weighting scheme advocated by Carey and Ames.

In the chapter's second section I present parameter estimates from the model, along with some corroborating evidence from the Senate's legislative debates. The parameter estimates from the statistical model portray a highly cohesive government coalition on the left opposed by an ideologically diffuse group on the right. Both the institutional senators and their elected counterparts of the right display substantial and statistically significant heterogeneity. These results permit rejection of the "bipolar model" and of the hypothesis that the institutional senators appointed by the Pinochet government advocated a common ideological agenda.

Carey's hypothesis that the *Concertación* and opposition electoral coalitions are effectively just two political parties is not rejected. The evidence of preference heterogeneity among the Labor Committee's elected opposition senators was due to differences among Senator Otero and his fellow members of the National Renovation party. Evidence presented in (Londregan 2000b) shows that on the Constitution Committee it is the *Concertación* that displays heterogeneity, mainly due to *intra*party differences among the Christian Democrats. The voting records of the *Concertación* and opposition senators are no more heterogeneous than the voting records of members of the less disciplined political parties in each coalition.

[7] Londregan (2000b) presents results for a larger set of committees.

Data and Methods

During Chile's democratic transition the Senate has been the legislative battlefield, where the governing *Concertación* coalition of parties that resisted the former military government, the opposition parties, and the Institutional Senators aligned with the former regime must resolve their differences. While the *Concertación* control the presidency, the lower legislative Chamber, and a majority of the elected seats in the Senate, the appointed Institutional Senators, combined with the elected senators of the opposition combine to form a majority in the upper Chamber. This has created a de facto policy veto for the opposition whenever the Institutional Senators and the opposition political parties unite, which they have done on most important legislation. While "roll-call" votes, in which the vote of each member is publicly reported, are rare occurrences on the Senate floor, Senate committee rules require that each amendment offered at the second reading of a bill must be subject to a roll-call vote within the committee. Moreover, any member may offer amendments at this stage, making it difficult for the majority or party leaders to restrict the content of the agenda at this stage. These votes constitute a very informative part of the public record and shed considerable light on committee members' issue positions.

The time frame for the analysis is the Aylwin administration, which lasted from March 1990 until March 1994, when Patricio Aylwin was replaced by his democratically elected successor and fellow Christian Democrat, Eduardo Frei. This was a period of intense legislative activity, as newly elected members of the *Concertación* parties sought to make good on their promise to change the policies left in place by Pinochet. The main stumbling block to these reforms was the upper Chamber of Chile's bicameral Congress: the Senate. There a combination of the electoral law, which favored the election of senators sympathetic to the military government, and the presence of "institutional" senators, appointed rather than elected to their posts, combined to create a narrow majority for the right, with *Concertación* senators occupying 22 of the Senates seats, while for most of the Aylwin administration the right controlled 24 Senate seats.[8] Narrow

---

[8] Initially the margin for the right was 25 to 22, but when Institutional Senator Ruiz Danyau, a retired Air Force general, died of natural causes on November 21, 1990, President Aylwin did not appoint a replacement, leaving the right with a 24 to 22 margin for the remainder of Aylwin's administration.

control of the Senate gave the right a de facto veto over legislation during the Aylwin years.[9]

While the Senate Labor Committee was not the only checkpoint on the road to reform, it was an important one, because of both the importance of labor legislation and the ability of the Senate to block proposed laws. Labor legislation is central to the differences separating parties of the political left and right throughout the world, and in Chile such proposals cannot be enacted without substantial support in the Senate.[10]

I have collected the votes taken at second readings of bills during the Aylwin administration by the Labor Committee. During this period, from March 1990 until March 1994, the legislative agenda in the Labor Committee was dominated by the executive. This committee held second readings of six presidential bills, each of which has since become law. The only member initiative that received a second reading was a bill introduced by Senators Fernández, Papi, and Ruiz De Giorgio, which grew out of a defeated amendment to one of the presidential bills and has not been ratified by the Chamber of Deputies. Of the six presidential bills, one dealt with the treatment of workers convicted of crimes related to their opposition to the military regime and subsequently exonerated. The remaining five bills dealt directly with the traditional labor issues that divide the left from the right in virtually every industrialized democracy. Two of these bills sought to favor unions, one dealt directly with working conditions, one with disability compensation for educators, and one provided more generous pensions for public employees.

Descriptive Statistics

We now turn to an overview of the data. This entails an examination of senator's voting records and the extent to which members of the same political coalition vote together. It also means taking a careful look at proposers, examining the reception given to the amendments that they offered. These descriptive findings point to several empirical regularities

[9] Indeed, at this writing an alliance of institutional and elected senators from the parties of the right remains able to block legislative proposals from the *Concertación*.

[10] Article XX of the Chilean Constitution does allow one mechanism for bypassing a Senate majority, but this can only be done with the assistance of a supermajority of the other house of Congress: the Chamber of Deputies. During the period under study, the parties of the right constituted a sufficiently large minority of the lower Chamber that such a supermajority could not be had without the participation of a substantial number of deputies from the right.

in the way in which senators on this five-member committee vote. First, there is a high rate of unanimity, with all five members of the committee frequently taking the same position. We also observed heterogeneous rates of "defection" on divided votes, with some senators much more prone to siding with the opposition and against the rest of their own party's committee contingent. Likewise there was heterogeneity among proposers, many of whom are not committee members, with some producing more votes along party lines while others were more successful at dividing the opposition.

The membership of the committee consisted of a Socialist, two Christian Democrats, one member of the National Renovation Party, and one of the Institutional Senators. Committee memberships belong to legislative caucuses and not to individuals; however, with the exception of the National Renovation Senators, the de facto membership of the committee was fairly stable. The parties differed in the degree to which they shared their committee seats. At one extreme, Socialist Senator Rolando Calderón was the sole member of his party to occupy the Socialists' seat on the committee. The Christian Democrats and Institutional Senators shared their seats more frequently. At one time or another the two committee slots belonging to the Christian Democrats were occupied by three senators, Ricardo Hormazábal, Humberto Palza, and José Ruiz. Of these three, Senators Palza and Hormazábal cast the greatest number of votes, with each voting on about three fifths of amendments considered by the committee, while Senator Ruiz's participation rate was about half that rate. Likewise the Institutional Senators Feliú and Thayer shared their caucus's committee seat, with Senator Thayer participating more than three times as often as Feliú. The National Renovation Party had the highest rate of sharing. Its seat was occupied at one time or another by seven of its thirteen senators, though Ignacio Pérez, Miguel Otero and Sergio Romero participated much more frequently than the others.

Given that the subject matter of the bills considered by the labor committee lies at the heart of longstanding controversies between right and left it is noteworthy that the amendments considered by the committee produced as little division among the committee's members as they did. Of the 244 amendments subject to votes at the second readings of the seven bills considered by the committee, 182 produced a unanimous response; 76 of these were unanimously approved, while the remaining 106 were rejected. While unanimous rejection may seem an odd occurrence, it should be borne in mind that amendments may be introduced by

Table 12.1. *Descriptive statistics: Labor Committee votes.*

Voter	#	Votes % Divided	Polar votes	Defections #	Defections %
Socialist/P.P.D. Caucus					
Rolando Calderón	186	26.88	25	1	4.00
Democrata Cristiano					
Ricardo Hormazábal	150	26.00	23	9	39.13
Humberto Palza	148	33.11	33	10	30.30
José Ruiz De Giorgio	84	7.14	4	0	0.00
Institutional Senators					
Olga Feliú	42	35.71	5	0	0.00
William Thayer	133	24.81	23	16	69.57
Renovación Nacional					
Miguel Otero	39	69.23	21	1	4.76
Other RN Senators	90	32.22	8	0	0.00

noncommittee members. None of the 106 amendments that were unanimously rejected were proposed by committee members.

Of the 62 votes that divided the committee, 28 split along coalition lines; 22 amendments were supported by the right and opposed by the *Concertación* and another 6 were supported by the *Concertación* against the opposition of the right. The remaining 34 votes divided one of the two delegations.

Table 12.1 presents some descriptive statistics for the committee's votes. As mentioned above, the seat controlled by the National Renovation Party was occupied at various moments by a total of seven of that party's senators. Because some of these senators voted very infrequently, they have been grouped together, with separate statistics reported only for Miguel Otero, who replaced Senator Jaime Guzmán after he was assassinated by terrorists in April 1991. Senator Otero was chosen from the Seventh Senate Circunscripción, which consists of the western half of metropolitan Santiago, and had a very conservative reelection constituency. Senators participated in the committee's business at very different rates, ranging from Socialist Senator Rolando Calderón, who voted on 186 amendments, to Senator Otero and the other members of his National Renovation Party.

Most of the votes for most of the senators were unanimous. Consulting the second column of Table 12.1 we observe that for all but two of the senators, Ruiz and Otero, divided votes accounted for only a moderate fraction (between about a quarter and about a third) of the roll-call votes in which they participated. The agenda considered while Senator Ruiz participated was even more consensual, with only 7% of the votes producing division. In contrast, the majority of votes cast by Senator Otero were votes on which the committee split.

The descriptive statistics presented here do not permit us to distinguish whether the higher rate of divided voting for Senator Otero is exogenously due to his having voted on a more polarizing set of proposals, or whether instead it is an endogenous consequence of his own ideological leanings leading him to differ from the *Concertación* voters on the committee more often than other members of his party. This question is addressed in the next section, using the theoretical framework developed in the following.

Even without a fully articulated analytical model, a gauge of the degree of ideological polarization can be had by examining the rate at which senators side with the opposition and against the remainder of their own political alliance. This enterprise is complicated somewhat by absenteeism; we only observe 109 roll calls with more than one senator from the right participating, while the corresponding number for the left is 217.[11] This means that without more information about these votes we cannot discriminate between a unanimous vote in which the lone senator on the right defects from the dominant tendency in her or his party and one in which the committee's vote corresponds to a genuine consensus in the Senate as a whole.

A preliminary measure of a senator's predisposition to defect to the opposition can be had by examining "polar" votes, on which the opposition senators all voted the same way, and on which at least one committee member from the senator's own alliance voted against the opposition position. For senators on the left I treat the *Concertación* as the senator's own alliance, while the RN and Institutional Senators are treated as the opposition, and for senators on the right these roles are reversed. For example, if Senator Palza participates in a vote on which Otero (RN) and Thayer (Inst.) cast negative votes, while Senator Hormazábal (DC) votes in favor and Senator Calderón (PS) is absent, we have a polar vote. Senator Palza can either join the other member of his delegation, Senator

---

[11] The higher number for the left is probably a result of the *Concertación* holding three of the committee's seats, while the right controlled only two.

Hormazábal, to vote in favor of the amendment, or he can "defect" and join opposition Senators Otero and Thayer in voting against the position of his fellow *Concertación* Senator, Ricardo Hormazábal.[12]

The third column of Table 12.1 shows the number of polarized votes in which each senator participated, ranging from 33 for Senator Palza to a mere 4 for Senator Ruiz. Each of these polar votes is an opportunity for us to catch the senator being "disloyal" to his political allies. The bipolar model would lead us to expect defection rates near zero, with all senators in the same coalition pursuing virtually the same policy goals. In a Senate made up of policy mavericks we might see much higher defection rates. Most of the defection rates are below 5%, as the bipolar model would lead us to expect. However, Christian Democrats Hormazábal and Palza both defected between 30% and 40% of their opportunities to do so, while Institutional Senator Thayer defected more often than he was loyal, siding with the *Concertación* position and against the remaining voter on the right on nearly 70% of his opportunities to do so. The parametric results presented in the next section provide some insights into the process driving these widely varying defection rates.

Before we turn to the parametric model, it is useful to take a quick look at some descriptive statistics for proposers. While most analyses focus on voters' policy preferences, it is also informative to examine the agenda presented by senators offering amendments. The amendment process is open to the entire Senate, plus the executive, but most senators only offer a few proposals. Thus proposers have been grouped by political party, with the exception of Senator Thayer, whose high desertion rate suggests that he may make proposals that are ideologically very different from those coming from the remainder of the Institutional Senators.

The most noticeable feature of Table 12.2 is the variation in the rate at which proposers are able to secure unanimous approval of their amendments. While less than a fifth of the amendments proposed by the Institutional Senators (*sans* Thayer) were unanimously approved, more than two-thirds of presidential proposals met with the approval of the entire committee. Conversely, while only about one-eighth of proposals made by members of the UDI party divided the voters on the committee, over two-

---

[12] If Senator Palza voted in favor of the measure, then it would also be treated as a polar vote for Senator Hormazábal; but if Palza sides with the opposition in voting "no," then it would be a polar vote for Senator Palza, but not for Senator Hormazábal. In this case, if Hormazábal also joined the right, the joint "defection" of both *Concertación* senators present would be indistinguishable from a consensus rejection of the proposal.

Table 12.2. *Descriptive statistics: Labor Committee proposers.*

Proposer	Number of Props	% Unan. "Yes"	% Split	% Unan. "No"
Socialist/P.P.D.	35	31.43	25.71	42.86
Democrata Cristiano (DC)	41	39.02	29.27	31.71
Executive	28	67.86	21.43	10.71
Institutional Senators				
Thayer	17	29.41	41.18	29.41
Other Institutional Senators	87	18.39	19.54	62.07
Renovación Nacional (RN)	60	35.00	20.00	45.00
Union Democrata				
Independiente (UDI)	56	30.36	12.50	57.14

fifths of the amendments sponsored or cosponsored by the Institutional Senator Thayer did so.

The consensual reception enjoyed by the majority of executive-sponsored amendments is not shared by proposals from the other *Concertación* Senate delegations. Fewer than two-fifths of the amendments offered by the Christian Democratic senators were unanimously approved, while proposals from the Christian Democrats and the Socialist/PPD caucus met with unanimous rejection far more often than their executive-sponsored counterparts.

It is somewhat surprising that executive proposals are unanimously accepted at almost twice the rate for proposals from the *Concertación* Senate delegation. We might expect proposals from the executive and from the political parties that helped him gain office to have similar ideological content. The greater tendency for executive proposals to meet with unanimous approval may be due to their having a higher "valence," to use the term coined by Stokes (1963) for issues about which there is consensus, such as highway safety. This possibility is discussed at greater length in the next section, as part of the presentation of the spatial voting model. The executive's superior staff resources might be expected to create such an advantage: While senators have but meager staffs, the executive can call on entire government agencies to assist in drafting legislation. Also potentially at work is the executive's monopoly over certain types of legislative proposal making, such as spending increases, conferred by Articles 62 and 64 of the Constitution. This at least occasionally leads the executive to

Table 12.3. *Proposals leading to divided votes.*

Proposer	Number	% of Divided Votes for Which:					
		a	b	c	d	e	f
Socialist/P.P.D.	9	11.11	33.33	44.44	0.00	11.11	0.00
Democrata Cristiano (DC)	12	25.00	16.67	25.00	8.33	16.67	8.33
Executive	6	16.67	50.00	0.00	33.33	0.00	0.00
Institutional Senators							
Thayer	7	57.14	14.29	14.29	0.00	14.29	0.00
Other Institutional							
Senators	17	17.64	58.82	23.53	0.00	0.00	0.00
Renovación Nacional (RN)							
Union Democrata	12	16.67	58.33	25.00	0.00	0.00	0.00
Independiente (UDI)	7	0.00	57.14	42.86	0.00	0.00	0.00

a = Own delegation was in favor, other delegation split.
b = Vote divided on party lines with own delegation in favor.
c = Own delegation was split, other delegation opposed.
d = Own delegation split, other delegation was in favor.
e = Own delegation was opposed, other delegation split.
f = Vote divided on party lines with own delegation opposed.

negotiate with all of the senators on the committee, and then to propose a compromise solution as an executive amendment. Such compromise amendments would obviously enjoy a high success rate.

Also noteworthy from Table 12.2 is the fact that no proposer seems immune from failure. One proposal in nine from the executive meets with unanimous rejection, and the failure rates are even higher for the various senators, up to a maximum of about five in eight for the Institutional Senators (excluding Thayer). This observation is easy to justify as the result of variation in the valence of proposals from each author; everyone has at least a few "bad ideas" that are discarded during deliberation. An explanation that did not rely on valence would have to contend that every legislator occasionally made ideologically extreme proposals, so extreme that at least one in nine is so far beyond the pale that no senator is willing to vote for it. While the internal logic of such an explanation is sound, the sporadic extremism that it requires professional politicians to exhibit seems implausible.

Table 12.3 provides more detail on the divided votes in response to proposals coming from various sponsors. While these descriptive statistics are only suggestive, we might expect to see extreme proposals generating lots of entries in column c, with even the proposer's own delegation divided while the opposition unites in opposition. Likewise, we might expect moderate proposals to divide the opposition while uniting the proposer's own coalition, the outcome tallied in column a. The entries of column b are the prototypic pattern of division that we would expect to observe from the "bipolar" model of voting, with the author's own delegation united in favor, while the opposition stands together in opposition.

The least intuitive voting outcome corresponds to column f: "reverse polarization," with the proposer's own delegation voting in contra, while the opposition is unified in support. Of the 62 divided votes analyzed here, only one, a proposal presented by the Christian Democrats, produced this odd pattern of voting coalitions; see Table 12.3 column f. The proposal by Christian Democrats Ricardo Hormazábal and Humberto Palza gave employers somewhat greater flexibility in assigning work schedules. This represented a loosening of the requirements outlined at the first reading of the bill that they sought to amend, and so met with the opposition of their fellow *Concertación* member, Socialist Senator Rolando Calderón, who sought to preserve the bill's initial language, while both senators on the right – Sergio Romero (RN) and William Thayer (Inst.) – cast favorable votes. While the right was quick to support this measure, they appeared to have wanted more: Senators Feliú (Inst.), Pèrez (RN), and Thayer (Inst.) unsuccessfully proposed yet further weakening of the proposed requirements on employers.[13]

In fact, for the executive and the DC, RN, and other institutional senators, the modal divided vote splits along coalition lines (see column b), though there was substantial variation in the rate at which they produced such divisions, with 57% of the divided votes on proposals from the UDI Party dividing the *Concertación* from the opposition, while only 17% of the divided votes on Christian Democratic proposals fall into this category.

While the number of proposals from Senator Thayer that produced divided votes is small, an examination of column a reveals that over half of them united the senators of the right while splitting the *Concertación* senators. This is the pattern that we would expect to see with ideologically moderate proposals, and it is a recipe for legislative success, drawing supporters from the opposition while retaining the support of the pro-

---

[13] Senado de Chile, March 30 1993.

posers' allies. While no other proposer approaches the high rate observed for Senator Thayer, a quarter of divided votes on proposals from the Christian Democratic senators divided the right while enjoying the support of the committee's *Concertación* senators. For the PS/PPD coalition, the modal divided vote combines unanimous opposition by the senators of the right with a divided reception among the *Concertación* senators; see column c.

The descriptive statistics presented above identify evidence of heterogeneity among the senators on the committee. While unanimous voting is the most common outcome, the data exhibit considerable heterogeneity in the reception of proposals from different authors, both in their rates of unanimous acceptance, with the executive enjoying a substantial advantage, and in the ways in which the voters split on divided votes, with proposals from the parties on the right, UDI and RN, and from the Institutional Senators (excepting Thayer) tending to divide the *Concertación* and the right (the outcome corresponding to column b of Table 12.3) at a much higher rate than proposals from the *Concertación* senators. A noticeable feature in the data is the idiosyncrasy of Institutional Senator Thayer, whose voting and proposing records exhibit a very different pattern from the remaining senators of the right. The spatial voting model can provide considerable insight about the process underlying these regularities, and it is to this model that we now turn.

A Spatial Model of Voting

The spatial model of voting represents policies as locations, and represents voters preferences over those policies using the distance between the location of a particular policy and the location of each voter's most preferred policy. While this is clearly an abstraction, it is one that has permeated both the informal discussion of politics, with its references to the political "left" and "right," and the formal modeling of legislative politics. The model of locations used here is based on the following utility function, which formalizes the spatial model of policy preferences:

$$U(p, q; x) = -(x - p)^2 + \alpha q. \tag{1}$$

Here policy is captured by the pair (p, q), while the parameters x and α characterize the individual's preferences. The parameter x represents a legislator's preferred outcome on the "position issue" of labor relations, with ideal points ranging from very pro-labor on the left to very pro-business

353

on the right, while p captures the issue content of a given proposal. The value of q represents the degree to which a proposal is recognized by all to be an improvement over the status quo. To use the terminology developed by Stokes (1963), if $\alpha = 0$, then all proposals are treated as pure "position issues" and individuals evaluate them solely in terms of the distance of the proposal position from their own most preferred outcome of x. On the other hand, in very consensual environments, with large positive values for α, individuals evaluate proposals as "valence" issues, focusing on the value of q. More generally, legislators will place significant weight on both sets of concerns.

To illustrate the factors at work, consider the hours of workers employed in public transportation. There is a powerful public interest in drivers being awake on the road, so that limits on the length of time that a driver is permitted to remain at the wheel between rest spells lead to consensus improvements in the public good of road safety, represented by a high and positive q in the model. At the same time, the right and the left disagree about the details of how to implement such hourly limits. Should the limits that apply to interurban bus drivers also apply to truck drivers? Should train crews be included in the limit? What about drivers in urban public transit? Should drivers be paid for the time that they spend in mandatory rest spells between turns at the wheel?

Let us suppose that, in the language of equation (1), Socialist Senator Calderón would like to see policy favor workers, even at the expense of employers, represented by a position like x_H in Figure 12.1, while National Renovation Senator Miguel Otero would prefer to see a pro-business policy, even if this came at the expense of workers, corresponding to a point like x_L in the diagram. Let the status quo legislation be represented by a policy location like p_0, farther left than Senator Otero would like to see and farther right than would be preferred by Senator Calderón. Likewise, let $q_0 = 0$ represent the consensus quality or "valence" of the status quo with its long and dangerous hours for transportation workers.

The set of policies that would be preferred to the status quo by Socialist Senator Calderón is represented by the union of regions A and B. Notice that the lower edge of this region to the right of p_0 curves upward. Therefore, any policy moving rightward of the status quo must compensate by an offsetting improvement in road safety to meet with the approbation of Senator Calderón, while policies moving leftward from p_0 may still appeal to this Socialist Senator, even if they represent a reduction in quality, provided that this decline is sufficiently small. Likewise, the set of

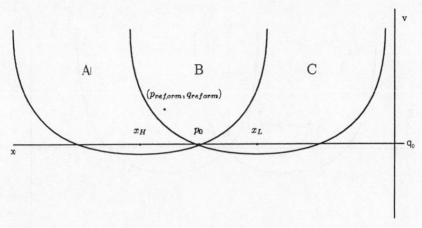

Figure 12.1 Hypothetical policy preferences: High salience on the valence dimension.

points preferred to the status quo by National Renovation Senator Otero corresponds to regions *B* and *C*. Policies lying within region *B* will appeal to both senators. Thus, a point like (p_{reform}, q_{reform}) in Figure 12.1, corresponding to a pro-labor position change combined with a substantial improvement in road safety, something like mandatory paid rest periods every four hours, would meet with the approval of both senators, with the improvement in road safety offsetting Senator Otero's dislike of the pro-labor shift in policy.

The α parameter in the model measures the weight placed on consensus concerns, such as safety, relative to the ideological content of labor policy. The higher the weight on consensus considerations, the greater the room for compromise, as measured by region *B*. Returning to the example of transportation policy, suppose that the senators placed less weight on safety vs. the ideological content of policy, represented by a lower value for α. Then instead of the preferences portrayed in Figure 12.1 we will observe something like Figure 12.2, where the preferred regions are bounded below by steeper curves and ideological considerations are more important relative to consensus concerns about safety. In contrast with the broad scope for consensus represented by region *B* in Figure 12.1, there is much less room for compromise, represented by region *B'* in Figure 12.2. The potential for agreement on policy reforms such as the one

355

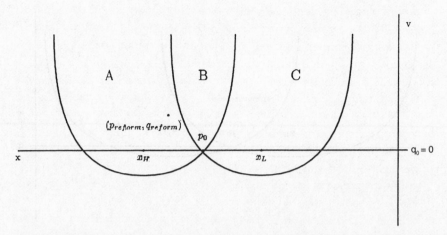

Figure 12.2 Hypothetical policy preferences: Low salience on the valence dimension.

represented by (p_{reform}, q_{reform}) is much more limited, and we can expect politics to be more polarized.

Given that legislators' preferences are represented by this model as summarized in equation (1), and given that each votes for the alternative that he or she prefers, it is straightforward to formalize the conditions for legislator v to vote for proposal p with position and quality (p_p, q_p). Substituting into equation (1), the proposal will result in a utility of $U(p_p, q_p; x_v)$ if it is approved, while the utility of maintaining the status quo is $U(p_{sq}, q_{sq}; x_v)$. The legislator will prefer the proposal to the status quo if and only if it results in greater utility:

$$U(p_p, q_p; x_v) > U(p_{sq}, q_{sq}; x_v).$$ (2)

Our next task is to convert this theoretical condition for voting for the proposal into a form that can be estimated statistically, completing the link between the theoretical model and observed legislative behavior. Here I provide a brief summary of the main features of such a model. Londregan (2000a) provides a more detailed explanation of the model used here, and of its foundations. Under certain conditions on the agenda being voted the inequality (2) is equivalent to:

$$g_{a(p)}x_v + c_{a(p)} + b_v + \alpha \varepsilon_p > \eta_{vp}.$$ (3)

Inequality (3) has the advantage that we can estimate it directly. In a sense it is the counterpart of a regression equation. While it is useful, inequality (3) requires a little explanation. The expression contains three sets of terms. The first, $\{x_v, b_v, \alpha\}$, pertains to the legislator casting the vote. A second set of terms, $\{g_{a(p)}, c_{a(p)}\}$, corresponds to the author of proposal p, denoted $a(p)$, while there are two random terms ε_p, which is unique to proposal p, and η_{vp}, which represents the idiosyncratic reaction of legislator v to proposal p.

Let us turn first to the terms that describe the voter. The x_v term represents the ideological content of legislator v's most preferred policy. The parameter α represents the relative weight accorded to the consensus aspects of policy. Higher values of α, all else held equal, correspond to a greater willingness on the part of voters to compromise their ideological goals in order to achieve policies with greater consensus appeal.

The author-specific parameter $g_{a(p)}$ represents the average distance that proposals sponsored by author $a(p)$ would move policy rightward from the status quo if they were approved. For legislators who systematically propose policies to the *left* of the status quo, $g_{a(p)}$ will be negative, while for authors consistently proposing reforms to the right of the status quo the $g_{a(p)}$ parameter will be positive. The second author parameter, $c_{a(p)}$, represents the average "consensus appeal" of proposals written by author $a(p)$.

A quick glance at inequality (3) reveals that, all else equal, the higher the value of $c_{a(p)}$, the larger the value on the right-hand side of the inequality, and so the more likely it is that a proposal will meet with acceptance. Similarly, we can see that proposals from an author who tends to propose rightward reforms, with $g_{a(p)} > 0$, will interact positively with the preferred policies of voters on the right, for whom $x_v > 0$, producing a larger value on the right-hand side of (3) and a greater disposition toward voting for proposals from $a(p)$. For legislators on the left, with $x_v < 0$, the interaction will be negative, reducing the tendency for voters on the left to vote for initiatives written by $a(p)$. For authors who tend to propose leftward reforms, with $g_{a(p)} < 0$, the interaction effects are in the opposite direction, with legislators on the left, with $x_v < 0$, and so for whom $x_v g_{a(p)} > 0$ being more favorably disposed towards the proposals than voters on the right, with $x_v > 0$, and hence for whom $x_v g_{a(p)} < 0$.

The random terms, ε_p and η_{vp} capture variation among proposals. The first of these affects all voters participating in the vote on proposal p, and I'll refer to it as "the valence shock." The latter random term, η_{vp}, calibrates the idiosyncratic part of the reaction of voter v to the proposal, controlling for the ideological content of the proposal and the ideological leanings of the voter. The b_v, parameter allows the average value for each voter's idiosyncratic shocks to differ from 0.

The model in (3) treats proposal authors as pursuing consistent ideological agendas across proposals, and $a(p)$ corresponds to the authorship of proposal p. The parameter $g_{a(p)}$ corresponds to the average ideological "displacement" of proposals advocated by author $a(p)$. The model is closed by positing normal distributions for ε_p and η_{vp}, while $c_{a(p)}$ can be thought of as the expected value of ε_p for proposals written by author $a(p)$. Moving from inequality (2) to its counterpart, inequality (3), is useful because the voter and author parameters, $\{x_v, b_v\}$, and $\{g_{a(p)}, c_{a(p)}\}$, can be estimated from voting data, closing the link between the theoretical model and observed behavior.

What Roll-Call Votes Can Tell Us

Roll-call votes are publicly reported votes on which the "aye," "nay," or "abstain" of each member present is reported, and not merely the totals in favor and opposed. As Barry Ames notes in another chapter in this volume, not all roll-call votes are created equal. Agendas can be manipulated, party delegations whipped, and swing voters bought off with the promise of a quid pro quo. But these factors do not always intervene. Some venues lend themselves to agenda manipulation, strategic voting, whipping, and vote buying, while others do not. In addition to their intrinsic importance, these common sources of strategic and instrumental voting are important because they affect the inferences that we can make from the record of public votes.

Suppose that members evaluated alternatives according to the spatial model of voting, with each alternative corresponding to a "location" along an ideological continuum. On labor policy the spectrum of alternatives might stretch from "extremely pro-labor" policies to those whose content is "extremely pro-business." The spatial model then characterizes each legislator's policy preferences in terms of his or her "most preferred outcome" along the same continuum, with each legislator always voting in favor of the alternative closer to his or her own preferred outcome. This hypothesis is sometimes referred to as "sincere voting."

If legislators vote sincerely, we can recover a great deal of information about both the legislators' most preferred outcomes and about the ideological content on the agenda on which they vote by carefully analyzing their roll-call voting records. Statistical techniques for accomplishing this have been developed and refined and are widely available. When analysts encounter roll-call voting data, they are sorely tempted to apply their roll-call voting computer software without giving a great deal of thought to whether legislators actually have any incentive to vote sincerely. Some legislative scholars, for example, Ames and Van Doren, argue persuasively that (a) legislators often have incentives to depart from sincere voting, and (b) when legislators do not vote sincerely, standard techniques for analyzing roll-call votes can lead to badly misleading inferences. In particular, party whip votes and executive offers of appointments and favors in return for a vote can lead analysts to overestimate both the degree of preference alignment within parties and the degree of polarization between them.

Excluding close votes may not remedy this situation. Groseclose and Snyder (1996) show that on votes that are expected to be close, legislative leaders using side payments, for example, promise of an amendment favorable to a member's districts and threats – ostracism from the party list in the next election – have an incentive to "buy" a lopsided majority. This is because the increased cost of having to bring more members into the voting coalition can be more than offset by a reduction in the bargaining power of individual coalition members. With a $k + 1$ to k majority, each member of the winning coalition can blackmail the leadership with the threat to single-handedly change the result. With a more lopsided margin it is harder for insurgents to make credible threats, and the spoils that they can extract from the leaders must be divided among more individuals, reducing the attractiveness of defecting. This implication differs from Riker's (1962) prediction of "minimum winning coalitions," which leads Ames to interpret lopsided voting margins on important bills in the Brazilian Congress as *prima facie* evidence against vote buying aimed at swing voters. This is not to say that Ames's conclusions are incorrect, merely that additional evidence will be needed to resolve the question of vote buying.

While the margins by themselves provide very little evidence on the question of whether legislators vote sincerely, the context can often provide better clues. We can usefully distinguish two kinds of departure from sincere voting: legislators who attempt to manipulate the agenda, and legislators who are coerced or enticed by the leadership to vote the "party line." An unpredictable agenda and public voting will tend to discourage the former, while we can test empirically for the latter.

First consider the incentives to cast an "insincere" vote for the less preferred of two alternatives. There are essentially only two reasons why it might serve a legislator to cast an insincere vote. First, an insincere vote might shift the agenda, and, second, it might deceive other members into supporting a proposal that they would have otherwise opposed. First, let us consider agenda manipulation. Denzau, Riker, and Shepsle (1985) analyze a prototypical case of this: voting on the Powell Amendment to the 1956 School Aid Bill in the U.S. House of Representatives. The bill was considered under a "closed rule," which set the agenda. First the House voted on whether federal funds for school construction could only be allocated to districts that refrained from racial discrimination. After that, the House was to vote on the bill as a whole, with no opportunity for further amendments. House Republicans opposed to the bill realized that many southern Democrats who would otherwise support the bill would vote against it if it included the equal access requirement contained in the Powell Amendment. At the same time, northern Democrats could not afford to oppose the Powell Amendment even if it meant that the bill would go down in defeat. Republicans thus decided to join northern Democrats in support of the Powell Amendment in order to ensure defeat for the entire bill on the following vote.

Notice that the Powell Amendment only worked because the agenda was predictable; if Republicans had been uncertain about subsequent amendments to the bill, or about the potential for a conference committee to strip the amendment from the bill, they would not have been able to ensure the bill's defeat by supporting the Powell Amendment. The Chilean Senate Labor Committee, whose voting is analyzed in this chapter, exercises little control over the agenda and is in a poor position to even predict what it will be. Any decision made by the committee at the second reading of a bill, when the roll-call votes are cast, can be revisited on the floor, and such revisions are common. Thus, the committee is not in a position to manipulate the agenda.

Deceptive voting is also dangerous, especially when roll calls are made public. To cast a deceptive vote a member would have to vote in favor of a more distant alternative, and thereby sway enough other members of the legislature to change their votes from the more distant alternative to shift the majority to the member's preferred outcome. Moreover, this will only make sense if the amendment being voted on is not subsequently reconsidered by informed legislators who will not be deceived by the individual's insincere vote. With an unpredictable agenda and an informed conference committee waiting "downstream," a legislator will be very uncertain about whether a deceptive vote will aid passage of the member's preferred alternative, while he or she can be sure that political opponents and journalists will comb through the member's record in search of embarrassing votes. The legislator will then have to explain the vote to constituents at the next election. Moreover, the only people likely to believe a pro-labor legislator who claims that he or she took a pro-business position in order to deceive other legislators will be the other legislators themselves. For senators voting in the Labor Committee, uncertainty about the subsequent agenda makes the benefits of a misleading vote highly uncertain, while the public nature of the committee's roll calls means that the costs of such a vote are swift and sure.

The same public roll-call voting that discourages strategic voting makes a party whip's job easier, whether the member complied with party orders or complied with her part of a "logroll" is indelibly recorded for all to see. However, detecting party "whip" votes is difficult because we are never entirely sure which votes are genuinely "whipped" and which are not. Hidden quid pro quo deals between swing voters and leaders or lobbyists outside one's party are even more difficult to identify.

Notwithstanding the difficulties inherent in finding the party whip votes, there is a means of testing for such behavior within the context of the spatial model. The potential for "extramural" pressure from beyond a legislator's party to sway moderates is harder to dismiss or test for, and the possibility that parameter estimates for the more moderate voters suffer from this source of bias needs to be taken seriously in any discussion of the estimates.

Do We Really Need All of This Math?

The preceding technical discussion raises the question of whether simpler descriptive statistics, such as Rice indices, or the more sophisticated weighted counting schemes, such as those employed in this volume by Ames and Carey, couldn't provide us with just as much information. The short answer to this is "no." The model used here makes more efficient use of the information contained in legislative voting records. The estimator used here automatically assigns weights to the different votes, and it does so on the basis of the estimated distance between the alternatives being voted, represented by the g parameter in the model. This is more appropriate than using the observed voting proportions as Ames and Carey do.

Why is this automatic weighting better? Consider two proposed amendments: On one the "aye" and the "nay" alternatives are far apart, something like "Resolved that Salvador Allende's birthday be declared a national holiday," proposed by a group of Socialist and PPD senators, and another that is barely ideological; "Resolved that farms receive priority access to water during droughts," coming from a hypothetical and ideologically neutral rural senator. It may be that the former would result in a less equal division of the legislature than the latter, a clean but lopsided division between the farther left and the center-left and right. An Allende holiday would nevertheless convey more information about senators' ideological sympathies than a closer but essentially nonideological "town vs country" vote. Yet the latter nonideological vote would receive greater weight in a scheme such as Carey's, which treats close votes as especially informative.

The maximum-likelihood estimation technique used here identifies highly ideological proposers. Votes on the stream of proposals coming from these more polarizing authors contain more information about voters' ideological dispositions than votes on proposals from more ideologically neutral authors, and the maximum liklihood technique automatically accords greater weight to these more informative votes. The rewards for the somewhat greater complexity of the model used here come in the form of a more realistic model and a more sophisticated weighting of the data, a weighting which recognizes that two proposals with equally narrow vote margins may contain very unequal amounts of information about legislator's ideological leanings.

Parameter Estimates

The model developed in the previous section provides a coherent framework for understanding the regularities identified by the descriptive analysis, including the high rate of unanimous voting, the heterogeneous defection rates on divided votes, and the considerable variation in the reception afforded the different streams of proposals coming from various sponsors. Thus, we now turn our attention to parameter estimates for the model. The parameter estimates exhibit two salient regularities of their own: a high value for the "consensus" element for policy, as calibrated by the α parameter that measures the importance of variation in the consensus quality of proposals, and a marked contrast between the homogeneous policy preferences of the senators on the left and the preference heterogeneity encountered among the senators of the right. This heterogeneity combined with the razor-thin margin by which the opposition controls the Senate offers an opening for the *Concertación* to propose legislation that is just barely acceptable to the leftmost of the opposition senators. While this legislation hardly goes as far as the *Concertación*, and presumably the majority of the electorate who support its candidates would prefer, it offers a wider window on reform than would be found if the senators of the right voted as a block with a shared ideal point closer to the center of the estimated preferred points for their senators on the Labor Committee.

Normalizations

Applying the model in equation (3) to the voting data from the Labor Committee requires one more detour before we can turn to the parameter estimates of Table 12.4. Those familiar with interest group ratings will have noticed that the "report card" scores preferred by most groups, with legislators' voting records receiving scores between 0% and 100% (politically) correct, are somewhat arbitrary: Those receiving scores near 100% from groups on the left receive scores near 0% from groups on the right, and vice versa.[14] Temperature scales are likewise arbitrary; a 32° outdoor temperature can either correspond to freezing or torrid conditions, depending on whether it is reported in Fahrenheit or Celsius. All of these scales require normalization. In the case of the Celsius scale, the freezing and boiling temperatures of water are arbitrarily normalized to equal 0 and 100°. Here I will adopt a convention similar to that used by Poole and Rosenthal for the U.S. Congress, arbitrarily setting $x_v = -1$ for the leftmost legislator and $x_{v'} = 1$ for the legislator farthest on the right.[15]

Because the model encompasses proposal authors as well as voters, a second pair of normalizations is required to identify the model. This can be achieved by choosing a "reference proposer" for whom the values of *g*

---

[14] This problem extends well beyond interest group scales. SAT scores run from 200 to 800, though the PSAT, which is designed to measure essentially the same attributes, has an upper limit of 240.

[15] Because the normalization is arbitrary, it is enough to first pick any pair of legislators, one to the left of the other, and then estimate the model. Once the most extreme legislators have been identified, one simply rescales the parameter estimates, with the extremes set to -1 and 1, respectively.

Table 12.4. *Parameter estimates for the Labor Committee.*

Participant	Parameter			
	x	b	g	c
Socialist/P.P.D.	–	–	–12.173	–9.608
	–	–	(4.832)	(4.822)
Rolando Calderón A.	–1.000	0.222	–	–
	–	(0.501)	–	–
Democrata Cristiano	–	–	–8.939	–8.973
	–	–	(4.297)	(4.188)
Ricardo Hormazábal S.	–0.895	1.302	–	–
	(0.084)[a]	(0.567)	–	–
Humberto Palza C.	–0.982	0.975	–	–
	(0.075)	(0.595)	–	–
José Ruiz De Giorgio	–0.997	0.672	–	–
	(0.094)	(0.618)	–	–
Union Democrata Independiente	–	–	2.205	–4.225
UDI	–	–	(3.225)	(2.974)
Institutional Senators	–	–	3.458	–3.376
	–	–	(4.020)	(3.463)
Olga Feliú S.	1.000	18.401	–	–
	–	(8.808)	–	–
William Thayer A.	–0.797	2.530	–8.685	–8.073
	(0.116)	(0.662)	(4.453)	(4.353)
Renovación Nacional (RN)	–0.595	3.869	0.000	0.000
	(0.184)	(0.806)	–	–
Miguel Otero L.	–0.012	8.956	–	–
	(0.434)	(2.308)	–	–
Executive Proposals	–	–	–9.692	–5.687
	–	–	(4.557)	(4.473)
Own Party Proposals	–	0.334	–	–
	–	(0.463)	–	–

[a] Estimated standard errors are shown in parentheses. $\tilde{\alpha} = 4.866$, $\check{S}d(\hat{\alpha}) = 0.562$, $\log(lik) = -280.622$, $n = 244$ amendments.

and c are set equal to 0. The remaining values for g and c can then all be interpreted relative to this value; proposers with $g > 0$ propose to the "right" of the reference proposer while those with $g < 0$, to the left of the reference proposer. Notice that the constellation of proposer parameters is anchored by the reference proposer, and not by the status quo! Finally, we can interpret the b_v parameters as calibrating the tendency of voter v to support initiatives from the reference proposer, which in this application is arbitrarily chosen to be the National Renovation Party on the political right.[16]

Results

The first column, headed by x, reports estimates of senators' most preferred policy outcomes. As described above, the preferred policy outcome of Socialist Rolando Calderón was normalized to equal −1, while the most preferred policy outcome of Institutional Senator Olga Feliú was normalized to equal 1. The remaining senators' estimates are all taken with reference to these two. On the left we encounter Senator Ruiz De Giorgio, a trade unionist, with an estimated preferred policy outcome of −0.997, which is virtually identical to the preferred outcome for Senator Calderón. Also on the left, and virtually indistinguishable from Senators Calderón and Ruiz, is Christian Democrat Humberto Palza, with an estimated preferred outcome of −0.982.

Additional evidence about the ideological preferences of these three senators is provided by their estimated values of b. As discussed previously, a legislator's value of b calibrates the probability that the legislator votes in favor of an amendment from the reference proposer, in this case the National Renovation Party, for which the proposal parameters g_{RN} and c_{RN} are normalized to equal 0. This means that in the context of Table 12.4 higher values for b imply a higher probability of voting for proposals from the National Renovation Party. The estimated value for $b_{Calderon}$ of 0.222 is lower than for any of the other senators on the committee and indicates a barely better than 50% chance that this Socialist senator would vote for a proposal written by a member of the National Renovation Party. However, Senators Ruiz and Palza, with estimated values of $b_{Ruiz} = 0.672$ and $b_{Palza} = 0.975$, have the next lowest probabilities of voting for proposals from the National Renovation Party.

While the estimates reveal the committee's *Concertación* senators to be very cohesive (the estimates for senators' preferred outcomes, the x's, are portrayed graphically in Figure 12.3), the opposition senators are anything but a homogeneous group. Most striking is the gigantic gap, illustrated in

[16] I chose the National Renovation Party because its members were active in making proposals to many committees, facilitating comparisons of parameter estimates in other related work; see Londregan (2000b).

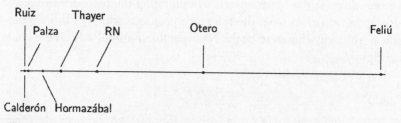

Figure 12.3 Estimated preferred outcomes.

Figure 12.3, between the two Institutional Senators Thayer, with an estimated preferred outcome of −0.797, and Feliú, with a preferred outcome normalized to equal 1. This gap is so large that it is important to remind ourselves that the positive estimated preferred outcome for Senator Thayer, and indeed for all of the opposition senators on the committee save Feliú, do not imply that all of these senators sympathize with proposals to move policy leftward. The estimates for b_v adjust to reflect the rightward leanings of these senators.

While the gap between the committee's two institutional senators is large, it is not the only evidence of heterogeneity among the senators of the opposition. As noted before, most of the National Renovation senators who served on the Labor Committee did so only briefly, and so they must be grouped to permit estimation. This means that only Senator Otero, who voted frequently, has an individually estimated set of preference parameters, while a common set of preference parameters are estimated for the remaining National Renovation senators. Like the Institutional senators, the members of the National Renovation Party do not take identical positions on labor policy, with Senator Otero's preferred policy position of −0.012 considerably to the right of the remaining members of his party, who are estimated to take a position of −0.595.

The estimated values for b, which calibrate legislators' predisposition to vote for proposals from the opposition National Renovation Party, provide further evidence of heterogeneity on the right. The parameter estimate for Senator Thayer of $b_{Thayer} = 2.530$ indicates that he is less likely than any of the other opposition senators to vote for a proposal from the National Renovation Party. Recall the very high desertion rate of almost 70% reported for this institutional senator in Table 12.1. In contrast with Senator Thayer's relative moderation, the estimated value of $b_{Feliú} = 18.401$ indicates that Senator Feliú is even more likely to vote for proposed amendments sponsored by members of the National Renovation than the party's own senators! Likewise, the estimated value of b for Senator Otero is substantially higher than for the remaining members of his party on the Labor Committee.

It is worth noting that the descriptive statistics reported in Table 12.1 capture part of the heterogeneity on the right, with the high desertion rate for Senator Thayer at least suggesting that this senator's ideological leanings differed from the remaining opposition committee members. However, the same descriptive statistics gave no hint of the also substantial heterogeneity among the RN senators, none of whom had a desertion rate above 5%. Moreover, the desertion rates for Christian Democrats Palza and Hormazábal *incorrectly* suggest that these two members of the *Concertación* pursued a different policy agenda than their fellow *Concertación* members, Calderón and Ruiz. As we shall see in the following, the high desertion rates for these senators probably came from Thayer's cunning at crafting reform proposals rather than from significant heterogeneity in the policy preferences of these senators.

Testing the Hypotheses

The preference parameter estimates indicate considerable heterogeneity on the right, in contrast with the "bipolar" hypothesis of a common policy position for the right as well as the left. Likewise, the large estimated gap between the preference parameter estimates for the two institutional senators appears inconsistent with the "Pinochet clones" hypothesis. The estimation framework used to estimate the preference parameters makes a statistical test of these two hypothesis straightforward.

The "bipolar" hypothesis predicts one pair of preference parameters, (x, b), common to members of the *Concertación* and another pair, (x', b'), shared by all members of the opposition. The first row of Table 12.5 reports the results of this hypothesis test.[17] The entry in the *p-value* column

---

[17] The Wald test statistic is of the form:

$$w = (R\tilde{\psi} - r)' \tilde{\Omega}^{-1}(R\tilde{\psi} - r),$$

where $\tilde{\psi}$ represents the k element column vector of parameter estimates for the model (the parameters reported in Table 12.4), $\tilde{\Omega}$ is the estimated variance-covariance matrix for these parameters, and the hypothesis can be written as: $R\psi = r$, where R is a $q \times k$ matrix of constants, r is a vector of constants, and ψ is the true parameter vector. Given the truth of the hypothesis, the asymptotic distribution for $\tilde{w}$ is χ_q^2.

Table 12.5. Test results.

Substantive Hypothesis	Formal Null Hypothesis	Asymptotic Distribution	Test Statistic	p-value
Bipolar Model	$x_i = x_j$ & $b_i = b_j$ for i, j in the same coalition	χ^2_{12}	2,597.6712	<0.0001
Bipolar Model (a)	$x_i = x_j$ & $b_i = b_j$ i, j in the *Concertación*	χ^2_6	7.4079	0.2847
Bipolar Model (b)	$x_i = x_j$ & $b_i = b_j$ for i, j in the opposition	χ^2_6	524.7232	<0.0001
Bipolar Model (c)	$H_0 : x_{Otero} = x_{RN}$ $H_0 : b_{Otero} = b_{RN}$	χ^2_2	8.0725	0.0177
Pinachet Clones	$H_0 : x_{Feliu} = x_{Thayer}$ & $b_{Feliu} = b_{Thayer}$	χ^2_2	414.6028	<0.0001
Bipolar Agenda	$g_i = g_j$ for i, j in the same coalition	χ^2_6	8.0285	0.1547

gives the probability of observing a value for the test statistic as large as the one realized, or larger. The test statistic reported for the bipolar hypothesis is literally off the charts, and it indicates rejection at all standard significance levels.

This raises the question of whether some variant of the bipolar hypothesis might be true. The second row of Table 12.5 shows that the data are consistent with a common set of preference parameters for the committee's *Concertación* senators, with the resulting *p-value* of 0.2847 indicating acceptance at all standard significance levels. At the same time, the results reported in column three indicate that we can reject the hypothesis of a shared set of preference parameters among the opposition senators. Pursuing the observed heterogeneity among the senators of the right even further, the results reported in the fourth row of Table 12.5 indicate significant differences even among the National Renovation party's senators on the committee; the large estimated gap between Senator Otero and the remaining legislators of his party to serve on the Labor Committee is also statistically significant.

The "Pinochet clones" hypothesis also fares badly. The test of the hypothesis that the two institutional senators share the same preference parameters leads to rejection at all standard significance levels.

The formal hypothesis tests bear out the picture painted by Figure 12.3, with a high level of cohesion among the senators on the committee's left but considerable heterogeneity among the senators on the right. What does this tell us about Carey's hypothesis that Chile has a de facto two-party system? While there is significant evidence of preference heterogeneity among the senators of the right, the differences among members of the National Renovation party, and especially between the two institutional senators, are greater than the differences between the average parameter values for the two groups of opposition legislators. Thus, in one sense, Carey's hypothesis is confirmed, at least for these data; the coalitions are no less cohesive than the underlying parties. As noted earlier, evidence from Londregan (2000b) shows that in the Constitution Committee it is the *Concertación* that displays heterogeneity, mainly due to *intra*party differences among the Christian Democrats, offering further confirmation that preference heterogeneity within each of the main coalitions is similar to within-party heterogeneity.

Proposal Parameters

Recall that the g parameters reported in Table 12.4 measure how far leftward or rightward the average proposal from a given author would move policy from the status quo. To identify the model the value of g was set equal to 0 for the stream of proposals coming from the National Renovation Party. This does not mean that the RN party necessarily sought to preserve the status quo. Instead, the ideological emphasis of the RN proposals is reflected in the estimated values of b_v for the various voters, with voters on the left receiving lower estimates for b than those on the right. For the remaining proposers g is informative, and it tells us whether an author proposes to the right (with $g > 0$) or to the left ($g < 0$) of the RN party.

Because of the relatively small numbers of proposals coming from each individual, it was not practical to estimate different values of the proposal parameters for each senator; hence most are grouped together with their parties' other authors. Because of the evidence about Senator Thayer's idiosyncratic preferences, an individual set of proposal parameters has been estimated for this senator. Even when they are grouped, the proposer parameters are not precisely estimated. While all of the point estimates for the proposal displacements are consistent with the findings for the preference parameters, very few of the estimated values differ significantly from one another. One of the estimates that is significant pertains to the Socialist/PPD coalition, whose estimated leftward displacement is −12.173. A test of the null hypothesis that the true coefficient for the PS/PPD coalition is actually equal to 0, the value for the National Renovation Party leads to a p-value of 0.0118, which is significant at the $\alpha = 0.05$ significance level, though not at $\alpha = 0.01$. The stream of proposals from the Christian Democratic senators and the executive are also estimated well to the left of the corresponding proposals from the National Renovation party, with p-values of 0.0375 and 0.03343, respectively, which are also significant at $\alpha = 0.05$ but not at $\alpha = 0.01$.

In keeping with the earlier estimates pertaining to Senator Thayer, the ideological displacement for the stream of proposals coming from this senator is a cypher; the estimated value for g_{Thayer} of −8.685 is only slightly to the right of that for the Christian Democrats. However, the precision of this estimate is lower. The p-value corresponding to the hypothesis that g_{Thayer} is really equal to 0 is 0.0511, just short of rejection. However, unlike the members of the *Concertación*, Thayer frequently co-authored proposals with other members of the opposition, moderating their ideological content, often by enough to attract votes from among the *Concertación* senators, as noted in Table 12.3, column a.

With the exception of Senator Thayer, all of the remaining proposers are more or less where we would expect, with the opposition clustering around 0, the ideological proposal parameter for the National Renovation party. Likewise, the *Concertación* members, including the executive, are also just above the threshold of being statistically significantly to the left of the opposition. It is straightforward to test the null hypothesis of a "bipolar agenda," that is, the hypothesis that all of the opposition senators share a common proposal parameter of 0, that is, that they make ideologically identical proposals, while all members of the *Concertación* share a common parameter of their own. The results of this test are shown on the last line of Table 12.5 and indicate acceptance of the null hypothesis at all standard significance levels. However, this acceptance is in part attributable to the low precision with which the proposal parameters are estimated; the data are almost as friendly to the hypothesis (mined from the data!) that proposals are bipolar with Senator Thayer sharing a preferred outcome with the Concertación rather than the opposition.[18] While the data do not

---

[18] The test statistic of 8.417 would correspond to an asymptotic p-value of 0.1347. Why is the p-value lower despite the closeness of Senator Thayer's location to the *Concertación*

refute the hypothesis of a "bipolar agenda," this is weak support given the imprecision of the parameter estimates. In the language of statistics, the test has "low power."

The estimated c_p parameters, also reported in Table 12.4, which capture the consensus appeal of the stream of proposals coming from a given author, are mostly similar, though the PPD, the Christian Democrats, and William Thayer have values that are just at the threshold of being statistically significantly lower than those of the National Renovation Party, with t-ratios of -2.142 for the CD, -1.993 for the PPD, and -1.885 for the NR Party. These estimates are also lower than those for the executive. Recall the high rate of unanimous approval of executive proposals reported in Table 12.2 and the lower rate for proposals from the *Concertación* senators.

The greater appeal of presidential proposals as compared with those coming from the other members of the *Concertación* may stem from the president's added bargaining power. With the president's monopoly proposal rights within the domains reserved by Article 62 of the Constitution the president is essentially able to act as an agenda-setter over an important set of issues. A little care in setting the agenda will result in a high approval rate for executive proposals relative to other, ideologically similar proposals made by legislators in issue domains in which the opposition is allowed to make counterproposals. Also likely to be at work here are the extra resources available to the executive. As noted earlier, the executive can tap the administrative resources of the entire government to assist in formulating legislation, while Senate staffs are measured in committees per secretary rather than secretaries per committee. It would be a surprise indeed if all of these extra resources did not at least somewhat increase the valence for executive proposals.

The high and statistically significant estimate for α of 4.866 indicates that variations in the consensus value of proposals swamp idiosyncratic preference shocks, whose variance has been normalized to equal 1. This parameter captures the intuitive notion that the stream of proposals from a given individual will be of uneven quality: The same proposer will come up with some "good ideas" and some "bad" ones. The higher the value of α, the more variation there is in the reception given to proposals sharing the same author. The high estimated value for α produces both a high

senators? Because this closeness is offset by the positive covariance between the estimated preferences of Senator Thayer and the *Concertación* senators, especially Socialist Rolando Calderón. The gap between Thayer's proposals and those of Calderón is estimated more precisely than the content of either stream of proposals.

fraction of unanimous votes in favor of some proposals and against others. However, $\alpha = 4.866$ is not so high that the ideological content of proposals is irrelevant.

A hypothetical example serves to illustrate the implications of the α parameter. Socialist Senator Rolando Calderón will be approximately indifferent between an average quality proposal from another Socialist senator and a proposal from a National Renovation senator whose quality is drawn from the top sixth of the distribution. While consensus quality matters, it takes a lot of it to overcome senators' ideological leanings.

Comparing the Parameter Estimates with the Descriptive Statistics

Three salient features of the data – the high rate of unanimity, the high defection rate for Senator Thayer on divided votes, and the high success rate for executive proposals – are all reflected in the parameter estimates of Table 12.4. The high value for α just discussed will tend to produce unanimous votes, notwithstanding substantial ideological polarization. Likewise, the relatively moderate policy preferences for Senator Thayer explain why he tends to vote with the *Concertación* on ideologically divided votes, deserting the remainder of the senators on the right. Another way of viewing this is that Senator Thayer is not really deserting, because, on labor relations issues, he is not really on the right. As discussed in the following, this policy moderation does not extend to his issue position on human rights!

Heterogeneous Policy Goals on the Right

One feature of the data not hinted at by the descriptive statistics is the tremendous heterogeneity of policy goals among the senators of the right. The enormous gap between Senator Feliú's issue position, normalized to equal 1, and all of the other senators is so great that it leaves even Senator Otero with an estimated preferred issue position to the left of 0, the middle of the scale. This means that, relative to the remainder of her colleagues on the Labor Committee, Senator Feliú takes a very polarized position. Except for Senators Feliú and Otero, whose preferred policy position is near 0, all of the remaining senators on the committee have ideal points well to the left of zero; even the National Renovation senators have an estimated preferred outcome of -0.595.

This does not mean that these legislators seek to implement a set of policies that most readers would identify as being "on the left." Recall that the normalization of preferred outcomes, choosing $x_{Calderon} = -1$ and $x_{Feliu} = 1$, was arbitrary. If we had instead anchored the right of the scale by setting the preferred outcome for Senator Thayer equal to 1, $x_{Thayer} = 1$, the estimated values for the proposes g and c parameters would have adjusted to preserve the initial fit of the model.[19] However, the model does tell us that the differences in policy preferences among the senators on the right is larger than the difference between the policies pursued by either Senator Thayer or the National Renovation senators and any of the senators of the *Concertación*. While we can change the units in which we measure these differences, the relative proximity between the *Concertación* and the more moderate members of the opposition is not an artifact of the scale used to measure preferences and will be preserved for any choice of units.

Thayer's more moderate position on labor issues has not passed unnoticed by the *Concertación*. From the perspective of Christian Democratic Senator Hormazábal, "Willy Thayer still has a little bit of a heart"[20] when it comes to labor issues, adding quickly that on the question of constitutional reform he marches in lockstep with the other institutional senators. Asked why he thinks Thayer takes what seem to be ideologically inconsistent positions on labor policy and constitutional reform, Hormazábal observes that as a former Minister of Labor for Eduardo Frei the Institutional Senator is a "prisoner of his history,"[21] a history that Senator Hormazábal is quick to recall in senate debates by quoting pro-labor passages from Thayer's *Manual de Derecho del Trabajo* (Senado de Chile, April 7, 1993).

That the Institutional senators do not represent a unified ideological position causes little alarm among the Institutional senators themselves. These senators see themselves as wise pragmatists who stand outside politics, if not necessarily above it. In Thayer's words, "I seek that I should

---

[19] For a proposer with an estimated parameter pair of (g_p^0, c_p^0) under the initial normalization of $x_{Calderon} = -1$ and $x_{Feliu} = 1$, the proposer parameters with the new normalization, $x_{Calderon} = -1$ and $x_{Thayer} = 1$, would simply change to:

$$(g_p^1, c_p^1) = \left(g_p^0(1 - x_{Thayer}), \ c_p^0 + \frac{1}{2} g_p^0(1 - x_{Thayer}) \right).$$

Of course, this is just another way of saying that the normalization of two voters is needed to identify the model.

[20] May 20, 1997, interview by the author with Ricardo Hormazábal in Valparaíso, Chile.
[21] May 20, 1997, interview by the author with Ricardo Hormazábal in Valparaíso, Chile.

have the most reasonable position"[22] rather than looking to defend a particular ideology. Discussing the ideological position of the institutional senators, Olga Feliú comments that, "There is not exactly, I would say, a clear position coinciding with the parties of the right."[23] While recognizing that "We Institutional Senators are not neutral,"[24] Senator Feliú describes an intellectual basis for her policy outlook favoring free markets and the ideal of a noninterventionist state. But it is clear that she does not view promoting this policy outlook as the fundamental mission of the Institutional senators.

While Senator Thayer sees himself as a nonideological pragmatist, his colleague, Senator Feliú, is correct in recognizing that the Institutional senators are not ideologically neutral. Instead, Thayer's self-perception is a part of his ideology. Near the center of the political spectrum on labor issues, pragmatic considerations will often serve to break "ties" between a status quo on the right and proposed reforms on the left, and so Thayer, like most ideological moderates, sees himself as making practical choices. Yet he is very much a creature of ideology, and it is his moderate outlook on labor relations that makes him pivotal on labor legislation.

One-Shot vs. Repeat Screening: The Institutional Senators

While elected legislators, and the parties that put them into office, face the continuous specter of the next election, appointees who cannot be dismissed have considerable extra leeway, especially when they are appointed for life or when they do not believe that their terms will be renewed. Constraining this tendency is the process of screening that is applied to longer term appointees. While the research of Lott (1992) indicates that congressmen who reach the stage of voluntary retirement continue to advocate the ideological positions that they have defended throughout their legislative careers, these legislators have been through a very thorough and continuous screening process; each election serves as an additional opportunity for parties to deny renomination, and for voters every election is an opportunity to reject an appeal for another term. Combined with careful vetting of first-time candidates by the parties, it is little wonder that Lott found so little ideological "shirking" by retiring members of Congress.

[22] May 22, 1997, interview by the author with William Thayer in Sangiago, Chile.
[23] May 26, 1997, interview by the author with Olga Feliú in Santiago, Chile.
[24] May 27, 1997, interview by the author with Olga Feliú Santiago, Chile.

Appointed senators in Chile, like Supreme Court justices in the United States, are subject to a single vetting, and we might expect that this single round of screening with little prospect for reappointment or subsequent election to a related office will lead to more substantial ideological shirking, that is, the taking of maverick positions of "conscience" not foreseen by those who chose them. This is what we observe with the Institutional Senators on the Labor Committee. It may be that part of the reason for this was that Pinochet cared more about his nominees' views on the democratic transition than he did about labor policy, so that Thayer's odd position on labor issues is really a reflection of Pinochet's indifference rather than any design.

There is evidence that Thayer's more moderate position on labor issues does not carry over to his views on the human rights issues surrounding the democratic transition. Although he did not sit on the Constitution Committee, Thayer did take a public position on the Cumplido Laws, specifically on the question of the jurisdiction of the military courts, saying that, while "one cannot pretend to have peace based on punishment for some and impunity for others . . . nevertheless this should not go to the other extreme of transferring to the ordinary courts mixed cases involving civilians and those in uniform. . . . " (*El Mercurio*, November 12, 1990). While this Institutional Senator took a moderate position on labor issues, his position on human rights issues cannot have given former President Pinochet much cause to regret having appointed him senator.

While the relative salience that Pinochet probably placed on not being brought to trial versus keeping the minimum wage low and the unions weak may help to explain his nomination of Thayer, it cannot be the whole story. After all, there were plenty of people around Pinochet who were on the right on both the transition and on labor issues, and who would have been more than willing to serve in Thayer's place. One is led to suspect that Pinochet's appointment of William Thayer to the Senate was, *ex post*, a mistake, that is, an error in forecasting the range of Thayer's issue positions.

Conclusions

The extreme institutions left in place as a part of the Faustian bargain struck by democrats with the departing Pinochet government in Chile provide a useful venue for testing several hypotheses about the coalition structure of Chilean politics.

Voting records from the Labor Committee of the Chilean Senate provide evidence against the "bipolar" hypothesis, which contends that the *Concertación*, and electoral among parties of the center and the left, and the opposition on the political right each take ideologically homogeneous positions on the issues. Nor do the data support the hypothesis that the senators appointed by Pinochet advocated a common issue position.

The evidence does lend qualified support for Carey's hypothesis that Chile's two coalitions, the *Concertación* and the opposition, constitute a de facto two-party system. However, if the coalitions are to be viewed as parties, they are parties with very loose discipline.

Control of elected officials stands on two pillars: the discipline provided by the prospect of reelection and the careful screening of those who reach office. Evidence from the United States suggests that by the end of their careers members of the U.S. Congress have been repeatedly screened by their parties and their constituents to such an extent that they are in fact committed to the issue positions that they advocate. Is careful screening sufficient to control public policy, even without the prospect of frequent elections?

The evidence from Pinochet's Senate appointees indicates that one round of screening may not be enough to achieve effective control. The extreme gap between the labor relations issues position advocated by Senator Thayer, who was appointed by Pinochet, and the positions advocated by the remaining senators on the right, including Senator Feliú, who was also appointed by the Pinochet government, indicates the difficulty of forecasting the true policy preferences of legislators and other political agents. Granted, the period between Pinochet's loss of the plebiscite in October 1988 and the handover of power to *Concertación* President Patricio Aylwin in March 1990 was a time of crisis for the military government, during which it made several political blunders, including the Gerrymander of the electoral districts for the Chamber of Deputies (Londregan 2000b). Nonetheless, the heterogeneity of opinion among the senators chosen by Pinochet reflects a more general difficulty in forecasting the true preferences of appointees who cannot be recalled and points to an avenue of further research on the relationship between the success at screening the preferences of political agents and the frequency with which their terms are renewed.

13

The Legal and Partisan Framework of the Legislative Delegation of the Budget in Mexico*

JEFFREY A. WELDON

The budget process in Mexico provides an excellent case study for how the party system interacts with constitutionally defined institutional relationships between the executive and legislative branches. The Constitution grants the Mexican Chamber of Deputies extraordinary powers over the budget. The Chamber has exclusive rights to approve the budget submitted by the president, and it may amend the budget. Moreover, according to the prevailing views of leading constitutional scholars, the president does not have the power to veto the budget.[1] The outcome of the budget game in Mexico, however, does not reflect this institutional bias toward Congress. Between 1928 and 1999, the Chamber of Deputies always approved the budget sent by the president, usually without amendments, and only in the last year with amendments unacceptable to Hacienda (the finance ministry). Furthermore, the president has been delegated enormous discretion over where the money is actually spent, so that budget authorizations rarely correspond to the actual expenditures. No one in Mexico doubts that the only actor who has had any real influence over the budget is the executive. This is an emphatic result of the "metaconstitu-

* A preliminary version of this chapter was presented at the 94th Annual Meeting of the American Political Science Association, Boston, September 6–8, 1998. The author thanks Federico Estévez, Gerónimo Gutiérrez, and Scott Morgenstern for their helpful comments, and is grateful for the excellent research assistance of Alejandro Díaz Domínguez, Marco Antonio Fernández Martínez, Karen García Valdivia, Liliana González Pantoja, Fernanda Mora Zenteno, María del Carmen Nava Polina, Juan Antonio Rodríguez Zepeda, and Jorge Yáñez López. ITAM and the Instituto de Investigaciones Legislativas of the Cámara de Diputados provided funding for the research for the *Enciclopedia Parlamentaria de México*.

[1] Furthermore, the Chamber of Deputies has extensive powers to review expenditures ex post, an issue that is not addressed here. See Ugalde (1997b, 2000), and Mendoza (1996).

tional" powers of the Mexican presidency, powers beyond the Constitution that are derived from the partisan powers of the president.

This chapter will examine why the president enjoys greater influence over the budget than what is granted him in the Constitution. The following section will explain how each of these conditions operate and when each condition has held over the past eighty years. The next section will explain the legislative procedures for the adoption of the federal budget, and demonstrate some important differences in the three budget laws that operated during the period. After that, I will demonstrate how the combination of the metaconstitutional conditions and the different budget laws have created different outcomes in the budget process, where the influence of the president over the budget process has varied over time. The last section will briefly explain how the budget process has operated in the current legislature, in which the first condition of metaconstitutional presidentialism, unified government, no longer holds. Furthermore, I will speculate how the other conditions of metaconstitutional presidentialism might begin to weaken in the near future.

Sources of the Metaconstitutional Powers of the Mexican President

The sources of congressional subordination to the presidency in Mexico have been discussed previously in this volume by Casar. I prefer to state the phenomenon of metaconstitutional presidentialism as requiring three conditions: unified government, party discipline, and the recognition of the president as party leader (Weldon 1997b).[2] If any of these conditions are relaxed, the president should lose some or all of his extraordinary powers and the Chamber of Deputies should exert a greater role over the budget.

There was not a unified party government in Mexico between 1917 and 1929, when former President Plutarco Elías Calles founded the Partido Nacional Revolucionario (Alvarado 1990; Garrido 1982, pp. 63–102; Lajous 1979; Loyola 1980). There was a short period of divided government during the term of Obregón (1920–1924), when there were sporadic partisan majorities in Congress organized against the president (José Valenzuela, forthcoming; Weldon 1997b); however, most of the time the partisan divisions between the two branches can best be described as unstructured, in which the president was not strongly identified with a particular party and no single party held a majority in the lower chamber

---

[2] I thank Juan Molinar for this simple formula. Cosío Villegas (1973, p. 29) first proposed the institutional connections between the party, the president, and Congress.

(Castro Martínez 1992, pp. 35–64; Garrido 1982, pp. 20–62; Meyer, Krauze, and Reyes 1977). As a result, the presidents enjoyed little legislative success in this period, and the Chamber of Deputies approved relatively few executive-sponsored bills (Molinar Horcasitas and Weldon, forthcoming; Weldon 1997c). Presidents Carranza (1917–1920), de la Huerta (1920), and Obregón (1920–1924) were particularly unproductive legislators (Marván, forthcoming).

After the formation of the PNR in 1929, unified government was secure. The official party controlled the presidency and majorities in both chambers of Congress between 1929 and 1997. In fact, before 1964, all senators, and virtually all deputies, had been members of the official party (renamed the Partido Revolucionario Institucional – PRI – in 1946). Minority-party representation was introduced in 1964 (Lujambio 1987; Molinar Horcasitas 1991). Guaranteed minority representation was increased to 25% of the whole Chamber in 1979, to 30% in 1988, to 37% in 1994, and finally to 40% in 1997 (Molinar Horcasitas and Weldon 2001). The 1988 and 1991 electoral laws also guaranteed a majority for the largest party, though the PRI held only 52% of the seats in the lower chamber for the 1988–1991 period. The PRI maintained about 60% of the seats under two different electoral laws between 1991 and 1997. In the 1997 election, the PRI won only 39% of the vote, and as of December 1999 the party held only 241 of the 500 seats in the Chamber of Deputies, though it still maintained a majority in the Senate.[3] Therefore, the condition of a unified government held between 1929 and 1997 but was not fulfilled in the periods 1917–1929 and 1997–2000.

The second condition is that there must be high discipline within the party that controls the Congress. If there is a unified government without strong party discipline, the deputies could vote against the executive's agenda, and the president would remain legislatively weak. There is not much evidence of low discipline in Congress in the first years of the PNR, but it is certainly true that there were major regional divisions in the party.[4] The PNR was a coalition of local political machines, and there was the danger that regional conflicts could arise, as they had repeatedly between 1917 and 1934. The regional divisions in the PNR were sometimes expressed through the representatives of the local political machines in

---

[3] At the beginning of the 57th Legislature (1997–2000), the PRI held 239 seats. This number fluctuated between 238 and 245 during the term.

[4] For regional political conflicts before the formation of the PNR, see Benjamin and Wasserman (1990).

Congress, and these deputies paid with life or liberty for the sins of their bosses in the rebellions of 1923, 1927, and 1929. However, after 1923, it is not so clear that regional divisions necessarily caused policy differences in the Chamber of Deputies.

Nonetheless, various institutional mechanisms were created during the *Maximato* (1928–1935) to decrease the strength of local party bosses and, in consequence, the autonomy of the deputies and senators in the federal Congress. One of the more dramatic reforms, if perhaps not the most important, was the prohibition of immediate reelection for deputies and senators. These constitutional reforms, passed by Congress in late 1932 and ratified in early 1933, also extended the no-reelection prohibitions to state legislators and mayors, where the impact was probably greater.[5] The prohibition on consecutive terms cut the electoral connections between the members of Congress and their electorate. Back then, when electoral fraud was commonplace, the "electorate" of a deputy was more likely his political boss and machine rather than ordinary voters; nevertheless, we should expect that the electoral connection between deputies and their bosses should diminish. The deputies should be less concerned over local issues and more likely to respond to cues from other political actors (Nacif 1995; Weldon 1997b).

The National Executive Committee (CEN) of the PNR was the natural source of these cues. It had already been taking an active role in the legislative process by presenting bills and seeking greater discipline among the deputies. At about the same time, the CEN of the PNR had begun centralizing the nominations process so that it could maintain greater control over who could use the party label. Also, in the 1933 national convention of the PNR, the local parties affiliated with the official party were formally abolished (though the process of exterminating them entirely would take the remainder of the decade). Since the CEN of the party now had greater control over access to important electoral posts, it was natural that deputies began to follow national party dictates rather than concern themselves with local issues.[6]

Reforms within the party in the late 1930s made sectoral organizations in the PNR (after 1938, the Partido de la Revolución Mexicana – PRM) as important as the geographical organizations. Political careers could be

---

[5] In this period, there was much more conflict between the executive and legislative branches at the local level than there ever had been at the federal level. See Weldon (1994).

[6] The CEN was also influential in local nominations, such as for governor, so loyalty to the national party might assist a politician who had immediate electoral concerns at the local level.

made in the PRM through the sectors, without ever having to worry about local politics. After the 1946 electoral reforms, which centralized the organization of elections at the federal Interior Ministry (*Gobernación*), the focal point of party discipline was even more highly concentrated at the national level.[7] These electoral reforms also contributed to the near certainty of a hegemonic party government, so that political careers outside of the official party (now the PRI) were not likely to prosper (Molinar Horcasitas 1991, pp. 29–56).

Therefore, the second condition for the maintenance of the metaconstitutional powers of the Mexican presidency, high party discipline, has been mostly in place since 1934, if not before.[8] Even today, discipline is extraordinarily high. During 1998–1999, party cohesion for PRI deputies was above 99% – that is, 99% of the party members voted with the majority of the party. Cohesion is also relatively high, above 90%, for the other two main opposition parties. Discipline in the future could decline if various electoral reforms are enacted. Probably opening ballot access through primaries would do the greatest damage to party discipline, even more than permitting reelection.

During the Maximato, the focal point of party discipline was not yet the president, because the latter was not yet recognized as the head of the official party. In the period beginning in 1928 and ending in 1935 or 1936, the acknowledged head of the party was former president Calles, known as the *Jefe Máximo*.[9] The Jefe Máximo was clearly the most important political figure in these years, and the presidents of the period, perhaps unfairly, were considered puppets of Calles. It was Calles, therefore, not the presidents of the Maximato, who was the beneficiary of the increased party discipline induced by the institutional reforms of those years. This dyarchy of president/Jefe Máximo was widely accepted.[10] The political actors who selected the centralizing reforms knew that this would strengthen Calles rather than the president.

[7] Before the electoral reform, the organization of elections was almost entirely at the municipal level, where mayors held enormous power over the registration of candidates and overseeing polling.

[8] In the pre-party era, 1917–1929, cohesion, if not discipline, among deputies was remarkably high, due in part to the threats of violence against members who acted against Chamber leadership.

[9] For the Maximato, see Córdova (1995); Dulles (1961); Medín (1982); Meyer (1978); and Meyer, Segovia, and Lajous (1978).

[10] In fact, other dyarchies had existed since the Revolution. See Meyer, Krauze, and Reyes (1977, pp. 126–127).

By 1936, however, President Lázaro Cárdenas (1934–1940) had sent Calles into exile. He also modified the structure of the party, increasing the power of the sectors, where his own supporters had been concentrated, and weakening the geographical organization, where old *callistas* might have remained influential. By the end of his term, Cárdenas held both posts of the dyarchy – the constitutional presidency and the metaconstitutional *jefatura máxima* – though this union was most likely an unintended consequence of the institutional reforms (Weldon 1997a). Now the president of the Republic could manipulate all of the discipline that had been focused in the party leadership. The president also had an ever-increasing number of appointed positions in the federal bureaucracy to hand out to loyal members of Congress when their terms ended.

Between the mid-1940s and the mid-1990s, the president remained the undisputed leader of his party. He generally held the power to nominate most candidates to elective office for the party, including the power to name his own successor. Without reelection, no one else in the party could build an independent geographical electoral base that might eventually challenge the authority of the national party leadership.[11]

This third condition for metaconstitutional powers, the unity of the presidency and the leadership of the party, was in full effect from the late 1940s to the beginning of the term of Ernesto Zedillo (1994–2000). Particularly in the first two years of his term, Zedillo was less involved in party matters and insisted on a "healthy distance" between the presidency and the PRI, claiming that he wanted to be merely a constitutional president.[12] Zedillo appeared to participate less in the nomination procedures for candidates for governor. This might have induced *priísta* deputies to look elsewhere for cues, and indeed there is some evidence that they were less obedient to the president on legislation during 1994–1997. For example, the social security reforms were significantly modified, the sale of the petrochemical plants of PEMEX was canceled, and the creation of the new federal controller was delayed for several years.[13] Nonetheless, no alternative, universally recognized Jefe Máximo emerged.

---

[11] See Mainwaring and Shugart (1997) for examples of the partisan effects on presidential power in other Latin American systems.

[12] This was prompted by the need to engage in all-party negotiations for electoral reform and to preserve the president's status as an honest broker.

[13] The bill that created the Entidad de Fiscalización Superior de la Federación was finally approved on Dec. 15, 1998.

The Legislative Delegation of the Budget in Mexico

In the months preceding the 1997 election, Zedillo had begun to act in a more partisan manner, and afterwards he was rewarded with strong support from his minority party in Congress. In 1999, for the first time ever, an open presidential primary was held to select the candidate for the PRI. Zedillo did not formally endorse a candidate, though most believe that the eventual winner, Francisco Labastida, was his favorite. Had he openly indicated that Labastida was his first choice, then the PRI would have considered that Zedillo had exercised his metaconstitutional prerogative over the succession.

All three factors of metaconstitutional presidentialism (unified government, high discipline, and president as head of the party) are necessary conditions. If any one of these fail, we should observe a depreciation of the power of the presidency. The Mexican president would still maintain his considerable constitutional powers, but he would have to share power with the other branches of government. Evidence demonstrates that the legislative success of the presidents follows this pattern remarkably. When there was a unified government for the first time, presidential legislative success increased dramatically. Once the president was also Jefe Máximo, there was another ratchet increase in the legislative success of the president (Molinar Horcasitas and Weldon, forthcoming; Weldon 1997c).

The resolution of the budget process, therefore, is influenced by these metaconstitutional mechanisms – these institutional arrangements that are defined outside of the Constitution and the laws – though they are highly dependent on legal institutions (such as the relationship between no reelection and high discipline). When the three conditions hold, we should expect that the president should have his budget passed with little interference from the Chamber of Deputies. If any of these conditions are lacking, then we should expect greater intervention by the Chamber: greater incidence of not approving the budget, greater incidence of amendments to the budget, longer time allowed to examine the budget, and so on.

In the next section I describe the formal legislative procedures for appropriations, which will define how the metaconstitutional powers of the president are expressed through the budget process. During the twentieth century there were different legal rules through which the partisan metaconstitutional arrangements were played out.

The Budget Process

The Chamber of Deputies actually has a remarkable scope of budgetary powers. Although the president may have a monopoly over presenting the unified budget, the Chamber of Deputies may modify the appropriations in any way, and the president (apparently) cannot veto these modifications.

The basic rules for the approval of the budget are found in the Constitution, principally in section IV of Article 74 and in Article 75. There were three budget laws in force in Mexico during the twentieth century: the Ley Orgánica del Presupuesto (1928),[14] the Ley Orgánica del Presupuesto de la Federación (1935),[15] and the Ley de Presupuesto, Contabilidad y Gasto Público Federal (1976).[16] Deputies from the National Action Party (PAN) proposed significant amendments to the 1935 budget law in 1947, but these were rejected by the PRI majority.[17] Legislative procedures for approving the budget vary only slightly from the rules regarding regular bills. These rules are found in the Ley Orgánica del Congreso General de los Estados Unidos Mexicanos and in the Reglamento para el Gobierno Interior del Congreso General de los Estados Unidos Mexicanos.[18]

The federal budget is composed of at least three different bills.[19] The Presupuesto de Egresos de la Federación is the federal appropriations law, approved only by the Chamber of Deputies. The Ley de Ingresos is the federal revenue law. It estimates revenue, given the current tax laws, and sets general spending and debt limits. The third element is the Miscelánea Fiscal, which is an omnibus bill that amends tax laws to conform to the Ley de Ingresos. Both chambers must pass the two revenue bills. The rest

---

[14] *Diario Oficial de la Federación (D.O.F.)*, May 28, 1928.

[15] *D.O.F.*, Dec. 26, 1935.

[16] *D.O.F.*, Dec. 29, 1976. The Reglamento of the budget law was published in the *D.O.F.* on Nov. 13, 1981. Budget matters are also discussed in the Ley Orgánica de la Administración Pública Federal and in the Ley General de Deuda Pública.

[17] *Diario de los Debates de la Cámara de Diputados (D.D.C.D.)*, Nov. 6 and Nov. 18, 1947.

[18] The Reglamento is antiquated, based on the original Reglamento of 1824. The current Reglamento dates to 1897, with only minor modifications in 1934 (*D.O.F.*, March 20, 1934), and a few amendments since. It is very short, only 204 articles, with very little detail on legislative procedures. There is much more detail on the rules of debate courtesy than on how a bill becomes a law. Amendment procedures are not specific. The Ley Orgánica was written in 1979 to enact changes in party and leadership structures that had become necessary when minority representation was increased (*D.O.F.*, May 25, 1979, amended, *D.O.F.*, July 20, 1994 and Sept. 3, 1999). The most recent reforms were substantial, but none of the amendments directly affected legislative procedure or the budget process.

[19] Recently, the budget package has also included the federal revenue sharing law, which provides the formula for the division among states.

of this chapter will deal with only the appropriations law, the Presupuesto de Egresos.

Introduction of the Budget

Current budget law appears to give the president a monopoly over the introduction of the budget, but this has not always been the case. The 1917 Constitution did not specify who should introduce the budget. The 1928 budget law, however, defined the budget as the set of documents prepared by the executive to be presented to the Chamber of Deputies for approval, and similar language reappeared in the 1935 and the 1976 laws. The 1935 budget law prescribed a unitary budget, where all *ramos* (major line items, corresponding roughly to executive departments) of the budget would be presented in one single appropriations bill. Before 1935, the ramos were often introduced separately.

The collection of budget requests and final preparation of the budget has nearly always been done in the executive branch. Before 1928, the process was controlled by Hacienda (the Finance Ministry). The 1928 budget law created a Budget Department, reporting directly to the president, which would have centralized the processing of budget requests. The new budget office would have the power to adjust appropriations requests from the agencies before submitting the budget to the Chamber of Deputies. Bureaucrats were prohibited from requesting adjustments from the Chamber's budget committee; all such requests had to be directed through the budget office. The 1928 law gave Hacienda until January 1932 to restructure itself and spin off the appropriations functions, though the transfer never occurred, and the presidential budget office never actually operated. The 1935 law reassigned appropriations to Hacienda.[20] The Secretary of Programming and Budget (SPP) supervised expenditures from 1976 to 1992, when these were transferred back to Hacienda.[21]

The fiscal year in Mexico runs from January 1 to December 31, and the budget must be passed before the end of the year prior to the fiscal year.

---

[20] The restrictions on communications between agencies and the budget committee were maintained. The only link was to be through Hacienda. The *panista* amendments to the 1935 budget law attempted to repeal this article (*D.D.C.D.*, Nov. 6, 1947).

[21] Salinas had been in charge of the SPP during the de la Madrid presidency (1982–1988), and Zedillo was the last secretary of the SPP before the demise of the ministry (he was transferred to the education ministry). For the fusion of the SPP and Hacienda, see *D.O.F.*, Feb. 21, 1992.

The 1917 Constitution did not specify a date for the introduction of the budget. The 1928 budget law set a submission date for November 1, and the congressional term ended on December 31, giving the Chamber of Deputies two months to resolve the question. In 1935, the date was moved to December 15, limiting deliberations to only two weeks. The *panista* amendments in 1947 attempted to move the submission date back to November 10, arguing that the Chamber needed more time to examine the budget.[22] In the 1976 budget law, the submission date was moved up to November 30. This was adjusted again to November 15 in 1982, the first time that a date had been specified in the Constitution.[23] In 1993, the congressional terms were modified, and the fall session now ends on December 15.[24] Therefore, current law gives the Chamber of Deputies one month to approve the budget. In 1998 and 1999, special sessions had to be called to pass the budget before the end of the year.

During the fiscal year, it is often necessary to increase the budget, or transfer money from one ramo to another. Under the 1928 budget law, if Congress passed a new law authorizing a program that needed appropriations, or if an agency required more money, they would inform the budget department so that it could prepare a supplemental appropriations bill that would be sent to the Chamber of Deputies. The budget department would also submit bills to transfer funds. Hacienda prepared bills to adjust current budgets under the 1935 budget law. The 1976 budget law permits the president to spend more money on projects if there is a budget surplus, and to transfer money between accounts. He only must inform the Congress the following year in his report of the public accounts.

Furthermore, it was common in the first couple of decades after the Revolution that deputies would introduce legislation for construction projects in their own districts or states, independent of the federal budgetary process overseen by the executive branch. Only the Chamber of Deputies approved these bills.

[22] They also argued that the Reglamento authorized the budget committee 30 days to examine the budget, in contradiction with the 15 days granted in the 1935 law. In its report, the PRI-controlled budget committee claimed that 15 days was more than enough time, and the differences between the Reglamento and the budget law had been resolved in a transitory article in the latter, which repealed any laws to the contrary (*D.D.C.D.*, Nov. 6, and Nov. 18, 1947).

[23] *D.O.F.*, Nov. 17, 1982.

[24] *D.O.F.*, Sept. 3, 1993.

Approval of Appropriations by the Chamber of Deputies

The appropriations law is approved only by the Chamber of Deputies. The 1824 Constitution, the first republican constitution of independent Mexico, granted the power to approve the budget to both chambers. The 1857 Constitution abolished the Senate, giving all legislative powers to the Chamber of Deputies. The Senate was restored in 1874, and most laws had to be passed by both chambers, though the Chamber of Deputies maintained exclusive powers over approving appropriations and examining the federal accounts (Tena Ramírez 1991, p. 702). Both chambers approved revenue legislation. The exclusion of the Senate from the appropriations process was continued in the 1917 Constitution (Tena Ramírez 1985, pp. 324–26).

The appropriations bill follows nearly the same path of legislative procedure as any other bill. All bills presented by the president, including appropriations, are sent directly to committee, unless the floor decides, by a two-thirds vote of members present, that the bill is of "urgent or obvious resolution." Under those circumstances, the bill is considered on the floor immediately.[25]

The budget bill has nearly always gone to committee. The PRI usually has been greatly overrepresented in committees, though recently committee assignments have been more proportional (Lujambio 1995, pp. 190–201; Martínez Gallardo 1998; Weldon 1998a). For the 57th Legislature (1997–2000), where no party held a majority of seats, deputies were assigned proportionally to committees. Although the majority party (when one exists) has always held a majority of seats on all committees, the chairs of the committees have recently been distributed to all parties. The PRI held more than its proportional share of chairs (Lujambio 1995, pp. 195–203), until the 57th Legislature, in which they were also been distributed proportionally.[26] Committee chairs have a double vote in case of ties, a *voto de calidad*.[27]

---

[25] Note that the two-thirds requirement is only to suspend the rules. After the suspension is authorized, the bill is passed by a simple majority vote.

[26] The chair of the budget committee was given to the opposition for the first time in the 57th Legislature, to the PRD. The 30-member committee has 14 members from the PRI, 7 each from the PAN and PRD, and 1 each from the PT and PVEM.

[27] The *voto de calidad* allows a chair to vote once as a regular member, and if there is a tie, she can vote a second time to break the tie. Nonetheless, final committee reports are signed, not voted, so the *voto de calidad* does not apply. See the discussion in Weldon (1998a). On the floor of the Chamber, if there is a tie, the vote is taken a second time; and if the tie persists, the vote is postponed for the next day. There is no tie-breaking rule on the floor.

Committees must report regular bills within five days, but the appropriations bill is an exception: The budget committee has 30 days to report the bill.[28] This special allowance is not of great importance, since the Chamber has only a month remaining on its calendar before adjournment, and only two weeks in inaugural years.

Amendments to Appropriations in Committee

Committees may amend bills, including the appropriations bill. The budget law of 1928 expressly permitted members of either chamber to submit proposed amendments to revenue or appropriations bills to the appropriate committees. This allowed senators to send amendments to the budget committee of the Chamber of Deputies (the Senate, of course, does not have a budget committee). On the other hand, no amendments to the committee report were allowed on the floor. This was modified in the 1935 budget law, so that only members of the Chamber of Deputies were allowed to submit amendment proposals to the budget committee. Again, floor amendments were prohibited. The *panista* reforms of 1947 tried to repeal this article as an unconstitutional restraint on the legislative powers of deputies.[29] The 1976 budget law does not restrict amendments to the budget in any way, though legislative procedures make floor amendments difficult.

Amendments to Appropriations on the Floor

Committee reports must be signed by a majority of the committee. Members of the committee may decline to sign the report and issue their own minority report – a *voto particular.* The *voto particular* is sent to the leader of the party of the dissenter and to the chairman of the committee. The former, "if he thinks it convenient," can send the *voto particular* to the president of the *mesa directiva* for purposes of possible debate. This gives the party leader a veto over any *voto particular* promoted by members of his party, and, in fact, it is usually the party leadership that writes up the minority reports. A *voto particular* can only be considered if the floor rejects

[28] Before the 1933 reform to the Reglamento, committees were allowed 15 days to report a bill. The 1999 reforms to the Ley Orgánica eliminate the deadline.
[29] The PRI argued that the mere regulation of a deputy's rights could not be interpreted as a constitutional restraint (*D.D.C.D.*, Nov. 18, 1947).

388

the majority report.[30] Therefore, these "amendments as substitutes" are rarely discussed on the floor and are not usually viable options for amendment.

The report of a bill is voted on twice on the floor. First, there is debate and a vote *en lo general*, which determines whether the Chamber is satisfied with the bill in general. If the report is rejected *en lo general*, there is a second vote on whether to send the report back to committee for amendment or to discard the bill entirely.[31] If it is approved *en lo general*, there is a further debate and set of votes *en lo particular* on specific articles of the bill that had been reserved by any deputy for further debate. Articles can be amended or deleted from the bill *en lo particular*. However, deletion of articles is not feasible in the appropriations bill, because in the quantitative section of the bill each article states the whole amount to be spent in each *ramo*. This would work only if the Chamber of Deputies wanted to eliminate an entire department.[32] The rule states that rejected articles are to be sent back to committee, where they might be amended or killed, but it is not clear who makes this final decision or whether the bill is formally allowed to continue toward passage without having resolved the fate of its rejected articles.

There is one other way of amending a bill on the floor. A deputy can propose modifications or additions to the text in debate *en lo general* or *en lo particular* (more often in the latter). The Reglamento is oddly worded

---

[30] If the rules are followed to the letter, this procedure will rarely develop, because the Reglamento states that *votos particulares* can be considered only if they had been presented at least one day before the report was discussed on the floor. Frequently, however, bills are discussed on the same day that they are reported. The 1997 parliamentary agreement on legislative procedures requires a report to be submitted 48 hours before debate is to begin ("Acuerdo parlamentario relativo a las sesiones, integración del orden del día, los debates y la votaciones de la Cámara de Diputados," *D.O.F.*, Nov. 11, 1997). However, a *voto particular* must also be published at least 48 hours before debate. The first rule was rarely followed in a strict sense during the 57th Legislature.

[31] This procedure was not followed on Dec. 4, 1997, when the Chamber, more or less by accident, rejected the Miscelánea Fiscal. The president of the Chamber for the day declared the bill "*desechada*," which killed the bill, and did not hold the second vote as stipulated by the Reglamento. This was a grave error, because the Constitution states that a bill that is rejected in its Chamber of origin cannot be considered until the next session, which would have been in March 1998. The Comisión de Regimen Interno y Concertación Política eventually found a way to revive the Miscelánea by presenting a second bill similar to the one rejected. This was approved by the Chamber on Dec. 12, 1997.

[32] At times, the budget has included all executive departments under a single article and all parastate companies under a second article.

and contradictory: "During the session in which a proposition or a bill is definitively voted upon, additions or modifications to the *approved* articles can be presented in writing."[33] The rules seem to permit amendments only to those articles that have already been approved *en lo particular* – obviating any amendments!

After a first reading, the author of the amendment is permitted to explain her reasons, and the amendment is put to a vote. If it is approved, it is sent to the reporting committee. This gives the reporting committee a veto over the amendment and would also require a suspension of floor debate while the committee convenes to discuss the amendment. In practice it is more common that the committee is asked on the floor whether it accepts the amendment.[34] If the committee agrees, the corrections are incorporated. The Reglamento does not specify what should happen if a committee does not accept the amendments "approved" on the floor.

Therefore, between 1935 and 1976, floor amendments to the appropriations bill were prohibited. Between 1976 and 1997, the budget was considered under a practically closed rule: A *voto particular* could be debated only after the majority report was rejected; modifications and additions required the assent of the budget committee; and finally, removing articles *en lo particular* was an alternative, but only a negative correction, and not a viable option for federal appropriations.

The November 1997 parliamentary agreement closed the amendment process more completely. Amendments contemplated under Articles 124 and 125 of the Reglamento can no longer be brought to debate. Instead, deputies can use hypothetical amendments as part of their arguments against a bill. If the articles are rejected *en lo particular*, they are sent back to committee, and the committee should take into account the arguments presented in the debate. The rest of the bill is frozen (it cannot be sent to the Senate or to the president) until a new report is issued on those articles. This rule is not followed to the letter, however, if the Comisión de Régimen Interno y Concertación Política (now the Junta de Coordinación Política) approves in advance a debate on specific amendments – something like a modified closed rule.

Voting in the Chamber of Deputies used to be by roll call, where each deputy announced his name and his vote, but these votes were not reported

---

[33] My emphasis.

[34] This was feasible in the past when committees were made up of only three members, but now committees have 30 members. As recently as the 55th Legislature (1991–1994), the budget committee had 77 members (Lujambio 1995, p. 196).

in any public documents. The 1997 parliamentary agreement authorized the purchase of an electronic voting system, which became operable in October 1998. A deputy can now see her vote appear next to her name on a large screen in the Chamber. Nonetheless, the votes are not published.

Presidential Veto of the Appropriations Bill

There is considerable debate over whether the president can veto the appropriations bill in Mexico.[35] Most constitutional scholars claim that the president does not have the power to veto the budget because the veto power is authorized in Article 72 of the Constitution, which describes the legislative process of bills that must be considered by *both* chambers. Since the budget is considered only by the Chamber of Deputies, the president cannot veto it (Burgoa 1994, p. 692; Carpizo 1978, pp. 86–87; Tena Ramírez 1985, pp. 263–267).

The intent of the writers of the Constitution is unclear. In the unicameral Congress of 1857, the president had lacked a meaningful veto over any legislation (the Chamber of Deputies could override with a majority vote). When the Senate returned in 1874, the Chamber of Deputies was given exclusive powers over appropriations. Article 71 of the 1857 Constitution described how bills should traverse the two chambers, and the strong veto (requiring a two-thirds vote in each chamber to override) was included as a clause within this article. Nothing in the article explicitly excludes the veto from resolutions passed by only one chamber, and I seriously doubt that the *constituyentes* meant to deny a veto to the president over such an important issue. The 1917 Constitution kept the text intact as Article 72.

The legal argument in favor of a presidential veto is that clause j of Article 72 explicitly denies the veto to the president on decisions of either chamber when they act in impeachment proceedings or as judge of their own elections.[36] Since these are inherently acts of single chambers, there should be no need to deny the veto. Also, Article 70 explicitly denies the veto on the *law* that establishes congressional rules. The Congress has adopted a Reglamento and an Organic Law. These are both laws in the strict sense, approved by both chambers, and are therefore examples of

---

[35] See Nava Polina, Weldon, and Yáñez López (1997).

[36] The reforms of 1874 to the 1857 Constitution included similar wording, denying the veto for when the Congress prorogued its sessions, judged its own elections, or was jury against government officials.

cases where the veto is disallowed to a law passed by both chambers. If it is necessary to specify cases of laws passed by one or two chambers in which the president does not have a veto, then perhaps these are the only cases where the veto is truly denied. Most constitutional scholars, however, are absolutely convinced that the president does not have a veto. Tena Ramírez (1985, p. 267) claims that clause j is superfluous and does not grant the veto power by explicitly disallowing it in specific cases. He even believes that the clause is dangerous, because it leads to "mistaken consequences." Carpizo (1978, p. 87) claims that the clause is "useless, for being absolutely inoperative."

The president, of course, would rather that the Constitution be interpreted so that he have a veto. Administration officials in 1997 and again in 1999 argued that the president indeed had a veto, thanks to clause j. Had the Chamber of Deputies modified the budget in such a way so that Zedillo were unsatisfied, he might have attempted a veto, and the Chamber of Deputies certainly would have taken the case to the Supreme Court. It should be noted that the judges on the Court come from the same school of interpretation as the constitutional scholars listed above, so had they decided to support the president they would have gone against their own long-held doctrine. The veto has not been required nor attempted, so the coin remains in the air.

What has been left out of the legal arguments is that the president in fact has vetoed appropriations numerous times. Between 1917 and 1933, there were 45 vetoes of appropriations bills: sometimes individual *ramos*, even the whole federal budget, but more often pork introduced by deputies. All of these bills had been passed by the Chamber of Deputies alone.

Reversion Point

The Constitution does not specify a reversion point in the event that the Chamber of Deputies does not approve the appropriations (or if the president vetoes). Some constitutional scholars claim that Article 75 implies that the reversion point is the spending levels of the previous year, but this is far from certain.[37] The 1928 budget law specified that the president's budget proposal would go into effect on January 1 until the Chamber of

---

[37] Article 75 states that the Chamber of Deputies cannot fail to appropriate funding for any government employment that has been created by law. If no appropriation has been assigned, then the levels of spending for that position should be the same as in the prior budget or in the law that created the office. This applies only to salaries.

Deputies revoked it later on with a substitute budget. This clause was repealed in the 1935 budget law, and there is no reversion point in the 1976 law, either. The parties in 1999 negotiated moving up the submission date and adding a reversion point, but the budget reform package was abandoned in the partisan shuffles over the budget itself at the end of the year.

The Influence of the Chamber of Deputies over Appropriations

The Chamber of Deputies has wide-ranging authority over the budget. The president has the exclusive power to present the annual budget, but the Chamber of Deputies can modify it however it wants, and the president may or may not have a veto. Given the clumsy amendment rules in the Reglamento, and the prohibition of floor amendments in the 1928 and 1935 laws, we should expect most amendments to occur in committee, not on the floor. However, what we observe is that, most of the time, the Chamber of Deputies has usually acted as if it had totally abdicated its authority over the budget to the executive branch. Only minor changes are made in committee, always with the approval of Hacienda (or the Budget Ministry, before it was absorbed into the former). The Chamber of Deputies appears to give the budget only a cursory look and approves the appropriations in short order. Even in the first legislature of Zedillo, when both chambers of Congress modified, delayed, or froze some major presidential bills, the Chamber of Deputies barely touched the budget.

Since the lack of influence of the Chamber of Deputies cannot be due to the legal structure of the budgeting process, we must find other justifications. There are two possible explanations for this apparent abdication of the Chamber of Deputies over the appropriations process. First, it is possible that the president has nearly perfectly anticipated the position of the median deputy in the Chamber, thus obviating the need for struggles between branches. This would require a great deal of information on the part of the president, which would be difficult to acquire when there is a 100% turnover in the Chamber every three years. Furthermore, this hypothesis is not testable without roll-call data for the period.

A second explanation would be based on the metaconstitutional powers of the Mexican presidency, which are derived from the partisan ties between the executive and legislative branches of government. When the conditions leading to a strong metaconstitutional presidency are lacking,

393

we should expect the Chamber of Deputies to take on a greater role in the appropriations process. When the conditions are present, we should expect the president to act more boldly and the Chamber of Deputies to abdicate its authority to the executive. Nonetheless, this story cannot be told independently of the legal history of the budget legislation. Different laws have given more or less leeway to the executive branch, and some laws have partially restricted the Chamber's authority over the budget.

This chapter will use comparative statics to demonstrate that the data fit with the predicted pattern derived from the metaconstitutional conditions and the legal environment. For example, in partisan terms, the current Chamber of Deputies resembles the legislatures of 1917–1924, but the legal rules are very different. Unfortunately, in most cases it is impossible to separate completely the partisan effects from the legal environment. For example, the 1928 law was approved just as the condition of unified government was fulfilled. The 1935 law closely corresponds with the unification of party leadership with the presidency. Nonetheless, we should get a good picture of how the budget process worked under different conditions.

During most of the first three decades of the period covered in this study, there was another method of appropriations that complicated the budget process. The president had extraordinary decree powers, based on the emergency clauses in Articles 29 and 49 of the Constitution. In fact, the first bill presented in the Chamber of Deputies after the promulgation of the Constitution in 1917 gave *facultades extraordinarias* to President Carranza in financial affairs.[38] The president immediately began to use these decree powers to issue revenue and spending laws. The *facultades extraordinarias* lasted until 1938, when constitutional reforms reiterated that such decree powers should be granted only when civil liberties are suspended during emergencies. An emergency was declared once more in 1942 for World War II, and decree powers were used by President Ávila Camacho for the duration of the war. No emergency decree powers have been authorized after 1946.

Relationship Between the Explanatory Variables

Table 13.1 gives a general review of key variables in the three budget laws, plus the two constitutional reforms that modified the submission and

[38] *D.O.F.*, May 15, 1917. See Marván (forthcoming) and Weldon (forthcoming) for details.

Table 13.1. *Review of budget laws (1917–1998).*

Law	Fiscal Years	Initiative	Submission Date	Session Ends	Amendments	Supplemental Appropriations	Reversion Point
None	1917–1928	No restriction	None	Dec. 31	No restrictions	No restrictions	None
1928 budget law	1929–1936	President	Nov. 1	Dec. 31	Committee only	Bills sent by executive to Chamber	President's bill
1935 budget law	1937–1977	President	Dec. 15	Dec. 31	Committee only	Bills sent by executive to Chamber	None
1976 budget law	1978–1982	President	Nov. 30	Dec. 31	No restrictions	Executive adjusts budget and informs Chamber	None
1982 constitutional reform	1983–1994	President	Nov. 15	Dec. 31	No restrictions	Executive adjusts budget and informs Chamber	None
1993 constitutional reform	1995–	President	Nov. 15	Dec. 15	No restrictions	Executive adjusts budget and informs Chamber	None

recess dates. In each case the fiscal years for which each budget law applied is given. Tables 13.2 through 13.4 (later) demonstrate the effects of the budget laws and the conditions for metaconstitutional presidentialism that applied in each period. The first three columns describe the different combinations of each dependent variable.[39]

The first 12 years of the study (covering fiscal years 1917–1928) correspond to the period when none of the three metaconstitutional conditions held. During exactly the same period, there was no budget law in force. However, all of the presidents could counteract obstructionist tactics from the Chamber of Deputies by using their extraordinary decree powers.

During the Maximato, which corresponds roughly to the fiscal years 1929–1936, the 1928 budget law was in effect. The PNR held a monopoly of seats in the Chamber, but party discipline was not totally secure, and the president was not yet the head of the party. The strongly presidentialist 1928 budget law was introduced by Obregón, as a candidate, remembering his own difficulties with Congress earlier in the decade. Shortly after it was approved, and days after Obregón was elected president for the 1928–1934 term, he was assassinated, and Obregón never personally benefited from his favorable budget law.

The 1935 budget law was in effect for fiscal years 1937–1977.[40] During the first ten years, the metaconstitutional conditions of unified government and party discipline certainly held, but the president was not yet the undisputed head of the party. After 1946, however, the dyarchy of president/*Jefe Máximo* was definitely united.

The 1976 law first went into effect for fiscal year 1978. During the period covering fiscal years 1978–1994, all of the conditions for metaconstitutional powers were in effect. During the four years of Zedillo's presidency, the third condition should have been relaxed somewhat. Although there was no *Jefe Máximo* to challenge the authority of Zedillo, the president had established a distance between himself and the PRI, promising to disengage himself from internal party affairs and nominations (and mostly keeping that promise). In 1997, the PRI lost its majority in the Chamber of Deputies, so the first condition is completely nullified for fiscal years 1998–1999.

[39] Dummy variables were created for each law and condition and used as explanatory variables in OLS and probit models. Unfortunately, there was too much multicollinearity among the explanatory variables for the models to work properly.

[40] The timing of this bill is not surprising. Several important *obregonista* laws were adjusted during and just after the Maximato.

Data

The data are from a database of all bills presented in the Mexican Chamber of Deputies from 1917 through 1999. The information has been gathered from the *Diario de los Debates de la Cámara de Diputados*, the official record of the Chamber (Cámara de Diputados 1994).[41] The legislative data presented in the tables include only the sections of the budget that refer to the executive branch. Frequently, the legislative and judicial branch appropriations are sent independently by the respective branches, and often these line items were approved on a different schedule.[42]

For data on the use of extraordinary decree powers by the president, all issues of the *Diario Oficial de la Federación* were consulted for the period 1917–1946. The president of Mexico makes all sorts of "decrees," including laws passed by Congress and rules and regulations derived from those laws, all decisions that he can make under constitutional authority. He can also decree laws directly under authority delegated by Congress during emergencies under Article 29 of the Constitution. Only the Article 29 cases have been recorded, and only spending decrees are included in the tables.

Hypotheses and Evidence

H1: When the conditions for metaconstitutional presidentialism are present, the president will submit a budget to the Chamber of Deputies instead of using decree powers.

This hypothesis applies only to the 1917–1945 period, when the use of *facultades extraordinarias* was possible. When the president is confident that the Chamber of Deputies will approve his budget, and not mutilate his proposal, he will submit a budget to the Chamber rather than act unilaterally.

For the 12 fiscal years between 1917 and 1928, covering the period before the metaconstitutional conditions had been met, the president sent a budget bill only seven times. The fiscal year 1922 budget was submitted

---

[41] The database was designed and created by the author with María del Carmen Nava Polina and Jorge Yáñez Lopez at ITAM. Much of the data from the 57th Legislature (1997–2000) has been published in *Reforma* (Mexico City) by Weldon with coauthors Nava, Yáñez, and Vidal Romero.

[42] The amendment data for 1982–1997 differ significantly from those presented by Ugalde (1997a).

by deputies only, and for fiscal years 1924–1927, the president did not send appropriations bills to the Chamber of Deputies, legislating instead through decrees. After the formation of the PNR, and once the 1928 budget law was approved, the president always has submitted appropriations legislation.[43] The 1928 budget law gave the president an incentive to send over the budget, because the reversion point was his proposed budget.

H2: When the conditions for metaconstitutional presidentialism are present, the president will introduce his budget on time.

If the president is certain that the Chamber of Deputies will approve his budget, he has less reason to play agenda games with the Chamber. When the metaconstitutional conditions are met, the Chamber is not likely to amend the president's budget and will likely only give it a cursory glance, so his submitting the budget on time is not likely to be a strategy that will backfire. On the other hand, when the Chamber of Deputies is likely to be more hostile, the president may send the budget late, forcing the Chamber to consider the bill on a fast track and giving the president more leverage. This is especially the case under the 1928 budget bill, where the reversion point is the president's bill. During the years of the Maximato, the executive learned that submitting regular bills in the last few weeks of the session greatly increased the likelihood of passage (Nava Polina and Yáñez López 1998; Weldon, forthcoming).

There have been four different deadlines, so the determination of whether the budget was submitted on time depends on the prescribed date. The evidence in Table 13.2 suggests that, before the 1976 law, the budget was rarely submitted on time. Before 1929, there was no deadline, but on average the president sent the budget on December 1, giving the Chamber less than one month to consider the bill.[44] Under the 1928 law, when only one of the metaconstitutional conditions were in effect (unified government), the budget was never submitted on time. The deadline was November 1, but on average it was submitted six weeks late.

Under the 1935 law, the budget was submitted before December 15 less than 42% of the time, but it varied according to the metaconstitutional

---

[43] The fiscal year 1947 budget was introduced on Dec. 30, 1946 by a deputy, the president of the *mesa directiva* (speaker pro-tem for the month of December). This was President Alemán's inaugural budget, and the irregularity in the procedures is likely due to time constraints during the succession.

[44] The figures given are means for the years when budgets were submitted in the period. Each fiscal year from 1917 to 1929 is the mean date of submission of the *ramos* for each budget.

Table 13.2. *Timing of submission and approval of budget (1917–1998).*

Fiscal Years	Budget Law	Metaconstitutional Conditions	Budget Submitted on Time?	Date of Submission (Mean)[a]	Approval Time (Mean, in Days)
1917–1928	None	Divided government, some party discipline, divided dyarchy	NA	Dec. 1[b]	13.4
1929–1936	1928 law	Unified government, some party discipline, divided dyarchy	0 of 8	Dec. 13	9.9
1937–1946	1935 law	Unified government, party discipline, some unity in dyarchy	1 of 10	Dec. 24	4.9
1947–1977	1935 law	Unified government, party discipline, unity in dyarchy	16 of 31	Dec. 15	10.7
1978–1982	1976 law	Unified government, party discipline, unity in dyarchy	4 of 5	Dec. 2	25.6
1983–1994	1976 law	Unified government, party discipline, unity in dyarchy	8 of 12	Nov. 16, Dec. 12	33.3
1995–1997	1976 law	Unified government, party discipline, some unity in dyarchy	3 of 3	Nov. 11, Dec. 9	25.3
1998–2000	1976 law	Divided government, party discipline, some unity in dyarchy	3 of 3	Nov. 12	42.3

[a] When two dates are listed, the first is for noninaugural years and the second for inaugural years.
[b] Excludes fiscal years 1917, 1922, and 1924–1927.

stature of the president. In the period covering fiscal years 1937–1946, the budget was submitted on time only once in ten years, and in an average year the budget was submitted on Christmas Eve, nine days late. When all three metaconstitutional conditions were met (1947–1977), the budget was submitted on time just over half of the time (16 out of 31 years), though the mean date of submission in this period was December 15.

The 1976 law has been more successful in inducing promptness on the part of the president, and most budget bills have been sent on time, or only slightly after the due date. The last 12 budgets have been submitted on time, and Zedillo in particular has been extremely punctual, despite his distance from the party.

H3: When the conditions for metaconstitutional presidentialism are present, it is more likely that the Chamber of Deputies will approve the budget.

Obviously, a tamed Chamber of Deputies will be more likely to support the president's budget. Here the evidence is very strong (Table 13.3). In the 12 budgets between 1917 and 1928, during the years before the first budget law, and when none of the metaconstitutional conditions applied, only twice was the budget approved in its entirety. The Chamber of Deputies did not approve the 1917 budget (which covered the second half of the year), and the president covered appropriations with decrees. The 1918 budget was passed, but the next three budgets were only partially approved. In these three years, only 12 of 59 total *ramos* were approved.[45] The fiscal year 1922 budget was submitted by deputies (and still only partially approved). President Obregón submitted the budget the next year, but the Chamber of Deputies did not approve 11 of the 28 *ramos*. The president did not submit the next four budgets. The fiscal year 1928 budget, however, was approved.

After the formation of the PNR, all budgets have been approved in their entirety. In the short term, the reversion point established in the 1928 budget law probably gave the Chamber of Deputies an incentive to enact the budget. It is also likely that the threat of the use of decree powers also pushed the Chamber into approving the budget, giving the deputies at least some influence over the budget process. By the mid-1940s, the metaconstitutional powers of the president had taken over to ensure the budget's passage.

[45] For fiscal year 1921, only 1 of 23 *ramos* was approved.

Table 13.3. *Budget approval, amendments, and vetoes (1917–1998).*

Fiscal Years	Budget Law	Metaconstitutional Conditions	Budget Approved?	Committee Amendments	Floor Amendments	Vetoes (Mean/Year)
1917–1928	None	Divided government, some party discipline, divided dyarchy	No: 1 of 12 In part: 5 of 12 Yes: 2 of 12 Not submitted: 4 of 12	6 of 7	5 of 7	1.3
1929–1936	1928 law	Unified government, some party discipline, divided dyarchy	Yes	7 of 8	1 of 8	3.6
1937–1946	1935 law	Unified government, party discipline, some unity in dyarchy	Yes	1 of 10	0 of 10	0
1947–1977	1935 law	Unified government, party discipline, unity in dyarchy	Yes	4 of 30 (1 obvia res.)	2 of 31	0
1978–1994	1976 law	Unified government, party discipline, unity in dyarchy	Yes	13 of 17	10 of 17	0
1995–1997	1976 law	Unified government, party discipline, some unity in dyarchy	Yes	2 of 3	0 of 3	0
1998–2000	1976 law	Divided government, party discipline, some unity in dyarchy	Yes	3 of 3	2 of 3	0

H4: When the conditions for metaconstitutional presidentialism are met, regardless of when the budget is introduced, but taking into account legal barriers, the Chamber of Deputies will approve the budget in less time.

This is a simple conclusion from the metaconstitutional powers of the presidency. A Chamber of Deputies that is subservient to the executive will spend less time examining his budget. However, the evidence is strongly biased by the submission dates. When the president is weak, he will send the budget late, so the Chamber of Deputies must rush its approval.

Before the 1928 budget law, the Chamber of Deputies approved the budget (when it in fact did so) in just under two weeks (Table 13.2).[46] Under the 1928 budget law, which corresponds to unified government but no other metaconstitutional condition, the budget was approved in ten days, near Christmas.

For the first ten years covered by the 1935 budget law, the Chamber of Deputies passed the budget in only five days. Not all of the metaconstitutional conditions were in effect during this period (the dyarchy of the president and party leader was still in its formative stages), but the president had left the Chamber very little time to approve the bill. In seven of the ten years the budget was approved on December 29 or later, twice on New Year's Eve. For the next 31 years of full presidentialism under the 1935 budget law, the Chamber approved the budget on average in less than 11 days. About a third of the time, the Chamber had resolved the budget before its Christmas break. This is an improvement, but one that is also predicated on the president's introducing the bill in a more timely fashion.

Under the 1976 law, regardless of the metaconstitutional conditions, the Chamber of Deputies has used almost all of the time available to examine the budget, approving the measure just before the end of the term. The fiscal year 1999 budget was not approved before the December 15 deadline, though the major disagreement was over the tax bill, which must be approved first. A special session was called for the last two weeks of December 1998, and the budget was finally approved on New Year's Eve. The fiscal year 2000 bill also required a special session. The tax packages, which were less controversial, were approved before December 15, but the appropriations bill was approved on December 28, 1999, after extensive negotiations and debate.

---

[46] Between 1918 and 1932, the approval dates from which the approval time is calculated are usually means among the *ramos*.

H5: When the conditions for metaconstitutional presidentialism are present, the Chamber of Deputies will approve the budget without amendments.[47]

The same argument follows as before. If the president has strong partisan ties to the Chamber, it is less likely that the deputies will modify the budget. During the whole period, committee amendments have been possible. Under the 1928 and 1935 budget laws, covering fiscal years 1929–1977, floor amendments have been prohibited. Before and after this period, floor amendments were permitted but the procedures were awkward.

In the first period, with no budget law and no metaconstitutional conditions in effect, of the seven budgets approved by the Chamber of Deputies, six were amended in committee and five on the floor (Table 13.3). Under the 1928 budget law, the committee amendments still prevailed (seven of eight years), but only one budget was amended on the floor. The addition of party discipline in the 1937–1946 period seems to have decreased the frequency of committee amendments: Only one of ten was modified in committee and none on the floor. This pattern continued under full presidentialism in the 1947–1977 period, under the 1935 budget law. The budget was amended in committee only 4 times out of 30, and only twice out of 31 occasions on the floor.[48]

The 1976 budget law permits floor amendments, and they have been relatively common, being approved in just over half of the years. Committee amendments have occurred in over 78% of the years under the 1976 law. The amendments in committee have occurred regardless of the metaconstitutional powers of the president. In the first three years of the Zedillo *sexenio*, two budgets were modified in committee but none on the floor. With a divided government in fiscal years 1998–2000, the appropriations bill has been heavily amended in committee, always with the participation of representatives from Hacienda. There were some minor amendments on the floor for the fiscal year 1998 bill.

In December 1999, there was extensive debate to increase revenue sharing in the states (favored by the PAN) and greater expenditures and

---

[47] It is not possible at this point to qualify amendments as significant or as merely minor corrections of style.

[48] The fiscal year 1947 budget (the one introduced by a deputy) was approved via *obvia resolución*, thus eliminating committee amendments. *Obvia resolución* does not prohibit amendments during consideration on the floor (though the budget law does), and this in fact is one of the two cases of floor amendments under the 1935 law.

debt limit in the Federal District (governed by the PRD). The PRI wanted to sustain funding for the bank bailout program, which the opposition parties opposed unless the files were opened to public scrutiny. One of the small parties supported the PRI's version in committee, creating a 15–15 tie, and no bill could be reported out of committee. It is important to remember that minority reports, under the rules, can be considered only when that section of a bill has been defeated *en lo particular*, which gives a strategic disadvantage to *votos particulares*. No one yielded, which led to the need for a special session. At first, the two small parties (PT and PVEM) appeared ready to vote with the PRI, but both had allied with one of the larger opposition parties for the presidential race in early December.

The committee finally reported out a bill on December 21, signed by the PAN, PRD, PT, and PVEM, and the PRI presented a minority report. The opposition report was defeated on the floor by a vote of 248 to 246, with 2 abstentions. The PRI's *voto particular* was then considered, and the first vote ended in a tie, 246 to 246, and in the second vote it was defeated, 248 to 247. The special session ended, and a new special session was called for the next week. A new committee report was issued, with substantial amendments, signed by all parties. A special rule, very unusual for the Chamber of Deputies, was written to allow the vote of this report without the required time limits, and to permit the vote of amendments under *obvia resolución*, so that the committee would not have to consider the amendments. This rule required a two-thirds vote, which was easily established. Then the Chamber voted on the report *en lo general*, and it passed 465 to 8, with 10 abstentions, as expected. The special rule allowed the parties to present *votos particulares* in debate *en lo particular*. The PRD amendment, on eliminating funds for the bank bailout, was defeated 243 to 140, with 106 abstentions. The PAN amendment, on opening the books on the bank bailout before authorizing funds to proceed, failed 246 to 245. One of the PRI amendments, increasing funds for the bank bailout, was approved 246 to 245, while another amendment by the PRI that would have shifted money among several social line items was defeated 248 to 245. With the special rule, the Chamber had found a way to bypass the difficult amendment procedures in the Reglamento.

H6: When the conditions for metaconstitutional presidentialism are present, there will be fewer appropriations bills from deputies (pork) introduced or approved.

Under strong presidentialism, especially when the ties that a deputy may have with his locality have been severed by the no-reelection rule, the deputies will expect the president to look after their districts. The budget laws are unclear on whether deputies can in fact present their own appropriations bills, but there is nothing in any of the three laws that explicitly prohibits this activity.

Data for this question are available for fiscal years 1917–1970. Despite the claims of constitutional scholars that such bills should be approved by both chambers, in practice the bills were approved only in the Chamber of Deputies and sent directly to the president (Carpizo 1978, p. 147; Tena Ramírez 1985, p. 325).

In the first period, before the 1928 budget law and before a unified government, there was a mean of 29.5 pork bills introduced per year, and over 12 on average were approved. The number drops remarkably in the Maximato. Under the 1928 budget law and with a unified government, 6.5 bills on average were introduced, and 5.3 were approved. The Chamber of Deputies is more efficient and is approving a greater percentage of the bills. What is most noteworthy is that only one and two pork bills were introduced in fiscal years 1934 and 1935, respectively; the no-reelection reform was approved in 1933, and these were the first deputies to be affected by the prohibition on reelection. They acted accordingly.

During the following period, with the 1935 budget law, a unified government, and higher party discipline (1937–1946), the mean number of appropriations bills introduced by deputies increased to 8.5, though the average number approved falls to 4. It appears that the factor that completely eliminated pork bills was the unification of the presidency and party leader. From fiscal years 1947 through 1970, only one bill was introduced, in 1948.[49] The legal situation was the same as the 1937–1946 period, so we can only assume that the third metaconstitutional condition was the factor that was most likely responsible.

H7: When the conditions for metaconstitutional presidentialism are present, the president should introduce fewer supplemental bills.

Supplemental bills cover extra expenditures that are not met in the regular annual appropriations law. These can be introduced during the fiscal year, or even a year or two later. We should expect the president to resort to supplemental bills more often when he does not have the total

---

[49] There is no reason to believe that any pork bills were introduced during the missing fiscal years 1971–1998.

loyalty of the Chamber of Deputies. Otherwise, he should be able to have articles placed in the annual budgets that authorize the transfer of funds among *ramos*.

In this case, there is strong evidence that the legal institutions have determined the number of supplemental bills sent by the executive. Before the 1928 law was in effect, the president sent on average 6.4 supplemental bills per year (Table 13.4). Under the 1928 law, which began to regulate the system of supplemental appropriations, the president sent 3.4 bills per year. Under the first ten years of the 1935 law, corresponding to the years before the dyarchy was completely fused, the president sent only 1.6 bills per year, and after 1947, the average number of bills fell to under one. Our data end for fiscal year 1969, but we should not expect any supplemental bills for years covered by the 1976 budget law, because the law permits the president to transfer funds more or less as he sees fit.[50]

H8: When the conditions for metaconstitutional presidentialism are met, it is less likely that the president will veto the budget or other appropriations bills.

This is a case where the legal institutions have not varied over the period in question. Most constitutional scholars have argued that the president does not have the power to veto appropriations bills, because these are considered by only one chamber. But the empirical evidence is to the contrary. Under strong presidentialism, we should not expect the Chamber of Deputies to modify the budget or send their own appropriations bills, so there is very little likelihood that the president will veto under these conditions.

Regardless of the constitutional debate, the president has issued a total of 45 vetoes over the budget or supplemental appropriations. When none of the conditions for metaconstitutional presidentialism were present, the president vetoed a mean of 1.3 appropriations bills per year (Table 13.3). During the Maximato (covering fiscal years 1929–1936) the executive vetoed on average 3.6 spending bills per year. The last veto was issued for fiscal year 1934. The Chamber of Deputies did not challenge the legitimacy of the veto over the budget; it received the vetoes and treated them as they would any other bill returned by the president, either accepting or overriding the vetoes. The Chamber did not override vetoes because they

---

[50] This power was restricted in the fiscal year 2000 law.

Table 13.4. *Pork, supplemental bills, and use of Facultades Extraordinarias (1917–1970).*

Fiscal Years	Budget Law	Metaconstitutional Conditions	Pork Introduced (Mean/Year)	Pork Approved (Mean/Year)	Executive Supplemental Bills (Mean/Year)	Decrees of *Facultades Extraordinarias* (Mean/Year)[a]
1917–1928	None	Divided government, some party discipline, divided dyarchy	29.5	12.4	6.4	143.6
1929–1936	1928 law	Unified government, some party discipline, divided dyarchy	6.5	5.3	3.4	78.9
1937–1946	1935 law	Unified government, party discipline, some unity in dyarchy	8.5	4.1	1.6	12.9[b]
1947–1970	1935 law	Unified government, party discipline, unity in dyarchy	0.04[c]	m.d.	0.7[d]	–

[a] Data missing for Feb. 1929 and Mar. 1936.
[b] 1937–1945.
[c] Only once, in 1948. Data on approval missing.
[d] 1947–1969.

were procedurally flawed, but rather on their merits. In no case were vetoes over appropriations forwarded to the Senate (as Article 72 would imply); the resolved vetoes were sent directly to the president.

H9: When the conditions are met, we should expect that the president use decree powers derived from *facultades extraordinarias* for appropriations less frequently.

If the president expects or experiences difficulties with the Chamber of Deputies, and he has already been delegated decree powers over the budget (which was the situation in 1917–1938 and 1942–1946), then he can skip the normal legislative process and publish his budget by decree. On the other hand, if the Chamber of Deputies has implicitly delegated its budget authority to the president, recognizing the president's meta-constitutional powers, it is not necessary to delegate decree powers as well.

This is a case where the budget laws do not intervene, and the use of decree powers should follow the course of metaconstitutional presidentialism. During the whole period, the president used his decree powers under *facultades extraordinarias* for budget matters a remarkable 2,470 times, a significant source of appropriations legislation (Table 13.4). In the period covering fiscal years 1917–1928, when none of the conditions were present, the president used his decree powers for appropriations measures on average nearly 144 times per year. The figures are especially high for Obregón (1920–1924), who faced a partisan majority in the first half of his term and a partisan plurality in the second half. The Chamber of Deputies even tried (unsuccessfully) to withdraw his decree powers (Weldon, forthcoming). During the Maximato, when there was a unified government but party discipline was not guaranteed and the president was not yet head of the party, the presidents issued a mean of just under 80 decrees per year. In fiscal years 1937–1946, when party discipline was high but the question of the dyarchy was not yet completely resolved, the executive issued under 13 decrees per year (including the fiscal years 1938–1942, when the Constitution made granting *facultades extraordinarias* more difficult, and there were thus very few decrees).

The game that presidents play with extraordinary decree powers runs simultaneously with the legislative games that they play with the Chamber of Deputies. Presidents can exchange low legislative success in Congress with decrees. On the other hand, the Chamber of Deputies can be forced into approving presidential bills, knowing that the president can often get what he desires through decrees anyway.

Conclusions

The evidence demonstrates that as presidents accumulated the three conditions necessary to control his party in the Chamber of Deputies, the budget process became more regular. As the metaconstitutional conditions were fulfilled, the presidents had to worry less about the outcomes of the budget process in the Chamber. When we take into account the various budget laws, which are not exogenous to the story of metaconstitutional presidentialism, the whole story of the budget process becomes clearer, and certain anomalies in the presidential theories can be better explained.

The conditions for metaconstitutional presidentialism match up only imperfectly with the model of static ambitious versus progressive springboard legislators (Morgenstern, this volume). Obviously, *priísta* deputies are springboard legislators, but it is also extremely important to identify whom they are courting. If the party leader is not the president, but instead a *Jefe Máximo*, then we should expect greater modification to the president's budget. Furthermore, the two conditions that create springboard legislators (party discipline and unified dyarchy) are inoperable without a unified party government. If the president's party does not hold a majority in the Chamber of Deputies, we should expect significant modifications to his budget, regardless of the characteristics of the legislators.

As the PRI has been moving toward the greater use of primaries to select congressional candidates (in 1998–1999 they were used on several occasions to select gubernatorial candidates), we should expect party discipline within the PRI to decline. Primaries not only make the winning candidate feel more personally responsible for his own nomination, they also reduce the ability of the party to salve the wounds of the candidates defeated in the primaries (in the past, unsuccessful candidates were often compensated with other positions before the announcement of the official candidate). Thus we should begin to see more open divisions within the PRI.

Moreover, it is not clear that the opposition deputies are springboard legislators in any meaningful way. Obviously, they have to spring over to some other position after their term is up, but whom they court varies significantly from *priísta* deputies. First, the head of the opposition party leaders do not have the bureaucratic posts available to reward loyalty. This may change now that the opposition governs about a third of the states. Second, until 1997, the great majority of opposition deputies had been elected from party lists instead of from single-member districts, unlike the PRI. By this alone we should expect greater discipline from opposition members than from the PRI, but this is not true. In the 57th Legislature (1997–2000) a majority of deputies from the PAN and PRD were elected in districts. There were frequent backbench revolts by *panista* members who had been elected in districts against their leadership, which had been almost entirely elected from the PR lists (and elected as parliamentary leaders by the NEC of the party). Third, the left-of-center PRD has been increasingly selecting candidates who openly disavow membership in the party, and their cohesion with the party is consequently much weaker.[51]

We have seen that a divided government in Mexico has led increasingly to greater difficulty in passing the budget. The learning process has favored the opposition parties. In 1997, the budget process was characterized by bad deals and rookie mistakes. In 1998, the opposition successfully held out against some taxes that they opposed. In 1999, the opposition took on the appropriations bill itself and made significant changes, both on amounts and on procedures for transfers.

Both the PAN and the PRD believe that a stronger legislative branch is necessary to weaken hyperpresidentialism. In the 57th Legislature (1997–2000), when they finally had the chance to strengthen the Chamber of Deputies, the opposition parties instead concentrated on reforms that strengthened the parties in the Chamber. They are still considering reforms that will balance powers between the Chamber and the president, but they have ignored changes that will make legislators more responsible to their electorate, such as the reinstitution of reelection.

[51] There cannot be closed primaries in Mexico because the IFE does not register voters by party preference, and the IFE has not been directly involved in the primaries sponsored by the PRD and the PRI in 1998 and 1999. The parties have to take a voter's word that she has not voted more than once in the primary, and that she is not intending to vote for another party in the general election. The 1999 nominating primary for the PAN's presidential candidate was closed to party affiliates, but there were too few of them in any party to make closed primary elections meaningfully democratic.

PART IV

Conclusions

14

Explaining Legislative Politics in Latin America

SCOTT MORGENSTERN

Instead of focusing on presidents, militaries, financial sector bureaucrats, or social actors, the preceding pages have placed the Argentine, Brazilian, Chilean, and Mexican legislatures at the center of democratic politics. While the authors all agree that the legislatures are potent, it is also clear that the legislatures take a less proactive role than does the U.S. Congress. In this chapter I draw on the previous chapters to argue that the legislatures take a generally reactive role, but within this role there is great variance in the way in which the legislatures assert their power and insert themselves into the policy process. I argue further that the chapters have also offered significant evidence that, as postulated in the introduction, many of the differences are explicable by institutional variation.

The country chapters are arranged to focus on substantive questions about executive–legislative relations and the role of parties in organizing the business of the legislature. In this conclusion I return to the thematic questions raised in the introduction about the importance of reelection rates, electoral systems, partisan alignments, and constitutional powers on legislative politics. In doing so, this chapter has two primary goals. First, a main methodological strategy of this book has been to borrow from the U.S. model in deriving descriptions of key pieces of the legislative process and explanations for legislative behavior in Latin America. But, we have also shown that the assumptions embedded in models of the U.S. Congress must become variables in a comparative context. In particular, in contrast to members of the U.S. Congress, many Latin American legislators are less focused on reelection, more reliant on party leaders, and/or concerned with intrapartisan rivals at election time, not members or opponents of a single majority party, and faced with distinct amalgamations of

413

constitutional powers. This chapter, therefore, reviews the range that these variables (*qua* U.S. assumptions) take in our four countries and discusses how the book's authors used them in our collective effort to move toward a comparative explanation of legislative behavior.

The second goal is to use these explanations to move us toward a typology of legislatures, which Gary W. Cox and I then apply in the succeeding chapter to a discussion about presidential reactions in the face of distinct legislative types.[1] The starting point for this typology is the assumption that democratic assemblies insert themselves into the policy-making process in one or more of three basic ways: (1) originative: making and breaking executives, who then shoulder most of the policy-making burden; (2) proactive: initiating and passing their own legislative proposals; and (3) reactive: amending and/or vetoing executive proposals. European parliaments are the primary examples of originative/reactive assemblies. The U.S. Congress and the assemblies of the U.S. states are the primary examples of proactive/reactive assemblies.

In Latin America, legislatures typically cannot get rid of presidents they dislike and lack the resources to fashion their own legislative proposals. Thus, they are neither originative nor proactive; they are merely reactive.

Within this general category legislatures can still range greatly, from "subservient" to "recalcitrant," with "workable" and "venal" options in between. These abstract ideal-types, which are developed in this and the succeeding chapter in more detail, are not meant as descriptions of our specific cases. The defined categories, however, do give us a starting point from which to understand and analyze the Latin American legislatures and the presidential reactions to them in a comparative context.

A typology of legislatures must take into account many factors. Twenty years ago Mezey (1979) created a simple categorization based on the democratic support of the legislative institutions and the legislature's policy-making power. Among the Latin American cases that Mezey considered, only the Costa Rican and Mexican (!) legislatures gained admittance to the "more supported" category, as those in the Southern Cone were all under dictatorial rule. On the axis differentiating policy-making power, Mezey then coded the Chilean, Uruguayan, and Costa Rican legislatures as "strong," while the others in Latin America were placed in the "modest" category (above some in Africa or under Soviet rule that were

---

[1] The succeeding discussion about legislative types comes directly from Cox and Morgenstern (2001).

considered to have little or no power). Today the legislatures of Argentina, Brazil, Chile, and Mexico (and most others in Latin America) would all fit into the "more supported" category. This book has shown that it also would be incorrect to code any of these legislatures as having only modest policy-making power. Each of the legislatures under study here clearly asserts itself and shapes the policy process. This does not necessarily require the proactive stance taken by the U.S. Congress. Although several chapters showed that the legislatures do initiate a significant number of bills, it is clear that their greatest role is in blocking unfavorable legislation or shaping outcomes by pressuring the president to change proposals or amending executive bills. My hypothesis for this chapter is that the manner in which these generally reactive legislatures play their roles is largely a function of the reelection drive, the party structure, the electoral system, and the constitution. Other factors that emerge from the chapters, including ideology, ties between the president and the parties, and the federal structure, also count, and I will therefore discuss these issues as well.

Static vs. Progressive Ambition and the Reelection Goal

In the United States around 90% of the lower house members seek reelection and at least 90% of them win, justifying the assumption that most U.S. legislators have static ambitions. In most of the Latin American cases, however, this assumption does not hold. Instead of taking great interest in constituent issues and building the infrastructure necessary for a legislature to fully analyze and create policy, legislators without a reelection drive should orient their time toward future careers. Progressively ambitious legislators, in short, should build very different types of legislatures.

Table 14.1 shows that our four countries differ markedly on the static–progressive scale. The Mexican legislators are at one extreme, as they are prohibited from immediate reelection. Chile provides the closest approximation to the U.S. pattern, as 76% of the incumbents were renominated and, of these, 78% won in 1993.[2] The overall turnover rate there, however, is more than twice that of the United States (41% versus 17%). Next in line is Brazil, where 70% of the legislators seek reelection but, of

---

[2] While the data here refer only to a single election, averages over the past few elections are very similar.

415

Table 14.1. *Reelection rates.*

Country	% seeking reelection	% winning (of those seeking	% returning to office	Length of term (years)
Argentina (1997)	26	67	17	4
Brazil (1995)	70	62	43	4
Chile (1993)	76	78	59	4
Mexico (1997)	0	–	–	3
United States (1996)	88	94	83	2

Data provided by Mark Jones for Argentina, David Samuels for Brazil, and John Carey for Chile.

those, only 62% won in 1995 (resulting in a 57% turnover rate). In Argentina, even fewer are reelected, 17%.[3]

Following Carey's suggestion, the final column of the table suggests that reelection rates are influenced by the length of terms. Since the Latin American legislators' terms are 50 or 100% longer than their U.S. counterparts, somewhat lower reelection rates should not be a surprise. Still, these data show that Latin American legislators face different career prospects than do their U.S. counterparts. As such, we cannot assume static ambition as we do in studies of the U.S. Congress.

These data also suggest an important impediment in the creation of a unified theory of legislative behavior. Since not all (or even almost all) legislators seek reelection, even within any given country it is incorrect to assume homogeneous legislators all driven by a similar motivation. Some seek reelection and build national level political careers. An important number seek reelection but fail. Others appear to use the legislature only as a stepping stone for building state or local political careers. Others still may join the legislature for a short break from their generally successful businesses and, after finishing a term or two, simply return to their enter-

[3] A party rule creates extra hurdles for incumbents seeking reelection in the Radical Party. In their regional primaries they use a list PR system, but primary lists that contain incumbents must receive two-thirds of the votes for their candidates to gain a place on the general election list. Most lists, therefore, are "pacted" to ensure such a high vote total, but the legislative leader of the Radicals (Jaroslavsky) was dumped due to this rule in the mid-1980s, and overall the Radicals return only 13% of their legislators to Congress. The Peronists also prefer fresh faces in the legislature. They reelected only 17% of their legislators.

prises. This inter- and intralegislature variance will challenge a general model of legislative behavior.

Varying the goals should alter legislative behavior in predictable ways. Polsby's (1968) work on the institutionalization of the U.S. House of Representatives is instructive. Until the twentieth century, after each election the House of Representatives was reconstituted with between 32 and 67% new membership. As a result, rules were informal and leadership unstable. As membership stability increased, the House developed rules (e.g., seniority) and "institutional complexity" increased (Polsby 1968, p. 99). That is, they developed committee jurisdictions, gave committees more oversight responsibilities, and increased staff. In addition to helping the members assure themselves of more power and perquisites, this allowed them to deal more effectively with the complex legislation that they faced. The power and expertise probably also led to their growing incumbency advantage.

The chapters in this book, as well as other studies, provide clear evidence that the static/dynamic distinction manifests itself in the varying rates of party unity, the subordination of the legislature to the executive, and the organization of the Congress.

For example, the Chilean legislature, which represents the high end of the Latin American scale for static ambition, shows how legislators seek voter recognition and work to professionalize their workplace. My own interviews in Chile found that legislators are very concerned with their case work and use the distribution of committee posts to their electoral advantage. The legislature is closed on Fridays and one week per month for legislators to spend in their districts. Every legislator I talked with stressed the importance of "local" politics, and all talked about spending significant amounts of time doing everything from raising money for a drug treatment center, making phone calls to help someone find a job, trying to speed up the hospital's surgery wait list, or pushing demands through the relevant ministry. Second, legislatures have organized their workplaces to aid their electoral needs. Legislative offices are not well staffed, but every party has a press officer who many claimed was crucial to their reelection. As in the United States, the legislators use committees to serve their reelection needs. Instead of giving many legislators permanent hold on chairmanships as in the U.S. Congress, the Chilean legislators aid their reelection-seekers by rotating important posts. This ensures that *all* of those in the majority coalition will hold committee presidencies or seats on the Chamber's governing board for at least some time during

417

the session. Carey's chapter shows that the legislators have also created a hierarchical committee system that helps legislators to develop another valuable reelection tool, expertise. Londregan's chapter shows that the Chilean Senate also has a well-developed committee system.

Chile also stands in stark contrast to Mexico, the country at the low end of the static ambition scale. Weldon argues that, without the prohibition on legislative reelection that cut the legislators' ties to the electorate, the president's dominance over the legislature would never have been secure. It is also clear that the forced progressive ambition structured the legislative business. Interviews there showed that legislators were relatively uninterested in district concerns, and, maybe to little surprise, the opposition has therefore had trouble holding on to its districts – even when its national level vote has risen.[4] Nacif explains that since the post-legislative careers of individual legislators depend on the party leadership, legislators act as agents of the leadership, not the reverse.

Since the Argentine and Brazilian cases lie between the extremes of Mexico and Chile (or the United States), the incentive structure is less clear. Since about two-thirds of Brazilian legislators seek reelection, it would be incorrect to ignore the static ambition among Brazilian legislators. Further, since reelection is so difficult to attain, it may be the case that Brazilian legislators work especially hard to serve their constituents. On the other hand, if the legislators understand that they face daunting odds in their attempts to win reelection, they may act more similar to the Mexican legislators and forego opportunities to build their institution. Either way, given the short legislative careers in these two countries, we should expect legislators to hedge their bets and concern themselves with post-legislative jobs.

Samuels uses the low reelection rates to justify his look at how Brazilian legislators use their posts to pursue their post-legislative careers. He argues that since many legislators seek future jobs in state-level politics, they structure committees and dole out state resources in ways that further their progressive ambitions. Ames' regression analysis is a particularly apt tool for distinguishing among types of legislators. In his analysis he finds that the goal of reelection, in combination with the degree to which a legislator must rely on the party for votes, is a significant factor in determining the predisposition of legislators to work with the executive or party leaders.

[4] These interviews were conducted and the data collected with Benito Nacif in 1997.

418

The authors dealing with Argentina also find that the reelection rates necessitate careful strategies by the president and party leaders. Mustapic uses the puny chance that legislators have to return to their posts in Argentina to motivate the potential for executive–legislative gridlock. Since legislators are unconcerned with reelection, she argues, they should be unconcerned with supporting their party's president. Jones then argues that the leaders' control of future jobs takes the place of nomination control in supporting leaders' ability to enforce discipline. Mustapic also argues that committee posts are intended as rewards or payments for service, not to give legislators new experience. The implication, then, is that low reelection rates work against professionalization of the legislature, which, in turn, dampen legislative opposition to the executive. Eaton agrees, arguing that limited experience and knowledge (as well as administrative support) hinders the legislators' influence. At the same time, since the legislators' progressive ambition implies a need to cultivate the president's favor, the legislators have little incentive to assert themselves. One can only speculate what their influence would be if reelection rates were higher, a seniority system for committee assignments were in place, and the legislators had access to better resources.

Electoral Strategies and Party (or Coalition) Unity[5]

Regardless of why someone seeks legislative office, all candidates must plan their campaign strategies around their particular electoral system. This basic idea has given rise to a large literature focusing on the effects of electoral systems on numerous aspects of party systems and the internal dynamics of parties.[6] One aspect of these studies that has a special bearing on legislative types is the effect of electoral systems on the unity of parties (or coalitions or even factions). They do this in part by influencing the degree of control that a party leader has in choosing candidates. When

[5] Though here I will frequently refer to the effect of electoral systems and other variables on parties, these effects influence coalitions or factions as well. In other work (manuscript), therefore, I argue that we should replace the term "party system" with "agent system."

[6] Primary examples of studies of the developed world include Duverger (1954) Lijphart (1984, 1994), Katz (1986), Grofman and Lijphart (1986), Cox and Rosenbluth (1994, 1996), and Cox (1997). On the lesser developed areas, see Ames (1987), Mainwaring (1991), Shugart (1995), Shugart and Carey (1992). These studies focus on representation, the number of parties, party factionalization, the president's support in the legislature, and many other issues.

Table 14.2. *Latin American electoral systems.*[a]

	Formula[b]	Ballot structure	District magnitude (M)	Control of nominations	Implied effect on unity
Argentina	PR	Closed list	Median $M = 3$; range 2–35	Provincial party leaders	+ (at least at provincial level)
Brazil	PR	Open list	Median $M = 11$; range 8–60	Candidates and governors	–
Chile	PR	Open list	$M = 2$[c]	Party and coalition leaders	?
Mexico	Mixed System of PR + SMD	Closed list SMD (voter has just one linked vote)	$M = 1$ for 300 seats; $M = 40$ for 200 seats	National party leaders	+

[a] Lower House.
[b] Proportional representation (PR) and single-member districts (SMD).
[c] First place list must win double the second place to gain both seats.
Source for district magnitude is Cox (1997).

leaders have this power, they can enforce *discipline* on the rank-and-file, who fear the hammer of future nominations. It can also affect *cohesion*, the ideological agreement among a party's members, as centralized control of nominations should lead to more careful screening of candidates.[7] The electoral system can also induce cohesion by setting up incentives for a party's legislative candidates to either compete with one another or to work as a team. This and the following sections therefore discuss party or coalition unity as a generic term that can result from either discipline or cohesion.

Theories about the effects of electoral systems have been thoroughly reviewed elsewhere, and thus it is not fruitful to do so here. Still, it is useful to review the expected impact of the electoral systems in these countries. Borrowing heavily from Mainwaring and Shugart (1997),[8] Table 14.2 sum-

[7] Ozbudun (1970) was the first to make the distinction between discipline and cohesion.
[8] See also Carey and Shugart (1995), Katz (1986), and Morgenstern (2001).

marizes the combination of electoral variables and includes predictions about party unity.

Briefly, the scheme devised by other authors predicts party unity when leaders control candidate nominations and there is no intraparty competition. As a result, closed lists (as in Argentina) generally increase unity and open lists (as in Brazil) hinder it. It is important to note, however, that this simple formula neglects the issue of conjoining several provincially led groups. In Argentina, for example, the closed lists are controlled by provincial leaders, thus implying discipline at the provincial, but not necessarily the national, level. Finally, assuming a fixed assembly size, unity and district magnitude, the number of seats available should move together under closed lists, since district magnitude (M) translates to the number of legislators who owe their posts to a nominator. But under open lists a larger M implies greater intraparty competition, which should decrease party unity (c.f. Carey and Shugart 1995).

The importance of intracoalitional competition and district magnitude to leaders' powers is clear in the case of Chile. Carey's chapter carefully describes the Chilean electoral law for the lower House and empirically shows that the coalitions sustain relatively high unity rates. In part, these rates are supported by the legislators' allegiance to the party and coalition leaders that put them on the ballot. But, the rates are considerably less than those reported by Jones for Argentina, arguably since the electoral rules force them to run against a fellow coalition (if not party) member. The Chilean system virtually guarantees that each coalition will run two candidates in each district, and each coalition will win just one of those seats in most districts. The real competition, therefore, is often among candidates within the coalitions, instead of among the coalitions. As a result, in spite of the leaders' control of the nomination process, their influence on the final party winners is considerably less than would be the case if there were no intraparty competition.[9] In other words, where voters cannot discriminate between the two intraparty (or intracoalition) candidates based on their party (coalition) affiliations, the candidates must differentiate themselves from their partisan (coalitional) affiliation, thus limiting the party's (coalition's) cohesiveness. The system also curtails the leaders' power over nominations, since they cannot credibly claim that the rank-and-file owe their elections to the support or reputation of the leadership.

[9] For an in-depth look at intraparty competition, see Katz (1986).

Other Variables Affecting Unity

The electoral system is helpful in explaining unity, but it offers a blanket effect on all legislative actors in a country. There is significant heterogeneity among the parties (and coalitions) in each country, however, implying a need for other explanatory variables. That is, if institutional variables were completely determinant, then all parties operating under the same rules would act similarly and look the same structurally. Since this is not the case, we must be careful not to ignore variables that explain intra-country differences, such as the value of a party's reputation in an election, ideology, and federalism.[10]

First, a party's reputation has a clearly positive relation with party leader strength and the resultant party unity.[11] If candidates are unconcerned with partisan labels, then they will find little value in making partisan appeals or working for the party. For example, until their recent reform Ecuador used a closed list system that we normally associate with tight discipline. But since voters apparently place little weight on the party label, legislators could dissent on votes, repel leaders' demands, and even switch parties without jeopardizing their electoral prospects. The limited importance of partisan labels similarly affects Brazilian politics. There the situation is exacerbated, since party leaders have limited control over the composition of their open lists and the nature of open lists virtually assures intraparty rivalry. Here again, the low importance that legislators place on partisanship manifests itself in Brazil's famous party jumping, as well as the constant rise and fall of new parties.[12]

One direct measure of the value of a party's label is the stability of partisan support or electoral volatility (see Coppedge 1998; Roberts and Wibbels 1999). Parties will rise and fall much more quickly where legislators place little value on party labels, and they will be much more stable where legislators are more concerned with maintaining the party's reputation. Roberts and Wibbels point to short-term economic fluctuations, institutions, and socio-economic cleavage structures as driving the degree

---

[10] This is not intended as an exhaustive list. One might also consider the relation of a legislative group to the president, ties to societal groups such as unions, and many other factors.

[11] Mainwaring and Shugart (1997) make a similar argument.

[12] The low importance that legislators place on partisanship is clearly tied to the low levels of partisanship amongst the electorate. Much of this discussion could, therefore, be reformulated as a discussion about low levels of partisan identification in the electorate.

of volatility. Still, high levels of volatility would not be possible without legislators and other politicians willing to abandon their party labels. Roberts and Wibbels employ the Pedersen index, which aggregates the parties' gains and losses (divided by 2) to measure volatility. These scores, as detailed in Table 14.3, therefore give an indication of the value of a party's reputation. Consistent with their low levels of unity, the statistics indicate much more volatility in Brazil than in other countries. However, like other variables discussed here, volatility may be a sufficient causal variable, but it is not a necessary factor in explaining low levels of party-line voting. The low levels of partisan unity in the United States, for example, could not be explained by volatility rates.

Second, I argued previously that centralized control of nominations can increase the ideological agreement among a party's (or coalition's) membership. It is clear, however, that coherent groups of legislators can come together for other reasons as well. Ideology thus has an independent effect on unity, as is clear in several chapters. Londregan's chapter on the Chilean Senate is a clear testament to the importance of ideology in explaining legislative (committee) voting, and Ames uses an ideological variable in his tests on Brazilian party unity. Ideology takes a less central, but still important role in other chapters. Mustapic notes that, while neither of the parties is ideologically coherent, ideological divides could generate dissent within the Peronist party. While Amorim Neto's model of coalition politics explains much about party unity, he argues that high party unity in several parties is the result of their radical positions. Jones notes that while the support of some provincial parties can be bought, the support of others is contingent on ideological stances. Carey's focus on the legislative voting in Chile suggests that a "moral obligation" supports coalition unity in the face of ideological tensions.

Table 14.3. *Pedersen index volatility scores, legislative elections, 1980–1997.*

Argentina	13.2
Brazil	27.7
Chile	10.0
Mexico	14.8

Source: Roberts and Wibbels (1999).
The Pedersen index is the sum of individual party gains and losses divided by 2.

Table 14.4. *Extremism, cohesion, and unity.*

		Relative Extremism	
		High	Low
Internal differences	High	Frep$_A$, UCEDE$_A$ PTB$_B$, PPB$_B$, Right$_C$, RN$_C$, UDI$_C$[a] PAN$_M$ PRD$_M$	PJ$_A$ UCR$_A$, PFL$_B$, PMDB$_B$, PSDB$_B$, PRI$_M$
	Low	PT$_B$, PPD$_C$, PS$_C$	Conc$_C$, PDC$_C$,

The subscripts refer to the four countries, Argentina, Brazil, Chile, and Mexico.
Extremism is defined as the absolute difference from median left–right self-placement within country (see appendix for details). The average across countries was an absolute difference of 1.06 from the mean. Countries were termed extreme if they were further than 1.06 from their country's mean. Internal differences are defined by a similar methodology, using the standard deviation for the ideological self-placements. The mean across countries for the SD was 1.26

[a] Discounting the one apparently incorrectly coded respondent.

These studies, then, suggest that both the relative extremism of a party (such as the PT in Brazil or the UDI in Chile) and general agreement among party members can drive unity. Table 14.4 measures these two dimensions of ideology using a survey of legislators undertaken by Manuel Alcantara and his team in 1997.[13] By using legislators' self-placement on a 10-point left–right scale, the table indicates relative extremism and internal ideological agreement (details are in Appendix Table 14A.1).

The lower left cell indicates the parties, like Brazil's PT and the Chilean Socialists, that should be the most unified; they have few internal differences and they are relatively extreme within their countries. As exemplified by Argentina's traditional parties (the Peronists [PJ] and the UCR) and Mexico's PRI, parties in the upper right cell should not be able to rely on ideology to generate party unity, since the legislators disagree with one another and are not bound by a general extremism. In the top left corner, parties are relatively extreme, but their unity may be hurt by internal differences. For example, while most members in Mexico's leftist opposition, the PRD, agreed that the party is left of center, few would argue that it

[13] The survey team has noted several sampling problems, but overall these data provide invaluable insights into the beliefs of Latin American legislators.

has a well-developed economic or social agenda. Chile's rightist coalition also falls into this box, as do the two main parties that make up that coalition. This is expected for the RN, which is a relatively loose grouping of legislators, but one aberrant legislator drives the unexpected placement of the UDI, an ideologically focused party that was organized by a vibrant and now-martyred leader.[14] Finally, members of Chile's center-left coalition, as well as the members of the primary party in that coalition, agree that they are centrist.

A final variable that several authors discuss as affecting the level of partisan unity is federalism. When legislators are closely tied to their home regions, some issues, such as those that divide rural and urban constituencies, will have the potential to cleave parties. Further, as noted previously, federal systems may distribute control of candidate nominations to provincial leaders, thus supporting discipline at the regional but not necessarily the national level. Federalism, in sum, affects cohesion through its tying of legislators on regional issues and discipline by moving control over electoral lists from the national to the provincial level.

This issue manifests itself in the chapters on Argentina and Brazil. For Brazil, Samuels explains how, in response to legislators' concerns with governors and state interests, state delegations trump partisan concerns in organizing committees and, consequently, in determining the division of resources. For Argentina, the role of federalism is a bit murkier, as the two main parties have generally overcome their divisions. Jones shows, in particular, that although the federal party officials have to concern themselves with provincial-level candidate nominations, the legislators' progressive ambition (which the national leaders influence), internal party rules, and legislative institutions still generate unity on roll-call voting in the parties. Eaton, meanwhile, forcefully argues that the Argentine provincial lawmakers have divided loyalties. While they owe loyalty to the national party and the president, the president has to work to overcome the legislators' interests in securing tax advantages for their home provinces.

---

[14] Actually there are two aberrant UDI legislators. Of the 12 UDI legislators, 10 listed their left–right placement as 5–8. The remaining two listed their ideology as far left (at 2). One of these legislators is clearly miscoded, since he or she lines up with the far left on every issue. That legislator has been excluded from the analysis. The remaining legislator is still included in the analysis, which yields the relative high score for the standard deviation on the left–right scale.

Determinants of Unity

In sum, partisan unity, which can result from either discipline or cohesion, is a function of a number of electoral and nonelectoral factors. These factors, it should be emphasized, are interactive, not additive. That is, a party leader who holds a monopoly over candidate nominations may be very weak if the party's reputation is not valuable to candidates. Similarly, as developed in the well-known distinction between the United Kingdom and the United States (see Cain, Ferejohn, and Fiorina 1987) the electoral formula tells us little until it is combined with the ballot structure and, especially in that case, the ties between the executive and the legislature. While it is beyond the scope of this chapter to define all of the permutations of the variables and their impacts on team orientation or leadership powers, Table 14.5 provides some of the information necessary to explain unity in our four cases.

Based on the previous discussion and tables, I have scored the Argentine electoral system as supportive of high unity rates, the Brazilian system as unsupportive, and the Chilean system as neutral. The Argentine coding may be a bit controversial, since nominations are not centrally controlled. Mexico's two-level system (300 single-member districts overlaid by 200 seats distributed by proportional representation) has opposing effects on unity, though the centralized control of nominations has so far overridden the negative effects of the single-member districts. The previous discussions suggest that only Brazil should earn a "–" for both the importance of the parties' labels and federalism. The coding for federalism is less clear for other countries. Formally the Mexican Constitution is federal, but in reality – at least until recently, when opposition parties have gained control of governorships – the states have been quite weak. Chile is not a federal state, but legislators do represent 60 different districts. Further,

Table 14.5. *Determinants of party unity.*

Country	Electoral System	Party Reputation	Federalism	Ideology	Partisan Unity
Argentina	+	+	–	–	High
Brazil	–	–	–	+/–	Low to high
Chile	0	+	0	+/0	Moderate to high
Mexico	+	+	+/0	–	High

426

mayors preside over administrative districts, which are quite distinct from one another. Thus, I have scored Chile a 0 instead of a "+" for the impact of federalism on unity. Argentina is again, perhaps, the most ambiguous case. Until recently the two main Argentine parties had had consistently strong and stable support, suggesting strong partisanship among the electorate (see Table 14.3). This earned Argentina a "+" on the party reputation variable, but the success of small provincial parties and the rise of the Alianza (which won the 2000 presidential election) implies a waning if not a historically limited role for parties' reputations or labels. Further, the provincial control of candidate lists suggests possible intraprovincial controversies. Finally, I have not scored any of the countries a "+" for ideology since no country features a full complement of strongly ideological parties. However, since several parties in Brazil and Chile are ideologically based, it would be incorrect to apply a single label to either country as a whole.

The final column in the table summarizes the results reported in other work and in earlier chapters.[15] Unity is high in Argentina and Mexico and moderately high in Chile. In Brazil, most parties have low unity, but members of the leftist Workers' Party (PT) vote together continually.

The different conjunction of variables that drive these patterns suggests that no factor is necessary, but any may be sufficient to support high unity rates. That is, the factors that support high unity in Argentina differ from the factors that help the PT or the Chilean parties.

The Argentine closed list electoral system would be the most propitious for partisan unity if federalism did not rob control of candidate nominations from the national leaders. Still, the national leaders' influence in the provinces, combined with the low party volatility, apparently work to overcome the divisive impacts of federalism and the lack of ideological consensus within the parties. In Brazil, the arrows all point toward low unity, as it uses open lists in a federal system, sports a "–" on the proxy for the importance of parties' reputations in Table 14.5, and its parties generally house ideological disparate members. It is therefore unclear which, if any, factor is determinant.

Next, Chile's double-member districts have conflicting impacts on party unity. Leaders have an important voice in candidate choice, but the intra-coalition competition for the seats could breed dissension. The only variable clearly working in favor of unity is the high value of party reputations,

---

[15] See also Morgenstern (n.d.) where I measure unity with roll-call data.

but ideological cohesion is also supportive. This case therefore shows a substantially different pattern than in Argentina, or our final case: Mexico.

Mexico combines a single-member district system, which could work against unity, with regional PR lists, which generally support unity. But, the personalism suggested by the single-member districts is overridden by the centralized control of nominations. The parties have begun to experiment with primaries for other elected offices in Mexico (including governors and the president), but congressional candidates are still chosen by central party leaders. This, plus the no-reelection clause that breaks the ties between legislators and voters, yields legislators loyal to leaders.

The Party System

The party system is a clear factor determining the expected lines of support and opposition – in short, the legislature's type. While the concept of a party system encompasses many factors, I will focus here on the existence of a coherent majority. There are two aspects of this concept: a solid party or coalition that controls at least 50% of the legislative seats, and at least a modicum of unity within that party (or coalition).

Models of U.S. legislative politics assume a partisan majority, though there are disagreements about how unified the majority has been and the effects of the partisan divisions. Thus, while partisan majorities in the U.S. Congress have control over the agenda, committee appointments, and other procedural issues, internal party divisions have limited the partisan agenda and have provided inconsistent support for presidents, even from their own party.

This majority-party model has some lessons for Argentina and pre-1997 Mexico, and Carey argues that the model is also correct for Chile's lower House, whose multiple parties are molded into two stable coalitions. However, for legislatures in which no single party has sufficient votes to run the house on its own (i.e., Brazil), this model needs some alteration. In these cases we expect party leaders to be severely hampered in their efforts to define collective agreements, allocate influential positions, and gain procedural (if not substantive) advantages for their members. We must therefore account for differing party arrangements in describing a legislature's type.

Table 14.6 details several statistics that together give an impression of the shape of political competition in our four cases plus the United States. By itself the composition of the majority can largely determine whether

Table 14.6. *Structure of partisan competition, lower House.*[a]

	Laakso and Taagepera index	Molinar index	% seats of president's party	% seats largest other party
Argentina (1989–1999)	2.83	1.86	49.6	31.1
Brazil (1990–1998)	7.98	6.13	12.1[b]	21.9
Chile parties (1989–1997)	4.89	3.44	31.9	23.3
Chile coalitions (1989–1997)	1.96	1.63	58.9	40.3
Mexico (1991–1994)	2.24	1.30	62.1	20.9
Mexico (1997–2000)	2.82	2.20	44.9	33.1
United States (1991–2001)	1.97	1.78	48.1	51.6

[a] Indices based on number of seats held by parties. The statistics indicate averages across years indicated, see text and footnotes for formulas.
[b] 1994–1998.

presidents will face a workable/compliant or a recalcitrant legislature. The final two columns in the table portray the size of the legislative contingent pertaining to the president's party and the size of the largest nonpresidentialist party. It shows that the Brazilian presidents have neither a solid supporting majority nor a solid opposition. The current president (Cardoso), for example, was first elected in 1994 with only about 12% of his co-partisans in the legislature. When he was reelected in 1998 his PSDB legislators won more seats, but they were still held under 20% of the lower House. In Argentina, Menem had a small majority in his final years, and the largest minority party has had over 40% of the votes. In Chile, the rightist coalition has held about 40% collectively, but the largest opposition party has only about one-fourth of the lower House. The Chilean presidents, in turn, have enjoyed large majority coalitions, but their own parties have held only relatively few seats (Frei's Christian Democrats had just 33% and Ricardo Lagos' Socialists won under 10%). The pre-1997 Mexican presidents, of course, had the most solid support, yielding a vastly different type of legislature than the one that has begun to emerge since the PRI's decline.

In addition to the existence of a coherent majority, the comparative politics literature attests that the legislative process is also shaped by the sheer number of different parties or coalitions (or factions) in the system. Downs (1957) and later Cox (1990) discussed how the number of parties alters the

429

centripetal versus centrifugal nature of party competition. One of Sartori's (1976) primary contributions was in arguing that "extreme" multipartism bred polarization that seriously theatened democracy. Mainwaring (1993) and later Jones (1995) argued about the relation between the number of parties and the president's legislative support as a determinant of executive legislative conflict and democratic survival.

In order to review this aspect of legislative politics, Table 14.6 reviews two indices for the number of parties. Both the Laakso and Taagepera (1979) and the Molinar (1991) indices weight the number of parties in the Congress by the number of seats that they hold, but the Molinar index applies an extra weight to majority parties, assuming that such parties will marginalize their smaller competitors.[16] Thus we see that while there are more than three parties in Argentina, competition is very much structured by a single large party there. Similarly, in pre-1997 Mexico, while there were three parties with significant numbers of legislative seats, the PRI's domination translates into a Molinar score of only 1.3. For Brazil both indices highlight the fragmented system, and for the United States both recognize two-party competition. For Chile the Molinar index rightly points us toward the *Concertacion's* dominance in the lower house, though the Laakso and Taagepera index correctly points us to the five principal parties and two coalitions.

One issue that has not received significant attention is the effect of multipartism on collective action. Although parties can be vehicles to organize legislators for collective action, a legislature may be immobilized when no party controls a majority of the house or senate seats. This is because organizing a minority party's members is insufficient for blocking or approving legislation; it also requires the assent of enough other legislators – who may have strategic or ideological reasons to resist a bargain – to create a majority bloc. Moreover, the literature on collective action explains that groups may be unmovable in spite of common interests (such as opposition to the executive) (Hardin 1982; Olson 1971).[17] Such was the

---

[16] The Laakso and Taagepera index is $N = 1/\Sigma_{i=1}^{n}P_i^2$, where P_i is the percentage of vote of the ith party squared, while the Molinar index is $NP = 1 + N[\Sigma_{i=1}^{n}(P_i^2 - P_L^2)/\Sigma_{i=1}^{n}P_i^2]$ and P_L is the percentage of the vote for the largest party. (Molinar retains the subscript i for the largest party vote as well.)

[17] It is interesting that this point is lost to Mayhew (1974), who assumes that legislators can overcome their collective action problems to create the structure that works so well in serving their individual interests. Similarly, Aldrich (1995) emphasizes the common interests of legislators in forming a majority party.

Table 14.7. *Partisan composition and legislative power.*

Partisan makeup	Incentive to assert institutional power	Ability to assert institutional power
No Unified Majority	?	Low
Unified majority supporting president	Low	High
Unified majority opposing president	High	High

case in Norway, where, as Strom (1994) describes in the "Presthus Debacle," the opposition parties had a clear interest in bringing down the government, and the power to do so, yet they failed to pass a no-confidence vote due to the parties' individual and ancillary interests.[18] This allegory of unused power appears apt for many of Latin America's multi-partisan legislatures, where, in spite of constitutions that parallel that of the United States in many ways, the legislatures have been unable to sustain high levels of proactivity relative to their executives.

As summarized in Table 14.7, only cohesive opposition parties (or coalitions) with majority control will have the means, method, and incentive to assert legislative authority.[19] If there is no cohesive majority, some parties may prefer to assert their power to push policy changes, though others may oppose beefing up the assembly's power for fear of how that power might be used. These oppositionists, however, should have little to fear, since conflicts of interest will make it quite difficult to form the coalition necessary for asserting such power.

The middle-left spot suggests that members of a majority party will have less interest in developing a professional legislature and asserting their authority if they support rather than oppose the president. The strength of the ties between the branches, however, is very important. As the U.S. case makes clear, a majority party supporting the president can still assert power. U.S. legislators have stronger ties to the electorate than to the president, and they therefore developed a seniority system and other mechanisms that help the legislators to attract constituents (or clienteles)

[18] For a similar example, see Huber (1996, ch. 5).
[19] For ease of exposition we will often talk about majority parties. As the case of Chile reminds us, however, it is important to note that cohesive majorities could be parties or coalitions.

431

by credibly claiming credit for affecting policy outcomes and channeling resources to voters and donors. In Latin America executives generally control tighter bonds to legislators in their parties, as epitomized by pre-1997 Mexico, where the legislators were completely subsumed by the president. Where the bonds are less tight, legislators should seek ways to use the legislature to further their career goals, and majority control can help them to do so. Still, it seems unlikely that a majority party that sides with the president would take as assertive a position as one that opposed the president. Moreover, a president who was the head of the majority party might well work to dampen legislative involvement, since it could weaken executive authority. Thus, while majority status by itself helps to reinforce a legislature's reactive status, proaction is a function of the strength of ties between the president and the members of the majority.

Although the conditions necessary for legislative assertiveness have been common in the United States, they have been uncommon in Latin America (Mainwaring 1993). There have been examples of cohesive assembly majorities in Latin America, but very few where the majority was in opposition to the president. Venezuela, a case that we unfortunately could not include in this volume, is one of the very few cases that has had significant experience with a unified opposition majority in the legislature.[20] The Congress that impeached and removed Venezuelan President Pérez from office was not controlled by the president's party, in contrast to the situation in Colombia, where President Samper's party, with a majority of the legislative seats, withstood pressure to do the same. It is important to note, however, that the opposition has frequently worked with the Venezuelan presidents as well. Crisp (1998) shows, for example, that the legislature has voted to delegate decree powers not only to presidents who wore the same color stripes, but also to two (relative) independents. The important difference, however, is that the presidents backed by a majority of their own partisans were given much more leeway than the others.

The pictures painted in this volume about Chile, Argentina, and Mexico all show how relatively unified majorities that support the executive severely restrict legislative proaction. Carey explains that the majority coalition has used its control of the Chilean legislature to maintain control of all committees, but Siavelis adds that, since the majority backs the pres-

---

[20] There has also been a single opposition party in control of at least one house of Congress in the Dominican Republic, in Colombia between 1982 and 1986, and the new Argentine President De La Rúa faces an opposition- (Peronist-) controlled Senate.

ident, the Chilean Congress has not asserted this control as a proactive policy maker. For Argentina, Eaton discusses how the Peronists monopolize policy making in the legislature and focuses on an issue where the president's majority opposes him, at least to a degree. He argues that legislators' regional interests led them to argue for tax policy that would benefit the areas from where the majority of the party's legislators had been elected. Crucial to this study is the finding that the legislators opposed Menem on this issue. On most issues Mustapic shows that Menem has been able to parlay his legislative support (and significant powers) into an almost dominant position. Next, in Mexico, Casar, Weldon, and Nacif all discuss how the PRI has dominated the system, leading to a very marginal legislature during most of the last 70 years. Weldon's historical look, however, is very instructive in showing that when the majority was less solid, the president was less dominant.

Finally, Brazil is a case where a lack of proactivity is partially explained by a lack of a cohesive majority. Ames argues that lack of support limits the presidents' ability to win approval for many initiatives, and Amorim Neto shows how the presidents' concern with the legislature has led them to try to cobble together support by strategically using cabinet appointments. There seems to be little legislative initiative, except, as Samuels shows, to ensure a generous supply of strategically directed pork.

Summarizing the Impacts of Party and Electoral Systems in Argentina, Brazil, Chile, and Mexico

In addition to, or as a result of, their general effects on party unity and legislative proactivity, the authors have explained how the party and electoral systems affect some very specific outcomes. Thus, before moving to the last assumption *qua* independent variable, it is useful to summarize these more precise contributions.

For Argentina, Mustapic explains how the presidents' near majority control of a disciplined party has helped Argentina to avoid almost certain gridlock. As I have explained, the closed list electoral system has not been the only key to party discipline, as the nomination procedure is not centralized. Without this tool at their disposal, the parties must shower the representatives with resources and leadership posts to combat this potential disunity. Still, the presidents' control of near majorities in the legislature allowed most executive bills to pass unobstructed and in an expeditious fashion.

Jones and Eaton focus on the strength of provincial leaders that results from the decentralized closed list system. Jones argues that, as a result of this system, the president has had to negotiate with provincial leaders to secure support on some key issues. Eaton's study of tax reform highlights this dynamic. He concludes that, although Peronist legislators supported reforms due to the importance of fiscal stability to their party, legislators also pushed for and sometimes gained modifications that benefited their provinces.

Brazil's open list electoral system leads to a contrasting story in that country. For Ames, the legislators' great independence from their leaders generates a high degree of interbranch conflict. Samuels explains that it also skews the distribution of public finances, as legislators try to channel funds to the state-level leaders who can influence legislators' careers.

Amorim Neto's interest is how the Brazilian party structure affects the style of presidential policy making. He first asks about the level of presidential support in the legislature. Presidents who have enjoyed support have built "coalitional" cabinets, in which the cabinet makeup reflects the partisan composition in the legislature. Presidents who plan on legislating through statutes use coalitional cabinets, Amorim Neto argues, to build legislative support. The converse situation was exemplified by President Collor, who had very little legislative support, filled his cabinet with cronies, and relied on decrees instead of statute to govern. The relationship between a president's legislative support and the style of governance is an important finding in light of the fact that Brazilian and other Latin American presidents frequently lack stable majorities, and the premonitions that O'Donnell (1994), Mainwaring (1993), and others have raised about the threat of unchecked presidential power to democracy.

A different aspect of the electoral system, the timing of elections, also enters into Amorim Neto's analysis. He finds that members of the governing coalition are much more highly disciplined early in the electoral cycle. But, "the value of holding ministerial posts declines over time as concerns with office seeking give way to vote maximization."

The party and electoral systems are also key ingredients in the chapters dealing with Chile. Siavelis, in a manner not dissimilar from Amorim Neto, argues that support in the legislature, which is affirmed by a careful distribution of cabinet seats, determines executive tactics. Unlike Brazil, however, the Chilean president has been backed by strong support in the lower house, and, as a result, the Chilean presidents have not resorted to strong-arm tactics. In the Senate, where the president lacks majority support, the president has had to employ other strategies. Siavelis notes that the president has refrained from proposing controversial legislation and at times has negotiated with the senators or their core supporters. As Jones (1995) suggests, a president's near majority makes this scheme possible. Since the Chilean presidents have only needed a few votes by members of the rightist coalition, and since some members of that coalition have been willing to cross coalitional lines, strong-arm tactics that could alienate the right would arguably have been a poor long-term strategy.

Carey's dependent variable, on which the electoral system bears directly, is the distinctive dual coalition arrangement of Chilean legislative politics. He states succinctly that "the stability and cohesiveness of the two main legislative coalitions: the *Concertación* on the center-left, and the coalition of the right . . . is a product of the $M = 2$ reform of the electoral system."

Londregan's study of the Senate shows that party and electoral – or in this case appointment – systems have very clear effects on Chilean politics. The distribution of seats in the Chilean Senate (and its committees) makes the appointed senators linchpins in the negotiation process. Londregan shows that they use their positions effectively; though they generally side with the right, sometimes they tip the balance to the left, even on controversial labor legislation. Their ideological affinities (which affected their decision to join one side or the other) are conditioned by the appointment process, which we could take as a distinctive electoral rule. The rules have generally favored rightists, since the outgoing president, Pinochet, held the power to directly appoint most of them. But although Londregan is not convinced of its importance, the rules may also have helped to produce some relative centrists. In particular, Pinochet's constitution stipulated that one appointed senator be a former university president. Few were available, and Pinochet's choice for this position was William Thayer, who in addition to his university experience was the Minister of Labor under the Christian Democratic administration in the 1960s. Londregan argues, therefore, that Thayer's moderate attitude towards labor, which allowed the Senate labor committee to approve many government-sponsored bills, could not have been a great surprise to Pinochet.

Finally, there is no doubt that partisan alignments have been key to explaining legislative politics in Mexico. In addition to the no-reelection clause, which Weldon argues helped to establish centralized control of nominations and thereby high party discipline, the dominant majority status has allowed the PRI to rule unencumbered by a pesky opposition.

Casar describes this in terms of the president's legislative powers. She notes that in spite of a constitution that balances the branches, the president's informal powers led to dominance until very recently. In her terms, the president's powers and the electoral/career incentives facing legislators reinforce one another. The PRI uses its dominant position to control the electoral process, and this obfuscation allows the executive unchallenged support in the legislature. Weldon generally agrees, offering an interesting view of how legislative politics looked before the PRI's dominance was complete. Finally, in the section on legislative organization, Nacif explains how the dominant party organized the legislature to prevent obtrusion by other parties. His look at how the committee and organizing structure of the legislature has changed as the PRI's dominance has waned are positive examples of the importance of the party system to legislative politics.

Constitutional Powers

Finally, legislatures are not equally empowered under their constitutions, thus altering from the U.S. model the legislature's role in the policy process and, by implication, how the legislators seek to organize themselves in pursuit of their policy or career goals. While some legislatures are armed with the ability to delay or amend presidential initiatives, revise the budget, overturn vetoes easily, or even amend the constitution, others face the mighty presidency with only small pebbles to protect their interests. For example, the Argentine and Brazilian legislatures are virtually powerless in response to presidential decrees.[21] The Chilean legislature has been hampered by the constitutional prohibition against their raising budget expenditures, and Siavelis's chapter highlights the importance of the president's constitutional right to determine the legislative agenda by declaring a bill urgent. In light of the suggestion by Mainwaring and Shugart (1997) and Shugart and Carey (1992) that strong executives are potentially dangerous to democratic stability, these differences could have ominous effects. The chapters here, however, have shown that the restrictions have not by themselves paralyzed the legislatures.

[21] On this point, with reference to Argentina, see Ferreira Rubio and Goretti (1998) and Jones (1997). Although the Argentine legislature challenged this power, the courts sided with the president, ruling that the legislature would have to write a new law – subject to a presidential veto – to overturn a decree. The 1994 constitutional revision called for a legislative committee to review decrees. It is uncertain, still, how much power this commission will hold.

Shugart and Carey (1992) were the first to carefully consider the range of presidential powers. On a scale of 0–4 (with 4 representing the strongest power), they evaluated the constitutions with respect to package and partial veto powers, decree provisions, budgetary powers, and the exclusive rights of the president to initiate bills and referendums. They then summed the scores to evaluate relative presidential powers. In adding across categories they assumed that each of the powers has equal weight, and thus though their results are generally on-track, they have been criticized for their methodology. A prime example of this problem would be the overriding importance of decree powers; it matters little that the Argentine president does not have a partial veto given that Menem and several Brazilian presidents have bypassed the legislature with decrees. This problem, however, should not detract from the instructive within-power comparisons, and thus Table 14.8 is only a slightly modified (and updated) version of the Shugart and Carey table.

Shugart and Carey discuss each of these powers except the final one, and therefore it is most useful to focus on urgency provisions, which take center stage in Siavelis's contribution to this volume.[22]

Urgency provisions are meant to help presidents overcome legislative bottlenecks. Sometimes these bottlenecks are truly the result of time-consuming legislative deliberations coupled with a limited capacity to deal with the numerous demands made by the executive, the public, political parties, and interest groups. At other times the bottlenecks are strategic; legislators may find it in their interest to tie up bills in committee instead of making explicit pronouncements. In response many constitutions include "urgency provisions" that force, or at least pressure, the legislatures to deal with presidential requests quickly.

Urgency provisions come in two basic types. In some countries the urgency provision is simply an agenda-setting tool. For example, in Brazil, the legislature must deal with bills that the president deems urgent within 45 days or they take precedence over every other legislative matter. In Colombia, it is even more stringent as there is no waiting period; all urgent bills immediately take precedence over other legislation. Although these

---

[22] Shugart and Carey also include referendums in their analysis, but this is not an issue for any of the countries under consideration here. They also discuss exclusive initiative, for which only the Brazilian Constitution has a provision. While this can be an important power since it can prevent certain bills from legislative action, this provision does not forbid amendments once a bill is initiated by the president.

Table 14.8. *Constitutional powers of the president.*[a]

	Package veto	Partial veto	Decree	Budget	Urgency powers
Argentina (1983–1994)	2	3[b]	4[c]	0	0
Argentina (post-1994)	2	3	3	0	0
Brazil	1	2	4	1	2
Chile	2	0	0	2	4
Mexico	2	0	0	−1[d]	0

[a] 0 is a weak presidential power, 4 implies maximum strength. See Shugart and Carey for specific description of values, except for urgency provisions, which are described in the text.
[b] Widely used in spite of no constitutional provision.
[c] Rated a 0 in Shugart and Carey, but a Supreme Court decision in 1990 asserted the presidential decree power.
[d] Rated 0 in Shugart and Carey, but since the president does not even have a veto regarding the budget, we rate this a −1.

measures do not force the legislature to approve executive requests (ending gridlock), they effectively create an express lane.

The stronger type of urgency provision also fails to necessarily end a stalemate, but it puts additional pressure on the legislature. In Chile and Uruguay, if the executive declares a bill urgent, the legislature must make a pronouncement within a specified (short) time period. The Chilean Constitution does not specify what happens if the Congress fails to act within that time frame, but in Uruguay inaction converts the bill into a law.[23] This is also true in Ecuador, but, unlike the former two countries, the Ecuadorian legislature can pass a bill that is *not* subject to a veto to rescind such legislation.

The studies in this and other volumes give ample evidence that differences in urgency powers and other constitutional provisions can have dramatic effects on executive–legislative relations, legislative organization, and the policy process more generally. But, none of the authors reported that constitutional (or paraconstitutional) provisions tipped the scales so far in favor of the president as to render the legislature insignificant. More-

[23] Though Article 71 of the Chilean Constitution requires congressional action within 30 days, there is no explanation of what happens if the Congress fails to act. Article 49 states that if the president asks for urgent treatment of a matter, then the Senate must act within 30 days or its assent is assumed. Since Article 49 does not discuss the lower house, and Article 71 does not express a reversion point, there is at least room to argue about the fate of urgent bills.

over, though almost unstoppable decree powers (as held by Argentine President Menem, Peruvian President Fujimori, and others) have led O'Donnell and others to question the institutionalization and quality of Latin American democracy, the authors in this volume have stressed that legislative politics are driven by other factors.

This is not to say that they ignore the importance of constitutional or paraconstituional powers. Mustapic, for example, emphasizes partisan and leadership resources within the context of crisis situations in explaining the lack of executive–legislative gridlock, but she also recognizes the importance of the Argentine president's "formidable institutional resources." Still, in most chapters constitutional provisions are secondary concerns in the analyses. Even for the other chapters on Argentina, the decree powers are far in the background. Eaton argues that the president is not always in a position to make use of the decree power, and when presidents want assurances that their policies will not be reversed in the future, they legislate through statute. Further, in showing that Menem was forced to accept some important changes, Eaton justifies his conclusion about the importance of the legislature and its sometimes-provincial leanings.

Amorim Neto argues that veto provisions, decrees (provisional measures), and other constitutional issues are "weapons that tempt [Brazilian] presidents to act unilaterally and to overstep their legislative powers." But, as noted previously, he interacts the Brazilian president's ability to decree legislation with his support in the legislature. Since the president has these two options for legislating, executive policy making is less problematic than may be predicted given Brazil's fragmented legislature. This is not to suggest, as Ames highlights, that the presidents can legislate freely. Indeed, a relatively small portion of executive initiatives make it to the legislative floor for debate, and "*practically nothing gets through the Congress without substantial modification*" (emphasis in original). Further, although Collor was somewhat of an exception, presidents have not been able to dictate decrees on controversial issues, such as the reelection of the president, administrative restructuring, or pension reform. Presidents can most effectively use decree powers when speed and secrecy of decisions is essential (such as decisions to freeze assets).[24]

In the final Brazil chapter, Samuels takes for granted an important constitutional restriction in his examination of how legislators use budget

---

[24] Ames made this argument in a personal communication, 11/30/1999.

amendments to feed their pork-hungry districts, apparently since the president and legislators have found a way around the restriction. The Brazilian Constitution forbids legislators from adding items to the budget, *unless* they also determine revenue sources. In response to their need to use pork to buy legislative support, the presidents have included about $1.5 billion (of the $100 billion dollar budget) in unrestricted funds for the legislators to squabble about.[25] The legislators use this money (capped at a limit of about $1.5 million per legislator) as the source of funds for their proposed amendments. This evasion is similar to the pre-Pinochet period in Chile that Agor (1970) describes, where legislators evaded a similar constitutional provision by pointing to the next year's budget for the necessary revenue. In contrast, Baldez and Carey (1999) argue that in current-day Chile, there are much more stringent restrictions on legislative budgetary amendments, thereby decidedly tipping the budgetary balance toward the president.

For Chile, as described by Siavelis, Pinochet bequeathed a very strong or "exaggerated" presidency on Chile. But, Siavelis reports, the two post-Pinochet presidents have restrained themselves in their application of such powers. Maybe as a result, the chapters by Carey and Londregan do not dwell on issues relating to the constitutional balance power. Siavelis' caution that in times of crisis presidents could resort to constitutional prerogatives, however, implies the importance of considering these powers.

Constitutional powers have played a smaller role in the Mexican case, at least prior to the recent changes. This limited importance, as Casar describes, was the result of the interaction between partisan and constitutional powers. As the chapters on Argentina and Chile show, the president does not always have to rely on his constitutional endowments to convert initiatives into law if the legislature is compliant. The Mexican president, who is not as strong on paper as other Latin American chief executives, has enjoyed the epitome of a subservient legislature. Now that partisan alignments have changed, however, the legislature has become much more involved in the policy process. For example, in the few short years since the opposition won control in 1997, the president has had to seek an alliance with the opposition to win general approval for his budget and some budgetary bills, including one dealing with the value added tax, were defeated.

---

[25] David Samuels provided this information.

In sum, while the chapters demonstrate the importance of constitutional variation to the executive–legislative balance and the policy-making process, formal powers alone are not determinant. Their interaction with legislators' ambitions and independence from the president, the partisan composition of the legislature, and the electoral system, however, are critical to an explanation of legislative politics.

Defining the Legislatures' Types[26]

This chapter has highlighted how the reelection drive, the party and electoral system, the Constitution, and other factors influence the means and motivations of legislators, and hence the legislatures' type. Strong binds between the legislature and the president, for example, can turn a potentially proactive legislature into a passive or at best reactive institution. The legislators' reelection motivations and the electoral system are related, in that they affect how strongly legislators are tied to their constituents. Legislators must contrast these sometimes competing motivations in their efforts to build a professional institution, seek spoils for their constituents, work with other legislators in pursuit of national policy goals, or simply follow executive directives. Legislators in Mexico, Argentina, and Brazil – where there were respectively 0, 20, and 35% of legislators returning to their posts in recent elections – should be looking to grab what they can and run. As argued in other chapters, such legislators should be particularly responsive to presidents (or others) who control resources that the legislators can use to line their pockets, improve their future career prospects, or pay off their patrons. While certainly interested in the electoral benefits of the pork-barrel, legislators who envision longer legislative careers (e.g., Chile, where about 70% of the lower House members generally return to their posts and another 10–15% attempt a move to the Senate) should also be worried about policy outcomes. This concern can be electorally motivated; since elections turn on a combination of candidate qualities and policy, reelection-minded legislators should involve themselves in the policy process.[27]

It is also important to note that, even if legislators are motivated to engage themselves in the policy process, not all enjoy the institutional framework to make their efforts fruitful. Some are hamstrung by

---

[26] Parts of this section were borrowed from Cox and Morgenstern (2001).
[27] See Cox and McCubbins (1993).

constitutions that limit, for example, significant changes to the budget. Others are cut short due to party factionalism or fragmentation (multi-partism) that slows collective action.

Aside from these institutional variables, partisan ideology has a clear effect on whether a legislature will be parochial or policy-oriented. Strong ideological parties should be less venal than a diverse coalition of politicians seeking fame, fortune, and power. Again, Chilean parties are distinctive. On the center-left, the two post-dictatorship Chilean presidents have enjoyed the support of a coalition banded together for its strong opposition to Pinochet. The Chilean right, alternatively, is strongly associated with Pinochet and his regime. One of the two main rightist parties, the UDI, is intensely ideological; many of its legislators were mayors during the Pinochet regime and many were personally trained by a charismatic and rabidly anti-communist recent martyr (Jaime Guzmán). UDI party members are unlikely to bend on crucial policy issues for an extra bridge in their district. In contrast, presidents in Argentina and Brazil are neither supported nor opposed by such ideologically driven and organized parties. In neither of these countries has any single party or group of parties won the anti-authoritarian banner, and the PT in Brazil, which currently has only 11% of the legislative seats, is the only significant class-based party.[28] The Peronists in Argentina had an ideological root based on their populist history, but Menem has effectively destroyed that party's legacy.

This discussion suggests that these factors orient the legislatures into several general categories. Leaving aside the proactive U.S.-style legislature, the two extremes of our reactive cases are marked by the *subservient* legislature, which bows to presidential dictates, and the *recalcitrant* legislature that blocks most presidential advances. In the middle are legislatures that are generally *workable*, frequently assenting to presidential bills but generally requiring compromises or payoffs in exchange for the assent.

The pre-1997 Mexican legislature fit pretty squarely into the subservient category. There the presidents faced legislatures filled with progressively ambitious politicians, a large majority of whom were highly disciplined and loyal to the president. Other cases do not fit as neatly into a single category, but the tendencies are clear. The post-Pinochet Chilean presidents have faced reelection-driven legislators with greater freedom

---

[28] There are several other small leftist parties, none of which approaches 10% of the legislature.

from the executive and stronger ties to their constituents. This independence is tempered, however, since the majority of these legislators have been in coalition with the president. At the same time, the Chilean legislature faces two important limitations: The majority coalition is composed of several competing parties, and it is constitutionally restrained in important ways. In sum, while some factors push the legislature toward proactivity, a number rein it in, thus yielding a generally reactive but *workable* legislature.

The Argentine and Brazilian legislatures also lie on this continuum. The Argentine Congress has been somewhat closer to the Mexican model, as the presidents have commanded progressively ambitious politicians and highly disciplined parties. But, Alfonsin, Menem, and now De la Rúa have not always enjoyed majority control in both Houses. The Argentine legislature has therefore not been subservient, but neither has it been as active as the Chilean legislature.

Finally, the Brazilian legislature is perhaps the most difficult to categorize, due to the heterogeneity of its membership. Many members do have static ambitions, but many are closely tied to state politicians and seek future jobs in state governments. The legislature is quite fractious, but some presidents have built working majorities. Others, however, have not been able to cobble together support. Further, the electoral system has helped to generate factious parties, which has favored pork payoffs to individual legislators over policy compromises among unified parties. This legislature, thus, has ranged between the *recalcitrant* and a relatively *venal* variety of a *workable* type.

By themselves these categories provide a summary of legislative politics in Latin America. They also imply something about politics more generally, as their titles insinuate interactions with the executive. This interaction is the subject of the succeeding epilogue.

Conclusion

In light of warnings about the dangers of presidentialism (Linz 1990), concerns with the strength of presidents vis-à-vis the legislature (Shugart and Carey 1992), and premonitions about the quality of delegated democracy (O'Donnell 1994), the role of the legislatures in consolidating democracy across Latin America has come under greater scrutiny.

In this book we have attempted to take a first step toward building an understanding of these institutions by addressing three empirical themes:

executive–legislative relations, the legislative structure, and the policy-making process. These have been perennial themes in the American literature, and we thus sought to apply the theoretical framework developed for studies of the U.S. Congress to our four cases. Further, we argued that the American model was appropriate, since Argentina, Brazil, Chile, and even Mexico are consolidating, if not fully consolidated, democracies, and all employ presidential rather than parliamentary forms of government. But, we found that even the assumption about legislators' desire for reelection, which drives much of the literature on the U.S. Congress, is inapplicable generally. We thus converted this – along with assumptions implicit in the U.S. model about the electoral system, the party system, and the Constitution – into independent variables. This process of defining a set of independent variables that can capture a diverse group of cases is an important step toward defining a general comparative model of legislative politics. As we have shown, this framework is useful in building theoretical explanations of why these legislatures look and function as they do.

In their explanations, the chapters have shown that the legislatures insert themselves into the policy process in a variety of ways. But, as a result of different legislator goals, constitutional power endowments, party arrangements, and other factors, the legislatures' structure and function are quite different from the proactive U.S. Congress. Even within this generally "reactive" category, the Latin American legislatures also differ amongst themselves, filling a typology that ranges from subservient to recalcitrant. In our epilogue, Gary W. Cox and I apply this typology to a discussion of the interaction of presidents with the different legislative types. We argue that presidents are keenly aware of the majority's construction, unity, and loyalty and condition their political strategies to the expected reaction of the legislature. This political dynamic rounds out our study of legislative politics.

Appendix

Table 14A.1. *Legislators' self-placement on 10-point left–right scale.*

	Mean	Abs Diff from country mean	Standard deviation	Number of legislators in sample
Argentina				
PJ	4.62	0.02	1.36	22
UCR	4.50	0.10	1.46	17
Frepaso	3.45	1.15	1.91	10
UCEDE	7.67	3.07	2.08	3
Avg/total[a]	4.60		1.70	62
Brazil				
PMDB	4.63	0.43	1.36	15
PFL	5.09	0.89	1.30	12
PSDB	4.22	0.02	1.39	9
PT	1.88	2.32	.64	8
PPB	5.80	1.6	1.64	6
PTB	6.33	2.13	1.52	3
Avg/total	4.20		1.31	66
Chile				
Concertación	3.96	1.04	1.11	55
PDC	4.52	0.48	0.93	31
PPD	3.60	1.4	0.70	11
PS	2.92	2.08	0.95	13
Right Total	6.48	1.48	1.46	35
RN	6.70	1.7	1.11	23
UDI[b]	6.45	1.45	1.86	12
Avg/total	5.00		1.16	
Mexico				
PRI	4.87	0.11	1.53	63
PAN	6.15	1.17	1.62	34
PRD	3.70	1.28	1.45	23
Avg/total	4.98	0.85	1.53	121
Overall		1.06	1.26	

Source: *1997 Survey of Parliamentary Elites of Latin America*, directed by Manuel Alcántara and financed by Spain's Comisión Interministerial de Ciencia y Tecnología.

[a] Average and totals include other parties as well; SD is average of listed parties.

[b] Excludes one respondent due to a probable coding error in the survey.

15

Epilogue: Latin America's Reactive Assemblies and Proactive Presidents*

GARY W. COX AND
SCOTT MORGENSTERN

The chapters in this book have shown that, although the Latin American legislatures are only reactive, they are not dysfunctional. Since they are reactive bodies, it is important to consider the force to which they are reacting, namely, the president. It is clear that at times this opposing force has dominated Latin American politics, but frequently the presidents do make policy concessions as a part of their overall strategy for getting their way. Even if one continues to view the president as the central actor in the civilian–political universe, his anticipation of a (possible) legislative veto should in theory condition most of his actions. The optimal strategy for even the most autocratically minded president is not to pretend that the legislature does not exist and propose whatever policies he likes, then react spasmodically when the legislature refuses its assent. Rather, the "cheapest" strategy will often be to cobble together as many legislative votes as possible purely on the merits, conserving other assets (such as pork and patronage) for securing any necessary marginal votes.

Our goal is to theorize within a rational choice framework about how Latin American legislatures operate when they are in the policy-bargaining mode, as opposed to the supine, venal, or horrified-onlooker modes. Our discussion revolves around three themes. First, the venerable "rule of anticipated reactions" makes even primarily reactive institutions, such as Latin American legislatures, relevant. Second, to the extent that Latin American presidents are continually anticipating legislative reactions, their strategies will vary depending on the type of legislature that they face. Third, the ordinary (noncrisis) policy-making process in Latin America is a distinctive form of a bilateral veto game, which in many ways

* A modified version of this chapter appeared in *Comparative Politics* (2001).

exhibits features intermediate between those characteristics of U.S. presidentialism and European parliamentarism. In developing these themes, we draw on the cases discussed throughout this book: Argentina, Brazil, Chile, and Mexico.

Anticipated Reactions and the Influence of Latin American Legislatures

Carl Friedrich's "law of anticipated reactions" expresses the simple idea that if X's actions will be subject to review by Y, with Y capable of rewarding good actions and/or punishing bad ones, then X will likely anticipate and consider what it is that Y wants (Friedrich 1963). In the end, X may not accommodate Y's desires. That depends on how large Y's potential rewards and punishments are relative to other considerations in X's decision. But Y will at least be considered.

A straightforward application of this idea suggests that an important role in the legislative process does not always require "proactive powers" – the ability to initiate legislation and set the agenda. It should also stem from the ability to shape or kill executive proposals. These "reactive powers," which seem to characterize the Latin American cases, invite anticipation by the president (Mainwaring and Shugart 1997).[1] If he finds it costly to dispense enough pork to buy every vote, or enough patronage to buy every legislator, or enough money to buy the election; and if it is also costly to rule by decree; then even authoritarian presidents should consider cutting a deal with the assembly.

We believe that there is evidence that Latin America's assemblies influence the policy process substantially – because the president sometimes attempts to rule through the legislature, rather than around it. This point is clearest in Chile, and it will be developed at greater length when we consider our following third theme. For now, it will suffice to note some examples from two countries where presidential anticipation and accommodation of legislative preferences might seem unlikely: Brazil and Mexico.

Brazil has gained fame for its decree-wielding presidents. Ames, however, makes clear that the legislature is instrumental in shaping the

[1] Mainwaring and Shugart (1997) discuss proactive and reactive presidencies. They focus on presidential types, but they also discuss legislative support for the president and the likely relationship between the two branches.

president's agenda. His extensive survey finds that almost no major proposal goes through Congress unchanged, and that many are rejected.

As regards Mexico, it is clear that the legislature made virtually no
attempt prior to 1997 to legislate on its own, and it was not much
more active in terms of modifying, much less rejecting, presidential
proposals. The formal powers of the legislature did not change, but its
political status changed considerably. As a consequence, the post-1997 legislature has rearranged its leadership structure (see the chapter by Nacif)
and it has had an important hand in shaping the banking insurance
law (FOBAPROA), the relationship with the Zapatista rebels, and even
the president's "secret" discretionary budget. Perhaps most strikingly, in
the budget adopted in December of 1997, legislative pressure led to a
rough doubling of the funds earmarked for transfer to state and local
governments.

Reactive Legislatures and Proactive Presidents: Latin American Variations on the Theme

In the remainder of this chapter we will focus on the broad category of
reactive legislatures and the subcategories defined in the previous chapter.
Our starting point is simply to note that assemblies and presidents in
Latin America are engaged in one or another of a distinctive subfamily
of bilateral veto games. In games of this subfamily the policy process is
asymmetric, in that (for the most part) only the president proposes. The
sequence of moves in the statutory process is typically as follows:

(1) The president proposes one or more new policies (bills).
(2) The legislature either accepts, amends, or rejects the president's
    proposals.
(3) If the legislature amends or rejects (some of) his proposals, the
    president can either bargain, take unilateral action, or seek to
    undermine the assembly's ability to veto proposals.

By bargaining we mean that the president makes actual concessions in proposed policies in order to gain legislative acquiescence or "buys" votes with
pork and patronage. By unilateral action we mean that the president emits
decrees, uses the rule-making authority of the bureaucracy, or uses other
unilateral powers to implement as many of his desired policies as possible.
By undermining the assembly's independence we mean that the president

seeks to win the next legislative election (by fair or foul means), control the career paths of assembly members, and so forth.

In the previous chapter Morgenstern discussed the set of variables that determine whether the majority in the legislature will tend toward one of four types: recalcitrant, workable, parochial-venal, or subservient. Although he also argued that legislatures seldom fit tightly into these ideal types, in what follows we shall simplify matters by imagining that the president anticipates one of these four legislative types and pursues a strategy that is optimal in light of such a legislature's likely responses to his initiatives. Recalcitrant majorities (very low percentages of members supporting the president) will reject essentially all of the proposals that the president really wants. Subservient majorities (very high percentages of members thoroughly beholden to the president) will accept essentially any proposal that the president makes. Between these extremes of support, the president can face two types of more manageable majorities, one that demands a seat at the policy table (workable) and the other that is willing to concede policy issues in exchange for access to pork or other resources (parochial-venal). Depending on which sort of assembly the president anticipates, he or she will undertake different strategies and use different institutional powers to implement those strategies. That is, strategy and tactics will oscillate with legislative type.

The previous chapter concluded that a legislature's type is a function of the Constitution, reelection drives of the legislators, the party system, and other factors. Aside from the Constitution (which is perhaps a less important ingredient), most of the other factors boil into the percentage of the legislature's seats occupied by members supporting the president. This implies that, in addition to the raw number of seats, a president takes account of the level of unity within the majority party or coalition. One additional factor that the president will notice is the percentage of legislators who pursue parochial over national interests (who see their careers as continuing at a local level and their duties as primarily the protection of local prerogatives). We view these variables as exogenous or pre-determined factors that the president cannot change in the short term but which materially affect the legislature's likely response to presidential initiatives. We do not wish to say that once a legislature is elected and these two percentages are fixed that the legislature never varies its strategy. But here we will take the legislature's type as a good enough clue to its likely strategy for presidents to act as "Stackleberg leaders" –

initiating legislation with a clear notion of, and in light of, the legislature's likely response.[2]

The Central Oscillation

In this section we explore the president's changing use of his constitutional and other powers, in response to changes in anticipated assembly support: the central oscillation in Latin American politics. Latin American executives typically have greater powers of unilateral action than U.S. presidents. They cannot dissolve the Congress, but they resemble European prime ministers as regards executive penetration of the legislative process within the assembly. They thus occupy an intermediate position between these two ideal types. As Mustapic argues for Argentina, this distinctive combination of institutional strengths, along two separate dimensions, leads to a distinctive "oscillation" in presidential strategy in response to variations in assembly types. In the following we consider first the president's changing use of "unilateral" powers and then the changing use of "integrative" powers.

Changing Use of Unilateral Powers One way in which presidents change their strategies has to do with their unilateral powers. By unilateral powers we mean something close to what Carey and Shugart mean by proactive powers: those powers that can be used (a) without the concurrence of the legislature to (b) change policy (Carey and Shugart 1998). The clearest examples are constitutional decrees, but other sorts of decrees, regulatory rule making, and even vetoes[3] can sometimes feature in pushing through a new policy.

The main point to make about presidential use of unilateral powers is just this: As numerous chapters in this book attest, when the president is politically weaker, he typically resorts more frequently to his unilateral powers; in contrast, when he is politically stronger, he resorts to these powers less often (Amorim Neto 1998; Cox and Kernell 1991; Tiefer 1994).

---

[2] A Stackleberg equilibria is a game-theoretic concept taken from the study of duopolies, in which after the leading firm moves, the other firm reacts in full knowledge of the first firm's move (see Fudenberg and Tirole 1991).

[3] In Argentina, for example, presidents can emit decrees that the Congress can only overturn with statutory proposals, those proposals themselves subject to the usual veto process.

This point can be illustrated by comparing the experiences of presidents in the four countries discussed in this book. In Brazil, politically weak presidents, such as Collor, have pushed the limits of the constitutional powers. Menem had the putative support of the largest single party in the Argentine system, but having reversed the field on several key issues, he could not rely on consistent support (see the chapter by Eaton). As Mustapic shows, Menem too ended up pushing the limits of his constitutionally defined powers, seeking only enough support in the assembly to prevent the override of his decrees. Frei, with a workable majority in Chile's lower House and a large minority in the upper House, avoided controversial use of his substantial unilateral powers (see the chapter by Siavelis) . Finally, as Weldon and Casar explain, during the long-lasting period of PRI dominance, Mexican presidents did not have to rely on unilateral powers because they derived power from "metaconstitutional" sources. President Salinas, for example, presiding over the last years of the one-party regime, could get whatever statutes he wanted – as soon as the ducks were lined up within the PRI – and so did not need executive decrees (which are not even included in the Mexican Constitution), vetoes, or other unilateral tools used by presidents in more competitive systems. Everything could happen off-stage, with the formal procedures a pro forma ratification of decisions made elsewhere.

The logic behind this declining use of formal constitutional powers as the president's legislative support increases can be indicated by considering presidential strategy at three levels of assembly support: weak (the president faces a hostile majority in the assembly), medium (the president has a workable majority), and strong (the president has a large and subservient majority). When the president faces a hostile majority in the assembly, he will often have no chance of implementing his policy goals via statutes. In these cases, his only recourse will be to take such unilateral action as he can manage, perhaps "pushing the envelope" of his powers in constitutionally provocative ways. When the president has a workable majority in the assembly, in contrast, he may be able to get his statutes passed with the aid of urgency provisions, the judicious allocation of cabinet positions to solidify legislative support, and a liberal distribution of pork. Since statutes can override conflicting decrees, are harder to overturn once enacted, and are constitutionally sounder instruments for many purposes, politically stronger presidents will more often prefer trying for statutes than issuing decrees. Finally, some presidents – e.g., those in Taiwan and Mexico until recently – may be able to count on a large and subservient majority in the assembly. These presidents – who typically appear only in authoritarian regimes for any extended length of time – can routinely expect to get just the statutes that they want and hence have no political need to employ vetoes or decrees. They may occasionally find it convenient to use decrees or administrative rule-making powers rather than statutes, but they are not usually constrained in this choice by any lack of support in the assembly. The separation of powers has been over-ridden, so to speak, by the president's political strength (usually based on his ability to control candidate selection and elections to the assembly, the distribution of pork to members of the assembly, and the post-assembly career prospects of sitting legislators).

Changing Use of Integrative Powers   Latin American presidents are not confined to unilateral powers. They also deploy powers, such as urgency decrees or the appointment of ministers, that can help the president to integrate himself into the legislative process of the assembly. As explained further in the following pages, integrative powers allow the president to set the policy agenda not just by sending proposals to Congress, but also by prioritizing bills in the internal procedures of Congress or empower-ing assembly allies. Use of potentially integrative powers for actually integrative purposes responds to variations in presidential support in the assembly in precisely the opposite pattern to that noted previously for unilateral powers: They are used more when the president is politically stronger and less when he is politically weaker. As this dimension of Latin American presidential power has received less attention in the previous literature, we expand on this topic in the following sections.

Evidence that Use of Powers Does Vary with Assembly Support   Evidence that Latin American presidents do vary their strategy in response to their prospects of support in the assembly and their institutional powers can be culled from the wealth of case studies in the Latin American literature. The best currently available systematic evidence is provided by Amorim Neto (1998), in a study of 75 cabinets appointed by 57 Latin American presidents from 10 countries over the period 1946–1995. The logic of Amorim Neto's study is that presidents who have decided to implement their policy goals via statutes will lay the groundwork for this by appoint-ing party leaders who can help to solidify assembly support. In contrast, those who seek to rule by decree can pack their cabinets with cronies and technocrats. Amorim Neto finds, among other things, that the percentage of partisan ministers in a president's cabinet increases: (1) as the percentage of seats held by the president's party in the assembly increases; and (2) as the president's decree powers decline. In other words, presidents with a better political base in the assembly, and with poorer institutional powers to pursue a unilateral strategy, are more likely to seek to govern through, rather than around, the assembly.

A Typology of Presidents and Assemblies In sum, a president's level of support in the assembly will have a large impact on his or her overall policy-making strategy – whether to seek a mostly statutory implementation of goals (governing through the assembly) or to seek a mostly nonstatutory implementation (governing around the assembly). This overarching strategic decision about the optimal mix of statutory and nonstatutory effort in turn influences presidential tactics – which powers to use and how to use them. These tactics are also influenced by the president's institutional powers, and thus, even for presidents in similar circumstances, the tactics could reveal presidents who range from impotent to imperial, as a comparison between Collor and Mitterand might show.

To encapsulate the gist of how presidents' strategies and tactics change with their anticipated level of assembly support, we employ the four adjectives discussed in the previous chapter and above that characterize the Latin American (and North American) legislatures: recalcitrant, workable, venal-parochial, and subservient. The president has a rather clear best response to each of these types, and thus we match the four legislative adjectives with four presidential adjectives. First, if the president believes that the assembly is recalcitrant – i.e., will reject most of his proposals and refuse to compromise – then (assuming he has unilateral powers at his disposal) his best strategy is to seek ways of getting around the assembly veto, by using his unilateral powers: This is the *imperial* president. (If he lacks such powers, he would be impotent.) At the other end of the scale, where the president believes that the assembly is subservient – i.e., will accept most of his proposals without the need of bargaining – then his best strategy is to dictate terms: This is the *dominant* president.

The third and fourth types of presidents face workable majorities and they bargain with legislative actors over the course of policy. The dividing line between these two types is what the presidents offer the legislators in return for their support. The type is therefore a function of how frequently the president uses four key bargaining chips: (1)

particularistic payoffs (pork and patronage); (2) positional payoffs (ministerial portfolios); (3) policy concessions; and (4) agenda-setting.

Where the president finds that his best response to a particular legislature is to buy support with pork and patronage, he is facing a venal or parochial assembly. These legislatures, maybe due to short legislative time horizons (i.e., low reelection rates) or career paths that reflect their pork-winning success, prefer the president to play a *nationally oriented* role, focusing on and taking the heat for national policy (Shugart 1998). Thus, in return for particularistic payoffs, we expect these legislatures to offer (in a manner that is probably closer to abdication than delegation) the president broad authority over policy through grants of decree powers, and to sponsor few important initiatives.

We have termed assemblies that are involved in the policy process – in the sense that (1) the president heads a coalition that includes assembly actors, (2) seeks to implement *coalitional* policies via statutes, and (3) designs the strategy for getting these statutes passed in consultation with his assembly allies – workable. Their foil, the coalitional president, may use some particularistic payoffs to clinch deals, but pork will be used to get the last few votes needed to clinch deals, not as the main bargaining technique. The coalitional president thus makes more extensive use of his other three bargaining chips, all of which involve the assembly more intimately in actual policy decision making. Clearly policy concessions bring the assembly into the policy process, but so do the allocation of ministerial portfolios to party leaders (these positions do not carry with them influence over pork alone) and the setting of the legislative agenda (which the president has influence over but can more effectively control with the help of assembly actors).

The four corresponding pairs of executive–legislative types – imperial-recalcitrant, nationally oriented-parochial, coalitional-workable, and dominant-subservient – are displayed in Table 15.1.[4] Every imperial president has a recalcitrant congress as his antagonist, whose actual or anticipated refusal to support his statutory initiatives drives him to use his unilateral powers. Every dominant president has a subservient congress that meekly acquiesces to most of his policies (typically because the president has previously established political dominance over the congress by control of nominations, elections, or post-assembly career options). And, finally, if the president believes that the assembly is workable – i.e.,

[4] We have excluded the impotent president here.

Table 15.1. *Presidential and assembly strategies.*

		Assembly Strategies		
		Reject	Bargain	Demand payments	Acquiesce
Presidential Strategies	Undertake unilateral action	Imperial president, Recalcitrant assembly			
	Bargain		Coalitional president, workable assembly		
	Pay Off			Nationally-oriented president, venal or parochial assembly	
	Dictate				Dominant president, subservient assembly

can be bargained with – then his best strategy depends on what bargaining mechanisms are most propitious. If he is better off using his integrative powers to work through the statutory process, he is a coalitional president. If, on the other hand, legislators are mostly after pork and the president can "buy" their support for his policies, then we call the president nationally oriented.[5]

---

[5] The preceding account was written to suggest optimal strategies and responses given certain pure types of legislatures and presidents. To specify the equilibria, we would have to take into account such variables as the varying range of unilateral and integrative powers available to the president, presidential preferences for quick action versus interbranch bargaining, how the party system affects the ability and willingness of the legislature to bargain, and the legislature's constitutional endowments of power (Mainwaring and Shugart 1997). Also, legislators do have varying interests across policy issues. For example, while Allende faced a consistently recalcitrant legislature and thus played a single strategy during his whole (shortened) term, other presidents face legislatures that are less consistently recalcitrant and vary their strategies accordingly.

The Amplitude of Oscillation

What distinguishes Latin American presidential systems from the U.S. model is not the existence of an oscillation in presidential strategy and tactics of the sort described previously, but rather its amplitude. Most Latin American presidents have greater powers of unilateral action than their American counterpart, greater ability to "penetrate" the internal legislative process of the assembly, and more variable political support. This combination of more variable legislative support with institutionally stronger presidencies (along two dimensions) has meant that many Latin American presidencies are outside the relatively narrow range of experience in the United States.

In the remainder of this section we discuss in greater detail the three key elements that jointly produce a greater amplitude of oscillation in the modality of presidential action in Latin America. The amplitude of oscillation is certainly greater in Latin America if one includes the cross-national variation – in which case one can range from the dominant presidencies of Mexico to the coalitional presidencies of Uruguay or Chile to the imperial presidencies of Argentina, Brazil, or Peru. We mean to assert also that the amplitude of oscillation is larger within many of these systems. Thus, for example, Allende pushed further in the imperial direction than did Nixon or Reagan, while Aylwin and Frei have pushed further in the coalitional direction than did Wilson.

Outside of Mexico, the oscillation throughout the Western hemisphere is mostly between imperial and coalitional presidencies, and so we shall focus on these types. We begin with the greater variability of presidential support in the assembly, the "engine" that drives variations in presidential strategy. We then consider the two sorts of institutional constraints discussed previously, those having to do with the president's powers to penetrate the internal legislative process of the assembly, and those that affect his or her powers to act unilaterally.

Variability in Presidential Support Some indication that Latin American presidents do experience greater variability in assembly support than their North American counterparts is given in Table 15.2. The table is based mostly on Deheza's attempt to identify the coalitions supporting each president in a number of Latin American countries (Deheza 1997). Although one might have qualms about her numbers in particular

Table 15.2. *Variability of presidential support in the assembly, 1950s–1990s.*

Country	Average support for president (N of periods)	Standard deviation of support for president	Minimum support for president in lower House	Maximum support for president in lower House
Argentina	50.64 (15)	8.56	35.9 (Illia)	71.1 (Frondisi)
Bolivia	49.60 (14)	21.43	22.3 (Siles Z)	85.9 (Paz E.)
Brazil	69.10 (15)	17.40	33.0 (Collor)	92.7 (Quadros)
Chile	42.35 (14)	11.87	15.6 (Frei)	58.7 (Frei)
Colombia	72.33 (15)	16.95	49.2 (Barco)	99.4 (Betancur)
Ecuador	32.10 (16)	16.18	01.4 (Hurtado)	52.0 (Arosmena)
France*	55.5 (8)	10.31	38.0 (Mitterand)	74.0 (Pompidou)
Peru	41.37 (7)	16.71	17.7 (Fujimori)	60.3 (Belaunde)
United States	50.66 (27)	9.92	36.3 (Reagan)	67.8 (Johnson)
Uruguay	56.90 (7)	14.74	41.4 (Sanguinetti)	80.3 (Bordaberri)
Venezuela	53.71 (13)	23.18	12.6 (Caldera)	95.7 (Pérez)

Source: Deheza (1997), Statistical Abstract of the US (1997), and historical statistics.

cases,[6] her work appears to be the best and most systematic available. As can be seen, in six of the nine Latin American countries covered in the table, the maximum assembly support for the president (observed over the period from the 1950s to the 1990s) is greater than the U.S. maximum; in seven of the nine cases, the minimum support is less than the U.S. minimum; and in eight of the nine cases, the standard deviation of presidential support in the assembly is greater than the U.S. figure. Thus, in most Latin American countries, presidential support in the assembly varies more widely than it does in the United States.

In terms of Table 15.1, what this means is that the Latin American cases vary more widely across the columns of the table. Thus, there are more cases of potentially dominant presidents (with particularly subservient legislatures) and more cases of potentially imperial presidents (facing particularly

[6] For example, Betancur's 99% level correctly implies that both primary parties gave some support to the president, but ignores the lack of party discipline and the intense interparty rivalry (Betancur won only 47% of the vote). Similarly, the 41% support of Sanguinetti overestimates his support, as factions in his party frequently withheld support. Her numbers do lend weight to our hypothesis of shifting powers, however, as she breaks presidencies into periods, showing changing levels of support for the same president.

recalcitrant assemblies). Whether these potential cases turn into the real thing depends both on the solidity of the nominal support levels reported by Deheza and on the institutional powers of the presidency in each case.

Executive Integration in the Legislative Process of the Assembly In parliamentary systems, the executive is deeply involved in the internal legislative process of the legislature. Simultaneous occupancy of ministerial and legislative offices is typically allowed. Even when it is not, ministers often appear personally in the legislature, participate in debate, answer questions, and so forth. Ministers also typically have superior abilities to set the legislative agenda of the assembly itself. In the United Kingdom, for example, only ministers can propose tax increases and the cabinet dominates the legislative agenda through such powers as the vote of confidence and the guillotine procedure.

These two factors – executive participation in, and executive agenda power over, the legislative process of the assembly – together indicate what we shall call the degree of executive integration in the legislative process. We shall discuss each in turn, contrasting the United States and the modal Latin American case.

The U.S. president cannot appoint a sitting member of Congress to his cabinet, unless that person chooses to relinquish his or her seat in Congress, because the Constitution (Article I, section 6) forbids the simultaneous occupancy of cabinet and legislative office. Although cabinet ministers in the United States do give testimony in congressional hearings, by custom they do not participate in debates.[7] These restrictions mean that executive personnel are not personally involved in the legislative process within Congress. They also make it difficult for a U.S. president to use cabinet appointments to build legislative support, as is routinely done in parliamentary systems.

In some Latin American cases, simultaneous occupancy of cabinet and legislative offices is not prohibited (e.g., under the Peruvian Constitution

---

[7] Even the one executive officer who has a constitutional mandate to participate in legislative affairs – the vice president (ex officio presiding officer of the senate) – is limited in his ability to participate. By constitutional prescription, the vice president can cast a vote only in the event of a tie and partly for this reason he rarely appears in the Chamber. Even when he does appear, however, the Senate has a long-standing custom that physically confines him to the dais. When Vice President Spiro Agnew unwittingly violated this rule, the Senate expressed its displeasure at this violation of the separation of powers by passing a resolution specifically enforcing this restriction on Agnew's whereabouts.

of 1933). In others, the *suplente* system – whereby an elected member of congress can yield his seat temporarily to a *suplente*, or replacement, but then reassume the seat later – means that a minister can reclaim his legislative seat at any time he or she wishes. In Brazil, ministers will occasionally resign their ministerial positions just before an important vote in the assembly, resume their legislative seats, vote, and then resign their legislative seats and resume their ministerial posts again. When one adds the possibility that *suplentes* may be pliant, Brazilian ministers can effectively be considered members of the assembly. Other cases in which a similar *suplente* system is used include Bolivia, Colombia (Hartlyn 1994, p. 301), El Salvador, Honduras, Paraguay, Uruguay, and Venezuela. Finally, Latin American presidents can sometimes appoint recognized party leaders who are not themselves elected legislators but still bring with them assembly support. In Argentina, for example, there is a quite pronounced pattern of legislative party leaders "graduating" to ministerial positions once their service in the legislature comes to an end. For example, the two Peronist bloc leaders in the lower Chamber became interior minister and vice minister, and clearly were used in the executive branch for their political skills and connections in Congress. Something similar seems to occur in Chile. Latin American presidents, unlike their U.S. counterpart, can thus more often use cabinet appointments as prime ministers do, to build legislative support.

The U.S. president does not have the right to directly introduce legislation in either house of Congress. Even the president's budget must be introduced by a member of Congress. In contrast, most Latin American chief executives have the power to introduce legislation directly, and some (in Brazil, Chile, Colombia prior to 1991, and Uruguay) have exclusive powers of introduction in designated areas. Latin American presidents' powers of initiative are thus closer to those typically wielded by prime ministers.

The U.S. president does not have the right directly to determine the measures that Congress will consider, to accelerate bills pending on congressional calendars, or to otherwise affect the legislative agenda. In contrast, Brazilian, Chilean, Colombian, and Peruvian presidents can send "urgent" bills to Congress that take precedence over every other legislative matter; while in Ecuador, Paraguay and Uruguay presidential urgency powers are even greater – the president's bill automatically becomes law if Congress does not formally reject it within a specified time period. Latin American presidents' powers of agenda-setting pale in comparison to those of the typical prime minister, who disposes of votes of confidence and (sometimes) other effective agenda-setting techniques, but they are nonetheless substantially greater than the U.S. president's.

All told, the separation of powers is much more thorough-going in the United States than it is in Latin America. The president can veto legislation, but he is not of much use in pushing legislation through the internal procedures of Congress. At best, he can "go public" and apply external pressure (Kernell 1986). The U.S. Congress' extraordinary abilities to initiate legislation have long been recognized. What is less well recognized is that the flip side of these abilities is the absence of executive powers to appoint legislators to the cabinet, initiate legislation, and control the congressional agenda.

In contrast, Latin American presidents can reach inside the assembly, appointing its members to his cabinet, directly proposing bills, and accelerating their consideration. Thus, when a president has good prospects of legislative support, cabinets are constructed to maintain that support, initiative powers and urgency provisions are used in concert with coalition partners, and the president relates to the congress more like a prime minister relates to a parliament.

Imperial Prerogatives When the president has little legislative support, however, cabinets are filled with cronies and technocrats, initiative powers and urgency provisions are used on an ad hoc basis, and the president relates to congress more like English monarchs used to relate to their parliaments. In the United States, where Congress regularly takes the legislative initiative, presidents with weak legislative support – i.e., those facing a divided government – make greater use of the veto power and more often attempt to implement policy without congressional authorization (Cameron 2000; Tiefer 1994). A similar syndrome is visible in Latin America, but presidents there start with wider unilateral powers and seem prepared to push the envelope of constitutional action harder.

In addition to reactive powers such as the veto, presidents can also wield proactive or unilateral powers (Carey and Shugart 1998). First, presidents almost always have rule-making or interpretative authority. Second, many constitutions also allow the president wide authority to appoint ministers, judges, and other high officials, though their appointments often need congressional assent. Third, explicit legislative delegations of power to the executive expand many presidents' repertoire of action. In these cases, the legislature will generally set a specific task and timeline for the executive, retaining the right to review or change the president's decisions. Fourth, some presidents are constitutionally endowed with decree powers. These provisions can include the power to suspend civil liberties and other parts of the constitution in time of emergency, in addition to making policy via decree. Finally, there are what Carey and Shugart call "paraconstitutional" decree powers, which can allow the president to change laws by using the pen or sword.

While there are important exceptions (see the chapter by Siavelis), Latin American presidents have generally taken much more advantage of their delegated, constitutional, and paraconstitutional powers than have U.S. presidents. There are certainly cases of presidential unilateralism in the United States, but presidents in Latin America regularly make policy decisions almost unilaterally. Presidents in Bolivia, Brazil, Chile, Colombia, Ecuador, Paraguay, Peru, Uruguay, and Venezuela have tremendous advantages in structuring the national budget, as the legislatures there are constitutionally restricted from making significant changes (Baldez and Carey 1999; Domingo and Morgenstern 1997). Moreover, Latin American legislatures are hindered by a lack of time, resources, and experience. This combination of constitutional and organizational limits has converted many Latin American presidents into virtual budget dictators. If we take into account paraconstitutional powers as well, we find even more presidential impositions. The Mexican president has frequently used his paraconstitutional powers to move funds among budget categories, remove irreverent governors, and impose tremendous policy shifts almost overnight (e.g., nationalization and then re-privatization of the banks). In Argentina, the limited delegation of power to President Alfonsín to deal with their economic crisis was later interpreted by Menem (and the courts) as an almost open-ended and very difficult-to-check power to decree whatever type of law that Menem preferred not to send to the legislature. Similarly, Fujimori and Collor made extremely free use of decree powers.

Coalitional Presidents and Workable Assemblies

Both dominant presidents and imperial presidents are more or less familiar types from the literature. What is more novel about the previous discussion is the characterization of presidents with intermediate levels of political strength in the assembly. Given the appropriate institutional strengths, presidents with supportive but not subservient majorities in the assembly can become what we have called coalitional presidents, integrating themselves into the legislative process of the assembly to a much greater degree than is typical in the United States. The corresponding assembly type, which is brought into some degree of partnership in the policy-making process, we call workable.

The coalitional president and the workable assembly are important and understudied types. We know a lot about Latin American failures – the dominant presidents who have managed to neutralize democratic checks and balances by virtue of their control over elections and the future career prospects of legislators; and the imperial presidents who emerge from the dangerous combination of political weakness and institutional strength. But we know much less about how these systems work when presidents attempt to forge coalitions with assembly actors. While the other modalities may meet a minimal definition of democracy, they call into question the ideals of functioning checks and balances and limited executives. In this section, we consider further some aspects of the more clearly democratic coalitional/workable pairing by comparing the Latin American experience to that in the United States and Europe.

Latin American Systems as Intermediate between Pure Presidentialism and Pure Parliamentarism The intermediate status of executive–legislative relations in Latin America can be seen by first sketching the main features of two polar opposites that we shall call pure parliamentarism and pure presidentialism.

In pure parliamentary systems, the head of government is chosen by, and can be dismissed by, the assembly. The second of these defining characteristics – the possibility of dismissal – leads to two corollary features of the legislative process and party system. First, because the government can be dismissed if it loses a vote of confidence, parties put a high premium on, and are generally successful at securing, unity in their voting behavior on the floor. Second, in order to attain and maintain the high levels of voting discipline required to avoid losing votes of confidence, parties in the majority coalition put a premium on, and are generally successful at securing, control of the legislative agenda in the assembly (Doring 1995).[8]

---

[8] In some parliamentary systems, such as Ireland, France, and the United Kingdom, the government's control over the parliamentary agenda is clearly established in the standing orders. In other cases the government's powers are less clearly delineated, but the govern-

Epilogue

In terms of Cox and McCubbins' (1993) terminology, these two points can be rephrased as saying that legislative parties in parliamentary systems have strong incentives to be unified as "floor voting coalitions" and can help to ensure such unity by also acting as "procedural coalitions" (Cox and McCubbins 1993). The first point has been widely noted in the literature; the second – which stresses that protecting members of the majority coalition from embarrassing votes, scheduling votes at the politically right times, and other abilities conferred by agenda power are important in preventing open disagreements within the majority coalition – has not.

The first defining feature of parliamentarism – the choice of the head of government by the assembly – has a profound impact on the organizational structure of political parties. In particular, parliamentary parties are fully integrated with the executive personnel in the party, whether ministers or shadow ministers. There is nothing like the separation visible in the United States, with one organization for the House of Representatives, one for the Senate, and one for the presidential wing of the party. Parliamentary parties thus unify the executive and assembly, reflecting both the greater confidence that the legislative rank-and-file can have in leaders that they choose (and who are dependent for their continuance in power on the aggregate electoral success of their followers) and the necessity to organize strongly in support of the executive. The natural consequence, in combination with the points made previously, is that ministers are often given substantial control over the legislative agenda of the assembly. Executive, as opposed to purely legislative, actors exert the agenda power.

A very different outcome ensues in a pure presidential system such as the United States. First, the head of government cannot be dismissed by the assembly (outside of impeachment proceedings). Thus, there is less need for voting cohesion on the floor and, hence, less need for strong agenda powers to support that cohesion. Second, the head of government is not chosen by the assembly and does not depend for continuance in office on the electoral success of his supporters in the assembly. Those supporters thus have need of their own leaders, and their own organization. With reference to Schlesinger's (1966) notion of party nuclei – the organizations devoted to securing particular offices – the separate election of the president naturally gives rise to two party-nuclei-in-government, one for the Congress and one for the president, where there had been only

ment nonetheless seems able to use its majority to dominate the agenda. Perhaps the case that least conforms to this generalization is Denmark (Doring 1995).

one in the parliamentary case.[9] Finally, putting these two points together, the natural locus of agenda power in a pure presidential system is within the congress. It will not be the president or his ministers who wield agenda power. Rather, it will be the leaders of the congressional parties – especially the majority – who wield it.[10]

Coalitional Presidents: Latin America and the U.S. Model Latin American polities do not differ much from the pure presidential system in terms of its two defining characteristics. Although the assembly in some Latin American systems (particularly Bolivia) has a substantial say in the selection of the president, in most the involvement is even less than it is in the U.S. case (where the possibility of presidential contests being decided by Congress exists). Similarly, although the theoretical possibility has existed in a few Latin American systems of removing the president other than by impeachment, in practice this has not amounted to much.

The real differences between the U.S. and Latin American styles of presidentialism – at least as regards the level of executive integration with the legislature – are that (1) ministers cannot sit in the assembly in the United States and typically are not appointed with an eye to building assembly support, whereas they can often sit in the assembly (practically speaking) in Latin America and are often appointed with an eye to solidifying assembly support; (2) ministers and the president wield important powers in setting the assembly's internal legislative agenda in Latin America but not in the United States; and (3) the integration of the executive and legislative branches of the parties is often greater in Latin America (e.g., Costa Rica, Uruguay, and Venezuela) than in the United States.[11]

These differences strongly affect the locus of political power, setting the Latin American legislatures in a category separate from the U.S. (ideal-

---

[9] The strength of the incentive to create separate party nuclei would appear to depend on the details of electoral law: Is the presidential election concurrent with the legislative? Is there a fused vote? And so on.

[10] Moreover, the purpose of agenda power will not be to help keep a government, since governments cannot fall on congressional votes. Instead, it will be to help establish a record on which the party can run in the next election (cf. Cox and McCubbins 1993).

[11] Other differences, noted previously, include the strength of the president's "imperial prerogatives."

typical) model. While certainly not irrelevant to the policy process, Latin American legislatures initiate less legislation than does the U.S. Congress, and their amendments are generally less weighty (see the chapters by Siavelis and Casar). Further, though in his chapter Ames shows the recalcitrance of the Brazilian Congress, the success rates for executive initiatives is generally quite high in Latin America (over 90% in Argentina, Chile, and Mexico), as contrasted with a low success rate for bills that start in the legislature. Clinton, on the other hand, won only 36.2 percent of his congressional battles in 1995.[12]

Coalitional Presidents: Latin America and the Eighteenth-Century British Model   Of the three features suggested previously as most clearly distinguishing Latin American from North American presidentialism, the value of ministerial appointments in securing support in the assembly is the most important. This feature, combined with the sometimes great power of the president, reminds one of the eighteenth-century British model of president-parliamentarism (in which the king played the role of president).[13] Although the British were famously fond of praising the balance of their Constitution, it was a balance that both king and Commons often sought to redress to their own advantage.

The king, saddled by past beheadings and constitutional settlements with a powerful and independent assembly, continually sought to control it by two methods entirely familiar to Latin American presidents: influencing legislative elections and "buying" support in the assembly with offers of employment and other favors. Foord reviewed some of the techniques of royal influence as follows:

Government funds were used to subsidize the ministerial press, to provide pensions, to purchase close boroughs, and to carry on such electioneering devices as parades, free beer for electors, and the patronising of local tradesmen. Patronage provided jobs for electors, employment for parliamentary placemen, and positions for the friends, relatives, and dependents of those who could supply the

---

[12] U.S. presidents cannot formally introduce legislation, but *Congressional Quarterly* does track presidential success rates. While success rates above 70% have been common, every president since Nixon, with the exception of Carter, has had success rates in the 50s or lower for one or more years.

[13] Following Shugart and Carey (1992), in president-parliamentary regimes the president has unilateral appointment and dismissal power, but cabinets must also maintain parliamentary confidence.

government with votes in parliament and the constituencies. Honours attracted the "many who cannot be caught by the bait of covetousness [but] are caught by the bait of vanity." ... Many of the most profitable contracts were under the management of the treasury, the headquarters for the distribution of government patronage, and the treasury's practice was to award contracts largely on the basis of political "recommendations." ... Financiers sought seats in Parliament, and when government credit was sound, they eagerly applied for a "slice" of governmental loans. ... [M]ore than eighty members of lords and commons rented royal property [needless to say, on favorable terms]. (Foord 1957, pp. 488, 495, 496)

From the Restoration (1660) through to the early decades of the nineteenth century, the House of Commons was constantly on guard against these royal tactics (Kemp 1957). To circumscribe the crown's ability to influence elections, the Commons sought to regulate the power of dissolution, the conduct of elections, the right of peers and crown officials to vote or interfere in elections, and even the right of the crown to participate in the market for the sale and purchase of rotten boroughs. To circumscribe the crown's ability to "buy" its members, the Commons passed a long parade of "place bills," forbidding those who had accepted crown offices from sitting in the legislature (or requiring them to resign and submit to reelection).

The king was not the only one actively seeking to redress the balance of the Constitution in his favor. Ministers increasingly parlayed their role as conveyors of votes in the Commons, and their obligation to countersign all royal acts, into political dominance. The king fades increasingly from the political scene until, by the nineteenth century, premier-presidentialism had given way to pure parliamentarism.

The inherent tension in eighteenth-century Britain's balanced Constitution between leaders of the assembly (attempting to force their way into the ministry and force the king to take their advice) and the king (attempting to control the assembly directly, so as to obviate the need for appointing assembly leaders as ministers) is similar to tensions observable in many Latin American cases. Consider two examples: Mexico and Peru.

The Mexican president used the same basic strategy as the British king but succeeded where the king failed. As Weldon (this volume) describes, both the electoral incentives of assembly members and their postassembly employment opportunities came increasingly to be dominated by the president until, eventually, an independent assembly ceased to exist.

The Peruvian Constitution of 1933 seems to have attempted to recreate the British polity in the immediate aftermath of the Glorious Revolution. It required that all official acts be countersigned by a minister and that ministers resign if censured by the assembly; at the same time, it explicitly allowed ministers to sit in the assembly. These constitutional stipulations did not, however, lead to any noticeable movement toward parliamentarism in Peru. The reason, suggested by an acute analysis by Needler, seems to be precisely the failure of Peruvian legislative elites to mount effective defenses to Peruvian presidents' pursuit of the same two strategies pursued by the British king and the Mexican president (Needler 1965). A key difference between most of Latin America and Britain is that civilian control of the military has not been established in the former cases but had in the latter case. But the central civilian tension in the systems is similar. Moreover, one does not have to be too Whiggish to argue that the best outcomes for these systems would entail either maintaining the balance between the executive and the legislative powers, or redressing it in favor of the assembly (moving more toward premier-presidentialism).

Conclusion

In this chapter we have argued that Latin America's executive–legislative relations typically take the form of a constitutionally distinctive bilateral veto game in which the president moves first, proposing most of the important legislation, but knows that the assembly will then have a chance to react. We have stressed three points. First, although Latin American assemblies are primarily reactive, this does not mean that they are necessarily impotent or unimportant. Presidents must anticipate what the assemblies that they face will accept and thus legislators have influence through anticipated reactions. It is only when the president has established political mastery over the assembly, as until recently in Mexico, that the assembly ceases to be a significant player. Second, to the extent that Latin American presidents do continually anticipate legislative reactions, their strategies vary depending on the type of legislature that they face. But Latin American executives have a unique combination of institutional powers, with both unilateral abilities (such as some forms of decree) and integrative abilities (such as urgency motions). Depending on the lay of the political land, they can choose either to end-run the assembly or to join it. In either decision, they are able to go much further than an American president would be able, producing a distinctive oscillation in Latin American executive–legislative relations. Third, Latin executives' combination of first-mover status with a distinctive set of institutional powers generates results, in terms of executive–legislative relations, that are often intermediate between those expected in the United States, with its more rigorous separation of powers, and in Europe, with its more complete fusion of powers.

References

Abal Medina (h.), Juan Manuel. 1998. "El Partido Frente Grande, Análisis de una Experiencia Inconclusa." *América Latina Hoy* 20: 101–110.

Abranches, Sérgio H. Hudson de. 1988. "Presidencialismo de Coalizão: O Dilema Institucional Brasileiro." *Dados* 31: 5–38.

Abrucio, Fernando L. 1998. *Os Barões da Federação: O Poder dos Governadores no Brasil Pós-Autoritário [The Barons of the Federation: The Power of the Governors in Post-Authoritarian Brazil].* São Paulo: Universidade de São Paulo/Editora Hucitec.

Acuña, Carlos H. and Catalina Smulovitz. 1995. "Militares en la Transición Argentina: Del Gobierno a la Subordinación Constitucional." In Carlos H. Acuña, ed., *La Nueva Matriz Política Argentina.* Buenos Aires: Nueva Visión.

Agor, Weston. 1971. *The Chilean Senate.* Austin: University of Texas Press.

1970. "The Senate in the Chilean Political System." In Allan Kornberg and Lloyd D. Musolf, *Legislatures in Developmental Perspective.* Durham, NC: Duke University Press.

Aldrich, John H. 1995. *Why Parties? The Origin and Transformation of Political Parties in America.* Chicago: University of Chicago Press.

Alonso, Guillermo V. 1998. "Democracia y reformas: las tensiones entre decretismo y deliberación. El Caso de la Reforma Previsional Argentina." *Desarrollo Económico* 38: 150 (July–September).

Altman Olin, David. 1998. "The Politics of Coalition Formation and Survival in Multiparty Presidential Democracies: The Case of Uruguay (1982–1997)." Paper presented at the annual meeting of the American Political Science Association, Boston.

Alvarado Mendoza, Arturo. 1990. "La Fundación del PNR." In Instituto de Estudios Políticos, Económicos y Sociales, ed., *El Partido en el Poder* (pp. 15–85). Mexico City: El Día/PRI-IEPES.

Ames, Barry. 1987. *Political Survival in Latin America.* Berkeley: University of California Press.

1994. "The Reverse Coattails Effect: Local Party Organization in the 1989 Brazilian Presidential Election." *American Political Science Review* 88, 1 (March): 95–111.

1995a. "Electoral Strategy Under Open-List Proportional Representation." *American Journal of Political Science* 39, 2: 406–433.

1995b. "Electoral Rules, Constituency Pressures, and Pork Barrel: Bases of Voting in the Brazilian Congress." *Journal of Politics* 57, 2: 324–343.

1997. *The Crisis of Governance in Brazil.* Manuscript.

2000. *The Deadlock of Democracy in Brazil.* Ann Arbor: University of Michigan Press.

Ames, Barry and Timothy Power. 1990. "Research Guide to Roll-Call Voting in Brazil's Constituent Assembly, 1987–88." Unpublished manuscript.

Amorim Neto, Octavio. 1994. "Formação de Gabinetes Ministeriais no Brasil: Coalizão versus Cooptação." *Nova Economia* 4: 9–34.

1995. "Party Politics and Cabinet Formation in Brazil." Paper presented at the 19th meeting of the Latin American Studies Association, Washington, DC.

1998. "Of Presidents, Parties, and Ministers: Cabinet Formation and Legislative Decision-Making Under Separation of Powers." Unpublished Ph.D. dissertation, University of California at San Diego.

Amorim-Neto, Octavio and Gary W. Cox. 1997. "Electoral Institutions, Cleavage Structures, and the Number of Parties." *American Journal of Political Science* 41: 149–174.

Amorim-Neto, Octavio and Fabiano Santos. 2001. "The Executive Connection: Presidentially-Defined Factions and Party Discipline in Brazil." *Party Politics* 7, 2: 213–234.

Anderson, Lee, M. Watts, and A. Wilcox. 1966. *Legislative Roll-Call Analysis.* Evanston, IL: Northwestern University Press.

Argento, Analía and Ana Gerschenson. 1999. *Quién es Quién en la Política Argentina.* Buenos Aires: Libros Perfil.

Arriagada, Genaro. 1984. "El Sistema Político Chileno (Una exploración del futuro)." *Colección Estudios CIEPLAN* 15: 171–202.

1992. "Después de los Presidencialismos . . . ¿Qué?" In Oscar Godoy, ed., *Cambio de Régimen Político.* Santiago: Ediciones Universidad Católica de Chile.

Azpiazu, Daniel and Eduardo Basualdo. 1990. *Cara y Contracara de los Grupos Económicos.* Buenos Aires: Cantaro Editores.

Baldez, Lisa and John Carey. 1996. "The Chilean Budget Process." Unpublished manuscript. Presented at the World Bank Conference on policy making in Latin America, University of California, San Diego, May 1996.

1999. "Presidential Agenda Control and Spending Policy: Lessons from General Pinochet's Constitution." *American Journal of Political Science* 43, 1: 29–55.

Barquín, Manuel, *La Reforma Electoral De 1986–1987 en México: Retrospectiva y Análisis,* Cuadernos de CAPEL no. 22. Costa Rica: CAPEL, 1987.

Barrera, Aglas Watson. 1994. "Aspectos Federativos das Relações Fiscais Intergovernamentais: Brasil 1988–92." In FUNDAP/IESP Project, *Balanço e Perspectivas do Federalismo no Brasil.* São Paulo: FUNDAP/IESP.

Barros e Silva, Fernando. 1995. "Pesquisa Revela que Há Fidelidade nos Partidos." *Folha de São Paulo,* July 17, pp. 1–8.

References

Becerra, Ricardo, Jesus Galindo, Manuel Palma, and José Woldenberg, 1996. *Así se Vota en la República*. México: Instituto de Estudios para la Transición Democrática, A.C.

Béjar, Luisa, 1995. *El Papel de la Legislatura en el Sistema Político Mexicano (1964–1978)*. Ph.D. dissertation, UNAM.

Beloch, Israel and Alzira Alves de Abreu. 1984. *Dicionário Histórico-Biográfico Brasileiro*, 4 vols. Rio de Janeiro: Forense Universitária.

Beltrán, Ulises. 1997. "Encuesta Nacional Sobre el Votante Mexicano; Primeros Resultados". *Política y Gobierno* 2: 407–470.

Benjamin, Thomas and Mark Wasserman. 1990. *Provinces of the Revolution: Essays on Regional Mexican History, 1910–1929*. Albuquerque: University of New Mexico Press.

Bernardes, Franco César. 1996. "Democracia Concentrada: Estrutura do Processo Decisório da Câmara dos Deputados." Unpublished Master's thesis, IUPERJ.

Bernardo, Paulo. 1997. World Wide Web page (http://www.sercomtel.com.br/bernardo).

Biblioteca del Congreso Nacional. *Sesiones del Senado*, April 7, 1993. Legislatura Extraordinaria 325, Sesion 40.

Bidart Campos, Germán. 1993. "El Federalismo Argentino desde 1930." In Marcello Carmagnani, ed., *Federalismos Latinoamericanos*. Mexico City: Fondo de Cultura Económica.

Birnbaum, Jeffrey H. and Alan S. Murray. 1987. *Showdown at Gucci Gulch: Lawmakers, Lobbyists, and the Unlikely Triumph of Tax Reform*. New York: Random House.

Blondel, Jean, et al. 1970. "Legislative Behaviour: Some Steps Towards a Cross-National Measurement." In *Government and Opposition*, Vol. 5. Reproduced in Philip Norton, ed. 1990. *Legislatures*. Oxford: Oxford University Press.

Bond, Jon R. and Richard Fleisher. 1990. *The President in the Legislative Arena*. Chicago: The University of Chicago Press.

Bowler, Shaun, David M. Farrell, and Richard S. Katz, eds. 1999. *Party Discipline and Parliamentary Government*. Columbus: Ohio State University Press.

Brady, David W. 1973. *Congressional Voting in a Partisan Era*. Lawrence: University of Kansas Press.

Brasil, Congresso Nacional. 1997. Comissão Mista de Planos, Orçamentos Públicos e Fiscalização. "Proposta Orçamentária da União para 1997: Reuniões Regionais." Brasília: Congresso Nacional.

Brasil, Senado Federal. 1991–1997. Secretaria-Geral da Mesa. "Commissão Mista de Planos, Orçamentos Públicos e Fiscalização." (Committee membership rolls) Brasília: SF/SGM.

1996. *Constituição da República Federativa do Brasil, 1988*. Brasília: Centro Gráfico do Senado Federal.

1997. "Emendas às Leis Orçamentárias Anuais, 1992–97" (Computer database). Brasília: PRODASEN.

Bravo-Lira, Bernardino. 1985. *De Portales a Pinochet*. Santiago: Editorial Jurídica de Chile.

Browne, Eric C. and Mark N. Franklin. 1973. "Aspects of Coalition Payoffs in European Parliamentary Democracies." *American Political Science Review* 67: 453–468.

Bruhn, Kathleen. 1993. *Taking on Goliath: The Emergence of a New Cardenista Party and the Struggle for Democracy in Mexico.* Ph.D dissertation, Stanford Univerity.

Budge, Ian and Hans Keman. 1990. *Parties and Democracy: Coalition Formation and Government Functioning in Twenty States.* New York: Oxford University Press.

Burgoa, Ignacio. 1994. *Derecho Constitucional Mexicano*, 9th ed. Mexico City: Porrúa.

Cain, Bruce E., John Ferejohn, and Morris Fiorina. 1987. *The Personal Vote: Constituency Service and Electoral Independence.* Cambridge: Harvard University Press.

Cámara de Diputados. 1994. *Diario de los Debates de la H. Cámara de Diputados.* Mexico City: INEGI/Cámara de Diputados, LVI Legislatura (CD-Rom version).

Cameron, Charles. 2000. *Veto Bargaining: Presidents and the Politics of Negative Power.* Cambridge: Cambridge University Press.

Camp, Roderic A. 1992. *Biografías de Políticos Mexicanos, 1935–1985.* México: Fondo de Cultura Económica.

1983. *Mexico's Leaders, Their Education & Recruitment.* México: Fondo de Cultura Económica.

Campos Harriet, Fernando. 1969. *Historia Constitucional de Chile.* Santiago: Editorial Jurídica de Chile.

Campos, Emma. 1996. "Los Legisladores del PRI de 1934 a 1977: La Perversidad de la No-Reelección." Paper presented at the conference, "La No Reelección Consecutiva en el Congreso: Sus Efectos en el Sistema Político Mexicano," Mexico, March 11–12.

Canales, René. 1998. Interview with Scott Morgenstern (August 6). Executive Secretary of the PPD, 1998. Santiago, Chile.

Cantón, Darío. 1966. *El Parlamento Argentino en Épocas de Cambio: 1890, 1916 y 1946.* Buenos Aires: Editorial del Instituto.

Cárdenas, Jaime, ed. 1997. *La Actualidad Constitucional en América Latina.* México: Editorial ProLiber.

Carey, John M. 1994. "Los Efectos del Ciclo Electoral sobre el Sistema de Partidos y el Respaldo Parlamentario al Ejecutivo." *Estudios Públicos* 55: 305–314.

1996. *Term Limits and Legislative Representation.* New York: Cambridge University Press.

1997. "The Impact of Constitutional Choices on the Performance of Presidential Regimes." Presented at the Conference on Constitutional Reform, Academia Sinica, May, Taipei, Republic of China.

2000. "Party and Coalition Unity in Legislative Voting." Working paper no. 376, Department of Political Science, Washington University at Saint Louis.

References

Carey, John M. and Matthew S. Shugart. 1995. "Incentives to Cultivate a Personal Vote: A Rank Ordering of Electoral Formulas." *Electoral Studies* 14, 4: 417–439.

1998. "Calling out the Tanks or Filling out the Forms." In John M. Carey and Matthew S. Shugart, eds., *Executive Decree Authority*. Cambridge: Cambridge University Press.

eds. 1998. *Executive Decree Authority*. Cambridge: Cambridge University Press.

Carey, John M., Octavio Amorim-Neto, and Mathew S. Shugart. 1997. "Outlines of Constitutional Powers in Latin America." In Scott Mainwaring and Matthew S. Shugart, eds., *Presidentialism and Democracy in Latin America*. Cambridge: Cambridge University Press.

Carpizo, Jorge. 1978. *El Presidencialismo Mexicano*. México: Siglo XXI.

Carpizo, Jorge and Jorge Madrazo, eds. 1984. *Memoria del III Congreso Nacional de Derecho Constitucional (1983)*. México: UNAM.

Casar, Ma. Amparo. 1998. "Los Sistemas de Comisiones en los Reglamentos Parlamentarios de América Latina. Un Estudio Comparado." Working paper no. 83, Department of Political Science, CIDE.

1997. "The Sources of Presidential Authority in Post-Revolutionary Mexico." Ph.D. dissertation, King's College, University of Cambridge.

Casar, María Amparo. 1999. "Las Relaciones Entre el Poder Ejecutivo y el Legislativo: El Caso de México." *Política y Gobierno* 1: 83–128.

Castro Martínez, Pedro. 1992. *Adolfo de la Huerta y la Revolución Mexicana*. Mexico City: Instituto Nacional de Estudios Históricos de la Revolución Mexicana.

Castro Santos, Maria Helena de. 1997. "Governabilidade, Governança e Democracia: Criação de Capacidade Governativa e Relações Executivo-Legislativo no Brasil Pós-Constituinte." *Dados* 41, 3: 335–376.

Cea Egaña, José Luis. 1992. "Presidencialismo Reforzado. Críticas y Alternativas Para el Caso Chileno." In Oscar Godoy, ed., *Cambio de régimen político*. Santiago: Ediciones Universidad Católica de Chile.

Centeno, Miguel Angel. 1994. *Democracy Within Reason. Technocratc Revolution in Mexico*. College Park: Penn State University Press.

Cetrángulo, Oscar and Juan P. Jiménez. 1996. *El Conflicto en Torno a las Relaciones Financieras entre la Nación y las Provincias. Segunda Parte: Desde la Ley 23.548 hasta la Actualidad*. Centro de Estudios para el Cambio Estructural, Serie de Estudios, no. 10 (February).

Cheresky, Isidoro. 1994. "La Innovación Política: Reflexiones a Partir de los Resultados Electorales del 10 de Abril de 1994 en Argentina." Working paper no. 1, Facultad de Ciencias Sociales, Instituto de Investigaciónes.

Clarín. Various issues.

Close, David, ed. 1995. *Legislatures and the New Democracies in Latin America*. Boulder, CO: Lynne Reinner.

Collie, Melissa P. 1984. "Voting Behavior in Legislatures." *Legislative Studies Quarterly* 9: 3–50.

Colosio, Luis Donaldo. 1994. "Intervention at the LXV Anniversary of the PRI," March 6.

Congreso Nacional de Chile. 1994. *Proceso Legislativo Chileno: Un Enfoque Cuantitativo*. Valparaíso: Congreso Nacional de Chile.

Constitución Política de los Estados Unidos Mexicanos, México: Colección Popular de la Ciudad de México, IIJ-UNAM y Procuraduría General de Justicia del Distrito Federal, 1997.

Cooper, Joseph, David W. Brady and Patricia A. Hurley. 1977. "The Electoral Basis of Party Voting: Patterns and Trends in the U.S. House of Representatives." In Louis Misel and Joseph Cooper, eds., *The Impact of the Electoral Process*. Beverly Hills, CA: Sage.

Coppedge, Michael. 1992. "(De)institutionalization of Latin American Party Systems." Paper presented at the annual meeting of the American Political Science Association.

1994a. "Venezuela: Democratic Despite Presidentialism." In Juan J. Linz and Arturo Valenzuela, eds., *The Failure of Presidential Democracy: The Case of Latin America*, Vol. 2. Baltimore: The Johns Hopkins University Press.

1994b. *Strong Parties and Lame Ducks: Presidential Partyarchy and Factionalism in Venezuela*. Stanford: Stanford University Press.

1997. "A Classification of Latin American Political Parties." Working paper no. 244, Kellogg Institute.

1998. "The Dynamic Diversity of Latin American Party Systems." *Party Politics* 4: 547–568.

Córdova, Arnaldo. 1995. *La Revolución en Crisis: la Aventura del Maximato*. Mexico City: Cal y Arena.

Corrales, Javier. 1997. "Domingo Cavallo as Technopol." In Jorge I. Dominguez, ed., *Technopols: Freeing Politics and Markets in Latin America*. College Park: Penn State University Press.

Cosío Villegas, Daniel. 1973. *El Sistema Político Mexicano*. Mexico City: Joaquín Mortiz.

Costa, Rossana. 1996. Interview (January). Economist for the Institute for Development and Liberty (Instituto Desarrollo y Libertad). Santiago, Chile.

Cox, Gary W. 1990. "Centripetal and Centrifugal Incentives in Electoral Systems," *American Journal of Political Science* 34, 4: 903–935.

1997. *Making Vote Count: Strategic Coordination in the World's Electoral Systems*. New York: Cambridge University Press.

Cox, Gary W. and Samuel Kernell. 1991. "Conclusion." In Gary W. Cox and Samuel Kernell, eds., *The Politics of Divided Government*. Boulder, CO: Westview Press.

Cox, Gary W. and Mathew D. McCubbins. 1993. *Legislative Leviathan: Party Government in the House*. Berkeley: University of California Press.

1999. "Agenda Power in the U.S. House of Representatives, 1877 to 1986." Revised version of a paper presented at the Conference on the History of Congress, January 15–16, Stanford, CA.

Cox, Gary W. and Frances Rosenbluth. 1994. "Reducing Nomination Errors: Factional Competition and Party Strategy in Japan." *Electoral Studies* 13, 1: 4–16.

1996. "Factional competition for the Party Endorsement: The Case of Japan's Liberal Democratic Party." *British Journal of Political Science* 26: 259–297.

References

CPDOC. N.d. *Ministros de Estado da República*. Rio de Janeiro: Fundação Getúlio Vargas.

Crespo, José Antonio. 1996. *Votar en los Estados. Análisis Comparado de las Legislaciones Electorales en México*. México: Porrúa.

Crisp, Brian. 1997. "Presidential Behavior in a System with Strong Parties: Venezuela, 1958–1995." In Scott Mainwaring and Matthew Soberg Shugart, eds., *Presidentialism and Democracy in Latin America*. Cambridge: Cambridge University Press.

——— 1998. "Presidential Decree Authority in Venezuela." In John M. Carey and Matthew S. Shugart, eds., *Executive Decree Authority*. Cambridge: Cambridge University Press.

Crónica del Gobierno de Carlos Salinas de Gortari.

Cuadernos de Apoyo, SIID, Comisión de Biblioteca e Informática, México: Cámara de Diputados, junio 1994 y julio 1997.

Cuello, Raúl. 1996. *Cinco Años de Convertibilidad*. Unpublished manuscript.

De la Garza, Rudolph. 1972. "The Mexican Chamber of Deputies." Ph.D dissertation, University of Arizona.

De Luca, Miguel, Mark P. Jones, and María Inés Tula. 2000. "Argentine Political Parties and Their Candidate Nomination Procedures: 1983–1999." Paper presented at the XXII International Congress of the Latin American Studies Association, March 16–18, Miami, FL.

De Riz, Liliana and Eduardo Feldman. 1989. *Guía del Parlamento Argentino. Poder Legislativo: Conformación, Naturaleza y Funciones*. Buenos Aires: Fundación Friedrich Ebert.

Deheza, Grace Ivana. 1997. "Gobiernos de Coalición en el Sistema Presidencial: America del Sur." Unpublished Ph.D. dissertation, European University Institute, Florence.

——— 1998. "Gobiernos de Coalición en el Sistema Presidencial: Américal del Sur." In Dieter Nohlen and Mario Fernández B., eds., *El Presidencialismo Renovado: Instituciones y Cambio Político en América Latina*. Caracas: Nueva Sociedad.

Denzau, Authur T., William Riker, and Kenneth Shepsle. 1985. "Farquharson and Fenne: Sophisticated Voting and Home Style." *American Political Science Review*, 79: 1117–1133.

Desposato, Scott. 1997. "Party Switching in Brazil." Paper presented at the annual meeting of the American Political Science Association.

Dias, José Luciano de Mattos. 1997. "Federalismo, Governos Estaduais e Políticas Públicas: Uma Análise das Instituições Federais no Brasil." Unpublished Ph.D. dissertation, Instituto Universitário de Pesquisas do Rio de Janeiro (IUPERJ), Rio de Janeiro.

Diniz, Eli. 1995. "Governabilidade, Democracia e Reforma do Estado: Os Desafios da Construção de uma Nova Ordem no Brasil nos Anos 90." *Dados* 38, 3: 385–416.

Dix, Robert H. 1994. "Incumbency and Electoral Turnover in Latin America." In Jorge I. Dominguez, ed., *Parties, Elections, and Political Participation in Latin America*. New York: Garland Publishing.

Documentos Básicos, PRI, Comité Nacional Ejecutivo, 1996.

475

Domingo, Pilar and Scott Morgenstern. 1997. "The Success Of Presidentialism? Breaking Gridlock In Presidential Regimes." Working paper no. 73, CIDE.

Döring, Herbert, ed. 1995. *Parliaments and Majority Rule in Western Europe*. Frankfurt: St. Martin's Press.

Dow, Jay K. 1998. "A Spatial Analysis of Candidate Competition in Dual Member Districts: The 1989 Chilean Senatorial Elections." *Public Choice* 97: 451–474.

Downs, Anthony. 1957. *An Ecnomic Theory of Democracy*. New York: Harper Collins.

Dromi, Roberto and Eduardo Menem. 1994. *La Constitución Reformada*. Buenos Aires: Ediciones Ciudad Argentina.

Dulles, John W. F. 1961. *Yesterday in Mexico: A Chronicle of the Revolution, 1919–1936*. Austin: University of Texas Press.

Durán, Viviana and Juan C. Gómez Sabaini. 1995. *Lecciones Sobre Reformas Fiscales en Argentina: 1990–1993*. CEPAL/PNUD, Serie Política Fiscal, no. 68.

Duverger, Maurice. 1954. *Political Parties: Their Organization and Activity in the Modern State*. Translated by Barbara North and Robert North. New York: Wiley.

Eaton, Kent. 2001a. "Political Obstacles to Decentralization: Evidence from Argentina and the Philippines." *Development and Change* 32, 1.

2001b. "Decentralization, Democratization and Liberalization: The History of Argentine Revenue Sharing," *Journal of Latin American Studies* 33, 1.

Forthcoming. *Legislating Adjustment: Politicians and Economic Reform in New Democracies*. University Park: Pennsylvania State University Press.

El Mercurio. 1993a. "Resultos Electorales." Santiago, Chile, December 13: C2–C5.

1993b. "Guía Electoral." Santiago, Chile, December 5: special supplement.

Estadísticas de las Elecciones Federales, México: Dirección Ejecutiva de Organización Electoral, Instituto Federal Electoral, 1994 y 1997.

Etchemendy, Sebastián and Vicente Palermo. 1998. "Conflicto y Concertación. Gobierno, Congreso y Organizaciones de Interés en la Reforma Laboral del Primer Gobierno de Menem (1984–1995)." *Desarrollo Económico* 37, 148 (January–March): 559–590.

Fennell, Lee C. 1974. "Reasons for Roll Calls: An Exploratory Analysis with Argentine Data." *American Journal of Political Science* 18: 395–403.

Ferreria Rubio, Delia and Matteo Goretti. 1996. "Cuando el Presidente Gobierna Solo. Menem y los Decretos de Necesidad y Urgencia Hasta la Reforma Constitucional (julio 1989–agosto 1994)." *Desarrollo Económico* 36, 141 (April–June): 443–474.

1998. "When the President Governs Alone: The Decretazo in Argentina, 1989–93." In John M. Carey and Matthew S. Shugart, eds., *Executive Decree Authority*. Cambridge: Cambridge University Press.

Figueiredo, Argelina Cheibub and Fernando Limongi. 1995. "Partidos Políticos na Câmara dos Deputados: 1989–1994." *Dados* 38: 497–524.

Figuereido, Argelina and Fernando Limongi. 1996. "Congreso Nacional: Organização, Processo Legislativo e Produção Legal." Cadernos de Pesquisa 5.

1997a. "O Congresso e as Medidas Provisórias: Abdicação ou Delegação." *Novos Estudos Cebrap* 47: 127–154.

References

1997b. "Presidential Power and Party Behavior in the Legislature." Paper presented at the 1997 Meeting of the Latin American Studies Association (LASA), April 17–19, Guadalajara, Mexico.

Figueiredo, Marcus. 1994. "A Lei de Ferro da Competição Eleitoral: A Aritmética Eleitoral ou Eleições Casadas, Resultados Solteiros." *Cadernos de Conjuntura IUPERJ* 50: 3–14.

Fiorina, Morris P. 1974. *Representatives, Roll Calls, and Constituencies*. Lexington, MA.: Lexington Books.

1989. *Congress: Keystone of the Washington Establishment*. New Haven: Yale University Press.

Folha de São Paulo. July 17, pp. 1–8.

Foord, A. S. 1957. "The Waning of 'The Influence of the Crown'," *English Historical Review* 62: 484–507.

Frei, Eduardo, et al. 1970. *Reforma constitucional 1970*. Santiago: Editorial Jurídica.

Frías, Pedro. 1980. *El Federalismo Argentino*. Buenos Aires: De Palma.

Friedrich, Carl J. 1963. *Man and his Government: An Empirical Theory of Politics*. New York: McGraw Hill.

Fudenberg, Drew and Jean Tirole. 1991. *Game Theory*. Cambridge: MIT Press.

Fuentes, José María. 1993. "La Alternativa Proporcional con Barreras de Entrada." *Estudios Públicos* 51: 269–302.

Garrido, Luis Javier. 1982. *El partido de la Revolución Institucionalizada*. Mexico: Siglo XXI.

1993. *La Ruptura: La Corriente Democrática del PRI*. México: Grijalbo.

Garza de la, Rodolfo. 1972. "The Mexican Chamber of Deputies and the Mexican Political System." Ph.D. dissertation, University of Arizona.

Gerchunoff, Pablo and Juan Carlos Torre. 1996. "La Política de Liberalización Económica en la Administración de Menem." *Desarrollo Económico* 36, 143 (October–December): 733–768.

Gibson, Edward L., Ernesto F. Calvo, and Tulia G. Falleti. 1999. "Federalismo Redistributivo: Sobrerepresentación Territorial y Transferencia de Ingresos en el Hemisferio Occidental." *Política y Gobiero* 6, 1: 15–44.

Gil, Federico. 1966. *The Political System of Chile*. Boston: Houghton Mifflin.

Gilligan, Thomas W. and Keith Krehbiel. 1990. "Organization of Informative Committees by a Rational Legislature." *American Journal of Political Science* 34: 531–564.

Gómez de la Fuente, Pedro and Carolina Pérez Colman. 1995. *Glosario Electoral Argentino*. Buenos Aires: Centro Editor Argentino.

Gómez Tagle, Silvia. 1990. *Las Estadísticas Electorales de la Reforma Política*. Cuadernos del CES del Colegio de México, México: El Colegio de México.

Gónzalez Casanova, Pablo. 1965. *La Democracia en México*. México: Ediciones ERA.

González Compeán, Miguel. 1996. *La Asamblea del PRI: México Bronco, México Manso*. Mimeo.

Goodspeed, Stephen S. 1955. "El Papel del Jefe del Ejecutivo en México." In *Problemas Agrícolas e Industriales en México*, Vol. VII, No.1. Enero–Marzo, México.

Goretti, Mateo and Mónica Panosyan. 1986. "La Eficacia del 'Ausentismo Activo' en las Comisiones Parlamentarias." In Liliana De Riz, Ana M. Mustapic, Mateo Goretti, and Mónica Panosyan, eds., *El Parlamento Hoy*. Buenos Aires: Centro de Estudios de Estado y Sociedad (CEDES).

Greggianin, Eugênio. 1997. "O Poder Legislativo e o Processo Orçamentário." Paper presented at the Conference "O Poder Legislativo e o Processo Orçamentário." Brasília: Câmara dos Deputados, Assessoria de Orçamento e Fiscalização Financeira.

Grofman, Bernard and Arend Lijphart, eds. 1986. *Electoral Laws and Their Political Consequences*. New York: Agathon Press.

Groseclose, T. and J. M. Snyder. 1996. "Buying Supermajorities." *American Political Science Review* 90, 2: 305–315.

Guinier, Lani. 1991. "No Two Seats: The Elusive Quest for Political Equality." *Virginia Law Review* 77, 8: 1413–1514.

Guzmán, Eugenio. 1993. "Reflexiones sobre el sistem binominal." *Estudios Públicos* 51: 303–325.

Hagopian, Frances. 1996. *Traditional Politics and Regime Change in Brazil*. New York: Cambridge University Press.

Hardin, Russell. 1982. *Collective Action*. Baltimore: Johns Hopkins University Press.

1998. *Constitutionalism, Liberalism, and Democracy*. New York: Oxford University Press.

Hartlyn, Jonathan. 1994. "Presidentialism and Colombian Politics." In Juan Linz and Arturo Valenzuela, eds., *The Failure of Presidential Democracy* (pp. 294–327). Baltimore: Johns Hopkins University Press.

Hernández, Rogelio. 1996. "El PRI entre la Competencia Electoral y la Indefinición Presidencial." Paper presented at the workshop, "Stability and Change in the Mexican Party System." November 28–29, London.

Huber, John D. 1996. *Rationalizing Parliament*. Cambridge: Cambridge University Press.

Hughes, Steven W. and Kenneth J. Mijeski. 1973. *Legislative-Executive Policy-Making: The Cases of Chile and Costa Rica*. Beverly Hills, CA: Sage.

INESC. 1993a. Informativo INESC. Volume 8(41).

1993b. Informativo INESC. Volume 7(32).

Jones, Charles O. 1968. "Joseph Cannon and Howard W. Smith: An Essay on the Limits of Leadership in the House of Representatives." *Journal of Politics* 30, 3: 617–646.

Jones, Mark P. 1995. *Electoral Laws and the Survival of Presidential Democracies*. Notre Dame, IN: University of Notre Dame Press.

1997a. "Evaluating Argentina's Presidential Democracy: 1983–1995." In Scott Mainwaring and Matthew Soberg Shugart, eds., *Presidentialism and Democracy in Latin America*. New York: Cambridge University Press.

1997b. "Federalism and the Number of Parties in Argentine Congressional Elections." *Journal of Politics* 59: 538–549.

Jones, Mark P., Sebastian Saiegh, Pablo Spiller, and Mariano Tommasi. 2000. "Professional Politicians – Amateur Legislators: The Argentine Congress in the

References

Twentieth Century." Paper presented at the Annual Conference of the International Society for New Institutional Economics, September 22–24, Tuebingen, Germany.

Jones, Charles O. 1968. "Joseph G. Cannon and Howard W. Smith: The Limits of Leadership in the House of Representatives." *Journal of Politics* 30: 617–646.

José Valenzuela, Georgette. Forthcoming. "Y Venían de una Revolución! De la Oposición Civil a la Oposición Militar (1920–1924)." In María Amparo Casar and Ignacio Marván Laborde, eds., *Episodios Republicanos: Experiencias de Gobierno Dividido en México a partir de 1867*. Mexico: Cide-Oceano.

Katz, Richard. 1973. "The Attribution of Variance in Electoral Returns: An Alternative Measurement Technique." *American Political Science Review* 67, 3: 817–828.

———. 1986. "Intraparty Preference Voting." In Bernard Grofman and Arend Lijphart, eds., *Electoral Laws and Their Political Consequences*. New York: Agathon Press.

Kernell, Samuel. 1986. *Going Public: New Strategies of Presidential Leadership*. Washington, DC. CQ Press.

Kiewiet, D. Roderick and Mathew D. McCubbins. 1991. *The Logic of Delegation: Congressional Parties and the Appropiations Process*. Chicago: University of Chicago Press.

King, Gary, Robert Keohane, and Sidney Verba. 1994. *Designing Social Inquiry: Scientific Inference in Qualitative Research*. Princeton, NJ: Princeton University Press.

Kingdon, John W. 1981. *Congressmen's Voting Decisions*, 2nd ed. New York: Harper and Row.

Kinzo, Maria D'Alva Gil. 1993. *Radiografia do Quadro Partidário Brasileiro*. São Paulo: Konrad Adenaur-Stiftung.

Krehbiel, Keith. 1990. "Are Congressional Committees composed of Preference Outliers?" *American Political Science Review* 84 (March): 149–163.

———. 1992. *Information and Legislative Organization*. Ann Arbor: University of Michigan Press.

———. 1993. "Where's the Party?" *British Journal of Political Science* 23: 235–266.

Kuschel, Carlos. 1998. Interview with Scott Morgenstern (August 6). Deputy for Renovación Nacional. Santiago, Chile.

La Época. 1997. "Jornada Electoral." http://200.9.122.8:80/default.htm

La Voluntad de Nuestro Pueblo, Memoria de la LV Legislatura, México: Chamber of Deputies, 1994.

Laakso, Marku and Rein Taagepera. 1979. "Effective Number of Parties: A Measure With Application to West Europe." *Comparative Political Studies* 12: 3–27.

Lajous, Alejandra. 1979. *Los Orígenes del Partido Único en México*. México: UNAM.

Lamounier, Bolivar. 1994a. "A Democracia Brasileira de 1985 à Década de 90: A Síndrome da Paralisia Hiperativa." In J. P. dos Reis Velloso, ed., *Governabilidade, Sistema Político e Violência Urbana*. Rio de Janeiro: José Olympio Editora.

Lamounier, Bolívar. 1994b. "Brazil at an Impasse." *Journal of Democracy* 5: 72–87.

479

Langston, Joy. 1996. "Why Rules Matter?: The Formal Rules of Candidate and Leadership Selection in the PRI, 1978–1996." Working paper no. 54, División de Estudios Políticos, Centro de Investigación y Docencia Económicas.

Laver, Michael and Norman Schofield. 1990. *Multiparty Government: The Politics of Coalition in Europe*. Oxford: Oxford University Press.

Laver, Michael and Kenneth A. Shepsle. 1990. "Coalitions and Cabinet Government." *American Political Science Review* 84, 3: 873–890.

1996. *Making and Breaking Governments: Cabinets and Legislatures in Parliamentary Democracies*. New York: Cambridge University Press.

León, Roberto. 1998. Interview with Scott Morgenstern (August 7). Deputy for Christian Democratic Party. Santiago, Chile.

Levitsky, Steven. 1998. "Crisis, Party Adaptation and Regime Stability in Argentina: The Case of Peronism, 1989–95." *Party Politics* 4: 445–470.

Ley Federal de Responsabilidades de los Servidores Públicos, Diario Oficial de la Federación, México D.F., December 28, 1963.

Lijphart, Arend. 1984. *Democracies: Patterns of Majoritarian and Consensus Government in Twenty-One Countries*. New Haven, CT: Yale University Press.

1994. *Electoral Systems and Party Systems: A Study of Twenty-Seven Democracies, 1945–1990*. New York: Oxford University Press.

Lima Junior, Olavo Brasil de. 1993. *Democracia e Instituições Políticas no Brasil dos Anos 80*. São Paulo: Edições Loyola.

Limongi, Fernando and Argelina Cheibub Figueiredo. 1995. "Partidos Políticos na Câmara dos Deputados: 1989–1994." *Dados – Revista de Ciências Sociais* 38, 3: 497–525.

1996. "Presidencialismo e Apoio Partidário no Congresso." *Monitor Público* 8, 3 (Jan/Feb/Mar): 27–33.

1998. "Bases Institucionais do Presidencialismo de Coalizão." *Lua Nova* 44: 81–106.

Linz, Juan J. and Alfred Stepan. 1996. *Problems of Democratic Transition and Consolidation: Southern Europe, South America, and Post-Communist Europe*. Baltimore: Johns Hopkins University Press.

Llanos, Mariana. 1998. "El Presidente, el Congreso y la Política de Privatizaciones en Argentina (1989–1997)." *Desarrollo Económico* 38, 151 (October–December): 743–770.

Londregan, John B. 2000a. "Estimating Legislators' Preferred Points." *Political Analysis* 8: 35–56.

2000b. *Ideology and Legislative Institutions in Chile's Transition Towards Democracy*. New York: Cambridge University Press.

Longo, Carlos Alberto. 1991. "O Processo Orçamentário no Brasil." *Revista de Economia Política* 11, 2: 78–91.

López Murphy, Ricardo et al. 1981. "Regimenes de Promoción en la Argentina." *Jornadas de Finanzas Públicas* 14.

Lott, John R. 1992. "Political Cheating." *Public Choice* 52: 169–186.

Lowi, Theodore J. 1969. *The End of Liberalism: Ideology, Policy, and the Crisis of Public Authority*. New York: Norton.

References

Loyola, Rafael. 1980. *La Crisis Obregón-Calles y el Estado Mexicano*. Mexico City: Siglo XXI.

Lujambio, Alonso. 1987. "La Proporcionalidad Política del Sistema Electoral Mexicano, 1964–1985." Unpublished thesis, Instituto Tecnológico Autónomo de México.

——— 1991. "Towards an Ambiguous Democracy. Electoral Laws and Democratization Process in Mexico." Mimeo.

——— 1995. *Federalismo y Congreso en el Cambio Político de México*. Mexico: Instituto de Investigaciones Jurídicas de la Universidad Nacional Autónoma de México.

Macón, Jorge. 1985. *Las Finanzas Públicas Argentinas*. Buenos Aires: Ediciones Maachi.

Magar, Eric, Marc R. Rosenblum, and David Samuels. 1998. "On the Absence of Centripetal Incentives in Double-Member Districts: The Case of Chile." *Comparative Political Studies* 31, 6: 714–739.

Mainwaring, Scott. 1991. "Politicians, Parties, and Electoral Systems: Brazil in Comparative Perspective." *Comparative Politics* 24: 21–43.

——— 1993. "Presidentialism, Multipartism, and Democracy: The Difficult Combination," *Comparative Political Studies* 26, 2: 198–228.

——— 1995. "Brazil: Weak Parties, Feckless Democracy." In Scott Mainwaring and Timothy R. Scully, eds., *Building Democratic Institutions: Party Systems in Latin America*. Stanford, CA: Stanford University Press.

——— 1997. "Multipartism, Robust Federalism, and Presidentialism in Brazil." In Scott Mainwaring and Matthew S. Shugart, eds., *Presidentialism and Democracy in Latin America*.. Cambridge: Cambridge University Press.

——— 1999. *Rethinking Party Systems in the Third Wave of Democratization: The Case of Brazil*. Stanford, CA: Stanford University Press.

Mainwaring, Scott and Aníbal Pérez Liñán. 1997. "Party Discipline in the Brazilian Constitutional Congress." *Legislative Studies Quarterly* 22, 4: 453–483.

——— 1997. "Party Discipline in the Brazilian Constitutional Congress." Working Paper, Kellogg Institute, University of Notre Dame.

Mainwaring, Scott and Timothy R. Scully. 1995. "Party Systems in Latin America." In Scott Mainwaring and Timothy R.Scully, eds., *Building Democratic Institutions: Party Systems in Latin America*. Stanford, CA: Stanford University Press.

Mainwaring, Scott and Matthew Shugart, eds. 1997. *Presidentialism and Democracy in Latin America*. New York: Cambridge University Press.

——— 1997. "Conclusion: Presidentialism and the Party System." In Scott Mainwaring and Matthew S. Shugart, eds., *Presidentialism and Democracy in Latin America*. Cambridge: Cambridge University Press.

Manzetti, Luigi. 1993. *Institutions, Parties, and Coalitions in Argentine Politics*. Pittsburgh: University of Pittsburgh Press.

Martínez Gallardo, Cecilia. 1998. "Las Legislaturas Pequeñas: La Evolución del Sistema de Comisiones en la Cámara de Diputados de México, 1824–2000." Unpublished thesis, Instituto Tecnológico Autónomo de México.

Marván Laborde, Ignacio. Forthcoming. "Ejecutivo Fuerte y División de Poderes: El Primer Ensayo de la Utopia Revolucionaria." In María Amparo Casar and Ignacio Marván Laborde, eds., *Episodios Republicanos: Experiencias de Gobierno Dividido en México a Partir de 1867.* Mexico: Cide-Oceano.

Mata, Manuel Antonio. 1998. Interview with Scott Morgenstern (August 13). Senator for Christian Democratic Party. Santiago, Chile.

Mayhew, David R. 1974. *Congress: The Electoral Connection.* New Haven, CT: Yale University Press.

McCubbins, Mathew D. 1991. "Government on Lay-Away: Federal Spending and Deficits under Divided Party Control." In Gary W. Cox and Samuel Kernell, eds., *The Politics of Divided Government.* Boulder, CO: Westview Press.

McCubbins, Mathew D. and Thomas Schwartz. 1984. "Congressional Oversight Overlooked: Police Patrols versus Fire Alarms." *American Journal of Political Science* 2, 1 (February): 165–179.

McGuire, James W. 1995. "Political Parties and Democracy in Argentina." In Scott Mainwaring and Timothy R. Scully, eds., *Building Democratic Institutions: Party Systems in Latin America.* Stanford, CA: Stanford University Press.

1997. *Peronism Without Perón: Unions, Parties, and Democracy in Argentina.* Stanford, CA: Stanford University Press.

Medín, Tzvi. 1982. *El Minimato Presidencial: Historia Política del Maximato.* Mexico City: Era.

Melero, Patricio. 1998. Interview with Scott Morgenstern (August). Deputy for UDI. Santiago, Chile.

Memoria del Proceso Electoral Federal de 1991. México: Instituto Federal Electoral, tomo IV, vols. 4–5, 1991.

Memoria Primer Periódo Ordinario de Sesiones. México: Chamber of Deputies, September 1988.

Mendoza Castillo, Leobardo Javier. 1996. "La Fiscalización de la Administración Pública en México: Análisis de la Propuesta del Ejecutivo de la Unión para Crear la Auditoría Superior de la Federación." Unpublished master's thesis, FLACSO-México.

Meneguello, Rachel. 1998. *Partidos e Governos no Brasil Contemporâneo (1985–1997).* São Paulo: Paz e Terra.

El Mercurio. Criticos Juicios Sobre "Presos Politicos": Plateamientos de Senador Thayer a "Leyes Cumplido", Santiago, November 12, 1990.

México, Presidencia de la República. Unidad de la Crónica Presidencial. 1987. *Diccionario Biográfico del Gobierno Mexicano.* México: Fondo de Cultura Económica.

1989. *Diccionario Biográfico del Gobierno Mexicano.* México: Diana.

1992. *Diccionario Biográfico del Gobierno Mexicano.* México: Fondo de Cultura Económica.

Meyer, Jean, Enrique Krauze, and Cayetano Reyes. 1977. *Estado y Sociedad con Calles,* vol. XI of *Historia de la Revolución Mexicana, 1924–1928.* Mexico City: El Colegio de México.

Meyer, Lorenzo. 1978. *El Conflicto Social y los Gobiernos del Maximato,* vol. XIII of *Historia de la Revolución Mexicana.* Mexico City: El Colegio de México.

References

Meyer, Lorenzo, Rafael Segovia, and Alejandra Lajous. 1978. *Los Inicios de la Institucionalización: La Política del Maximato*, vol. XII of *Historia de la Revolución Mexicana*. Mexico City: El Colegio de México.

Mezey, Michael. 1979. *Comparative Legislatures*. Durham, NC: Duke University Press.

Mizrahi, Yemile. 1999. "Los Determinantes del Voto en Chihuahua: Evaluación del Gobierno, Identidad Partidista y Candidatos." Working paper no. 106, División de Estudios Políticos, Centro de Investigación y Docencia Económicas.

Molinar, Juan. 1991. "Counting the Number of Parties: An Alternative Index." *American Political Science Review* 85, 4: 1383–1391.

Molinar Horcasitas, Juan. 1991. *El Tiempo de la Legitimidad: Elecciones, Autoritarismo y Democracia en México*. Mexico City: Cal y Arena.

Molinar Horcasitas, Juan and Jeffrey A. Weldon. 2001. "Reforming Electoral Systems in Mexico." In Matthew Soberg Shugart and Martin P. Wattenberg, eds., *Mixed-Member Electoral Systems: the Best of Both Worlds?* Oxford: Oxford University Press, pp. 209–230.

Forthcoming. *Los Procedimientos Legislativos en la Cámara de Diputados, 1917–1964*, series I, vol. I, tomo 2 of the *Enciclopedia Parlamentaria de México*. Mexico City: Instituto de Investigaciones Legislativas, Cámara de Diputados.

Molinelli, Guillermo. 1986. "Relaciones Presidente-Congreso: El Ejercicio del Veto y la Insistencia en Argentina, 1862–1985." Ph.D. dissertation, Facultad de Derecho y Ciencias Sociales, Universidad de Buenos Aires.

1991. *Clase Política y Reforma Electoral*. Buenos Aires: Grupo Editor Latinoamericano.

Molinelli, N. Guillermo, Valeria Palanza, and Gisela Sin. 1999. *Congreso, Presidencia y Justicia en Argentina*. Buenos Aires: CEDI-Temas. Cuadro 2.206, p. 434.

Morgenstern, Scott. 1997. "The Selectoral Connection: Electoral Systems and Legislative Cohesion." Working paper no. 65, División de Estudios Políticos, Centro de Investigación y Docencia Económicas.

N.d. *Legislative Politics and Democracy in the Southern Cone*. Manuscript.

2001. "Organized Factions and Disorganized Parties: Electoral Incentives in Uruguay." *Party Politics* 7, 2: 235–256.

Morgenstern, Scott and Pilar Domingo. 1997. "The Success of Presidentialism? Breaking Gridlock in Presidential Regimes." Working paper no. 73, CIDE.

Morgenstern, Scott, Daniel Nielson, and Steven Swindle. 1998. "The Electoral Disconnection? A Comparative Look at Reelection Rates." Paper prepared for delivery at American Political Science Association, Boston.

Mustapic, Ana M. and Sebastián Etchemendy. 1998. "El Papel de la Insistencia en el Sistema Político Argentino. Un Estudio de Caso." Mimeo.

Mustapic, Ana M. and Natalia Ferretti, 1995. "El Veto Presidencial Bajo Alfonsín y Menem." Paper presented at the XXV LASA Congress, September 28–30, Washington, DC.

Mustapic, Ana María and Matteo Goretti. 1992. "Gobierno y Oposición en el Congreso: La Práctica de la Cohabitación Durante la Presidencia de Alfonsin (1983–1989)." *Desarrollo Económico* 32, 126 (July–September): 251–269.

Nacif Hernández, Benito. 1995. "The Mexican Chamber of Deputies: The Political Significance of Non Consecutive Reelection." PhD dissertation, University of Oxford.

1996. "La Rotación de Cargos Legislativos y la Evolución del Sistema de Partidos en México." *Política y Gobierno* 1: 115–148.

1997. "Political Careers, Political Ambitions and Career Goals." Working paper no. 51, División de Estudios Políticos, Centro de Investigación y Docencia Económicas.

Nava Polina, María del Carmen and Jorge Yáñez López. 1998. "Legislar en la postrevolución, 1917–1946." Unpublished thesis, Instituto Tecnológico Autónomo de México.

Nava Polina, María del Carmen, Jeffrey A. Weldon, and Jorge Yáñez López. 1997. "Veto al Presupuesto: Interpretación Jurídica y Evidencia Histórica." *Reforma* (*Enfoque* 204), Mexico City (7 Dec.).

Needler, Martin. 1965. "Cabinet Responsibility in a Presidential System: The Case of Peru." *Parliamentary Affairs* 18 (Spring): 156–161.

1995. "Conclusion: The Legislature in a Democratic Latin America." In David Close, ed., *Legislatures and the New Democracies in Latin America*. Boulder, CO: Lynne Reinner.

Nef, Jorge and Nibaldo Galleguillos. 1995. "Legislatures and Democratic Transitions in Latin America: The Chilean Case." In David Close, ed., *Legislatures and the New Democracies in Latin America*. Boulder, CO: Lynne Reinner.

Nicolau, Jairo. 1994. "Breves Comentários sobre as Eleiçoes de 1994 e o Quadro Partidário." *Cadernos de Conjuntura IUPERJ* 50: 15–18.

Nicolau, Jairo Marconi. 1996. *Multipartidarismo e Democracia: Um Estudo sobre o Sistema Partidário Brasileiro (1985–94)*. Rio de Janeiro: Fundação Getúlio Vargas.

Nohlen, Dieter. 1993. *Enciclopedia Electoral Latinoamericana y del Caribe*. San Jose, Costa Rica: Instituto Interamericano de Derechos Humanos.

Norton, Philip. 1994. "Representation of Interests: The Case of the British House of Commons." In Samuel C. Patterson and Gary W. Copeland, eds., *Parliaments in the Modern World: Changing Institutions*. Ann Arbor: University of Michigan Press.

Novaro, Marcos. 1998. "El Gobierno y La Competencia Entre los Partidos Argentinos en los '90: Una Perspectiva Comparada." Paper presented at the XXI International Congress of the Latin American Studies Association, September 24–26, Chicago, IL.

Nuñez Minana, Horacio and Alberto Porto. 1982. "Coparticipación Federal de Impuestos: Distribución Primaria." *Jornadas de Finanzas Públicas* 15.

1983. "Coparticipación Federal de Impuestos. Distribución Secundaria." *Jornadas de Finanzas Públicas* 16.

O'Donnell, Guillermo. 1994. "Delegative Democracy." *Journal of Democracy* 5, 1: 55–69.

References

Olivera, Héctor Ricardo. 1995. *La Caída del Radicalismo*. Buenos Aires: Ediciones Corregidor.

Olivero, Roberto H. 1994. *El Financiamiento de Partidos Políticos en la Argentina: Un Problema de Cultura Política y Valores Sociales*. Buenos Aires: Ediciones I Y and Instituto Internacional de Investigaciones Interdisciplinarias.

Olson, Mancur. 1971. *The Logic of Collective Action: Public Goods and the Theory of Groups*. Cambridge, MA: Harvard University Press.

Orozco Henriquez, Jesus J. 1993. "Comentario al Artículo 49 de la Constitución." In *Constitución Política de los Estados Unidos Mexicanos*, México: Colección Popular de la Cuidad de México, IIJ-UNAM Y Procuraduría General de Justicia del Distrito Federal.

———. 1988. "El Sistema Presidencial en el Constituyente de Querétaro y su Evolución Posterior." In Madrazo, Jorge et al., *El Sistema Presidencial Mexicano (Algunas Reflexiones)*. México: Instituto de Investigaciones Jurídicas, UNAM.

Orpis, Jaime. 1996. Interview with Lisa Baldez (January). Deputy for the Independent Democratic Union (UDI). Santiago, Chile.

———. 1998. Interview with Scott Morgenstern (August 14). Santiago, Chile.

Özbudun, Ergun. 1970. *Party Cohesion in Western Democracies: A Causal Analysis*. Beverly Hills, CA: Sage Publications.

Padgett, Vincent. 1966. *The Mexican Political System*. Boston: Houghton Mifflin.

Página 12. Various issues.

Palermo, Vicente. 1995. "Reformas estructurales y régimen político." *Agora* 3 (Invierno): 95–113.

Palma, Andrés. 1996. Interview with Lisa Baldez (January). Chilean deputy for the Christian Democratic party. Santiago, Chile.

Paoli Bolio, Francisco José. 1997. "Instalación y gobierno de la Cámara de Diputados." *Juridíca; Anuario de derecho de la Universidad Iberoamericana* 27: 233–250.

Paya Mira, Darío (1998). Interview with Scott Morgenstern (August 17). Deputy for UDI. Santiago, Chile.

Pellet Lastra, Arturo. 1992. *El Congreso Por Dentro: Desde 1930 Hasta Nuestros Dias*. Buenos Aires: Sainte Claire Editora.

Pessanha, Charles. 1997. "Relações Entre os Poderes Executivo e Legislativo no Brasil: 1946–1994." Unpublished Ph.D. dissertation, University of São Paulo, Brazil.

Peterson, Mark. 1990a. *Legislating Together: The White House and Capitol Hill From Eisenhower to Reagan*. Cambridge, MA: Harvard University Press.

———. 1990b. "Developing the President's Program: The President as a Strategic Player." Paper presented at the Annual Meeting of the Midwest Political Science Association, Chicago.

Pinheiro, Vinícius Carvalho. 1996. "Inflação, Poder e Processo Orçamentário no Brasil – 1989 a 1993." *Revista do Serviço Público* 120, 1: 141–165.

Pírez, Pedro. 1986. *Coparticipación Federal y Descentralización del Estado*. Buenos Aires: Centro Editor de América Latina.

Polsby, Nelson. 1968. "The Institutionalization of the U.S. House of Representatives." *American Political Science Review* 62, 2: 144–168.

Porto, Alberto. 1990. *Federalismo Fiscal: El Caso Argentino*. Buenos Aires: Editorial Tesis.

Power, Timothy. 1997a. "Neoliberal Orientations among Brazilian Politicians: A Research Note." Paper prepared for delivery at the annual meeting of the Southern Political Science Association, November 5–8, Norfolk, VA.

1997b. "Parties, Puppets and Paradoxes: Changing Attitudes Toward Party Institutionalization in Post-Authoritarian Brazil." *Party Politics* 3, 2: 189–219.

Power, Timothy J. 1998. "The Pen is Mightier Than the Congress: Presidential Decree Power in Brazil." In John M. Carey and Matthew S. Shugart, eds., *Executive Decree Authority*. New York: Cambridge University Press.

2000. *The Political Right in Postauthoritarian Brazil: Elites, Institutions, and Democratization*. College Park: Penn State University Press.

Proceso, No. 915, May 16, 1994.

Rabkin, Rhoda. 1996. "Redemocratization, Electoral Engineering, and Party Strategies in Chile, 1989–1995." *Comparative Political Studies* 29: 335–356.

Reforma. Various issues.

Rehren, Alfredo. 1997. *Elites Parlamentarias Iberoamericanas*. Chile: Universidad de Salamanca.

Republic of Chile. 1980. *The Political Constitution of the Republic of Chile, 1980*.

República Argentina. 1989. Cámara de Diputados: Su Composición y Comisiones (Secretaría de la Honorable Cámara, Imprenta del Congreso Nacional).

Boletín Oficial, various issues.

Cámara de Diputados. *Diario de Sesiones de la Nación*, various issues.

Reglamento del Honorable Senado de la Nación.

Senado. *Diario de Sesiones de la Nación*, various issues.

Rice, Stuart A. 1925. "The Behavior of Legislative Groups." *Political Science Quarterly* 40: 60–72.

Riker, William H. 1959. "A Method for Determining the Significance of Roll Calls in Voting Bodies." In John C. Wilkie and Heinz Eulau, eds., *Legislative Behavior: A Reader in Theory and Practice* (pp. 377–384). Glencoe, IL: The Free Press.

1962. *The Theory of Political Coalitions*. New Haven, CT: Yale University Press.

Roberts, Kenneth M. and Erik Wibbels. 1999. "Party Systems and Electoral Volatility in Latin America: A Test of Economic, Institutional, and Structural Explanations." *American Political Science Review* 93: 575–590.

Rodríguez Araujo, Octavio. 1985. "Partidos Políticos y Elecciones en México." In *Revista Mexicana de Sociología*, Año 47, num. 1. México: UNAM, Enero-Marzo.

Rohde, David W. 1991. *Parties and Leaders in the Postreform House*. Chicago: University of Chicago Press.

Romer, Thomas and Howard Rosentahal. 1978. "Political Resource Allocation, Controlled Agendas, and the Status Quo." *Public Choice* 33: 27–44.

Rose, Richard. 1984. "Electoral Systems: A Question of Degree or of Principle?" In Arend Lijphart and Bernard Grofman, eds., *Choosing an Electoral System: Issues and Alternatives*. New York: Praeger.

Saiegh, Sebastián. 1997a. "Las Instituciones Políticas Argentinas y su Reforma: Una Agenda de Investigación." Working paper no. 1, Centro de Estudios para el Desarrollo Institucional (CEDI), Buenos Aires.

References

1997b. "Conservas el Cargo con el Sudor de Tu Frente: El Control Electoral Como Mecanismo de Incentivos Compatibles." Paper presented at the III Congreso de Ciencia Política of the Sociedad Argentina de Análisis Político, November 5–8, Mar del Plata, Argentina.

Samuels, David J. 1998. "Careerism and its Consequences: Federalism, Elections, and Policy-Making in Brazil." Unpublished Ph.D. dissertation, University of California at San Diego.

Samuels, David. 2000. "Ambition and Competition: Explaining Legislative Turnover in Brazil." *Legislative Studies Quarterly* 25, 3: 481–497.

Samuels, David J. and Fernando Luiz Abrucio. 1997. "The New Politics of the Governors: Subnational Politics and the Brazilian Transition to Democracy." Paper presented at the meeting of the International Political Science Association, Seoul.

Sanches, Oswaldo Maldonado. 1993. "O Ciclo Orçamentário: Uma Reavaliação à Luz da Constituição de 1988." *Revista de Administração Pública* 27, 4: 54–76.

1995. "Processo Orçamentário Federal: Problemas, Causas e Indicativos de Solução." *Revista de Administração Pública* 29, 3: 122–156.

1996. "A Participação do Poder Legislativo na Análise e Aprovação do Orçamento." *Revista de Informação Legislativa* 33, 131: 59–77.

Santiago Times Online (1999). "Senate Rejects Landmark Labor Reform." December 2 (subscribers@santiagotimes.chip.mic.cl).

Santos, Fabiano. 1995. "Microfundamentos do Clientelismo Político no Brasil." *Dados* 38: 459–496.

1997. "Patronagem e Poder de Agenda na Política Brasileira." *Dados* 40: 465–491.

Sartori, Giovanni. 1976. *Parties and Party Systems*. New York: Cambridge University Press.

1997. *Comparative Constitutional Engineering: An Inquiry into Structures, Incentives and Outcomes*, rev. ed. New York: New York University Press.

Sawers, Larry. 1996. *The Other Argentina: The Interior and National Development*. Boulder, CO: Westview Press.

Schattschneider, E. E. 1935. *Politics, Pressures, and the Tariff*. New York: Prentice-Hall.

Schinelli, Guillermo Carlos. 1996. *Reglamento de la Cámara de Diputados de la Nación: Comentado*. Buenos Aires: Dirección de Información Parlamentaria, Honorable Cámara de Diputados de la Nación.

Schlesinger, Joseph A. 1966. *Ambition and Politics: Political Careers in the United States*. Chicago: Rand McNally.

1991. *Political Parties and the Winning of Office*. Ann Arbor: University of Michigan Press.

Schmitt, Rogério. 1999. "Coligações Eleitorais e Sistema Partidário no Brasil." Unpublished Ph.D. dissertation, Instituto Universitário de Pesquisas do Rio de Janeiro.

Schofield, Norman and Michael Laver. 1985. "Bargaining Theory and Portfolio Payoffs in European Coalition Governments 1945–83." *British Journal of Political Science* 15: 143–164.

Schumpeter, Joseph A. 1942. *Capitalism, Socialism, and Democracy*. New York: Harper & Brothers.

Schuttemeyer, Suzanne S. 1994. "Hierarchy and Efficiency in the Bundestag: The German Answer for Institutionalizing Parliament." In Samuel C. Patterson and Gary W. Copeland, eds., *Parliaments in the Modern World: Changing Institutions*. Ann Arbor: University of Michigan Press.

Scully, Timothy R. 1995. "Reconstituting Party Politics in Chile." In Scott Mainwaring and Timothy R. Scully, eds., *Building Democratic Institutions: Party Systems in Latin America* (pp. 100–137). Stanford, CA: Stanford University Press.

Scully, Timothy and Samuel Valenzuela. 1993. "De la Democracia a la Democracia: Continuidad y Variaciones en las Preferencias del Electorado y en el Sistema de Partidos en Chile." *Estudios Públicos* 51: 195–228.

Serra, José. 1993. "As Vicissitudes do Orçamento." *Revista de Economia Política* 13, 4: 143–149.

Serra, Jose. 1994. *Orçamento no Brasil*, 2nd ed. São Paulo: Atual Editora.

Shepsle, Kenneth A. 1991. *Models of Multiparty Electoral Competition*. New York: Harwood Academic Publishers.

Shugart, Matthew S. 1995. "The Electoral Cycle and Institutional Sources of Presidential Government." *American Political Science Review* 89: 327–343.

1998. "The Inverse Relationship between Party Strength and Executive Strength." *British Journal of Political Science* 28 (January): 1–29.

Shugart, Matthew and John Carey. 1992. *Presidents and Assemblies*. New York: Cambridge University Press.

Siavelis, Peter. 1993. "Nuevos Argumentos y Viejos Supuestos: Simulaciones de Sistemas Electorales Alternativos para las Elecciones Parlamentarias Chilenas." *Estudios Públicos* 51: 229–267.

1997a. "Continuity and Change in the Chilean Party System: On the Transformational Effects of Electoral Reform." *Comparative Political Studies* 30, 6: 651–674.

1997b. "Executive/Legislative Relations in Post-Pinochet Chile: A Preliminary Assessment." In Matthew Shugart and Scott Mainwaring, eds., *Presidentialism and Democracy in Latin America*. New York: Cambridge University Press.

2000. *The President and Congress in Post-Authoritarian Chile: Institutional Constraints to Democratic Consolidation*. University Park: Pennsylvania State University Press.

Siavelis, Peter and Arturo Valenzuela. 1996. "Electoral Engineering and Democratic Stability: The Legacy of Authoritarian Rule in Chile." In Arend Lijphart and Carlos Waisman, eds., *Institutional Design in New Democracies*. Boulder, CO: Westview Press.

Sin, Gisela and M. Valeria Palanza. 1997. "Partidos Provinciales y Gobierno Nacional en el Congreso (1983–1995)." *Boletín SAAP* 3, 5: 46–94.

Sinatra, Mauricio and Mónica Veléz. 1994. *Quorum: Perfil de los Legisladores*. Buenos Aires: Grupo de Comunicación.

Sistema Integral de Información – Comité de Biblioteca e Información de la Cámara de Diputados. 1997, Iniciativas Presentadas al Congreso 1994–1997. Cuadernos de Apoyo, July.

References

Smith, Peter H. 1974. *Argentina and the Failure of Democracy: Conflict Among Political Elites 1904–55.* Madison: University of Wisconsin Press.

——— 1979. *Labyrinths of Power: Political Recruitment in Twentieth-Century Mexico.* Princeton, NJ: Princeton University Press.

Smith, Steven and Christopher Deering. 1990. *Committees in Congress.* Washington DC: Congressional Quarterly.

Sorauf, Frank J. 1992. *Inside Campaign Finance: Myths and Realities.* New Haven, CT: Yale University Press.

Souza Junior, Homero de. 1997. "Do Julgamento das Contas do Presidente da República." Paper presented at the conference "O Poder Legislativo e o Processo Orçamentário." Brasília: Câmara dos Deputados, Assessoria de Orçamento e Fiscalização Financeira.

Stokes, Donald. 1963. "Spatial Models of Party Competition." *American Political Science Review*, 57: 368–377.

Stokes, Donald E. 1965. "A variance components Model of Political Effects." In John M. Claunch, ed., *Mathematical Applications of Political Science.* Dallas: Southern Methodist University.

——— 1967. "Parties and the Nationalization of Electoral Forces." In Walter D. Burnham and William N. Chambers, eds., *The American Party Systems: Stages of Political Development.* New York: Oxford University Press.

Stokes, William. 1959. *Latin American Politics.* New York: Crowell.

Strom, Kaare. 1990a. *Minority Government and Majority Rule.* New York: Cambridge University Press.

——— 1990b. "A Behavioral Theory of Competitive Political Parties." *American Journal of Political Science* 34: 565–598.

——— 1994. "The Presthus Debacle: Intraparty Politics and Bargaining Failure in Norway." *American Political Science Review* 88: 112–127.

Sullivan, Terry. 1987. "Headcounts, Expectation, and Presidential Coalitions in Congress." *American Journal of Political Science* 87: 567–589.

Taachi, Carlos. 1995. "Revolución Tributaria en la Argentina," *Boletin de la DGI* 500 (August).

Taagepera, Rein and Matthew S. Shugart. 1989. *Seats and Votes: The Effects and Determinants of Electoral Systems.* New Haven, CT: Yale University Press.

Tanzi, Vito. 1995. *Taxation in an Integrating World.* Washington, DC: The Brookings Institution.

Tapia Videla, Jorge. 1977. "The Chilean Presidency in a Developmental Perspective." *Journal of Interamerican Studies and World Affairs* 19, 4: 451–481.

Tena Ramírez, Felipe. 1985. *Derecho Constitucional Mexicano*, 21st ed. Mexico City: Porrúa.

——— 1991. *Leyes Fundamentales de México, 1808–1991*, 16th ed. Mexico City: Porrúa.

Thibaut, Bernhard. 1996. *Präsidentialismus und Demokratie in Lateinamerika: Argentinien, Brasilien, Chile und Uruguay im Historischen Vergleich.* Oplade: Leske and Budrich.

——— 1998. "El Gobierno de la Democracia Presidencial: Argentina, Brasil, Chile y Uruguay en una Perspectiva Comparada." In Dieter Nohlen and Mario

Fernández B., eds., *El Presidencialismo Renovado: Instituciones y Cambio Político en América Latina*. Caracas: Nueva Sociedad.

Tiefer, Charles. 1994. *The Semi-Sovereign Presidency: The Bush Adminstration's Strategy for Governing without Congress*. Boulder, CO: Westview Press.

Torre, Juan Carlos. 1996. "Argentine: Le Péronisme, Solution et Problème de la Crise." *Problèmes d'Amérique Latine* 20 (Janvier–Mars): 41–46.

Tsebelis, George. 1990. *Nested Games: Rational Choice in Comparative Politics*. Berkeley: University of California Press.

1995. "Decision Making in Political Systems: Veto Players in Presidentialism, Parliamentarism, Multicameralism and Multipartyism." *British Journal of Political Science* 25: 289–325.

Ugalde, Luis Carlos. 1996. "El Poder Fiscalizador de la Cámara de Diputados en México." Paper presented at the seminar "La No Reelección Consecutiva en el Congreso: Sus Efectos en el Sistema Político Mexicano." March 11–12, México D.F.

1997a. "La Aprobación del Presupuesto." *Reforma* (*Enfoque* 190), Mexico City (31 Aug.).

1997b. "Los Aspectos Legislativos del Gasto Público en México, 1970–1996." *Perfiles Latinoamericanos* 10 (Jan.–June): 75–99.

1997c. "La Aprobación del Presupuesto: El Poder de la Bolsa, 1970–1997." *Perfiles Latinoamericanos*. México: FLACSO, junio.

2000. *The Mexican Congress: Old Player, New Power*. Washington: The CSIS Press.

Valenzuela, Arturo. 1977. *Political Brokers in Chile: Local Government in a Centralized Polity*. Durham, NC: Duke University Press.

1978. *The Breakdown of Democratic Regimes: Chile*. Baltimore: Johns Hopkins University Press.

1994. "Party Politics and the Crisis of Presidentialism in Chile: A Proposal for a Parliamentary Form of Government." In Juan J. Linz and Arturo Valenzuela, eds., *The Failure of Presidential Democracy* (pp. 91–150). Baltimore: The Johns Hopkins University Press.

Valenzuela, Arturo and Peter Siavelis. 1991. "Ley Electoral y Estabilidad Democrática: Un Ejercicio de Simulación para el caso de Chile." *Estudios Públicos* 43: 27–88.

Valenzuela, Arturo and Alexander Wilde. 1979. "Presidential Politics and the Decline of the Chilean Congress." In Joel Smith and Lloyd Musolf, eds., *Legislatures in Development: Dynamics of Change in New and Old States*. Durham NC: Duke University Press.

VanDoren, Peter M. 1990. "Can We Learn the Causes of Congressional Decisions from Roll-Call Data?" *Legislative Studies Quarterly* 15, 3: 311–340.

Veléz, Mónica. 1997. *Quorum: Perfil de los Legisladores II*. Buenos Aires: Proyecto Quorum.

Warwick, Paul V. 1994. *Government Survival in Parliamentary Democracies*. New York: Cambridge University Press.

Weldon, Jeffrey A. 1994. "Congress, Political Machines, and the *Maximato*: The No-Reelection Reforms of 1933." Paper presented at the 18th International Congress of the Latin American Studies Association, March 10, Atlanta.

References

1997a. "El Crecimiento de los Poderes Metaconstitucionales de Cárdenas y Ávila Camacho: Su Desempeño Legislativo." *Diálogo y Debate* 1, 1 (April–June): 11–28.

1997b. "The Political Sources of *Presidencialismo* in Mexico." In Scott Mainwaring and Matthew Shugart, eds., *Presidentialism and Democracy in Latin America* (pp. 225–258). Cambridge: Cambridge University Press.

1997c. "El Presidente como Legislador, 1917–1934." In Pablo Atilio Piccato Rodríguez, ed., *El Poder Legislativo en las Décadas Revolucionarias, 1908–1934*, serie I, vol. I, tomo 3 of *Enciclopedia Parlamentaria de México* (pp. 117–145). Mexico City: Instituto de Investigaciones Legislativas, Cámara de Diputados, LVI Legislatura.

1998a. "Committee Power in the Mexican Chamber of Deputies." Paper presented at the 21st International Congress of the Latin American Studies Association, September 24, Chicago.

1998b. "Acumulan Diputados Trabajo en Iniciativas". *Reforma*, June 24, Section A: 18.

Forthcoming. "Las Estrategias del Presidente con Gobierno Dividido." In María Amparo Casar and Ignacio Marván Laborde, eds., *Episodios Republicanos: Experiencias de Gobierno Dividido en México a Partir de 1867*.

Weldon, Jeffrey and Vidal Romero. 1998. "Considerable Trabajo Legislativo." *Reforma*, December 19, Section A: 4.

Wilkie, James W. 1967. *The Mexican Revolution: Federal Expenditure and Social Change Since 1910*. Berkeley, CA: Univerity of California Press.

World Bank. 1990. *Argentina: Provincial Government Finances*. Washington, DC: The World Bank.

1993. *Argentina: From Insolvency to Growth*. Washington DC: The World Bank.

Yazbeck Jozami, Mora. 1999. "Legisladores Oficialistas y Poder Ejecutivo en Argentina: La Construcción de la Disciplina. Un Estudio de Caso." B.A. thesis, Universidad Torcuato Di Tella.

Zedillo, Ernesto, Intervention at the XVII PRI Assembly, September 22, 1966.

Author Index

Author Index

Ugalde, Luis Carlos, 133, 377, 397

Valenzuela, Arturo, 83, 100, 105, 106, 222, 223, 226, 228, 229, 230, 253, 378

VanDoren, Peter M., 359

Weldon, Jeffrey A., 13, 14, 15, 121, 123, 132, 231, 254, 280, 313, 377–380, 382, 383, 387, 391, 394, 397, 398, 408, 418, 433, 435, 436, 451, 466

Wilde, Alexander, 83, 100, 222, 223

Author Index

General Index